ALZHEIMER'S DISEASE TREATMENT AND FAMILY STRESS

ALZHEIMER'S DISEASE TREATMENT AND FAMILY STRESS

Directions for Research

Edited by

Enid Light, Ph.D.
Barry D. Lebowitz, Ph.D.
National Institute of Mental Health

⊙HEMISPHERE PUBLISHING CORPORATION
A member of the Taylor & Francis Group

New York   Washington   Philadelphia   London

This permanent edition contains the complete text of the U.S. Department of Health and Human Services report, *Alzheimer's Disease Treatment and Family Stress: Directions for Research.*

DISCLAIMER: The views expressed in this volume are those of the authors and do not necessarily reflect the opinions or official position of the National Institute of Mental Health or any other part of the U.S. Department of Health and Human Services.

Library of Congress Cataloging-in-Publication Data

Alzheimer's disease treatment and family stress : directions for
  research / [edited] by Enid Light and Barry D. Lebowitz.
      p.   cm.
    Reprint. Originally published: Rockville, Md. : U.S. Dept. of
Health and Human Services, Public Health Service, Alcohol, Drug
Abuse, and Mental Health Adinistration, National Institute of
Mental Health : Washington, D.C. : For sale by the Supt. of Docs.,
U.S. G.P.O. [1989]
    Includes bibliographical references.

    1. Alzheimer's disease.   2. Alzheimer's disease — Patients — Family
relationships.   3. Stress (Psychology)   4. Alzheimer's disease —
Social aspects.   I. Light, Enid.   II. Lebowitz, Barry.
    [DNLM: 1. Alzheimer's Disease — nursing.   2. Family.   3. Mental
Health Services.   4. Stress, Psychological.   WM 220 A477823 1989a]
RC523.A3884   1990
362.1'96831 — dc20
DNLM/DLC
for Library of Congress   90-4801
                                                              CIP

ISBN 1-56032-137-7

Contents

Part II. Caregiver Stress: Research Issues in the Mental Health/Health Interface

Part III. Research Issues in the Treatment and Management of Alzheimer's Disease Patients

vi

Part IV. Issues and Directions for Mental Health Services Research

Foreword

Alzheimer's disease is a chronic, degenerative, dementing illness of unknown etiology. Despite the tremendous explosion in our understanding of the biology of this disorder, there is no known cure or intervention to stop the progression of this disease. An estimated 2 million older Americans are afflicted with Alzheimer's disease, and, as the elderly segment of the U.S. population sharply increases over the next four decades, the number and proportion of afflicted individuals can be expected to rise dramatically. The impact of this disease on individuals and their families is both tragic and severe. The National Institute of Mental Health (NIMH), in recognizing both the demographic and humanitarian imperative brought about by this illness, is focusing national attention on the development of a comprehensive research agenda to address the *immediate* care needs of the Alzheimer's disease victims and their families. This volume underscores the NIMH commitment and leadership toward achieving this goal.

A great deal of scientific excitement is evident throughout this volume. These reflective state-of-the-science papers, written by highly regarded researchers in the field, bring together both knowledge and theoretical perspectives. They converge in suggesting that advances can be made in treatments designed to both reduce excess disability and enhance spared capabilities associated with the emotional, behavioral, and psychosocial impairment of Alzheimer's disease patients and in understanding and helping families cope with the stresses of caregiving.

This volume marks the recognition of a tremendous opportunity to advance the care of Alzheimer's disease patients and their families. It is therefore with much appreciation that we acknowledge the contributions of each of the authors for their knowledge, their insight, and their guidance toward a new generation of research.

Lewis L. Judd, M.D.
Director
National Institute of Mental Health

ix

Preface

Research on Alzheimer's disease has enormously expanded our understanding of how to better direct current services and how to better design new studies on improving the treatment of this most serious disorder. Research has shown us that while Alzheimer's disease is a devastating brain disorder, so much of its symptomatology for so much of its clinical course is behavioral. Pathological, neurochemical, and neuroanatomical changes in Alzheimer's disease translate into abnormal behavioral phenomena–i.e., cognitive dysfunction (e.g., memory and intellectual impairment), problem behaviors (e.g., wandering and agitation), disturbed psychological states (e.g., depression and delusions), and adverse psychosocial consequences (e.g., family stress and societal costs).

A number of the behavioral and psychosocial concomitants in Alzheimer's disease cause what is referred to as excess disability states, where the patient or family confronts problems that are greater than those caused by the dementia of Alzheimer's disease alone. Hence, an Alzheimer's disease patient with compounding delusions will do worse than one without such disturbed thinking; similarly, the family will have a harder time helping a member with Alzheimer's disease who is also delusional than one who is not. Treatment of excess disability states in Alzheimer's disease allows us to alleviate patient suffering, reduce family burden, and diminish societal costs. Treatment of excess disability states also allows us to maximize coping capacities of both the patient and the family at given points along the course of the disorder. Part of the treatment research agenda for Alzheimer's disease is to come up with better treatment modalities and intervention strategies for dealing with excess disability states.

Combined with the treatment research agenda is a clinical services research agenda that addresses another key aspect of Alzheimer's disease. Because Alzheimer's disease is a progressive disorder, the nature of symptoms and problems it causes for both the patient and the family change over time. Hence, different service needs and different mixes of various needed services are required at different times during the course of the disorder. A challenge to services researchers is to come up with optimal designs for individual services as well as for specific combinations of services that appropriately respond to the natural history or progression of Alzheimer's disease.

This volume addresses all these issues. It addresses the needs of both the patient and the family afflicted with Alzheimer's disease. It addresses the treatment and clinical services issues that must be considered in the development of a comprehensive approach to helping both patients and their families. It addresses the relationships between brain and behavior and between health and mental health in treating Alzheimer's disease. Finally, it addresses the research recommendations that have emerged from the Secretary's Task Force and Council on Alzheimer's Disease in the areas of treatment and services for patients and families confronting Alzheimer's disease.

Gene D. Cohen, M.D., Ph.D.
Associate Director for Aging
Division of Clinical Research
National Institute of Mental Health
and
Executive Secretary
Council on Alzheimer's Disease, and the
Advisory Panel on Alzheimer's Disease
Department of Health and Human Services

Introduction

Alzheimer's disease and related disorders have come to be recognized as a major public health problem in both the United States and the world. More than 2 million older Americans are afflicted with this disorder, which has a progressively downward clinical course with increasing behavioral, cognitive, emotional, and psychosocial impairment. An estimated 1.5 million Americans suffer from severe dementia (e.g., they are incapacitated to the point of needing others to care for them continually), and the number of individuals with severe dementia is expected to increase 60 percent by the year 2000. The impact of Alzheimer's disease is both tragic and severe on the patient and the family. This illness also poses a considerable burden on the system of health care.

Alzheimer's disease is one of the major challenges to geriatric research. In the long range, the objectives of research are to develop more effective ways of characterizing the disorder and its subtypes, to identify its etiology, and to develop effective treatment and prevention strategies. In the short run, the research objectives (in the absence of a cure and prevention) are to reduce patient excess disability and to maximize individual functional level and family coping through the development of behavioral treatments, family supportive interventions, and models of family, community, and institutional care. The ultimate goal of such short-term research is to advance the development of research-validated clinical and services approaches that address the *immediate* needs of Alzheimer's patients and their families.

This volume brings together a collection of papers that focus attention on these short-term research objectives. The overall goal of this volume is to stimulate research on the development of effective treatment, management, and service delivery models for patients with Alzheimer's disease and related disorders and to increase our understanding of and ability to reduce the negative health/mental health consequences experienced by many family caregivers of dementia patients.

This volume is divided into four sections that address research on

Alzheimer's disease and the family, caregiver stress, the treatment and management of Alzheimer's disease patients, and services. Each section brings together chapters representing a range of theoretical perspectives that address many of the complex methodological issues inherent to such research.

Each of the chapters in this volume embodies information that is relevant to both the other chapters within its section and the chapters in other sections. This highlights the need for researchers to take a multidisciplinary approach to study designs.

We wish to gratefully acknowledge the efforts of each of the authors who made this book possible. Their thoughtful, scholarly, and creative approaches to these extremely complex problems will hopefully lead to a new generation of productive research on Alzheimer's disease treatment and family stress.

Enid Light, Ph.D.

Barry D. Lebowitz, Ph.D.

Part I

Issues in Alzheimer's Disease and Family Research

It has been well-documented that the family is the primary source of short- and long-term emotional help and instrumental services to individuals with Alzheimer's disease and related disorders. The family, particularly the spouse, plays a major role in maintaining Alzheimer's disease patients in the community and preventing or delaying their institutionalization. For some families, caregiving functions may extend 10 years or more.

The initial studies in this field examined family caregiving descriptively. In general, studies were conducted to describe families in terms of the following: who provided care (spouse/child/sibling); the nature, type, and extent of care provided (financial/activities of daily living); living arrangements between caregiver and Alzheimer's patient; extent of disability of Alzheimer's patient; and length of time spent caregiving. Most of these initial studies focused attention almost exclusively on the primary caregiver rather than on the family as a whole.

A new generation of research, exemplified by the following chapters, focuses on the family as a total system and emphasizes the need to firmly ground such research in current social-psychological theory. These chapters also emphasize the recognition of family differences (at both the individual and cultural level) and the need to adopt lifespan perspectives in conducting research.

These second generation caregiving studies suggest that, in a number of areas, the existing knowledge base is sufficient to support theory-based predictive studies. Such predictive research may ultimately lead to the identification and increased understanding of dysfunctional family situations and form the basis for the development of family-based interventions.

Chapter 1

The Family at Risk

Elaine M. Brody, M.S.W.

A major philosophical thrust of this century has been recognition of the interrelationships and interdependence of the members of the family; the homeostasis of the family as a whole is affected by a disturbance in any of its parts. That understanding is illustrated in bold relief when a family member is stricken with Alzheimer's disease. The afflicted individual's need for care sets up reverberations affecting every member of the family. Theoretical understanding of the impact on the entire family has not been fully operationalized, however, in research on family caregiving to the elderly in general or, in particular, in research on caregiving to the patient with Alzheimer's disease. A copious literature documents the mental and emotional strains experienced by the individual characterized as the primary caregiver. But there has been little exploration of the effects on other family members, their perceptions of the caregiving situations, the interactions of the various people on the family scene, or how those interactions affect the caregiver's mental health.

Despite major gaps in knowledge, available data together with a deluge of descriptive reports lead to the inescapable conclusion that the occurrence of Alzheimer's disease does indeed directly affect all members of the family and the family as a whole. Moreover, the concrete caregiving activities required and the emotional concomitants and consequences have unique aspects that may strain the family to an extraordinarily painful level. In short, when an older person becomes demented, it is a family event, and the family is at risk of mental health problems.

Excellent comprehensive reviews of the literature on family caregiving are available (e.g., Doty 1986; Horowitz 1985). This chapter, therefore, includes only a brief summary, highlighting information that casts some light on the special aspects of caregiving when the family member has Alzheimer's disease or a related disorder. Data and case material from Philadelphia Geriatric Center (PGC) studies illustrate selected issues of family caregiving, specifically the effects on family members other than the caregiver (spouse, children, and siblings) and their roles, attitudes, and perspectives.

The PGC research concerned caregiving families of a particular type in which the primary caregiver was a married daughter and the care receiver was a widowed elderly mother. Daughters were selected because they are the main helpers to older people who care for impaired spouses, the main caregivers to the widowed elderly, and the major caregivers to the most severely impaired (Stone et al. in press). Since greater disability and dementia are associated with advanced old age, and most people in advanced old age are widowed, daughters are likely to predominate in caring for the oldest and most demented elderly (most of whom are women).

Filial care by married daughters is not the only important form of care. Each pattern of family caregiving has special features and effects on family members; each deserves more research and clinical exploration that can lead to appropriate interventions.

Research on Family Caregiving

Research has yielded such a consistent body of information that certain facts can be accepted as givens. Families of disabled older people are dependable in providing care. As the "informal" system of care, they provide the vast majority of medically related and supportive health and social services–assistance with activities of daily living (ADL) e.g., bathing, feeding, dressing, toileting; and instrumental activities of daily living (IADL), e.g., laundry, household chores, managing money, transportation, shopping (Comptroller General of the United States 1977; Shanas 1979a, 1979b, 1980; Stone et al. in press).

Recent data from the 1982 Long-Term Care Survey show that less than 15 percent of all "helper days of care" for people needing help with ADL (an extreme form of caregiving) are provided by the "formal" or nonfamily system (Doty et al. 1985). Moreover, only 4 percent of old people who need such help have any part of it paid for by government. The results of a PGC study of daughter-caregivers were similar: most nonfamily help was not subsidized but was purchased by the older people and their families (Brody and Schoonover 1986).

Despite the difficulties of caregiving, the formal support system does not encourage families to shirk caregiving, but complements and supplements family services (Horowitz 1982; Zimmer and Sainer 1978). In general, older people are placed in nursing homes only after strenuous and prolonged family efforts to maintain them in the community (see Brody 1985a for review).

Families perform many services that are not usually counted in surveys. They respond in emergencies, provide intermittent acute care, and implement professional recommendations for rehabilitation procedures. Most importantly, they give emotional support (concern, affection, socialization, and a sense of having someone to rely on), the most universal family service and the one most wanted by the old. The family also mobilizes, coordinates, and monitors family and formal services, a form of help often regarded as the province of professionals and characterized as "case management."

While some caregivers manage well, others experience a host of strains and mental health symptoms such as depression, nervousness, anxiety, sleeplessness, frustration, and lowered morale. In data from many studies, the proportion who suffer moderate or severe negative effects of that kind hovers at about 50 percent. These mental health problems are related to such factors as restrictions on time and freedom, interference with social and recreational activities, income, plans for vacations and for the future, privacy, and use of space in the home. Many daughters feel "caught in the middle" of multiple competing demands on their time and energy such as responsibilities to their husbands, children, households, and jobs (Brody 1981).

Alzheimer's disease makes special and particularly arduous demands on caregivers. The disabilities associated with this affliction go beyond those of other diagnoses and are not measured by most systems of functional assessment. Round-the-clock surveillance may be required because of disruptive, even dangerous, behaviors such as wandering, nighttime wakefulness, or turning on the stove or water faucets and leaving them untended. The patient may have sudden and upsetting emotional outbursts.

The Alzheimer's patient's resistance and need for special management techniques often make the tasks of assisting with ADL more time consuming and problematic than for patients with other conditions. Embarrassing behaviors may discourage caregivers from having visitors in the home or taking the patient out. Particular distress is caused the caregiver when the patient no longer recognizes her and cannot provide her with feedback and appreciation for her efforts. Families often fear that the disease can be inherited.

Many studies, beginning with the classic Grad and Sainsbury research in the 1960s (1966), identified the care of mentally impaired older people as the most stressful to caregivers. Most of the symptoms predictive of caregiver strain are characteristic of Alzheimer's patients–incontinence and the need for considerable help because of multiple deficits in ADL, for example. Dementia per se does not produce stress, but rather the disruptive behavioral manifestations of that ailment (Horowitz 1985; Deimling and Bass 1986).

Sharing a household with a disabled older person is a strong predictor of strain. While mildly demented individuals may begin by remaining in their own homes, such arrangements cannot be sustained as the ailment progresses; virtually all noninstitutionalized Alzheimer's patients ultimately live with a caregiver. In the PGC respite care study of 634 caregivers of Alzheimer's patients, only 8 percent of the older people lived alone at baseline (Lawton et al. 1988).

A study by George (1984a) found that, in comparison to the general population, caregivers to Alzheimer's patients experienced more stress, took more prescription psychotropic drugs, participated in fewer social and recreational activities, and reported three times as many stress symptoms. Female caregivers (wives and daughters) were worse off than males on all of those effects. While spouse caregivers were more likely to use psychotropic drugs, to have financial problems, and to give up leisure, the filial caregivers (most of whom were daughters) reported higher levels of stress and unhappiness.

Data from the PGC study of working and nonworking daughter caregivers also speak to the effects on the lives and well-being of those caring for a parent with Alzheimer's disease. Reports of depression among working women were related to having elderly mothers with poor cognitive functioning and worry about being able to meet the mothers' future needs (Kleban et al. 1984).

More than one-fourth of nonworking daughters had quit their jobs to take care of their disabled parents, and a similar proportion of working daughters were "conflicted" in that they had cut back on their working hours and/or were considering quitting because of parent care. The mothers of these women had poorer cognitive functioning than the mothers of the other daughters in the study, and these daughters reported more problems and lifestyle disruptions (Brody et al. in press).

In short, the weight of the accumulated evidence suggests that care of the demented patient is the most difficult form of family help, produces the most strain for caregivers, interferes most with the caregivers' work lives (Brody et al. in press), and has more negative effects on family lifestyles. It has been called the most socially disruptive of all ailments (Brody 1967), and is more damaging to family relationships and the mental well-being of the primary caregiver than physical disability (Noelker and Poulshock 1982). The proliferation of support groups for families of Alzheimer's patients and the publication of several books offering information and counsel

5

to such families (i.e., Cohen and Eisdorfer 1986; Mace and Robins 1981; Safford 1986) also attest to the severe problems such caregivers experience.

The characteristics of the family have long been known to influence institutionalization as much as the characteristics of the older person (see Brody 1985a for review). Specifically, while those in institutions are older, more disabled mentally and physically, and predominantly female, they also have fewer social supports than their counterparts in the community. The role of the family in maintaining older people in the community is highlighted by the fact that the vast majority (88 percent) of the institutionalized aged are not married (widowed, divorced, or never married), about half are childless, and those with children have fewer children, older children, and children who are more geographically distant than the noninstitutionalized (Brody 1981).

Though demented older people are overrepresented in nursing homes, constituting 50-60 percent of the total nursing home population, an equal number live in the community. Whether in the community (Mace and Robins 1981) or in the nursing home (Brody et al. 1984), they are the ones likely to need the most time-consuming care. Community care is often described as a less costly "alternative" than a nursing home, but it is not cheaper in dollars and does not avoid nursing home placement for severely impaired people such as Alzheimer's patients (Weissert 1985).

Nursing home placement is often assumed to relieve caregiver strain. Contrary to popular belief, the family does not cease its supportive activities when the older person enters an institution (Brody 1981). Nor do family strains disappear, though they may derive from different factors. Many clinical reports describe the continuation of family concern, interest, and contacts with institutionalized older people. They talk to nursing home personnel about the patient, worry, feel guilty about having placed the patient (no matter how clearly placement was dictated), are sad about the older person's continuing decline, and are depressed and anxious about their own aging. They may be upset about the quality of care or staff attitudes, but afraid to complain because they fear retaliation on the patient. When the patient has Alzheimer's disease, that fear is intensified because the older person is relatively helpless, cannot communicate needs to staff, and cannot report any negative treatment received.

George found no significant differences in mental health, stress symptoms, and physical health between caregivers whose Alzheimer's patients resided in long-term care facilities and those whose patients lived in the caregivers' households. When the same families were followed up a year later (George 1984b), caregivers who had placed

6

the patient in a nursing home during the past year were more likely to be taking psychotropic drugs than were caregivers whose patients were in the community or had died. Those who had placed the patient equaled the people who were caring for the patient in their own homes in reporting stress symptoms and low levels of life-satisfaction and emotional well-being.

Little research has focused on the family relationships of institutionalized older people with Alzheimer's disease. One set of findings from a treatment project for cognitively impaired elderly women who lived in the PGC's nursing home indicated that such relationships remain important to both the older people and their family members. The elderly women's emotional investment in their families had risen in relative importance between their middle years and old age (Kleban et al. 1971), perhaps because other sources of emotional supplies had become depleted. Moreover, the relationship of the elderly people with their families improved with counseling intervention (Brody et al. 1971). Family visits to the more deeply impaired institutional residents were as frequent as to those with milder impairment, but were shorter and less enjoyable to the family member. Most of the relatives reported worrying about the old person and discussing her frequently with other family members (Moss and Kurland 1979).

Neither the George study nor the PGC study compared families of Alzheimer's patients with those whose elderly relatives had other diagnoses. Two NIMH-sponsored investigations are now underway at the PGC on the differential strains on families whose institutionalized relatives have different types of disabling mental and physical conditions.

Members of the Family

The focus of this chapter now shifts to family members other than the primary caregiver–her husband, her children, and her siblings– using selected portions of data from the PGC studies. The illustrative case excerpts were developed in an indepth qualitative study of a subsample of families who participated in the larger survey. Then one aspect of the complex relationship between the disabled mother and her caregiving daughter is discussed. (After all, the elderly person is the central figure around whom the caregiving scenario is enacted.) Finally, some of the excerpts about these various family members are assembled into three "whole" families, to which they belong, to demonstrate the kinds of interventions needed. The reader should note that those designated as Families G, A, and C in the case excerpts reappear later in the "whole families."

Most studies have examined caregiving from the perspective of the primary caregiver, who may provide information about the roles of other family members. Such investigations found that the actual amount of other family help did not buffer the caregivers' stress, but their strain was lessened when they felt supported by spouses, siblings, and other relatives (George in press; Horowitz 1982; Sussman 1979; Zarit et al. 1980). At the same time, the potential exists for the attitudes and behavior of family members to exacerbate caregivers' strains (Brody and Spark 1966; Spark and Brody 1970).

Household Configuration

The pattern in which older people live with adult children or other relatives (other than a spouse) is atypical and usually occurs after the elderly people have grown quite old. In the main, the very old move into their children's households because of disabilities that prevent them from managing independently or because of poor economic status. Moreover, contrary to popular notions about the past, the prevalence of such households was low in the late 19th century, as it is now. In 1975, only 3.9 percent of elderly males and 13.4 percent of elderly females shared a home with an adult child. Widowed elderly people are much more likely than their married peers to live with a child, particularly in advanced old age when disability precludes continued independent living (see Mindel 1979 for review). The effect of disability has a significant effect only on the odds of living with children, particularly with daughters (but not other family members) relative to living alone (Shanas et al. 1968; Wolf and Soldo 1986).

At any given time, the proportion of older people living in three-generation households is very small. Soldo's analysis of a national data set indicates, for example, that cross-sectionally 2.16 percent of all people aged 65 and over live in the homes of daughters between the ages of 40 and 59 who have both a parent and a child under 18 in those households (Soldo 1980). Since those figures do not include three-generation households of sons, those in which the daughter is under 40 or over 60, or those containing children over 18, a conservative estimate is that 4 percent or about one million older people live in three-generation households at any given time.

Because information on two- and three-generation households is cross-sectional, however, it obscures the fact that over time some older people who can no longer live alone move in with adult children. That is, a much larger proportion of the aged live in an adult child's home at some time during their lives. It follows, then, that more of them live in three-generation households. In the 1982 Long-Term Care Survey, one-quarter of daughter-caregivers had children under 18

8

years of age living at home. Thirty-six percent of the extremely disabled elderly (those who needed help with activities of daily living) lived with an adult child, most of them with a daughter. Sixty percent of the caregiving daughters shared their homes with the parent, and one-third of those (20 percent of the total) had both the disabled elderly parent and at least one child under 18 in their homes (Stone et al. 1987). A rough calculation indicates that there are about 250,000 households of filial caregivers (sons and daughters) containing both a severely disabled older person (i.e., in need of ADL help) and at least one child (either under or over 18).

An analysis of one portion of the PGC data compared the effects of parent care in three different household configurations: the disabled older person, her daughter and son-in-law (no children present because, in the main, they had "left the nest"); the older person, her daughter, son-in-law, and their child(ren) (who ranged in age from preschoolers to young adults in their twenties); and the elderly mother in her own separate household. (See Brody et al. in press for a complete report of this analysis.)

The caregiving daughters whose elderly mothers lived in separate households fared better than those who shared a household, a finding that supports those of previous studies. As might be expected, these mothers were younger and were the most capable functionally and cognitively. Fewer daughters in this group experienced caregiving strain, limitations on space, privacy, and social activities, or interference with time and relationships with their husbands, children, and friends. In fact, they did not exceed the shared-household caregivers on any strain variable.

In the two-generation households, both the disabled elderly mothers and their daughters were older than their counterparts in the other two groups. More of these mothers evidenced symptoms of Alzheimer's disease and sensory impairment (hearing and vision), and they received more hours of help each week than those in the other two household types. More of the daughters reported strain from their caregiving roles. They also felt less in control of their lives and were more likely to report interference with time for themselves, interference with the family budget, and problems with their husbands related to the caregiving situation. Theoretically at the "empty nest" phase of life, these daughters and their husbands exemplify the concept of the "empty nest refilled" (Brody 1978).

The daughters whose "nests" contained both their own children and the disabled elderly parent had the poorest mental health and reported the most symptoms of depression, restlessness, and feelings of isolation and missing out on something because of caregiving. In addition, they were more likely to rate their elderly mothers as

9

complaining and critical of the sons-in-law and grandchildren. Three-generation households, of course, have a greater potential for not only problems of space and privacy, but for interpersonal conflicts and for the caregiver's role-strain in meeting the needs of husband, child(ren), and parent.

Limitations of this study relate to the nature of the sample and its cross-sectional design. As stated above, all of the older people in the sample were disabled widowed women and the caregiving daughters were all married. The findings, therefore, cannot be generalized to all multigenerational households. Nor should the sharing of households be confounded with the poor functional capacities of the older people who live in them as a predictor of strain. More studies are needed of sons, daughters-in-law, and children of both sexes whose marital statuses differ as their caregiving occurs in the context of different living situations. Moreover, the effects to which caregivers in any category are vulnerable may change over time in response to changes in their own and their elderly parents' health and situational factors. The data reported, however, do identify the household types in which adult daughters are at risk of specific kinds of mental health and interpersonal problems.

Sons-in-Law

Though most caregiving daughters are married, the roles and perceptions of their husbands–the sons-in-law–have been virtually ignored. Obviously, however, when daughters report negative effects of caregiving on their family lives and lifestyles, their husbands are also experiencing many restrictions–interference with social and leisure activities, vacations, and privacy, for example.

Data from interviews with those sons-in-law confirm the vast body of literature showing repercussions throughout the family system from the experiences of individual family members. (See Kleban et al., submitted 1988, for complete report). Though the husbands of caregiving daughters in the PGC study played minor roles in the day-to-day provision of concrete services to their elderly mothers-in-law (Brody and Schoonover 1986), most of the men were under strain because of the caregiving situation, some of them for many years. They, too, reported the lifestyle restrictions so often mentioned by caregivers themselves (e.g., Brody et al. in press; Danis 1978; Frankfather et al. 1981; Kleban et al. submitted 1988).

Substantial minorities of the sons-in-law reported interference with time for themselves, time with their wives, their social lives, family vacation plans, and work that needed to be done around the house. Almost one-quarter of the husbands had experienced work

10

interruptions to help their mothers-in-law, while 10 percent had actually missed work.

Despite reports that significant numbers of caregivers view the caregiving situation as having negative effects on their family relationships (Adams et al. 1979, for example), few sons-in-law in the PGC study reported relationship problems with their wives and children as effects of care. Moreover, although almost half the men said they argued with their wives at times about the caregiving situation, very few thought it had driven them apart. Most said it had made no difference in their relationship, suggesting that the basic quality of long-standing marital relationships endures despite the strains of parent care and problems that may arise.

It is of special interest here that many of the negative consequences reported by the sons-in-law were associated with sharing their households with the mothers-in-law, and with the poor cognitive functioning and great disability of those elderly women. The husbands in shared households also perceived their wives' caregiving burdens to be greater when the impaired parent lived with them.

To compare the daughters' and sons'-in-law distinctive perspectives on caregiving situations, some sections of the questionnaires administered to the spouses were identical. Analysis of the responses indicates both similarities and differences in the perceptions of the wives and their husbands. The spouses agreed about the kinds of disruptions that can be observed with some objectivity–to vacation plans, to the family budget, and to household chores, for example. The wives, however, were much more likely than their husbands to report that caregiving interfered with the time they spent with each other, caused problems in the marital relationship itself, and interfered with relationships and time with the couple's children. The women also thought that these interferences occurred more frequently than their husbands did. On the other hand, the husbands were more likely to cite interference with relationships in the extended family.

In addition to perceiving less marital disruption from parent care, the men reported less marital tension than their wives did. Such findings are consonant with literature to the effect that men are more likely than women to repress or deny their emotional reactions (e.g., Walum 1977). Also, family life may be more central to women, and therefore they may be more sensitive to relationship problems. However, the sensitivity of the wives in this study may have been heightened because the dependent elderly women were *their* mothers, and the daughters therefore felt somewhat responsible when problems occurred. This suggestion is supported by the fact that 40 percent of the men viewed their wives as being "caught in the middle" between them and their mothers-in-law. The husbands also viewed the parent-care situation to be more burdensome to their wives than the women did themselves. The men, it appears, were quite aware of their wives' problems.

It deserves emphasis that the vast majority of couples felt that the caregiving situation had not affected their basic relationship. Nevertheless, the quality of the marital relationships and the interpersonal interaction patterns varied greatly and, as the case excerpts indicate, undoubtedly affected the ways in which care was provided.

Excerpts from interviews in the qualitative substudy illustrate both positive and negative aspects of the sons'-in-law attitudes and roles in the caregiving situation.

The wives in most situations described their husbands as emotionally supportive and helpful, upholding the observation that many sons-in-law are "unsung heroes" (Brody 1985b).

> *The G Family.* For 3 years, Mr. G (the son-in-law) stopped in every day to check on the old people. "He did even more than I did," says Mrs. G. Finally, Mr. G said, "Why don't you move in?" (into the Gs' home). Mrs. G says: "Our relationship has not been affected (by caregiving) because it was established long before. We had our ups and downs, but we have weathered it."

> *Family 2.* "My husband is very understanding," says Mrs. P. "I don't think my mother could have come here to live if he hadn't been. When there were a lot of health problems with my mother, if it hadn't been for him being so understanding, I wouldn't have been able to say 'Come and live with us.' He would do a lot more if she would let him. I'm thankful my husband is like he is."

> *Family 3.* "My husband did her handyman work. He would check on her every night after work so I didn't have to check on her every day. My husband was there to help and support me and do things for her so I didn't have to run down there all the time. My husband has been a support. He is always willing to go up and visit her with me. If your husband pulled you in another direction you couldn't do it."

> *The A Family.* "When we were both working, my husband would get off work early to pick my mother up at day care. He took it as vacation time. She was up all night, we weren't sleeping, it was terrible. My husband was working then. I was between the two of them. He was wonderful when he retired, he would babysit mother. When I reduced my work hours, my husband was all for whatever would help."

> *Family 4.* My husband is the balancing point. When things get

on my nerves about the help I give to my mother, I go to him and he calms me. If anything happened to him, I would have no support and I would go crazy."

Family 5. "My husband would help her. At night he would care for her completely. It was rough on him, and she's not even his mother. I am very grateful for this."

There were also situations with considerable marital tension:

Family 6. "My husband moaned, groaned, and complained. He said we should put her in a nursing home. My husband complained about the constant bickering between my mother and I."

The C Family. "My first husband took no responsibility. I would beg my husband and say we had to do something with Mom. He would just go and have another drink. Mr. C (caregiver's second husband) began to work overtime to pay for these things (the elderly mother's needs). My mother has ruined our sex life. Twice she went out of the house at night and laid down in the roadway. My husband did not ask me to remove my mother from our home. Some day (resignedly), I'll have his mother here. I know it."

Some husbands sent their wives conflicting messages:

Family 7. Mrs. H, age 67, is exhausted from many years of caregiving. Her elderly mother refuses placement in a nursing home. Mrs. H. says, "If *only* my husband had said 'Enough. Your mother must go to a nursing home.' But what he says is 'She wouldn't like it. She's not that sick yet'." Nevertheless, he often complains to friends and family in his wife's hearing that he can't go away on vacation or go out socially because of his mother-in-law.

Certainly, much more exploration of the experiences and roles of sons-in-law is indicated. However, just as studies of caregiving daughters have allowed us to see their parent care experiences through their eyes, these data begin to delineate experiences of their husbands. (For the complete report of PGC research on sons-in-law, see Kleban et al. 1988).

Grandchildren

Virtually no research exists about the effects on grandchildren when an older person receives family help or the caregiving roles grandchildren may play. Yet the vast majority of filial caregivers have children of their own, all of whom witness the caregiving situation and are invariably affected themselves to some extent. Some of those grandchildren live or have lived under the same roof as the disabled grandparent while others have not, either because the grandparents maintained their own households or the children had already left the nest when the grandparent moved in.

Most studies involving three-generation family relationships focused on issues such as the transmission of values (e.g., Bengtson 1975) or the roles, styles, and meaning of grandparenthood (see Bengtson and Robertson 1985 for a collection of papers about grandparenthood). In the majority of these studies, the grandparents concerned were primarily the younger cohorts of older people, including those who had not yet reached the age of 65. The grandparent's health and functional capacities were rarely addressed, although one study did include the grandparent's health as a variable in the contacts of grandchildren and grandparents (Cherlin and Furstenberg 1985), and another as it related to the happiness or distress of grandchildren (Troll and Stapley in press).

The PGC studies were not designed to examine the roles and perspectives of grandchildren in helping their disabled grandparents or the effects for good or ill on those grandchildren. Some of the findings, however, are relevant to those issues. (See Brody et al. 1988 for complete report.)

The ages and stages of the grandchildren varied greatly, and their roles varied accordingly. The help they provided was not negligible, and was more apparent in the qualitative than in the quantitative data. The discrepancy probably is due to the way the survey questions were framed. That is, the questions about "who helps" the older person referred to routine help with tasks related to the older persons' chronic ADL and IADL incapacities. But some adult grandchildren or those in their late teens appear to serve as a "backup" reserve of assistance (as did their fathers). Sometimes their help was direct to the grandparents and sometimes indirect through assistance to their mothers. It ranged from adult grandchildren's advice and emotional support to their caregiving mothers to extensive instrumental help. Some cleaned and cooked for the grandparent at times of special need or helped them move from one home to another. Some did "sitting" to allow their mothers respite to take a vacation or to go to work, or to fill in when the caregiver was sick.

In the following case excerpts, the daughters speak from their own perspectives about their children's roles:

> **The G Family.** Mrs. G., who took both of her elderly parents into her home, says "My children have really helped. When I was sick, my eldest daughter took care of things. My youngest

14

daughter would stay with my parents so that we could go out to a movie. Our middle daughter sometimes stays with Mother. When my parents moved here, my daughters did all the unpacking and arranged the furniture."

Even when the grandchildren were not active in providing concrete help, they were involved emotionally.

Family 8.   Mrs. F is divorced and has two grown children. She and her mother live together, and the care of the older woman is getting unmanageable because Mrs. F must work to support them both. In addition, the elderly woman is controlling and critical so that the daughter has no peace at home. When Mrs. F talks of finding a nursing home for her disabled mother, the grandson says, "Do it!," but the granddaughter says, "Don't! How could you do it to her?"

Teenagers and young adults often found their social lives disrupted; they couldn't play music or have parties for their friends, or the grandmothers' behavior was irritating or embarrassing when boyfriends came to call. Some grandchildren were upset by the bickering between elderly mother and her daughter or resented the burdens their mother was carrying and the reduction in the time she spent with them.

The C Family.   Mrs. C has two teenage children from a first marriage and a 5-year-old and a 7-year-old from the second. When Mr. and Mrs. C married, they agreed that she would not work. Mrs. C felt she had neglected her older children because she had to work. But the elderly mother's care strains the family's finances. Mr. C began to work overtime. Mrs. C worked on the afternoon-evening shift so that the younger children could be cared for by the older children after school. The teenagers cared for their grandmother as well, but complained of all the responsibility. They had no time of their own. "It isn't fair," they said. They can't even bring friends home because the behavior of the elderly woman is disruptive and embarrassing. The oldest daughter is now receiving psychiatric care.

Family 9.   Mrs. M's extremely disturbed and disturbing mother lives with Mr. and Mrs. M and several grandchildren. A granddaughter is tearful. She cannot bring her suitor home because the grandmother makes embarrassing noises.

Some adult grandchildren were not deeply involved.

The A Family.   "My children really couldn't help because they were married and live far away, but they were always very good to my mother. They are good children and grandchildren.

15

Some caregiving daughters felt they were setting a model of how their children should care for them in their own old age. "I want to set an example," said one. Another stated, "I hope my children will treat me the same way." Others tried to protect their children from involvement. One daughter sent the granddaughter away to school so that she wouldn't become the "grandparent-care person," and another said, "I hope this isn't a turnoff for them."

In some situations, the daughters were caught between their elderly mothers and their children. "I was always in the middle, trying to keep grandmother off the kids and the kids off of grandmother." Some women are "in the middle" in feeling that they must mediate conflicts among various family members–not only between elderly mother and husband but also between elderly mother and grandchildren.

While grandchildren may be involved in care of the elderly when their parents become caregivers, an unknown number of them find themselves in the role of primary caregiver to grandparents when death or illness of their parents leaves a gap in the generational caregiving chain. Some become responsible for two generations of disabled older people–their parent(s) and grandparent(s). If the values and attitudes of today's young women are indications of their future behavior, grandchildren will be reliable helpers to older people when they are needed. (See, for example, Brody et al. 1983, 1984). But the actual effects they experience and the roles they play have not been explored.

Siblings

Most research on family caregiving has had a *vertical* perspective–that is, it has examined parent-child relations during the phase of the family life cycle when the elderly parent(s) need help. This attention to the intergenerational aspects of family relationships has not been matched by study of the *horizontal* relationships at that phase of family life–that is, among the adult siblings who have a disabled parent. Moreover, what information does exist derives from reports of the primary caregiver rather than from the siblings themselves. Thus, little information exists about the interactions of the siblings, what siblings other than the primary caregiver actually do, the strains they may experience, or their perspectives on the situation.

Middle-aged siblings (even those who have lived relatively separate lives) may need to interact to a greater extent and in unrehearsed ways when a parent becomes disabled. The illness of a parent may constitute a "critical event" in the sibling relationship, with the possibility of a positive or negative outcome (Ross and Milgram 1982).

Because the disability of a parent is a family crisis, family problems and strengths stand out in bold relief, with the older person becoming the focal point.

Clinical reports have described the stimulation and reactivation of sibling relationship problems when an elderly parent is at risk of institutionalization (Brody and Spark 1966; Simos 1973; Spark and Brody 1970). Much anecdotal material from support groups of adult children highlights siblings' conflicts about parent care (e.g., Saline 1982). In an Australian study, deteriorated sibling relationships were reported as effects of parent care by 90 percent of the children in whose homes an impaired, elderly parent lived (Kinnear and Graycar 1982). Research rarely explores the positive aspects of sibling interaction, however; social supports (when mentioned at all) are referred to in general terms.

In another PGC study, the principal caregivers and their local sib-lings were interviewed and a survey was mailed to geographically distant siblings.

Local Siblings

One section of the data compared the caregivers and their local siblings on the help each provided, the effects of care they experienced, and the hassles and uplifts in their interactions with each other. (See Brody et al. 1988 for details.)

The caregivers spent many more hours each week helping the mother (almost 23 hours), followed by their sisters (10 hours) and brothers (almost 4 hours). The differences obtained with respect to almost all instrumental tasks and personal care, with the sons contributing the least time to most of these tasks and the local sisters providing slightly more time than their brothers. Exceptions to this pattern were that the sisters were closer to the caregivers than to the brothers in the amount of time spent as the mother's confidant and that the brothers provided more financial help to the mothers than either group of daughters.

The principal caregivers experienced the most overall strain from helping the mother, the brothers the least strain, and the sisters fell in between.

As expected, the daughters who were the principal caregivers reported the most negative effects of caregiving on their mental health, physical health, and lifestyles. Brothers consistently reported the least negative effects, and again the sisters fell in between. It was the caregivers, for example, followed by their sisters and brothers, who most frequently felt drained, nervous, frustrated, overwhelmed, pulled in different directions, had difficulty in setting priorities, and

17

experienced interference with their family responsibilities. Particularly salient for caregivers as compared with both groups of siblings were lifestyle disruptions such as interference with privacy, social activities, vacation, time with spouse, and time with friends. The caregivers also reported more problems with their spouses because of the parent-care situation and, to a greater extent, reported feeling angry and resentful as a result.

As for the siblings' feelings about their roles in parent care, both groups of daughters exceeded the brothers in feeling guilty when they became angry with their mothers, while the brothers more often felt that they did not spend enough time talking with their mothers. The sisters outdid the caregivers in the frequency with which they felt guilty about not doing more for their mother and in wishing that they weren't so busy so they could assist their mother more. More sisters than brothers felt that distance made it difficult for them to help their mothers, though all respondents in both groups lived less than 50 miles away. As might be expected, the caregivers were the ones who most resented the fact that siblings were doing less than they were.

As for the intersibling hassles and uplifts, the caregivers exceeded both groups of their siblings in feeling hassled about ways in which their siblings were meeting parent-care responsibilities. For example, two-thirds of the caregivers thought that a sibling had not visited the mother enough, had waited to be asked before helping, or could have helped more; more than half felt that a sibling had not called enough or had not done a fair share of parent care. It is striking, however, that the sisters exceeded both the caregivers and the brothers in complaining that siblings had tried to make them feel guilty for not helping more, had tried to have the mother appreciate what they did more than what she did, had complained of doing more than she did, or had said how burdened they felt. One interesting difference was that more of the caregivers than their brothers felt that a sibling was the mother's favorite even though the caregiver helped more.

Even where the groups did not vary significantly, hassles appear to be prevalent phenomena. For instance, half of the principal caregivers, one-third of the local sisters, and a third of local brothers reported that their sibling(s) did not take enough interest in the elderly mothers' situation. Likewise, 32 percent of primary caregivers, 44 percent of local sisters, and 40 percent of the local brothers said that their sibling(s) thought they knew what was best for the mother.

While it had been anticipated that the caregivers would be the most "hassled," the sisters experienced about the same number of hassles (though somewhat different ones) as the caregivers did. Brothers were the least troubled by the intersibling parent-care interaction, reporting significantly fewer hassles and significantly less strain from those hassles than either group of sisters. For example, 30 percent of the men reported no hassles at all, and only 6 percent of them experienced "a great deal" or a "fair amount" of strain as compared with 29 percent of the caregivers and 39 percent of the sisters.

Most of the principal caregivers and both groups of local siblings reported many parent care uplifts. For instance, 79 percent of principal caregivers, 90 percent of local sisters, and 83 percent of local brothers felt that their sibling(s) were dependable about helping their mother. Similarly, over 85 percent of each group (85 percent, 93 percent, and 87 percent, respectively) said their siblings understood the effort they make in helping their mother.

There were, however, some significant differences between the groups of local children. Sisters experienced more uplifts and felt more benefited by those uplifts than the caregivers. In particular, the sisters were the ones who felt uplifted when permitted to share decisions about the mother. While large proportions of caregivers experienced uplifts, many of those uplifts were the obverse of the hassles they had expressed--specifically, they missed social support from their siblings when it was not forthcoming and felt uplifted when it was. Less than both groups of siblings, these caregivers felt uplifted when siblings visited, phoned, or offered to help without being asked.

When the hassles and uplifts were factor analyzed, two hassles factors and one uplifts factor emerged for the principal caregivers and the same number for their siblings. These factors were labeled "nonfeasance," "malfeasance," and "uplifts," and proved to be a useful analytic tool for understanding the nature of the siblings' parent-care interactions.

For the caregivers, the nonfeasance factor was first to emerge. As the label suggests, it is composed of items indicating complaints that their siblings do not do enough things such as visiting, calling, helping in general, doing a "fair share," and showing an interest in their mother. The malfeasance factor comprises items describing more active negative behaviors by the siblings, such as criticizing the caregiver or trying to make her feel guilty. In the third, or uplifts factor, the caregiver felt uplifted primarily by items indicating that she received emotional and moral support from siblings, had a sympathetic listener to whom she could talk frankly, and the sense that she could rely on a sibling if help should be needed.

The malfeasance and nonfeasance factors of the local siblings contain most of the same items plus several more. The factors emerged in the reverse order, however, indicating that nonfeasance was more salient to caregivers and malfeasance to the siblings. The siblings felt uplifted by all of the emotional support variables appearing in the caregivers' uplifts factors and, in addition, they appreciated

19

the approval of their siblings and the willingness to share decisions with them.

Thus, the study identified some of the repercussions on adult siblings other than the principal caregiver and on the relationships among siblings when confronted with parent care responsibilities. Not only the daughters who were the principal caregivers, but also their local brothers and sisters participated in care (though not to the same extent as the main caregivers) and experienced strains in varying degrees (again to a lesser extent). Although the sibling interaction was often problematic, it also often was supportive and positive.

The reports of the local siblings confirm, from their perspective, what has been reported in previous research only from the perspective of the primary caregivers. Specifically, the adult daughter who becomes the main caregiver provides the bulk of care, while her siblings provide significantly less help. It is not surprising, therefore, that those daughters experienced the most negative effects in terms of many emotional symptoms, interference with lifestyle, overall strain, and deterioration of their physical health as compared with their local sisters and brothers.

The caregivers were candid in expressing resentment about their siblings' doing less parent care than they were. They were the ones most hassled by siblings' failure to give them emotional support or to meet certain parent-care responsibilities (nonfeasance) and when the siblings evidenced more active negative behaviors such as being critical of the caregivers' efforts (malfeasance). On the other hand, the caregivers were "uplifted" when siblings did give them emotional support and understood their efforts, indicating the importance to them of such social support. It is of special interest that the intersibling interactions caused the local sisters to be as hassled and to experience as much strain from the relationships as the principal caregivers.

The caregivers' local brothers clearly were the group who provided the least instrumental help and emotional support to the elderly mother. That financial help was an exception to this pattern of the men doing less is, of course, consistent with the ways in which males and females are socialized to their expected roles in life. The brothers also were the ones whose emotional and physical health were least negatively affected by their parent-care activities, who experienced the least strain, and who were the least hassled by intersibling interactions about parent care.

The local sisters of the principal caregivers are a particularly interesting group. They provided considerably less help than the caregivers, but more than the brothers, and also fell in between the other two groups in reporting overall strain and specific negative emotional and physical consequences of caregiving. As stated above, they equaled the principal caregivers in reporting strain from and in being hassled by the intersibling interactions. The sisters appeared to be particularly sensitive to any implication that they were not meeting their parent-care responsibilities. They, much more than the caregivers and brothers, complained that a sibling had tried to make them feel guilty for not helping more or had tried to have the elderly mother appreciate their siblings' contributions to parent care more than their own efforts. But they were particularly appreciative when included in decisions about the mother's care. The salience of uplifts to the sisters emerge as well in their sense of overall uplift from positive interactions with their siblings.

It was also the local sisters who felt guilty about more matters than the caregivers or the brothers. They were the ones who more often than the caregivers felt guilty about not doing more for their mothers, and who most often wished they weren't so busy so that they could do more. They joined the caregiver in feeling guilty more often than the brothers when they became angry with the mothers, and they joined the brothers in feeling guilty more often because they were doing less parent care than the principal caregiver.

The overall feeling conveyed by the data is the discomfort of the local sisters, but not the brothers, about being in the role of secondary caregiver, even though in reality they provided more help than did those brothers. Aware that they were doing less than the caregivers, the sisters were appreciative when their efforts were recognized and approved.

The caregivers describe their intersibling hassles:

Family 10. My sister took mother for a period of time but felt very resentful about it. We were not communicating very well.

Family 11. I'm not satisfied with the amount of help they give Mother. They take her for weekends but have to be reminded that she sat home for some weekends in a row. With eight of us, it shouldn't be that way.

Family 12. My brother and sister used to help, but when Mother moved in with us they considered the problem solved.

Family 13. My mother is critical and demanding and gives us a hard time. But when by brother visits, she's a different person.

Family 14. My sister stopped coming to see my mother for 2 years. I'm almost 70. I couldn't take it any more. So we placed Mom in a nursing home. Somehow my sister heard about it and went and took her out.

21

Sometimes the parent-care responsibilities are genuinely shared.

The G Family. When the mother had a heart attack and the disabled father went to a nursing home, Mrs. G's brother went back and forth several times. At a family conference, it was arranged that the elderly couple would move to an apartment in Philadelphia. A brother-in-law and a friend went to Chicago to do the packing and help manage the move. The brother is very supportive and appreciative. He visits three or four times a year so the Gs can go away for a week, and he calls every week.

Family 18. My sister and I both work. We really tried to share the responsibilities of my mother and we still share them. We are better at doing different things. I'm better at talking to the staff at the nursing home and getting mother's needs met because I'm more assertive. My sister was much better at filling out all the forms at the nursing home. We really try to share. There is no resentment that one does more than the other. If there was a difficulty, if one wasn't satisfied or something, we would just talk about it.

Family 19. There had been a number of years early when my mother was a widow that my sister lived close by and had taken more responsibility than we had. Without talking about it with great explicitness we sort of agreed it was our turn to have the responsibility and that was fine.

Geographically Distant Children

Though there has been considerable attention recently to older people's geographically distant children, their experiences remain relatively unexamined by research. The thrust of social and demographic change undoubtedly will render distant children increasingly significant in the lives of elderly parents. Not only do today's elderly have fewer descendants upon whom to rely for help than used to be the case, but more of the children of future cohorts of the elderly may live at a geographic distance. The trend today is toward greater rather than less residential separation between older parents and children (Treas and Bengtson 1982). While in most cases it is children who move away from parents, the elderly themselves are migrating in increasing numbers. Longino et al. (1984) noted that over the past decade, there was a 54-percent increase in the number of Americans of retirement age who migrated from State to State. It is therefore important to gain some understanding of the problems and perspectives of caregivers' siblings who are geographically distant and there-

22

fore functionally limited in their ability to provide regular and sustained instrumental support to an aged, impaired parent.

The questionnaire mailed to geographically distant children in the PGC study compared male and female distant siblings on their attitudes toward the mother's need for help, the amount of help they provide to and their social contact with the mother, the effects of the caregiving situation on them and their families, and their reports of intersibling problems and uplifts related to the mother's care. In addition, their opinions on the specific problems of such caregiving situations were elicited by means of open-ended questions. (See Schoonover et al. 1988 for complete report.)

Some significant differences emerged between geographically distant sons and daughters. Daughters were more likely than sons to express feelings of guilt about the mother's situation—in particular, about not doing enough for the mother and the fact that a sibling was doing more, about living far away, and about getting angry or losing patience with the mother at times. The daughters were also more likely to express the desire to spend more time with the mother, and to want to live closer so that they could provide more help.

While these geographically distant daughters were more likely than sons to express such reservations about the adequacy of the help and attention they gave the parent, most felt that their mother was receiving the assistance that was necessary. About 20 percent felt that the mother would receive better care if they lived close to her, however, and 30 percent thought that they would be the ones to provide the most help if that were the case.

No significant differences emerged between the sons and daughters regarding the amount of help they provided to and their social interaction with the mothers. Sixty percent of the sample said they helped their mothers only "a little." Financial support provided by the distant siblings was very modest, with approximately 90 percent contributing less than $10.00 per month to their mother's living expenses and care. Two-fifths of these children visited their mothers several times a year, and 38 percent did so once a year or less; approximately 11 percent saw the mother once or twice a month. About a third of the sample called their mothers once or twice a week, another third did so once or twice a month, and the final third phoned several times a year.

The daughters more frequently reported certain negative emotional effects of the caregiving situation such as feeling helpless, drained, overwhelmed, and having difficulty in setting priorities. They also reported higher levels of strain deriving from the mother's situation and from living far away from her.

The majority (80 percent) of the total group of distant siblings reported no interferences in family finances or activities caused by the mother's situation. More than half sometimes felt helpless and nervous about the mother's need for help, about three-fifths reported frustration, about a third reported feeling depressed and drained, and about one-quarter reported feeling overwhelmed, tired, and pulled in different directions by the mother's need for help.

Relatively small percentages of these distant siblings experienced intersibling hassles. Overall, about 20 percent of the sample reported at least some strain deriving from intersibling problems, but the sisters were more likely than brothers to report strain caused by the "hassles" that did occur. Similarly, the sisters of caregivers were more likely than brothers to respond that a sibling had complained of doing more for the mother than they had, and to report that a sibling had not understood how much help the mother needs. Approximately 15 percent reported that a sibling tried to make them feel guilty about not doing more, had not done his or her fair share, and about 20 percent of the sample said that a sibling had criticized what they did to help the mother, had complained of doing more, had not visited the mother enough, and did not understand how much help the mother needs. The intersibling hassle most frequently reported was that one-third said a sibling thought he or she knew better what was best for the mother.

In terms of "uplifts," fairly large percentages responded favorably as to the social and emotional support provided by their siblings, and there were no significant group differences. Between two-thirds and four-fifths of the sample said that a sibling had been really dependable about helping when needed, had made them feel that they could talk about their feelings, had visited and called the mother as often as they should, had given them moral support, had been there when they needed them, and had understood the effort the distant sibling made to help the mother. Overall, four-fifths felt that the uplifts from siblings were helpful.

Almost all of the distant children responded to an open-ended question concerning what they felt were the main problems or concerns facing an adult child who lives at some distance from an impaired parent needing help. The responses of the male and female siblings were similar and certain themes recurred in their answers. These were their inability to respond to the mother's needs in a timely fashion or on a regular basis because of family obligations and/or financial restraints; feeling cut off and left out of decisionmaking and uninformed as to the mother's day-to-day conditions; feelings of guilt for not being able to do more or to relieve the sibling providing the help; and the competing demands of their own families and careers. The daughters wrote:

I feel sad and guilty both for my mother and my sister's always being 'on call'; I worry about being unable to get there on time when needed, and I worry a lot about responsibilities of my own here and the stress of not being able to accept a commitment that might be interrupted, or unfulfilled, should I be needed at my mother's side. . .

It takes a major effort to visit her, particularly as my children get older. These visits are usually instead of a family vacation. When she is here, we give up our room, as space is limited, and arrange our lives around her. All of this puts a strain on my family and I feel guilty that I can't please them or help mother enough.

The major problem is not being able to provide help, and not being sure what is really wrong or what is taking place. I never really am able to feel secure about my mother.

Sons expressed similar sentiments:

Major problems are finding ways to provide something like a fair share of the help while living at a distance; feeling that I have little right to assert my views of her needs because others are providing most of the care. There is little sense of a sustained relationship that makes a large difference toward her comfort instead of a periodic one that makes little difference on the whole. . .

. . .not being able to visit or invite her on a regular basis; helping to make financial decisions when she is not able to do this; the feeling of being almost helpless when certain situations arise.

Other themes emerged in response to a question about what they felt were the main problems among siblings when an elderly parent needs help. These were the equitable sharing of responsibility among siblings, problems with communication, disagreements over the mother's needs and care, and, for some, unresolved sibling rivalries:

Her care is unlikely to be equally shared, which leads to guilt and resentment. Children may have different ideas about what is most important in her care and how she should be treated; those who are not primarily caretakers have little voice in what happens to her. (daughter)

Problems with siblings and rivalry come up with conflicts over who does more for mother. This creates tension and often hostility and resentment; jealousies emerge. (daughter)

The problem is finding ways to work out an equitable sharing of the help so that old family patterns are not simply reinforced;

25

also, coping with the ways in which different values or different senses of mother's real needs can create tension and distance rather than cooperation and closeness. (son)

The main problems are the unequal degrees to which siblings help (or are perceived to help), the differing extents to which siblings are able to help, and indifference on the part of some siblings. (son)

The distant siblings were also asked if there were any other ways in which the mother's needs affected them and their families. Both sisters and brothers described arrangements whereby they attempted to participate in and relieve their sister's caregiving burden, as well as the ways in which these arrangements affected their and their families' lives. In addition, some described the effects of their parent's condition on their own children. For example:

I have developed a pattern of making visits to relieve my sister and brother-in-law several times a year. That is, I take over for a few days and let them get away. This has been very beneficial to me as well as to them. (son)

We do feel responsible for emotional support and for frequent visits; these visits are wrenching and a strain for the whole family. My children have a pessimistic view of aging and the terrible changes it works on people they love. We often feel caught between the needs of helpless parents and siblings who take the major burden. We feel guilty about taking vacation time for ourselves. Our jobs are often stressful and we need time for ourselves. It's horrible to see people you love lose so much of their personality and dignity. (daughter)

Finally, the siblings were asked if they had any advice to offer others who are in, or anticipate being in, their situations. The dominant themes emerging for both sons and daughters focused on planning, communication and cooperation, and flexibility among siblings:

Set it up front what is to be shared and include the older person, then all will know what was said. Remember, what you wanted to do in 1976 you may not want to do in 1984. Also, have all meet with the doctor so all hear the same story. (daughter)

Be prepared! Understand well in advance what might happen. Attend any and all information meetings, seminars, whatever, concerning older parents and their effects on children. (daughter)

Talk to each other. Try to state needs and limits clearly and without placing blame. (daughter)

Obtain agreement in advance between siblings as to the sharing of responsibilities. (son)

Be patient, sympathetic, and permissive towards the other members of the family in terms of their reactions and emotional needs. (son)

The responses of the geographically distant children in this sample reinforce other research (Marshall and Rosenthal 1985; Mercier et al. 1987; Shanas 1973) documenting the persistence and durability of emotional bonds between parents and their adult children despite the barrier of geographic distance. Indeed, the data attest to the high level of interest and affective solidarity on the part of both the distant sons and daughters. It is apparent that emotional bonds linking elderly parents and their adult offspring transcend geographic distance, though the degree of social interaction and nature of help they provide is necessarily different from that of proximate siblings.

The personal insights volunteered by the distant siblings testify to the far-reaching nature of parent-care responsibilities, both geographically and in terms of the family system itself. Despite living far away, both the sons and daughters reported emotional strains and worries, as well as disruptions to their own family lives because of the mothe.'s situation. At the same time, both the sons and daughters cited problems with their siblings deriving from the mother's need for help. While the results of this and other research are evidence that family bonds endure, it is obvious that such ties may transmit intrafamily tensions as well, particularly when a family crisis, such as a parent requiring help, revives longstanding or dormant family conflicts.

It should be remembered that all of the adult children in this study had a sister who lived close to their disabled mother and was the primary caregiver. Undoubtedly, distant children whose parents do not have a proximate adult child experience more pressing and distressing problems. Nonetheless, the study, though small, illuminates the enduring bonds between elderly parents and their distant children, as well as the nature of the problems these offspring experience.

Who Becomes "Principal Caregiver"?

Data from the survey cast some light on how, from among the various children in the family, the caregiver had been "elected" to that role. Caregivers were asked: "Thinking about the help your mother required as she grew older, what would you say is the main reason the chief responsibility for seeing to her needs fell on you?" More than half the caregivers offered one of three reasons: geographic proximity (23.5 percent); she felt responsible and volunteered or felt better able

27

to provide the care (16.3 percent); or gender or birth-order (14.3 percent) dictated her role. Only slightly more than 8 percent of the daughters were already sharing their homes with the mothers when the latter began to need care. An equal proportion attributed their role to having more appropriate housing, money, or time than her siblings. Small percentages noted reasons such as the mother's preference, work-related factors, or emotional closeness to the mother.

Of those caregivers whose mothers shared their households, the largest group stated that the mother had moved in because she had become disabled. Others cited reasons such as the mother's loneliness or her financial inability to live alone.

> *The C Family*. Mrs. C is the youngest of six siblings. They strongly advised Mrs. C against moving the mother into her home (they knew what she was like), but she did so anyway. Once, when Mrs. C was on the verge of a breakdown, her sister took the mother. After a couple of weeks, the brother-in-law put the elderly woman in a taxi and sent her back to the C's home. When Mrs. C did have a breakdown, her older sister said firmly, "This is the end of the road. Mom must go to a nursing home."

> *Family 15*. After my mother retired it just happened that I made the offer for my mother to come and live with us, and I became the principal caregiver. I don't know if my sister would have made the offer or not. It really didn't enter into my decision.

> *Family 16*. Maybe mother chose to live with me because growing up she and I got along the best of the four children.

> *The A Family*. I didn't mind being the principal caregiver. My other sisters and my mother never got along. I never faulted them. One of my sisters was never a giver and that was all right. My other sister was willing but couldn't manage mother.

> *Family 17*. She is my mother and she's got sensitivity and she cares. She cares about me, nobody else, just me. Maybe my brothers but not so much because they aren't with her. Anybody else could do the same things that I do for my mother, but it wouldn't be the same and it wouldn't satisfy her. I've taken care of her that many years.

Mothers and Daughters

The subject of mother/daughter relationships is enormous and could not be dealt with comprehensively here, even if it were fully understood. However, two aspects of those relationships will be mentioned that stood out in the PGC studies: the gender differences in the reactions of sons and daughters to the caregiving situations, and the struggle for control between the elderly mother and the daughter who was her principal caregiver.

Gender differences occur consistently in comparisons of strains experienced by sons and daughters of the disabled elderly, with the women almost invariably experiencing more strains. Such gender differences have been found in comparisons of sons and daughters who were primary caregivers (Horowitz 1985b). In the PGC study, those gender differences appeared in the comparison of geographically distant sons and daughters (Schoonover et al. 1988) and in the comparison of sons and daughters who live proximate to the mother (Brody et al. 1988).

It is suggested here that the fundamental reason that daughters experience more strain than sons is that it is women on whom the demand is made to fulfill the role of family nurturer. Socialization to that role begins early in childhood (See Cohler and Grunebaum 1981). Women, therefore, have expectations of themselves in the caregiving role that often are not or cannot be achieved. They are painfully aware of a disparity between what they actually are doing and what they feel they should do, a disparity that exacerbates their emotional strains and often leads to guilt (Brody 1985). Even being the principal caregivers who do far more than the other siblings does not exempt many such daughters from guilt.

Whatever the experiences and roles of other family members, however, it is clear that the daughter who is the primary caregiver does the most, experiences the most stress, and is the one most "in the middle." Understanding her inner experience of parent care is unfinished business on the research/clinical agenda, as is understanding the older person's inner experience of becoming dependent.

A theme that appeared again and again and speaks to the tension between mother and daughter focused on the struggle between them for control of the caregiving situation. This struggle for power is inherent to a lesser or greater degree in all helping relationships. It underlines the difficulties involved in the shift in the balance of dependence/independence that occurs when the disabled mother receives help from the daughter. Each expects to be in control. The elderly mother wants her care provided in ways that permit her to control the situation in accordance with her own preferences and the continuation of her lifestyle. For her part, the daughter feels that, since she is the one doing the various tasks and the caregiving is arduous, she has the right to do it her way and in a manner that fits in with her lifestyle and other responsibilities. And, at some level, both women expect their roles to be reversed–that the daughter

29

should care for the mother as completely as the mother had cared for the daughter as a young child (see Brody 1985*b* for fuller discussion).

The daughters' voices are heard here, but a glimpse is provided of the feelings and experiences of the elderly mothers as well.

The C Family. The mother had always been a difficult woman. But when her father was on his deathbed, he extracted a promise from Mrs. C that she would always take care of "Mommy." "I thought it would be role-reversal, but she fights everything I do."

Family 20. It's so different now. I look at my mother in a certain way. It's hard to cope with when she's childish. I'm the disciplinarian now, but she's still my mother. My mother is a different person now from the mother I knew.

The A Family. She fought getting into bed. I tried to encourage her to go the bathroom like the book says, but she wouldn't listen. Toward the end, she refused to sit on the toilet. It was a fight every night to get her to go to bed. At night I would give her the capsule. But then I realized she wasn't taking them. She was hiding them in the bed.

Family 21. She has always felt that she knows best. That control thing—she is the mother and I am the child. I can never do anything right. She was used to being the mother. Now it's turned around the other way. She can't accept it. She just wouldn't stop telling me what to do. A lot of mothers are that way. They won't let go.

Family 22. No matter what I do, it isn't enough or it isn't right. When I wash her feet, I sort of automatically begin with her (the mother's) left foot. She gets angry and criticizes me. She wants me to do her right foot first.

There are, of course, situations in which mother and daughter are considerate of each other, discuss issues openly, and sustain the good relationships they have always enjoyed.

The G Family. Now Mrs. G (the elderly mother) is often seriously ill. She stays in her room a lot to give the Gs privacy. She is very grateful for the care the family provides and is very supportive of Mrs. G. The daughter says, "I take care of Mother because I can give her better care (than a nursing home) and I love her. She knows that if she needs 24-hour care and we can't provide it, she may have to go into a nursing home. It's no big secret. We discuss it all with her."

Though the vast majority of adult children are well motivated, their attempts to take over may be resisted and resented by the parent.

Caregiving of a parent means assuming a new role, for which the daughter's major prior rehearsal was having cared for her own children. Then she was in control; it was her parental prerogative to be the decisionmaker. The situation is further compounded because the older person also has a new and unrehearsed role. Though now disabled and dependent on the adult child, psychologically the elderly mother is still parent to the child she had parented and controlled. Being expected to become child to one's child adds insult to the injury of becoming disabled and losing autonomy. An additional frustration for the parent may be remnants of the unresolved but inevitable loss of control over the child. At the same time, the daughter may have vestiges of her own ambivalent struggle toward independence.

Yet, on some level, the daughter also feels that she should provide care the way the parent wants it. She therefore feels guilty if she becomes angry, even when the mother is demanding, controlling, or critical—the more so because the old person, being disabled, is seen as helpless, pitiable, and, therefore, deserving of patience and kindness.

To the extent that the parent is compliant and grateful and the daughter is sensitive to the parent's need to be involved in decisions, things may go smoothly (the G family). The struggle for control may be exacerbated when the older person has Alzheimer's disease (the A family). Now, the caregiver must protect the parent and insist on doing things to ensure that parent's very survival. The mother, for her part, is struggling against the devastation and panic of losing control—the erosion of her autonomy. Determining the points at which various decisions must be transferred from patient to caregiver is a delicate matter.

The Family as a Whole

The complexities of viewing caregiving with a wide-angle lens cannot be overemphasized. Looking at different family members separately with tunnel-vision focus does not illuminate the complex manner in which various sets of relationships are layered and intricately interwoven. The family situation also interacts with the socioeconomic context and the service environment in which caregiving occurs, a context that plays a major role in determining how care is provided and the mental health effects on family members.

To illustrate the multidimensional nature of caregiving situations, three case summaries are presented. They are a "best case" scenario, a "worst case" scenario, and a narrative that depicts the long process of caring for an Alzheimer's patient. The reader is reminded that embedded in these case descriptions are vignettes that have already been used to illustrate sons-in-law, grandchildren, siblings, or mother/daughter relationships. Those excerpts appear in *italics*. Factors relating to formal services and the socioeconomic context of caregiving are highlighted in CAPITAL LETTERS.

The Green Family.   Mr. and Mrs. Green have three children and several grandchildren. Mrs. Green's parents, Mr. and Mrs. Harris, lived in Chicago until 11 years ago. When the mother had a heart attack and the disabled father went to a nursing home, *Mrs. Green's brother went back and forth from his home in Detroit several times. At a family conference, it was arranged that the elderly couple would move to an apartment in Philadelphia.* Mr. and Mrs. Green both went out to Chicago to get them. *A brother-in-law and a friend went to Chicago to do the packing and to help manage the move.* A granddaughter did all the unpacking and arranged the Harris' furniture to get things ready for them in their new home while they were driven to Philadelphia by the Greens.

During the next 3 years, *Mr. Green stopped in every day to check on the old people. "He did even more than I did," said Mrs. Green.* She and her daughter did all the housekeeping and a VISITING NURSE CAME ONCE WEEKLY. Then both the Harrisses began a series of hospitalizations, including several surgeries. When Mrs. Harris was in the hospital, *her husband stayed with the Greens. When Mr. Harris was hospitalized, the granddaughter stayed with her. Finally Mr. Green said "Why don't you move in?" They had deliberately planned their home to accommodate the older people.* "We knew it would happen sooner or later." *A niece and nephew helped with the move.* THERE WAS NO FINANCIAL STRAIN BECAUSE THE HARRISES HAD ENOUGH MONEY TO SUPPORT THEMSELVES, AND THE GREENS WERE WELL OFF.

The elderly couple continued to be in and out of the hospital. When the father was incontinent and comatose, Mrs. Green took him back to her home and cared for him. She arranged PHYSICAL THERAPY, HOMEMAKER SERVICE, A VISITING NURSE, AND GOT ALL THE EQUIPMENT. He improved amazingly and was cared for in that way until his death 5 years ago. *Now Mrs. Harris is often seriously ill. She stays in her room a lot to give the Greens privacy. She is very grateful for the care the family provides and is very supportive of Mrs. Green.* The daughter says, "I take care of Mother because I can give her better care (than in a nursing home) and I love her. *She knows that if she needs 24-hour care and we can't provide it, she may have to* go into a nursing home. It's no big secret. We discuss it all with her."

MRS. GREEN HAD GIVEN UP WORK WHEN SHE HAD CHIL-DREN. "Back then you did what your husband wanted you to do." She went back to work part-time later. "I enjoyed it, it was supplementary income, and the children were proud that I did something besides just being a mother. I was still there for them and could be home." After her parents moved to Philadelphia, Mrs. Green did not return to work. "I felt I was investing my time in them."

Mrs. Green says *"My children have really helped. When I was sick, my eldest daughter took care of things. My youngest daughter would stay with my parents so that we could go out to a movie. Our middle daughter sometimes stays with Mother. My brother is very supportive and appreciative. He visits three or four times a year so we can go away for a week, and he calls every week.* His daughters visit and call. Even my husband's family is supportive. My husband is a saint, and I try not to slight him. We are very close. *Our relationship has not been affected because it was established long before. We have had our ups and downs, but we have weathered it."*

Mrs. Green occasionally feels fatigue, frustration, or being pulled in different directions. She feels it's very important to know what you can and can't do where your parents are concerned. "A lot of it has to do with personality. It's an individual matter. If everyone was complaining it would have been different. I am very lucky." She adds wistfully, "The only thing is, we are missing out on the Empty Nest syndrome."

The Carter Family. For Mrs. Carter, it started with her "doing food shopping, visiting, doctors, laundry," etc., for her parents. Her father was "definitely senile," so could not drive a car. Once in a while a sister would help, but not very often. When her father was on his death bed, he extracted a promise from Mrs. Carter that she would always take care of "Mommy." "I would have died for Daddy," Mrs. Carter says. The mother had always been a very difficult woman. *The other siblings strongly advised Mrs. Carter against moving the mother into her home (they knew what she was like), but she did so anyway.*

Mrs. Carter is the youngest of six siblings. *Now married for the second time, she has two teenage children from the first marriage and a 5-year-old and a 7-year-old from the second. When Mr. and Mrs. Carter married, they agreed that she would not work.* Mrs. Carter says she had a dream—"I guess everyone

33

has a dream." Hers was to be a "regular" mother. *She felt she had neglected her older children because she had to work.* But the ELDERLY MOTHER'S CARE STRAINS THE FAMILY'S FINANCES BECAUSE SHE MUST HAVE A DIABETIC DIET AND HER INSULIN IS EXPENSIVE. MR CARTER BEGAN TO WORK OVERTIME TO PAY FOR THESE THINGS. FINALLY, HE TOLD HIS WIFE RELUCTANTLY, "YOU'LL HAVE TO GO TO WORK. WE'RE DROWNING. WE COULD LOSE THE HOUSE."

Mrs. Carter worked on the afternoon-evening shift as a waitress so that *the younger chi¹dren could be cared for by the older children after school. The teenagers cared for their grandmother as well, but they complained of all the responsibility. They had no time of their own. "It isn't fair," they said.*

Mrs. C said *"My first husband took no responsibility. I would beg my husband and say we had to do something with Mom. He would just go and have another drink. Mr. C (caregiver's second husband) began to work overtime to pay for these things (the elderly mother's needs). My husband did not ask me to remove my mother from our home. Some day (resignedly), "I'll have his mother here. I know it."*

When the elderly woman moved into the Carter home, she made the daughter "nuts." At times she was "shuffled around" among the sisters, but they wouldn't keep her. One sister refused to have anything to do with the situation.

Someone has to be in the same room with her almost all of the time. You had to leave the door open when taking a bath. The elderly woman presents extraordinary difficulties that have been getting worse. The whole family eats diabetic food because she ferrets out and gobbles up anything with sugar in it. She embarrasses her daughter in the supermarket by grabbing sweet things off the shelves, stuffing them into her mouth and telling the other shoppers that Mrs. Carter starves her. *If the children or the Carters bring friends to the house, she is nasty to them, so there are no more visitors. She has turned night into day. If they shut their bedroom door, she bangs on it. Twice, she went out of the house at night and laid down in the roadway.* "We are lucky she wasn't run over," says Mrs. Carter.

The older children can't even bring friends home because the behavior of the elderly woman is disruptive and embarrassing. The teenage granddaughter begged for a high school graduation party. She had never had a party before. Mrs. Carter agreed and planned to send her mother to another daughter's house. But the mother, in order to thwart the plan, pulled "one of her little tricks." She only pretended to take her insulin for several days before the party and went into shock. There was no party. *The girl is now receiving psychiatric care.*

AT ONE TIME, THE STATE SOCIAL WORKER FOUND A DOMICILIARY CARE HOME, BUT THE MOTHER GAVE THEM A TERRIBLE TIME. "SHE WOULD RUN AWAY JUST LIKE SHE DID HERE, BUT THEY WEREN'T USED TO CALLING THE STATE POLICE TO LOOK FOR HER. THEY SAID THEY COULDN'T DEAL WITH IT." The sisters tried to have her with them, but she caused so much trouble they would bring her back to Mrs. Carter. Mr. Carter started not coming home. "He deserted us mentally. He tuned out."

Once, when Mrs. Carter was on the verge of a breakdown, her sister took the mother. After a couple of weeks, the brother-in-law put the elderly woman in a taxi and sent her back to the Carters.

Mr. Carter did not urge removal of his mother-in-law from the home. "Some day," says Mrs. Carter resignedly, "I'll have his mother here. I know it." Finally, Mrs. Carter did break down and needed psychiatric care. *Her older sister said fu nly, "This is the end of the road. Mom must go to a nursing home."* BUT IT WAS MANY LONG MONTHS BEFORE A MEDICAID BED COULD BE FOUND. Mommy is now in a nursing home. Mrs. Carter says "It's better without her. It's being able to go to the bathroom and take a shower. It's not having the TV on full blast all day and all night." But she adds despondently, "I think Daddy is looking down and is angry with me. But it ruined my life. I can understand why two of my sisters don't see Mom at all."

The Anthony Family. Mrs. Anthony is now 64 years old. Her caregiving career has lasted many years. She took care of her mother for more than 6 years before the older woman entered a nursing home. Before that, she had helped to take care of her father.

"I guess we didn't notice a lot of things while my Dad was alive. Soon after he died, the first symptom we noticed was that she (the elderly mother) didn't know the time. I was working full-time and I'd ask her to meet me at a certain time and she wouldn't be there. I'd come home and find her and she would say she waited for me all afternoon. She had no idea what time it was. She would try to go to the bank on Sunday morning or she would pay the same bills three times. We would stop by her house every day. She would come and stay the night with us and in the morning she would be gone.

Then one of my mother's neighbors called and said she was

going out of the house at 2:00 a.m. She came back, but the neighbor was frightened for her. I knew she was going around to the grocery to check what time it was. She wasn't afraid. She'd go out and come right back. When we went to visit our children in Columbus or Washington, we would take her with us. When she came back, she couldn't remember where she had been.

I was beside myself because I didn't know what to do with her. I didn't know which way to turn. I SAW AN AD IN THE PAPER ABOUT A MEETING TO HELP PEOPLE DEALING WITH THE ELDERLY. BUT I COULDN'T ATTEND THE MEETING BECAUSE I WAS WORKING FULL-TIME. BUT WHEN I CALLED, THEY SUGGESTED THAT WE GO TO A CLINIC THAT DIAGNOSED PEOPLE LIKE MY MOTHER. SO I DECIDED WE WOULD GO THERE. RIGHT AROUND THIS TIME, I WENT PART-TIME IN MY JOB. IT WAS A VERY STRESSFUL TIME–WORKING FULL-TIME AND DEALING WITH HER, GOING BACK AND FORTH. I TOLD MY HUSBAND I COULDN'T HANDLE EVERYTHING, SO I WENT PART-TIME.

Between my job, my mother, and my husband, I was going baloney. So I went part-time. I always enjoyed my work. It was an interesting job, a nice job and very well paid. I think if it hadn't been for my mother, I would have stayed full-time. But that was the last straw. The work was very important. I enjoyed it. I just couldn't take it all–work, mother, and husband. I thought I would explode. Before I reduced my hours, I thought of my work as a career. I really enjoyed it and was good at it. Now that I work part-time, it is just a job.

WE WENT TO THE CLINIC. She was really confused. They were very lovely. They diagnosed her. Physically she was in good shape. My husband and I went to the final evaluation. It was Alzheimer's disease. They said she wouldn't get any better. They don't call it senility anymore. They ruled out all physical problems.

She stayed with us more and more after that. *She was up all night, we weren't sleeping, it was terrible. My husband was working then. I was between the two of them.* He would ask her if she was going to go to bed sometime today. I would try to calm him down, because he had to go to work and was trying to handle her. She wouldn't do what you told her. That was very difficult, because I was in between there, and then it got bad.

I asked my sister in Chicago, who wasn't working, if she could take her. She said she could take her for 2 months. We put her on the plane. After 3 weeks, my sister couldn't wait to get her on the plane to get her back to us.

PRIOR TO THIS WAS OUR FIRST EPISODE WITH THE

POLICE. We came home from work and she wasn't there. She used to stay with us, though she still had her own house. When we got home, all the lights were out and the doors were wide open, but she wasn't home. We went to her house, but it was dark, so she didn't go home. I said to my husband that I bet the police have her. She probably got confused and started walking. They sort of regress to previous years. Maybe she went back to when she walked to my other house and helped me when my children were babies. I called the police. They had found her, but she couldn't remember where she lived. She showed them. But she didn't have a key. So they took her to a neighbor. When I called the police, they knew what I wanted and where she was. So we went and got her.

That did it. I called my sister in Chicago and asked her to take her until we could catch our breath. I was frightened and exhausted. We weren't sleeping, and I had the tension between my husband and my mother. It was right around then that we decided she couldn't be by herself. That's what they told me at the clinic. We couldn't leave her all day because it was dangerous. We didn't know what to do.

THE DOCTOR SUGGESTED A DAY CARE CENTER AT A NURSING HOME. So that is what we decided to do. She couldn't be left alone. Otherwise, we would have to come home to an empty house and the fright. SO WE APPLIED FOR DAY CARE, BUT WE HAD TO WAIT A FEW WEEKS BEFORE SHE COULD START. I was still working part-time. We got someone to babysit on the days I worked. But my mother was very bad, and the woman quit. We still had one more week before my mother could start day care. So my brother and sister-in-law (my husband's brother) took her for the days I worked. They just did this for 1 week.

THEN SHE STARTED DAY CARE. She gave them a run-around. They told me she needed some medication. The doctor prescribed some medicine, Haldar. All the medicine did was make her doze. When she was awake, she was still the same. It didn't change her. I told the doctor that one of us needed a prescription. So the doctor tried one medication for the day and one for the night. That worked. *She fought getting in bed*. It quieted her and made it so that at least we could exist. It helped when she was at the day care—before, she had been very bad and uncooperative. That continued for awhile.

My mother had two more trips to Chicago. One time she visited my other sister and another time I went with her. At least it was a different set of walls.

We tried and gave it our best. I was very afraid they were going to put her out of the day care. They were really good.

Then she started to be incontinent. *I tried to encourage her to go to the bathroom like the books say, but she wouldn't listen.* I spent my days worrying about the fact she wasn't going to the bathroom. Another time, my mother told me not to call her Mother because I wasn't her mother. So I started calling her Mary. *I tried to get her to go to the bathroom, but she refused and* invariably would wet the carpet. *Toward the end she refused to sit on the toilet.* That was a continuing stress. I was always worried. At the end I was just satisfied if she would stay in her room. *It was a fight every night to get her to go to bed.* Sometimes she wouldn't, and I would blow up. That went on for awhile. I counted it good if I could get her to her room.

She was still supposedly taking the medicine. *At night I would give her her capsule. But then I realized she wasn't taking them.* She was hiding them in the bed. THE WOMAN AT THE DAY CARE SUGGESTED I PUT THE MEDICATION IN A COOKIE. I TRIED IT AND IT SEEMED TO WORK.

One time we went on a short trip and I fought with her all day to get her to go the bathroom. I was going bananas. In a restaurant, I finally got her into a stall, but she wet herself. She was soaked. I had a change of clothes with me, but then she fought me when I tried to help her change. It was a hassle. She also refused to bathe. But they wouldn't keep her at day care unless she was clean. WE GOT A HOME HEALTH AIDE. One time she cooperated, but never again. She couldn't understand. That was the big problem–lack of communication. So the home health aide didn't work out. Every time I tried to give her a bath, my stomach would turn over. At the end, my husband had to pick her up and carry her to the tub. This was horrible. Every week we had to go through this.

I was off the wall. I was never myself. I was never me. I was always concerned with her. Our whole lives revolved around her. If she had a decent day, we had one too. At the end, we couldn't take her out. At the shopping center she wouldn't stay with us. She would take off. It was bad. I was getting to the point where I didn't know what to do. I was concerned that they were going to say no more day care, but they didn't complain.

I DIDN'T CARE WHAT HAPPENED THE REST OF THE WEEK IF WE COULD GET HER IN SHAPE FOR THE DAY CARE. THAT WAS WHAT WE REVOLVED AROUND. At the end, it was a real fight to get her clothes off for bed, and my husband had to hold her.

MY SISTERS MUST WORK FOR A LIVING. My mother visited several times with my sister in Chicago. The other sister is in Baltimore. The sister in Baltimore would occasionally babysit so we could go away. She always said, "I'll give money, but count me out." I had suggested we take turns—each of us caring for mother for 4 months. My sister in Baltimore said absolutely no. My sister in Chicago at one point said I was having a hard time, so I could send Mother out and she would manage somehow. But I knew she couldn't manage. She is really sick. If I sent my mother out there, I would have had to go out and bring her home again. It would have been impossible. That's why that sister never got involved. When my sister in Baltimore cared for her, mother always got away. The same thing happened in Chicago. MOTHER GOT TO KNOW THE POLICE IN BOTH PLACES BECAUSE THEY ALWAYS PICKED HER UP.

The whole thing prevented my husband and I from taking vacations or seeing our friends. But the whole thing has made me appreciate my husband even more.

My children really couldn't help because they were married and lived far away, but they were always very good to my mother. They are good children and grandchildren.

I didn't mind being the principal caregiver. All our lives my mother was my friend. She was a nice woman and didn't have much of a life with my father. *My other sisters and her never got along.* I never faulted them. *One of my sisters was never a giver and that was all right. My other sister was willing but couldn't manage mother.* No one was making me do it. (A brother is not mentioned as a potential caregiver.) I could have put her in a home before. I didn't feel resentful, and here we are. We were always friends besides being mother and daughter. We were able to communicate. That was the worst, when we couldn't communicate anymore. That was the greatest strain.

My sisters and others said why don't you put her away? They said this long before. I said the day she doesn't know me is the day I will put her away. But our lives became impossible, and I couldn't take care of her. My mother said she hated me.

I felt the time had come. She was unhappy here and she hated me, because I was the one dealing with her. At the end, she wouldn't let me do anything for her. It was impossible. So we started looking around. We were wondering how to go about it and what to do. WE WERE IN TOUCH WITH A SOCIAL WORKER. I realized I couldn't handle it. She was fighting with me, and I couldn't let it go. I could deal with it, but not when she wouldn't let me. That was horrible.

39

BEFORE THAT, I HAD SENT AWAY FOR SOME BOOKLETS ON NURSING HOMES. ONE BOOKLET GAVE A LISTING OF NURSING HOMES THAT WERE RUN WITH THE PATIENT IN MIND AND DID NOT MAKE A PROFIT. In the private ones, if you can pay for 2 years, they take you in and, depending on how many people they have on Medicaid, when you run out of funds, they may keep you and put you on Medicaid. I got a lot of feedback from the girls at work who had to place relatives in nursing homes.

So we sent for some literature on some of these homes, and the three of us visited some of these places. ONE CONSIDERA-TION WAS FINANCIAL–HOW MUCH MONEY MOTHER HAD TO PUT DOWN. She had $35,000. I tried to look at the places through her eyes.

I had investigated a nonprofit religious home for my father before he died. I thought it would be a good spot for her. To be a resident, you needed $38,000. We had already filled out forms for another place, but something in me made me want to call the nonprofit home. The woman was very nice. My husband and I went there, and when I got there I said to my husband, "This is it!" MY MOTHER HAS AN INCOME OF $8,000 A YEAR UNTIL SHE DIES, PLUS $35,000 IN CASH. THEY FIGURED SHE HAD ENOUGH TO FULL PAY FOR 3 YEARS. But they wanted to meet my mother. Thank G–my mother was good. She was "Miss Congeniality." My husband and I were saying, "Thank you, Whoever!" that she was so well behaved. They said she would get the first available space. We were delighted.

But the time wore on, and we were having our hassles with bathing and the whole thing. She was still going to day care. *By this time my husband was retired, so he babysat her. Before, when we were both working and she went to day care, he would get off of work early so he could pick her up. He was wonderful. It was great. At the end, so his bosses wouldn't complain, he took it as vacation time.*

AFTER 3 MONTHS, WE GOT A CALL AND THE NEXT DAY WE TOOK HER IN TO THE NURSING HOME. I didn't know what to do. I wanted to explain it to her. I couldn't tell her because she couldn't understand. My husband and I were there. I asked the Director of Nurses what we should do. I didn't know how long to wait before visiting her. She told me to do whatever I wanted. I stayed away for 3 days. She was fine.

But I worried about the care. For anyone to get care, you need one on one, and where are you going to get it? You get it when it's yours, like I gave it to her. I thought she won't get her daily piece of fruit. I wondered what would happen, because she can't communicate about anything. That's really hard. I figured they knew what they were doing.

One afternoon the Director of Nursing told me she was fist fighting with all the attendants. She won't cooperate about anything. They had her on a lot of drugs. She wound up on Thorazine, so she is really spaced out. If I hadn't lived through it, I would be very dissatisfied with that. I know how it is. They have their routines. They have to fight with her to make her do. This is one of the problems with her. They are very nice, and she was never alone. I am very satisfied.

In the beginning, I went every day. We would walk inside or sit outside. I told my husband I would love to bring her home, but I was afraid it would upset her when I took her back. I didn't know what to do. But I figured I'd chance it. We did it, and she was happy. I took her back, and she didn't say anything, but her face was glum. Since then, I bring her home once a week. It's been fine. She is not as lively because of the medicine. This last Sunday, she didn't know me. I was glad in a way, because it lets me off the hook a bit. If she's got complaints, it's not me they're directed to as the daughter. One time she confused me with my sister. She must come in and out. This last time there was no recognition of me or my husband. It will be interesting to see if she knows me next time, but she wasn't antagonistic and she seemed glad to get back to the home. She may be going into another stage.

My mother right now has enough money to support herself for 3 years in the home. When she only has $1,500 left, the rest will be covered by Medicaid. The nursing home will take her checks and use them toward the cost of care, and the rest will be paid by Medicaid. This is all arranged now, so mother will not be put out of the home.

Implications for Interventions

The families in the PGC studies were diverse in their socioeconomic status, ethnic backgrounds, and educational levels. The caregiving daughters were homemakers, waitresses, secretaries, health professionals, artists, and college professors. They ranged from 36 to 70 years of age, from being pregnant, to having young children, to marrying off their children, to being grandmothers. The quality of relationships among caregivers, their husbands, children, siblings, and mothers also varied greatly.

The effects of caregiving on the lives of the caregivers and their families and the emotional and mental effects they experienced need not be underlined. The women themselves described them vividly. What is emphasized here is that the quality of family relationships, economic status, and the availability of formal services influence the caregiving situation directly.

The Green family had good interpersonal relationships and cooperative behavior among members of the extended as well as the nuclear family. The mother's personality and understanding eased the situation. Plans were discussed openly, and help from both informal and formal sources was mobilized and orchestrated in an orderly manner. The financial status of parents and children permitted the creation of an appropriate environment for the parents (a room was added to the Green's house), and whatever supportive services were needed could be purchased. Even in this "best case" scenario, however, Mrs. Green had reluctantly given up the job she enjoyed, was not free of emotional symptoms, and felt that she and her husband were missing out on the "empty nest syndrome."

By contrast, the chaotic Carter situation was characterized by disorder and conflict between the extraordinarily difficult mother and everyone else in the family. The caregiver was driven to a nervous breakdown, both of her marriages suffered, and she was depressed and guilty after the elderly mother went to a nursing home. All this was aggravated by the family's poor economic status. Mr. Carter had to work overtime, and Mrs. Carter had to get a job to pay for things her mother needed that were not covered by Medicare. In turn, additional problems were created for the grandchildren. Appropriate services and facilities were not available, even when Mrs. Carter was ready to use them. The domiciliary home sent the mother back to the Carters, and the Medicaid nursing home was not available for many months. The family needed an array of supports: therapeutic counseling, thorough assessment services, professional case management to mobilize and monitor services, economic support, resources and services to supplement or substitute for family help, and education in techniques of management of the resistive parent. The importance of long-term care insurance and continuity of care is amply demonstrated by this situation.

The Anthony family is a striking example of a prolonged odyssey of caregiving to a mother deteriorating because of Alzheimer's disease, a situation that went beyond the family's limits of endurance. The ordeal was long, but the Anthonys sought and used help along the way. Mrs. Anthony was willing and able to secure services (a diagnostic workup, day care, an in-home worker, a support group, social work counseling, and educational information about management of the parent). But, ultimately, the services did not work because of the mother's incontinence and disordered behavior. As often happens, not only the older woman's intractable behavior and the exhaustion of her caregivers, but finally, her inability to communicate or even to recognize her daughter prompted nursing home placement. Community alternatives are not really alternatives in such situations; the real alternative is access to a good nursing home. Fortunately, there was enough money so that the elderly woman was accepted by such a nursing home, and both she and her daughter were able to adapt to their new situations.

Mrs. Anthony's story is classic in its description of the development and progression of Alzheimer's disease. It also illustrates many findings from the PGC and other studies. Mrs. Anthony suffered severe stress effects. Caregiving competed with her job; she had to cut back on her work hours and give up her career. Her husband, too, was deeply affected and under strain, and at one point he even changed his work hours in order to help. Though he was "wonderful," at times Mrs. Anthony was "caught in the middle" between him and her mother as well as between her job and her mother. Her mother's premorbid personality and their good relationship were among the reasons why (in contrast to her sisters) she became the caregiver and endured the situation so long. Despite the horrors caregiving entailed, her longstanding, good relationship with her husband was not damaged. When caring for her mother was no longer within the realm of possibility, Mrs. Anthony did not "dump" the older woman, but was careful to find a nursing home that she felt would give good care. After placement, she did not abandon her mother but still worried about her, visited faithfully, and took her home on visits frequently.

Taken together, the research data and case studies show that each family has different needs. Each member of the family has different inner resources in the form, for example, of personality and mental and physical health. Each family is also different in the availability of other family members, their geographic proximity, and the assistance they give to each other. Each family has different income, housing, and available services. Each family has its own set of religious and cultural values. Families are subjected to different strains and in differing degrees, depending in part on the amount and types of help they provide, on the condition, behavior, and personality of the disabled older person, and on the other responsibilities they carry. The sense of burden they experience and the mental health status of the caregiver and the family as a whole depend on *all* of these.

In that light, no one intervention serves all families or can proceed

43

independently of other interventions. Rather, various services must be assembled in individualized packages designed to meet the unique needs of the particular family. Mental health services are critical to the well-being of the older people who are afflicted with Alzheimer's disease or other disabling conditions and to the well-being of all generations in the family. Just as critical are the concrete services and facilities so desperately needed at times. Questions to be answered thoughtfully by professionals and society are: For any given family, at what point is the goal to encourage continued caregiving no matter the psychological and social cost to the family and its members? At what point do our values dictate that we help them *reduce* the amount of care they provide?

Not all strains are preventable or remediable, of course, and there is no panacea. But mental health services, together with income supports and an appropriate and available system of long-term care, can do much to prevent families at risk from going beyond the limits of human endurance.

Acknowledgments

Most of the Philadelphia Geriatric Center research described in this chapter was financed by NIMH Grant #MH35252, Elaine Brody, Principal Investigator. The case studies were financed by The Fredrick and Amelia Schimper Foundation of New York.

Acknowledgment is made of the assistance of the project staff in collecting and analyzing the data: Morton H. Kleban, Co-Principal Investigator, and Christine Hoffman, Claire Schoonover, Karen Hammer, and Jeanette Dickerson-Putmar.

References

Adams, M.; Castor, M.; and Danis, B. "A Neglected Dimension in Home Care of Elderly Disabled Persons: Effect on Responsible Family Members." Paper presented at 32nd Annual Meeting of the Gerontological Society, Washington, DC, 1979.

Bengtson, V.L. Generation and family effects on value socialization. *American Sociological Review* 40:358-371, 1975.

Bengtson, V.L., and Robertson, J.F., eds. *Grandparenthood*. Beverly Hills, CA: Sage Publications, 1985.

Brody, E.M. The mentally-impaired aged patient: A socio-medical problem. *Geriatrics Digest* 4:25-32, 1967.

Brody, E.M. The aging of the family. *Annals of the American Academy of Political and Social Science* 438:13-27, 1978.

Brody, E.M. "Women in the middle" and family help to older people. *Gerontologist* 21:471-480, 1981.

Brody, E.M. The role of the family in nursing homes: Implications for research and public policy. In: Harper, M.S., and Lebowitz, B., eds. *Mental Illness in Nursing Homes: Agenda for Research*. NIMH. Washington, DC: Supt. of Docs., U.S. Govt. Print. Off., 1985*a*. pp. 234-264.

Brody, E.M. Parent care as a normative family stress. The Donald P. Kent Memorial Lecture. *Gerontologist* 25:19-29, 1985*b*.

Brody, E.M.; Hoffman, C.; Kleban, M.H.; and Schoonover, C.B. Parent care and sibling relationships: Perceptions of caregiving daughters and their local siblings. *Gerontologist*, 1988 (submitted).

Brody, E.M.; Johnsen, P.T.; and Fulcomer, M.C. What should adult children do for elderly parents? Opinions and preferences of three generations of women. *Journal of Gerontology* 39:736-746, 1984.

Brody, E.M.; Johnsen, P.T.; Fulcomer, M.C.; and Lang, A.M. Women's changing roles and help to the elderly: Attitudes of three generations of women. *Journal of Gerontology* 38:597-607, 1983.

Brody, E.M.; Kleban, M.H.; Hoffman, C.; and Schoonover, C.B. Parent care: Adult daughters and a comparison of one- two- and three-generation households. *Home Health Care Services Quarterly*, in press.

Brody, E.M.; Kleban, M.H.; Johnsen, P.T.; Hoffman, C.; and Schoonover, C.B. Work status and parent care: A comparison of four groups of women. *Gerontologist* 27:201-208, 1987.

Brody, E.M.; Kleban, M.H.; Lawton, M.P.; and Silverman, H. Excess disabilities of mentally impaired aged: Impact of individualized treatment. *Gerontologist* 11:124-133, 1971.

Brody, E.M.; Lawton, M.P.; and Liebowitz, B. Senile dementia: Public policy and adequate institutional care. *American Journal of Public Health* 74:1381-1383, 1984.

Brody, E.M., and Schoonover, C.B. Patterns of parent-care when adult daughters work and when they do not. *Gerontologist* 26:372-381, 1986.

Brody, E.M., and Spark, G. Institutionalization of the aged: A family crisis. *Family Process* 5:76-90, 1966.

Cherlin, A., and Furstenberg, F.F. Styles and strategies of grandparenting. In: Bengtson, V.L., and Robertson, J.F., eds. *Grandparenthood*. Beverly Hills, CA: Sage Publications, 1985. pp. 97-116.

Cohen, D., and Eisdorfer, C. *The Loss of Self: A Family Resource for the Care of Alzheimer's Disease and Related Disorders*. New York: W.W. Norton and Company, 1986.

Cohler, B.J., and Grunebaum, H.U. *Mothers, Grandmothers, and Daughters: Personality and Childcare in Three-Generation Families*. New York: Wiley and Sons, 1981.

Comptroller General of the United States. Report to Congress on Home Health, *The Need for a National Policy to Better Provide for the Elderly*, U.S. GAO, HRD-78-19, Washington, DC: December 30, 1977.

Danis, B.G. "Stress in Individuals Caring for Ill Elderly Relatives." Paper presented at the annual meeting of the Gerontological Society, Dallas, TX, 1978.

Deimling G.T., and Bass, D.M. Symptoms of mental impairment among elderly adults and their effects on family caregivers. *Journal of Gerontology* 41:778-784, 1986.

Doty, P. Family care of the elderly: The role of public policy. *The Milbank Quarterly* 64(1), 1986.

Doty, P.; Liu, K.; and Wiener, J. An overview of long-term care. *Health Care Financing Review* 6:69-78, 1985.

Frankfather, D.; Smith, M.J.; and Caro, F.G. *Family Care of the Elderly: Public Initiatives and Private Obligations*. Lexington, MA: Lexington Books, 1981.

George, L.K. Caregiver burden: Conflict between norms of reciprocity and solidarity. In: Pillemar, K., and Wolf, R., eds. *Conflict and Abuse in Families of the Elderly: Theory, Research, and Intervention*. Boston, MA: Auburn House, in press.

George, L.K. *The Burden of Caregiving, Center Reports on Advances in Research*. Vol. 8, No. 2. Durham, NC: Duke University Center for the Study of Aging and Human Development, 1984a.

George, L.K. *The Dynamics of Caregiver Burden*. Final report submitted to the AARP Andrus Foundation, December 1984b.

Grad, J., and Sainsbury, P. Problems of caring for the mentally ill at home. *Proceedings of the Royal Society of Medicine* Section of Psychiatry 59:20-23, 1966.

Horowitz, A. "Predictors of Caregiving Involvement Among Adult Children of the Frail Elderly." Paper presented at Annual Meeting of the Gerontological Society of America, Boston, MA, 1982.

Horowitz, A. Family caregiving to the frail elderly. In: Eisdorfer, C.; Lawton, M.P.; and Maddox, G.L., eds. *Annual Review of Gerontology and Geriatrics*. Vol. 5. New York: Springer, 1985a. pp. 194-246.

Horowitz, A. Sons and daughters as caregivers to older parents:

Differences in role performance and consequences. *Gerontologist* 25:612-617, 1985*b*.

Kinnear, D., and Graycar, A. *Family Care of Elderly People: Australian Perspectives.* Social Welfare Research Centre, University of New South Wales, SWRC Reports and Proceedings, No. 23, May 1982.

Kleban, M.H.; Brody, E.M.; and Lawton, M.P. Personality traits in the mentally impaired aged and their relationship to improvements in current functioning. *Gerontologist* 11:134-140, 1971.

Kleban, M.H.; Brody, E.M.; Schoonover, C.B.; and Hoffman, C. Sons'-in-law perceptions of parent care. *Journal of Marriage and the Family,* in press.

Kleban, M.H.; Brody, E.M.; Schoonover, C.B.; and Hoffman, C. "Some Effects of Parent Care: Patterns of Strain for Working and Nonworking Adult Daughters." Paper presented at 37th Annual Meeting of the Gerontological Society of America, San Antonio, TX, 1984.

Lawton, M.P.; Brody, E.M.; and Sapterstein, A. A multi-service program for caregivers of Alzheimer's patients. *Gerontologist,* in press.

Lawton, M.P.; Moss, M.; Fulcomer, M.C.; and Kleban, M.H. A research- and science-oriented multilevel assessment instrument. *Journal of Gerontology* 37:91-99, 1982.

Longino, C.F.; Biggar, J.C.; Flynn, C.B.; and Wiseman, R.F. "The Retirement Migration Project: A Final Report to the National Institute on Aging." Center for Social Research on Aging, University of Miami, Coral Gables, FL, 1984.

Mace, N., and Robins, P. *The 36-Hour Day: A Family Guide to Caring for Persons with Alzheimer's Disease, Related Dementing Illnesses and Memory Loss in Later Life.* Baltimore, MD: Johns Hopkins University Press, 1981.

Macken, C.L. A profile of functionally impaired elderly persons living in the community. *Health Care Financing Review* 7:33-49, 1986.

Marshall, V.W., and Rosenthal, C.J. "The Relevance of Geographical Proximity in Intergenerational Relations." Paper presented at 38th Annual Meeting of the Gerontological Society of America, New Orleans, LA, 1985.

Mercier, J.M.; Paulson, L.; and Morris, E.W. "The Effect of Proximity on the Aging Parent/Child Relationship." Paper presented at 40th Annual Meeting of the Gerontological Society of America, Washington, DC, 1987.

Mindel, C.H. Multigenerational family households: Recent trends and implications for the future. *The Gerontologist* 19:456-463, 1979.

Moss, M., and Kurland, P. Family visiting with institutionalized mentally impaired aged. *Journal of Gerontological Social Work* 1:271-278, 1979.

Noelker, L.S., and Poulshock, S.W. "The Effects on Families of Caring for Impaired Elderly in Residence." Final Report, AoA Grant #90-AR-2112, Benjamin Rose Institute, Cleveland, OH, 1982.

Ross, H.G., and Milgram, J.J. Important variables in adult sibling relationships: A qualitative study. In: Lamb, M.E., and Sutton-Smith, B., eds. *Sibling Relationships: Their Nature and Significance Across the Lifespan.* Hillsdale, NJ: Lawrence Erlbaum Associates, 1982. pp. 225-250.

Safford, F. *Caring for the Mentally Impaired Elderly: A Family Guide.* New York: Henry Holt, 1986.

Saline, C. Our parents, ourselves. *Philadelphia Magazine* 73(July):114-117, 158-167, 1982.

Schoonover, C.B.; Brody, E.M.; Hoffman, C.; and Kleban, M.H. "Parent Care and Geographically Distant Children." Paper presented at 40th Annual Meeting of the Gerontological Society of America, Washington, DC, 1987.

Shanas, E. Family-kin networks and aging in cross-cultural perspective. *Journal of Marriage and the Family* (Aug.):505-511, 1973.

Shanas, E. Social myth as hypothesis: The case of the family relations of old people. *Gerontologist* 19:3-9, 1979a.

Shanas, E. The family as a social support system in old age. *Gerontologist* 19:169-174, 1979b.

Shanas, E. Older people and their families: The new pioneers. *Journal of Marriage and the Family* 42:9-15, 1980.

Shanas, E.; Townsend, P.; Wedderburn, D.; Friis, H.; Milhoj, P.; and Stehouwer, J., eds. *Old People in Three Industrial Societies.* New York: Atherton Press, 1968.

Simos, B.G. Adult children and their aging parents. *Social Work* 18:78-84, 1973.

Soldo, B.J. "The Dependency Squeeze on Middle-Aged Women." Paper presented at Meeting of the Secretary's Advisory Committee on Rights and Responsibilities of Women, DHHS, Washington, DC, 1980.

Spark, G., and Brody, E.M. The aged are family members. *Family Process* 9:195-210, 1970.

Stone, R.; Cafferata, G.L.; and Sangl, J. Caregivers of the frail elderly: A national profile. *Gerontologist* 27:616-626, 1987.

Sussman, M. "Social and Economic Supports and Family Environment for the Elderly." Final Report to AoA, Grant #90-A-316, January 1979.

Treas, J., and Bengtson, V.L. The demography of middle and late-life transitions. *Annals of the American Academy of Political and Social Science* 464:11-21, 1982.

Troll, L.E., and Stapley, J. Elders and the extended family system: Health, family salience, and affect. In: Munnich, J.M.A., ed.

Lifespan and Change in a Gerontological Perspective. New York: Academic Press, in press.

Walum, L.R. *The Dynamics of Sex and Gender.* Chicago, IL: Rand McNally, 1977.

Wiessart, W.G. Seven reasons why it is so difficult to make community based long-term care cost effective. *HSR: Health Services Research* 20:423-431, 1985.

Wolf, D.A., and Soldo, B.J. "The Households of Older Unmarried: Micro-Decision Model of Shared Living Arrangements." Paper presented at annual meeting of the Population Association of America, San Francisco, CA, 1986.

Zarit, S.H.; Reever, K.E.; and Bach-Peterson, J. Relatives of the impaired aged: Correlates of feelings of burden. *Gerontologist* 20:649-655, 1980.

Zimmer, A.H., and Sainer, J.S. "Strengthening the Family as an Informal Support for Their Aged: Implications for Social Policy and Planning." Paper presented at the 31st Annual Meeting of the Gerontological Society of America, Dallas, TX, 1978.

Chapter 2

Caring for Family Members With Alzheimer's Disease

Bertram J. Cohler, Ph.D., Leslie Groves, Ph.D.,
William Borden, Ph.D., and Lawrence Lazarus, M.D.[1]

Alzheimer's disease represents one of the major sources of impairment among older persons. An illness with unknown origins and an unpredictable course, its early symptoms are often difficult to detect, preventing an accurate diagnosis. As the illness progresses, the patient's sense of judgment and memory become impaired, leading to a diminished capacity for self-care that places insuperable burdens on those significant others expected to provide their care. Indeed, eventual failure even to recognize a long-time spouse or adult offspring, together with accompanying destruction of personality, is terrifying testimony to the ravages of this illness.

Study of the impact of Alzheimer's disease upon the family is significant in three quite different respects: first, comparative study of families with and without impaired elders highlights factors related to relationships within the family in later life; second, since patients with Alzheimer's disease are involved in protracted relations with hospitals, nursing homes, and other community institutions, study of family involvement in this illness provides additional information regarding changes in the relationship of the family to other institutions across the life course; finally, study of family response to caretaking demands may lead to better understanding of processes determining adult socialization, including induction of offspring into the role of caretaker and socialization into grief.

This chapter discusses research on the impact of Alzheimer's disease upon the family, reviewing findings from both clinical and systematic observational study of family caretakers and integrating these findings with those from normative study of relations within the family of later

50

adulthood. It should be noted that findings reported to date were based on relatively small opportunity samples and often failed to consider the stage of the illness or the gender and generation of the caretaker. Further, many studies on the mental health of care-givers did not report findings regarding perceived burden and coping strategies for dealing with this burden, or separate mental health outcomes by patients with Alzheimer's disease and other illnesses or by gender and family role of caregiver. The distinctive nature of this illness affects the caregiver's definition of the situation in particular ways, further qualified by caretaker role within the family.

Alzheimer's Disease: Degenerative Processes in Later Life

Origins and Course of the Illness

Identification of a "progressive, age-related, chronic cognitive dys-function" known as Alzheimer's disease (Schneck et al. 1982) was the result of cumulative studies by a number of European investigators. Discovery of cerebral "plaques" by Blocq and Marinesco (1892) was followed by Alzheimer's (1907) reports on the relationship between autopsy findings of brain neuropathology and the occurrence of psychiatric symptoms during the illness, and Simchowicz's (1910) report of a relationship between these "senile plaques" and behavior characteristic of dementia. Subsequently, Kraepelin began the tradition of using Alzheimer's name for this progressive dementia. More recent investigations by Roth (1955) and Corsellis and Evans (1965) further clarified this syndrome, distinguishing between dementias resulting from cerebrovascular disease and those specifically caused by the formation of brain abnormalities, including neurofibrillary tangles and degenerating nerve endings or neuritic plaques (Katzman 1986; Schneck et al. 1982).

Studies by Kidd (1963) and by Terry, Gonatas, and Weiss (1964) showed that so-called presenile dementia and senile dementia associated with Alzheimer's disease could be attributed to similar neuropathology. Blessed, Tomlinson, and Roth (1968) showed that behavioral changes among elderly patients are significantly correlated with later autopsy findings: increased evidence of plaque formation in the cortex is associated with both intellectual deterioration and, in particular, impairment in everyday functioning among afflicted elderly patients.

From the social science perspective, Alzheimer's disease presents several features that are unique among neuropsychiatric disorders. In the first place, the symptoms of this illness defy our culturally defined view of behavior as intentional. Western psychiatry has long emphasized that people are generally responsible for their own actions. In contrast with other cultures, in which unacceptable and deviant behavior may be attributed to jealous spirits or demonic possession, Western culture tends to view psychiatric illness as a moral failing. Even when biological components can be identified as contributing to the origin and course of such disorders as schizo-phrenia, the subsequent course of the disorder is believed to be largely a consequence of patient actions. Patients with Alzheimer's disease display behavior that is socially unacceptable and inappropriate, and yet is completely beyond the realm of the patient's responsibility.

In the second place, the course of the illness, while progressive, is also completely unpredictable. For reasons not yet clear, some patients die within a relatively few years after first symptoms appear, while others live for decades. The uncertainty associated with changes in symptoms or course of the illness (negative life events that relatives cannot predict or control) is a major reason for the particular adversity reported by caregivers of relatives with Alzheimer's disease (Gubrium 1987; Pagel et al. 1985).

To date, no cure, or even palliative treatment, has been discovered that can alter the inevitable, destructive course of brain degeneration. For family and friends who care for the patient with Alzheimer's disease, learning the diagnosis begins the process of mourning. The process of working through grief associated with the death of a loved one is made more difficult by both the unpredictable course of the illness and the perplexing, socially disruptive, symptoms that characterize the later stages of the illness.

Often, in an effort to resolve conflicting feelings evoked by these bizarre symptoms, caretakers redouble their heroic efforts to care for the ill family member, attempting to maintain their usual routine while accepting responsibility for care. Although adaptive in terms of the patient's need for care, these efforts to deal with emotions through frantic caretaking activity may postpone resolution of feelings about the elder patient's deterioration, leading to increased difficulty in resolving these issues after the relative's death. The caretakers' denial of their own needs out of feelings of loyalty may lead to exhaustion and personal depletion.

Finally, one of the most tragic and difficult symptoms of this disorder is the inability to remember significant family relationships that have evolved over a lifetime. Occasional forgetfulness, often an early symptom of this disease, is later expressed as lack of orientation to person and place, and still later as an inability to recognize spouse, children, and close friends. Memory for relationships is central to being human: the failure to acknowledge others is among the most painful and crushing responses that persons can show to each other. To date, little research has looked at the impact of this failure to acknowledge another upon the caretaker, showing once again the importance of studying Alzheimer's disease as a means for understanding both psychological health and illness.

In her discussion of the psychology of parenthood, Benedek (1973) observed that one is a parent as long as there is active memory. Benedek anticipated the problems posed for the parent of no longer remembering the fact of parenthood; serious problems are posed for adult offspring when their impaired parent no longer acknowledges the relationship. No single aspect of caring for a relative with Alzheimer's disease may be quite as upsetting as the parent's failure to remember and acknowledge this relationship. For the caretaker, most often a spouse of many years, this lack of acknowledgment is experienced as a blow to self-esteem and a major break in empathy.

Family Study and Alzheimer's Disease

Alzheimer's disease shares with other chronic illnesses significant problems for the patient's family. The relevant family unit includes immediate relatives, such as adult offspring, and relatives more distant in terms of genealogy and geography. As both Cohler (1983) and Pruchno, Blow, and Smyer (1984) noted, life events are not independent; when one family member is confronted with adversity, others are affected as well.

In the first place, the lives of family members are disrupted as a result of caretaking. For example, when the mother of young children is hospitalized, other relatives are called upon to provide babysitting and housekeeping help (Grunebaum et al. 1983). Disruption due to family obligations affects women more than men since women are the primary kin-keepers in our society (Firth et al. 1970; Komarovsky 1950, 1956).

In the second place, family members inevitably become concerned and emotionally involved in the course of a close relative's debilitating illness. An accident to a grandchild, the illness of a parent-in-law, or psychiatric illness in a niece or nephew all have impact upon the morale of other family members. Concern regarding the well-being of the afflicted relative may sap vitality and feelings of personal well-being. While social support from other family members may be significant for those presently confronting adversity, the need to provide support spreads the adversity throughout the family, just as a stone thrown into the water causes ripples (Pruchno et al. 1984). The support and assistance that helps one family member may have significant emotional costs for other family members (Cohler and Lieberman 1980).

Among all major illnesses, Alzheimer's disease is unusual in the extent to which it may affect the extended family unit. It presents all the symptoms of the most debilitating forms of illness, including the need for others to assume the most intimate aspects of self-care. At the same time, patients with this disease will sometimes present with symptoms of the most virulent forms of psychiatric illness, including hallucinations, rage toward well-meaning caretakers, and loss of orientation to person, place, and time.

Not only are patients with Alzheimer's disease difficult to manage, but in the later stages of the illness, they may require relocation into institutional residence because of the insuperable burden of care. However, stigma is attached to nursing home placement; patients are sometimes aware enough to understand the implications of placement. Further, family members may feel guilty about this decision. As a consequence, continuing demands are made on the morale and financial resources of the larger family unit. Other family members worry about both the emotional demands made upon caregivers and the patient's decline in health. The unpredictable course of the illness, including changes in both symptoms and rate of decline, means that turmoil for the larger family unit may continue for many years, further taxing the ability of family members to deal with the patient's inevitable placement.

Caretaking and Intergenerational Relations: Normative Perspectives

The task of caring for dependent family members, either the very young or the very old, is at least formally voluntary in ways that are unknown in societies with extended family households, where generations live together (Nydegger 1983). Questions such as the degree of strain imposed on adult offspring caring for elders are irrelevant among societies where such caretaking is intrinsic to family life. Even within our own society, aging is expected to bring with it the "right" to be dependent on others for at least some aspects of care (Blenkner 1969). Family members have the unique responsibility of providing this care and support (Blenkner 1965; Brody 1981).

Study of provision of care for older family members raises important questions for both caretakers and dependent elders themselves. The older family member has questions about the means for obtaining such services at time of need. The caregiving family members have important questions regarding the nature and extent of both the strains imposed by providing such care and the accompanying rewards and satisfactions.

Family Relations and Beliefs About Caretaking Responsibilities

Caring for dependent family members is among the central functions of the family. However, as Hagestad (1982) suggested, quite different demands are made by caring for dependent offspring early in the family life cycle and caring for dependent elders much later in the family life cycle. Further, much less is known about relations within the family in later life than in young to middle adulthood.

After the first postpartum weeks, it is considered inappropriate for parents of infants to seek assistance with their care (Fischer and Fischer 1963). Indeed, as Cherlin and Furstenberg (1986), Cohler and Grunebaum (1981), and Robertson (1977) all suggested, childcare issues become significant issues to be negotiated between adult offspring and their middle-aged and older parents. Grandparents in contemporary society often regard requests from their adult children for assistance with babysitting as an intrusion upon their own busy schedules. It is considered somewhat appropriate for older parents unable to manage tasks of everyday life to expect help from their adult offspring, and for offspring caring for older parents to expect assistance from each other, as well as from others in the family circle.

It is an accepted belief in our society that family members should care for each other during periods of illness (Brody 1985; Brody et al. 1983). This feeling of obligation is largely independent of affection. As Horowitz and Shindelman (1983), Isaacs (1971), Jarrett (1985), Lowther and Williamson (1966), and Walker and Thompson (1983) all suggested, family members are able to separate feelings of intimacy and caring from obligatory caretaking for other family members. One need not even particularly like another family member in order to provide expectable care and assistance at times of need although, as Horowitz and Shindelman (1983) showed, positive affection appears to mitigate at least some of the strain involved in caretaking.

Findings from a number of studies (Blenkner 1965, 1969; Brody et al. 1983; Niederehe and Frughe 1985; Schoor 1980; Zarit et al. 1985) showed that adult offspring share a common belief with members of both the parental and grandparental generations that offspring have a filial obligation or responsibility toward their own now elderly parents. Findings reported by Sauer (1977) and Seelbach and Sauer (1977) showed that increased offspring commitment to these

55

norms of responsibility is negatively associated with morale. However, these findings are based on a study of black elders and may reflect the "amoral familism" (Banfield 1958; Stack 1974) characteristic of families living in poverty who fear that demands made by other family members will deplete precious financial resources. These differences in attitudes toward parental morale as a function of social status and ethnicity point to the importance of including variation in social composition in studies of caretaking within the family.

The literature regarding performance of caretaking responsibilities is consistent with Boszormenyi-Nagy and Spark's (1973) discussion of the invisible loyalties that bind a family together. As Cohler and Stott (1987), O'Brien and Wagner (1980), and essays edited by Heller, Sosna, and Wellberry (1986) emphasized, the reality of relational interdependence in our society conflicts with the value of individualism and personal autonomy. Not only is care and assistance provided to relatives regardless of personal cost, but this care is provided for extended periods. One need not feel love toward relatives needing care to obtain a sense of enhanced self-regard from providing such care, consistent with the shared value of helping family members in distress (Kohut 1971, 1977).

Much of the literature on caretaking for dependent family members, from studies of the transition to and problems of parenthood to studies of caring for dependent elders, emphasizes feelings of role strain, overload, and personal depletion (Croog 1970). Provision of care for a loved one is presumed to lead only to a sense of burden and depletion. Much less often recognized are the personal gains realized from acting in accordance with what one believes to be proper in helping others. Further, findings suggest that although the strains initially derived from providing care are high, over time some individuals adapt to the caretaking process, which leads to a reduced sense of strain and burden.[2]

Expectable Family Relations and the Impact of Caretaking

Findings from studies of urban families consistently showed continuing, high rates of interaction across the generations, with frequent visiting and telephone contact (Cohler and Grunebaum 1981; Firth et al. 1970; Litwak 1960a, 1960b, 1965; Shanas 1961, 1979a, 1979b; Sussman 1954, 1965). Largely as a result of earlier efforts at understanding social change accompanying urbanization, sociology had assumed that population shifts from small communities with continuing face-to-face interaction to city life would necessarily lead to feelings of alienation and the breakdown of traditional family ties

(Park et al. 1925; Simmel 1898; Wirth 1938).[3] In fact, as Haller (1961) noted, urbanization fosters maintenance of the extended family unit since younger family members need not move away in order to find employment. Further, findings such as those reported by Fischer and his colleagues (1977, 1982) refuted earlier assumptions regarding the breakdown of the moral order and increased alienation accompanying urbanization.

Findings from a number of survey studies supported the initial formulations of Litwak (1960a, 1960b) and Sussman (1954, 1959, 1965) that the *modified* extended family is the modal family structure in contemporary urban society. While family members may no longer live together in a common household, they share resources and provide assistance for each other. Mutual interdependence is fostered by the ease of transportation and communication possible in contemporary urban society.

Although figures regarding living arrangements vary by age, sex, and marital status, among persons aged 65-74, only 6 percent of men and 14 percent of women live with relatives; among those over age 75, 10 percent of men and 24 percent of women live with relatives (U.S. Senate: Special Committee on Aging 1986).

Even though living with relatives is somewhat infrequent, older persons living separately are likely to live near their relatives. Shanas' (1979b, 1980) survey findings showed that about 80 percent of persons over age 65 had visited with an adult offspring within the past week, and more than half had seen an adult child within the prior day. Shanas (1961, 1980) reported that more than half of these older persons with children live within a few blocks of their offspring. Among those few never-married childless older persons, more than 75 percent had visited with a brother or sister in the prior week. Cantor (1979) reported more than half of her elderly respondents had at least one intimate friend, and nearly 40 percent had seen this confidant within the past day, while more than two-thirds had seen this confidant within the past week.

As both Cohler and Grunebaum (1981) and Rosenmayr and Kockeis (1963) showed, the issue for older persons is not accessibility to relatives but their preference for a more formal relationship, characterized by "intimacy at a distance" (Rosenmayr and Kockeis 1963). Indeed, older persons enjoy their personal freedom and prefer not to live with relatives. Findings from a recent Harris (1987) survey for the Commonwealth Fund showed that 75 percent of older persons have children with whom they could live, but less than 1 percent would prefer such living arrangements.

This becomes a serious issue for older persons suffering cognitive impairment to such a degree that they are unable to live inde-

57

pendently. At least for some parents, the loss of morale associated with giving up one's own home and moving into an intergenerational household may accentuate cognitive decline and depressive symptoms in a manner parallel to relocation into residential care. Little is known about factors accounting for individual differences in response.

The significance of confidants for the morale of older persons was shown in Lee's (1979) study of friendship ties and morale in later life: even phone contact with one or two confidants is a major source of positive morale among older persons. In fact, as Cohler and Grunebaum (1981), Cohler and Lieberman (1980), Lee and Ihlinger-Tallman (1980), and Strain and Chappell (1982) showed, confidants are far more important than offspring as a source of positive morale among older persons.

Findings reviewed by Bengtson and DeTerre (1980) and by Troll, Miller, and Atchley (1979) documented the high levels of visiting and telephone communication among middle-aged adults and their parents. At the same time, as virtually every study has shown (Brody 1978; Cohler and Grunebaum 1981; Firth et al. 1970; Horowitz 1985; Komarovsky 1962; Longino and Lipman 1985; Soldo and Myllyuoma 1983; Sweetser 1963, 1964), daughters and daughters-in-law are differentially expected to engage in kin-keeping and to care for ill or infirm family members. Consistent with Shanas' (1979a) principle of substitutability, daughters are most often called upon to help with caretaking when the spouse is unable to provide such assistance (Stoller 1983). Considering the impact of such roles in the portfolio as housewife, wife, and mother upon such caretaking, Stoller (1983) reported that husband's employment and wife's marital status, not the number of still-dependent children at home (in contrast to findings reported by Liebowitz (1975)) both reduce time spent in caring for parents. Stoller's (1983) findings, together with those reported by Lang and Brody (1983), suggested that, at present, single adult women, either widows or never married, are overrepresented among these helpers.

Findings reported by Brody and Schoonover (1986), in contrast to those reported by Stoller (1983), showed little association between women's employment and provision of assistance to older family members. These findings are consistent with other reports regarding the role of women in contemporary society (Cohler 1984). Where work demands are a "legitimate" justification for men's problems in assisting in household tasks as diverse as childcare and parentcare, among women, work is regarded as secondary and discretionary (Lopata and Norr 1980). Feelings of role strain and overload created by work are not considered legitimate justification for reducing the time devoted to household tasks, which are still assumed to be essential components of the wife-mother role.

Study of exchange of aid within the multigeneration family is a complex process. Social status appears associated with patterns of exchange. As Rosenberg (1970) showed, working-class families frequently exchange technical assistance, including advice on home maintenance and auto repairs, and babysitting services. Within middle-class families, cash and goods are most often exchanged, at least in part to assure that offspring will be able to maintain the same lifestyle as their parents. Findings from Cantor's (1975) survey study of the elderly in New York, the Harris national surveys (1975), and Hill's (1970) Minnesota intergenerational study of consumer panels all showed that even among very old parents, nearly half are still making financial and other gifts to their now middle-aged offspring. Further, older persons are often willing to undergo considerable privation to conserve economic resources that may be inherited by the next generation.[4]

Caretaking as an Expectable Task

Reviewing studies of adult family processes, Elder (1984) observed that structural-functional perspectives, as pioneered by Parsons (1949), may be less relevant for family study than symbolic interactionist perspectives, as formulated by Blumer (1938, 1962, 1969), Stryker (1981), Turner (1981), and others. Symbolic interactionism assumes that actions are structured by the social encounter, based on shared interpretations of the situation. Responses in particular situations can only be understood in terms of the meaning that persons attach to these situations. Central to this concept of personal definition of the situation is the person's beliefs about the reciprocal manner in which they should act with regard to particular others, at particular times, and in particular situations, together with the manner in which others should respond reciprocally (Burr et al. 1979).

While this symbolic interactionist perspective has implications for study methods that are beyond the concern of this chapter (see Blumer 1969), it does focus concern on understanding the situation from the perspective of each family member. For example, it is less important to know that older persons have ready access to help from other family members than to understand the circumstances defined by particular family members as appropriate for seeking such help. Within contemporary society, a premium is placed on individual autonomy and independence; living with relatives is viewed as limiting personal freedom and mobility and is to be avoided at all costs.

Therefore, as long as older people are able to manage their daily activities, they are determined not to seek help from offspring, siblings, or other relatives (Bengtson and DeTerre 1980; Bengtson and Treas 1980).

Role theory (Biddle and Thomas 1966; Gross et al. 1958) assumes that strain and overload are an inevitable consequence of providing care for relatives, particularly among those persons termed the "generation in the middle" by Brody (1970, 1978). The time, effort, and expense required to care for older relatives is presumed to add to the strain of continuing support for unmarried children still living at home or away at college (Brody 1981; Menaghan 1978). Cicirelli's (1983b) path analysis findings suggest that adult offspring increase their scrutiny of parents well in advance of parental need for support in preparation for providing assistance.

Family members in our society supply virtually all the services and supports that older persons require for their daily round, with little additional assistance expected or required from the community (Brody 1981; Cantor 1985). While the importance of adult offspring in the care of their now dependent parents has been well documented, relatively few studies looked at how older persons without children manage or obtain such assistance. As Shanas (1979a) noted, most often elderly husbands and wives provide this care for each other; when a parent is widowed, care is then provided by an offspring, most often a daughter or daughter-in-law.

Perhaps the most detailed and succinct overview of caretaking within our own society was provided by Brody (1981) who noted the increasing frequency of three- and even four-generation modified extended families in our society. Particularly significant is the large number of older persons whose own parents are still living. Not only the persons needing care, but also their caretakers, are among the older persons in our society.

Much of the literature on intergenerational relations within the family of adulthood was devoted to the problems posed for each generation by the provision of care by adult offspring for their parents, including such issues as role reversal (Glasser and Glasser 1962) in which offspring find themselves responsible for their parents rather than being recipients of care. Continuing efforts by adult offspring to resolve longstanding resentment over failures of empathy by the parents of early childhood, unresolved rivalry with the same-sex parent, and envy or jealousy of the parental relationship, all lead to additional problems in being able to assist dependent parents (Kahana and Levin 1971).

At least one reason for lowered morale associated with caretaking is the increased opportunity for interpersonal conflict. For example,

Johnson and Bursk (1977) showed that parental decline in health is associated with increased conflict between the generations, creating additional strain for both offspring caretaker and dependent parent. Raising an issue intrinsic to study of social attitudes (Brown 1965/1985), Brody (1981) suggested that little is to be gained from examining attitudes about filial responsibility apart from the impact of caretaking on each generation. Indeed, Cicirelli (1983*b*) reported that most offspring perform relatively few caretaking actions. Further, attitudes toward filial responsibility are only indirectly related to caretaking actions and are mediated by both feelings of closeness to parents and actual caretaking behaviors. Expectations may be greatly altered by the reality of caretaking, including the adjustment that persons apparently make to maintain morale even when confronted by feelings of role strain and overload.

When care is required for the opposite-sex parent, guilt at finally realizing early childhood ambitions to replace the father or mother may make it particularly difficult to provide care (Lansky 1984; Savitsky and Sharkey 1972). While daughters may be particularly attentive to their widowed fathers, this care may be accompanied by renewed stimulation of wishes long out of awareness. Sons find it particularly difficult to assist in their mothers' bodily care. If men and women continue to harbor competitive, resentful feelings toward the parent of the same sex, increased feelings of distress may accompany caretaking.

Some findings suggest that middle-aged and older daughters are better able than young adult daughters to realize satisfying relationships with their mothers, and obtain increased comfort from maintaining close ties, with lessened concern about maintaining psychological separateness (Cohler 1986; Low 1978). Other studies report that daughters continue to have difficulty realizing psychological separateness across the course of life, including oldest age (Simos 1973). Finally, among both men and women, increased involvement in care of their own parents leads to increased awareness of the finitude of life (Munnichs 1966) and the personalization of death (Neugarten and Datan 1974; Robinson and Thurner 1979).

Ironically, although much of the literature on expectable caretaking for older family members focused on adult offspring, principally daughters and daughters-in-law, the majority of older persons are cared for by their elderly spouses (Cantor 1983). Spouses are particularly likely to be understanding and to feel that the burden of caretaking during times of illness or other adversity is part of a lifetime commitment (Cantor 1983). Among the young-old, principal caretaking is likely to be among women caring for a spouse during a last illness. Concern over the spouse's illness and prognosis for recovery, together with worries about managing finances and the transition to widowhood, are likely to be major sources of strain (Lopata 1979). To the extent that such caretaking is socially "on-time" and the widow has at least a convoy of support from other women experiencing such adversity, the long-term adverse impact of such caretaking and its outcome may be reduced (Bankoff 1983; Hagestad and Neugarten 1985; Neugarten and Hagestad 1976).

The reality of the spouse's own aging may make caretaking particularly difficult. Cantor (1983) reported that more than four-fifths of older spouse caretakers were, themselves, in poor health. These problems are intensified when, as often happens among older couples, the caretaker is the husband. Husbands find caring for wives to be more inconsistent with their prior marital relationship and socially valued skills than do wives caring for husbands. Further, men lack anticipatory socialization into caretaking as well as a convoy of support from others in a similar situation, so important in successfully resolving this developmental task of the adult years (Neugarten and Hagestad 1976). As both Kohen (1983) and Lopata (1979) have noted, widows remain involved in the same social support systems as before widowhood, relying particularly upon their children during time of need.

Childless married persons, particularly men, are markedly more socially isolated than never-married persons (Johnson and Catalano 1981). Never-married men are somewhat more at a disadvantage than married men when requiring help with the activities of daily living. These men rely on formal community resources to a greater extent than ever unmarried childless persons, who are more likely to rely on siblings and other relatives, as well as formal community resources. Childless married persons are required to depend more directly upon friends and neighbors and formal community resources than married persons with children, and are particularly at risk for relocation into institutional care (Gubrium 1975; Johnson and Catalano 1981; Kivett and Learner 1980; Morycz 1985; Ward 1978). As Kalfayan (1987) showed, adjustment in later life is more positive among persons who never married than among widowed but childless persons. Callahan, Diamond, Giele, and Morris (1980) reported that more than 85 percent of nursing home residents are divorced or widowed. Never-married patients comprise more than a fifth of all nursing home residents.

Some reports suggested that older never-married women may be particularly resourceful in providing for themselves (Longino and Lipman 1985). Further, Johnson and Catalano (1981) reported that unmarried persons showed the same rate of interaction with relatives that Shanas (1979a) reported among older married persons. Although this issue has received little detailed study, unmarried persons have probably long since developed alternative (nonfamily) sources of help during times of need. However, Hess and Saldo (1985) and Ross and Kedward (1977) reported that unmarried elders living alone in the community are particularly socially isolated and in need of formal community services. Grad and Sainsbury (1963) reported that elderly people living alone, rather than in some sort of group quarters such as a boardinghouse, tended to make greater demands upon their families and were reported by the family to be a more significant source of problems. These more isolated elders rely upon siblings and close friends for services generally performed by spouse and offspring among their married counterparts (Johnson and Catalano 1981), but do not appear to find much solace in such caretaking.

Cicirelli (1985) noted that older unmarried men who were assisted by their sisters felt more secure about the resources that could be provided than older sisters who relied on brothers. This gender difference once again reflects shared expectations regarding the role of women as kin-keepers in our society, and their "expressive" or nurturant role within the family.[5] At the same time, as already noted, these never-married persons are overrepresented among users of formal services, including institutional care (Gubrium 1975; Kivett and Learner 1980).

Cicirelli (1980, 1985) also noted that the relationship of siblings in later life is among the least carefully studied of family relations and aging. Consistent with Schneider's (1968) discussion of kinship in contemporary society, Cicirelli distinguished between geographic and social distance. Older siblings can be geographically available as a resource for support and assistance, and yet be socially unavailable because of a longstanding family feud. Indeed, as George (1980) noted in her discussion of adult social roles, we focus too much on the formal attributes attached to such roles and too little on the meaning of persons for each other. Siblings feel closer to each other than to other relatives and yet can maintain longstanding quarrels unknown to the rest of the family. Jealousy of brothers and sisters, particularly those of the same sex, may be maintained from earliest childhood across the life course (Flugel 1921; Ross et al. 1980; Sutton-Smith and Rosenberg 1970), although findings to date are contradictory on the extent to which such jealousy is maintained into later life (Allan 1977; Cicirelli 1985; Laverty 1962).

Friends are particularly important as a source of caregiving in later life. Over the past decade, a large number of studies documented the significance of social support systems or convoys (Kahn 1979; Kahn and Antonucci 1980) in reducing stress through buffering the effects of such eruptive, unpleasant life changes as serious personal illness, the illness or death of a loved one, a job loss, or marital disruption (Cobb 1976, 1979; Thoits, 1981, 1983). Much of this literature has been reviewed (Dean and Linn 1977; Greenblatt 1984; Hammer 1983; Henderson 1980; Lin et al. 1986; Mueller 1980; Pearlin et al. 1981; Thoits 1983).

The presence of a convoy of support is significant in preserving morale and health for both older persons and other family members involved in caretaking activities. However, as Larson (1978), Lowenthal and Robinson (1976), and Ward (1985) all observed, little is known about how such buffering works to increase morale. Experimental studies (Schachter 1959) showed that the physical presence of others was important in reducing levels of physiological arousal while waiting to participate in a psychological experiment. However, it has been difficult to translate such findings into real social situations. At least to some extent, factors such as anticipatory socialization and tangible advice and assistance provided by a social convoy serve to reduce uncertainty accompanying adverse life changes. The literature attempted such distinctions as expressive versus instrumental support and social contact versus exchange of services. Factors such as density of social network, pairs unacquainted, and frequency of contact (Bott 1955/1971) were studied in relation to issues such as morale and adjustment. However, most of these findings emerged from multivariate studies.

The very modest relationships between nature of social ties and feelings of well-being reported in most studies suggest that to understand the significance of social support, increased attention must be paid to how persons experience the situation, including subjectively defined role strain and adversity. As Lowenthal and Robinson (1976) noted in their review, and as Ward (1985) noted in his integration of findings in this area, little is known about how social support affects morale, increasing resilience when confronted by adversity. For example, although adult children are the most likely sources of social support, confidants are the most significant sources of increased morale among persons in each generation. Instrumental assistance and friendship function in some interrelated manner to affect morale. Future research must carefully distinguish between these two aspects of social support.

A number of studies reviewed the significance of friends or confidants as sources of caretaking for older persons. Ward (1978) suggested that friends are better suited than family members as long-term caretakers, particularly among widows who have retired to communities far away from relatives, where other widows, confidants, and friends have relatively few other long-term caretaking obligations and fewer ambivalent feelings. Ward (1985) also noted the important contributions that friends make to morale and sense of self, quite apart from specific instrumental functions during times of need.[6]

As already noted, Lee and Ihlinger-Tallman (1980) and Strain and Chappell (1982) showed that access to a few confidants is among the most significant factors contributing to morale in later life. However, as Babchuk (1978) and Lowenthal and Haven (1968) noted, among very old persons there is little association between maintenance of intimate ties and morale. Cantor (1979), Hess (1972), and Peters and Kaiser (1985) all showed that access to friends is markedly reduced in later life; death and relocation of older persons into long-term care facilities leave many elderly persons cut off from these ties.

Frail elderly are likely to be constrained by health problems and energy in the amount of visiting that is possible (Babchuk 1978; Riley and Foner 1968). These much older persons become increasingly preoccupied with the inner world and with issues of life review; they increasingly seek solace from representations and memories of the past, rather than from continuing interpersonal relationships. The very concept of friendship shows marked variation across studies as diverse as small-town midwestern elderly and underclass urban black elderly, and among older men and women (Babchuk 1978; Lowenthal and Haven 1968; Powers and Bultena 1976; Strain and Chappell 1982).

At least among inner-city elderly, the distinction between friend and neighbor blurs in later life. Issues of balance in exchange of assistance and support appear to be more salient among neighbors than friends. Again, consistent with Shanas' (1979a) concept of substitutability, Cantor (1979), Hess (1972), and Lawton and Simon (1968) reported that older persons look to somewhat younger persons for assistance, and tend to use neighbors and friends as a source of support only when children or other relatives are not available.

Caretaker Burden and Role Strain

Illness of family members is among the life changes believed to have the greatest impact upon physical and mental health of the caretaking family members. Because of both its implications for loss (Marris 1975) and its impact upon a large circle of relatives, chronic illness taxes the family's emotional and financial resources (Cook 1983; Cook and Cohler 1986). Illness accentuates many of the expectable problems related to caretaking by other family members for the frail elderly, including support for spouses caring for each other and for offspring caring for widowed parents.

65

Earlier work by Hill (1949) and associates on the stress on the family evoked by separation and reunion with the husband and father during the Second World War, and by Parsons and Fox (1953) on the social significance of illness for the family, revealed the complex problems involved in the study of family response to such adversity. Following the Viet Nam War, McCubbin and Patterson (1982) replicated Hill's work on military service and the family and extended the model to the study of illness in young children. This approach may be generally useful in the study of adverse life changes and the family.

Hill and his associates (Hill 1949; Hansen and Hill 1964; Klein and Hill 1979) initially formulated a so-called ABCX model of stress and social systems in which some event, usually adverse and unexpected (A), interacts with the family's ability to cope with that event, including available resources and sources of social support (B), and the family's particular understanding of that life change, including both objective and subjectively defined elements (C), resulting in the cre-ation of what at least some family members view as a crisis, discussed in this chapter as role strain, overload, and conflict (X).

Although Hill documented a number of alternative means for resolving the crisis resulting from separation and reunion of ser-vicemen and their families, McCubbin and Patterson (1982) maintained that Hill's initial model was too static and did not allow for change and response to life changes over time. The work of McCubbin and his associates supplemented the initial ABCX model with a "double" ABCX model that more explicitly allows for study of change. The double "A" in this model comprises the initial adverse life change event, other changes within the family, both associated with the initial event and independent of this event, and significant additional changes resulting from the process of confronting stress. The double "B" in the revised model represents available family resources, including social support, initial family coping resources as well as those which the family mobilizes in response to the change events, and available community supports. As Young (1983) observed, illness may mobilize previously unrealized coping resources within the family.

The double "C" includes the family's definition of the initial change event, together with other associated and independent events that are defined as "stressful." This double "C" is often referred to in studies of caretaking among relatives of Alzheimer's patients as caretaker sense of "burden," including both objective burden, such as the amount of nighttime supervision the patient requires, and subjective burden, such as feeling housebound with little time for oneself (Blumenthal and Morycz 1979; Clark and Rokowski 1983; George 1986; George and Bearon 1980; George and Gwyther 1986; Gilhooly 1984; Hoening and Hamilton 1966, 1967; Lezak 1978; Montgomery

66

et al. 1985; Niederehe and Fruge 1985; Platt 1985; Poulshock and Deimling 1984; Robinson 1983; Robinson and Thurner 1979; Zarit et al. 1985; Zarit et al. 1980).

Gilhooly (1984) showed that negative rather than positive aspects of the caretaker's definition of the situation may be particularly important determinants of experience of strain. Hirschfeld (1983) observed that caretaking based on longstanding love and intimacy, such as between husband and wife, leads intrinsically to positive construction of meaning that helps to buffer feelings of strain and overload.

Young (1983) also noted positive outcomes from the situation; while the illness may create increased conflict, it may also unite the family, leading to increased congruence of experience and purpose across generations within the family providing care as well as for elderly family members requiring such care. Montgomery, Gonyea, and Hooyman (1985) reported a relatively low relationship between objective and subjective burden, with caretaker feeling of constraint on time the single most significant aspect of burden or definition of the situation. It should also be noted that burden is not independent of life changes associated with adversity; as a result of their definition of the situation, family members may experience additional problems that become intertwined with the set of family-based life changes.

Finally, the double X in the ABCX model refers to sense of strain viewed over some interval of time. Klein and Hill (1979) and McCubbin and Patterson (1982) suggested replacing the concept of crisis with that of adaptation, allowing for specification of both positive and negative outcomes as well as the relative success realized by the family in response to the initial set of life changes. For example, summarizing findings from a survey of caregivers for Alzheimer's patients, including spouses, adult offspring, and other relatives, George and Gwyther (1986) reported marked feelings of role strain, lowered levels of life satisfaction, and increased rates of physical illness among caregivers, as compared with noncaregiving counterparts. However, as Thoits (1981) showed, there is a problem in assuming a necessary relationship between life changes and deleterious health outcomes. Negative health outcomes may be incidental to life event stress or may confound the results because health events are included both in the pileup of adverse life events, or "A" in the model, and in the response to this adversity, or the "X." Correlations do not necessarily reflect causality.

This double ABCX model was used in a number of studies, including those concerning the impact of illness within the family upon family members, although, to date, much of the initial research by McCubbin and his associates, who developed the model, focused on the "A" component, showing the extent to which adversity represents not just a single event but the pileup of events. McCubbin and colleagues (1982) reported on life changes in terms of the "pileup" of related events, studying families of children with cerebral palsy. Patterson and McCubbin (1983a, 1983b) and McCubbin et al. (1983) reported on a study of families with a child having cystic fibrosis—an illness governed by genetic factors and nearly always fatal after a decade or more of considerable investment in trying to make the child comfortable. Just as in Alzheimer's disease, while the prognosis is certain, the course of the illness itself is much less certain. Parents report both lowered morale and increased feelings of depression, as well as psychophysiological changes, in response to the child's illness.

Patterson and McCubbin documented the extent to which life events pile up in determining overall adversity; consistent with Pruchno, Blow, and Smyer's (1984) emphasis on the interdependence of events in defining overall adversity, the child's illness led to parental need to shift working hours; just as Cook (1983) and Cook and Wimberley (1984) reported in a study of families of childhood cancer patients, rearrangement of parental work hours, particularly in response to periodic rehospitalizations, affects the well-being of other children in the family. As brothers and sisters of the ill child become more distracted, leading to increased problems at school and with friends, parents become increasingly torn between the needs of the ill child and well brothers and sisters. These problems of siblings further contribute to overall family adversity, showing the manner in which adverse life changes are interactive and compound misfortune. This additional adversity within the family negatively affects the illness course of the ill child, further intensifying overall family stress.

This pileup of negative life events (A) interacts with available social support systems, such as community resources and help from other relatives and friends, coping mechanisms (B), and family definition of the situation, including experience of burden (C) in determining the extent of role strain reported by caretaking family members. As in so many situations of adversity, the more prolonged the illness, the more family members withdraw from potential sources of assistance available within the community (Grunebaum et al. 1975/1982).

As Patterson and McCubbin (1983b) noted, the more the family views chronic illness as a challenge, the greater their effort to cope with its impact. Parents appear to cope with the illness in ways governed by the sex-role expectations of society (Gutmann 1987; Parsons 1955). Increased adaptation (X) is attained through increased efforts by the wife and mother to foster family integration and stability, complemented by the husband-father's efforts to support his wife's efforts (Patterson and McCubbin 1983a, 1983b). Similar findings, less explicitly shaped by this model but also focused on the impact of life events, were reported by Patterson (1984) among mothers of antisocial children.

To date, the work of McCubbins and the Minnesota family stress research group is important principally as a means of focusing on the impact of adversity upon family functioning. Important but difficult areas of the paradigm, particularly measurement of the family's definition of the situation and shared coping techniques, were less carefully studied than either tabulation of life event pileup (A), available resources, including prevailing family coping style (B), or family definition of the situation (C).

The Double ABCX Model and Alzheimer's Disease

Life Event Issues Unique to Alzheimer's Disease

Considering the "A" factor, or pileup of life events, in the double ABCX model, Alzheimer's disease represents a life change of unparalleled magnitude for both caretaker and family. It shares with cancer and other terminal illnesses the quality of finality that demands anticipatory mourning by the family. However, Alzheimer's disease also resembles other chronic degenerative diseases in which the patient lingers for years in poor health, with marked effects on the caregiver's morale. Further, this illness presents not only with a complex series of interrelated physical symptoms, but also with symptoms of serious psychiatric illness, including severe anxiety, hallucinations and delusions, and aberrant irrational behaviors. The specific stages of Alzheimer's disease (Cohen and Eisdorfer 1986; Cohen et al. 1984) pose different and unique demands for caretakers (Ware and Carper 1982).

The marked loss of memory occurring in the middle and later phases of Alzheimer's disease is frightening for both patient and family members, adversely affecting family members' attitudes in caring for the patient. Feelings of responsibility and filial obligation are difficult to maintain when the patient does not recognize or respond to caretakers. Loss of speech and control over body functions make it difficult to understand the patient's needs, and also becomes embarrassing and uncomfortable for caretakers who are now required to provide the most intimate details of ordinary self-care. Finally, when institutional care is required, family members often feel ambivalent and guilty, even though they may have tolerated problems that would

69

have justified earlier institutional placement (Reifler et al. 1981). Although more systematic study is required, family members often report that health care professionals provide little specific information about or help with the problems confronted by caretakers (Chenoweth and Spencer 1986; Glosser et al. 1985).

The unpredictable course of the illness makes it difficult for family caretakers to plan for the future, or even to begin to anticipate and grieve over the ill family member's eventual death. Rakowski and Clark (1985) showed that the greater the patient's impairment and the greater the caretaker's report of strain, the less able are family members to consider the future. Considerable financial costs may be involved, such as incurred by placement into long-term care. Even when traditional medical intervention provides little or no relief for the patient, concurrent psychiatric and social work intervention may be especially helpful in supporting the family in carrying out its responsibilities to the patient.

Ultimately, coping resources are taxed to the limit, sometimes leading to crisis and, inevitably, leading to family strain, as expressed in lowered family morale, increased depression, and even physical illness among relatives caring for the patient for many months (Wilder et al. 1983). However, over time, family members appear to adapt to the illness, with signs of strain greater in the first months after beginning caretaking than after several years (Hoening and Hamilton 1967; Zarit et al. 1986).

Finally, family caretakers are concerned about the implications of the patient's diagnosis for their own aging. There is some evidence (Heston et al. 1981) that first-degree relatives, particularly offspring, of elders with early onset Alzheimer's disease may be at greater risk for this illness than the population as a whole. Just as with Huntington's disease (Falek 1979), relatives are forced to live with anxiety about the future, facing a possible biological time bomb over which they have no control, and with unknown outcome. One obvious means for coping with these implications of the illness is to avoid contact with the afflicted relative.

The magnitude of the resources required to care for relatives with Alzheimer's disease was described by Callahan, Diamond, Giele, and Morris (1980). These authors noted that responsibility for the care of the patient includes financial obligation for doctor and nursing bills, help with the activities of daily living, and support through socializing and providing encouragement. Again, although these authors assumed that particular caretakers carried most of the burden, the impact of this responsibility may involve a number of relatives.

Home care may be a cost-effective alternative to institutional placement, and may be particularly important in maintaining the older patient's morale and vitality (Brody 1966; Brody et al. 1978; Callahan et al. 1980; Kent and Matson 1972). However, reimbursement for home-care expenses is very limited, in spite of the fact that home care is far less expensive than residential care. Community institutions provide very little respite for caretakers, such as relieving them by using home visiting staff and short-term hospital stay. As Crossman, London, and Barry (1981), Fengler and Goodrich (1979), Grad and Sainsbury (1968), and Sainsbury and Grad de Alarcon(1970) all observed, failure to provide respite for family caretakers increases caretaker personal distress, possibly leading to increased rates of untreated psychiatric illness in the community.

Indeed, Rabins, Mace, and Lucas (1982) reported feelings of frustration, fatigue, and depression among more than 85 percent of family caregivers of Alzheimer's patients evaluated at a single point in time. Pratt, Schmall, Wright, and Cleveland (1985) noted that four-fifths of respondents interviewed on health status reported that caring for a patient with Alzheimer's disease had negatively impacted caretaker physical health. However, Chenoweth and Spencer (1986) reported that nearly a quarter of caregivers showed physical illness or depression following the relative's placement into long-term care, suggesting that the subjective burden of responsibility for the care of an elder relative, regardless of the setting, may be the critical factor associated with lowered caretaker morale and increased health problems.

Coping With the Caretaking Task

The double ABCX model clarifies factors contributing to increased sense of burden, and use of particular coping techniques, in determining the extent to which assumption of the caretaker role for the patient with Alzheimer's disease is perceived to be a source of role strain. Measurement of coping presents particular problems in applying the double ABCX model to the study of family caretaking for those patients. Too often, studies of family adaptation to crisis use models of coping based on individual difference personality research, rather than those which are family centered (Folkman and Lazarus 1980; Lazarus and Folkman 1984).[7]

Discussing techniques used by caretakers for adapting to the caregiving demands of Alzheimer's patients, Johnson (1983) reported a high frequency of either psychological distancing from the patient or the opposite pattern in which the patient's relatives become totally involved in caretaking, withdrawing from other relationships and focusing all remaining energy on the patient. However, this coping strategy may lead to withdrawal from the very community resources that might be particularly helpful for both patient and caretaker in the relief of strain, ultimately increasing family stress (Levine et al. 1983).

In addition to Johnson's pioneering study, at least four other researchers have looked at coping techniques used by caretakers of Alzheimer's patients. In an effort to provide more effective skills for family caretakers, Levine and his colleagues (1983) surveyed coping skills used by caretakers who differed in the amount of reported role strain. Although the findings are not separated by spouse and off-spring caretakers or men and women within each generation, those best able to cope with caretaking demands attempted specific strategies for solving such caretaking problems as wandering or improving capacity for self-care. Prayer and an increased sense of self-worth and personal congruence as a consequence of following through on their own ideals proved to be particularly important in permitting these "good copers" to function effectively.

Religion also proved effective as a means of dealing with the ravages of Alzheimer's disease in Pratt, Schmall, Wright, and Cleveland's (1985) study of caretakers. Again, findings were not disaggregated according to generation and sex of caretakers, limiting understanding of factors differentially accounting for selection of particular coping techniques. Further, while the double ABCX model includes both family resources and coping styles as resources, the study by Pratt and her colleagues included resources as a coping factor, rather than as a separate but related aspect of available resources (B in the ABCX model). Religiosity was significantly related to reduced feeling of burden (C in the ABCX model), as was the presence of help from the extended family. Greater availability of friends and neighbors was not related to lesser sense of burden.

Futurity, or the capacity to see beyond the present illness, was reported by Coppel, Burton, Becker, and Fiore (1985) and Rakowski and Clark (1985) to be associated with lessened sense of role strain among caregivers of patients with Alzheimer's disease. However, neither study reported findings disaggregated by age and gender of caretaker. Coppel and associates found that those caregivers report-ing lower levels of coping skills were more likely to attribute their lack of success to external constraints such as lack of financial resources or time available for caretaking, although lower levels of coping were not associated with greater depressive feelings. Further, as Pagel, Becker, and Coppel (1985) showed, greater depression was related to more unstable course of the illness, leading to greater feelings of loss of control.

These findings point again to the need for a more specific under-standing of adverse life events, such as differences in the natural progression of an illness as a factor related to definition of burden, use of particular coping techniques, and resulting role strain. In particular, as Pagel, Becker, and Coppel (1985) noted, it is important to determine the caregivers' understanding of symptom changes in studying the impact of caregiving upon caregivers' mental health. Some caregivers view increased impairment as a relief from the demands made upon them by the patient earlier in the course of the illness.

Burden Assumed by Spouse and Offspring

To date, much of the research regarding the impact of Alzheimer's disease on the family has remained at a descriptive level. For example, in determining the source of the burden so often reported among caretakers of Alzheimer's patients, Grad and Sainsbury (1963, 1968) reported that lowered patient mood and other evidence of patient personal distress had a greater impact on caretaking family members than such problems as performing self-care tasks that patients could no longer handle. However, other clinical investigators (Chenoweth and Spencer 1986; Deimling and Bass 1986; Groves 1987; Sanford 1975; Sheldon 1982) reported patient night wandering, incontinence and problems of managing the patient to toilet facilities, personal irresponsibility, and disruptive behavior to be particularly difficult problems for caretakers. Zarit, Reever, and Bach-Peterson (1980) found neglect of self-care and restlessness to be the most frequently encountered problems.

Two groups of researchers attempted systematic reviews of previous findings in an effort to tally reported descriptions of the experience of burden (Niederehe and Fruge (1985) attempted a much more limited tally). Blumenthal and Morycz (1979) reported the following specific patient behaviors that are particularly burdensome: wandering, dangerous patient actions, falling and accidents, incontinence, bedfastness and immobility, blindness, disturbed sleep, medication problems, need to have meals prepared and lack of competence for feeding oneself, frailty and malnutrition, inability to bathe and to dress, need for personal care, fearfulness and agitation, lack of cooperation and restlessness, demanding behavior, psychosis and catastrophic reactions, aggression, depression, need for transportation, assistance with finances, embarrassing behavior, and need to have laundry done. Bedfastness/immobility, patient sleep disturbance, and patient aggression were most frequently cited.

These burdensome aspects of patient care led to the following subjective sources of burden among caretakers: depression, anxiety, reduced life satisfaction, secondary caretaker illness, back strain, em-

embarrassment at having to provide intimate care for the patient, fatigue, inadequate space for caretakers to move around, financial strain, marital conflict, time lost from work, inadequate strength, loss of income, reduced social activities, reduced leisure activities, family conflict, and fear of the caretaker's own impaired mental health.

Blumenthal and Morycz (1979) noted the complex, interrelated nature of objective (patient) symptoms and caregiver (subjective) burden. Patient, caretaker, and caretaker environment are all important components of overall defined burden.

Clark and Rakowski (1983) further elaborated this list of objectively and subjectively experienced burdens. They differentiated burden as (1) direct assistance in performing activities of everyday life, (2) coordination of patient, family, and society (principally the patient's physician and other health professionals), and (3) personal challenges posed for caregivers by this process (subjective burden).

Included under subjectively defined burdens are issues of emotional drain from continual performance of duties, loss of time for oneself, problems in learning about the illness, and drain on one's own health as well as problems in dealing with inevitable guilt for feeling angry at and resentful of the patient, attempting to make up for time lost due to caregiving, readjusting personal routines, dealing with inevitable loss of sleep, accepting the terminal nature of the diagnosis and anticipatory grieving, accepting changes in the relationship with the patient, dealing with issues of "why" this illness, assuming both present and projected financial costs of the illness, dealing with possible patient relocation to long-term care, accepting reduced relations with friends and confidants, maintaining caring concern for the patient even when confronted with patient behaviors difficult to contain or to accept including personality changes, and resolving uncertainty about the caretaker's own caretaking skills. Clark and Rakowski (1983) maintained that energy drain, loss of time for self, and guilt over imposition on caretaker time and energy are among the most significant subjective sources of burden.

Few empirical reports and even fewer studies attempt to develop a model of the relationship between adversity stemming from the pileup of life events due to Alzheimer's disease, family definition of the situation, family coping strategies, and outcome in terms of role strain among caretakers. Also, few studies compare caretaking burden and both caretaker and patient outcomes over long periods of time, although Johnson (1983) reported that when patient dependence upon the family increases over time, relations within the family deteriorate, leading to increased conflict between the generations.

As generally found in studies of caretaking among older persons, the primary caretaker is most often the spouse (Cantor 1983;

Johnson 1983; Stoller and Earl 1983; Tobin and Kulys 1980). Coppel, Burton, Becker, and Fiore (1985) reported greater depression among caretakers of patients with a more variable course, and within families in which caretakers were less able to make specific plans for coping with caregiving tasks. As Grad and Sainsbury (1968) and Kraus et al. (1976) showed, believing that the patient would be better treated at home than elsewhere, spouses labor to prevent hospitalization regardless of the personal costs involved. Characteristically, the ill spouse in these families was markedly impaired, well beyond what would justify institutional care.

Caring for an older spouse, particularly one who shows marked cognitive impairment, is experienced as a burden which, accompanied by problems in coping with this burden, leads to increased role strain, psychological symptoms, and impaired physical health (Farkas 1980; Groves, 1987; Klein et al. 1967). Coppel, Burton, Becker, and Fiore (1985) reported an association between the belief that the illness would continue in a similar pattern over the ensuing 3 years and both greater impact of the patient's illness on the spouse's life and more reports of depression among the spouses of Alzheimer's patients. Caretaking spouses of patients living at home differed very little from spouses of patients in institutional care. Regardless of placement, those caretaking spouses feeling least able to cope with the problem and most responsible for the patient's illness also reported the greatest depression.

Beyond showing an association between spouse definition of the situation and psychological symptoms, research on the spouse as caretaker has generally not disaggregated findings by gender. While men are becoming increasingly accepted as caretakers, caretaking has traditionally been defined as a woman's role. Even considering the normative "tilt" toward the woman's role as kin-keeper (Sweetser 1963, 1966), the lack of systematic study of the roles of men and women as caretakers, particularly for their spouses, is surprising.

Focusing on the issue of gender differences and caretaking for an ill spouse, Fitting and Rabins (1985) and Fitting, Rabins, Lucas, and Eastham (1986) reported few differences in the manner in which older men and women experienced the burdens of caretaking, although the morale of the women caretakers was initially more adversely affected by caregiving.

Reporting on the older wives of ill men, although not necessarily those with Alzheimer's disease, Fengler and Goodrich (1979) also found that wives expressed lower morale. The wife's morale level was best predicted by the morale of the spouse, largely independent of the severity of the husband's condition, except for the most impaired, aphasic men. The inability to communicate with one's spouse, a

75

problem accentuated in Alzheimer's disease, appears to affect care-taking spouse morale to a greater extent than constraints on free time and ability to tend to personal chores. Zarit (1982) also reported that the morale of women caretakers is more adversely affected than that of men, noting that men are more likely to hire housekeepers and also to seek the assistance of other (woman) relatives, who are drawn into the caretaking process in the manner portrayed by Cohler (1983), Cohler and Grunebaum (1981), Firth, Hubert, and Forge (1970), and Pruchno, Blow, and Smyer (1984). Gender differences in reporting distress may partially account for these findings: women are both more aware of their feelings and more willing to talk about them. Following these patients and caretakers over a period of 2 years, Zarit, Todd, and Zarit (1986) reported that initial differences in morale diminish over time. This finding suggests that family members do adapt to the caretaking demands, although how this adjustment takes place is not well understood.

Anecdotal evidence suggests that, with the passage of time, wives begin to adopt an instrumental orientation toward their ill husbands that is much like that initially reported by the husbands of ill wives. Increased concern with decisionmaking within the family serves as a "psychological distancing technique" very similar to that reported by Johnson (1983) as an adaptive technique.

Study of burden and coping responses is made more difficult by the often unpredictable progression of Alzheimer's disease. Johnson (1983) reported that some patients showed increased impairment across the 2 years of the study, while others showed little symptom change. The uncertainty and changes in caregiving demands over time as factors relating to caregiving role strain have received little discussion. Johnson (1983) reported that the most distressed spouses are more likely to have had their ill husband or wife put in residential care during the intervening 2 years. Unfortunately, the study did not mention any association between caretaker gender and outcome, nor discuss the significance of increased distress associated with caretaking as a factor in relocation to institutional care.

Noelker and Wallace (1985) also reported that the mental health of women caretakers is more adversely affected than that of men; while the two sexes devote about equal time and effort to caretaking, women report greater strain than men regarding caretaking and experience caretaking as more restricting and confining. Women are also more likely to appreciate the serious nature of the patient's distress. Consistent with Johnson's (1983) findings that men are more likely to obtain assistance in caretaking, women relatives are more likely to respond to requests from men, who are presumed not to deal with these tasks, than from other women, who are presumed to be adequate caretakers.

Grunebaum, Gamer, and Cohler (1983) reported similar findings based on a study of housekeeping arrangements when the wife and mother is hospitalized for psychiatric illness.

The other cardinal role in caretaking of family members with Alzheimer's disease is played by the middle-aged woman in the second generation, most often the daughter, but sometimes the daughter-in-law. A large descriptive literature reports increased feelings of burden associated with assuming the role of caregiver, although few of these studies focus specifically on offspring caring for patients with Alzheimer's disease. Also, few systematic studies contrasted gender and relationship of offspring caretakers. Sons and daughters or daughters-in-law clearly define the caretaking situation in quite different ways.

Studying caregiving for older persons, but not specifically focusing on family members with Alzheimer's disease, Horowitz (1985) reported that sons may be more involved in caretaking than is commonly realized. Offspring caretakers lived no further away than an hour's drive, and one-quarter shared a common household with the ill parent. Women offspring generally lived closer to their parents than men did, and were more dutiful in maintaining at least daily phone contact. Not surprisingly, men were less immediately involved in caretaking for their parents, relying on their spouses for caregiving services.

Horowitz (1985) reported that caregiving women offspring expected little more than tacit understanding from their husbands. Wives of men providing care were expected to take over this caregiving role within the family, and consequently, reported much less role strain attendant upon caregiving than was reported by women offspring. Johnson (1983) also reported a "pass through" effect in which men turn to their sisters or wives to provide major caregiving for parents. This finding is consistent with normative findings regarding gender differences in caregiving for elderly parents, reviewed in this chapter, particularly problems faced by women offspring in the middle generation (Brody 1981).

Townsend and Poulshock (1986) interviewed both parental and offspring generations, including both the impaired elder (thereby excluding significantly impaired elders) and caretakers within widowed families and those in which both members of the older couple were still alive. This report, confined almost exclusively to issues of the structure of the decisionmaking network within the family, is notable largely for showing that the older generation remains active in making decisions about care arrangements, with offspring often seeing themselves as more significant in the caretaking process than their parents do. Widowed elders created more diverse support systems than couples still living together, maintaining active control over events of daily life. Overall, older couples in this study particularly wanted to avoid becoming dependent upon offspring and to avoid even the appearance of frailty.

Several studies contrasted the significance of the spouse and offspring as caregivers for patients with Alzheimer's disease. Stoller and Earl (1983) noted that the spouse is the primary source of assistance. Offspring are relied upon only when no well spouse is available for providing care. Consistent with the principle of substitutability (Johnson 1983; Shanas 1979a), families in which offspring rather than spouses provide care show greater impairment within the parent generation, suggesting problems in generalizing from families with offspring as primary caretakers to other family caretaking situations. Zarit, Reever, and Bach-Peterson (1980) reported few differences in the extent of reported burden between spouse and offspring; within each generation, greater caretaking responsibility was associated with greater feelings of burden.

George and Gwyther (1986) showed that the increased sense of burden and accompanying feelings of strain were associated with having an impaired family member, rather than with the length or severity of the impairment. In contrast with findings reported by Rankin and Pinkston (1985) that offspring felt greater role strain than caretaking spouses, George and Gwyther showed marked levels of personal distress among both spouse and offspring caretakers; caretaking spouses reported more than twice the level of strain than was shown by offspring. George and Gwyther also showed that strain evident in restricted social relations differentially affects caretaking spouses and offspring.

Among spouse caretakers, club membership and outside employment are sacrificed for caregiving, while among offspring caretakers, visiting with family and friends is sacrificed, as is time spent simply relaxing. Both spouse and offspring caregivers report a markedly lower level of life satisfaction than other relatives who provide care and support for elders in nursing homes or living with relatives. George and Gwyther's findings suggest that the role of caregiver, whether spouse, child, or other relative, is intrinsically burdensome, even apart from such other factors as living arrangement (ill family member living in the same household or apart) or ill relative's placement (long-term care or still living in the community).[8]

Contrasting families in which either offspring or spouse provides care for the impaired elderly (although not limited to patients with Alzheimer's disease), Parmelee (1983) noted that caregiving spouses are particularly likely to be in conflict with the spouse for whom care is provided; this conflict is also acknowledged by the ill spouse.

However, Johnson (1983) reported that the ambivalence expressed by offspring caretakers is particularly likely to lead to conflict with the parent for whom such caretaking is being provided. In contrast with Johnson's findings, Parmelee reported that conflict is not as apparent in the relationship of caretaking offspring and their ill parents, perhaps in part because adult offspring rely on resources outside the family for additional assistance. Johnson (1983) showed that, when contrasted with offspring, caretaker spouses rely much less upon outside support. Regardless of their generation, respondents in Johnson's (1983) study reported not only the experience of burden, but an outcome characterized by marked role strain; however, spouses were more willing than offspring to accept burden and to endure strain without resentment. Offspring are willing to undertake caregiving but do so with markedly greater reluctance than the spouse.

Conclusion

Alzheimer's disease is a frightening, lingering illness, principally afflicting late middle-aged and older persons, ultimately destroying consciousness itself. While the patient suffers terribly from the impact of the disease—from the first awareness of loss of memory through progressive loss of awareness of self—this illness has unusual impact upon other family members. Particularly during the middle and later phases of the illness, patients gradually lose the ability to perform even the most basic self-care activities. This loss of function requires increased caretaker effort and poses severe constraints on caretaker time and energy. Further, it is particularly distressing for offspring to see their parent lose the ability to perform even the most essential aspects of self-care. This pain is enhanced by the patient's loss of memory and increasing problems in recognizing persons known over a lifetime.

While the spouse feels a degree of commitment based on longstanding marital ties—and most caretaking *is* provided by the spouse—at the same time, the spouse is also likely to be elderly and in frail health, requiring assistance from other family members (Groves 1987). However, such support is more likely to be forthcoming for men caring for their ill wife than for women caring for their ill husband. Such caretaking is often assumed to be continuous with the wife's caretaking career over a lifetime. This same tilt toward women as caretakers has been reported among offspring caretakers as well. Daughters care for their ill parents, requiring only tacit support from their husbands; sons relinquish caretaking in favor of their wives,

79

who are expected to assume this caretaking burden in addition to housekeeping, childcare, and career.

Supplemental caretaking follows what Shanas (1979a) described as the "principle of substitutability," with those relatives closest to the patient first called upon to provide support and assistance. As Cohler (1983), and Pruchno, Blow, and Smyer (1984) noted, the need for caretaking spreads out from the immediately afflicted patient to an ever-expanding, interdependent circle of relatives. And the relatives do perform such caretaking, even in the absence of particular affection for the patient or others in the family circle. While caretaking may not be explicitly mandatory in the manner prescribed within an extended family living in a common household (Nydegger 1983), bonds of invisible loyalty (Boszormenyi-Nagy and Spark 1973) are maintained in contemporary urban society.

Studies of families with Alzheimer's patients have not, in general, been guided by the extent of theory that has informed normative study of older persons, caretaking, and family relations. Normative study of the family of later life has relied on such diverse perspectives as role theory (Hagestad 1984; Troll et al. 1979), exchange theory (Bengtson and Dowd 1980-81), and network theory (Ward 1985).

Theory guides the formulation of the research problem and is useful in integrating findings. For example, in this chapter, the family stress theory, as initially formulated by Hill (1949) and enlarged by McCubbin and his colleagues (McCubbin et al. 1983), is relied on in an effort to integrate findings reported to date. As Gubrium (1986) and Gubrium and Lynott (1984) noted, few researchers have examined the social meaning of the diagnosis of Alzheimer's disease. Much remains to be learned about the complex interaction between the experience of aging in our society and the onset of disease processes, particularly Alzheimer's disease, which itself is a caricature of shared beliefs regarding the process of growing old. However, it is impossible to enlarge the metaperspective until more detailed findings are available on the family's engagement and response to this illness. Study of the meaning of this illness for society and response among family members must proceed in tandem.

There have been problems in extending concepts and methods from normative study of older persons and their caretakers to study of families with elders afflicted with chronic illnesses such as Alzheimer's disease. An extensive literature shows that, at least at the beginning of the caretaking process, both spouse and offspring define caretaking as burdensome and lack resources to cope with the impact of this illness, presumably leading to impairment in caretaker health and morale. However, much less systematic study has been done on caretaking and its outcome over extended periods of time.

Recognizing that, at least initially, caretakers do feel burdened and do experience some loss of morale, at least some studies suggest processes of accommodation over time that enable caretakers to gradually adapt to the demands of caretaking.

While detailed study has been devoted to more precise measurement of both objectively defined and subjectively experienced burden (Harel and Deimling 1984; Montgomery et al. 1985; Platt 1985; Poulshock and Deimling 1984; Robinson 1983; Schwartz 1983; Townsend and Poulshock 1986; Zarit et al. 1980), little study has addressed how family caretakers adapt to this burden, with only a few studies even indirectly addressing issues of coping and adaptation (Coppel et al. 1985; Levine et al. 1983; Pratt et al. 1985). The value of most descriptive studies is limited by failure to disaggregate caretakers by sex and generation within the family, as well as by failure to include the stage of the illness. Little is to be gained by including much older husbands of ill patients together with middle-aged daughters or daughters-in-law in studying perceptions of burden and response within the family. Even where efforts are made to present findings by sex and generation of caretaker, the number of families studied is so small and, often, so unrepresentative, that it is difficult to interpret the findings.

We have tried to summarize findings to date in tabular form (please see table 2-1). This table shows classes of patient, caregiver, family, and environmental characteristics believed to influence caregiver functioning on the basis of theoretical, clinical, and empirical findings to date. As section A shows, there has been considerable descriptive study of illness characteristics believed to be important for caregiver mental health. However, these studies failed to document significant relationships between specific illness characteristics and caregiver distress. Perhaps of greater importance is the caregiver's understanding of symptom and course as related to caregiving, including the degree of uncertainty caregivers experience over the course of the illness. The patient's premorbid personality and coping style should also be considered as factors related to response to symptoms, particularly in the early and middle stages of the illness.

While individual differences in caregiver personality have been studied (section B), including issues of self-efficacy, little specific consideration of coping behaviors and health status of caregivers appears in work to date. Sections C and D summarize findings regarding the impact of family structure and social context upon caregiving response. Variation in functional characteristics, such as adaptability, family cohesiveness, and extent to which family roles are defined in a traditional manner, all appear related to outcome. Future study must take into consideration the pileup of family life events

Table 2-1. Determinants of caretaker health and morale

A. PATIENT CHARACTERISTICS	RESEARCH

I. Health status

Dementia	Hoening & Hamilton 1966;
—Time since diagnosis	Grad & Sainsbury 1968;
—Global severity of disorder	Sainsbury & Grad 1970;
- cognitive deficits	Sanford 1975;
- physical impairment	Ross & Kedward 1977;
- behavioral disturbance	Godber 1977;
—Caregiving needs	Blazer 1978;
- physical care needs	Gurland et al. 1978;
- mental care needs	Koopman-Boyden & Wells 1979;
Health problems unrelated to	Rabins, Mace, & Lucas 1982;
dementia	Gelleard & Boyd-Watts 1982;
	Johnson & Johnson 1983;
	Wilder et al. 1983;
	Poulshock & Deimling 1984

II. Psychological characteristics

Premorbid personality features	Anecdotal clinical accounts; not
Perception of illness	yet systematically investigated
Perception of spousal and	in empirical study
family relationships	
Perception of social support	
Coping strategies	

III. Social characteristics

Age	Fengler & Goodrich 1979;
Sex	Johnson 1979;
Race	Hirschfeld 1983;
Ethnicity	Cantor 1983;
Religion	Poulshock & Deimling 1984
Occupation prior to disability	
or retirement	
Income level	

Table 2-1. (Continued)

B. CAREGIVER CHARACTERISTICS RESEARCH

I. Health status

Mental conditions	Blumenthal & Morycz 1980;
Physical conditions	Zarit, Reever, & Bach-Peterson 1980

II. Psychological characteristics

Personality features	Niederehe & Fruge 1982;
Perception of illness	Groves et al. 1984;
Perception of patient	Lansky 1984;
response to illness	Zarit, Orr, & Zarit 1985;
Perception of caregiver tasks	George & Gwyther 1986;
—Physical tasks	Brody 1979;
—Mental tasks	Fitting et al. 1986;
—Social norms and roles	Hudson 1986;
Perception of spousal and	Zarit et al. 1986;
familial relationships	Coppel et al. 1985;
Perception of social support	Pagel et al. 1985;
Coping strategies	Johnson 1983;
	Levine et al. 1983

III. Social characteristics

Age	Fengler & Goodrich 1979;
Sex	Hirschfeld 1983;
Race	Cantor 1983;
Ethnicity	Poulshock & Deimling 1984
Religion	
Occupation	
Income	

Table 2-1. (Continued)

C.   FAMILY CHARACTERISTICS   RESEARCH

I. Family constellation

II. Family functioning*

   Problemsolving   Bruhn 1977;
   —Instrumental   Blazer 1978;
   —Affective   Koopman-Boyden & Wells 1979;
   Communication   Groves et al. 1984;
   Roles   Lansky 1984;
   Affective responsiveness   Niederehe & Fruge 1985
   Behavioral control
   Adaptability
   Cohesion

III. Family response to illness

   Perception of disorder
   Perception of caregiver needs
   Degree of involvement in
      caregiving tasks

IV. Family life stage
      (Developmental issues)

V. Family life events

----

*Selection of such characteristics has been based on models of family functioning described by Epstein, Bishop, and Baldwin (1982) and Olson and Associates. See Walsh (1987) for comprehensive review of family issues in later life.

Table 2-1. (Continued)

D. SOCIAL-ENVIRONMENTAL CHARACTERISTICS	RESEARCH
I. Living arrangements	
Physical setting	Sanford 1975
–Home	
–Institution	
Caregiving constellation	
Geographical factors	
II. Caregiving context	
Informal social structure (family, friends)	Fengler & Goodrich 1979; Zarit, Reever, & Bach-Peterson
Formal social structure (health and supportive services)	1980; Kahn & Tobin 1981; Johnson 1983; Cantor 1983

and developmental tasks related to family life stage on caregiver responses. The nature of supportive services and informal social structure also shows some relationship with caregiver maintenance of morale.

Future research on family caretaking and Alzheimer's disease could well be guided by such recent exemplary efforts as Noelker and Wallace's (1985) comprehensive study of intergenerational households and caretaking processes, Morycz's (1985) study of the determinants of the decision to institutionalize a patient with Alzheimer's disease, Townsend and Poulshock's (1986) study of decisionmaking and support networks in the family of Alzheimer's patients, George and Gwyther's (1986) comparative, multidimensional study of caregivers for Alzheimer's patients and community counterparts not involved in such caregiving, and Zarit, Todd, and Zarit's (1986) longitudinal study of caregiving in families with Alzheimer's patients, one of the few to focus explicitly on changes in caregiver perception of burden and mental health over time.

Significantly, these theoretically informed and methodologically appropriate studies have all appeared in print over the past 2 years.

Study of family caretaking response is both more inclusive and more methodologically sophisticated than in the past, promising greater understanding of the impact of Alzheimer's disease on family processes and of the variations in caretaking for the impaired elder with this terrifying and mysterious disease.

Notes

1. The authors wish to thank Judith Cook for her suggestions regarding issues of family, caretaking, and stress and illness discussed in this chapter.

2. Emphasis upon provision of care for others in the family, based on feelings of responsibility and obligation, regardless of feelings of love and affection, must be differentiated from the view, advocated by exchange theory in the social sciences (Bengtson and Dowd 1980-81; Blau 1964; Homans 1964/1974), that persons deliberately follow a policy of rational selection or choice based on concepts of enlightened self-interest. As Sussman (1985) notes in reviewing conceptual frameworks for studying the family life of older persons, interpersonal relations may often reflect lack of equity in exchange. A variety of factors lead persons to care for each other beyond simple economic calculation. Feelings of satisfaction based on acting according to valued goals, and realization of the implicit but delayed exchange of caring for older family members in expectation that such care will one day be available for the caretaker as well, are among the many factors determining caretaker agreement to assume responsibility for older family members. Sussman (1985) also observes that issues of distributive justice may be present as well. That is, persons who provide extra care to older relatives assume that they will be entitled to more than their share of a later inheritance as a reward for extraordinary caretaking services. While the concept of equity is undoubtedly a factor motivating caretaking, this concept, in turn, rests on normatively structured understandings of fairness in relationships within our society. However, that is not to imply that such economic motivation is the basis for caretaking activities. For example, the daughter who assumes particular responsibility for care of a frail, elderly mother may be encouraged by brothers or sisters to elect to receive particular heirlooms, but such caretaking is not necessarily motivated by this concern.

3. Based on this assumption, Parsons (1949) suggested that this social change had led to structural change in the family. Parsons has been misread as believing that social change resulted in destruction of the

extended family unit; his only claim was that the urban family need not continually work together as a unit since family members do not tend a farm in common.

4. At the present time, there is continuing controversy regarding the role of government in protecting this intergenerational transfer. For example, there is continuing question whether Social Security should provide financial assistance for older persons in nursing homes as long as there are family resources available to purchase such care. There appears to be consensus on the "right" of families to receive such inheritance, as well as the obligation of government to assist in protecting this inheritance through financial assistance for catastrophic illness and the expenses of long-term care.

5. While Guttman (1977, 1988) suggests that there is a reversal of gender roles after midlife, with women becoming more instrumental and men becoming more expressive and nurturant, this presumed reversal does not appear to take place in the roles assigned to men and women within the family of later life.

6. Elder (1984) has observed that structural-functional perspectives are far less significant than those based on symbolic interactionism as a perspective on understanding family relations. Formulations such as those of Kahn (1979) and Kahn and Antonucci (1980), Fischer (1982), Thoits (1982), and Ward (1985) point to the very real contributions of the distinction between expressive and instrumental activities in understanding the role of social supports as factors contributing to morale across the adult life course.

7. Considerable research has been done on family-centered approaches to family problems in the study of schizophrenic young adults and their parents (Mishler and Waxler 1968; Reiss 1981; Waxler 1974; Wild and Shapiro 1977; Wild et al. 1977). Consistent with Burgess' (1926) emphasis on the family as the "unity of interacting personalities," this work has focused on observation of the family as a group, working in concert to solve a problem. However, this study has been concerned principally with the process of communication regarding problem solving, and has been less explicitly concerned with the outcome of decisionmaking. Important advances in this area could be realized by the integration of family approaches to study of problem solving with those developed by Lazarus, Pearlin, Moos, and others for the study of individual personality. Work of Moos (1984), Menaghan (1983), and Pilisuk and Parks (1983) points the way to the development of better techniques for measuring coping styles at the family level of measurement.

8. While beyond the scope of this chapter, it is interesting to note that

George and Gwyther's findings regarding the burden and resulting strain of placement of an elder in long-term care, while stressful for the older impaired relative who is placed, appears to affect caregivers less adversely than has been suggested. While there is little systematic data regarding family response to placement in long-term care, findings from George and Gwyther's study suggest that having an impaired elder living in the same household results in markedly greater impairment in mental health than having an elder placed into care; family-living impaired elders appear particularly to affect opportunities for visiting or other activities outside the household; time and effort must be devoted largely to caretaking activities. Although some relatives appear to thrive when confronted with such caretaking responsibilities, most find such provision of care to be a source of burden, leading to notable experience of role strain and overload, with accompanying reduction in life satisfaction and increased symptoms of psychiatric distress and physical illness.

Although many studies have documented the serious problems involved in placement and subsequent visits (Brody and Spark 1966; Cath 1972; Ross and Kedward 1977; Savitsky and Sharkey 1972; Soyer 1972; York and Calsyn 1977), noting guilt over placement and lack of satisfaction derived from visits in the nursing home as prominent concerns, other studies report that the decision for placement may enhance relations within the family and provide an opportunity for renewed closeness when relatives are no longer burdened with issues of providing care which is beyond their emotional resources (Dobrof and Litwak 1977; Treas 1977). Smith and Bengtson (1979) suggest that when interviews with family members are carried out prior to admission, such as in Tobin and Lieberman's (1976) report, issues of conflict and guilt are more apparent than when family relations are evaluated following placement, when each generation has had an opportunity to adjust to this relocation into long-term care. Smith and Bengtson's clinical observations beg for replication in systematic, longitudinal study of placement and its aftermath.

References

Allan, G. Sibling solidarity. *Journal of Marriage and the Family* 39:177-184, 1977.

Alzheimer, A. Uber eine eigenartige der hirnrinde (On a peculiar disease of the cerebral cortex). *Allegemeiner Zeitschrift fur*

Psychiatrie 64:146-148, 1907. Wilkine, R., and Brody, I., trans. *Archives of Neurology* 21:109-110, 1969.

Babchuk, N. Aging and primary relations. *Aging and Human Development* 9:137-151, 1978.

Banfield, E. *The Moral Basis of a Backward Society.* New York: Free Press/Macmillan, 1958.

Bankoff, E. Social support and adaptation to widowhood. *Journal of Marriage and the Family* 45:827-839, 1983.

Benedek, T. Parenthood as a developmental phase: A contribution to the libidio theory, and discussion. In: Benedek, T., ed. *Psychoanalytic Investigations.* Chicago: Quadrangle Books, 1959/1973. pp. 377-407.

Bengtson, V., and DeTerre, E. Aging and family relations. *Marriage and Family Review* 3(1/2):51-76, 1980.

Bengtson, V., and Dowd, J. Sociological functionalism, exchange theory, and lifecycle analysis: A call for more explicit theoretical bridges. *International Journal of Aging and Human Development* 12:55-73, 1980-81.

Bengtson, V., and Treas, J. The changing family context of mental health aging. In: Birren, J., and Sloane, B., eds. *Handbook of Mental Health and Aging.* Englewood Cliffs, NJ: Prentice Hall, 1980. pp. 400-428.

Biddle, B., and Thomas, E. *Role Theory: Concepts and Research.* New York: John Wiley, 1966.

Blau, P. *Exchange and Power in Social Life.* New York: John Wiley, 1964.

Blazer, D. Working with the elderly patient's family. *Geriatrics* 117-123, Feb. 1978.

Blenkner, M. Social work and family relationships in later life with some thoughts on filial maturity. In: Shanas, E., and Streib, G., eds. *Social Structure and the Family: Generational Relations.* Englewood Cliffs, NJ: Prentice Hall, 1965. pp. 46-59.

Blenkner, M. The normal dependencies of aging. In: Kalish, R., ed. *The Dependencies of Old People.* Ann Arbor, MI: The University of Michigan-Wayne State University Institute of Gerontology, 1969. pp. 27-38.

Blessed, G.; Tomlinson, B.; and Roth, M. The association between quantitative measures of dementia and of senile change in the cerebral gray matter of elderly subjects. *British Journal of Psychiatry* 114:797-811, 1968.

Blocq, P., and Marinesco, G. Sur les lesions et al pathogenie de l'epilepsie dite essentielle (On the lesions and pathogenesis said to be essential to epilepsy). *Seminars in Medicine* (Paris) 12:445, 1892.

Blumenthal, M., and Morycz, R. "Late Life Brain Disease and Family

Burden: Some Theoretical Perspectives." Unpublished manuscript, School of Medicine, University of Pittsburgh, 1979.

Blumer, H. Social psychology. In: Schmidt, E.P., ed. *Man and Society.* New York: Prentice Hall, 1938. pp. 144-198.

Blumer, H. Society as symbolic interaction. In: Rose, A.M., ed. *Human Behavior and Social Processes.* Boston: Houghton Mifflin, 1962. pp. 179-192.

Blumer, H. *Symbolic Interactionism: Perspective and Method.* Berkeley: University of California Press, 1969/1976.

Boszormenyi-Nagy, I., and Spark, G. *Invisible Loyalties: Reciprocity in Intergenerational Family Therapy.* New York: Harper and Row, 1973.

Bott, E. *Family and Social Network.* Rev. ed. London: Tavistock, 1955/1971.

Brody, E. The aging family. *Gerontologist* 6:201-206, 1966.

Brody, E. The etiquette of filial behavior. *International Journal of Aging and Human Development* 1:87-97, 1970.

Brody, E. The aging of the family. *Annals of the American Academy of Political and Social Science* 438:13-27, 1978.

Brody, E. "Women in the middle" and family help to older people. *Gerontologist* 21:471-480, 1981.

Brody, E. Parent care as a normative family stress. *Gerontologist* 25:19-29, 1985.

Brody, E.; Johnsen, P.; Fulcomer, M.; and Lang, A. Women's changing roles and help to elderly parents: Attitudes of three generations of women. *Journal of Gerontology* 38:597-607, 1983.

Brody, E., and Schoonover, C. Patterns of parent-care when adult daughters work and when they do not. *Gerontologist* 26:372-381, 1986.

Brody, E., and Spark, G. Institutionalization of the aged: A family crisis. *Family Process* 5:76-90, 1966.

Brody, S.; Poulshock, W.; and Masciocchi, C. The family caring unit: A major consideration in the long-term support system. *Gerontologist* 18:556-561, 1978.

Brown, R. *Social Psychology.* Rev. ed. New York: Free Press, 1965/1985.

Bruhn, J. Effects of chronic illness on the family. *Journal of Family Practice* 4:1057-1060, 1977.

Burgess, E. The family as a unity of interacting personalities. *Family* 7:3-9,1926.

Burr, W.; Leigh, G.; Day, R.; and Constantine, J. Symbolic interactionism and the family. In: Burr, W.; Hill, R.; Reiss, D., eds. *Contemporary Theories About the Family.* Vol. I. New York: Free Press, 1979. pp. 42-111.

Callahan, J.; Diamond, L.; Giele, J.; and Morris, R. Responsibility of families for the severely disturbed elders. *Health Care Financing Review* Winter:29-48, 1980.

Cantor, M. Neighbors and friends: An overlooked resource in the informal support system. *Research on Aging* 1:435-463, 1979.

Cantor, M. Strain among caregivers: A study of experience in the United States. *Gerontologist* 23:597-604, 1983.

Cantor, M. The interface between informal and formal supports: A systems approach to social care for the elderly. International Congress of Gerontology, New York, 1985.

Cath, S. The institutionalization of a parent—A nadir of life. *Journal of Geriatric Psychiatry* 5:25-51, 1972.

Chenoweth, B., and Spencer, B. Dementia: The experience of family caregivers. *Gerontologist* 26:267-272, 1986.

Cicirelli, V. Sibling relationships in adulthood. In: Poon, L.W., ed. *Aging in the 1980s*. Washington, DC: American Psychological Association, 1980. pp. 455-462.

Cicirelli, V. Adult children's attachment and helping behavior to elderly parents: A path model. *Journal of Marriage and the Family* 45:815-825, 1983.

Cicirelli, V. The role of siblings as family caretakers. In: Sauer, W., and Coward, R., eds. *Social Support Networks and the Care of the Elderly: Theory, Research and Practice*. New York: Springer, 1985. pp. 93-107.

Clark, N., and Rakowski, W. Family caregivers of older adults: Improving helping skills. *Gerontologist* 23:637-642, 1983.

Cobb, S. Social support as a moderator of life stress. *Psychosomatic Medicine* 38:300-314, 1976.

Cobb, S. Social support and health through the life course. In: Riley, M., ed. *Aging from Birth to Death: Interdisciplinary Perspectives*. Boulder, CO: Westview Press, 1979. pp. 93-106.

Cohen, D., and Eisdorfer, C. *Loss of Self: A Family Resource for the Care of Alzheimer's Disease and Related Disorders*. New York: W.W. Norton, 1986.

Cohen, D.; Kennedy, G.; and Eisdorfer, C. Phases of change in the patient with Alzheimer's disease: A conceptual dimension for defining health care management. *Journal of the American Geriatrics Society* 32:11-15, 1984.

Cohler, B. Autonomy and interdependence in the family of adulthood: A psychological perspective. *Gerontologist* 23:33-39, 1983.

Cohler, B. Parenthood, psychopathology, and child care. In: Cohen, R.; Cohler, B.; and Weissman, S., eds. *Parenthood: A Psychodynamic Perspective*. New York: Guilford, 1984. pp. 119-148.

Cohler, B. "The Adult Daughter-Mother Relationship: Perspectives From Life-Course Family Study and Psychoanalysis." Paper presented at Annual Meetings, Boston Society for Gerontologic Psychiatry, 1986.

Cohler, B., and Grunebaum, H. *Mothers, Grandmothers and Daughters: Personality and Child-Care in Three Generation Families.* New York: John Wiley, 1981.

Cohler, B., and Lieberman, M. Social relations and mental health among three European ethnic groups. *Research in Aging: A Quarterly of Social Gerontology* 2:445-469, 1980.

Cohler, B., and Stott, F. Separation, independence, and social relations across the second half of life. In: Feshbach-Moore, J., and Feshbach-Moore, S., eds. *Separation and Individuation Across the Life-Cycle.* San Francisco: Jossey-Bass, 1987. pp. 165-204.

Cook, J. A death in the family: Parental bereavement in the first year. *Suicide and Life-Threatening Behavior* 13:42-61, 1983.

Cook, J., and Cohler, B. Reciprocal socialization and the care of off-spring with cancer and with schizophrenia. In: Datan, N.; Greene, A.; and Reese, H., eds. *Life-Span Developmental Psychology: Intergenerational Relations.* Hillsdale, NJ: Laurence Erlbaum and Associates, 1986. pp. 223-244.

Coppel, D.; Burton, C.; Becker, J.; and Fiore, J. Relationships of cognitions associated coping reactions to depression in spousal caregivers of Alzheimer's disease patients. *Cognitive Therapy and Research* 9:253-266, 1985.

Corsellis, J., and Evans, P. The relation of senosis of the extracranial cerebral arteries to mental disorder and cerebral degeneration in old age. *Proceedings of the Fifth International Congress of Neuropathology.* The Hague, The Netherlands: Mouton, 1965. p. 546.

Croog, S. The family as a source of stress. In: Levine, S., and Scotch, N., eds. *Social Stress.* New York: Aldine, 1970. pp. 19-53.

Crossman, L.; London, C.; and Barry, C. Older women caring for disabled spouses: A model for supportive services. *Gerontologist* 21:464-470, 1981.

Deimling, G., and Bass, D. Symptoms of mental impairment among elderly adults and their effects on family caregivers. *Journal of Gerontology* 41:778-784, 1986.

Dobroff, R., and Litwak E. *Maintenance of Family Ties of Long-Term Care Patients.* (ADM)77-400. Washington, DC: Supt. of Docs., U.S. Govt. Print. Off., 1977.

Elder, G. Families, kin, and the life course: A sociological perspective. In: Parke, R., ed. *Review of Child Development Research: Volume 7: The Family.* Chicago: University of Chicago Press, 1984. pp. 80-136.

Epstein, N.; Bishop, D.; and Baldwin, L. McMaster model of family functioning. In: Walsh, F., ed. *Normal Family Processes*. New York: Guilford, 1982. pp. 115-141.

Falek, A. Observations on patient and family coping with Huntington's disease. *Omega* 10:35-42, 1979.

Farkas, S. Impact of chronic illness on the patient's spouse. *Health and Social Work* 5:39-46, 1980.

Fengler, A., and Goodrich, N. Wives of elderly disabled men: The hidden patients. *Gerontologist* 19:175-183, 1979.

Firth, R.; Hubert, J.; and Forge, A. *Families and Their Relatives*. New York: Humanities Press, 1970.

Fischer, C. *To Dwell Among Friends: Personal Networks in Town and City*. Chicago: University of Chicago Press, 1982.

Fischer, C.; Jackson, R.; Stueve, C.; Gerson, K.; and Jones, L., with Baldassare, M. *Networks and Places: Social Relations in the Urban Setting*. New York: Free Press, 1977.

Fischer, J., and Fischer, A. The New Englanders of Orchard Town. In: Whiting, B., ed. *Six Cultures: Studies of Childrearing*. New York: Wiley, 1963.

Fisher, J.; Nadler, A.; and Whitcher-Alagna, S. Recipient reactions to aid. *Psychological Bulletin* 91:27-54, 1982.

Fitting, M., and Rabins, P. Men and women: Do they give care differently? *Generations* 10:23-26, 1985.

Fitting, M.; Rabins, P.; Lucas, M.; and Eastham, J. Caregivers for dementia patients: A comparison of husbands and wives. *Gerontologist* 26:248-252, 1986.

Flugel, J. *Psychoanalysis of the Family*. London: Hogarth Press and the Institute for Psychoanalysis, 1921.

Folkman, S., and Lazarus, R. An analysis of coping in a middle-aged community sample. *Journal of Health and Social Behavior* 21:219-239, 1980.

George, L. *Role Transitions in Later Life*. Monterey, CA: Brooks/Cole, 1980.

George, L. Caregiver burden: Conflict between norms of reciprocity and solidarity. In: Pillemer, K., and Wolf, R., eds. *Elder Abuse: Conflict in the Family*. Dover, MA: Auburn House, 1986. pp. 66-90.

George, L., and Bearon, L. *The Quality of Life of Older Persons: Meaning and Measurement*. New York: Human Sciences Press, 1980.

George, L., and Gwyther, L. Caregiver well-being: A multidimensional examination of family caregivers of demented adults. *Gerontologist* 26:253-259, 1986.

Gilhooly, M. The impact of caregiving on caregivers: Factors associated with the psychological well-being of people supporting a demented relative in the community. *British Journal of Medical Psychology* 57:35-44, 1984.

Gilleard, C.; Boyd, W.; and Watt, G. Problems in caring for the elderly mentally infirm at home. *Archives of Gerontology and Geriatrics* 1:151-158, 1982.

Glasser, P., and Glasser, L. Role reversal and conflict between aged parents and their children. *Marriage and Family Living* 24:46-51, 1962.

Glosser, G.; Wexler, D.; and Balmelli, M. Physicians' and families' perspectives on the medical management of dementia. *Journal of the American Geriatrics* Society 33:383-391, 1985.

Godber, C. Planning services of the elderly demented patient. *Age and Aging* 6:100-103, 1977. (Supplement: Anderson, W.F., and Carlton-Ashton, J.R., eds. *Brain Failure in Old Age*).

Grad, J., and Sainsbury, P. Mental illness and the family. *Lancet* 544-547, March 9, 1963.

Grad, J., and Sainsbury, P. The effects that patients have on their families in a community care and a control psychiatric service—A two-year followup. *British Journal of Psychiatry* 114:265-278, 1968.

Greenblatt, M. Social networks and mental health: An overview. *American Journal of Psychiatry* 139:977-984, 1984.

Gross, N.; Mason, W.; and McEachern, W. *Explorations in Role Analysis: Studies of School Superintendency Role*. New York: Wiley, 1958.

Groves, L. "Psychological Distress of Caregivers to Spouses With Alzheimer's Disease." Unpublished doctoral dissertation, Northwestern University, 1987.

Grunebaum, H.; Gamer, E.; and Cohler, B. The spouse in depressed families. In: Morrison, H., ed. *Children of Depressed Parents: Risk, Identification and Intervention*. New York: Grune and Stratton, 1983. pp. 139-158.

Grunebaum, H.; Weiss, J.; Cohler, B.; Hartman, C.; and Gallant, D. *Mentally Ill Mothers and Their Children*. Rev. ed. Chicago: University of Chicago Press, 1975/1982.

Gubrium, J. *Oldtimers and Alzheimer's: The Descriptive Organization of Senility*. Greenwich, CT: JAI Press, 1986.

Gubrium, J. Structuring and destructuring the course of illness: The Alzheimer's disease experience. *Sociology of Health and Illness* 9:1-24, 1987.

Gubrium, J., and Lynott, R. Alzheimer's disease as biographical work. In: Peterson, W.A., and Quadagno, J., eds. *Social Bonds in Later Life: Aging and Interdependence*. Beverly Hills, CA: Sage, 1984. pp. 349-367.

Gutmann, D. The cross-cultural perspective: Notes toward a comparative psychology of aging. In: Birren, J., and Schaie, K.W., eds. *Handbook for the Psychology of Aging.* New York: Van Nostrand-Reinhold, 1977. pp. 302-326.

Gutmann, D. *Reclaimed Powers: Towards a Psychology of Men and Women in Later Life.* New York: Basic Books, 1987.

Hagestad, G. Parent and child: Generations in the family. In: Field, T.; Huston, A.; Quay, H.; Troll, L.; and Finley, G., eds. *Review of Human Development.* New York: Wiley, 1982. pp. 485-499.

Hagestad, G. The continuous bond: A dynamic, multigenerational perspective on parent-child relations between adults. In: Perlmutter, M., ed. *Minnesota Symposia on Child Development.* Hillsdale, NJ: Earlbaum and Associates, 1984. pp. 129-158.

Haller, A. The urban family. *American Journal of Sociology* 66:621-622, 1961.

Hammer, M. 'Core' and 'extended' social networks in relation to health and illness. *Social Science and Medicine* 17:405-411, 1983.

Hansen, D., and Hill, R. Families under stress. In: Christensen, H., ed. *Handbook of Marriage and the Family.* Chicago: Rand-McNally, 1964. pp. 782-819.

Harel, Z., and Deimling, G. Social resources and mental health: An empirical refinement. *Journal of Gerontology* 39:747-752, 1984.

Harris, L., and Associates. *The Myth and Reality of Aging in America.* Washington, DC: National Council on the Aging, 1975.

Heller, T.; Sosna, M.; and Wellbery, D. *Reconstructing Individualism: Autonomy and the Self in Western Thought.* Stanford, CA: Stanford University Press, 1986.

Henderson, S. A development in social psychiatry: The systematic study of social bonds. *Journal of Nervous and Mental Disease* 168:63-69, 1980.

Hess, B. Friends and neighbors. In: Riley, M., and Foner, A., eds. *Aging and Society.* Vol. 1. New York: Russell-Sage, 1972. pp. 561-576.

Hess, B., and Saldo, B. Husband and wife networks. In: Sauer, W., and Coward, R., eds. *Social Support Networks and the Care of the Elderly: Theory, Research, and Practice.* New York: Springer, 1985. pp. 67-92.

Heston, L.; Mastri, A.; Anderson, E.; and White, J. Dementia of the Alzheimer type. *Archives of General Psychiatry* 38:1085-1090, 1981.

Hill, R. *Families Under Stress.* Greenwood, CT: Greenwood Press, 1949.

Hill, R. *Family Development in Three Generations.* Cambridge, MA: Schnekman, 1970.

Hirschfeld, M. Homecare versus institutionalization: Family caregiving and senile brain disease. *International Journal of Nursing Study* 20:23-31, 1983.

Hoening, J., and Hamilton, M. Elderly psychiatric patients and the burden on the household. *Psychiatry and Neurology* 152:281-293, 1966.

Hoening, J., and Hamilton, M. The burden on the household in an extramural psychiatric service. In: Freeman, H., and Farndale, J., eds. *New Aspects of the Mental Health Services*. New York: Pergamon Press, 1967. pp. 612-635.

Homans, G.C. *Social Behavior: Its Elementary Forms*. Rev. ed. New York: Harcourt, Brace, and World, 1964/1974.

Horowitz, A. Sons and daughters as caregivers to older parents: Differences in role performance and consequences. *Gerontologist* 25:612-617, 1985.

Horowitz, A., and Shindelman, L. Reciprocity and affection: Past influences on current caregiving. *Journal of Gerontological Social Work* 5:5-20, 1983.

Isaacs, B. Geriatric patients: Do their families care? *British Medical Journal* 4:282-286, 1971.

Jarrett, W. Caregiving within kinship systems: Is affection really necessary? *Gerontologist* 25:5-10, 1985.

Johnson, C. Dyadic family relations and social support. *Gerontologist* 23:377-383, 1983.

Johnson, C., and Catalano, D. Childless elderly and their family support. *Gerontologist* 21:610-618, 1981.

Johnson, E., and Bursk, B. Relationships between the elderly and their adult children. *Gerontologist* 17:90-96, 1977.

Kahana, R., and Levin, S. Aging and the conflict of generations. *Journal of Geriatric Psychiatry* 4:115-162, 1971.

Kahn, R. Aging and social support. In: Riley, M., ed. *Aging from Birth to Death: Interdisciplinary Perspectives*. Boulder, CO: Westview Press, 1979. pp. 77-91.

Kahn, R., and Antonucci, T. Convoys over the life course: Attachment, roles, and social support. In: Baltes, P., and Brim, O.G., Jr., eds. *Life-Span Development and Behavior*. Vol. 3. New York: Academic Press, 1980. pp. 253-286.

Kahn, R., and Tobin, S. Community treatment for aged persons with altered brain function. In: Miller, N., and Cohen, G., eds. *Clinical Aspects of Alzheimer's Disease and Senile Dementia*. New York: Raven Press, 1981.

Kalfayan, S. "The Differential Effect of Marital and Parental Status on the Well-Being of Elderly Women." Unpublished doctoral dissertation, University of Chicago, 1987.

Katzman, R. Alzheimer's disease. *New England Journal of Medicine* 314:964-973, 1986.

Kent, D., and Matson, M. The impact of health on the aged family. *The Family Coordinator* 21:29-36, 1972.

Kidd, M. Paired helical filaments in electron microscopy of Alzheimer's disease. *Nature* 197:192-193, 1963.

Kivett, V., and Learner, R.M. Perspectives on the childless elderly: A comparative analysis. *Gerontologist* 20:708-716, 1980.

Klein, D., and Hill, R. Determinants of family problem-solving effectiveness. In: Burr, W.; Hill, R.; Nye, F.I.; and Reiss, I., eds. *Contemporary Theories about the Family*. New York: Free Press-Macmillan, 1979. pp. 493-548.

Klein, R.; Dean, A.; and Bogdonoff, M. The impact of illness upon the spouse. *Journal of Chronic Disease* 20:241-248, 1967.

Kohen, J. Old but not alone: Informal social supports among the elderly by marital status and sex. *Gerontologist* 23:57-63, 1983.

Kohut, H. *The Analysis of the Self.* New York: International Universities Press, 1971.

Kohut, H. *The Restoration of the Self.* New York: International Universities Press, 1977.

Komarovsky, M. Functional analysis of sex roles. *American Sociological Review* 15:508-516, 1950.

Komarovsky, M. Continuities in family research: A case study. *American Journal of Sociology* 62:42-47, 1956.

Komarovsky, M. *Blue Collar Marriage*. New York: Random House, 1962.

Koopman-Boyden, P., and Wells, L. The problems arising from supporting the elderly at home. *New Zealand Medical Journal* 89:265, 1979.

Kraus, A.; Spasoff, R.; Beattie, E.; Holden, D.; Lawson, S.; Rodenburg, M.; and Woodcock, G. Elderly applicants to long-term care institutions. I. Their characteristics, health problems, and state of mind. *Journal of the American Geriatrics Society* 24:117-125, 1976.

Lang, A., and Brody, E. Characteristics of middle-aged daughters and help to their elderly mothers. *Journal of Marriage and the Family* 45:193-202, 1983.

Lansky, J. Family psychotherapy of the patient with chronic organic brain syndrome. *Psychiatric Annals* 14:2, 1984.

Larson, R. Thirty years of research on the subjective well-being of older Americans. *Gerontologist* 33:109-125, 1978.

Laverty, R. Reactivation of sibling rivalry in older people. *Social Work* 7:23-30, 1962.

Lawton, M.P., and Simon, B. The ecology of social relationships in housing for the elderly. *Gerontologist* 8:108-115, 1968.

Lazarus, R., and Folkman, S. *Stress, Appraisal, and Coping*. New York: Springer, 1984.

Lee, G. Children and the elderly. *Research on Aging* 1:335-360, 1979

Lee, G., and Ihinger-Tallman, M. Children and the elderly: Interaction and morale. *Research on Aging* 2:367-391, 1980.

Levine, N.; Dastorr, D.; and Gendron, C. Coping with dementia: A pilot study. *Journal of the American Geriatrics Society* 31:12-18, 1983.

Lezak, M. Living with the characterologically altered brain injured patient. *Journal of Clinical Psychiatry* 39:592-598, 1978.

Liebowitz, A. Women's work in the home. In: Lloyd, C., ed. *Sex, Discrimination, and the Division of Labor*. New York: Columbia University Press, 1975.

Lin, N.; Dean, A.; and Ensel, W. *Social Support, Life Events, and Depression*. New York: Academic Press, 1986.

Litwak, E. Occupational mobility and extended family cohesion. *American Sociological Review* 25:9-21, 1960a.

Litwak, E. Geographic mobility and extended family cohesion. *American Sociological Review* 25:385-394, 1960b.

Litwak, E. Extended kin relations in an industrial society. In: Shanas, E., and Streib, G., eds. *Social Structure and the Family: Generational Relations*. Englewood Cliffs, NJ: Prentice Hall, 1965. pp. 290-323.

Longino, C., and Lipman, A. The support systems of women. In: Sauer, W., and Coward, R., eds. *Social Support Networks and the Care of the Elderly: Theory, Research, and Practice*. New York: Springer, 1985. pp. 219-233.

Lopata, H. *Women as Widows: Support Systems*. New York: Elsvier-North Holland, 1979.

Lopata, H., and Norr, K. Changing commitments of American women to work and family roles. *Social Security Bulletin* 43:3-14, 1980.

Low, N. "The Relationship of Adult Daughters to Their Mothers." Paper presented at the Annual Meeting, Massachusetts Psychological Association, 1978.

Lowenthal, M., and Haven, C. Interaction and adaptational intimacy as a critical variable. *American Sociological Review* 33:20-30, 1968.

Lowenthal, M., and Robinson, B. Social networks and isolation. In: Binstock, R., and Shanas, E., eds. *Handbook of Aging and the Social Sciences*. New York: Van Nostrand-Reinhold, 1976. pp. 432-456.

Lowther, C., and Williamson, J. Old people and their relatives. *Lancet* 1459-1460, Dec. 31, 1966.

Marris, P. *Loss and Change*. New York: Doubleday, 1975.

McCubbin, H.; McCubbin, M.; Patterson, J.; Cauble, E.; Wilson, L.; and Warick, W. CHIP—Coping health inventory for parents: An assessment of parental coping patterns in the care of the chronically ill child. *Journal of Marriage and the Family* 43:359-370, 1983.

McCubbin, H., and Patterson, J. Family adaptation to crises. In: McCubbin, H.; Cauble, A.E.; and Patterson, J., eds. *Family Stress, Coping, and Social Support.* Springfield, IL: Charles Thomas, 1982. pp. 26-47.

McCubbin, H., and Patterson, J. The family-stress process: The double ABCX model of adjustment and adaptation. *Marriage and Family Review* 6:7-38, 1983.

Menaghan, E. Individual coping efforts and family studies: Conceptual and methodological issues. *Marriage and Family Review* 6:113-136, 1983.

Mishler, E., and Waxler, N. *Interaction in Families: An Experimental Study of Family Processes and Schizophrenia.* New York: John Wiley, 1968.

Montgomery, R.J.V.; Gonyea, J.; and Hooyman, R. Caregiving and the experience of subjective and objective burden. *Family Relations* 34:19-25, 1985.

Moos, R. Context and coping: Toward a unifying conceptual framework. *American Journal of Community Psychology* 12:5-36, 1984.

Morycz, R. Caregiving strain and the desire to institutionalize family members with Alzheimer's disease. *Research on Aging* 7:329-361, 1985.

Mueller, D.P. Social networks: A promising direction for research on the relationship of the social environment to psychiatric disorder. *Social Science and Medicine. Part E, Medical Psychology (Oxford)* 14(2):147-161, 1980.

Munnichs, J. *Old Age and Finitude: A Contribution to Psychogerontology.* New York: Karger, 1966.

Neugarten, B., and Datan, N. The middle years. In: Arieti, S., ed. *American Handbook of Psychiatry. I: The Foundations of Psychiatry.* New York: Basic Books, 1974. pp. 592-606.

Neugarten, B., and Hagestad, G. Age and the life course. In: Binstock, R., and Shanas, E., eds. *Handbook of Aging and the Social Sciences.* New York: Van Nostrand-Reinhold, 1976. pp. 35-55.

Niederehe, G., and Fruge, E. Dementia and family dynamics: Clinical research issues. *Journal of Geriatric Psychiatry* 17(1):21-60, 1984.

Noelker, L., and Wallace, R. The organization of family care. *Journal of Family Issues* 6:23-44, 1985.

Nydegger, C. Family ties of the aged in cross-cultural perspective. *Gerontologist* 23:26-32, 1983.

O' Brien, J., and Wagner, D. Help seeking by the frail elderly: Problems in network analysis. *Gerontologist* 20:78-83, 1980.

Olson, D., and Associates. "Circumplex Model of Marital and Family Systems." Unpublished manuscript. Department of Family Social Science, The University of Minnesota.

Pagel, M.; Becker, J.; and Coppel, D. Loss of control, self-blame, and depression: An investigation of spouse caretakers of Alzheimer's disease patients. *Journal of Abnormal Psychology* 94:169-182, 1985.

Park, R.; Burgess, E.; and McKenzie, R. *The City*. Chicago: University of Chicago Press, 1925/1967.

Parmelee, P. Spouse versus other family caregivers: Psychological impact on impaired aged. *American Journal of Community Psychology* 11:337-349, 1983.

Parsons, T. The social structure of the family. In: Anshen, R., ed. *The Family: Its Function and Destiny*. New York: Harper and Row, 1949. pp. 173-201.

Parsons, T. Family structure and the socialization of the child. In: Parsons, T., and Bales, R.F. (with Zelditch, M., and Slater, P.), eds. *Family, Socialization and Interaction*. New York: Free Press, 1955. pp. 35-134.

Parsons, T., and Fox, R. Illness, therapy, and the modern urban American family. *Journal of Social Issues* 8:31-44, 1953.

Patterson, G. Stress: A change agent for family processes. In: Garmezy, N., and Rutter, M., eds. *Stress, Coping and Development in Children*. New York: McGraw-Hill, 1984. pp. 235-264.

Patterson, J., and McCubbin, H. Chronic illness: Family stress and coping. In: Figley, C., and McCubbin, H.I., eds. *Stress and the Family. Volume II: Coping with Catastrophe*. New York: Brunner/Mazel, 1983a. pp.21-36.

Patterson, J., and McCubbin, H. The impact of family life events and changes on the health of a chronically ill child. *Family Relations* 32:255-264, 1983b.

Pearlin, L.; Lieberman, M.; Menaghan, E.; and Mullan, J. The stress process. *Journal of Health and Social Behavior* 22:337-356, 1981.

Pilisuk, M., and Parks, S.H. Social support and family stress. *Marriage and Family Review* 6(1/2):137-156, 1983. Also in McCubbin, H.; Sussman, M.B.; and Patterson, J., eds. *Social Stress and the Family: Advances and Developments in Family Stress Theory and Research*. New York: Haworth Press, 1983.

Platt, S. Measuring the burden of psychiatric illness on the family: An evaluation of some rating scales. *Psychological Medicine* 15:383-393, 1985.

Powers, E., and Bultena, G. Sex differences in intimate friendships of old age. *Journal of Marriage and the Family* 38:739-747, 1976.

Poulshock, S.W., and Deimling, G. Families caring for elders in residence: Issues in the measurement of burden. *Journal of Gerontology* 39:230-239, 1984.

Pratt, C.; Schmall, V.; Wright, S.; and Cleveland, M. Burden and coping strategies of caregivers to Alzheimer s patients. *Family Relations* 34:27-33, 1985.

Pruchno, R.; Blow, F.; and Smyer, M. Life events and interdependent lives. *Gerontologist* 27:31-41, 1984.

Rabins, P.; Mace, N.; and Lucas, M. The impact of dementia on the family. *JAMA* 248:333-335, 1982.

Rakowski, W., and Clark, N. Future outlook, caregiving, and care-receiving in the family context. *Gerontologist* 25:618-623, 1985.

Rankin, E., and Pinkston, E. "Family Caregivers and Burden: A Developmental Perspective." Paper presented at Annual Meetings, The Gerontological Society, New Orleans, 1985.

Reifler, B.; Cox, G.; and Hanley, R. Problems of mentally ill elderly as perceived by patients, families, and clinicians. *Gerontologist* 21:165-170, 1981.

Reifler, B., and Larson, E. Alzheimer's disease and long-term care: The assessment of the patient. *Journal of Geriatric Psychiatry* 19:9-25, 1986.

Reiss, D. *The Family's Construction of Reality*. Cambridge: Harvard University Press, 1981.

Riley, M., and Foner, A. *Aging and Society. Volume I: An Integration of Research Findings*. New York: Russell-Sage, 1968.

Robertson, J. Grandmotherhood: A study of role conceptions. *Journal of Marriage and the Family* 39:165-174, 1977.

Robins, L., and Tomanec, M. Closeness to blood relatives outside the immediate family. *Marriage and Family Living* 24:340-345, 1962.

Robinson, B. Validation of a caregiver strain index. *Journal of Gerontology* 38:344-348, 1983.

Robinson, B., and Thurner, M. Taking care of aged parents. *Gerontologist* 19:586-593, 1979.

Ross, H.; Dalton, M.; and Milgram, J. "Older Adults' Perceptions of Closeness in Sibling Relationships." Paper presented at Annual Meeting, The Gerontological Society, San Diego, 1980.

Rosenberg, G. *The Worker Grows Old: Poverty and Isolation in the City*. San Francisco: Jossey-Bass, 1970.

Rosenmayr, L., and Kockeis, E. Predispositions for a sociological theory of action and the family. *International Social Science Journal* 15:410-426, 1963.

Ross, H., and Kedward, H. Psychogeriatric hospital admissions from the community and institutions. *Journal of Gerontology* 32:420-427, 1977.

Roth, M. The natural history of mental disorders in old age. *Journal of Mental Science* 102:281-301, 1955.

Sainsbury, P., and Grad de Alarcon, J. The psychiatrist and the geriatric patient: The effects of community care on the family of the geriatric patient. *Journal of Geriatric Psychiatry* 4:23-41, 1970.

Sanford, J. Tolerance of debility in elderly dependents by supports at home: Its significance for hospital practice. *British Medical Journal* 3:471-473, 1975.

Sauer, W. Morale of the urbanized: A regression and analysis by race. *Journal of Gerontology* 32:600-608, 1977.

Savitsky, E., and Sharkey, H. The geriatric patient and his family: Study of family interaction in the aged. *Journal of Geriatric Psychiatry* 5:3-25, 1972.

Schachter, S. *The Psychology of Affiliation.* Stanford, CA: Stanford University Press, 1959.

Schneck, M.; Reisberg, B.; and Ferris, S. An overview of current concepts of Alzheimer's disease. *American Journal of Psychiatry* 139:165-173, 1982.

Schneider, D. *American Kinship: A Cultural Account.* Englewood Cliffs, NJ: Prentice Hall, 1968.

Schoor, A. *"Thy Father and Thy Mother...": A Second Look at Filial Responsibility and Family Policy.* (SSA)13-11953. Washington, DC: Supt. of Docs., U.S. Govt. Print. Off., 1980.

Schwartz, G. Development and validation of the geriatric evaluation by relative's rating instrument (GERRI). *Psychological Reports* 53:479-488, 1983.

Seelbach, W., and Sauer, W. Filial responsibility expectations and morale among aged parents. *Gerontologist* 17:492-499, 1977.

Shanas, E. Living arrangements of older people in the United States. *Gerontologist* 1:27-29, 1961.

Shanas, E. The family as a social support system in old age. *Gerontologist* 19:169-174, 1979a.

Shanas, E. Social myth as hypothesis: The case of the family relations of old people. *Gerontologist* 19:3-9, 1979b.

Shanas, E. Older people and their families: The new pioneers. *Journal of Marriage and the Family* 41:9-15, 1980.

Sheldon, F. Supporting the supporters: Working with the relatives of patients with dementia. *Age and Aging* 11:184-188, 1982.

Simchowicz, T. Histologische studeien aber the senile demenz (Histological studies of senile dementia). *Histological und Histopathologie Arbeiten* 4:267, 1910.

Simmel, G. The persistence of social groups. *American Journal of Sociology* 3:662-698, 1898.

Simos, B. Adult children and their aging parents. *Social Work* 18:78-85, 1973.

Smith, K., and Bengtson, V. Positive consequences of institutionalization: Solidarity between elderly parents and middle-aged children. *Gerontologist* 19:438-447, 1979.

Soldo, B., and Myllyluoma, J. Caregivers who live with dependent elderly. *Gerontologist* 23:605-611, 1983.

Soyer, D. The geriatric patient and his family: Helping the family to live with itself. *Journal of Geriatric Psychiatry* 5:52-76, 1972.

Stack, C. *All our Kin: Strategies for Survival in the Black Community.* New York: Harper and Row, 1974.

Stoller, E. Parental caregiving by adult children. *Journal of Marriage and the Family* 45:851-858, 1983.

Stoller, E., and Earl, L. Help with activities of everyday life: Sources of support for the noninstitutionalized elderly. *Gerontologist* 23:64-70, 1983.

Strain, L., and Chappel, N. Confidants. *Research on Aging* 4:479-502, 1982.

Stryker, S. Symbolic interactionism: Themes and variations. In: Rosenberg, M., and Turner, R., eds. *Social Psychology: Sociological Perspectives.* New York: Basic Books, 1981. pp. 3-29.

Sussman, M. Family continuity: Selective factors which affect relationships between families at generational levels. *Marriage and Family Living* 16:112-120, 1954.

Sussman, M. The isolated nuclear family: Fact or fiction. *Social Problems* 6:333-340, 1959.

Sussman, M.B. Relationship of adult children with their parents in the United States. In: Shanas, E., and Streib, G., eds. *Social Structure and the Family: Generational Relations.* Englewood Cliffs, NJ: Prentice Hall, 1965. pp. 62-93.

Sussman, M.B. The family life of older people. In: Binstock, R., and Shanas, E., eds. *Handbook of Aging and the Social Sciences.* 2d ed. New York: Van Nostrand-Reinhold, 1985. pp. 415-449.

Sutton-Smith, B., and Rosenberg, B. *The Sibling.* New York: Holt, Rinehart, and Winston, 1970.

Sweetser, D. Asymmetry in intergenerational family relationships. *Social Forces* 41:346-352, 1963.

Sweetser, D. Mother-daughter ties between generations in industrialized societies. *Family Process* 3:332-343, 1964.

Sweetser, D. The effect of industrialization on intergenerational solidarity. *Rural Sociology* 31:156-170, 1966.

Terry, R.D.; Gonatas, N.K.; and Weiss, M. Ultrastructural studies in Alzheimer's presenile dementia. *American Journal of Pathology* 44:269, 1964.

Thoits, P. Undesirable life events and psychophysiological distress: A problem of operational confounding. *American Sociological Review* 46:97-109, 1981.

Thoits, P. Conceptual, methodological, and theoretical problems in studying social support as a buffer against life stress. *Journal of Health and Social Behavior* 23:145-159, 1982.

Thoits, P. Dimensions of life events that influence psychological distress: An evaluation and synthesis of the literature. In: Kaplan, H.B., ed. *Psychosocial Stress: Trends in Theory and Research.* New York: Academic Press, 1983. pp. 33-103.

Tobin, S., and Kulys, R. The family and services. In: Eisdorfer, C., ed. *Annual Review of Geriatrics and Gerontology.* New York: Springer, 1980. pp. 370-399.

Tobin, S., and Lieberman, M. *Last Home for the Aged.* San Francisco: Jossey-Bass, 1976.

Townsend, A., and Poulshock, W. Intergenerational perspectives on impaired elders' support networks. *Journal of Gerontology* 41:101-109, 1986.

Treas, J. Family support systems for the aged. *Gerontologist* 17:486-491, 1977.

Troll, L.; Miller, S.; and Atchley, R. *Families in Later Life.* Belmont, CA: Wadsworth-Brooks/Cole, 1979.

Turner, J. Social support as a contingency in psychological well-being. *Journal of Health and Social Behavior* 22:357-367, 1981.

U.S. Senate: Special Committee on Aging. *Developments in Aging: 1985.* Vol. 3. Washington, DC: Supt. of Docs., U.S. Govt. Print. Off., 1986.

Walker, A., and Thompson, L. Intimacy and intergenerational aid and contact among mothers and daughters. *Journal of Marriage and the Family* 45:841-849, 1983.

Walsh, F. The family in later life. In: Carter, E., and McGoldrick, M., eds. *The Family Life Cycle.* Rev. ed. New York: Gardiner Press, in press.

Ward, R. Limitations of the family as a supportive institution in the lives of the aged. *Family Coordinator* 27:365-373, 1978.

Ward, R. Informal networks and well-being in later life: A research agenda. *Gerontologist* 25:55-61, 1985.

Ware, L., and Carper, M. Living with Alzheimer disease patients: Family stresses and coping mechanisms. *Psychotherapy: Theory, Research, and Practice* 19:472-481, 1982.

Waxler, N. Parent and child effects on cognitive performance: An experimental approach to the etiological and responsive theories in schizophrenia. *Family Process* 13:1-22, 1974.

Wild, C., and Shapiro, L. Mechanisms of change from individual to family performance in male schizophrenics and their parents. *Journal of Nervous and Mental Disease* 165:41-56, 1977.

Wild, C.; Shapiro, L.; and Abelin, T. Communication patterns a role structure in families of male schizophrenics: A study using automated techniques. *Archives of General Psychiatry* 34:58-70, 1977.

Wilder, D.; Teresi, J.; and Bennett, R. Family burden and dementia. In: Mayeux, R., and Rosen, W.G., eds. *The Dementias*. New York: Raven Press, 1983. pp. 239-251.

Wirth, L. Urbanism as a way of life. *American Journal of Sociology* 40:1-20, 1938.

York, J., and Calsyn, R. Family involvement in nursing homes. *Gerontologist* 17:500-505, 1977.

Young, R. The family-illness intermesh: Theoretical aspects and their application. *Social Science and Medicine* 17:395-398, 1983.

Zarit, J. "Predictors of Burden and Distress for Caregivers of Senile Dementia Patients." Unpublished doctoral dissertation, University of Southern California, Los Angeles, 1982.

Zarit, S.; Orr, N.; and Zarit, J. *The Hidden Victims of Alzheimer's Disease: Families Under Stress*. New York: New York University Press, 1985.

Zarit, S.; Reever, K.; and Bach-Peterson, J. Relatives of the impaired elderly: Correlates of feelings of burden. *Gerontologist* 20:649-655, 1980.

Zarit, S.; Todd, P.; and Zarit, J. Subjective burden of husbands and wives as caregivers: A longitudinal study. *Gerontologist* 26:260-266, 1986.

Chapter 3

Psychological Paradigms for Understanding Caregiving

Richard Schulz, Ph.D., David Biegel, Ph.D.,
Richard Morycz, Ph.D., and Paul Visintainer, Ph.D.

Introduction

The literature on caregiving can be characterized as an attempt to link some antecedent variables to outcomes assessing the well-being of individuals who provide support to elderly relatives. A typical independent variable in this conceptualization might be the functional or behavioral status of the patient; a representative dependent variable could be any one of a number of measures of the psychosocial status or physical and mental health of the caregiver, such as morale, life-satisfaction, depression, or perceived strain or burden. Sandwiched between the independent and dependent variables are a large number of individual and situational variables characteristic of all stress-coping models, such as age, gender, socioeconomic status, type and quality of the relationship between caregiver and patient, social support, and a number of personality characteristics of the caregiver, such as self-esteem and locus of control. This basic model has been elaborated by a number of researchers (e.g., Montgomery et al. 1985; Schulz et al. 1987; Schulz et al. in press). On the whole, these models provide a convenient framework for organizing the large number of variables relevant to understanding the caregiving process.

As one would expect in the early stages of a new research area, the empirical literature has focused primarily on the social-structure correlates of caregiver well-being (e.g., gender, age, type of relationship, living arrangement) and to a lesser extent on psychological parameters such as coping strategies and affective ties between patient and caregiver. Although this literature is a rich source of descriptive data concerning caregiving and provides a firm foundation for future research, it is also fair to conclude (see Ory et al. 1985; Horowitz 1985; Gallagher 1985) that it suffers from a number of important shortcomings. Studies were often based on small numbers of subjects, the range of variables investigated in any one study was frequently very limited, and, with few exceptions, researchers rarely used multivariate analytic strategies. As a result, we can point to a large number of variables that seem relevant to understanding the well-being of caregivers, but we can say little about the importance of a given variable in relation to others. Morever, there exist almost no longitudinal studies (for exceptions, see Schulz et al. in press; and Zarit et al. 1986), making it difficult to examine the temporal dynamics of caregiving.

In contrast to the inductive approach to the study of caregiving inherent in the existing empirical literature, our goal in this chapter is to examine caregiving deductively. We attempt to identify fundamental questions and relevant psychological theories that should be useful in understanding caregiving and providing direction for future research. We begin by asking a question that has not been addressed directly by researchers in this area, namely, why do people help? Next we examine a number of fundamental psychological theories relevant to understanding caregiving, and finally, we deduce from our analysis questions for future research.

Why Do People Help?

Much of the literature on caregiving is aimed at dispelling the "illusion of the Golden Past" (Kent 1965; Brody 1985), the myth of the idyllic three-generation household in which, in contrast to current practice, the oldest generation was diligently cared for by younger generations. As Brody (1985, p. 21) pointed out in her review of this literature, it is ironic that this myth persists despite the fact that "nowadays adult children provide more care and more difficult care to more parents over much longer periods of time that they did in the good old days."

Although abundant data document the validity of Brody's analysis, few researchers have attempted to answer the appropriate followup question: Why do people provide such large quantities of help, particularly in view of the apparent personal costs often associated with providing care? To some, the answer may be self-evident. As the demand for care changes, so does the amount of care provided because of the strong normative expectations in our culture to help our kin. This explanation obviously tells us little of psychological significance in understanding caregiving and invites further speculation about the motives of caregivers. The purpose of this section is to address this question from a psychological perspective.

For almost two decades, experimental social psychologists have been developing theory and a data base to answer the questions, why and when do people help? Interest in these questions was kindled by the tragic stabbing death of Kitty Genovese in 1964, who was repeatedly attacked over a period of 37 minutes in the presence of 38 witnesses, none of whom helped, and only one of whom finally called the police. Many experts and members of the press blamed the onlookers for their failure to get involved, suggesting that they were cruel and selfish; others suggested they lacked moral compunction or were cowards. Some social scientists had no ready explanation for the behavior of the onlookers and decided to systematically investigate the giving and receiving of help as a form of social behavior.

Given the circumstances surrounding the murder of Kitty Genovese, it is not surprising that much of the early research in this area focused on finding out why and when people are willing to help strangers in emergency situations. This is obviously far removed from a family caregiving situation, but some of the findings of this research may be relevant nevertheless. For example, one phenomenon documented in a series of studies (Latane and Darley 1970) was the *bystander effect*: the more people present, the less likely a given individual is to help. The presence of others may result in the *diffusion of responsibility* and cause an individual to feel that others will take care of the problem, or it may make individuals feel apprehensive because others will be evaluating their performance as helpers.

When applied to a family caregiving situation, the bystander effect raises some interesting questions that have not yet been addressed in the caregiver literature. For example, although we know that eldest daughters and wives are most often cast in the caregiving role, we know little about how caregiving responsibilities are negotiated and shared as a function of family size, how this process affects satisfaction with the caregiving role, and how caregiving behavior and satisfaction is affected by the caregivers' concerns regarding evaluations of their performance by others.

Another series of studies showed that the victims' personal attributes are powerful determinants of helping. Individuals are more willing to help people in need who are physically attractive (Harrell 1978), dressed attractively (Kleinke 1977), and have no stigmatizing physical characteristics, such as unattractive birthmarks (Piliavin et al. 1975), eye patches, or scars (Samerotte and Harris 1976). People are also more willing to help others who are similar to themselves on such attributes as attitudes, political beliefs, nationality, race, and the way they dress (Dovidio 1984). Applied to the family caregiving context, these findings point to another set of variables that have been neglected in the caregiving literature. To date, the patient characteristics more frequently studied include physical functioning, cognitive abilities, and perceived personality changes, but little attention has been paid to physical appearance changes associated with a debilitating illness. Similarly, the helping literature suggests that caregiving should be less stressful for both caregiver and patient when they share similar attitudes and perspectives.

Motives for Helping

Attempts to identify specific motives for helping yielded two types of explanations. One assumes that helping serves an *egoistic or self-serving motive*, while the other centers on *empathy and altruism* (Batson and Coke 1983).

The egoistic explanation argues that helping is motivated by the anticipation of rewards for helping and punishment for not helping. Individuals may help another for obvious reasons such as the expectation of payment (Fischer 1963), gaining social approval (Baumann et al. 1981), avoiding censure (Piliavin et al. 1975), receiving esteem in exchange for helping (Hatfield et al. 1978), complying with social norms (Berkowitz 1972), seeing oneself as a good person (Bandura 1977), or avoiding guilt (Hoffman 1982). For example, caring for a relative to prevent institutionalization can be interpreted in terms of avoiding censure, complying with social norms, and/or seeing oneself as a good person (Brody et al. 1978).

Guilt and indebtedness are the motives alluded to by the often heard comment made by caregivers, "I know I'm doing everything I can for my mother, but somehow I still feel guilty" (Brody 1985, p. 26), or in the idea that caretaking is repayment in kind for care provided by the parent at an earlier age. Guilt may also be the motivating force for individuals who feel they must atone for past sins (e.g., neglect, bad treatment) against their spouse or parent.

A theoretical basis for indebtedness as a motive was provided by Greenberg (1980), who stated that feeling indebted has motivational properties such that the greater its magnitude, the greater the resultant arousal and discomfort, and hence, the stronger the ensuing attempts to deal with or reduce it. Feelings of indebtedness should be higher to the extent that an individual feels the help provided him was based on altruistic motives on the part of the helper, help was given in response to requests or pleas for help from the recipient, and the helper incurred costs in providing the help. All of these factors apply to spousal and parent-child relationships and may be worthy of attention in our efforts to understand who becomes the caregiver, the magnitude of the costs the caregiver is willing to incur in providing help to a relative, and the amount of residual guilt experienced by the caregiver.

A substantially different perspective on human nature is provided by a theory of helping based on purely altruistic motivation. According to this view, individuals help others because they are able to adopt the perspective of the other and experience an emotional response—empathy—congruent with the other's welfare; empathic emotion evokes a desire to reduce the other's needs. The magnitude of the altruistic motivation is assumed to be a direct function of the magnitude of the empathic emotion. Unlike the egoistic perspective, the primary goal of empathically evoked altruism is to benefit the other and not the self, even though benefits to oneself may be a consequence of helping (see Batson and Coke 1983 for a review of the relevant literature). It seems reasonable to assume, although it has not been demonstrated empirically, that the ability to empathize may be based on such variables as kinship, similarity, prior interaction, attachment, or some combination of these variables, all of which are relevant to the intrafamilial caregiving situation. This suggests that higher levels of similarity, attachment, and prior positive interaction would result in greater levels of caregiving.

Although helping an elderly relative is likely to be based on both altruistic and egoistic motivation, it would be interesting to know whether the two motives differentially affect caregiver well-being. Since emotions are a central feature of altruistic helping, one might hypothesize that the emotional status of the patient plays an important role in determining the amount of help provided and the affect of the helper. Moreover, the nature of the cognitive declines associated with Alzheimer's disease suggests that altruistic motivation may be more relevant to the early stages of the disease when cognitive function is still more or less intact and the caregiver can readily empathize with the patient, and that egoistically motivated helping is the driving force in later stages of the disease when cognitive function is debilitated.

Social Norms and Helping

Sociological explanations for why people help frequently emphasize the role of social norms, such as *reciprocity, equity,* or *social responsibility.* The reciprocity norm enjoins us to pay back what others give to us, while the equity norm underscores the importance of costs and rewards in a relationship. Simply stated, a relationship is equitable if those involved benefit in proportion to their investment in it. According to the social responsibility norm, helping others in need—the sick, infirm, or very young—is a duty not to be shirked, although the manner in which and how much we help another may depend on our beliefs about who or what is responsible for the cause and solution of the recipient's problem (see Brickman et al. 1982).

The notion of social norms is obviously relevant to understanding caregiver behavior. For example, norms may be useful in predicting caregiving behavior among successive cohorts of caregivers. But the existence of norms do not in themselves explain why people adhere to them. We still need to answer the questions, why do these norms exist or where do they come from? To address these questions we need to examine some underlying characteristics of human beings.

Sociobiology of Helping

The social-psychological theories of helping described above are based on the notion that social behavior in humans is developed through experience and learning, rather than through instinct. A new theoretical approach that can have direct relevance for understanding the helping process, *sociobiology*, challenges this orthodoxy. Sociobiology suggests that the fundamental goal of the organism is not mere survival, or survival of its offspring, but "inclusive fitness"—to pass on the maximum number of genes to the next generation (Hamilton 1964). Sociobiology believes that human helping can only be understood in terms of the human evolutionary past—close relatives help each other, even at risk of their lives, to increase the chance that their genes will survive in their relatives (Forsyth 1986). Thus, sociobiology takes a positive view of human nature, believing that human beings are innately helpful to each other albeit for a "selfish" purpose, the preservation of the gene pool.

To date, tests of this theory, which relied on research with non-humans only, indicate that helping is much more common among close relatives than among strangers and in dense rather than dispersed communities (Barash 1982). Applying this theory to family caregiving, it can be argued that, in general, intrafamilial helping behaviors enhance the survival of the familial gene pool. Thus, intrafamilial helping of all types is desirable. However, this general rule likely has at least one qualification: When resource constraints demand that priorities be set among those who can be helped, we would predict that resources will be allocated to the young rather than the old, if the choice has to be made.

Our discussion of why people help raises a number of important

111

questions about the instigation and perpetuation of intrafamilial helping, but it does not directly address questions concerning predictors of patient and family outcomes associated with caregiving. To address this issue, we turn next to a number of psychological perspectives on how humans cope with challenging situations.

Psychological Models for Predicting Caregiver Outcomes

Much of the social-psychological literature on aging in the last decades has emphasized the importance of predictability (Schulz 1976), control (Schulz 1976; Schulz and Hanusa 1978, 1980; Schulz 1986; Rodin and Langer 1977, Rodin et al. 1985), and autonomy as central theoretical constructs that help us understand individual functioning when confronted with difficult challenges. One of our fundamental beliefs about human nature is that there exists "within each of us a need for considerable influence over the people, events, and situations that have a substantial impact on our well-being and valued life pursuits" (Renshon 1979, p 49). Predictability and control are preferred to their absence, and their presence is beneficial to human beings as well as animals. The rationale behind these ideas is found in a variety of theories regarding the origins of the need for control, ranging from natural selection and basic instincts to childhood socialization, and in a substantial empirical literature.

Predictability

How are these constructs relevant to caregiving? Some of the central features of Alzheimer's disease are the inability to predict who will get it, the difficulty of diagnosing it, and the unpredictable nature of its course. Although we do not know what causes Alzheimer's disease, we do know that the probability of its occurrence increases with age and that it has a gradual onset. These facts alone may contribute to feelings of uncertainty and low-level anxiety as elderly individuals attempt to discriminate between normative and nonnormative cognitive and behavioral symptoms associated with growing old. Even after a diagnosis has been made, our limited knowledge of how the disease progresses makes it difficult to predict in any given case the exact nature and severity of symptoms to be expected, or the rate at which they will appear. Finally, some of the symptoms of the disease, such as memory loss and bizarre emotional expressiveness, severely disrupt the routine of life established over a period of several decades.

To date, the empirical literature on caregiving has paid little attention to the role of the unique attributes of Alzheimer's disease and their effect on the caregiver. We know little about the relative impact of communication and memory difficulties, socially inappropriate behaviors, and patient affect and personality changes on the caregiver. Other factors likely to play a role in caregiver response to disability include *nature of onset* (sudden or insidious), *prognosis* (recuperative, degenerative, stable, or terminal), *visibility* (physically or behaviorally stigmatizing such as dementia or cancer or nonvisible and nonstigmatizing such as heart disease) and *time since onset*. Investigating the impact of these variables requires us to examine multiple diseases simultaneously. For example, the role of onset and prognosis could be studied by comparing dementias caused by stroke, in which onset is sudden and the prognosis stable, with Alzheimer's dementia, in which onset is gradual and the course of the disease is degenerative. One may also wish to examine diseases such as cancer for which prognosis is also uncertain and physical disfigurement is a central feature of the disease.

Although experimental psychologists for many years have studied the impact of negative unpredictable events on laboratory animals, it is difficult to imagine a laboratory analog that would capture the chronic uncertainty inherent in a caregiver-dementia patient relationship. It should come as no surprise to us that information and time-out from vigilance (e.g., respite) are two of the major needs of caregivers.

Control and Learned Helplessness

The reduction of uncertainty is beneficial for a number of reasons, including the fact that it enhances the organism's chances for exerting control. For example, a caregiver who knows that in 6 months the patient will be too disabled to be cared for at home can investigate appropriate institutional options and be prepared to act when the time comes.

The construct of control has a long history in the annals of experimental psychology. Early research demonstrated that the perception of control facilitated coping with a variant of stressors (Glass and Singer 1972) and that the absence of control or the lack of contingency experiences may bring about feelings of helplessness and depression.

In the last decade, the construct of control has evolved to become a central feature in learned helplessness theory (Abramson et al. 1978) and self-efficacy theory (Bandura 1977, 1982). According to the current version of learned helplessness theory, once people perceive that they are unable to control important outcomes, they attribute their helplessness to a cause. This cause can be stable or unstable, global or specific, and internal or external. The particular attribution chosen determines whether feelings of helplessness are likely to persist, the range of situations one is likely to feel helpless in, and whether helplessness will lower self-esteem. This theory was recently applied to caregiving in a study carried out by Pagel, Becker, and Coppel (1985). They found that perceived loss of control over important events related to a spouse's illness combined with a tendency to attribute loss of control to internal causes is positively related to severity of depression.

The concept of control also was used as a dispositional attribute and found to be related to caregiver coping (Levine et al. 1983). Caregivers who scored as internals on the Rotter Locus of Control scale (Rotter 1966) were judged to be more skillful in coping with the demands of caregiving than individuals who scored as externals. Unfortunately, the small sample size of 10 caregivers precluded multivariate analysis of the data. As a result, it is difficult to conclude from this study whether a personality attribute such as internal/external control is useful in predicting caregiver outcomes. Even if control is predictive, one has to question its pragmatic value since personality attributes are, by definition, not easily changed through intervention strategies.

Self-Efficacy

While learned helplessness focuses on outcome expectancies, the belief that a given behavior will lead to certain outcomes, self-efficacy theory is concerned primarily with efficacy expectations, the conviction that one can successfully carry out the behavior required to produce outcomes. Thus, individuals may know that a particular course of action produces certain outcomes, but feel that they are incapable of performing those actions. Such an individual would have low levels of perceived self-efficacy and would be expected to exhibit impaired coping when confronted with obstacles and aversive experiences.

Expectations of personal efficacy are derived from four principal sources: performance accomplishments, vicarious experience (e.g., observing others' performance), verbal persuasion (e.g., suggestion), and physiological state (e.g., emotional arousal). Intervention strategies used with caregivers, such as those developed by Gallagher, Lovett, and Zeiss (in press), are based on the premise that the self-efficacy of caregivers can be enhanced. Research indicates that the most effective way to enhance efficacy expectations is through ex-

114

perience-based inductions that demonstrate to individuals that they possess relevant competencies.

Participants in the Gallagher et al. study were taught a set of specific skills designed to enhance coping and were encouraged to practice these skills in the home setting. They were then provided with performance feedback and encouraged to adjust their behaviors accordingly. Preliminary results suggest that both efficacy expectations and coping ability are enhanced by this intervention and a variety of others (e.g., Davis 1983; Gwyther and Blazer 1984; Selan, and Schuenke 1982; Glosser and Wexler 1985; Kahan et al. 1985; Aronson et al. 1984, Schmidt and Keyes 1985).

Although the existing intervention research holds promise for the future, it is unlikely to yield generalizable results because it is not sufficiently theory driven. For example, according to self-efficacy theory, it is important to distinguish between efficacy expectations and outcome expectations; applied to caregiving, it is important to know whether people give up trying because they lack a sense of efficacy in executing the required behaviors for a particular outcome or because they expect their behavior to have no effect in a given situation.

Clinical observation of caregivers suggests that one of the most frustrating aspects of caregiving is the discovery that behaviors that were effective in the past no longer produce the outcomes desired. Changing

> efficacy-based futility requires development of competencies and expectations of personal effectiveness. By contrast, to change outcome-based futility necessitates changes in prevailing environmental contingencies that restore the instrumental value of the competencies that people already possess. (Bandura 1977, p. 205)

Designing an effective intervention program initially requires the assessment of both self-efficacy and outcome beliefs. When a sense of personal efficacy and outcome expectations are both high, we would expect assured, opportune action (see figure 3-1). Such an individual should exhibit intense and persistent effort when confronted with the obstacles and challenges associated with caregiving. In contrast, individuals who have a low sense of personal efficacy and who believe that no amount of effort by themselves or similar others is likely to produce results should demonstrate resignation and apathy. Despondency and self-devaluation are likely to result when individuals see themselves as ineffectual when compared to similar others who are successful in dealing with problems similar to their own. Finally, persons who perceive themselves as efficacious and judge the en-

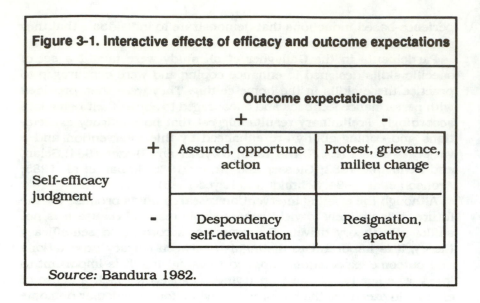

Figure 3-1. Interactive effects of efficacy and outcome expectations

		Outcome expectations	
		+	-
Self-efficacy judgment	+	Assured, opportune action	Protest, grievance, milieu change
	-	Despondency self-devaluation	Resignation, apathy

Source: Bandura 1982.

vironment to be unresponsive are likely to intensify their efforts and try to change the environment, sometimes through protest, social activism, and grievance.

Given the complexity of the demands placed on caregivers and the fact that the demands change significantly over time, we would expect a given individual to occupy different cells of the four-cell matrix described above at different times and/or occupy different cells simultaneously, depending on the particular challenge being evaluated. A maximally effective intervention program should be able to identify the exact location of each participant, both globally and/or with respect to specific problems and challenges, and it should be capable of making such assessments on a continuing basis as the status of the patient and the accompanying caregiving tasks change. We believe that intervention research with caregivers will have to adopt the kind of microanalytic approach described here if we hope to significantly affect the lives of caregivers.

Conclusion and Future Research

We have identified a number of psychological theories and applied them to the caregiving context. These theories have, in turn, led to a number of specific variables and hypothetical constructs deserving further investigation.

The theoretical literature on helping raises a number of intriguing questions regarding family interaction and structure and their relation to caregiving. We know very little about the relationship between family size and caregiving. Does the availability of more adult children increase the amount of help provided to a frail parent or does the responsibility become diffused, resulting in less care overall? Although we know that spouses and the older adult female child carry the largest burden in providing care, we know little about how caregiving responsibilities are negotiated when more than one potential caregiver is available.

The literature on sociobiology sensitizes us to the possible conflict between caring for one's dependent children and caring for one's parents. When finances, time, and energy are abundant, such conflicts are unlikely to arise. In fact, adults with dependent children may provide more support to their frail parent because they have a stake in modeling behavior that may benefit them when they become frail. However, when resources are constrained, adult children may find themselves having to make difficult choices, and a sociobiological perspective would predict that these choices be made in favor of the younger generation.

One of the underlying themes in the caregiving literature is the idea that feelings of indebtedness, or guilt, and empathy are powerful mediators of the behavior and well-being of caregivers. If this is true, then prior help received should be predictive of help given. Perceived discrepancies between help received and help given may, in turn, be predictive of feelings of guilt. Similarly, the similarity and attachment between caregiver and recipient and the nature of their prior interactions should be related to the level of empathy the caregiver experiences and, hence, the quantity and quality of help provided. On the whole, hypothetical constructs such as guilt and empathy, although frequently mentioned, have not been explored empirically.

Illness-related factors such as the nature of its onset, prognosis, visibility, and behavioral symptomatology are also relatively unexplored. We know that physical symptoms alone are not particularly predictive of caregiver well-being and that behavioral changes such as the occurrence of bizarre and disruptive behaviors are especially devastating, but we know little beyond these broad generalizations. Attaining a more detailed perspective on these variables requires quasi-experimental strategies that compare the impact of illnesses that differ on key features. In general, we strongly recommend that researchers focusing on caregiving for Alzheimer's patients closely examine and take advantage of the existing literature based on other illnesses such as cancer, heart disease, and stroke.

Interventions for caregivers are more likely to succeed when they are based on a microanalysis of the caregiver's knowlege and beliefs about the behaviors needed to achieve desired outcomes and their ability to carry out those behaviors. In addition, intervention strategies should be designed to assess and address the changing needs of the caregiver as the patient declines. We already have detailed behavioral analyses of caregiving behaviors; they should be expanded to provide efficacy-relevant information and then rigorously tested with caregivers.

Finally, one of the underlying themes of this chapter has been the need for better research methods. We have more than enough descriptive accounts of caregiving based on small, heterogeneous samples. Future research efforts should focus on large, preferably more homogeneous, samples (e.g., caregivers dealing with the early stages of dementia) that are followed longitudinally. Moreover, such studies should include the full range of variables relevant to understanding caregiving and should take advantage of the multivariate structural modeling techniques available to analyze these data.

Acknowledgment

Preparation of this manuscript was in part supported by grants from the National Institute on Aging (AGO 5444) and the National Institute of Mental Health (MH 41887). The authors also wish to express their appreciation to Chris Curnow for her able assistance in the preparation of this manuscript.

References

Abramson, L.Y.; Seligman, M.E.P.; and Teasdale, J.D. Learned helplessness in humans: Critique and reformulation. *Journal of Abnormal Psychology* 87:49-74, 1978.

Aronson, M.K.; Levine, G.; and Lipkowitz, R. A community-based family/patient group program for Alzheimer's disease. *Gerontologist* 24(4):339-342, 1984.

Bandura, A. *Social Learning Theory*. Englewood Cliffs, NJ: Prentice-Hall, 1977.

Bandura, A. Self-efficacy mechanism in human agency. *American Psychologist* 37:122-147, 1982.

Barash, D.P. *Sociobiology and Behavior*. 2d ed. New York: Elsevier, 1982.

Batson, C.D., and Coke, J.S. Empathic motivation of helping behavior. In: Cacioppo, J.R., and Petty, R.E., eds. *Social Psychophysiology: A Sourcebook*. New York: Guilford Press, 1983.

Baumann, D.J.; Cialdini, R.B.; and Kenrick, D.T. Altruism as hedonism: Helping and self-gratification as equivalent responses. *Journal of Personality and Social Psychology* 40:1039-1046, 1981.

Berkowitz, L. Social norms, feelings, and other factors affecting helping and altruism. In: Berkowitz, L., ed. *Advances in Experimental Social Psychology*. Vol. 6. New York: Academic Press, 1972.

Brickman, P.; Rabinowitz, V.C.; Karnza, J., Jr.; Coates, D.; Cohn, E.; and Kidder, L. Models of helping and coping. *American Psychologist* 37:368-384, 1982.

Brody, E.M. Parent care as a normative family stress. *Gerontologist* 25(1):19-29, 1985.

Brody, S.J.; Poulshock, S.W.; and Masciocchi, C.F. The family caring unit: A major consideration in the long-term support system. *Gerontologist* 18(6):556-561, 1978.

Davis, J.L. Support groups: A clinical intervention for families of the mentally impaired elderly. *Journal of Gerontological Social Work* 5(4):27-35, 1983.

Dovidio, J.F. Helping and altruism: An empirical and conceptual overview. In: Berkowitz, L., ed. *Advances in Experimental Social Psychology*. Vol. 17. New York: Academic Press, 1984.

Fischer, W.F. Sharing in preschool children as a function of amount and type of reinforcement. *Genetic Psychology Monographs* 68:215-245, 1963.

Forsyth, D.R. *Social Psychology*. Monterey, CA: Brooks/Cole, 1987.

Gallagher, D.E. Intervention strategies to assist caregivers of frail elders: Current research status and future research directions. In: Lawton, M.P., and Maddox, G., eds. *Annual Review of Gerontology and Geriatrics*. Vol. 5. New York: Springer, 1985. pp. 249-283.

Gallagher, D.; Lovett, S.; and Zeiss, A. Interventions with caregivers of frail elderly persons. In: Ory, M., and Bond, K., eds. *Aging and Health Care: Social Science and Policy Perspectives*. New York: Tavistock, in press.

Glass, D.C., and Singer, J.E. *Urban Stress: Experiments on Noise and Social Stressors*. New York: Academic Press, 1972.

Glosser, G., and Wexler, D. Participants' evaluation of educational/support programs for families of patients with Alzheimer's disease and other dementias. *Gerontologist* 25(3):232-236, 1985.

Greenberg, M.S. A theory of indebtedness. In: Gergen, K.J.; Greenberg, M.S.; and Willis, R.H., eds. *Social Exchange: Advances in Theory and Research*. New York: Plenum, 1980. pp. 3-26.

119

Gwyther, L.P., and Blazer, D.G. Family therapy and the dementia patient. *American Family Physician* 29(5):149-156, 1984.

Hamilton, W.D. The genetical evolution of social behaviour: I and II. *Journal of Theoretical Biology* 7:1-52, 1964.

Harrell, A.W. Physical attractiveness, self-disclosure, and helping behavior. *Journal of Social Psychology* 104:15-17, 1978.

Hatfield, E.; Walster, G.W.; and Piliavin, J.A. Equity theory and helping relationships. In: Wispe, L., ed. *Altruism, Sympathy, and Helping: Psychological and Sociological Principles*. New York: Academic Press, 1978. pp. 115-139.

Hoffman, M.L. Development of prosocial motivation: Empathy and guilt. In: Eisenberg, N., ed. *The Development of Prosocial Behavior*. New York: Academic Press, 1982. pp. 281-313.

Horowitz, A. Family caregiving to the frail elderly. *Annual Review of Gerontology and Geriatrics*. Vol. 5. New York: Springer, 1985. pp. 194-246.

Kahan, J.; Kemp, B.; Staples, F.R.; and Brummel-Smith, K. Decreasing the burden in families caring for a relative with a dementing illness. *Journal of the American Geriatrics Society* 33(10):664-670, 1985.

Kent, D.P. Aging—fact or fancy. *Gerontologist* 5:2, 1965.

Kleinke, C. Compliance to requests made by gazing and touching experiments in field settings. *Journal of Experimental Social Psychology* 13:218-223, 1977.

Latane, B., and Darley, J.M. *The Unresponsive Bystander: Why Doesn't He Help?* New York: Appleton-Century-Crofts, 1970.

Levine, N.; Dastoir, D.; Gendron, C. Coping with dementia: A pilot study. *Journal of the American Geriatrics Society* 31:12-18, 1983.

Montgomery, R.J.V.; Stull, D.E.; and Borgatta, E.F. Measurement and the analysis of burden. *Research on Aging* 7:137-152, 1985.

Ory, M.G.; Williams, T.F.; Emr, M.; Lebowitz, B.; Rabins, P.; Sallowan, J.; Sluss-Radbaugh, T.; Wolff, E.; and Zarit, S. Families, informal supports and Alzheimer's disease: Current research and future agendas. *Research on Aging* 7:623-644, 1985.

Pagel, M.; Becker, J.; and Coppel, D. Loss of control, self-blame, and depression: An investigation of spouse caretakers of Alzheimer's disease patients. *Journal of Abnormal Psychology* 94:169-182, 1985.

Piliavin, I.M.; Piliavin, J.A.; and Rodin, J. Costs, diffusion, and the stigmatized victim. *Journal of Personality and Social Psychology* 32:429-438, 1975.

Reis, H.T., and Gruzen, J. On mediating equity, equality, and self-interest: The role of self-presentation in social exchange. *Journal of Experimental Social Psychology* 12:487-503, 1976.

Renshon, S.A. Control in political life: Origins, dynamics and implications. In: Perlmuler, L.C., and Monty, R.A., eds. *Choice and Perceived Control*. Hillsdale, NJ: Erlbaum, 1979. pp. 41-63.

Rodin, J., and Langer, E.J. Long term effects of a control-relevant intervention with the institutionalized aged. *Journal of Personality and Social Psychology* 35:897-902, 1977.

Rodin, J.; Timko, C.; and Harris, S. The construct of control: Biological and psychosocial correlates. In: Lawton, M.P., and Maddox, G., eds. *Annual Review of Gerontology and Geriatrics*. Vol. 5. New York: Springer, 1985. pp. 3-55.

Rotter, J.B. Generalized expectancies for internal versus external control of reinforcement. *Psychological Monographs* 80(1, whole No. 609), 1966.

Samerotte, G.C., and Harris, M.B. Some factors influencing helping: The effects of a handicap, responsibility, and requesting help. *Journal of Social Psychology* 98:39-45, 1976.

Schmidt, G.L., and Keyes, B. Group psychotherapy with family caregivers of demented patients. *Gerontologist* 25(4):347-350, 1985.

Schulz, R. The effects of control and predictability on the physical and psychological well-being of the institutionalized aged. *Journal of Personality and Social Psychology* 33:563-573, 1976.

Schulz, R. Successful caregiving: Balancing primary and secondary control. *Adult Development and Aging News* 13:2-4, 1986.

Schulz, R., and Hanusa, B.H. Long-term effects of predictability and control enhancing interventions: Findings and ethical issues. *Journal of Personality and Social Psychology* 36:1194-1201, 1978.

Schulz, R., and Hanusa, B.H. Applications of experimental social psychology to aging. *Journal of Social Issues* 36:30-47, 1980.

Schulz, R., Tompkins, C.A., and Rau, M.T. A longitudinal study of the psychosocial impact of stroke on patients and support persons. *Journal of Social Issues*, in press.

Schulz, R.; Tompkins, C.A.; Wood, D.; and Decker, S. The social psychology of caregiving: Physical and psychological costs of providing support to the disabled. *Journal of Applied Social Psychology* 17:401-428, 1987.

Selan, B.H., and Schuenke, S. The late life care program: Helping families cope. *Health and Social Work* 7(3):192-197, 1982.

Zarit, S.H.; Todd, P.A.; and Zarit, J.M. Subjective burden of husbands and wives as caregivers: A longitudinal study. *Gerontologist* 26(3):260-266, 1986.

121

Chapter 4

Cultural and Ethnic Issues in Alzheimer's Disease Family Research

Ramon Valle

Culture and Ethnicity: A Working Model for Alzheimer's Disease Research

The focus of this chapter is the delineation of a working model for assessing the impact of culture on the later life dementias with the intent of guiding Alzheimer's disease family research. The concept of *culture* as used here, even though applied to specific populations which retain their culture-of-origin beliefs and practices within a host culture, must be understood as extending to all persons at all points in the life course. *Ethnicity*, the identifiable expressed heritage of a specific cultural group, is likewise applicable to all persons including those who are considered representatives of the mainstream or host society.

Not enough attention has been paid to the important role of culture in the field of aging research, particularly in the area of Alzheimer's disease research where all possible coping resources, including those of one's ethnic heritage, need to be brought to bear. From the research standpoint, therefore, it is important to document differential human response to the same phenomena, namely Alzheimer's disease and related disorders, based on culturally varied normative outlooks and caretaking practices. It is time to focus attention on the manner in which response to catastrophic illness is filtered through differing ethnic groups' belief systems and practices.

Admittedly, Alzheimer's disease by itself presents a complex enough research phenomena without adding a cultural assessment requirement. The disease remains difficult to diagnose, demanding a differential diagnosis process operating at multiple levels, with the final determination made by excluding other possible conditions--and more than 70 neurologically degenerative, vascular, viral, and psychological/affective states can cause or simulate this organic brain disease (Katzman et al. 1987; U.S. Congress, Office of Technology Assistance 1987). The research task increases in complexity when we consider that not only the affected person requires assessment. Alzheimer's disease and the related dementias have considerable impact beyond the affected individual, extending into the patient's primary group/significant other caretaker network and reaching into the long-term care/formal human service sector.

The research task is especially difficult because culture is dynamic, ever modifying itself. A continual acculturation process is taking place even within the most traditional societies. Second, the problem, from the researcher's perspective, is not just that it will not hold still, but that culture behaves both as a dependent and an independent variable. As Kluckhohn (1962, p.73) has indicated, cultural systems may "on one hand be considered as products of action, and on the other as conditioning influences upon future action." A third and even more serious difficulty is the lack of consensus on an accepted model for making cultural assessments (Holzberg 1982; Markides 1982). How then to proceed?

Culture-Free/Culture-Fair Instrumentation and Procedures

The problem is not insurmountable. A feasible initial step would be to apply the *culture free* and *culture fair* conceptualization, as suggested by Gurland (1986), to the Alzheimer's disease and related disorders research and clinical assessment. The term culture-free applies here to the development of research instrumentation and/or clinical protocols, as well as components of such instruments, that, when translated and backtranslated, can be used with certainty across cultures. For example, the request for one's name and residence in the research or clinical interview could be considered a culture-free item applicable to data gathering efforts across cultures. A health examination protocol could likewise be considered a culture-free procedure, applicable across cultures whether the procedure is administered by an orthodox (Western trained) physician or health professional or a traditional (indigenous) healer/cultural health practitioner. The shaman, the natural healer, and the Western-trained physician all have protocols that they follow. The issue is not how adequate the assessment process may be, or whether the indigenous health examination is better, but rather the universality of certain processes across cultures. Documenting these types of common human experience could serve as a culture-free or transcultural "knowledge bridge" within the Alzheimer's disease/dementia research process–and, specifically, the Alzheimer's disease family research arena.

From a broader perspective, the driving forces behind the culture-free concept are the worldwide acculturation and modernization/social change processes pressing all societies. Culture-fair content, though, has a different connotation. In this instance, research instruments and procedures, or their components, while different, could be made equivalent across cultures. Within the culturally fair rubric, an idiomatic expression and/or point of reference may not be translatable into a different linguistic/communicational format, or the two cultures may not have the same referent, so an analog is employed. For example, although every cultural group is familiar with some form of health examination, the exact health questions and the manner and sequence in which these questions are asked might only approximate each other across cultures.

An example of a culturally fair equivalency would be the substitution of an ethnic-appropriate phrase for "no ifs, ands, or buts" within the Folstein et al. (1975) Mini Mental Status Examination (MMSE). Spanish has no exact translation of this English idiomatic turn of phrase, which is used to assess possible apraxia. The translation issue is made all the more complex as it must not only (1) combine a mixture of consonants and vowels, mixing labials and aspirants, (2) use prepositions, but also (3) make some idiomatic sense (Goodglass and Kaplan 1983). A number of alternatives have been used in a variety of Spanish as well as other language translations, not all of which have met the criteria for this item on the MMSE. The problem for the researcher or clinician is that there is *no* exact culture-free translation and a search must be undertaken for a *culture-fair* equivalent. Some idiomatically acceptable Spanish-language alternatives have been developed such as "no hay pero que valga" (there is nothing that is not of worth) and "si no bajo, entonces me subo" (If I do not go down, then I will go up). While these may meet the criteria, they do not have the complete ease of the English phrase.

The same attention has to be applied to other items in the MMSE, such as asking the name of the current and recent past President of the United States. Even though the question may be linguistically translatable, many elderly from other ethnic cultures may be unfamiliar with the U. S. referent. Therefore, given the core intent of the item, the culturally fair approach would permit the use of a validated alternative. In this context, Flaherty (1987) suggested that, in addition to content equivalence, the translator seek conceptual, criterion, and technical equivalence–this latter affecting "pencil and paper" type data collection relative to groups that have considerable illiteracy within their ranks, or whose written/symbolic tradition differs from Western societies, where much of the social research instrumentation has been normed.

Not all researchers agree with the possibility of attaining a culture-free methodology and accompanying instrumentation (Murphy 1984; Williams 1987), the issue being that all cultures contain an inherent bias that only permits the application of the culture-fair construct. The position taken here is that both the culture-free and culture-fair components of the suggested strategy have to be attempted, allowing the research experience and attendant findings to help decide the issue. The problem in the worldwide interpenetration of cultures is all the more pronounced when a specific ethnic cohort exists as a subgroup within a host society, as is the case of U.S. ethnic populations. Figure 4-1 summarizes the core notion of achieving a culturally syntonic assessment of individuals in relation to their core ethnic/traditional orientation.

A Dual Axis

Indeed, because of the complexity surrounding the clinical as well as research assessment of Alzheimer's disease and related demen-

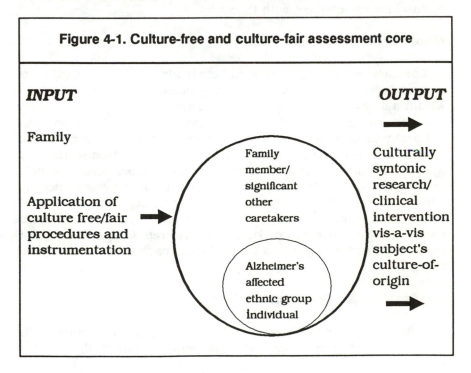

Figure 4-1. Culture-free and culture-fair assessment core

INPUT

Family

Application of culture free/fair procedures and instrumentation

Family member/ significant other caretakers

Alzheimer's affected ethnic group individual

OUTPUT

Culturally syntonic research/ clinical intervention vis-a-vis subject's culture-of-origin

tias, the cultural component cannot stand alone. For purposes of our working model, it is better to see the research assessment/differential diagnosis and the cultural assessment as operating along two different axes. Figure 4-2 extends the proposed cultural assessment working model and places the cultural component along a plane complementary to the comprehensive Alzheimer's disease/dementia research and clinical assessment process. The research assessment and/or the clinical differential diagnosis, probing for the type as well as extent of the dementia on the affected individual, and/or the level of stress and burden accruing to the family caretakers, can be said to move along the vertical axis. The cultural component can be seen proceeding along the horizontal axis.

It helps if we reflect for a moment on the fact that every research or clinical assessment, whether biophysiological, psychosocial, and/or epidemiological in scope, has a cultural correlate. Whenever a demographic profile is drawn, a social history taken, or a family assessment made, the cultural correlate is present as an integral part of the Alzheimer's disease research and clinical assessment/treatment process, whether it is recognized or not. The discussion to follow necessarily centers on the lateral acculturation (cultural) continuum aspects of the framework. The differential assessment components along the vertical axis are not ignored, though, particularly as the cultural issues intersect with them.

Mixed Methods

The framework being suggested here lends itself to the application of both advanced statistical and ethnomethodological techniques within a single research design, as recommended by Sieber (1973), and can capture both cohort generalizable data and the ordinary, culturally unique cognitive and behavioral patterns of ethnic elder dementia patients within their natural social environments. This approach is more proximate to the actual circumstances constantly facing the Alzheimer's disease and related disorders researcher and clinician alike, who are constantly sifting through subject-specific information while searching to establish cohort generic criteria, be these biological markers or behavioral referents. Figure 4-2 incorporates the notion of a mixed methods approach within the research design.

The Acculturation Continuum

A further conceptual refinement is needed, though, to move the working model ahead. The horizontal cultural axis in figure 4-2 is

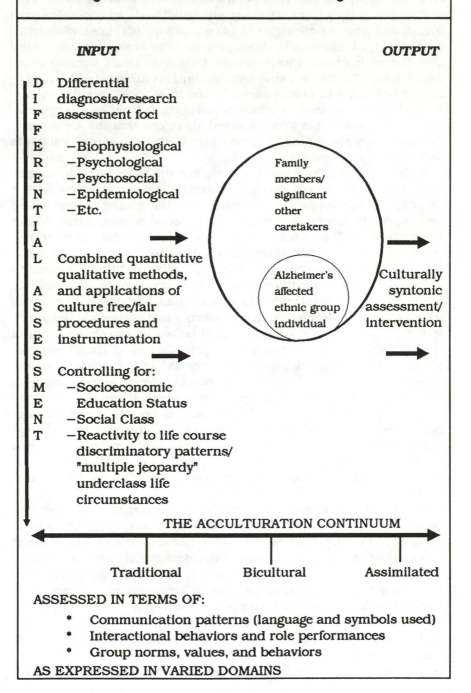

Figure 4-2. A cultural assessment working model

INPUT
OUTPUT

D   Differential
I   diagnosis/research
F   assessment foci
F
E   −Biophysiological   Family
R   −Psychological   members/
E   −Psychosocial   significant
N   −Epidemiological   other
T   −Etc.   caretakers
I
A
L   Combined quantitative
    qualitative methods,   Alzheimer's   Culturally
A   and applications of   affected   syntonic
S   culture free/fair   ethnic group assessment/
S   procedures and   individual   intervention
E   instrumentation
S
S   Controlling for:
M   −Socioeconomic
E   Education Status
N   −Social Class
T   −Reactivity to life course
     discriminatory patterns/
     "multiple jeopardy"
     underclass life
     circumstances

THE ACCULTURATION CONTINUUM

Traditional   Bicultural   Assimilated

ASSESSED IN TERMS OF:
  *   Communication patterns (language and symbols used)
  *   Interactional behaviors and role performances
  *   Group norms, values, and behaviors
AS EXPRESSED IN VARIED DOMAINS

better understood if cast in terms of an *acculturation continuum* (Gordon 1964; Fabrega 1969; Clark et al. 1976; Favazza 1980). This continuum ranges from ethnic group individuals who demonstrate *traditional* (culture-of-origin) orientations through those who maintain *bicultural* outlooks to those persons who are quite *assimilated* into the mainstream (host) society (Romano 1969; Cuellar et al. 1980). It is difficult to see any specific ethnic group member remaining totally isolated and uninfluenced by the host society's culture, particularly when one looks at cultural phenomena from an intergenerational perspective. It is to be expected, therefore, that the Alzheimer's disease family researcher will encounter a mix of acculturation levels within any ethnic cohort.

With this said, ethnic group elderly are still more likely to remain close to the traditional end of the continuum, particularly as the dementia progresses and cognitive as well as behavioral regression occurs. Family members, though, may be found scattered throughout the continuum. This is not to discount the fact that, despite their own personal relative assimilation into the host society, many family/significant-other caretakers will revert to more traditional modes in deference to the dementia-affected ethnic group elder. An example would be the bicultural and/or assimilated family members' hesitancy to use exogenous formal helping resources and systems in deference to the traditional elder's customs and beliefs that problems should remain within the confines of the primary group itself, however stressful the circumstances. In the context of the working model suggested here, *traditionalists* can be considered as persons with homeland-of-origin beliefs and practices who maintain themselves in separate relational systems parallel to the host U.S. cultural ambience. *Biculturalists* represent a mix or fusion of cultures, though not at the expense of either their traditional culture or the mainstream society. *Assimilateds*, on the other hand, have for the most part stopped identifying with their cultural past (Romano 1969; Valle 1986).

To help maintain this more flexible approach to understanding ethnic-specific cultural phenomena and, for that matter, the cultural dynamics of all populations, the researcher should keep in mind that several, and at times countervailing, developmental forces are at work within these groups. On one hand, within each U.S. ethnic cohort we have traditional enclaves represented by "long-time, local community" resident elderly. These long-time residents may reflect immigrant elderly who came to this country in their youth. They could also include individuals who have lived for several generations within the U.S. cultural ambience but who retain many of their culture-of-origin ethnic group/normative outlooks and practices. One need only look

128

to the Amish and Mennonite (religious/philosophical) societies to see this at work. A similar situation can be found in the Appalachian regions of the country. The fact of the matter is that, in all sectors of U.S. society, one can encounter traditional, culture-of-origin orientations among individuals of Euro/Anglo ethnic heritage overriding a number of the normative outlooks and practices of the host society (Cohler and Lieberman, 1980).

The same dynamic can be even more pronounced in other, more defined ethnic populations. For example, in rural areas of New Mexico and Colorado, some fifth or sixth generation elderly retain their traditional Mexican heritage orientations and still use Spanish as their primary language. Similar patterns can be found in Southern rural black communities. English may be the primary language, but it has been modified to a local or regional ethnic cultural idiom. Allegiance to traditional folk medicine can also be encountered. Such enclaves of long-time residents who communicate in their language of origin can be found in urban/metropolitan areas among the large, ethnically diverse elderly populations (Shanas 1973; Cantor 1976; Valle 1981; Colen 1983; Zuniga 1983; Becerra 1984; Lockery 1986) and in institutional settings (Chee and Kane 1979).

At the same time, intergenerational variance in acculturation can be expected even within the staunchest representatives of a specific ethnic group. The obvious issue here for Alzheimer's family dynamics is that a single ethnic group caretaking family will reflect various mixes of orientations along the acculturation continuum. To some extent, this circumstance can be understood in the context of the structural changes that have taken place in the makeup of the family within the host society as well as by the varying patterns of migration and immigration to be encountered within the different ethnic groups themselves (Vega et al. 1983). Much of the literature on ethnic groups, though, has described the more traditional *extended family* mode, with several generations living under one roof or on the same property. Indeed, it may well be that a significant portion of some ethnic group elderly are living alone without apparent recourse to an extended family/significant-other caretaking system (Weeks and Cuellar 1981).

Other ethnic group elderly can be found in *modified extended* families. Here, not all of the family/significant others reside in the same dwelling or even the same community but remain in primary contact around the caretaking function. Still others will be part of more *nuclear families*. These variances notwithstanding, the researcher and clinician alike may well encounter dementia in ethnic group elderly who still value the "affectively remembered" family caretaking modality and look for its comforting presence in some surrogate form.

In brief, when interacting with persons and/or groups who retain their culture-of-origin orientations, we must be alert to and work with ethnocultural identity constructs that persist over time and that probably become more pronounced as the dementing disease progresses.

Documenting Cultural Behaviors

An individual's position along the acculturation continuum can be assessed in three ways. First, the researcher or clinician can assess cultural phenomena through knowledge of or familiarity with the language and symbols distinct to the individual's specific ethnic group. As is readily evident, many ethnic groups in the United States still retain their language of origin as their primary means of communication, with English serving as a second language. Familiarity with these languages can often provide clues to the nature of the family's mutual relationships, caretaking practices, and group values. Hence, language provides the initial point of entry to cultural phenomena (Sapir 1921; Whorf 1971).

Second, the researcher or clinician can assess a specific culture through documentation of the ethnic group's primary interactional behaviors (Cantor 1976; Blau 1978; Cohler and Lieberman 1980; Weeks and Cuellar 1981). The problem for the researcher or clinician is that the ethnic group family may be less forthcoming with the more private, primary level information until a bond of trust has been established. Therefore, the initial information gathered may be more peripheral than integral to the ethnocultural caretaking situation. Engaging in somewhat elaborate trust building activity may be difficult for the researcher or clinician, particularly in the face of the caretaking emergency represented by the all-pervasive catastrophic nature of Alzheimer's disease and related dementias. The logical assumption would be that, under such duress, the caretakers and/or the affected individual would drop these ethnocultural veils. However, these ethnic, in-group response patterns have, in the past, most likely served a positive protective function. The researcher or clinician may simply be seeing the residuals of old roles and norms operating in the elder's and the family's response to their present circumstances, despite their less productive outcomes. New but culturally syntonic stratagems have to be developed, and here the culture-free/culture-fair principles can be brought to bear.

Long-held ethnic group values and beliefs are a third avenue for tracking the individual and the family member along the acculturation continuum (Kardiner 1939; Seward and Marmor 1956; Spicer 1971; Herskovitz 1972; Lerner 1972; LeVine and Padilla 1980). The

130

researcher and clinician may need to be prepared with some advance knowledge of the cultural background of the ethnic group with which dementia patients and their families identify. Some understanding of the individual's ethnic group history, both past and current, is required (Osako 1979). Admittedly, this is a formidable task for any single research group, particularly in view of the variety of ethnic subgroups found in the United States. In most instances, though, the task is manageable, since community and professional experts are usually available who can readily provide the necessary cultural orientation and knowledge for the research effort and/or clinical program.

These three factors can combine to yield considerable insight into Alzheimer's disease/dementia-affected elders and their help-accepting attitudes, as well as the family's mutual assistance styles and coping capabilities.

The Issue of Behavioral Domains

To view the acculturation continuum appropriately, the researcher and clinician must take into account a further dynamic. Culture is not only expressed with considerable variation along a continuum, but also unevenly within distinct domains of daily living where individuals and groups act out their lives. The concept of domain as used here follows the Pearlin and Schooler (1978) formulation indicating that behavioral and coping responses will vary within different social environments such as the home, the workplace, and the broader community. As noted earlier, the investigator may well find that bicultural or even quite assimilated significant others will be much more traditional in their caretaking roles and practices at home, particularly with regard to their traditionally oriented elders.

Controlling for Possible Confounds

When undertaking cultural assessments, the researcher/clinician should avoid confusing cultural variables with socioeconomic status factors (Valentine 1968; Casavantes 1969; Leacock 1971; Attunes et al. 1974; Holzberg 1982; Lee 1984; Mutran 1984). For example, when engaged in ethnic-specific research, there may be a tendency to relate *all* service utilization difficulties to ethnocultural behaviors. In many instances, such problems result from a lack of money, or transportation, or knowledge of how to access these resources (Torres Gil 1978). These factors must be accounted for within the research design before determining that the study findings indeed indicate cultural variance.

A second possible problem facing the researcher in studying

specific ethnic populations is confusing reactive behaviors emerging from experiences of discrimination and overt racism with culture-of-origin dynamics (Mirowsky and Ross 1984). Whereas low socioeconomic status often leads to lifelong patterns of episodic use of health and related services, including applying for services at the more advanced, less tractable stages of a disease or disorder (Weaver 1976; Torres Gil 1978), the experience of discrimination creates a certain, equally lifelong feeling of unease or apprehension about treatment outside one's accustomed family and community. The lingering residual effects of discrimination cannot be easily discounted. The obvious issue for the researcher, particularly in the area of Alzheimer's disease and related dementias, is to also properly distinguish these factors from the culture-of-origin behavioral dynamics.

Application

Some of the concepts of the suggested cultural research framework might be better seen in the context of a specific research problem— for example, the use of cognitive screening instruments with a specific ethnic cohort.

A number of mental status examinations are currently used with the elderly. Whether one is using the Folstein, Folstein, and Mchough (1975) MMSE or its counterparts, such as the the Goldfarb (Kahn et al. 1963) and the Blessed, Tomlinson, and Roth (1968) mental status tests, the Pfieffer (1975) Short Portable Mental Status Questionnaire, or others, these cognitive screens are a crucial first tier in the assessment of the late onset dementias. A central problem that immediately surfaces in the use of these screens is their validation with other than U.S. English-speaking populations. A further difficulty is controlling for socioeconomic and educational status within the validation. The literature reports much about the strong culture-of-origin allegiance of the Hispanic ethnic cohort; this group, therefore, can serve to illustrate both of these concerns.

Developing Culture Free/Fair Assessment Tools

A number of mental status examinations have been used with Hispanic populations. The most common of these, the Folstein,

Folstein, and Mchough (1975) MMSE has been translated into Spanish and used either intact or in a modified form in a variety of studies with this ethnic group. For example, Lopez-Aqueres et al. (1984) used a modified version of the MMSE as imbedded within the Gurland et al. (1977) and Gurland and Wilder (1984) CARE instrument package.

The MMSE was also employed in the University of California at Los Angeles Epidemiological Catchment Area Project, where it received its most extensive validation to date with reference to Hispanics (Escobar et al. 1986). Escobar and his colleagues interviewed 3,117 adult respondents in two Los Angeles mental health catchment areas. Of those, 40 percent were Mexican-heritage Hispanics, 42 percent Euro/Anglo/White, 6 percent Hispanics of other descent, and 12 percent blacks and Asian Americans. Of the Hispanic subjects, 47 percent chose to take the interview primarily or entirely in Spanish, and 53 percent in English. The prevalence rates of definite or possible severe cognitive dysfunction were 1.7 percent for the Mexican-heritage Hispanic cohort and 0.4 percent for the non-Mexican-American subjects.

The researchers undertook item analyses to explore the excessively high Mexican-heritage Hispanic rate. Their analyses assumed that the percentage incorrect on an item would be correlated primarily with age if the item were working appropriately. An attempt was made to determine whether errors might be more a function of education and/or ethnicity and language. The researchers reported that language and ethnicity significantly affected the error rate on the MMSE orientation item of State of residence. Education/ethnicity/language affected the orientation items of season of the year and county of residence, the memory item of serial 7s, and the language item of "repeat no ifs, ands, or buts." Age, along with education, ethnicity, and language, was implicated in the memory item of "spell world backwards." These findings suggest that a large portion of the high rates of cognitive impairment found for Mexican-heritage Hispanics in the Los Angeles ECA study may be due to factors such as ethnicity and language differences, along with education, rather than to a higher prevalence of cognitive impairment within the cohort. One could speculate about possible differences in the response patterns if a *culture-free/culture-fair* mental status screen were used. Reports on the use of the MMSE in Puerto Rico underscore these concerns. Bird et al. (1987) indicated excessively high rates of cognitive dysfunction for Puerto Ricans when the instrument was administered in Spanish, with education being heavily implicated in the outcomes. It is clear that much work remains to be done.

133

The acculturation continuum construct presents the researcher and clinician alike with still other tasks. The investigator seeking to place Hispanic Alzheimer's disease/dementia patients and their family members/significant others appropriately along the continuum looks to gather pertinent information relative to the ethnic group members' language and communication patterns, interactional behaviors, and underlying values and beliefs. The literature draws a composite profile of the cultural characteristics of Hispanic elderly (though not specific to the Alzheimer's disease/dementia arena). In the main, (1) this cohort of elderly favors Spanish as their language of choice; (2) they apparently prefer intergenerational contacts–taking into account that a number of elderly from the Hispanic group may lack such contacts (Weeks and Cuellar 1981); and (3) as a group, these elders can be put into the traditional sectors of the *acculturation continuum* with regard to their help-accepting beliefs and caretaking attitudes. Table 4-1 provides a glimpse of some relevant attitudes that might support the researcher making such an assessment from the perspective of underlying values that govern help-seeking and help-taking behaviors.

At this point in the process, though, a very real danger arises of stereotyping the members of any ethnic cohort, thereby skewing the analysis, particularly in the sensitive area of Alzheimer's disease family research. A case example might assist in illustrating the concern.

> Senora L., a 72-year-old Hispanic of Central American origin, had been demonstrating signs of confusion and forgetting. She had been brought to the clinic for an assessment. The family had become concerned with the clinic's diagnosis of probable Alzheimer's disease. They and, in particular, the husband wondered if she had been properly assessed and even though they had not at first asked that the testing be conducted in Spanish, they asked for a reevaluation. The writer was called into the case. Some of the background information indicated that she had come to the United States at the age of six and had functioned in a bilingual mode for most of her life. The husband, an individual of Euro/Anglo background, had no command of Spanish and indicated that part of the problem now was that Sra L. was talking more in Spanish and he felt he was having trouble communicating, as were other English-speaking-only family members. This seemed to be adding to the confusion and stress all were feeling in trying to communicate with her.

Table 4-1. Terminology of significant expectations of elders

How to treat elders	Qualities valued in person(s) first turned to for help	Qualities valued in agency people
*Con respeto** With respect *Con dignidad* With dignity *Con delicadeza* Gentleness *Con comprension* Understanding *Con consideracion* Consideration *Con cartno* Affection *Con paciencia* Patience	*Siempre dispuestos a ayudar* They are always ready to help *Me quieren* They care for me *Son muy atentos* They are very attentive *Son comprensivos* They are under-standing *Me Conocen* They know me	*Nos trata con respeto* He/she treats us with respect *No nos da prisa, pero se pueda dar prisa si lo necesitas* He or she doesn't hurry, but will hurry if there is a need to *Todo lo que se le ofrece a uno, lo hace. Es muy complido* Whatever he/she offers, he or she does, follows through *Si no lo puede hacer llama a alguien quien lo haga* If he/she cannot provide, he or she secures someone who can *Viene a la casa. Puede ayudar fuera de la oficina* He/she comes to the house. Can help outside the office *Nos saluda por nombre* He/she greets us by our name *Uno puede llamar a cualquier hora* One can call on him or her at any time *Sabe ayudar con problemas* Knows how to solve problems

NOTE: Terms are arranged in relative order of frequency.
* The term respeto was universally mentioned by the respondent group.
Source: Valle and Mendoza 1978. Reprinted with permission.

The retest involved the clinic's extensive psychological/psychometric battery. At the point of the exam, the writer communicated conversationally in Spanish with Sra. L. to determine if indeed this language capability was current and whether the process whereby the question in English was translated verbally into Spanish would work. Once into the test, it became obvious that she was having more trouble with the questions worded in Spanish, rather than in English. In fact, she began to score lower in Spanish, and the testing reverted to English with results proximate to the first assessment.

On the suggestion to the clinic outreach staff that another dynamic might be present, information emerged that there was a longstanding marital problem present, and even though Sra. L. was a probable Alzheimer's disease victim, her resorting to Spanish at home had, at this moment, another possible origin, more related to the longstanding marital and family strain than to the current progress of the disease. It could also be that Sra. L. would eventually revert more to Spanish as the disease progressed but it was clear that, at this point, Spanish was contraindicated in the clinic and perhaps with regard to her current interactions with the Long Term Care System and its providers—although, as the disease progressed, staff would have to be alert to the signs that Sra. L's reversion to her original learned language of Spanish would indeed now be more reflective of the progress of the disease than to the underlying family conflict. (Valle 1985)

As is evident, despite some of the information originally provided by the collateral informants, a further assessment at the point of the clinical process indicated the need to place Senora L. closer to the *assimilated* or English-speaking side of the acculturation scale–at least in her relations with the exogenous service delivery, clinical environment.

The Alzheimer's disease/dementia research effort may become stymied at this point and unable to proceed further if the background knowledge and cultural research expertise needed to accomplish the cultural assessment task are not present. As a consequence, much vital information may be lost. A pragmatic step has already been suggested to assist in overcoming this possible barrier, namely, to hire the cultural assessment expertise either on a consultative basis or as an integral part of the overall undertaking.

At the same time, it should be noted that the scarcity of cultural research expertise may be more assumed than actual. The difficulty rests more in the fact that Alzheimer's disease/dementia-related research does not usually include cultural assessment as an integral part of the research design, although the cultural component is present every time a sociodemographic profile is drawn, a patient's medical and family history is taken, or a psychosocial assessment is elicited. But, as argued here, it is not just personnel or expertise that is a problem. The lack of an appropriate framework impedes focusing on these data from a cultural perspective. Unfortunately, therefore, the empirical definition of the acculturation continuum within the proposed working model remains very tentative and preliminary. Even in recent studies, language and other ethnocultural variables still remain mixed with socioeconomic/social status factors. Again, caution is indicated against stereotyping, as many ethnocultural groups, such as the Chinese, Japanese, and Jewish peoples, have a long history of literacy. The same could possibly be said about upper-class ethnic minority group members, who may retain their culture-of-origin orientations. In many instances, these latter individuals will have been exposed to higher levels of formal education within the "host" society. The issue here is that the cognitive screens may well be affected by the respondent's educational attainment and not just by culture-of-origin factors.

The possibility of the educational level skewing specific items on the MMSE has been raised by a number of investigators, such as Holzer et al. (1984), Escobar et al. (1986), and Bird et al. (1987), with regard to the "serial 7s" item (the subject is requested to count backwards by 7s beginning at 100). Applying the MMSE within the New Haven Epidemiological Catchment Area survey, the researchers questioned whether serial 7s might not be inappropriately difficult for less well-educated subjects. The Blessed et al. (1968) "counting backwards from 20" item may well be more suited to elderly individuals with elementary school (or less) education regardless of ethnicity. As indicated, considerable research distinguishing the impact of socioeconomic factors from cultural variables remains to be done.

Distinguishing Ethnocultural Factors From Multiple Jeopardy Status

The problem of sorting cultural variables from other status factors is made even more difficult by the underclass position of certain ethnic population groups within the host society. For over four decades in the general literature, four cohorts have been identified as ethnic minority populations. These include persons of American Indian/Native American, Asian American, black, and Hispanic/Latino heritage (Yin 1973; Solomon 1974, 1982; Bell et al. 1976; Chunn et al. 1983; McNeely and Colen 1983; Lum 1986).

The more limited use of the terms ethnic minority or just minority elderly to designate members of U.S. populations of color is quite consistent with a practice dating back some four decades, reflecting the actual underclass status of these groups within the larger society (National Urban League 1964; White House Conference 1971; Stanford 1974; Solomon 1974; Bell et al. 1978; Jackson 1980; Manuel 1980; Valle 1981; Moore 1971, 1973; Markides 1982; McNeely and Colen 1983; Lockery 1987). As noted by Holzberg (1982), this designation may be an artifact of the civil rights movement starting in the early 1950s. However, the members of the above four noted population groups clearly fit the generally cited Wirth (1945, p.347) definition of minority group membership, namely, persons who

> because of their physical (and/)or cultural characteristics are singled out from others in the society in which they live for differential and unequal treatment and who therefore regard themselves as objects of collective discrimination.

Two core issues are at stake here. First, we must recognize that while not all U.S. ethnic group populations have been discriminated against—noting here that there is great "ethnic variation" among persons of Euro/Anglo heritage (Scandinavian, Germanic, Eastern European, English, etc.), certain ethnic elderly, specifically those identified as ethnic minority group members, have experienced discrimination whose residual effects still linger. Second, the research effort must be able to distinguish those responses arising as reactions to discrimination from those emerging from within the matrix of culture-of-origin value and belief constructs.

The available data show that the largest portion of the elderly members of the four designated ethnic minority groups are in the lower economic strata of the society so as to overbalance the respective cohorts in this direction (White House Conference 1971; Bell et al. 1976; Weaver 1976; Jackson et al. 1982; McNeely and Colen 1983). Individual and family economic and social resources for the elderly members of these groups are, to say the least, insufficient, placing greater burdens on their caregivers, and especially on the caretakers of the elderly affected with Alzheimer's disease and related disorders. For this reason, the concept of *double jeopardy* was introduced by the National Urban League (1964) to describe the varied effects of discrimination on these populations and was subsequently expanded into the concept of multiple hazards and/or multiple jeopardy with regard to ethnic minority elderly (Lindsay 1971; Jackson 1972; Saenz 1972; Jeffries 1972; Manuel 1982). Here, the concept of minority status becomes enmeshed with the ascription of ethnicity to specific subgroups.

The research issue at stake is that learned or acquired cognitive and behavioral response patterns arising from longstanding discriminatory influences within the host society need to be accounted for within the inquiry. It may well be that the underclass victimization response patterns, more than culture-of-origin beliefs and practices, can help explain the differential access to formal services by ethnic minority groups, and, particularly, the elderly from these groups as reported in the literature (Manuel 1982).

For example, to counterbalance the view that resistance to and/or underutilization of formal services by ethnic minority populations and their elderly might be primarily due to cultural factors are those reported successes in providing services to minority elderly dementia-affected individuals and their caretaking significant others (On Lok Senior Health Services 1982; Yee 1983; Zawadski and Ansak 1983; Aranda 1984) and in using support group strategies (Henderson 1987). These Alzheimer's disease successes in linking long-term care services to ethnic minority populations point to the fact that differential access can be bridged. They also illustrate the possibility that culture-free and culture-fair syntony can be attained by segments of the service provision and research sectors.

A Further Issue: The Designation of Minority Status

The combination of minority and underclass status encountered by the four ethnic cohorts identified above leaves the field of aging with still another problem, namely, the strategic inclusion of these populations within Alzheimer's disease and related disorders research. It is important to indicate here that the focus of the concern being voiced is not one of *overt* discrimination against, or maltreatment of, Alzheimer's disease-affected ethnic minority elderly and/or their caretakers by the field of aging. Rather, the issue is one of the systematic bypassing or ignoring of these four groups within the field of dementia research as evidenced by the absence of these populations in the literature (Valle 1981; Lockery 1986).

Admittedly, the field of gerontology is not completely comfortable conferring minority status somewhat exclusively on certain aging cohorts and prioritizing research directed to them (Holzberg 1982). Several reasons account for this discomfort, the first being that minority status could be accorded other population groups for a variety of reasons. For example, the elderly as a whole have often been identified as a minority group vis-a-vis their status within the broader society (Steib 1965). Elderly women can likewise be considered as a minority within their own age group when their socioeconomic status

139

is compared to that of elderly males—even though they outnumber males. The term could likewise be applied to persons affected with Alzheimer's disease and related disorders, who are in the minority within the total cohort of the aged. Lastly, as some gerontologists (Holzer 1982) maintain, focusing on minority group status has tended to skew research away from a broader based, ethnocultural investigative agenda within aging as espoused by Clark (1967), Kiefer (1971), Gelfand (1982), and others.

However, if the conceptual distinctions are clearly maintained, it is not clear how the designation of some specific ethnic populations as minority groups excludes research opportunities relative to other ethnic populations, including any of the Euro/Anglo ethnic cohorts identifiable within the host U.S. culture. The studies of Cohler and Lieberman (1980) and Cohler (1982) highlight comparative cultural study of several Euro/Anglo ethnic populations, as does the work of Gelfand and Fandetti (1980) and Gelfand (1982). Nor, for that matter, does this designation preclude ethnocultural analysis of family values as related to the mainstream U.S. elderly, such as presented by Nydegger (1983).

Implications for Action and Recommendations for Research

The multilevel complexities surrounding the diagnosis, treatment, and societal impact of Alzheimer's disease and related disorders have, more than perhaps any other single area of aging inquiry, brought about multidisciplinary collaboration. This collaboration now needs to incorporate cultural assessment as an integral part of the research and intervention strategy. There is no lack of appropriate ethnocultural theory to accompany Alzheimer's disease treatment and family stress research. For example, one can look to methodological support from the social sciences as a whole (Seward and Marmor 1956; Kaplan 1961; Murphy and Leighton 1965; Lofland 1966; Webb et al. 1966; Garfinkel 1967; Cicourel 1968; Schatzman and Strauss 1973; Sieber 1973; Truzzi 1974; Price-Williams 1975; Meyers 1977; Weiss 1977; Wright et al. 1983; Yu 1985). One can likewise find support from specialty social science research areas, such as designing culturally syntonic translation strategies (Werner and Campbell 1970; Brislin et al. 1973; Brislin 1980; Triandis 1978; Aday et al. 1980; Marcos and Trujillo 1981; Burnam et al. 1983; Karno et al. 1983; Guthrie 1984). The field of aging itself has its own cultural research tradition as represented by a host of investigators (Clark and Anderson 1967; Clark 1967; Kiefer 1971; Moore 1971, 1973; Ragan 1973; Bengston 1979; Cuellar 1974; Cantor 1976; Valle and Mendoza 1978; Fry 1979; Cohler and Lieberman 1980; Markides 1980, 1982; Gelfand 1982; Holzer 1984). The problem is elsewhere and relates more to barriers of research prioritization as well as to the perceived lack of sufficient expertise to undertake such inquiry.

Comparative Studies

Studies are needed in both the field and the clinic on possible differential responses to Alzheimer's disease and related disorders among ethnic group members who retain culture-of-origin orientations. In reality, because so little cultural information exists in the Alzheimer's disease treatment and family stress research area, each of the topical themes noted here could be approached from the standpoint of a specific ethnocultural/ethnic minority group. A comparative approach is suggested to expedite knowledge development relative to ethnic populations.

There is a dearth of information on family structure and caretaking functions across ethnic groups related to the impact of Alzheimer's disease and the other late-onset dementias. Popular theory has placed the ethnic elder, and in particular, the ethnic minority elder, within a type of intergenerational, extended family. Is this the actual situation, or does this reflect an affectively desired preference? Reports show that some ethnic elderly are without such supports. Some ethnic groups, such as the Chinese and the Filipinos, were not permitted to bring family members when they immigrated and, hence, are alone in their elderhood without family caretaking resources— and more problematic yet, they are without these resources when struck with one of the dementing diseases. In other instances, ethnic families may be experiencing changes similar to mainstream U.S. families.

It would be important to document the configuration of the non-mainstream Alzheimer's disease/dementia-affected family across ethnic groups. One hypothesis to test, among many, would be that ethnic elders who have maintained their culture-of-origin orientations would prefer an intergenerational extended family caretaking context, despite their actual present circumstances. If such preferences are verified through research, a number of treatment and service implications follow with regard to simulating this desired state.

Study is likewise needed on the extent of the caretaking burden and possible cultural mediators. The impact of the Alzheimer's disease burden on the family/significant other caretakers is well documented for the mainstream population (Zarit 1980; Wilder et al. 1983;

141

George 1984; Poulshock and Deimling 1984). With the exception of Morycz et al. (1987), almost no research has been undertaken on how this burden is experienced across different cultural groups. Do some ethnic groups provide more social network support to offset the perceived as well as actual burden? Do some value and/or belief configurations lessen the feeling of burden? Or is the reverse true? Could it be that a greater burden is felt by a larger number of caretakers/significant others within the culture-of-origin retaining ethnic elders for many of the socioeconomic and multiple jeopardy factors outlined above? Focused research could serve to clarify these questions.

Also needed are research approaches that document culturally related coping strategies along with studies that would highlight culturally specific aspects of handling loss, bereavement, and depression both during the disease process and after it has run its course with the family's loved one.

The whole area of ethnocultural variance relative to cognitive, behavioral, psychotherapeutic, and environmental intervention modalities within the Alzheimer's disease/dementia process awaits investigation. Many existing methodologies are probably adaptable to non-English-speaking, culturally unique dementia-affected ethnic elderly and their significant others. What is unclear are the cross-cultural parameters of such interventive approaches, as well as the cultural modifications that need to be made.

Epidemiological and Services Research

Existing Alzheimer's disease/dementia prevalence data, while cross-cultural in nature (Cross and Gurland 1987), primarily compares Northern European and U.S. Euro/Anglo populations. We have little basic scientific information on the course of the dementing diseases among the other ethnically diverse populations. The NIMH-funded Epidemiological Catchment Area projects broke some ground in cross-cultural comparative assessment of cognitive dysfunctions using the the MMSE as the core measure (Holzer et al. 1984; Escobar et al. 1986; Bird et al. 1987). This can only be considered a preliminary step. A major, across-the-board epidemiological research effort is required. What is important from the standpoint of the cultural concerns expressed herein is that nonmainstream ethnics be targeted on a priority basis within any future epidemiological studies undertaken. Without some urging from funding sources, though, it is not certain that such will occur serendipitously within the research community.

Services present still another major area of inquiry with regard to

Alzheimer's disease/dementia-affected ethnic elderly and their family/significant other caretakers. Much has been written regarding the problems and barriers that ethnic minority elderly, in particular, encounter in accessing formal services. As noted throughout this discussion, the problem at hand is to clarify whether the barriers encountered by the members of these groups are due more to socioeconomic constraints or their minority/underclass status, or in actuality due primarily to ethnocultural beliefs and help-seeking/help-accepting practices. All may be involved, but it is necessary at this juncture to distinguish among the relative influence of the different classes of variables.

A central difficulty is the fact that the services research area in general has focused only peripherally on non-English speaking, nonmainstream U.S. ethnic cohorts with regard to Alzheimer's disease and related disorders. Without some priority attention, Alzheimer's disease/dementia-affected persons from these groups are unlikely to receive services research attention commensurate with need, particularly when similarly afflicted elderly and their caretakers in the general population are themselves pressing for research notice.

Basic Biomedical Research

The charge to the writer has been the exploration of cultural factors related to Alzheimer's disease treatment and family stress research. This is not to say that the biomedical research arena is exempt from the need for cultural analyses. There are a host of genetic, neurological, metabolic, and immune system function, as well as environmental impact and basic science questions about Alzheimer's disease requiring study from the cultural perspective, particularly as applied to those groups identified as Third World peoples, who, in actuality, are the elder cousins of many of the U.S. ethnic populations. An important direction to take in the cross-cultural study of Alzheimer's disease and related phenomena would be that suggested by Kleinman (1977), namely, to engage in research that distinguishes clearly between the disease entity and the illness process. As Lefly (1985) further indicates, the medical or disease model may exist side by side with traditional culture-of-origin coping/caretaking beliefs and behaviors. With this said, recognition is given to the fact that the basic science issues at this level are so broad and complex that a separate extended discussion is needed so as to properly frame the biomedical research questions within the cultural context.

Closing Methodological Note

The preceding discussion has, by intent, illustrated rather than exhausted all possible cultural and ethnic issues related to Alzheimer's disease treatment and family research. In fact, there are more gaps in the extant knowledge base than relevant findings. This places all the more urgency on the research community to undertake the necessary inquiry. As indicated, whether formally recognized or not, the cultural dimension is present the moment the investigator or clinician engages the patient and begins eliciting information about the life-course context of the disease, as well as about the ways in which the individual and his/her significant others have coped.

Clearly, diverse ethnic groups, and particularly those designated as ethnic minority groups, can be expected to increase in the United States both in number and with regard to health needs (Allan and Brotman 1981). The researcher and the clinician, in turn, can expect to encounter many more Alzheimer's disease/dementia-affected elderly from these groups. The problem for the investigator and clinician alike will be the fact that these elderly and their caretakers will be communicating in languages other than English and following traditions that differ from those of the mainstream population. The lack of familiarity with ethnocultural variances by investigators and clinicians alike may lead to serious misunderstandings at the point of intervention, no matter how well intended. It is hoped that the working notions provided here will facilitate further study in this vital area.

The microscope may eventually demonstrate the absence of variance in diseased brain tissue across cultures. The clinic and the community, though, will continue to attest to the variety of human response around the devastating impact of Alzheimer's disease and related disorders, and here the ethnic and cultural phenomena begin to assume vital research importance.

The framework suggested at the outset in figure 4-2 is offered as an approach to the task at hand and lends itself to the application of both advanced statistical and ethnomethodological techniques within a single research design. Figure 4-3 summarizes a series of considerations implicit in operationalizing a cultural assessment research strategy specifically aimed at those elderly whose culture-of-origin identification, distinct from mainstream U.S. society, persists over time. It should be kept in mind that, while the various steps are delineated serially, continuous interaction among them is the norm.

It is difficult to think of a part of the country where ethnic variety cannot be encountered. And, although a case has been made for the possible focusing of study on certain ethnic cohorts identified as eth-

┌───┐
│ **Figure 4-3. Operationalizing the cultural assessment research strategy** │
└───┘

Step 1. The researcher has mastery of own core discipline attendant technology; maintains multidisciplinary capability ⟷ *Step 3.* The researcher applies the culture-free/fair framework and gathers data re: the ethnic group's language/ communication systems; interactional behaviors; norms, values, and beliefs

A COMBINED QUANTITATIVE AND QUALITATIVE RESEARCH STRATEGY

Step 5. Culturally syntonic research assessment and intervention outcome

*Step 2.*The researcher has developed a cultural assessment framework to include culture-free/fair technology and has included an acculturation continuum component ⟷ *Step 4.* The researcher develops an appropriate socioeconomic/educational social status/multiple jeopardy profile distinguishing same from cultural variables

nic minority populations, ethnocultural research herein has been defined in the broadest possible context to include all groups clustering around specific culture-of-origin beliefs and practices differing from U.S. mainstream society. Investigators, therefore, need to examine their research strategies to see if their projects are indeed reflective of the cultural and ethnic group diversity to be found within their own research environments. In this context it is difficult to exempt any project from the need to include culturally diverse samples.

A simpler discussion would have been preferable. Unfortunately, cultural phenomena remain complex.

References

Aday, L.A.; Chiu, G.Y.; and Anderson, R. Methodological issues in health care surveys of the Spanish heritage population. *American Journal of Public Health* 70(4):367-374, 1980.

Allan, C., and Brotman, H. *1981 Chartbook on Aging in America.* Washington, DC: White House Conference on Aging, 1981.

Aranda, M.P. Caring for Our Elders. *Calmecac* 1:7-12, 1984. (Supplemented by site visit and in person conferences May 1984.)

Attunes, G.; Gordon, C.; and Gaitz, C.M. Ethnicity, socioeconomic status and the etiology of psychological distress. *Social Science Research* 4(58):361-368, 1974.

Becerra, R.M., and Shaw, D. *The Hispanic Elderly: A Research Reference Guide.* New York: University Press of America, 1984.

Bell, D.; Kasschau, P.; and Zellman, G. *Delivering Services to Elderly Members of Minority Groups: A Critical Review of the Literature.* Santa Monica, CA: Rand Corporation, 1976

Bengston, V.L. Ethnicity and aging problems and issues in current social science inquiry. In: Gelfand, D.E., and Kutzik, A.J., eds. *Ethnicity and Aging: Theory, Research, and Policy.* New York: Springer, 1979.

Bird, H.R.; Canino, G.; Stipec, M.R.; and Shrout, P. Use of the Mini-Mental State Examination in a probability sample of a Hispanic population. *Journal of Nervous and Mental Disease* 175:731-737, 1987.

Blau, Z.S. *Aging and Social Class and Ethnicity. Leon and Josephine Winkelman Lecture Series.* Ann Arbor, MI: School of Social Work, University of Michigan, 1978.

Blessed, G.; Tomlinson, B.E.; and Roth, M. The associations between quantitative measures of dementia and of senile change in the cerebral grey matter of elderly subjects. *British Journal of Psychiatry* 114:797-811, 1968.

Brislin, R.W. Translation and content analysis of oral and written materials. In: Triandis, H.C., and Berry, J.W., eds. *Handbook of Cross-Cultural Psychology-Methodology.* Vol 2. Boston: Allyn and Bacon, 1980. pp. 389-444.

Brislin, R.W.; Lonner, W.J.; and Thorndyke, R.M. *Cross Cultural Research Methods.* New York: Wiley and Sons, 1973.

Burnam, M.A.; Karno, M.; Hough, R.L.; Escobar, J.I.; and Forsythe,

A.B. The Spanish diagnostic interview. *Archives of General Psychiatry* 40:1189-1196, 1983.

Cantor, M.H. Effect of ethnicity on life styles of the inner-city elderly. In: Monk, A., ed. *The Age of Aging: A Reader in Social Gerontology.* New York: Prometheus Books, 1976.

Casavantes, E.J. *A New Look at the Attributes of the Mexican American.* Washington, DC: ERIC Document Reproduction Service, No. ED 028 010, 1969.

Chee, P., and Kane, R. Cultural factors affecting nursing home care for minorities: A study of Black American and Japanese American groups. *Journal of the American Geriatrics Society* 31:109-112, 1979.

Chunn, J.C.; Dunston, P.J.; and Ross-Sheriff, F., eds. *Mental Health and People of Color: Curriculum Development and Change.* Washington, DC: Howard University Press, 1983.

Cicourel, A.V. *Method and Measurement in Sociology.* New York: Free Press, 1968.

Clark, M., and Anderson, B.G. *Culture and Aging.* Springfield, IL: Charles C. Thomas, 1967.

Clark, M.; Kaurman, S.; and Pierce, R.C. Exploration of acculturation: Toward a model of ethnic identity. *Human Organization* 35:231-238, 1976.

Cohler, B. Stress or support: Relations between older women from three European ethnic groups and their relatives. In Manuel, R.C., ed. *Minority Aging: Sociological and Social Psychological Perspectives.* Westport, CT: Greenwood Press, 1982.

Cohler, B., and Lieberman, M. Social relations and mental health among three European ethnic groups. *Research on Aging: A Quarterly of of Social Gerontology* 2:445-469, 1980.

Colen, J.N. Facilitating service delivery to the minority aging. In: McNeely, R.L., and Colen, J.L., eds. *Aging in Minority Groups.* Beverly Hills, CA: Sage Publications, 1983.

Cross, P.S., and Gurland, B.J. *The Epidemiology of Dementing Disorders.* Contract Report Office of Technology Assessment, Springfield, VA: National Technical Information Service, U.S. Department of Commerce, 1987.

Cuellar, I.; Harris, L.C.; and Jasso, R. An acculturation scale for Mexican American normal and clinical populations. *Hispanic Journal of Behavioral Sciences* 2:199-217, 1980.

Cuellar, J.B. On the relevance of ethnographic methods: Studying aging in an urban Mexican American community. In: Bengston, V., ed. *Gerontological Research and Community Concern: A Case Study of a Multidisciplinary Project.* Los Angeles: University of Southern California Gerontology Center, 1974.

147

Escobar, J.I.; Burnam, A.; Karno, M.; Forsythe, A.; Lansverk, J.; and Golding, J.M. Use of the Mini-Mental State Examination (MMSE) in a community population of mixed ethnicity. *Journal of Nervous and Mental Disease* 174:607-614, 1986.

Fabrega, H. Social psychiatric aspects of acculturation and migration: A general statement. *Community Psychiatry* 10:314-329, 1969.

Favazza, A.R. Culture change and mental health. *Journal of Operational Psychiatry* 11:101-119, 1980.

Flaherty, J.A. Appropriate and inappropriate research methodologies for Hispanic mental health. In: Gaviria, M., and Arana, J.D., eds. *Health and Behavior: Research Agenda for Hispanics*. Chicago, IL: Simon Bolivar Hispanic-American Psychiatric Research Institute and Training Program, University of Illinois, 1987.

Folstein, M.F.; Folstein, S.A.; and Mchough, P.R. Mini Mental State: A practical method for grading the cognitive state of patients for the clinician. *Journal of Psychiatric Research* 12:189-198, 1975.

Fry, C.L., ed. *Aging in Culture and Society: Comparative Viewpoints and Strategies*, New York: James Bergin Publishers, 1979.

Garfinkel, H. *Studies in Ethnomethodology*. Englewood Cliffs, NJ: Prentice Hall, 1967.

Gelfand, D.Z. *Aging: The Ethnic Factor*. Boston, MA: Little Brown, 1982.

George, L.K. *The Dynamics of Caregiver Burden*. Final report submitted to AARP Andrus Foundation, 1984.

Goodglass, H., and Kaplan, E. *The Assessment of Aphasia and Related Disorders*. Philadelphia: Lea and Febiger, 1983.

Gordon, M.M. *Assimilation in American Life*. New York: Oxford University Press, 1964.

Gurland, B.J. The North Manhattan Aging Project (working document). New York: Columbia University Center for Geriatrics and Gerontology, 1986.

Gurland, B.J., and Wilder, D. The CARE interview revisited: Development of an efficient, systematic clinical assessment. *Journal of Gerontology* 39:129-137, 1984.

Gurland, B.; Kuriansky, J.; Sharp, L.; Simon, R.; Stiller, P.; and Birkett, P. The Comprehensive Assessment and Referral Evaluation (CARE) rationale, development and reliability: Part II. A factor analysis. *International Journal of Aging and Human Development* 8:9-42, 1977.

Guthrie, G.M. The problems of measurement in cross-cultural research. In: Mezzich, J.E., and Berganza, C.E., eds. *Culture and Psychopathology*. New York: Columbia University Press, 1984.

Henderson, J.N. Mental disorders among the elderly: Dementia and its sociocultural correlates. In: Silverman, P., ed. *Older People*,

Modern Pioneers: An Interdisciplinary View of Aging. Bloomington, IN: Indiana University Press, 1987.

Herskovitz, M. *Cultural Relativism: Perspectives in Cultural Pluralism.* Herskovitz, F., ed. New York: Vintage Books, 1972.

Holzberg, C.S. Ethnicity and aging: Anthropological perspectives on more than just minority elderly. *Gerontologist* 22:249-257, 1982.

Holzer, III, C.E.; Tischler, G.L.; Leaf, P.J.; and Myers, J.K. An epidemiologic assessment of cognitive impairment in a community population. *Research Communication and Mental Health* 4:3-32, 1984.

Jackson, J.J. Black aged in quest of the Phoenix. In: *Triple Jeopardy: Myth or Reality.* Washington, DC: National Council on Aging, 1972. pp. 27-40.

Jackson, J.J. *Minorities in Aging.* Belmont, CA: Wadsworth Publishers, 1980.

Jackson, M.; Kolody, B.; and Wood, J.L. To be old and black: The case for double jeopardy on income and health. In: Manuel, R.C., ed. *Minority Aging: Sociological and Social Psychological Perspectives.* Westport, CT: Greenwood Press, 1982.

Jeffries, D. Our aged Indians. In: *Triple Jeopardy: Myth or Reality.* Washington DC: National Council on Aging, 1972. pp. 7-10.

Kahn, R.L.; Goldfarb, A.I.; Pollock, M.; and Peck, R. Brief objective measures for the determination of mental status in the elderly. *American Journal of Psychiatry* 117:326-328, 1963.

Kaplan, B. *Studying Personality Cross Culturally.* New York: Harper & Row, 1961.

Kardiner, A. *The Individual and His Society.* New York: Columbia University Press, 1939.

Karno, M.; Burnam, M.A.; Escobar, J.I.; Hough, R.L.; and Eaton, W.W. Development of the Spanish language version of the National Institute of Mental Health Diagnostic Interview Schedule. *Archives of General Psychiatry* 40:1183-1188, 1983.

Katzman, R.; Lasker, B.; and Bernstein, N. *Accuracy of Diagnosis and Consequences of Misdiagnosis of Disorders Causing Dementia.* Springfield, VA: U.S. Department of Commerce, National Technical Information Service, 1987.

Kiefer, C. Notes on anthropology and the minority elderly. *Gerontologist* 11:194-198, 1971.

Kleinman, A.M. Depression and somatization and the "New Cross-Cultural Psychiatry." *Science and Medicine* 11:3-10, 1977.

Kluckhohn, C. *Culture and Behavior.* Kluckhohn, R., ed. New York: Free Press, 1962.

LeVine, E., and Padilla, A. *Crossing Cultures in Therapy: Pluralistic Counselling for the Hispanic.* Belmont, CA: Wadsworth, 1980.

Leacock, E.B., ed. *Culture of Poverty: A Critique*. New York: Simon and Schuster, 1971.

Lee, R.P.L. The causal priority between socioeconomic status and psychiatric disorder: A prospective study. In: Mezzich, J.E., and Berganza, C.E., eds. *Culture and Psychotherapy*. New York: Columbia University Press, 1984.

Lefly, H.P. Families of the mentally ill. In: Cross-Cultural Perspective. *Psychosocial Rehabilitation Journal* 8(4):57-75, 1985.

Lerner, B. *Therapy in the Ghetto*. Baltimore: Johns Hopkins University Press, 1972.

Lindsay, I.B. *Multiple Hazards of Race and Age: The Situation of Black Aged in the United States*. Report of the Senate Special Committee on Aging. Washington, DC: Supt. of Docs., U.S. Govt. Print. Off., 1971.

Lockery, S.A. *Impact of Dementia within Minority Groups*. Contract report for the Office of Technology Assessment, U. S. Congress. Springfield, VA: National Technical Information Service, U.S. Department of Commerce, 1986.

Lofland, J. *Analyzing Social Settings*. Belmont, CA: Wadsworth Publishing, 1966.

Lopez-Aqueres, W.; Kemp, B.; Plopper, M.; and Staples, F.R. Health needs of the Hispanic elderly. *Journal of the American Geriatrics Society* 32:191-198, 1984.

Lum, D. *Social Work Practice and People of Color*. Monterey, CA: Brooks/Cole Publishing, 1986.

Manuel, R.C. Leadership factors in service delivery and minority aging utilization. *Journal of Minority Aging* 5:218-232, 1980.

Manuel, R.C., ed. *Minority Aging: Sociological and Social Psychological Perspectives*. Westport, CT: Greenwood Press, 1982.

Marcos, L.R., and Trujillo, M.R. Culture, language, and communicative behavior: The psychiatric examination of Spanish Americans. In: Duran, R.P., ed. *Latino Language and Communicative Behavior*. Newark, NJ: Alex Publishing, 1981.

Markides, K.S. Ethnic differences in age identification. *Social Science Quarterly* 60:659-666, 1980.

Markides, K. Ethnicity and aging: A comment. *Gerontologist* 22:467-470, 1982.

McNeely, R.L., and Colen, J.L., eds. *Aging in Minority Groups*. Beverly Hills, CA: Sage Publications, 1983.

Meyers, V. Survey methods for minority populations. *Journal of Social Issues* 33:11-19, 1977.

Mirowsky, J., and Ross, C.R. Minority status, ethnic culture, and distress: A comparison of blacks, whites and Mexican Americans. *American Journal of Sociology* 86:474-495, 1984.

Moore, J.W. Situational factors affecting minority aging. *Gerontologist* 11:88-93 (Part II), 1971.

Moore, J.W. Social constraints on sociological knowledge: Academics and research concerning minorities. *Social Problems* 21:65-77, 1973.

Morycz, R.K.; Malloy, J.; Bozich, M.; and Martz, P. Racial differences in family burden: Clinical implications for social work. In: *Gerontological Social Work with Families*. New York: Haworth Press, 1987.

Murphy, H.B.M. Handling the cultural dimension in psychiatric research. In: Mezzich, J.E., and Berganza, C.E., eds. *Culture and Psychopathology*. New York: Columbia University Press, 1984.

Murphy, J., and Leighton, L., eds. *Approaches to Cross Cultural Psychiatry*. Ithaca, NY: Cornell University Press, 1965.

Mutran, E. Intergenerational family support among blacks and whites: Response to culture or to socioeconomic differences. *Journal of Gerontology* 40:382-389, 1984.

National Urban League. *Double Jeopardy: The Older Negro in America Today*. New York: National Urban League, 1964.

Nydegger, C. Family ties of the aged in cross cultural perspective. *Gerontologist* 23:26-32, 1983.

On Lok Senior Health Services. A case study. *Health Services Integration: Lessons for the 1980s*. Vol. III. Final Report. DHHS Contract No. 282-89-0043-SW T.O. 2. Publication IOM-82-03C, 1982.

Osako, M.M. Aging and family among Japanese Americans: The role of ethnic tradition in adjustment to old age. *Gerontologist* 19:448-455, 1979.

Pearlin, L., and Schooler, C. The structure of coping. *Journal of Health and Social Behavior* 19:2-21, 1978.

Pfeiffer, E. A short portable mental status questionnaire for the assessment of organic brain deficit in elderly patients. *Journal of the American Geriatrics Society* 23:433-441, 1975.

Poulshock, S.W., and Deimling, G. Families caring for elders in residence: Issues in measurement of burden. *Journal of Gerontology* 39:230-239, 1984.

Price-Williams, D.R. *Explorations in Cross-Cultural Psychology*. San Francisco: Chandler and Sharp, 1975.

Ragan, P.K. *Aging Among Blacks, Mexican Americans and Anglos: Problems and Possibilities of Research as Reflected in the Literature*. Los Angeles: Andrus Gerontology Center, University of Southern California, 1973.

Romano, O. The historical and intellectual presence of Mexican-Americans. *El Grito* 2:13-26, 1969.

Saenz, D. Triple jeopardy: Myth or reality. In: *Triple Jeopardy: Myth or Reality*. Washington, DC: National Council on Aging, 1972. pp. 1-5.

Sapir, E. *Language*. New York: Harcourt Brace Javanovitch, 1921.

Schatzman, L., and Strauss, A. *Field Research Strategies for a Natural Sociology*. Englewood Cliffs, NJ: Prentice Hall, 1973.

Seward, G., and Marmor, J. *Psychotherapy and Culture Conflict*. New York: Ronald Press, 1956.

Shanas, E. Family kin networks and aging in a cross cultural perspective. *Journal of Marriage and the Family* 35:505-573, 1973.

Sieber, S. The integration of fieldwork and survey methods. *American Journal of Sociology* 78:1335-1358, 1973.

Solomon, B.B. Growing old in the ethno system. In: Stanford, E.P., ed. *Proceedings of the Institute on Minority Aging*. San Diego: Campanile Press, 1974.

Solomon, B.B. Ethnic minority elderly in long term care: A historical perspective. In: Stanford, E.P., and Lockery, S.A., eds. *Minority Aging and Long Term Care*. San Diego: Campanile Press, 1982.

Spicer, E.H. Persistent cultural systems: A comparative study of identity systems that can adapt to contrasting environments. *Science* 174:785-800, 1971.

Stanford, E.P., ed. *Proceedings of the Institute on Minority Aging*. San Diego: Campanile Press, 1974.

Steib, G.F. Are the aged a minority group? In: Neugarten, B.L., ed. *Middle Age and Aging*. Chicago: University of Chicago Press, 1965.

Torres Gil, F. Age, health, and culture: An examination of health among Spanish speaking elderly. In: Montiel, M., ed. *Hispanic Families*. Washington, DC: National Coalition of Spanish Speaking Mental Health Organizations (COSSMHO), 1978.

Triandis, H. Approaches toward minimizing translation. In: Brislin, R., ed. *Translation: Applications and Research*. New York: Wiley/Halstead, 1978. pp. 229-243.

Truzzi, M., ed. *Verstehen: Subjective Understanding in the Social Sciences*. Reading, MA: Addison Publishing, 1974.

U.S. Congress, Office of Technology Assessment. *Losing a Million Minds: Confronting the Tragedy of Alzheimer's Disease and Other Dementias*. OTA-BA-323. Washington, DC: Supt. of Docs., U.S. Govt. Print. Off., 1987.

Valentine, C. *Culture and Poverty: Critique and Counter Proposals*. Chicago: University of Chicago Press, 1968.

Valle, R. Natural support systems, minority groups and the late life dementias: Implications for service delivery, research and policy. In: Miller, N., and Cohen, G.D., eds. *Clinical Aspects of Alzheimer's Disease and Senile Dementia*. New York: Raven Press, 1981. pp. 277-299.

Valle, R. "Senora L: Case Analysis Report." Prepared for the Alzheimer's Disease Research Center, California Alzheimer's Disease Diagnostic Treatment Center (also SOCARE), 1985.

Valle, R. Cross cultural competence in minority communities. A curriculum implementation strategy. In: Miranda, M.M., and Kitano, H.H.L., eds. *Mental Health Research and Practice in Minority Communities*. National Institute of Mental Health. DHHS Publication No. (ADM) 86-1466. 1986.

Valle, R., and Mendoza, L. *The Elder Latino*. San Diego: Campanile Press, 1978.

Vega, W.A.; Hough, R.L.; and Romero, A. Family life patterns of Mexican Americans. In: Powell, G.P., ed. *Psychosocial Development of Minority Group Children*. New York: Brunner/Mazel Publishers, 1983.

Weaver, J. *National Health Policy and the Underserved Ethnic Minorities, Women, and the Elderly*. St. Louis: C.V. Mosby, 1976.

Webb, E.J.; Campbell, D.T.; Schwartz, R.D.; and Schrest, L.B. *Unobstrusive Measures: Nonreactive Research in the Social Sciences*. Chicago: Rand McNally, 1966.

Weeks, J.R., and Cuellar, J.B. The role of family members in the helping networks of older people. *Gerontologist* 24:23-30, 1981.

Weiss, C.H. Survey researchers and minority communities. *Journal of Social Issues* 33:20-35, 1977.

Werner, C., and Campbell, D. Translating, working through interpreters, and the problem of perceiving. In: Narrd, R., and Cohen, R., eds. *A Handbook of Methods in Cultural Anthropology*. New York: Natural History Press, 1970. pp. 398-420.

White House Conference on Aging. *Special Concerns Session Reports*. Washington, DC: Supt. of Docs., U.S. Govt. Print. Off., 1971.

Whorf, B.L. *Language, Thought, and Reality*. Carroll, J.C., ed. Cambridge, MA: MIT Press, 1971.

Wilder, D.; Teresi, J.A.; and Bennett, R.G. Family burden and dementia. In: Mayeux, R., and Rosen, W.G., eds. *The Dementias*. New York: Raven Press, 1983.

Williams, C.L. Issues surrounding psychological testing of minority patients. *Hospital and Community Psychiatry* 38:184-196, 1987.

Wirth, L. The problem of minority groups. In: Linton, R., ed. *The Science of Man in World Crisis*. New York: Columbia University Press, 1945.

Wright, R.; Saleeby, D.; Watts, T.; and Lecca, P. *Transcultural Perspective in the Human Services: Organizational Issues and Trends*. Springfield, IL: Charles C. Thomas, 1983.

Yee, D. Community based long term care. In: Stanford, E.P., and Lockery, S.A., eds. *Minority Aging and Long Term Care*. San Diego: Campanile Press, 1983.

Yin, R.L. *Race, Creed, Color, or National Origin: A Reader on Racial and Ethnic Minorities in American Society.* Itasca, IL: F.E. Peacock, 1973.

Yu, E.S.H. Studying Vietnamese refugees: Methodological lessons in transcultural research. In: Owan, T.C.; Bliatout, B.; Lin, K-M; Liu, W.; Nguyen, T.D.; and Wong, H.Z., eds. *Southeast Asian Mental Health: Treatment, Prevention, Services, Training, and Research.* DHHS Publication No. ADM 85-1399, 1985.

Zarit, S.H.; Reever, K.E.; and Bach-Peterson, J. Relatives of the impaired elderly: Correlates of feelings of burden. *Gerontologist* 20:649-655, 1980.

Zawadski, R.T., and Ansak, M-L. Consolidating long term care: Early returns from the On Lok demonstration. *Gerontologist* 23:364-369, 1983.

Zuniga, M. Social treatment with the minority elderly. In: McNeely, R.L., and Colen, J.L., eds. *Aging in Minority Groups.* Beverly Hills, CA: Sage Publications, 1983.

Chapter 5

Guardianship of the Cognitively Impaired Elderly: Directions for Research

George T. Grossberg, M.D., George H. Zimny, Ph.D., and
Leslie J. Scallet, J.D.

Introduction

One of the major consequences of dementing illnesses such as Alzheimer's disease in the elderly may be incompetence, that is, inability to handle one's personal and financial affairs in an appropriate and reasonable manner. Inability to make appropriate decisions in matters of medical care, transportation, nutrition, personal hygiene, housing, and finance can result in adverse consequences ranging from overpayment of a bill to accidental death. Providing those elderly persons who are incompetent with protection from adverse consequences is the responsibility of the families of those persons, of guardians, or of appropriate State agencies.

One type of protective service that can be provided for cognitively impaired elderly is surrogate management. Informal surrogate managers in the form of a family member, friend, or long-time banker or attorney may be able to help the minimally impaired person in making some decisions. However, as the degree of impairment increases and decisions become more serious and more fraught with legal consequences, informal surrogate managers may become unwilling or unable to provide the type and degree of help needed. One very important recourse available to families and agencies in this situation is surrogate management in the form of guardianship and/or conservatorship.

155

Guardianship and conservatorship involve a complex process on which relatively little nonlegal research has been conducted. As background for the research questions presented at the end of this chapter, there follows a description of the guardianship process, a brief review of some previous research, a description of a recent research study of the guardianship process, and two detailed case histories of elderly persons for whom guardianship was sought.

Guardianship Is a Matter of Law

Guardianship and conservatorship are legal matters (Brakel et al. 1985) prescribed in the laws of each of the 50 States and the District of Columbia. The guardianship law specifies the process by which a court can appoint a surrogate manager--a guardian and/or conservator--for persons adjudicated by the court as being incompetent to handle their own affairs. The purpose of the law is to protect those legally determined to be unable to protect themselves.

A guardian or conservator is made responsible for and empowered to act on behalf of the incompetent person, for example, by making decisions about medical treatment or disposal of property. Assuming that the guardian acts conscientiously and prudently, it is often advantageous for the incompetent person to have someone who is legally responsible acting on his behalf. It is also advantageous for institutions and agencies such as psychiatric hospitals, State divisions of aging, banks, and nursing homes to be able to turn to the legally appointed guardian for decisions that incompetent persons are unwilling or unable to make in their own best interests.

Despite these advantages, guardianship does involve a number of difficulties and limitations in the areas of costs of the legal process, evidence of competency/incompetency, and the consequences of guardianship.

Costs of the Legal Process

One difficulty of guardianship is the cost in time, effort, and money required to complete the legal process that leads to a decision by the court on whether to appoint a guardian for an aged person. The legal process involves a series of steps that are set down in the State guardianship law. Carrying out these steps generally involves the time and effort of a number of people, including the petitioner for guardianship, the aged person for whom guardianship is being sought, persons who conduct competency/incompetency evaluations, attorneys, witnesses, and court personnel. Months may elapse between the time a petition for guardianship is submitted and the court decides whether to appoint a guardian. Financial costs include filing fees, charges for evaluation of competency/incompetency, attorney's fees, travel by witnesses, and court costs, which may include posting of a bond by the appointed guardian.

Since guardianship is a State law concern, the steps and the specific requirements for each step in the legal process differ depending upon where guardianship is being sought. In addition, changes in the guardianship law can be made during any session of a State legislature, so that year-by-year variations in the guardianship law of any State may occur. For example, Schmidt, Miller, Bell, and New (1981) reported that 12 States had guardianship legislation pending in the spring of 1979, and 8 of the 12 States were proposing legislation aimed at updating their current law to a significant degree.

Evidence of Competency/Incompetency

The decision of the court as to whether to appoint a guardian for an aged person is based principally on the court's judgment of the competency of the aged person for whom guardianship is being sought. Adjudication of incompetency ordinarily leads to appointment of a guardian but, without such adjudication, appointment of a guardian will be refused by the court. The standard by which the court determines incompetence is legal rather than scientific and is formulated in each State law. Some laws focus on general mental status and others on the ability to function in society (Brakel et al. 1985).

The court determines whether the person meets the standard in the relevant State law on the basis of information presented in evidence by the petitioning person or organization, the aged person, witnesses called by each side, or by depositions and other such documents. This information is based upon evaluation of the aged person made by one or more individuals or organizations.

Because of the crucial role played by evidence of competency/incompetency, the court is concerned about the nature and quality of the information presented. The court may thus inquire about the qualifications of the person or organization providing the information and the nature and length of their relationship with the aged person, the methods used to assess competency/incompetency, the kind of information obtained, and the irreversibility of the conditions that are claimed to produce incompetency. The nature and quality of

157

information that can be presented as evidence in court can vary considerably. Clearly, the more thorough and comprehensive the assessment of competency/incompetency, the more likely the assessment information is to be accepted as meeting the standard of evidence required by the court and used in the adjudication.

Consequences of Guardianship

The principal legal consequence for the aged person who is adjudicated incompetent by the court and assigned a guardian is the loss of the right to control major aspects of life. Regan (1983) noted that "the consequences of the appointment of a guardian are drastic" and added that the "guardian may assume complete control and even title to the ward's property and decide where the ward will reside." In recent years, many States have created levels of "limited guardianship" designed to give the guardian control only in specific areas (Brakel et al. 1985).

The personal consequences for the aged person in the form of anger, disappointment, shame, fear, and negatively altered self-concept may also be drastic. Personal reactions like these could well occur in aged persons who are informed by the court that guardianship is being sought for them or that the court has decided that they are not able to handle their own affairs and control has been legally given to someone else.

Two other difficulties with guardianship might be mentioned. One is the possibility of abuse of the guardianship law. The legal literature contains reports of guardianship cases in which the decision of the probate court to appoint a guardian was reversed because, in the opinion of the appellate court judge, the purpose of seeking guardianship was to gain control of the aged person's estate rather than to protect the person's welfare. Some relatives, well-meaning or not, may use guardianship as a mechanism to institutionalize an aged family member who has become a family or economic burden. The other difficulty is the limited availability of acceptable persons willing to serve as guardians of aged persons. This difficulty is especially acute for aged persons without family or friends who become clients of public agencies. Persons without significant estates–which generate income that can pay for a guardian's service–often have no access to guardians. Some States have established "public guardian" agencies to address this need (New 1984).

158

Research on Guardianship of the Mentally Impaired Elderly

For a number of reasons, a large body of writings (as contrasted with research) on guardianship exists. Guardianship is a complicated and evolving matter of law. It relates to many specific and broad issues in medicine (refusal of treatment), mental health (commitment to psychiatric hospitals), and social programs (deinstitutionalization) (Scallet 1986). Guardianship may apply to minors, the mentally retarded, the mentally ill, and the aged.

Given the complex, multidimensional, multirelational, and evolving nature of guardianship, it is not surprising that a lot of people have had a lot to say about it over the years. For example, in 1963, Lehmann and Mathiasen wrote a book entitled *Guardianship and Protective Services for Older People* and, in 1984, Apolloni and Cooke authored *A New Look at Guardianship*. The difficulties and limitations of guardianship are often noted in writings, one example being the paper by Gutheil, Shapiro, and St. Clair (1980) entitled "Legal Guardianship in Drug Refusal: An Illusory Solution." The American Bar Association has sponsored reports, including "Substituted Judgment for the Disabled: Report of an Inquiry into Limited Guardianship, Public Guardianship and Adult Protective Services in Six States" (Axilbund 1979) and a "Statement of Recommended Judicial Practices" (Wood 1986) adopted by a National Conference of the Judiciary on Guardianship Proceedings for the Elderly.

Some research has been conducted on guardianship. Although not limited to guardianship, a landmark study was the Mental Competency Study initiated in 1962 with grant support by NIMH and conducted by The George Washington University Institute of Law, Psychiatry, and Criminology (Allen et al. 1968). Two excerpts from the report of the study indicate the purpose and the method.

> The focus of concern of the Mental Competency Study has included: proceedings that may lead to appointment of a guardian or conservator; adjudications of "incompetency" without appointment of a guardian; de facto and de jure incompetency resulting from hospitalization; the effect of determinations by governmental agencies of the incapacity of a beneficiary to manage benefit payments; the myriad of ad hoc legal determinations of competency. . . ; and devices employed to meet the contingency of mental impairment other than through initiation of formal legal proceedings. . . .
>
> Empirical techniques employed included: structured and un-

structured interviews with lawyers, judges, clerks of court, public officials, institutional superintendents and other personnel, psychiatrists, psychologists, social workers, county clerks, officers of trust companies, banks and title companies, and boards of professional and occupational licensure and accreditation; examination of court file records; and observations of judicial and administrative proceedings. In areas which did not lend themselves well to empirical research, monographs were prepared based largely on reported appellate cases. . . .

In more recent years, at least a few studies of various aspects of the complex process involved in guardianship of the cognitively impaired elderly have been undertaken. Two such studies were conducted in Florida. The Dade County Grand Jury (1982) studied 200 randomly selected guardianship cases heard between 1979 and 1981 and found that 170 (85 percent) were over 60 years of age and 116 (58 percent) were over 75 years of age. Peters, Schmidt, and Miller (1985) reported on a study of all 42 guardianship cases, excluding guardianship for minors, referred to the circuit court in Tallahassee for the 5-year period from 1977 to 1982. The ages ranged from 18 to 96 years, but 37 (88 percent) of the respondents were at least 60 years of age.

In an effort to promote research on guardianship of the cognitively impaired elderly, the Center for Studies of the Mental Health of the Aging (CSMHA) of NIMH contracted with the Division of Geriatric Psychiatry, Department of Psychiatry and Human Behavior, St. Louis University Medical Center to analyze data and prepare a monograph on the "Clinical and Legal Aspects of Guardianship of the Aged Encountered in a Geropsychiatry Center." One part of this project consisted of an empirical investigation of the guardianship of the aged cases in which the Division of Geriatric Psychiatry was involved. A shortened version of the report (Grossberg and Zimny 1984) of this study is included here. In addition to the results, the study demonstrates how information can be obtained about the major steps involved in the guardianship process and the outcomes of that process.

Guardianship Cases Encountered In a Geriatric Psychiatry Center

Purposes of the study. The purposes of the study were:
- to determine the number of guardianship cases encountered in one geriatric psychiatry center and the nature of the information provided as evidence in those cases by examining the

160

depositions submitted by the center in guardianship of the aged cases, and

- to obtain information about the major aspects of the legal process and outcome of those cases for which the center provided depositions by examining the public court records.

Method. The study was conducted at one geriatric psychiatry center, namely, the Division of Geriatric Psychiatry of the Department of Psychiatry and Human Behavior of the St. Louis University Medical Center. The full-time staff of the Division consists of three geriatric psychiatrists, a geriatric psychiatry nurse practitioner, a geriatric social worker, a research assistant, and a secretary-coordinator. A full complement of nursing and support personnel staff the 10-bed inpatient unit of the Division. In addition, consultants from a wide variety of health disciplines provide specialized diagnostic and treatment services for Division patients.

The subject population for this study consisted of the 705 new patients evaluated by the Division during the period from January 1, 1983 through December 31, 1984. A guardianship case was defined as a patient evaluated by the Division for whom a notarized deposition was completed by a Division geriatric psychiatrist. Depositions completed by the Division are made a part of the patient's records on file in the Division.

The data analyzed in this study were drawn from two sources. The first source was the depositions, or series of questions to be answered, completed by Division geriatric psychiatrists. The answers constitute data for analysis. Of particular interest are the answers dealing with (a) the diagnoses of the aged person (patient) and the symptoms upon which the diagnoses are based and (b) the incapabilities of the aged person and the need for appointment of a guardian and/or conservator.

The second source of data was the public court records of those guardianship cases that actually went to court. These records commonly include the petition for guardianship, the notice of hearing sent to the respondent, depositions, any motion for withdrawal of petition for guardianship, inventory and appraisal of the respondent's property, and the court order.

Results

Guardianship cases in the center. During the 2-year period of the study, 17 notarized depositions were completed by geriatric psychiatrists in the Division and sent to attorneys representing individuals or agencies planning to submit petitions for guardianship/conservatorship. Thus, depositions were completed for 2.4 percent of the Division's new patients. Nine depositions were completed at the request of attorneys representing individuals and eight for attorneys representing agencies.

Of the 17 depositions, 14 were filed as evidence for the petitioner with the probate division of the circuit court. One deposition was not filed because the patient died, and in two cases, the agency decided not to submit the petition for guardianship.

Thirteen cases were heard in court. The remaining petition did not receive a court hearing because the agency withdrew its request after the petition had been filed with the court; however, the deposition completed by the Division was submitted by the agency as evidence in its motion to withdraw. Thus, 13 (77 percent) of the 17 patients for whom depositions were completed by the Division received hearings in court. This constituted 1.8 percent of the Division's 705 new patients.

Analysis of depositions. Analysis of the depositions completed by geriatric psychiatrists in the Division revealed the number of patients with particular diagnoses to be as follows:

Primary degenerative dementia of the Alzheimer's type (3 patients)

Dementia, Alzheimer's type (3)

Diagnosis not specified but symptoms listed (2)

Dementia (1)

Primary degenerative dementia (1)

Dementia, probably degenerative type, diabetes mellitus of the adult onset type (1)

Primary degenerative dementia of the Alzheimer's type with secondary paranoid symptomatology (1)

Senile dementia, mild diabetes mellitus, arthritis of both hands (1)

Senile dementia–Alzheimer's type, hypertension, Parkinson's disease (1)

Delirium secondary to metastatic carcinoma of the colon and liver failure (1)

Hyperthyroidism, blindness secondary to glaucoma, mild cognitive impairment, syncope, inability to take care of herself, history of affective disorder (1)

Severe grief reaction (1)

Dementia was included in the diagnosis in 12 (71 percent) of the depositions. Both guardianship and conservatorship were recommended in all of these depositions. Overall, the depositions made 14 (82 percent) recommendations for both guardianship and conservatorship, 2 (12 percent) recommendations for conservatorship alone, and 1 (6 percent) recommendation favoring neither guardianship or conservatorship.

162

In addition to a diagnosis, the depositions asked for the symptoms upon which the diagnosis was based. Examination of the large number and variety of symptoms indicated that they fell into seven general categories. These were, in order from the largest number of symptoms cited, memory impairment, cognitive and intellectual impairment, difficulties of judgment and decisionmaking, general inability to care for self, specific inability to care for self, difficulties in orientation, and mental/emotional problems. In addition, five depositions specifically cited the likelihood of progressive impairment or degeneration over time.

Two other questions contained in the depositions were also analyzed. The first asked whether the respondent is of unsound mind and incapable of managing his/her affairs. An affirmative answer was given to this question in 16 of the 17 depositions. The negative answer was given in the one deposition which recommended neither guardianship nor conservatorship. The other question asked whether it is in the respondent's best interest to have a guardian and/or conservator. Affirmative answers were given in the same 16 depositions and a negative answer in the remaining ones.

Characteristics of petitioners.   The analysis of the characteristics of the petitioners was based upon the information contained in the 14 petitions that were filed with the court. Nine petitions were filed by attorneys representing individual petitioners. Two of these petitions involved copetitioners filing jointly. Thus, a total of 11 individuals petitioned the court—7 (64 percent) were men, and 4 (36 percent) were women. All the petitioners were related to respondents: 5 (46 percent) were sons, 4 (36 percent) were daughters, 1 (9 percent) was a brother, and 1 (9 percent) was a nephew.

Five petitions were filed by attorneys representing agencies—four by the Division of Aging of the Department of Social Services of the State of Missouri and one by the St. Louis Area Agency on Aging's Volunteer Guardianship/Conservatorship Program.

Bases for petitions.   The bases for petitions are the reasons given in the petition for seeking guardianship/conservatorship of the aged person. These reasons generally consist of statements or descriptions of the mental and physical impairment of the respondent. Over two-thirds of the bases given in the petitions included the terms senility, Alzheimer's disease, or dementia. These terms thus describe the principal basis for seeking appointment of a guardian and conservator. The petitions also usually included statements that the aged person was not able to care for self and not able to manage finances, and specific examples of each statement were often given.

Guardian requested by petitioner. The guardian requested by the petitioner may be the petitioner or someone else. All nine of the petitions filed with the court by individuals requested appointment of the petitioner as the guardian and conservator (singly or, in two instances, jointly). The four petitions for both guardianship and conservatorship filed by agencies requested appointment of the public administrator for the county in which the court hearing took place.

The one petition for conservatorship alone was filed by a volunteer guardianship/conservatorship agency and requested that a volunteer from the agency be appointed as the conservator.

Characteristics of the aged persons. For the depositions that led to petitions being filed in court, the respondents ranged in age from 62 to 89 years with a mean of 77 years. Twelve (86 percent) of the respondents were women, and two (14 percent) were men.

When the petitions were filed with the court, nine of the respondents were domiciled at residential care facilities, one was an inpatient of the Division of Geriatric Psychiatry, and four were living in their own homes or in the home of the petitioner.

The values of real property cited in the court records for 13 of the 14 respondents ranged from nothing to $73,707, with a mean of $16,462. No value was cited for the other person. The cited values of personal property for 12 of the aged persons ranged from nothing to $295,865, with a mean of $65,667; no value was cited for two respondents.

Court hearings in guardianship cases. For all 13 cases heard in probate court, the right to a trial by jury was waived by the attorney for the respondent. Two (15 percent) of the aged persons were present at their court hearings, and 11 (85 percent) were not present but were represented by attorneys. Ten (77 percent) petitioners appeared at the court hearing, and three (23 percent) were not present but were represented by attorneys.

Three separate probate court sessions were observed in the City of St. Louis at which guardianship cases were heard. A description of the general court proceedings is provided in the full report (Grossberg and Zimny 1984) of the study.

Court decisions and bases. Of the 13 petitions that received court hearings, 12 (92 percent) resulted in a decision by the court that the aged person was both incapacitated and disabled. In the guardianship law of the State of Missouri (Revised State Statutes of Missouri 1983), incapacitated refers to inability to care for self and results in appointment of a guardian. Disabled refers to inability to

164

care for finances and results in appointment of a conservator. The court appointed both a guardian and a conservator for each of the 12 persons. The remaining person was adjudicated disabled, and a conservator was appointed. The court thus granted the requests made in all of the petitions.

The bases for the court's decision are given on the order adjudicating the aged person as incapacitated and/or disabled and authorizing appointment of a guardian and/or conservator. The bases given by the court for 10 (83 percent) of the 12 aged persons adjudicated both incapacitated and disabled included the terms senility, dementia, or Alzheimer's disease. For the remaining two persons and the one adjudicated only disabled, mental illness was included in the bases given by the court.

Characteristics of appointed guardians/conservators. Nine of the petitions were submitted by individuals requesting that they be appointed as guardians and conservators. These requests were granted in every instance; thus these appointed guardians and conservators are described in the section on characteristics of petitioners.

Three petitions submitted by an agency (Division of Aging) and requesting that the public administrator in the aged person's county of residence be appointed as the guardian and conservator were granted by the court. The one petition for conservatorship only was submitted by a volunteer guardianship/conservatorship organization and requested that a specific member of the organization be appointed conservator. Although the court appointed a member of the organization as a conservator, it was not the member requested in the petition.

Conditions of appointment. The court order appointing a guardian and/or conservator ordinarily contains three additional instructions or stipulations: placement of the aged person (now called a ward or protectee), the bond to be secured by the appointed guardian and/or conservator, and the fee for the aged person's attorney.

In 9 (75 percent) of the 12 cases in which a guardian and a conservator were appointed, the placement of the aged person (ward) was addressed in the court order. In six cases, the court order stated that "Guardian authorized to admit ward to continued care and treatment at ____." In three cases, the court order stated that "He/She requires placement in a supervised living situation with complete supervision." The three orders also stipulated that "His/Her financial resources require complete supervision."

Twelve (92 percent) of the 13 court orders specified the bond to be secured by the appointee and the fee for the respondent's attorney.

The amount of bond required ranged from nothing to $280,000 with a mean of $66,750. The fees ranged from $100 to $300 with a mean of $176. In 11 of these 12 court orders, the attorney's fee was taxed to the estate of the aged person; in the other case, the fee was taxed to the City of St. Louis because the respondent was indigent.

Case Studies

Two actual cases of competency evaluation for the purpose of the guardianship made by the Division of Geriatric Psychiatry are described below. Data that would permit identification of the patients have been eliminated or modified. Each case includes the conditions that raised the issue of guardianship, the competency evaluation that was conducted, and the adjudication made by the court.

Case 1

Mrs. B, a 73-year-old white female, was referred to the Division by her daughter to corroborate a prior diagnosis of Senile Dementia of the Alzheimer's Type (SDAT) and for treatment of suspected depression.

Though diagnosed as having SDAT approximately 1^{1}/2 years before, until 8 weeks prior to referral, Mrs. B had been driving her own car and doing volunteer work at a local hospital. Unfortunately, 8 weeks prior to referral, Mrs. B slipped on a stairway in her home and required brief hospitalization for a pelvic fracture, followed by a 1-month stay in an extended care facility. After discharge from the facility, Mrs. B's daughter arranged for a nurse's aide to spend 4 hours per day with the patient in her home.

According to the patient's daughter, Mrs. B "became more confused" in the nursing facility and her forgetfulness worsened. After discharge to her home, Mrs. B was noted by her daughter and the nurse's aide to be "frustrated and misplacing things," more "confused," and "depressed all the time." She had frequent crying spells, was afraid to be left alone, and paced the floors at night. She complained of "losing her mind." Secondary to the above changes, the patient's daughter had made arrangements for Mrs. B to live in a small boarding facility.

Mrs. B presented herself to the Division, accompanied by her daughter, 2 weeks after an initial telephone evaluation/interview. Prior to her appointment, records from her two recent hospitalizations—the one 18 months before that resulted in the SDAT diagnoses and the

166

one 10 weeks before for the pelvic fracture–were reviewed. In addition, nursing reports from the extended care facility were evaluated, and telephone interviews were held with the nurse in charge at the nursing facility as well as with the manager of the boarding facility in which the patient was now residing.

During the initial evaluation of the patient at the Division office, a more detailed clinical history, past medical history, family history, and developmental, social, and functional history were obtained from the patient's daughter. A list of Mrs. B's present prescribed as well as over-the-counter medications was reviewed. Importantly, the latter review revealed that the patient's thyroid supplement had not followed her from the hospital to the nursing facility. Additional medications the patient was taking were digitalis, hydrochlorothiozide, and potassium.

On Mental Status Evaluation, Mrs. B appeared to be an age-appropriate, neat, well-dressed, moderately obese white female in a wheelchair. She claimed she used a walker in her apartment but now was too weak to walk. Mrs. B's affect was somewhat flat, and she showed mildly decreased psychomotor activity. However, her speech was clear, and at times she would smile and joke appropriately. There was no evidence of psychosis or major depression.

On cognitive screening, which she was reluctant to participate in, Mrs. B was oriented to self only and guessed wrongly at the month and year. Her recall for events in the distant past, e.g., birthdate and prior hospitalizations, was well preserved, but she showed problems in recent recall and, in particular, immediate recall. On the Cognitive Capacity Screening Test, her score was 14/30, placing her in the significantly impaired range.

Her neurologic screen failed to show evidence of focal deficit with the exception of mild lower extremity weakness bilaterally and significant cognitive deficits.

Based on clinical history, record review, and office evaluation, a tentative diagnosis of SDAT with a dysthymic disorder, possibly due to hypothyroidism, was made. A thyroid screen showed the patient to be hypothyroid and supplementation medication was reinstituted in the boarding facility.

For the next several months, Mrs. B did quite well in the boarding facility with a good remission of her dysphoric symptoms. She was walking well and posed no management problem. However, she required admission to the St. Louis University Geriatric Psychiatry Inpatient Unit after progressive increase in agitation and paranoid symptoms made her a management problem at the boarding facility.

After a brief hospitalization, Mrs. B returned to the boarding facility on small doses of a neuroleptic. She again did fairly well, but 6 months later was rehospitalized at the Geriatric Psychiatry Inpatient Unit with a diagnosis of delirium, secondary to hepatotoxicity from the neuroleptic and pneumonia.

Though Mrs. B's delirium cleared, her underlying dementia had quite obviously progressed and she required more supervision and assistance than the boarding facility could provide. A functional evaluation by occupational and activity therapy revealed that she needed help with even basic activities of daily living. During this hospitalization, a recommendation for intermediate care postdischarge was made to the family. At this time, with the assistance of the Division of Geriatric Psychiatry, the family took steps to seek guardianship for Mrs. B.

Guardianship proceedings were initiated separately by Mrs. B's daughter and Mrs. B's son. Each sought to be appointed guardian/conservator. Each petition was filed with the Probate Division of the Circuit Court. The petition filed by the attorney for Mrs. B's daughter stated that Mrs. B was in need of a guardian/conservator by reason of Alzheimer's disease. The reasons given in the petition filed by the attorney for Mrs. B's son were mental illness and Alzheimer's disease.

Upon receipt of each petition, a notice was sent by the court to Mrs. B notifying her of the initiated guardianship/conservatorship proceedings, the hearing date, and the name, address, and phone number of her court-appointed attorney.

The date of the hearing was postponed and reset five times. During this time, Mrs. B's daughter and son agreed to work as copetitioners and seek appointment as coguardian/conservator.

The hearing occurred 145 days after the first petition was filed and the first notice issued. Mrs. B's son and daughter were both present at the hearing and represented by attorneys. They testified that Mrs. B was not able to feed or dress herself and was suffering from some memory impairment. They also gave an accounting of her assets as they knew them. The deposition of George Grossberg, M.D., was entered into evidence for the petitioners. The attorney for Mrs. B stated that he had visited her at home and found her confused, unable to make decisions, and of limited physical ability. He stated that Mrs. B had no understanding of her assets. He recommended that a guardian/conservator be appointed. The judge ordered, by reason of senility, that Mrs. B's son and daughter be appointed coguardian/conservator.

Case 2

Mrs. J, a 79-year-old white female, was referred for evaluation by her son secondary to his concerns regarding the patient's increased "hostility, belligerence, and forgetfulness." He was also quite concerned about the patient's "abuse of her medications."

Apparently, Mrs. J had done quite well until approximately 3 years before the evaluation when her son began to notice some mild forgetfulness. Though this continued to progress, the patient was able to live independently in a senior housing complex. However, over the prior several months, Mrs. J became increasingly disoriented, accusatory, and suspicious. She threatened her neighbors and did not clean her apartment. Her personal hygiene began to suffer. The manager of the senior apartment threatened to evict her and recommended psychiatric evaluation.

Mrs. J's past medical history was unremarkable with the exception of repair of a hip fracture 2 years prior to evaluation and a vague history of "nerve problems" over the years with a questionable "overdose" 25 years back. She disliked physicians and had not visited a doctor's office for the past 2 years.

Her medications at the time of the evaluation included Diazepam, Secobarbital, and aspirin.

Three days after the initial telephone interview and screening, Mrs. J was seen by a geriatric psychiatrist at the office of the Division of Geriatric Psychiatry for evaluation. She came accompanied by her son and daughter-in-law.

Additional history from the family revealed that the patient's course had declined precipitously during the prior 2 months. She was now confusing her son with her father and was calling her daughter-in-law constantly. Apparently, her other children refused to have "anything to do with her," with one daughter saying "she needs to be committed to State Hospital." Her son was reluctant to take this approach, preferring to give Mrs. J "another chance at living alone."

On Mental Status Evaluation, Mrs. J proved to be an angry and hostile woman. She was upset that her family had brought her and felt that nothing was wrong with her. She was a very thin, age-appropriate, plainly dressed, ambulatory white female who talked clearly. Her main theme was: "I have only a few more years left. I want to be left alone." She unknowingly repeated herself on a regular basis and looked suspicious and bewildered. At times she was hyperalert, while at other times she appeared withdrawn. She was not grossly psychotic and denied delusions or hallucinations. There was no evidence of major depression. Importantly, she was quite forgetful about her medication usage.

On cognitive screening, she was oriented to year, place, and person, but not month or day of the week. She showed problems in recent recall and current information as well as in continuity in level of alertness. Her Cognitive Capacity Screening score was 11/30 which is clearly suggestive of cognitive impairment.

Neurologic exam showed some fluctuation in level of alertness but no focal neurologic deficits.

The patient was hospitalized on the Geriatric Psychiatry Inpatient Unit with a tentative diagnosis of delirium secondary to iatrogenic drug toxicity. A secondary consideration was to rule out progressive dementia.

During the 22 days the patient was in the hospital, her medications were phased out, and she received a complete physical and neurological workup and finally a dementia workup. Though her functioning improved following clearing of the delirium, nursing observations, formal functional assessment, and psychometric testing showed that the patient would require a structured, highly supervised environment to ensure her safety and well-being. At that time, guardianship proceedings were initiated by her son to relocate her to an intermediate care facility. Her discharge diagnoses were drug-induced delirium-cleared and SDAT.

A Petition for Appointment of a Guardian and Conservator was filed by the attorney for Mrs. J's son with the Probate Division of the Circuit Court. The petition stated that Mrs. J was unable to take care of herself and/or her business affairs. The petition additionally specified that Mrs. J was at times a danger to herself, i.e., she forgot to turn appliances off and she wandered outside at night. The petition requested that Mrs. J's son be appointed guardian/conservator.

When the petition was filed, a notice was sent by the court to Mrs. J informing her of the initiated guardianship proceeding. The notice included the date of the hearing and the name, address, and phone number of her court-appointed attorney.

The guardianship hearing took place 55 days following the filing of the petition. The son of Mrs. J and his attorney were present. Mrs. J's son testified as to his mother's inability to care for herself. The testimony included information concerning her misuse of electrical appliances, her tendency to wander at night, and her inability to pay bills and handle a checkbook. The deposition of George Grossberg, M.D., was entered into evidence for the petitioner. Mrs. J was not present at the hearing. Her attorney was present and stated that she had visited Mrs. J and found her totally incapacitated and disabled. She stated that Mrs. J was disoriented as to time and place and required the appointment of a guardian and conservator. The judge found Mrs. J incapacitated and disabled by reason of senility and ordered Mrs. J's son appointed guardian/conservator.

170

Directions for Research

The study and the two case histories described in this chapter demonstrate some of the complex legal, personal, and clinical aspects of guardianship of the cognitively impaired elderly and give some indication of the importance of guardianship. Many groups and organizations have a legitimate and often practical need to obtain more information about guardianship of the impaired elderly—family members, lawyers, judges, physicians, psychologists, sociologists, public and private agency personnel, nursing home administrators, and government officials at local and national levels.

With so many interested parties, research can take many different directions. Without attempting to include all legitimate interests, listed below are four general areas or aspects of guardianship of the impaired elderly and some specific questions in each area toward which research can be directed. No attempt is made to prioritize the areas or questions because priority levels will vary from group to group. Where the priorities of groups or organizations overlap, interdisciplinary research should be undertaken. In light of the legal nature of guardianship, cooperative research involving members of the legal profession and of other disciplines seems particularly advisable.

Decision To Seek Guardianship

Cognitive impairment in the elderly is a matter of degree, and various types of surrogate management are available in addition to guardianship.

What kinds and degrees of cognitive impairment warrant a family's or agency's decision to seek surrogate management of an elderly person? What types of surrogate management are available, and what are the pros and cons of each type? How is a decision made as to which type of surrogate management to seek? What various types of guardianship and conservatorship are provided by the law of the State? What resources are available to a family or agency wanting guidance in making a decision to seek guardianship?

Assessment of Competency/Incompetency

An assessment of competency/incompetency serves as a basis for the decision to seek guardianship and for evidence in a court hearing for guardianship. Evidence, in turn, is the basis for the adjudication made by the court.

171

With regard to evidence, what is and what should be assessed in the elderly person? What assessment procedures and materials are used? Who uses them? How valid and reliable are the procedures and materials? What improvements can be made in the assessment process? Is it possible to develop a reasonably simple, valid, reliable, and standardized assessment instrument that would be generally accepted throughout the country? What factors affect the acceptability of assessments as evidence in a court of law? How do judges use assessments in arriving at an adjudication? What information about assessments is provided in appellate court cases of guardianship and conservatorship?

Financial Costs

Financial costs are involved in assessing competency/incompetency and in seeking guardianship in a court of law.

What are the mean, median, and range of costs of assessment of competency/incompetency and of each step in the legal process? Who pays or is expected by law to pay what costs? What exceptions are made in the law as to who pays what costs? What effect does cost have on the decision to seek guardianship?

Guardians and Conservators

The purpose of the guardianship law is to provide for appointment of a guardian and/or conservator for those adjudicated by the court as incompetent. The guardian and conservator are given the responsibility and the legal power by the court to make binding decisions for the impaired elderly in those areas in which they are judged to be incompetent. Guardians and conservators thus play a very important and powerful role in the lives of the impaired elderly.

What functions do guardians and conservators actually serve for the impaired elderly? How well are each of the functions served to the benefit of the elderly? What abuses of functions occur? What additional functions might be served? Who are the guardians and conservators appointed by the court? What problems and potential solutions exist with respect to the characteristics of appointed guardians and conservators? What are some major additional sources of guardians and conservators?

In conclusion, it should be noted that, despite an abundance of questions and directions for research on guardianship of the cognitively impaired elderly, there is a dearth of research.

172

References

Allen, R.C.; Ferster, E.Z.; and Weihofen, H. *Mental Impairment and Legal Incompetency.* Englewood Cliffs, NJ: Prentice-Hall, 1968.

Apolloni, T., and Cooke, T.P. *A New Look at Guardianship.* Baltimore: Brookes, 1984.

Axilbund, M.T. *Substituted Judgment for the Disabled: Report of an Inquiry into Limited Guardianship, Public Guardianship and Adult Protective Services in Six States.* Washington, DC: Commission on the Mentally Disabled, American Bar Association, 1979.

Brakel, S.J.; Parry, J.; and Wiener, B.A. *The Mentally Disabled and the Law.* 3rd ed. Chicago: American Bar Association, 1985.

Dade County Grand Jury. *Final Report of the Grand Jury.* Miami: Office of the State Attorney, 1982.

Grossberg, G.T., and Zimny, G.H. Guardianship cases encountered in a geropsychiatry center. Contract No. 84M029501701D, CSMHA, NIMH, April 26, 1984.

Gutheil, T.G.; Shapiro, R.; and St. Clair, R.L. Legal guardianship in drug refusal: An illusory solution. *American Journal of Psychiatry* 137:347-352, 1980.

Lehmann, V., and Mathiasen, G. *Guardianship and Protective Services for Older People.* Washington, DC: National Council on Aging Press, 1963.

New, B.E. *Final Report of the Public Guardianship Pilot Program.* Tallahassee: Office of the State Courts Administrator, 1984.

Peters, R.; Schmidt, W.C.; and Miller, K.S. Guardianship of the elderly in Tallahassee, Florida. *The Gerontologist* 25:532-538, 1985.

Regan, J.J. Protective services for the elderly: Benefit or threat. In: Kosberg, J.I., ed. *Abuse and Maltreatment of the Elderly.* Boston: John-Wright-PSG, 1983.

Revised State Statutes of Missouri, 1983. (Senate Bills Nos. 44 and 45, 82nd General Assembly).

Scallet, L.J. *Mental Health Care in Nursing Homes: Legal and Policy Issues.* Washington, DC: Policy Resources, Inc., 1986.

Schmidt, W.C.; Miller, K.S.; Bell, W.G.; and New, B.E. *Public Guardianship and the Elderly.* Cambridge: Ballinger, 1981.

Wood, E.F., compiler. *Statement of Recommended Judicial Practices.* Washington, DC: American Bar Association Commission on Legal Problems of the Elderly and the National Judicial College, American Bar Association, 1986.

Chapter 6

Alzheimer's Disease and Families: Methodological Advances

Rachel A. Pruchno, Ph.D.

Introduction

While the past decade has witnessed tremendous growth in the professional and scholarly pursuit of knowledge regarding the impact of Alzheimer's disease and related disorders on caregivers (e.g., Sainsbury and Grad de Alarcon 1970; Isaacs 1971; Lezak 1978; Morycz 1980; Zarit et al. 1980; Colerick and George 1986; George 1983; Noelker and Poulshock 1982), little attention has been directed toward exploring the impact of Alzheimer's disease on the family or the role played by characteristics of family members (e.g., coping styles) or family units (e.g., degree of cohesion, adaptability, communication) in determining the mental health of the primary caregiver.

That families should be affected when one of its members develops Alzheimer's disease, and that characteristics of people in families and of families per se should affect the mental health of the primary caregiver, have been well documented. Pruchno et al. (1984) presented a "life event webs" image in which, because

> the lives of individuals (in families) are intricately linked and entangled, people must change, adapt to, or resist the impact of events and change which occur in the lives to which they are interlinked.

Similarly, Brody and Spark (1966) suggested that

> as each person in the family experiences the repercussions of a problem with respect to an elderly family member, shifts in the

174

balance of individual roles and responsibilities, as well as changes in family lifestyle, frequently occur.

The purpose of this chapter is not to review the extensive literature regarding caregivers (for an excellent review, see Horowitz 1985). Rather, it is to highlight those empirical studies that focus on families and to draw upon and evaluate the usefulness of existing theoretical thought and methodological techniques that may be of value to researchers concerned with understanding the dynamics of families involved in caregiving.

Family Caregivers: State of the Art

Recognizing that the household provides the context for a great deal of caregiving, and that shared housing influences both the caregiving process and the stress experienced by family members, Noelker and Poulshock (1982) sought to purposively sample the population to obtain a representative number of one-, two-, and three-generation households. Data analysis revealed that a more precise delineation of household configuration was necessary to better understand differences in caregiving patterns and stress effects. They identified seven household types: (1) one-generation families in which either older wives were caring for husbands or husbands were caring for wives (50 percent); (2) two-generation households in which either: (a) an unmarried child lived alone with an aging parent (16 percent); (b) a married child and his/her spouse lived with the aging parent (11 percent); or (c) an unmarried adult child, the aging parent, and at least one other relative (e.g., a sibling of the caregiver) were living together (3 percent); and (3) three-generation families in which either: (a) an adult child caregiver resided with a spouse and child along with the impaired elder (16 percent) or (b) a currently unmarried adult-child caregiver lived with his/her children and an impaired elderly parent (4 percent). Furthermore, they found that regardless of the household type, the primary caregiver reported five or six proximate relatives, most of whom were involved to some degree in meeting the elder's needs.

The respondents in the above study were the impaired elder's primary caregivers, identified by the referral source, the impaired elder, head of the household, or the elder's spouse or adult child as the person who supplied the elder with the greatest amount of concrete or direct care and assistance. The study found that the numerous, diverse, and time-consuming tasks entailed in the elders' care were primarily assumed by this one person—the primary caregiver. While this is not surprising, additional evidence indicated that although other family members had minimal involvement in "hands on" care of the elder, they did assume some responsibility for helping with household tasks and transportation. The question which comes to mind is: "If other people in the household had been asked about caregiving activities and their effects, what would their stories have been?"

Noelker and Poulshock (1982) also reported that primary caregivers feel that interpersonal relations of household members are relatively unaffected by the presence of a physically disabled elder, whereas a mentally impaired or disturbed elder within the home is likely to damage family roles and relationships. Other factors less highly associated with caregiver reports of disrupted family relationships were onerous tasks, household size, and a three-generational household composition. Noelker and Poulshock postulated that these associations may have occurred because the presence of more persons in the household provided greater opportunities for interpersonal problems or because competing demands were made on the caregiver by more household members. In addition, the caregivers in the three-generation households were generally younger, employed, and had multiple roles competing with the demands of caregiving. These findings only hint at the potential effect that caring for a dependent mentally impaired elder may have on family members.

From a different perspective, Kleban, Brody, Schoonover, and Hoffman (in press) studied the effects of parent care on both the caregiving daughters and the daughters' husbands (sons-in-law). While findings regarding daughters are reported elsewhere (Brody and Schoonover 1986; Brody et al. 1987, in press), findings regarding sons-in-law are briefly described here. Sixty-six percent of sons-in-law experienced strain because of the help they gave to their mothers-in-law; 29 percent reported that elder care interfered with time for themselves; 21 percent reported that care interfered with their social lives; 23 percent of the men who were working reported that helping their mothers-in-law had caused interruptions in their work; 33 percent of sons-in-law reported interference with family vacation plans; 30 percent believed that care usurped the time they were able to spend with their wives; 21 percent said that care interrupted work that had to be done around the house; 46 percent of those men who shared households with their mothers-in-law reported interference with family privacy as a problem. This research provides important information about the "web-like effects" of caregiving.

The few research studies that have begun to address the effects of caregiving beyond the level of the caregiver, combined with the more voluminous clinical evidence (see Brody's chapter), urge that for the sake of understanding how families operate as well as for suggesting appropriate models for intervention, this topic must be given more serious thought.

To proceed on a new course, it is often useful to reflect on why these measures have not yet been taken. A simplistic, yet useful explanation is that such research is more difficult to do than research focused solely on the caregiver. From a data collection perspective, it requires cooperation from multiple family members, significantly increasing the time required to collect data, as well as the cost.

A host of new data analytic issues arise as information is collected from multiple family members, including: What differences in responses mean and how to handle such differences; the wisdom of creating family scores; the physical organization of data sets; and the appropriate methods of data analysis. These complexities resulted in the following statement by Fisher (1982), which summarizes the situation:

> At the risk of being overly simplistic, it appears that on the one hand families seem considerably more complex and subtle than are reflected in present methods of assessment, whereas on the other hand, diving into the complexity often yields a mass of variables from which little meaningful structure can be derived. (p. 313)

Hints from Family Research

While the study of multiple family members is relatively new to gerontologists, researchers from more traditional family sociology backgrounds have long been concerned with this topic. Despite this, a number of questions regarding how to conduct this type of research remain unanswered. To build on the accomplishments of family researchers, a brief description of the state of that art follows.

Most research about the family has been grounded in theory with the family as its unit of concern. While theoretical models, for example, predict how families will respond to the various challenges that present themselves, a gap remains between theory and empirical research, especially quantitative research. Much of the reason for this deficiency rests with problems in "unit parity" across the domains of research and with inappropriate generalizations made beyond the purview of the research.

Empirical research about families has tended to focus almost exclusively on the individual. Fisher (1982) stated "most researchers designate the person, who also happens to be a family member, as the object of study and not the family as a unit." This statement is supported by Hodgson and Lewis' (1979) analysis of all studies published between 1969 and 1976 in *Family Process, Family Coordinator*, and *Journal of Marriage and the Family*. The family was the object of study in only 7 percent of the published studies, and the marital dyad was the object in only 10 percent. In contrast, the individual was the subject of study in 56 percent of the "family studies."

Following this perspective, the individual is generally the sampled unit, and data are collected from the individual. Data are then generally organized in data sets with the individual as their unit. Individuals are assigned identification numbers, and variables in the data set include demographic information such as age and religion as well as the individual's reported perceptions of self and other family members, similarity or differences between self and other family members, and family relationships. Statistical analyses typically assess the similarities or differences between individuals on variables of interest. Results from such studies are then discussed in terms of how well they support theories about families.

Depending on what the individual reports are intended to represent, such research may or may not be considered true "family" research. If the intention is either (1) to represent an objective reality, implying that the report is independent of the individual's view, such as the number of family members, length of time a marriage has existed, or presence/absence of characteristics that can be corroborated by an outside observer or (2) a subjective individual reality that is interpreted as one family member's perception of himself, his family, or other family members, then the data collected from individuals represent research about families. If, however, the intention is to use one family member's subjective perceptions to characterize a whole family or to try to represent a family's objective reality beyond the confines of its physical and demographic characteristics, gathering information from only one family member is insufficient.

Research that has sampled individual family members' perceptions and then generalized results to families as a whole has not been sensitive to the issue of unit parity. The unit shifted from family (at the theoretical level) to individual (at the empirical level) and then back to family. The problems inherent to this lack of parity have not gone unnoticed. In 1969, for example, Safilios-Rothschild criticized family sociology for being "wives" family sociology—that is, the study of family life based on information provided exclusively by wives. Further evidence of this trend is provided by Ruano, Bruce, and McDermott (1969), whose analysis of 444 empirical articles from 12

178

journals related to the family revealed that "mother (as reporter) was used six times as often as her male counterpart."

Characteristic of this research is Herbst's (1952) study of marital structure, tension, and balance in which the reports of children aged 10-12 years were used to describe their family's hierarchy of responsibilities. While these self-reports were useful statements about the child's view of division of labor within families, accurate statements about the family itself cannot be extrapolated from these opinions (Fisher et al. 1985).

Researching Multiple Family Members: Problems and Promises

The past decade has witnessed an interesting development in family research, as scientists have begun to study more than one member of a family. The impetus for this derives from two diverse theoretical underpinnings: (1) the feeling that each person's portrait of a relationship may be biased in a systematic fashion (differences as error) and (2) the belief that the family is greater than the sum of its individuals and, therefore, knowledge about a family requires information from more than one of its members (differences as true differences).

While including more than one family member in a research project may represent a step forward, the majority of these studies have been plagued by lack of unit parity in at least one of the study domains. Typically, the family is the sampling unit, and data are collected by conducting separate interviews with men and women who are married to each other. Once the data are collected, however, the majority of studies from this genre lapse back to focusing on the individual. Data sets are organized and analyzed using each individual as a separate case. Often data from husbands are put in one data set and kept separate from the wives' data set.

When researchers considered responses from husbands and wives using an aggregate analysis procedure, they found that data collected from males and females tended to have similar distributions or mean score responses (Bokemeier and Monroe 1983). Such aggregating techniques, however, do not treat the male and female respondents as matched couples, and information about a particular husband and wife cannot be linked. When the matched responses of husbands and wives are analyzed as a unit, inconsistency increases considerably (Granbois and Willet 1970; Jaco and Shepard 1975; Price-Bonham 1977; Szinovacz 1983). Furthermore, as Downs (1977) suggested, the aggregate analytic method masks the existence of individual patterns of responses among couples. Once data have been analyzed at the individual level, the focus of discussion reverts back to the family level. Conclusions are then phrased in terms of husbands and wives when, in reality, males and females were studied. Inappropriate generalizations are made from aggregate level data to the family or couple level, another example of lack of parity between units of research.

Maintaining Unit Parity: Differences as Error Versus Differences as Reality

Family research that has maintained unit parity across the domains of sampling, data collection, and conceptualization of variables has been plagued by difficulties in interpreting differences between husband and wife responses. Although some empirical studies reported agreement in husband and wife responses (e.g., Blood and Hamblin 1958; Heer 1968), the majority of studies reported considerable differences in spouses' responses (Quarm 1981; Wilkening and Morrison 1963; Scanzoni 1965). These discrepant reports were interpreted differently depending on whether the researcher viewed multiple family responses as useful for minimizing response bias or error, or providing helpful information about true differences. Some researchers tried to explain away discrepancies as the result of poor questions or inappropriate wording of questions (Wilkening and Morrison 1963). Others argued that husbands and wives (within couples) might have different scores in individual cases, but these differences would disappear when large numbers of cases were considered (Blood and Wolfe 1960).

The tendency to deemphasize family differences and treat divergent responses as error or bias, which has characterized most family research, was explained by Safilios-Rothschild (1969). She contended that it results from our concept of the ideal American family as sharing activities, decisions, opinions, and beliefs. Such sharing should lead husbands and wives to hold the same view of said activities, decisions, opinions, and beliefs, and any differences between husband and wife responses to interview questions must be attributable to error on the part of the research instrument.

In contrast, some researchers explain these differences as true differences reflecting two separate subjective realities, the husband's and the wife's (Safilios-Rothschild 1969). These two perspectives demand different methodologies.

The differences as error philosophy requires responses from several family members to reduce the error bias. Once data are collected from husbands and wives, second-order data are created, generally by combining individual husband-wife scores. Discrepancy scores, correlations, agreement coefficients, ratios, conditional probabilities, sums, and averages are among the techniques used to create a single score from multiple responses (Thompson and Walker 1982). On the other hand, the differences as true differences philosophy requires that the individual perceptions from husbands and wives be maintained separately. The former philosophy allows data sets to be organized by assigning an identification number to each family, and data are entered as summed, averaged, or correlated scores derived from individual responses. The latter philosophy, however, necessitates creating data sets that assign a unique identification number to each family, but then include as data the individual husband and wife scores. From this, family typologies are created and compared along various dimensions with one another.

Generating and Using Relational Data: Differences as Error

Both the differences as error and differences as true differences perspectives have as their goal the creation of information reflective of an attribute or characteristic of the family unit. Following the differences as error philosophy, derived scores no longer reflect a single family member, but instead are summaries that describe the combined products of individual family members. Fisher et al. (1985) devoted great effort to investigating the benefits and problems associated with the various methods of creating "relational data." These are summarized below, with the caveat that the prospective researcher make decisions about the usefulness of each technique based on the theoretical assumptions and questions at hand.

Arithmetic Mean

The arithmetic mean of two or more individual scores, while easy to compute and representative of the arithmetic center of a distribution of family member scores, has the following problems:

1. The mean score may lack conceptual significance. Mean scores, for example, don't reflect differences among family members based on age or developmental stage.

2. Regression to the mean and reduced score variance characterize the use of arithmetic mean scores. By reducing the distribution's variance, the influence of deviant families in the

sample, as well as deviant members within families, is reduced. Also, the larger the number of family members, the less impact each deviant member will have on the arithmetic mean.

3. The arithmetic mean does not take into account the differences among contributing scores. For example, if one couple scored 48 and 2 on a scale from 0 to 50, and the second couple scored 26 and 24, both would end up with the same couple mean score of 25.

4. The arithmetic mean does not reflect the order of scores; information about whether the husband or wife had the highest score is lost.

Fisher et al. (1985) concluded that although mean scores severely reduce the information contained in original scores, and potentially distort the data if used alone, they may be valuable if used and interpreted appropriately. For example, the mean is a good indicator of family scores when the discrepancy between family members is small. It is also useful if the purpose is to classify families on level of response alone.

Olson, Russell, and Sprenkle (1983) presented a more radical interpretation. They contended that a couple or family mean score may be an important measure even when it washes out individual differences. The average may reflect the unit in a way that other scores cannot. For example, when the discrepancy between spouse perceptions is sizable, the collective assessment of the couple as represented by the mean score represents a compromise somewhere between the individual positions.

Sum of Scores

The sum of scores is another technique for deriving family scores. The advantages and disadvantages are similar to those described for means, except that score sums may increase the range and variance of family scores. While this can be particularly useful in scales where the range of scores is small, problems emerge in the interpretation of such scores.

Maximized Couple Scores

Olson et al. (1983) suggested a variant of the simple sum of scores, termed the "maximized couple score," which is the sum of nonredundant responses. A list of life events is administered separately to all family members. A potentially stressful event is scored as occurring in the family if at least one member acknowledges it. The rationale for this type of score is that if one member is forced to cope with a situation, that, in turn, is likely to affect the rest of the family. Such

182

a scoring procedure could also be helpful in documenting the number of disagreements in a family, complaints, events such as doctor visits, work changes, or contacts with social service agencies. These scores serve to document discrete situational events or circumstances rather than family members' views or opinions.

Extreme Scores

Deviant or extreme scores within a family can also be informative. Klein and Hill (1979), for example, entered into their analysis the score of the family member who was least satisfied with the solution in a family problemsolving task. They argued that

> the effectiveness of a problem solution depends on its consequences for family functioning, and that one sufficiently disenchanted family member is enough to upset the effective implementation of a solution. (p.520)

Fisher et al. (1985) suggested that extreme scores may be helpful if extreme reactions are to be noted, variations among family scores are high, or they fit the conceptual model being tested.

Discrepancy Scores

Discrepancy or congruence scores reflect differences or similarities among family members. Discrepancy scores are problematic because:
1. They do not reflect score level. For example, a couple with scores of 38 and 48 and another couple with scores of 4 and 14 would have the same discrepancy score of 10. Depending on the question at hand, such scores may be conceptually misleading.
2. The distributions of discrepancy scores have less variance, are less reliable than their contributing scores, and are characterized by some degree of attenuation.
3. Discrepancy scores do not contain information above and beyond what is already present in the correlation between separate family member scores.

Correlation Scores

To circumvent some of the problems with discrepancy scores, several authors use the correlation between spouse scores instead of the raw difference scores (Stephen and Markman 1983; Van der Veen et al. 1964). The rationale is that high correlations imply low discrepancy, and low correlations imply high discrepancy. Fisher et al. (1985) cautioned that scatterplots of scores should be explored, since high correlation may, in fact, represent a high degree of covariation within the respective ranges of husband and wife scores and may not reflect couple agreement.

Combined Scaling Techniques

Another technique for creating family scores is combined scaling. Fisher et al. (1985) discussed the possibility of combining the magnitude of each family member score with the differences between scores into a single, combined score. This can be done either by weighting the mean couple score by the discrepancy score or, alternatively, by weighting the discrepancy score by the mean couple score. If the focus of concern is to account for differences between family members at different levels of the scale, in addition to level and disagreement, a contingency table approach may be useful. This tactic helps to partition couples or families into convenience types for further analysis. The two drawbacks to this approach, highlighted by Fisher et al. (1985), are (1) important information can be lost when continuous data are reduced to categories, and (2) this lost information reduces power and the chances of obtaining statistical significance.

Method Comparisons

Olson et al. (1983) computed couple scores using a variety of methods and compared the results. Their study employed the EN-RICH inventory, which has 12 subscales, each comprising 10 items. The response scale for each item ranges from 1 to 5; thus, the scores for each subscale range from 10 to 50. The subscales assess such components of the marital relationship as communication, conflict resolution, financial management, and marital satisfaction.

Olson et al. (1983) found high levels of agreement between couple mean scores and positive couple agreement scores (determined by identifying couple agreement on all the items that represent positive aspects of the relationship). This high correlation was particularly surprising because the correlation between all husband and wife scores on the ENRICH subscales was a modest .43. These data, therefore, support the idea that the mean score is a robust and reasonably accurate summary of the positive agreement between spouses.

Another consistent finding was the lack of correlation (r=.05) between the couple mean scores and the couple discrepancy scores. This finding indicates that the two are measuring different and relatively independent aspects of a couple's relationship. Also, a negative

184

correlation (-.21) was found between positive couple agreement and the couple discrepancy score.

Generating and Using Relational Data: Differences as True Differences

If the differences as true differences perspective is followed, alternative data analytic techniques are required. Several methods are described below.

Repeated Measures Analysis

One of the most appealing data analysis techniques was suggested by Ball, McKenry, and Price-Bonham (1983). They contended that repeated measures designs are appropriate to family study. The procedure parallels the traditional repeated measures design in which the same individual is observed more than once; a series of observations constitute the levels of within-subject factor. In this case, a family is repeatedly observed by collecting information from more than one of its members. For example, husband score and wife score are treated as two levels of the factor known as family. Instead of several measurements being made on one individual, several individuals within a family are measured.

Multiple Regression

Multiple regression procedures that include level, discrepancy, and order scores from multiple family members in an equation to predict a dependent variable permit the independent contributions of each variable or type of variable to be assessed separately. In this manner, any shared variance is not duplicated. Fisher et al. (1985) pointed out, however, that although this technique accounts for the quantitative properties of the family's scores, it is often atheoretical. The method's strong point is that it reflects the actual empirical relationships among the variables, but the researcher may be at a loss to explain the theoretical reason for a score's predictive power.

Scatterplot Regression

Draper and Leik (1985) suggested a modification of the basic regression format called scatterplot regression. Rather than using a least-square fit to a given line as in traditional regression analysis,

185

this technique calls for using a "least-square fit between the appropriate points of two standardized bivariate normal distributions which share a common point of origin." They recommended standardizing husband and wife scores separately, plotting wives' scores along the Y axis, husbands' scores along the X axis, and using the score along the line between the two spouse scores that is closest to the origin of the two axes. This score, they contended, "preserves the unique information about each couple."

Canonical Correlation

Canonical correlation analysis, a technique designed to provide a summary measure of the relationship between two sets of variables, has the potential to be very useful to family researchers. The model can simultaneously create two linear composites, one from each set of variables, that maximize the correlation between the two sets of variables. The canonical model shows the structure of relationships across the two sets of variables, thus reducing the dimensionality of the measures studied. McLaughlin and Otto (1981) illustrated the usefulness of the canonical correlation approach by taking indicators of the husband's evaluation of his wife's competence as predictor variables, and the wife's evaluation of her husband's competence as criterion variables. These investigators interpreted the two sets of canonical variates as follows: The first represents an "expressive" dimension along which family roles are exchanged, while the second canonical variate characterizes an "instrumental" dimension along which reward is exchanged.

Cluster Techniques

Cluster or factor analytic techniques are also useful for classifying families into typologies based on individual members' scores. Although themselves atheoretical methods, if used in combination with such strategies as confirmatory factor analysis and structural modeling, the atheoretical nature of these methods can be circumvented. Thomson and Williams (1982), for example, suggested the LISREL technology for assessing multiple measures of a construct. Both the exploratory and confirmatory models used by LISREL are specifically designed to allow for the correlated errors that may result from multicolinearity characterizing data collected from multiple members of a family. The technique allows the researcher to identify specific measures that should share common method variance and analyze them appropriately.

186

Alternative Data Collection Techniques

An alternative approach to collecting data from individuals is to collect data from families or couples. Such a procedure was used by Belsky, Spanier, and Rovine (1983) in a study on the marital relationship. Joint couple interviews were administered. They found that spouses rarely disagreed by more than a single point in responding to questions posed to them at the same time. Whenever disagreements did occur, couples were required to reach consensus and provide a single response.

While such a procedure can distort the process a family goes through to reach consensus, it may be a useful approach for some research questions. If, however, the issue is identifying families characterized by conflict versus those characterized by harmony, the research methodology would have to be modified. One suggestion would be to ask the family to try to reach consensus, while the interviewer records what is actually going on within the family as it tackles this task.

Using a similar method, Stetz, Lewis, and Primomo (1986) collected information about family coping strategies through structured interviews with 125 families in which the mother was diagnosed with either nonmetastic breast cancer, diabetes, or fibrocystic breast disease. The mother, her partner, and all children aged 6 to 19 residing in the home were interviewed using the Problem Centered Family Coping Interview instrument developed by Lewis, Woods, and Ellison (1983), based on the work of Pless and Satterwhite (1973). The families were asked to identify a problem or challenge experienced during the previous month and to discuss the strategies they used to handle the problem. Responses were then content analyzed. The important contribution of this study was that it focused on the same unit from theoretical conceptualization through measurement to analysis.

Parent Care from a Family Perspective

The remainder of this chapter describes how future research could pursue these ideas by focusing, for example, on describing, explaining, and optimizing development among families who are caring for a parent suffering from Alzheimer's disease. However, the principles discussed are generalizable beyond the content of parent care.

The theoretical and empirical domains of research approach the

187

problem using the family as unit of focus. One theory with the family as its foundation is Hill's (1949) classic ABCX theory of family stress based on war-induced separation and reunion. Hill's theory has been only slightly modified (Burr 1973; Hanson and Hill 1964; Hill 1958) over the past 30 years. The theory holds that A (the event and related hardships) interacting with B (the family's crisis-meeting resources) interacting with C (the family's definition of the event) produces X (the crisis). The hardship of the event, which comprises the first determinant, lies outside the family per se and includes attributes of the event itself. The second and third determinants, the family resources and family definition of the event, lie within the family itself and must be seen in terms of the family's structure and values. The X factor of the model denotes variation in the amount of disruption or disorganization experienced by the family system.

Additions to the theory were suggested by McCubbin and Patterson (1982). Their version, known as the Double ABCX Model, predicts the longitudinal changes that families are expected to experience over time. The theory is particularly useful for a discussion of family unit parity since it includes constructs that can be conceptualized at a variety of levels.

Within this theoretical framework, the sampling unit, whether selected randomly or for convenience, would be the family. Family could be defined by the researcher in a number of ways. For our example, we will define family as husband, wife, and one teenage child; unmarried adults would be excluded from the study. Similarly, families in which the husband, wife, or teenager refuse or are unable to participate in the research would not be included in the potential sample pool.

Data collection would also use the family unit. Data could be collected separately from husbands, wives, and teenagers using standard interview or questionnaire formats. Another technique, used frequently by clinicians but rarely by researchers, is to gather data from the family collectively. In this manner, an interviewer might pose questions to the family and record only those answers agreed upon by the family. Similarly, one questionnaire could be given to a family along with instructions for them to record a "best answer" for them as a family.

The family stress theory also helps conceptualize variables for study. The first determinant, A, the hardship of the event, includes attributes of the event itself and is defined as being outside the family. As such, it is perceived as an objective rather than subjective reality. One approach to operationalizing this variable at the level of the family would be to select one member of each family as reporter. Additional reports gathered from other family members could be used to test the reliability of the original report. Discrepancies among reports would be considered measurement error, which could be incorporated into a test of the model. The researcher could also choose to sum or average multiple reports from a family into a family score.

One aspect of construct B, the family's crisis-meeting resources, is conceptualized as family cohesion and adaptability and is perceived as a subjective reality. Since the goal is to understand the family, a report from one member would not suffice. Rather, all members must be queried. Discrepancies between views would no longer represent pure measurement error, but would become valid, reliable (given that the instrument used was reliable) subjective reality distinctions between family members.

C, the family's definition of parent care, is also concerned with subjective reality. An approach similar to that suggested for B might be used. An alternative method would be to have all members of the family define the sense of burden they are experiencing as a family. Incorporated within the instrument might be questions about how much burden husband, wife, and teenager feel wife alone is experiencing, husband alone is experiencing, teenager alone is experiencing, and the family together is experiencing.

The X component of the model, the degree of crisis the family is experiencing, could be defined in a number of ways. From the most objective perspective, one member of the family could report on the use of verbal or physical abuse within the home within the past week. From the perspective of mental health as subjective reality, husband, wife, and teenager could report on their own levels of depression or anxiety and their perceptions of the depression and anxiety experienced by others in the family.

Regardless of the type of data collected, the data set would use the family as the unit of focus, and each family would be assigned a unique identification number. Variables would be set up to maximize the use of the data collected. For example, with regard to family cohesiveness and adaptability, variables would include husband's, wife's, and teenager's scores on the instrument. From these raw data, typologies reflecting combinations of scores could be created, and families reflecting the different typologies compared. The flexibility that results from setting up data sets using the family as unit is helpful for understanding differences between families as well as differences within families over time. Typologies offer an opportunity to describe families as something qualitatively different from the summation of characteristics of that family's individual members.

A similar approach was used by McCubbin and Patterson (1982) in studying families of children with cerebral palsy. In these families, all members must respond to the ever-changing needs and demands dictated by the disorder. Family responsibilities and tasks shift and change in response to the child's changing functioning capacities as well as to their normative developmental changes. Postulates derived from the Double ABCX Model helped identify those families most likely to be vulnerable to crisis, i.e., those families who experienced a pileup of life event strains before either the mother or the father had developed coping behaviors to manage the stressors.

Intervention From a Family Perspective

The challenge to research presented by approaching the study of families using family as the unit of analysis is great. Establishing and obtaining unit parity between theory and research is of utmost importance.

In addition to the previously discussed issues, the problems researchers often encounter in convincing individuals to participate in their studies may be compounded when they are faced with including multiple family members. Yet, the return on this investment may be substantial. A richer understanding of families and family trajectories offers the possibility of more appropriate interventions.

Danish, Smyer, and Nowak (1980) suggested that human development interventions can be arrayed along two dimensions: timing of intervention and level of intervention. This discussion is most central to the level of intervention. Rather than focusing interventions at the traditional level of the individual, the family of the Alzheimer's patient now becomes the level of focus. Similar views have been suggested by family therapists.

To follow through on the example of the stresses associated with caring for a parent who has Alzheimer's disease, it may be most useful to focus education and therapeutic efforts not solely on the identified caregiver, but on the spouse and children as well. One could envision developing educational programs to help families anticipate the changing emotional conditions and economic resources that will be available to each member as the older generation changes its demands on the support system. In addition, research about families may result in an understanding of family typologies such that families at risk for dysfunction could be identified. Such an approach could provide clues to clinicians as scarce mental health resources are allocated to families.

Interventions aimed at families extend beyond age-related disciplines such as child psychology or gerontology. When working with three or four generations, for example, a focus from an age-related discipline may put blinders on the therapist. Maintaining a lifespan orientation, on the other hand, allows various developmental tasks and their crises to be included in both problem definition and solution.

The developmental perspective reminds us that individual family members, in the midst of fulfilling various developmental tasks themselves (Havighurst 1948; Erikson 1968), may be unprepared for the demands placed on them by changes in the lives of other family members. For example, when a middle-aged woman returns to work, we may see an increase in acting out on the part of her young son, or resentment on the part of her husband. The problem is neither the middle-aged woman, her son, nor her husband. Rather, the problem is defined by the unique coalescing of lives developing in conjunction with one another. Treating any of the three actors separately misses the point and may, in fact, have negative results.

Conclusions

The need to advance theoretical concepts and methods for studying caregiving families beyond the level of the individual is crucial. Specific techniques must be selected carefully, recognizing that the various methods have their benefits as well as their problems. No one method is applicable to all types of family research, and selection depends on the statistical properties of the scale, the specific question being addressed, and the predictive utility or appropriate generalizability of the method.

That the family is "greater than the sum of its parts" is no longer at issue. Now the challenge is to develop and use methods that capture the unique intricacies of families. Expanding caregiving research beyond the primary caregiver to encompass the other family members will provide a more holistic perspective on the stresses associated with caregiving as well as suggest more appropriate directions for intervention.

References

Ball, D.; McKenry, P.C.; and Price-Bonham, S. Use of repeated-measures designs in family research. *Journal of Marriage and the Family* Nov.:885-896, 1983.

Belsky, J.; Spanier, G.B.; and Rovine, M. Stability and change in marriage across the transition to parenthood. *Journal of Marriage and the Family* Aug.:567-577, 1983.

Blood, R.O., and Hamblin, R. The effect of the wife's employment on family power structure. *Social Forces* 36:347-352, 1958.

Blood, R.O., and Wolfe, D.M. *Husbands and Wives*. Glencoe, IL: The Free Press, 1960.

Bokemeir, J., and Monroe, P. Continued reliance on the respondent in family decision-making studies: A content analysis. *Journal of Marriage and the Family* Aug.:645-652, 1983.

Brody, E.M.; Kleban, M.H.; Hoffman, C.; and Schoonover, C.G. Adult daughters and parent care: A comparison of one-, two- and three-generation households. *Home Health Care Services Quarterly*, in press.

Brody, E.M.; Kleban, M.H.; Johnsen, P.T.; Hoffman, C.; and Schoonover, C.G. Work status and parent care: A comparison of four groups of women. *Gerontologist* 27(2):201-208, 1987.

Brody, E.M., and Schoonover, C.G. Patterns of parent-care when adult daughters work and when they do not. *Gerontologist* 26:372-381, 1986.

Brody, E.M., and Spark, G. Institutionalization of the aged: A family crisis. *Family Process* 5:76-90, 1966.

Burr, W.R. *Theory Construction and the Sociology of the Family*. New York: John Wiley and Sons, 1973.

Colerick, E.J., and George, L.K. Predictors of institutionalization among caregivers of patents with Alzheimer's disease. *Journal of the American Geriatrics Society* 34:493-498, 1986.

Danish, S.J.; Smyer, M.A.; and Nowak, K.C. Life-span development and life skills. In: Baltes, P.B., and Brim, O.G., eds. *Life-Span Development and Behavior*. Vol. 3. New York: Academic Press, 1980.

Downs, P.E. Intra family decision making in family planning. *Journal of Business Research* 5:63-74, 1977.

Draper, T.W., and Leik, R.K. "On the analysis of dyadic data." Paper presented at the 13th Annual Family Demographic Research Institute: The Measurement of Dyadic and Group Properties in Families. Provo, UT: Brigham Young University, 1985.

Erikson, E.H. *Identity: Youth and Crisis*. New York: W.W. Norton, 1968.

Fisher, L. Transactional theories but individual assessment: A frequent discrepancy in family research. *Family Process* 21:313-320, 1982.

Fisher, L.; Kokes, R.F.; Ransom, D.; Phillips, S.; and Rudd, P. Alternative strategies for creating "relational" family data. *Family Process* 24:213-224, 1985.

George, L.K. "Caregiver well-being: Correlates and relationships with participation in community self-help groups." Final report submitted to the AARP Andrus Foundation, 1983.

Granbois, D., and Willett, R. Equivalence of family role measures based on husband and wife data. *Journal of Marriage and the Family* 32:68-72, 1970.

Hanson, N.R., and Hill, R. Families under stress. In: Christensen, H.T., ed. *Handbook of Marriage and the Family.* Chicago: Rand-McNally, 1964.

Havighurst, R.J. *Developmental Tasks and Education.* New York: David McKay Co., 1948.

Heer, D.M. The measurement and bases of family power: An overview. *Marriage and Family Living,* 25:133-139, 1968.

Herbst, P.G. The measurement of family relations. *Human Relations* 5:3-36, 1952.

Hill, R. *Families Under Stress.* New York: Harper, 1949.

Hill, R. Sociology of marriage and family behavior, 1945-56: A report and bibliography. *Current Sociology* 7:1-98, 1958.

Hodgson, J.W., and Lewis, R.A. Pilgrim's Progress III: A trend analysis of family theory and methodology. *Family Process* 18:163-174, 1979.

Horowitz, A. Family caregiving to the frail elderly. In: Eisdorfer, C.; Lawton, M.P.; and Maddox, G.L., eds. *Annual Review of Gerontology and Geriatrics.* Vol. 5. New York: Springer, 1985. pp. 194-246.

Isaacs, B. Geriatric patients: Do their families care? *British Medical Journal* 4:282-286, 1971.

Jaco, D.K., and Shepard, J.M. Demographic homogeneity and spousal consensus: A methodological perspective. *Journal of Marriage and the Family* 37:161-169, 1975.

Kleban, M.H.; Brody, E.M.; Schoonover, C.G.; and Hoffman, C. Family help to the elderly: Sons'-in-law perceptions of parent care. *Journal of Marriage and the Family,* in press.

Klein, D.M., and Hill, R. Determinants of family problem-solving effectiveness. In: Burr, W.R.; Hill, R.; Nye, F.I.; and Reiss, I.L., eds. *Contemporary Theories About the Family.* Vol. 1. New York: Free Press, 1979.

Lewis, F.M.; Woods, N.F.; and Ellison, E. *The Family Impact Study.* Seattle, WA: University of Washington, 1983.

Lezak, M.D. Living with the characterologically altered brain injured patient. *Journal of Clinical Psychology* 39:592-598, 1978.

McCubbin, H.I., and Patterson, J.M. Family adaptation to crises. In: McCubbin, H.I.; Cauble, A.E.; and Patterson, J.M., eds. *Family Stress, Coping, and Social Support.* Springfield, IL: Thomas, 1982.

McLaughlin, S.D., and Otto, L.B. Canonical correlation analysis in family research. *Journal of Marriage and the Family*, Feb.:7-16, 1981.

Morycz, R.K. An exploration of senile dementia and family burden. *Clinical Social Work Journal* 8:16-27, 1980.

Noelker, L.S., and Poulshock, S.W. "The effects on families of caring for impaired elderly in residence." Final report submitted to the Administration on Aging. The Margaret Blenkner Research Center for Family Studies, Benjamin Rose Institute, Cleveland, OH, 1982.

Olson, D.H.; Russell, C.S.; and Sprenkle, D.G. Circumplex model of marital and family systems: VI. Theoretical update. *Family Process*, 69-83, 1983.

Pless, I.B., and Satterwhite, B. A measure of family functioning and its application. *Social Science in Medicine* 7:613-621, 1973.

Price-Bonham, S. Marital decision making: Congruence of spouses' responses. *Sociological Inquiry* 47:119-125, 1977.

Pruchno, R.A.; Blow, F.C.; and Smyer, M.A. Life events and interdependent lives: Implications for research and intervention. *Human Development* 27:31-41, 1984.

Quarm, D. Random measurement error as a source of discrepancies between reports of wives and husbands concerning marital power and task allocation. *Journal of Marriage and the Family* 43:521-535, 1981.

Ruano, B.J.; Bruce, J.D.; and McDermott, M.M. Pilgrim's Progress II: Recent trends in family research. *Journal of Marriage and the Family* 31:688-698, 1969.

Safilios-Rothschild, C. Family sociology or wives' family sociology? A cross-cultural examination of decision-making. *Journal of Marriage and the Family* 31:290-301, 1969.

Sainsbury, P., and Grad de Alarcon, J. The psychiatrist and the geriatric patient: The effects of community care on the family of the geriatric patient. *Journal of Geriatric Psychiatry* 1:23-41, 1970.

Scanzoni, J. A note on the sufficiency of wife responses. *Pacific Sociological Review* 8:109-115, 1965.

Stephen, T., and Markman, H. Assessing development of relationships: A new research. *Family Process* 22:15-25, 1983.

Stetz, K.M.; Lewis, F.M.; and Primomo, J. Family coping strategies and chronic illness in the mother. *Family Relations* 35:515-522, 1986.

Szinovacz, M. Using couple data as a methodological tool: The case of marital violence. *Journal of Marriage and the Family* Aug.:633-644, 1983.

Thompson, L., and Walker, A.J. The dyad as the unit of analysis: Conceptual and methodological issues. *Journal of Marriage and the Family* Nov.:889-900, 1982.

Thomson, E., and Williams, R. Beyond wives' family sociology: A method for analyzing couple data. *Journal of Marriage and the Family* 44:999-1008, 1982.

Van der Veen, F.; Huebner, B.; Jorgens, B.; and Neja, P. Relationships between the parents' concept of the family and family adjustment. *American Journal of Orthopsychiatry* 34:45-55, 1964.

Wilkening, E.A., and Morrison, D.E. A comparison of husband and wife responses concerning who makes family and home decisions. *Marriage and Family Living* 25:349-351, 1963.

Zarit, S.H.; Reever, K.E.; and Bach-Peterson, J. Relatives of the impaired elderly: Correlates of feelings of burden. *Gerontologist* 20:649-655, 1980.

Part II

Caregiver Stress: Research Issues in the Mental Health/Health Interface

Although the existing body of literature is clear in its implication that many caregivers experience deleterious effects from caregiving, the level, extent, and nature of these effects has just begun to be examined. The overarching research questions being raised by the chapters in this section include: Are there negative short- and long-term mental health/health outcomes associated with caregiving stress? What psychological, social, and biological factors may mediate adverse health/mental health consequences of caregiving stress, and can vulnerable caregivers be identified? What impact does the chronic stress of caregiving have on the development or exacerbation of different disease processes?

In directing research toward these issues, these chapters suggest the need for longitudinal, multidisciplinary research that examines the morbidity and mortality of individuals exposed to the chronic stress of caregiving.

Chapter 7

Coping and the Mediation of Caregiver Stress

Leonard I. Pearlin, Ph.D., Heather Turner, and Shirley Semple

Stress research has been guided in recent years by a central question: Why do the same life problems have different effects on different individuals? To rephrase the query in terms of the concerns of this chapter, we may ask how the trials and vicissitudes of giving care to Alzheimer's disease victims have a more deleterious effect on some caregivers than on others. In considering this question, it quickly becomes apparent that many factors have a potential role in regulating or mediating the impact of caregiving, and we examine some of these in the course of our discussion. However, our principal focus is on coping. Coping, along with social support, has come to be recognized over the past two decades as a major mediator in the stress process. It certainly deserves the attention of people interested in identifying conditions that can soften the impact of the harsh and endless demands experienced by Alzheimer's disease caregivers.

Because relatively little is known about how people cope with the exigencies of Alzheimer's disease caregiving, we conducted our own pilot study. Much of the material of this chapter is organized around what was learned from this small inquiry. We describe some of the strategies that people use to cope with the caregiver role. However, we believe that the study of coping is inseparable from the study of what people are coping with. Consequently, we present in this chapter a description of the kinds of stressors people encounter as Alzheimer's disease caregivers as well as the coping strategies they employ in contending with the stressors.

When coping is viewed in relation to the problems caregivers have to contend with, it becomes quickly evident that the efficacy of coping is not always equal to the magnitude of the problems caregivers face.

For this reason, we also address the apparent limitations of coping and the conditions under which caregivers' coping seems to be most effective. The substantive sections of the chapter, then, are concerned with the dimensions of strains found in the caregiver role, the coping repertoires used in dealing with the strains, and the limitations of individual coping. Before taking up these matters, aspects of the conceptual framework that guides much of our thinking needs to be explicated.

Conceptual Issues in the Study of Caregiver Coping

Despite the attention it has received—or perhaps because of it—coping is still surrounded by a number of unsettled conceptual issues. Two of these are directly relevant to coping with the stress of caring for patients with Alzheimer's disease and warrant attention here. One concerns the generality or specificity of coping and the other the functions of coping.

Generality Versus Specificity of Coping

Should coping be regarded as a general behavior cross-cutting different situations or as a behavior tailored to specific situations? Some scholars (e.g., Valliant 1967) tend to regard coping as embodying a general style of dealing with the world and the tasks it entails. This view, with its roots in psychoanalysis, emphasizes modes of internalized adaptive strategies and defenses that are activated when the individual faces threatening situations. Coping repertoires are seen as reflecting deeply embedded defenses, such as denial, that are triggered by stressful circumstances. According to this orientation, individuals are disposed to cope with different threats in similar, characteristic ways.

In contrast to this view, which emphasizes the general use of established coping dispositions, is that which sees coping as shaped by the stressful situation being confronted and the specific exigencies encompassed by the situation (Lazarus and Folkman 1984). According to this approach, we may learn little or nothing of how individuals cope with marital problems from knowledge of how they cope with problems in the work setting. Similarly, the understanding of how people deal with Alzheimer's caregiver stress may not be illuminated by how they deal with other problems.

Our own position is more in accord with arguments supporting

199

specificity (Pearlin and Schooler 1968), although we suspect actual coping behavior typically combines situationally unique responses with those that are dispositionally internalized. We raise the issue of generality versus specificity, not because it will be definitively settled here, but because it has important and sobering methodological implications for how one approaches the study of coping with Alzheimer's caregiver stress—or any other specific stressful situation. Concretely, if we wish to know how people cope with the Alzheimer's caregiver role, we need to develop measures that will specifically assess coping responses to problems in that role. Measures developed to evaluate coping behavior in other situations or designed to evaluate general dispositions are not likely to be wholly appropriate to the study of coping with the particular demands and threats that one encounters in caring for an Alzheimer's patient. If we are to learn how Alzheimer's caregivers cope, we have to study Alzheimer's caregivers.

Yet, it is not necessary to start completely afresh. Although we believe that coping is most accurately discerned within the context of specific situational problems and threats, each new situation we study need not and should not be treated as a tabula rasa. Indeed, accumulated knowledge ideally should enrich each new undertaking. In particular, conceptual frameworks are available to guide new inquiries. Though concrete coping behaviors vary across situations, our underlying theoretical orientations to these behaviors should not.

Coping Functions

Our own efforts to understand the coping of Alzheimer's disease caregivers have benefited from a conceptual schema developed several years ago (Pearlin and Schooler 1968). Essentially, this schema is built around four *functions* of coping. The notion of function calls attention not to specific behavior but to the potential consequences of the behavior for avoiding or minimizing stress (Pearlin and Aneshensel 1986). The four functions that can be distinguished are (1) prevention of the stressful situation, (2) management of the situation, (3) management of the meaning of the situation, and (4) management of stress symptoms.

For two reasons, little or nothing is known of the first of these functions of coping—prevention. First, with rare exceptions (e.g., Menaghan 1982), researchers typically focus their studies on problems that have already taken their place in people's lives, not those they have succeeded in avoiding because of their coping acumen. Second, some stressful situations are impervious to preventive activities; that is, their occurrence cannot be precluded as a result of individual or collective behavior. Alzheimer's disease

200

and the patient's need for care are obvious and unfortunate examples. No amount of anticipatory coping can prevent Alzheimer's disease and the caregiving it requires. However, abundant evidence exists of coping actions around the other three functions. We briefly discuss these functions here, leaving until later a description of some of the concrete coping behaviors through which these functions are performed.

Coping behavior that functions for the management of the situation involves efforts aimed at reducing the demands of caregiving or making them easier to perform. The ultimately effective way to manage a stressful situation is to eliminate the situation itself. In the case of Alzheimer's disease caregiving, this is not possible, even when the patient is institutionalized. Instead, situational management, where it occurs, is limited to decreasing the level of burden that the caregiver must bear. Later, we describe some of the coping techniques of this genre that were reported to us in our pilot study.

In situations that are inherently difficult to eliminate or modify, the modes of coping that are most likely to be adopted function primarily to manage the *meaning* of the situation. Past research has shown that not only the objective properties of a situation determine its stressfulness, but also how the situation is perceived and understood. Because of differences in the way people are able to perceive a given situation, the degree to which the situation is experienced as problematic and threatening may vary widely. The perceptions and understandings of the situation are similar to what Lazarus (1966) refers to as appraisal. In our view, appraisal is more than a detached, objective evaluation of the situation. It involves the motivated and selective use of perceptual and cognitive devices that shape the meaning of the situation so it comes to be seen as less ominous and more within the capacity of the individual to forbear. As we shall see, Alzheimer's disease caregivers employ a number of devices that potentially function in this manner.

The final function of coping entails the management of stress symptoms. Symptoms of which we are aware are virtually always unpleasant. Anxiety, muscular tensions, and dysphoria, for example, are noxious states from which we typically seek relief. Indeed, coping efforts are often aimed at easing these states. The alleviation of tensions and depressed affect is certainly a positive outcome, particularly to the extent that this kind of coping frees the individual to engage in other coping behavior having different functions. By itself, of course, it does not alter the stressful situations in which individuals' lives are embedded, nor does it shape the meaning of such situations. Nevertheless, it can keep individuals from being over-

201

whelmed by the stresses they experience and, in doing so, enables them to mobilize and divert their coping energies elsewhere.

In the actual course of coping with life problems, the different coping functions take on a more dynamic character than is conveyed by these brief descriptions. First, they are not mutually exclusive; coping behavior does not necessarily involve one function or another but, instead, may encompass multiple functions. Indeed, our earlier work indicated that the more people's coping repertoires varied and the more functions they entailed, the more effective were their coping efforts (Pearlin and Schooler 1968).

Second, and very important, there is reason to believe that coping repertoires are very fluid; that is, the way in which people cope with a problem at any moment in time may be quite different from how they coped with it in the past or will in the future. Particularly when persistent, chronic stressors are involved, coping efforts can be expected to change over time. They change not only as a reflection of a trial and error process but also because the array and intensity of stressors change as the situation passes through its natural history. As these changes evolve, they call forth different coping responses. This can be clearly illustrated in the case of Alzheimer's disease caregiving, where the problems the caregiver confronts at an early stage of the disease may evoke coping behavior that would be less appropriate at a late stage of the disease. The point to be borne in mind is that the coping function prominent at one period of observation may very well recede to a less salient place later, its position taken by another coping function. The particular mix of behaviors bearing on the management of the situation, on its meanings, or on the stress symptoms it creates can be assumed to shift as people test different coping responses, discarding some and adding others, and as the nature of the problems they must deal with evolve.

In sum, we would argue on the side of the specificity of coping behavior. The research implication of this position is that with each distinctly different problematic situation we study, it is necessary to develop coping measures tailored to that situation. Measures developed to assess coping in one situation may very well fail in a different situation to assess coping accurately or in sufficient detail. When we treat coping as an expression of general dispositions, we may fail to capture the coping behaviors specific to the situation under study. However, while it is desirable to create new measures of coping each time a new stressful situation is studied, it is not necessary to create de novo the conceptual framework that guides the inquiries.

The framework we find particularly useful is built around the functions of coping and their dynamic interrelationships. Without a conceptual framework, it would be difficult to identify coping behaviors or to discern the manner in which they are structured in people's actions. Moreover, it would not be possible to develop a theoretical view of coping that cuts across specific situations. In the area of Alzheimer's disease caregiver stress, we might note, little research effort can be found that encompasses either a desired level of specificity or an overarching conceptual framework. These shortcomings were among the considerations that prompted us to undertake our limited pilot inquiry.

But first, it is necessary to explicate the fundamental assumption that we have been arguing: the ways that people cope with a situation depend on the character of the stressors that they encounter in that situation. If, in fact, coping does tend to be a specific set of responses to a specific situation, then the study of caregiver coping is inseparable from the study of the stressful circumstances they find in their roles as caregivers.

The Context of Coping: Dimensions of Caregiver Strain

In identifying the potentially stressful elements of the caregiver role, we emphasize those stressors that tend to be built into the role itself. Because they are aspects of the caregiver role, they are relatively persistent and enduring. This type of stressor involves what we refer to as role strains (Pearlin 1983), in contrast to eventful or ephemeral stressors. Their continuing presence in people's lives makes these strains particularly stressful (Pearlin and Lieberman 1969).

Whereas relatively little has been done to develop measures of coping specific to Alzheimer's disease caregiving, a fairly substantial literature describes and attempts to measure the strains that can criss-cross the caregiver role. We had the opportunity in our pilot work to both construct new measures of strain and reconceptualize some existing measures. This work, it should be noted, was particularly concerned with caregiving by spouses and adult children to noninstitutionalized patients. Our discussion, therefore, is not relevant to situations where informal caregivers provide auxiliary care to institutionalized patients.

One way to distinguish the strains that caregivers face is in terms of the demands inherent in the condition and needs of the patient. Simply put, how much care must caregivers provide because the patients are unable to provide it for themselves? This can be determined quite directly and objectively by assessing the daily and instrumental activities for which the patient depends on the caregiver. The assumption here is that the greater the range and number of such dependencies, the greater will be the strain experienced by the caregiver. Similarly, certain problem behaviors, while not involving the functional needs of the patient, represent a substantial demand on the energies of the caregiver and contribute to the level of strain experienced by the caregiver. These problematic behaviors include sleep disruption, wandering, the use of obscenities, inappropriate sexual behavior, misuse of appliances, and so on. Such behaviors may require unflagging vigilance and the exercise of constant controls and constraints. The enormous demands that they impose on the time and energies of the caregivers come to constitute important sources of strain.

Yet, some research indicates that the relationship between the objective demands of the role and the subjectively felt burdens are quite imperfect (Zarit et al. 1980). That is, some caregivers appear to function quite well under very adverse conditions and others do less well under less adverse conditions. The assessment of caregiver strain, therefore, cannot rely entirely on assessments of objective role demands. It must also take into account the ways in which these demands are subjectively experienced. The sheer sense of role overload is part of this objective experience, and caregivers discussed this in our pilot interviews. Indeed, frequent references by caregivers to elements of overload provide abundant items for its measure. Going to bed completely exhausted, not having time to look at the paper, having to do the work of two people, working hard but seeing no progress are a few of the indicators of overload. Again, while we think that the sheer volume of demands in the role is a core element of caregiver strain, similar demands do not necessarily result in similar levels of role overload.

Still another dimension of strain involves the sense of *loss*. In our interviews, it became evident that caregivers may experience three distinct, albeit related, types of loss: the loss of joint social and leisure activities, the loss of affectionate exchange, and the loss of the patient's former self. Although some shared activities are usually maintained, such as watching television, a dramatic constriction in the number and range of treasured pursuits that were once enjoyed together is typical. These might involve dining out, family gatherings, travel, participation in clubs and voluntary associations, getting together with friends, and so on. Spousal caregivers, in particular, often look back at these activities as representing part of a cherished life that is lost, never to be regained.

This can be even more poignantly true in the second type of loss, that entailing affective exchange. Here the spouse may be called upon to give relentlessly to a person who can never again reciprocate, to be a source of affection without being its object, or to be no longer cared about by the one who is cared for. Not only the expressions of love and affection are lost, but also the reciprocity of exchange on which the relationship with the patient was built. These are painful losses, indeed; and when they are experienced by caregivers, they are powerful sources of strain.

Along with the loss of shared activities and affective exchanges, caregivers commonly have to minister to patients who possess only faint traces of their former selves. Alzheimer's disease and other diseases that produce cognitive impairments can be profoundly transforming. Those attributes and dispositions that previously were distinctively characteristic of the patient are no longer in evidence. The impairment in a very literal sense can create the diminishment or disappearance of the quintessential person. Continued caregiving to a person who in large measure is now a stranger only serves to accentuate the awareness that the former person no longer exists.

These components of the caregiver role, then, represent different dimensions of strain; they are among the elements of the situation that impose hardships and problems on the caregiver. When we speak of caregivers' coping, therefore, these are the core things they are coping with; they are among the threats that caregivers must deal with to survive and continue in the role. But they are not all the problems with which caregivers might have to contend. The demands and problems of caregiving are likely to create problems in other areas of life, and these problems must also be faced and handled. We refer to the problems that come to be clustered around caregiving as "associated strains."

Associated strains can be observed in the roles and social relations inherently interconnected with caregiving. For example, it has been noted (Niederehe and Fruge 1984; Rabins et al. 1982; Wilder, Tenes, and Bennett 1983) that family conflict is a familiar concomitant of caregiving. Thus, one family member may feel that another is not attentive to the patient or sufficiently helpful to the principal caregiver; opinions may differ with regard to maintaining the patient at home or in an institution; some might display impatience or a lack of compassion for the patient; and so on. Unfortunately, there is no shortage of ways in which Alzheimer's disease and the caregiving it necessitates can create family disharmony and diversion.

For those caregivers who are employed outside the household, the demands of caregiving may conflict with those of the job. Employed caregivers report that they are more tired on the job since the onset of the patient's illness, less able to concentrate, more often absent, and—as a result of these problems—experience more insecurity about their occupational futures. Interestingly, however, even those exposed to these kinds of job pressures may be reluctant to give up work. As difficult as it may be, the job gives some caregivers a bit of relief from the day-to-day tedium and hardships of caregiving.

A final associated strain concerns economic resources. Taking care of a cognitively impaired person can be costly, sometimes devastatingly so. In addition to the expense of health care and related services, a severe loss of income may result from the inability of the patient or caregiver to work. Economic deprivation, in turn, has repeatedly been shown to have potent stressful consequences (Pearlin et al. 1981; Catalano and Dooley 1983).

We have gone into some detail to describe the various strains to which caregivers may be exposed, because they form the necessary background to an understanding of caregiver coping. These strains are presented in a simple paradigm in figure 7-1. The figure is designed to highlight several aspects of the caregiver stress process. First, it portrays the depth and scope of the potential adverse effects on the lives of caregivers. The caregiving role itself may be host to a variety of strains, each capable of exerting deleterious consequences for mental and physical health. Moreover, the caregiving strains have dislocating effects on other areas of life, leading to associated strains in family relations, job, and finances. Because these strains are likely to occur in important roles and because they tend to be persistent and chronic, they become independent sources of stress for the caregiver. Thus, to look only at the caregiver role could lead to an underestimation of the nature and range of stressors that actually confront the caregiver.

These aspects of the caregiver stress process reveal multiple points and junctures at which coping needs to be strategically aimed. Specifically, coping may minimize the presence and intensity of the various core strains found within the caregiver role. It may be aimed at constraining the diffusion of strains into associated roles or at minimizing their intensity, or it may be aimed at preventing or reducing the stressful impact of the antecedent strains. As yet, there is but little empirical research organized in a way that would permit the observation and assessment of coping at different strategic points of the stress process (see Pearlin et al. 1981). Were such studies available, we would better understand why individual coping may not be equal to the variety of tasks and threats that caregivers have to face. Hypothetically, one might cope very effectively with some problems along the process but not with others and, therefore, still suffer adverse psychological and physical effects. In our pilot interviews, we were impressed by the ways that people coped with the caregiver role.

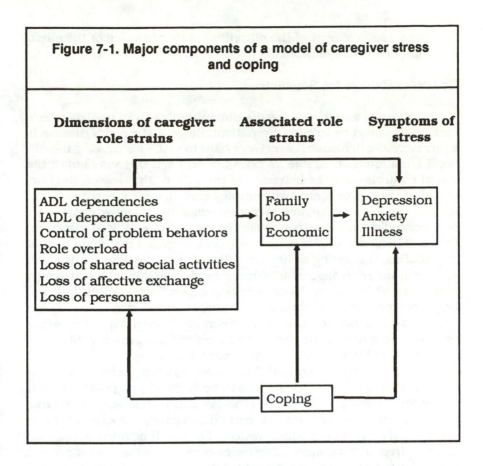

Figure 7-1. Major components of a model of caregiver stress and coping

Dimensions of caregiver role strains

Associated role strains

Symptoms of stress

ADL dependencies
IADL dependencies
Control of problem behaviors
Role overload
Loss of shared social activities
Loss of affective exchange
Loss of personna

Family
Job
Economic

Depression
Anxiety
Illness

Coping

But when the entire range of stressors to which people are potentially exposed is considered, it is fanciful to assume that this alone could shield one from stress and its health concomitants.

The Coping Repertoires of Caregivers

Considerable time was devoted in our pilot interviews to coping. Because our prior research informed us of coping strategies in relation to family, occupational, and economic strains (Pearlin and Schooler 1968), these interviews limited their focus to how people dealt with caregiver strains proper. Caregivers' responses to our questions about their ways of dealing with caregiving problems can be organized around our conceptual distinctions of the three coping functions: management of the situation, of the meaning of the situation, and of stress symptoms.

Coping to Manage the Situation

The ultimate way to manage the difficulties involved in Alzheimer's caregiving would be to cure the patient. Since Alzheimer's disease is an irreversible dementia, caregivers have to settle for making the difficult situation as bearable as possible. In part, this may entail the use of controls over the behavior of the patient that lessen the burden of the caregiver. Caregivers employ such diverse measures as enforcing a prescribed regimen of tranquilizers, the selective expression of anger or forcefulness to activate the patient in a desired direction, the establishment of priorities when all caregiving demands cannot be satisfied, the telling of lies or half-truths to assuage or head off agitation, the rearrangement of household furnishings, the strategic placement of locks on doors, seeking expert information, and anticipatory planning for future legal and financial exigencies. These coping devices do not necessarily eliminate hardship; they serve primarily to harness the demands to make them less urgent, more easily satisfied, and less laden with uncertainty.

No matter how creative and diverse one's coping devices are, it is unlikely that the level of demand can be lowered to a point where it no longer poses a problem. Nevertheless, coping that serves to make the situation more manageable can be extremely important. It can result, first of all, in the conservation of scarce time and energy, and it can help people be more effective in performing tasks that are not discretionary. Moreover, to the extent that these techniques succeed, caregivers may also enjoy the secondary benefit of having their own hard-pressed sense of mastery reinforced.

Coping to Manage Meaning

In general, when people face stressful situations that are intractable or highly resistant to change, their coping strategies are largely directed toward functions other than managing the situation. Giving care to one who suffers from a severe and progressive cognitive impairment represents precisely such a situation. Although important practical and logistical measures can be taken to ease the situation, the caregiver role remains irreversibly formidable and wearing, fundamentally impervious to individuals' coping repertoires. In such instances, a major, expected direction of coping will be toward constructing a meaning of the situation that reduces its threat. Essentially, if people are bound to an onerous situation they cannot change, they will search for ways to live with it. This search motivates caregivers to perceive the caregiving role and the demands that impinge on it in ways that help them to survive and continue in the role.

Some of the perceptual and cognitive coping devices that people employ have been observed in other studies. One of these, positive comparisons (Pearlin and Schooler 1968; Taylor 1983), may involve invidious estimates of whether one is better off than others. One does not wish another ill but simply takes some psychic comfort in knowing from the plight of others that things could be worse than they are. Some positive comparisons do not involve others but are temporal, involving comparisons across time. Thus, a caregiver might see the patient's impairment as plateauing—no worse this year than last. The future as well as the past may be compared to the present, as when caregivers try to convince themselves that "next year will not be worse than this year." It does not matter whether these are accurate appraisals; what does matter is that they are seized upon selectively as positive elements in an otherwise bleak situation.

The future, however, is something that caregivers do not always want to contemplate; because it can be ominous and threatening, some may seek to screen it from clear view. Thus, they make a deliberate effort "to think about the present rather than the future" or "I just try to get along day by day." The day-to-day theme is familiar and represents an attempt to avoid the deeply discouraging prospect of conditions progressively worsening over time. The future for these caregivers can only generate a profound sense of futility. To maintain the motivation necessary to continue in the role, therefore, caregivers blot out what lies ahead. Thinking too closely about the next year may prevent them from dealing with the next hour.

Just as some caregivers cope by obliterating the future, others cope by holding on to the past. As we discussed earlier, Alzheimer's disease can be transforming, changing the victims in ways that leave little trace of their former personas. In response, the caregiver might try to recreate part of the past, or when traces of the person do occasionally occur, to seize upon and magnify them. Thus, people may spend an extraordinary amount of time reflecting on "all the good years we had together." Or they might try to find whatever vestige remains of "the things I always liked and admired in her," such as flashes of a former sense of humor. As brief and intermittent as these vestiges of the past may be, they constitute reminders of characteristics once prized. They become desperately sought indicators that not everything that was good in the past is lost to the present.

To the extent that caregivers cling to a happier past, they cannot maintain the same set of expectations that previously characterized

209

their relationship with the patient. This would result only in disappointment and disillusionment. Survival with the profoundly changed patient and the losses these changes entail depends somewhat on being able to abandon former aspirations and expectations. Simply put, the caregiver will "try to accept my spouse as she is, not as I wish she could be." A somewhat different expression of the same sentiment is, "I try to accept that my parent is now a different person." One way, then, in which caregivers strive to avoid the pain that comes from unfulfillable expectations is by changing these expectations to fit the behavioral realities of the situation.

Even humor is a way of coping. Caregivers will occasionally laugh at their own plight or find something lighthearted in the behavior of the patient. Used in this way, humor dispels the heavy, ubiquitous grimness that can so easily hang over the lives of caregivers. Poking fun at distressing elements of the situation expresses defiance and contempt of its deadly seriousness and, in so doing, perhaps makes it more bearable.

One would think that the storehouse of cognitive coping mechanisms would have some mode of explaining why a loved one has been victimized by a terrible affliction. Why us, why our household? Is it because of something we did or failed to do? Could it have been avoided? These seem to be important questions, but they are questions more often eschewed than pursued. There seems to be a deliberate effort to see the debilitating disease of the patient as a phenomenon without reason, without design. If Alzheimer's or related diseases are seen by caregivers as maladies that purposefully seek out their victims, then caregivers are forced to wonder if they or the victim might bear some responsibility for the awesome state. Understandably, then, to the extent that caregivers are drawn to any explanation, they are likely to hold to naturalistic views rather than those that imply purpose or distributive justice. They are apt to disavow the statement, "I try to figure out why this happened to us" and to subscribe, instead, to the view that "no one is to blame for my spouse's illness; it could happen to anyone" or "I try to accept the illness without making sense of it."

Although most people do not attempt to find reason or purpose, many use prayer to ask for divine intervention. Alzheimer's disease or similar maladies may not be created by a divine act, but a divine act, nevertheless, is believed to be capable of providing some alleviation. A number of respondents in our pilot inquiry said they prayed, and examination of their reports revealed interesting differences in the kind of intervention they called for. For example, one may pray for a cure, that the patient's health be restored to its former state. Another prayer, this one directly in behalf of the caregiver rather than the patient, seeks the strength to carry on in the role or for guidance in performing it. Caregivers might also use prayer to be able to accept better their new and difficult lot in life. Aside from whether prayer provides what it seeks, the very act asserts that a channel of action exists that might lead to relief. For some, then, praying assumes that the situation is not altogether beyond hope.

Another coping strategy, quite different from those we have described, involves active engagement in organizations concerned with Alzheimer's disease. People become members of such organizations or active in their affairs and leadership for many reasons. Some either seek such involvement or adventitiously find that it provides an avenue for converting personal tragedy into a social cause. Whatever else they might gain from their active involvement, these caregivers are using their own hardships for the benefit of a larger collectivity. In so doing, of course, they are creating a new meaning of the affliction and its effects on their own lives. In investing themselves in the benefits of a large collectivity, they are able to feel that some good may result from their own difficult experiences. For these caregivers, the relevance of their struggles reaches beyond the boundaries of their own families into the households of others. Organizational involvement can help caregivers endow their efforts with a sense of mission.

In brief, many perceptual and cognitive devices function to create a less stark and less threatening understanding of the situation than would otherwise be the case. This understanding may be helped (1) by the way in which the caregiver invokes positive comparisons, both across time and across appropriate reference figures; (2) by screening out of view a dismal future so that one need contend only with the present; (3) by restructuring one's levels of expectations so that they are more consistent with the patient's behavior; (4) by the use of humor to demean the rule of the situation over one's life and emotions; (5) by rejecting any explanation of the patient's condition as part of a purposive design or as something that could have been avoided; (6) by discerning in the behavior of the patient positive traces of the past; (7) by exercising and reinforcing hopefulness through prayer; and (8) by investing themselves in the broad objectives of organizations concerned with Alzheimer's disease. Undoubtedly, other coping responses of this genre exist, but they all have in common a potential for perceptually reshaping a relentlessly difficult situation into a less stressful and more endurable one.

Coping for the Management of Symptoms

An entirely different set of coping responses are those that func-

211

tion primarily for the management and control of the stress symptoms that arise from caregiving. This function is, in some respects, the most difficult to describe in concrete terms because of the almost limitless range of behaviors that potentially serve the function. Virtually any behavior that assists caregivers in eliminating or reducing awareness of the distress they bear can be regarded as having this function. However, whether a particular behavior represents a coping response cannot be determined from the behavior alone; it depends also on how the behavior is being used. One person might use alcohol, for example, because it is an expected pattern of sociability in his membership group, and another may drink because it eases his psychic pain.

Fortunately, most people are able to report whether they do something because "it makes me feel better." Among the behaviors that caregivers refer to as making them feel better are drinking alcohol, eating more, smoking, sleeping, exercising, increased use of drugs and medications, marathon television watching, reading, yelling and other emotional "safety valve" outbursts, occasional solitude, and immersion in work. Undoubtedly, many other behaviors are put to the service of keeping distress under control. They can be useful coping functions to the extent that they keep people from being immobilized by emotional disorder and to the extent that the relief of pressure enables caregivers to bring responses having other functions into their coping repertoires. Used exclusively, however, this type of coping can create additional long-run problems that do not compensate for the benefits they yield in the short run. This was demonstrated in the case of alcohol consumption (Pearlin and Radabaugh 1966; Aneshensel and Huba 1983), and there are probably other devices that lead both to immediate relief and, with time, to further damage to one's capacities.

Looking back at what we have learned about the coping behavior of caregivers, a rich array of responses has been identified. Yet, as in other potentially stressful situations, an underlying order can be discerned when we consider not only the concrete coping act but also its apparent function. Now it can be seen that caregivers are likely to adopt a number of coping strategies, including those that serve to ease the demands on time, energy, and vigilance, that help caregivers experience and interpret their situations in ways that make them less onerous and that provide some immediate relief from the distress and tensions engendered by caregiving. At this stage of our knowledge, it is not possible to point to one response or group of responses as representing the best way to deal with the strains of caregiving. We can assume, at least provisionally, that caregiving is similar to other stressful situations in that coping effectiveness increases with the richness of coping repertoires and the number of functions they embody (Pearlin and Schooler 1968). However, even the most effective coping might not succeed in sparing the caregiver the mental and physical tolls exacted by the role.

The Limitations of Individual Coping

Active coping is likely to help Alzheimer's disease caregivers continue to perform the most formidable duties and tasks. We can confidently assume that people are better off when they cope, and they are even better off when they cope well. But the best individual coping might not be enough. Indeed, we would predict that if caregivers were left alone to cope as best they could with the caregiver role, they would very quickly succumb to the awesome hardships inherent in the role. Coping, in our view, is most effective when accompanied by other resources. More specifically, if caregivers are cut off from informal supports and access to and the use of formal facilities and services, their individual coping efforts will probably not bear the burdens of sustained caregiving for very long. Although we need to know more about strategies of coping with caregiver stress, an even more urgent need is to examine the optimum mix of formal resources, informal support, and personal coping strategies.

Survival in the role, we submit, depends on the presence of all three, and while this may appear to be self-evident, it needs to be underscored. Otherwise, we may misattribute the success of a caregiver to the coping ingenuity of the individual when, in fact, coping ingenuity itself may depend on having an ample supply of resources and support on which to draw. The coping of people who are isolated from family and friends and alienated from their communities is not likely to be creative. Creativity notwithstanding, coping by itself cannot bear the weight of caregiving. Thus, those interested in coping and convinced of its efficacy should recognize that it emerges most firmly as a barricade against stress when the caregiver is not abandoned by his friends, relatives, and community. The strength and durability of coping very much depends on the presence of other conditions that also mediate the stress process.

In trying to gauge the strength and limitations of individual coping, it is useful to keep in mind the range of threats and strains that may impinge on the caregiver. Within the caregiver role itself may be multiple dimensions of problems and hardships, and each of these, in turn, may be differentially responsive to different coping strategies. In addition, strains associated with caregiving but not directly a part of it may develop. As portrayed in figure 7-1, when these associated

213

strains surface in key areas of life, such as family relations, job, and economic resources, they come to stand as powerful and independent sources of stress. This proliferation of life strains around caregiving has serious implications for coping and how we judge its efficacy.

Briefly, one might cope quite well with the caregiving role and its strains and still be host to intense symptoms of stress. The explanation is suggested by figure 7-1 and the junctures along the stress process where coping is potentially engaged. The hypothetical caregivers who cope satisfactorily with patients' dependencies, who succeed in controlling problem behavior and avoiding overload, and who contend with their losses without being desolated by them may still face family, job, and economic problems that exceed their coping capacities. If we were to look solely at the ability of these caregivers to deal adequately with the caregiver role proper, we might be surprised to discover that they are emotionally devastated. One reason for this, we submit, lies in the inability of caregivers to prevent the development of associated strains or to temper the severity of these strains. Thus, if caregivers are to be truly efficacious, they must be efficacious in coping not with one role, however central it might be, but with all roles in which they face serious threat. For many caregivers, it is unrealistic to expect their own coping resources to be sufficient to stretch across the entire spectrum of life problems they may be facing. We would like again to emphasize a point that is probably obvious, namely, that the availability of formal services and informal support is no less important to success in coping with associated strains than with strains residing within the caregiver role.

There are caregivers who, despite valiant efforts, have been psychologically and physically assaulted by their ordeal. This tempts us to wonder if any attempt to cope with a role that harbors as many hardships as caregiving is not doomed to defeat at the outset. On the other hand, we are led to marvel at the power of coping when we observe the many caregivers who maintain vigor and determination in the midst of the continuous demands that beset them.

At some point we must move beyond asking what coping strategies caregivers use and which of them seem to be effective and to ask, instead, under what *conditions* particular coping strategies may or may not be effective. The two conditions we have emphasized as regulating the efficacy of coping are, first, the formal and informal social resources that are combined with individual coping and, second, the range and intensity of the associated strains. On prima facie grounds alone, each of these appears quite capable of governing the outcomes of individual coping.

Conclusions

Alzheimer's disease and other similarly debilitating illnesses associated with old age are destined to become more common as old age itself becomes more common. Just as predictably, an increasingly large number of people will be cast into the role of caregiver. Most of them, moreover, will be family members—spouses and adult children—who will bear the brunt of the role while providing care in the household. It might be noted in passing that caregiving rather strikingly affirms the persisting power of family bonds and commitments and belies the notion that our contemporary society is directed to narcissistic pursuits. At any rate, it behooves us to identify those circumstances that enable people to respond to the endless needs of others with minimal damage to themselves.

Coping represents one of these circumstances. Unfortunately, our ability to recognize how people cope with caregiver stress is helped only to a limited extent by our recognition of how people cope with other problems. While the functional character of coping transcends situational boundaries, if we want to know the behavioral repertoires of people as they cope with a situation, it is necessary to look specifically at that situation. Coping, in other words, is inseparable from the situational contexts in which it occurs and the threats and strains that reside in those contexts.

The pilot interviews we conducted were designed both to examine the interiors of the caregiver role—that is, the role as perceived by the caregiver—and the ways that people attempt to deal with the demands of the role. We found several features of the role that make it stressful, indeed. However, we also found a varied and extensive array of coping responses to these demands. Additional work is needed before we shall be able to know which constellations of responses are most effective. Nevertheless, as a group, caregivers are clearly not passively resigned to their unchangeable fates but, instead, are actively and creatively engaged in their own survival as well as that of the patient.

The formation of social policies regarding caregiving should not assume that the caregivers' own coping resources can long sustain them in the role, however energetic and creative they may be. These policies need to contribute to the economic and social resources that are the necessary adjuncts to individual coping. Moreover, policymakers need to take a broad perspective on the life of the caregiver. If they focus exclusively on the caregiver role, they could very well neglect other, associated problems that also beset caregivers. It is a tall order, but one worth filling. Its payoffs are in the economic well-being of the society, the health of the caregiver, and the humanitarian care received by the patient.

References

Aneshensel, C.S., and Huba, G. Depression, alcohol use, and smoking over one year: A four-wave longitudinal causal model. *Journal of Abnormal Psychology* 92(2):134-150, 1983.

Catalano, R., and Dooley, D. Health effects of economic instability: A test of economic stress hypothesis. *Journal of Health and Social Behavior* 24:46-60, 1983.

Lazarus, R.S., and Folkman, S. Coping and adaptation. In: Gentry, W.D., ed. *The Handbook of Behavioral Medicine.* New York: Guilford, 1984. pp. 282-325.

Lazarus, R. *Psychological Stress and the Coping Process.* New York: McGraw-Hill, 1966.

Menaghan, E. Measuring coping effectiveness: A panel analysis of marital problems and coping efforts. *Journal of Health and Social Behavior* 23(3):220-234, 1982.

Niederehe, G., and Fruge, E. Dementia and family dynamics: Clinical research issues. *Journal of Geriatric Psychiatry* 17:21-56, 1984.

Pearlin, L.I. Role strains and personal stress. In: Kaplan, H.B., ed. *Psychosocial Stress: Trends in Research and Theory.* New York: Academic Press, 1983.

Pearlin, L.I., and Aneshensel, C. Coping and social supports: Their functions and applications. In: Aiken, L.H., and Mechanic, D., eds. *Applications of Social Science to Clinical Medicine and Health.* New Brunswick, NJ: Rutgers University Press, 1986.

Pearlin, L.I.; Lieberman, M.L.; Menaghan, E.; and Mullan, J. The stress process. *Journal of Health and Social Behavior* 22:337-356, 1981.

Pearlin, L.I, and Lieberman, M.L. The social sources of emotional distress. In: Simmons, R., ed. *Research in Community and Mental Health.* Greenwich, CT: JAI Press, 1969. pp. 217-248.

Pearlin, L.I., and Schooler, C. The structure of coping. *Journal of Health and Social Behavior* 19:2-21, 1968.

Pearlin, L.I., and Radabaugh, C.W. Economic strains and the coping functions of alcohol. *American Journal of Sociology* 82:652-663, 1966.

Rabins, P.V.; Mace, N.L.; and Lucas, M.J. Impact of dementia on the family. *JAMA* 243:333-335, 1982.

Taylor, S.E. Adjustment to threatening events: A theory of cognitive adaptation. *American Psychologist* 38:1161-1173, 1983.

Valliant, G.E. *Adaptation to Life*. Boston: Little, Brown, 1967.

Wilder, D.E.; Tenes, J.A.; and Bennett, R.G. Family burdens and dementia. In: Mayeaux, R., and Rosen, W.G., eds. *The Dementias*. New York: Raven Press, 1983.

Zarit, S.; Reeves, K.; and Bach-Peterson, J. Relatives of impaired elderly: Correlates of feelings of burden. *Gerontologist* 20:649-655, 1980.

Chapter 8

Depression and Other Negative Affects in Family Caregivers

Dolores Gallagher, Ph.D., Amy Wrabetz,
Steven Lovett, Ph.D., Susan Del Maestro, Ph.D.,
and Jonathon Rose, M.S.

In this chapter, we review what is known about the negative emotions, including depression, anger, and anxiety, experienced by family caregivers. We also present some data from our own ongoing longitudinal research regarding this issue. The chapter closes by raising unanswered questions and suggesting future research needs.

Our aim is to underscore the importance of careful assessment and treatment of caregivers' emotional status as one critical, but often neglected, aspect of their well-being. Families having relatives diagnosed with dementia of the Alzheimer's type (DAT) live in an atmosphere of emotional ups and downs (Power and Courtice 1983; Zarit et al. 1985); learning to understand and cope with these emotions is a continual struggle for most.

Common Negative Emotions in Family Caregivers

Much has been written from a clinical perspective about the emotional distress that typifies DAT caregivers. For example, the U.S. Department of Health and Human Services Secretary's Task Force on Alzheimer's Disease (1984) stated that the extremely debilitating,

NOTE: Preparation of this chapter was supported in part by grants MH37196-04 and MH40041-03 (Alzheimer's Disease Clinical Research Center) from the National Institute of Mental Health, and by grant #AG04572 from the National Institute on Aging.

218

chronic nature of DAT places tremendous burdens on family caregivers, especially in terms of altered lifestyles (including social isolation); psychological problems such as stress, anxiety, and depression; and stress-induced physical problems such as high blood pressure (p. 48). However, few references were cited to provide empirical data to support these clinical observations.

Similarly, Oliver and Bock (1985) said that caring for a person with DAT places "an enormous emotional burden" on the caregiver, leading to responses such as denial, anger, guilt, self-pity, and depression. These negative emotions are thought to exacerbate the difficulties of caring for the relative while, at the same time, causing acute discomfort to caregivers themselves. A similar message is given by Powell and Courtice (1983), who devote chapters to denial, anger, depression, and guilt in their popular self-help book for DAT family caregivers.

Other researchers have found that precisely these emotional stresses associated with caregiving are the most difficult to deal with, compared to the physical or financial aspects of the situation (Cantor 1983; Cicirelli 1981; George and Gwyther 1986). George and Gwyther's (1986) survey of 510 caregivers of memory-impaired older adults is particularly compelling in this regard. They found that patient illness characteristics were minimally related to caregiver well-being, while the presence of symptoms of stress, negative affects, and low life satisfaction were related.

A unique feature of their study was the comparison of caregiver data with normative information available from several surveys of older adults' well-being, using essentially the same measures. This comparison showed that, in terms of physical health, caregivers did not use more medical services or rate their health worse than random community samples. However, wide discrepancies appeared on the mental health indicators. Caregivers averaged nearly three times as many stress symptoms as the other samples, along with low levels of affect balance and life satisfaction. From these data, George and Gwyther (1986) concluded that "caregivers are an at-risk population who are especially vulnerable to emotional discomfort" (p. 259).

Still others, studying mainly DAT caregivers, found that caregiving appears to produce negative effects on the mental health of family members, including development of symptoms such as resentment and guilt (York and Calsyn 1977), low morale (Fengler and Goodrich 1979), feelings of burden (Zarit et al. 1980; Zarit and Zarit 1982; Zarit et al. 1986), and depression and anxiety (Coppel et al. 1985; Gallagher et al. 1986; Kahan et al. 1985; Snyder and Keefe 1985; Rabins et al. 1982). Severe depression, leading to psychiatric hospitalization, was reported by Goldman and Luchins (1984) for three spouses of demented partners subsequent to the increasing burden of care they

faced. Although this outcome is not frequently reported in the literature, it is noteworthy that these three cases occurred within 6 months
in the authors' clinic. They suggest that severe depressions may be
more common than we realize in DAT caregivers, and aggressive treatment may be needed if the affected individuals are to care for their
demented partners more effectively.

One of the earliest studies on the prevalence of these negative affects in DAT caregivers was done by Rabins et al. (1982), who surveyed the primary caregivers of a group of demented patients and
found that 87 percent reported chronic depression, fatigue, and/or
anger when asked about their emotional state. Similarly, Snyder and
Keefe (1985) reported on a survey conducted by the Older Women's
League that found that 47 percent of the sample of 117 DAT caregivers
endorsed feelings of tension, anxiety, burn-out, and/or self-doubt, and
22 percent specifically stated they had problems with depression.
While these data are impressive, a stronger argument is made when
more standardized measures of depression are used (rather than subjective rating scales). When this was done, studies found much higher
rates of depression among DAT caregivers than among the general
aging population. Two studies addressed this point directly.

First, in a study by Coppel et al. (1985), 68 Alzheimer's caregivers
were interviewed by trained clinicians using a slightly abbreviated
version of the Schedule for Affective Disorders and Schizophrenia
(SADS) (Endicott and Spitzer 1978). This interview is considered the
"gold standard" in psychiatric research on affective disorders; its usefulness and appropriateness with older adults are reviewed in Gallagher (1986a). Information from the SADS is used to formulate
diagnoses of depressive disorders based on the Research Diagnostic
Criteria (RDC) (Spitzer et al. 1978), which is similar to DSM-III criteria
(American Psychiatric Association 1980) but in some ways more strin-
gent; for that reason, RDC criteria are commonly used by clinical
researchers.

Coppel et al. (1985) found that 27 caregivers currently met the
criteria: one had a major depressive disorder, and 26 had minor or
intermittent depressive disorders at the time of the interview (Jo
Becker, personal communication, 1985). Thus, 40 percent were clinically depressed.

The most recent data from NIMH's Epidemiological Catchment
Area (ECA) survey indicated that for both 6-month and lifetime
prevalence, between 1 and 2 percent of persons over age 65 at three
participating study sites (New Haven, Baltimore, and St. Louis)
qualified for the diagnosis of major depressive episode. In addition,
between 1 and 3 percent met criteria for dysthymic disorder, which
is equivalent to chronic depression. For both types of diagnosis,

women had higher prevalence than men (see Myers et al. 1984 for further information on the 6-month prevalence data; see also Robins et al. 1984 for lifetime prevalence data).

Blazer and colleagues, reporting on an older sample (as part of the same ECA study in the Piedmont area of North Carolina) found that 27 percent of more than 1,300 adults 60 years of age and older reported current depressive symptoms. However, only 0.8 percent met criteria for major depression and only 2 percent for dysthymia. The remainder experienced mild dysphoria and/or other symptoms of depression, but not of sufficient magnitude to reach a diagnosis (Blazer et al. in press).

From these data, it is apparent that the prevalence reported by Coppel et al. (1985) for depressive disorders in DAT caregivers was very significantly higher than rates in the general older population. Part of this discrepancy may be due to the nature of the assessment process: Coppel et al. (1985) used the SADS interview whereas the ECA study used the Diagnostic Interview Schedule (DIS) (Robins et al. 1981). No data have been published on the validity or reliability of the DIS with elders, and it has been criticized for some of the content (particularly the extensive sections on sociopathy, alcoholism, and drug abuse) that may be offensive to the current cohort of older adults (Gallagher 1986a). Thus, the DIS may tend to underreport the prevalence of depression in older persons. Nevertheless, the large discrepancy between these rates—and others previously published by Gurland (1976) and Blazer and Williams (1980)—and the rates found in caregivers probably cannot adequately be accounted for by differences in how depression was assessed.

Second, pilot work in our laboratory at the Palo Alto Veterans Administration Medical Center, using the SADS interview and RDC criteria, found prevalence of depressive disorders in both Alzheimer's and non-Alzheimer's caregivers to be closer to Coppel's data than the ECA data (Gallagher et al. 1986). We found that about 25 percent of DAT caregivers were diagnosable as being in a current major or minor depressive episode, while an additional 26 percent had depressive features that were present but not sufficient to be diagnosed (total N at that time was 39). Results of this work with a somewhat larger sample is reported below.

Finally, Kahan et al. (1985) used the Zung Self-Rating Depression Scale (Zung 1965) to measure pre/post change in a cognitive-behaviorally oriented group intervention program offered to 40 DAT caregivers. They noted that 18 of the 40 scored above 50 on the scale at the outset; this is the usual cutoff used to signify a clinical level of depression. Thus, 45 percent of these caregivers were at least somewhat depressed.

Also, Kahan et al. (1985) found a significant decrease in symptoms of depression on the Zung scale from pre to post, suggesting that the intervention was helpful to participants and that depression could be alleviated through relatively inexpensive means. This latter finding agrees with our own experience conducting intervention research with family caregivers; a significant reduction in pre/post depression can be achieved through psychoeducationally oriented small group interventions (Gallagher et al. 1986).

Interestingly, no other common emotions (such as anger, irritability, frustration, anxiety, or fear) that one observes clinically when working with DAT caregivers have been systematically measured, using standardized instruments, in this group. With the exception of very brief mention of the fact that hostility and anxiety were assessed in the DAT caregivers studied by Becker's group (which is noted in a separate publication, Pagel et al. 1985), no other published reports could be found that assessed these emotions in measurable and/or standardized ways. It is impossible at present to know, in an epidemiological sense, just how common the full spectrum of negative affects is in DAT caregivers. While clinical experience suggests that such feelings are quite common (cf. Powell and Courtice 1983; Zarit et al. 1985), researchers in this field have been slow to address the issue.

A final point concerns the fact that negative emotions may be experienced and/or expressed differently by male and female DAT caregivers. For example, Snyder and Keefe (1985) asked about the types of services used by the caregivers surveyed and found that at least one type of caregiver service was being used by over 80 percent of this sample. Women used mainly counseling or support groups (presumably to deal with emotional issues) whereas the male caregivers most often acquired homemaker or home nursing services. Snyder and Keefe (1985) speculated that males have been socialized to be independent of others and emotionally restrained; however, they do seem to experience the same kinds of negative emotions that female caregivers do. How these feelings are handled is an important, and poorly researched, topic.

Other recent surveys found a strong relationship between caregivers' mental health status and the eventual institutional placement of the relative. In a study of 152 DAT caregivers, Chenoweth and Spencer (1986) found that 72 percent gave as the primary reason for institutionalization their feeling of being overwhelmed. Similarly, Colerick and George (1986) found that high caregiver stress was a very significant predictor of subsequent institutionalization in a sample of 209 caregivers who were studied longitudinally. In fact, caregiver well-being and caregiver characteristics (e.g., relationship to patient) were more significant predictors than patient characteristics (e.g., extent of disability or amount of care required) in both studies.

In summary, numerous reports in the literature suggest that caregivers have to cope with a high frequency of negative affects. Relatively strong data exist indicating that clinical depression, in particular, is quite common. Other studies, based primarily on clinical observation or very broad surveys, have found that anger, resentment, frustration, and anxiety are also typical. These are reported for both DAT and non-DAT caregivers and appear to be related to the decision for institutional placement. Thus, increasing our understanding of what these emotions are, and how they can be managed, should be a high priority for those interested in maintenance of caregivers' mental health and delay or prevention of permanent institutional placement whenever possible.

Current Research

For the past 3 years, our research group has been attempting to make a systematic study of the frequency and intensity of at least some of the negative emotions commonly associated with being a caregiver.

Sample and Methodology

We have examined data from a volunteer sample of caregivers who sought treatment for distress related to their caregiving situation in a psychoeducational program conducted by our center. The focus of the program is on improving skills for coping with caregiving, such as increasing time for pleasant events and learning effective ways to problem-solve. To date, 190 family caregivers have enrolled in the program; somewhat more than half (N = 112) were caring for a relative with Alzheimer's disease or a related disorder with significant cognitive impairment. The remainder (N = 78) were caring for a relative with heart disease, bleeding disorders, severe mobility problems, and the like, but with no evidence of cognitive impairment. Table 8-1 provides demographic data for these two subgroups.

The two samples were very comparable in terms of ages of the caregiver and care-receiver, educational level, caregivers' self-reported physical health status, and proportion of husbands, wives, sons, daughters, and others who were fulfilling the caregiving role. In terms of length of time as a caregiver, there was a trend for those of

Table 8-1. Sociodemographic information for caregivers

Variable	Cognitive status of relative					
	Impairment (N=112)		No impairment (N=78)		t test	p
	Mean	SD	Mean	SD		
Caregiver's age	59.5	11.1	58.8	11.3	.415	.679
Relative's age	74.8	11.3	74.7	11.6	.087	.931
Caregiver's education	14.3	2.0	14.1	2.4	.516	.606
Relative's education	11.9	3.6	12.3	3.2	.721	.472
Number health problems[a]	1.54	1.59	1.64	1.50	.437	.662
Number medicines used[a]	2.19	2.11	2.14	1.75	.160	.873
Caregiver's health rating[b]	3.17	.64	3.04	.67	1.35	.176
Time as caregiver (months)	45.1	52.7	59.9	58.3	1.73	.085

	Percent	N	Percent	N
Relationship to relative				
Husband	12.5	14	15.4	12
Wife	38.4	43	35.9	28
Son	6.3	7	7.7	6
Daughter	38.4	43	35.9	28
Other	4.5	5	5.1	4
Marital status				
Married	69.6	78	73.1	57
Single	30.4	34	26.9	21
Caregiver gender				
Female	83.0	93	80.8	63
Male	17.0	19	19.2	15

[a] *pertains to caregiver;* [b] *1=Poor, 2=Fair, 3=Good, 4=Excellent*

the noncognitively impaired group to have been caregivers longer (about 5 years versus a little under 4 years for those caring for a cognitively impaired relative). Gender and marital status were comparable between the two groups.

As has been reported in many prior studies, females comprised the majority of respondents (about 82 percent). They were well-educated, averaging 2 years beyond high school, and they were in reasonably good health (the self-rating of overall health was in the "good" to "excellent" range, with an average of between one and two current health problems and about two regularly taken medications in each subgroup).

Prevalence of clinical levels of depression in these caregivers was determined by the SADS interview and application of RDC criteria, and a widely used self-report measure of depression, the Beck Depression Inventory (BDI; Beck et al. 1961). The BDI has excellent reliability and validity with older adults (see Gallagher 1986*b* for review). The scale contains 21 categories of symptoms and attitudes; each category describes a specific manifestation of depression (cognitive, behavioral, or vegetative). Each category has four response choices; respondents indicate which is most accurate (the usual timeframe is the past week, including today).

Results

Depression. Table 8-2 shows that in both groups a comparable number of caregivers was clinically depressed—46 percent and 47 percent for the cognitively impaired and noncognitively impaired groups, respectively. Of these, about 25 percent in each group were experiencing a current episode of major depression; about 20 percent were experiencing a current episode of minor depression; and another 2 percent and 6 percent, respectively, had been depressed on and off for the 2 years preceding their interview. These rates are very much higher than what would be expected in an older population in general (see Blazer et al. in press; Blazer and Williams 1980). Most prior studies, using similar methodology and criteria for diagnosing depression, reported rates between 1 percent and 10 percent in the general older adult population. Thus, clinical depression is, unfortunately, all too common among caregivers—both those caring for an Alzheimer's disease relative, and those caring for someone with severe physical disabilities but without cognitive impairment.

Table 8-2 also indicates the results from the self-report measure. It can be seen that, among caregivers caring for a cognitively impaired relative, there was somewhat greater agreement between self-reported depression and interviewer-assessed depression than among caregivers of the noncognitively impaired. Although the overall mean scores were lower for the BDI than would be anticipated in both groups, given the high level of clinical depression, there were no significant differences between them in patterns of response on the BDI.

These findings about the frequency of depression are somewhat surprising, even though this was totally a help-seeking sample, be-

Table 8-2. Prevalence of depression in caregivers grouped according to cognitive status of relative

	Impairment Percent	N	No impairment Percent	N
Diagnosis by clinical interview using the SADS				
Major depressive episode	23.5	24	26.4	19
Minor depressive episode	20.6	21	15.3	11
Intermittent depressive disorder ..	2.0	2	5.6	4
Not depressed	53.9	55	52.7	38
Total		102		72
Diagnosis by self-rating using the BDI				
Moderate to severe depression (score > 16)	23.4	25	17.1	13
Mild (score 11 to 17)	25.2	27	18.4	14
Not depressed (score < 11)	51.4	55	64.5	49
Overall BDI mean (SD)	11.2 (7.3)		9.7 (6.8)*	
Total		107		76

SADS = Schedule for Affective Disorders and Schizophrenia
BDI = Beck Depression Inventory
* t test = 1.41, p > .10

cause our interview team took special care in evaluating symptoms of depression so as not to have a spuriously elevated rate. On the basis of earlier pilot work, our clinical research team adopted an explicit decision rule to help us be as accurate as possible in this regard. We wanted to only attribute symptoms to depression when their presence and/or intensity was not explainable on the basis of the caregiving situation itself. For example, insomnia may be considered a "normal" part of caregiving when an Alzheimer's patient is in a more advanced stage of the disease, with frequent nighttime wandering, since the caregiver cannot afford to sleep soundly. However, should insomnia be regarded as "normal" if it occurs in caregivers whose impaired relative does not wander at night? Similarly, low energy may be due to keeping up with all the chores and errands that are part of caregiving, or it can be due to depression. It is more likely to reflect the latter if the person is unable to "get going" versus being on the go so much that fatigue (and subsequent low energy, often for taking care of oneself) results.

Thus, our primary decision rule involved evaluating whether symptoms typically associated with depression were, in fact, explainable as part and parcel of the caregiving situation, or if they occurred over and above what would be expected for someone in that role. We decided not to count as "present" those symptoms in the former category and to count only those symptoms that, in the judgment of the interviewer and the subject, were in the latter category. This rather conservative position should permit few "false positives." Yet, despite this method, around 45 percent of the sample were diagnosed as depressed (and self-reported this as well). It should be noted that adequate interrater reliability was achieved among the various interviewers. Their average percent agreement across diagnostic categories ranged from 90 to 95, as evaluated through random selection and rating of SADS interviews, both "live" and on audiotapes.

Other negative affects. We also examined items on the SADS that asked about emotions such as anger (both angry feelings and angry expressions), anxiety, worry, etc. Although these affects were not studied as thoroughly (because the SADS contains, at most, 1 or 2 items about each, in contrast to the 15 or so about depressive symptoms), we were able to draw some conclusions about the frequency with which they were endorsed by caregivers.

Table 8-3 presents the "top 25" SADS items, ranked according to the frequency with which they were rated at a clinical level or beyond, for the two groups. (Rankings were made on the basis of the percentage clinically endorsing the item among caregivers of the cognitively impaired.) A clinical level on a SADS item refers to a rating of 3 or greater on a 7-point intensity scale for the item. This way of examining the data indicates which affects are prominent among family caregivers.

These caregivers clearly experienced a wide range of affects. Caregivers of the cognitively impaired group endorsed angry feelings to a very large extent: about 68 percent of them said they felt anger "more than called for by the situation." Those with higher ratings on the item were affirming that they felt very angry most or all of the time. Although fewer caregivers of the noncognitively impaired group endorsed having a problem with angry feelings, this was still the most frequently indicated negative affect for them as well.

Depressed feelings, worrying, discouragement, expression of anger, and guilt and anxiety feelings comprised the remainder of the top 10 negative affects. Two somatic symptoms of depression (low

227

Table 8-3. Prevalence of negative affects and depressive symptoms in caregivers based on proportions of SADS items rated at clinical levels*

SADS item	Cognitive status of relative	
	Impaired (N=102) Percent	Not impaired (N=72) Percent
1. Angry feelings	67.75	53.52
2. Depressed feelings	46.08	46.48
3. Worrying	45.10	39.44
4. Discouragement	44.12	42.25
5. Expression of anger	41.18	40.00
6. Lacks energy	37.25	35.21
7. Sleep disturbance	32.35	33.80
8. Somatic anxiety	31.37	26.76
9. Guilt feelings	29.41	29.58
10. Anxiety feelings	27.72	21.13
11. Weight gain	26.47	21.43
12. Reduced concentration	26.47	28.17
13. Inadequacy feelings	25.49	21.13
14. Social withdrawal	22.55	22.54
15. Lower interest/pleasure	19.61	14.08
16. Terminal insomnia	19.61	23.94
17. Increased appetite	16.67	16.90
18. Health worries	15.69	9.86
19. Indecisiveness	12.75	12.68
20. Suicide ideation	8.82	7.04
21. Low reactivity	7.84	4.35
22. Panic attacks	6.86	8.45
23. Alcohol dependence	6.86	1.41
24. Decreased appetite	4.90	8.45
25. Sleeps more	4.90	2.82

* *Clinical level refers to a rating of 3 or more.*

energy and sleep disturbance) were also endorsed by more than 30 percent of both groups. Ranking of the affects between the two groups was virtually identical; the Spearman rank order correlation coefficient was 0.94. This very strong correlation indicates that caregivers, in general, will commonly experience similar negative affects—although caregivers of those with cognitive impairment will more often be angry about it.

Next, the rankings of these caregivers were compared to a sample of noncaregiving older adults who were normal volunteers given the SADS interview in another study (Dessonville et al. 1982). Although the pattern of rankings between caregivers of the cognitively impaired relatives and the noncaregiver volunteers was similar, the magnitude of the correlation was not as high (rho = 0.67). The difference between these two correlation coefficients was then tested using Fisher's z test and was statistically significant ($t=3.70$; $p < .01$), indicating that the two groups of caregivers we have been reporting on were more similar to each other than the caregivers of the cognitively impaired were to the noncaregiving group.

Clear differences between caregivers and noncaregivers in endorsement patterns appeared on items about negative affect, including depressed mood, discouragement, worrying, and somatic and psychic anxiety, with more caregivers endorsing these items at or beyond the clinical level of distress. Unfortunately, data were not retrievable for the angry feelings and angry expression items in the noncaregiving sample. However, the same general finding would probably hold, namely, that caregivers are more likely to endorse these than noncaregivers of approximately the same age and sociodemographic background.

Finally, looking at the sample of caregivers of the cognitively impaired only, we wanted to determine how these negative affects clustered together in this group. We found that 28 percent of them were high (e.g., at or above the clinical level on the SADS item) on items pertaining to the three major negative affects we examined: dysphoria, anger, and anxiety. An additional 25 percent were high on two of the three (dysphoria and anger). This suggests that the negative affects of depression and anger, in particular, tend to cluster in caregivers. This is an interesting finding and challenges most notions about how depression originates and is maintained. It also suggests that psychologically oriented treatments for caregivers may need to focus on *both* these disturbing affects without assuming an independence between them. While this poses a theoretical challenge (particularly to psychodynamic theorists, who would argue that an inverse relationship between anger and dysphoria would be more common), further understanding of the dynamics operating here will be a valu-

229

able addition to our conceptualizations about depression and about caregiving.

Summary of key findings. Through study of the responses of this large sample of caregivers who were seeking assistance to cope better with their situation, we have learned several things about the nature and frequency of negative affects in family caregivers. First, depressive disorders (both acute and chronic) are very common. As determined by the SADS/RDC system, 46 percent and 47 percent of those interviewed met criteria for clinical depression among those caring for cognitively impaired and noncognitively impaired relatives, respectively. Although conservative decision rules were used during the interview process in an attempt to minimize false positives, these proportions are *much* higher than would be expected in a sample of older adults randomly selected from the population. Second, their self-reports of depression, as indexed by the BDI, tended to be in reasonably good agreement with the interview data, although there was less agreement among those caring for a relative who was cognitively intact. This may be due to the fact that some caregivers, at least, need to "look good" on measures of psychological distress because of anxiety about acknowledging their own distress. For many, the interview situation seemed to provide more of an opportunity to be open and frank about their difficulties than completing the self-report questionnaire did.

Third, we found that anger is, by far, the most common negative affect among caregivers of Alzheimer's disease and related disorder victims. Sixty-seven percent of this sample of more than 100 endorsed frequent feelings of anger, compared to only 46 percent endorsing dysphoria, and fewer endorsing worrying, feelings of guilt and anxiety, and overt expression of their anger. Although caregivers of the physically disabled also endorsed the same general ranking of affects, they acknowledged less anger. Yet, for them as well, angry feelings were the most prominent negative emotion that was expressed. This suggests that the combination of anger and depression may be more common than has been realized among family caregivers, who may need help coping with both kinds of feelings to successfully maintain themselves in their role.

A fourth finding is that somatic symptoms of depression (e.g., insomnia, low energy, and the like) were less common than the negative affects we have been discussing. In fact, worry and discouragement (which can be viewed as cognitive/emotional accompaniments of depressed mood) were more common in DAT caregivers than were somatic symptoms. Nevertheless, problems with sleeping, eating, and maintaining an adequate energy level were reported by more than 30 percent of the sample—not a trivial number. This suggests that not only psychological assistance, but also participation in programs emphasizing health care (e.g., nutrition and exercise) could potentially be very beneficial for DAT caregivers.

Implications for Treatment

The high frequency of depression in family caregivers should not necessarily be cause for alarm, since a number of effective treatment intervention programs are available, and some have already been used with DAT caregivers.

Cognitive/behavioral therapies, as outlined by Rush (1982) and Thompson, Davies, Gallagher, and Krantz (1986), were shown to be effective both in the short and long run with younger and older persons in a depressive episode, some of whom were family caregivers. Zarit et al. (1985) gave clear and detailed information about how to apply cognitive/behavioral theory and procedures to DAT caregivers, using individual and group counseling and family meetings in an integrated approach to the problem. Effective use of brief psychodynamic psychotherapy, both with depressed elders in general and with caregivers in particular, was reported by Lazarus and Groves (in press) and Groves, Lazarus, Newton, Frankel, Butmann, and Ripeckyj (1984).

Judicious use of antidepressant medication can be very helpful, used either independently or adjunctively with counseling (see Veith 1982 for discussion of important considerations when doing pharmacotherapy with older persons). Several studies have reported that use of psychoeducational programs (e.g., classes in "Coping with Caregiving") can measurably reduce depression in family caregivers (Gallagher et al. 1986; Kahan et al. 1985).

Pinkston and Linsk (1984) provided data on the efficacy of behavioral training for the caregiver to reduce problematic behaviors in the DAT patient, including symptoms of depression, and Teri and Uomoto (1986) described the reduction in caregiver depression that accompanies improvement in mood in the DAT patient. Finally, numerous papers on the value of caregiver support groups have appeared in the literature. Although most do not address the issue of how these groups affect depression per se, the general conclusion is that support groups help in the expression and management of negative affects (see Gallagher 1985 for a review of this issue).

Much less literature has accumulated in gerontology on therapeutic interventions for management of anger and its as-

231

sociated feelings and behaviors. Given that caregiving is often viewed as a normative family stress (cf. Brody 1985) that causes both interpersonal and intrapsychic tensions, and given the realities of the problems that typify a victim of Alzheimer's disease, it should not be surprising that anger is a significant part of the daily life of caregivers and of their clinical profiles. However, more conceptual work is needed on this topic since there is no taxonomy for anger disorders and no hard and fast way to draw the line between normal and abnormal "amounts" of anger. Thus, it may be helpful to speculate upon possible sources of caregiver anger, whom it is likely to be directed at, what distinguishes caregivers who experience clinical levels of anger (and depression) from those who do not, and how to intervene.

One explanation for the presence of clinical levels of anger in caregivers can be found in what Burns (1981) described as the "just world" hypothesis. Most individuals form and carry with them expectations and goals for each stage of life. They may believe that if they work hard and fulfill "their side of the bargain," they will then be rewarded with what they deserve—their expectations will be met and their plans realized. When a close relative is diagnosed with Alzheimer's disease, this belief in a "just world" is shattered. Caregivers must abruptly come face to face with the fact that their plans, goals, and expectations for this point in their lives may never be met. Specific thoughts such as: "It's not fair that this is happening to me now"; "I don't deserve this, I've been a good person my whole life"; and "I've been cheated" probably arise. These thoughts of injustice, in turn, stimulate feelings of anger. Other caregivers may view the illness of their relative as a punishment they deserve because of past mistakes. This belief can obviously lead to feelings of guilt and depression.

Another source of negative feelings among caregivers may be the sense of loss of control over their lives. A dilemma is intrinsic to the caregiving situation: caregivers see the Alzheimer's victim suffering and in need of help and yet are unable to remediate the situation. Help brings only temporary relief or amelioration of symptoms; the underlying problem remains the same. Also, if caregivers view their task as one of bringing about positive *changes* in the Alzheimer's patient's condition, they set themselves up for failure and are likely to be frustrated and angry as well-intentioned efforts fail. Emotionally healthy caregivers may be able to differentiate between their control over other aspects of their lives and their lack of control over curing their relative, and come to accept the latter rather than react against it.

The quality of the relationship between caregiver and demented relative prior to the patient's illness may also explain the anger some caregivers feel (e.g., unresolved issues between the two individuals may surface). Those who have a history of a good relationship will probably have less difficulty with anger, which may be temporary and quickly pass; those with a poor history may have established angry exchanges as part of their relationship over the years, so that new anger arising because of he demented person's behavior is seen as continuation of an already established pattern.

On the other side of the coin are the caregivers who are angry because the Alzheimer's victim has deserted them by no longer being the person the caregiver knows. Caregivers often describe this kind of anger (when they first experience it) as irrational. Yet this reaction is very common as Alzheimer's disease progresses. It is particularly widespread in the later stages of the disease when the patient's personality is gone and the "anticipatory grief" reaction of the caregiver has begun (Tensink and Mahler 1984). However, in the meantime, caregivers often feel guilty about these kinds of angry feelings; they may turn their anger inward, causing negative self-evaluation and depressed fellings. This, in turn, may lead to further anger at the Alzheimer's victim who keeps them trapped in the situation, thus causing a self-perpetuating cycle of anger > guilt > depression > more anger > more guilt, and so forth. Future research may test this hypothesis by investigating the sequence of emotions that caregivers experience.

Several behaviorally based intervention programs for anger management were reviewed by Novaco (1985). These included classical and operant conditioning approaches (used with acting-out children and adolescents, in the prison system, and with socially awkward adults) and the social skills/assertion training approach, which uses behavioral techniques such as modeling and role playing to teach appropriate skills for handling interpersonal conflict. Novaco developed his own program (1975) based on the notion that cognitive factors (particularly expectations and appraisals) determine anger. His program is best regarded as a cognitive/behavioral approach because he focuses on both thought processes and behavioral skill training. To the knowledge of the authors, his approach has not been used with family caregivers, although it certainly seems promising in that regard.

We recommend study of caregivers' cognitive distortions as well as their appraisal of threat and how to deal with it, so that ideas such as the "just world" hypothesis can be aired and challenged. Also, family caregivers most likely need to normalize a certain amount of the anger experienced. It is an appropriate emotion, given the situation, and the caregiver needs to recognize this so that the anger can be modulated. If it is denied, it cannot be worked with in any modality of therapy.

Although aggression is a central concept in psychodynamic therapy, little has been written within that framework specifically about treatment of the anger/aggression problems of adults. Behavior therapy programs were forerunners in this regard. One could speculate that anger toward an Alzheimer's relative could spring from early unresolved conflicts in the family, from the stresses of the role reversal that is occurring, and/or from challenges to one's self-esteem that are inherent in the powerlessness of the situation. These issues could be dealt with, using a psychodynamic psychotherapeutic model; of interest is the work of Horowitz and Kaltreider (1979) on time-limited dynamic therapy, which has recently been used to treat older adults experiencing bereavement reactions and episodic depressions (Horowitz et al. 1984; Thompson et al. in press). More research is needed on the efficacy of this approach with DAT caregivers.

A final point about how the data we reported relate to clinical practice concerns the somewhat lower prevalence of anxiety in the caregiving samples than in the normal volunteers. Given the constellation of anger, irritability, depression, worry, and discouragement regarding the future, one would expect anxiety to be highly endorsed as well. One very reasonable possibility is that the construct is not being well measured. Although a few SADS items would apply, no unique anxiety measures were used.

As noted in a recent review on the problems of measuring affect in older adults (Gallagher 1987), precious little data exist on the evaluation of anxiety disorders in the elderly. Also, no existing interview or self-report scales have published psychometric information for the elderly. Thus, these data must be viewed with caution. Anxiety may be a much more cardinal feature of the caregiving situation that we would learn more about if we approached the topic in a better way. For about a fourth of the DAT caregivers in our study, elevated anxiety *did* accompany high dysphoria and high anger; but for the majority, somatic signs of anxiety were particularly low, with psychic anxiety reported by only a little more than one-fourth of the samples.

Another possible explanation for these results is that caregivers live in an everyday world of almost chronic anxiety, which comes to be experienced as "second nature" and is not complained about. Given the ups and downs of the disease process and the fact that no one can exactly predict the course of deterioration for any given patient, this explanation is at least plausible, but clearly in need of further study.

234

Implications for Future Research

We hope the data reported here will stimulate considerable new research on the evaluation and treatment of the affective components of caregiving, for DAT caregivers in particular. Although we saw virtually no differences in patterns of affective distress between DAT and non-DAT caregivers in this research, we did see that caregivers were different in some measurable ways from their noncaregiving counterparts. Specifically, they more strongly endorsed symptoms of anger, dysphoria, discouragement, and related affective distress items. They seemed to have a much higher prevalence of depression than noncaregiving adults, along with elevated anger and, for some, anxiety.

However, these data must be interpreted with careful reference to the samples from which this set of information was obtained. Both the longitudinal ADCRC sample of DAT caregivers and the help-seeking sample composed of DAT and non-DAT caregivers contained well-educated persons (the average was 14 years of education) who were volunteering for these research and clinical service projects. The majority were self-referred, with a small percentage referred from other professionals. They were willing to complete a variety of interviews and questionnaires tapping their most personal feelings, and generally were very aware of the fact that their participation in the research was valuable to increase the knowledge base in this field. Thus, they were probably not the typical caregiver one finds in most community surveys. They were "responders"; nonresponders may have a very different psychological profile. Overall, they also rated their relationship with the care-receiver as "excellent"; those with very poor relationships probably did not volunteer for these types of research projects.

It will be very important to find out if these findings replicate with less well-educated caregivers and samples garnered in such a way that they are less obviously research volunteers. What about caregivers with a poor relationship with their Alzheimer's relatives? Will their affective distress manifest itself in the same ways? One would expect to find some differences based on variation in these factors in future research. Also, gender differences should be examined. We have too small a sample of male caregivers in the current project to make any statements on this topic, but a wealth of literature points to differences in the kinds of emotions men experience and how they handle them.

A related question for future research concerns how the pattern of affective distress, and the prevalence of depression, may *change* over the course of the disease. The rate of deterioration of the Alzheimer's relative is variable and erratic, so the caregiver never knows how long the patient will stay at any one level or when the patient may suddenly show drastic deterioration. It is reasonable to assume that the caregiver's emotional status will change as these peaks and valleys in the disease occur. Longitudinal research that carefully follows caregivers and patients through the entire course of the disease is really necessary to address this point in depth.

One could speculate (following the phase model proposed by Cohen et al. 1984) that levels of anger and depression vary as a function of how well the caregiver is coping overall at different plateaus in the disease process. In the early stage, for example, anger may be the most dominant emotion, whereas over time (and with increasing acceptance of realities), depression may become more prominent. If institutional placement is eventually needed, grief and guilt may take over as the major feelings the caregiver needs to cope with, perhaps accompanied by a sense of relief and freedom if the placement is reasonably successful. These hypothesized trends could be tested through longitudinal research that looked for nodal points of change, as well as for periods of relative stability, within the disease progression.

Controlled studies of the efficacy of various types of interventions are clearly needed. Cognitive/behavioral therapy is effective for reducing depression and other components of caregivers' affective distress. A variety of approaches within the overall cognitive/behavioral framework (including individual, group, and family modalities) can appropriately be studied. Short-term psychodynamic psychotherapy also appears to hold promise for DAT caregivers, as do various kinds of psychoeducational interventions. Medication and support groups are also widely used to help with affective ups and downs.

What is noteworthy is that no published studies exist at the present time on the comparative efficacy of any two or more of these approaches. The clinical literature has numerous examples of the effectiveness of each of them, but very few empirical studies have been done. Although intervention research is a costly and time-consuming process, it is also a very reasonable way to proceed. The major goal would be to determine if certain interventions are superior to others, either in the amount of time needed for improvement or in the kind of improvement generated.

A second important goal would be to identify which kinds of caregivers have a positive response to which kinds of interventions (e.g., emotionally distressed non-DAT caregivers may do as well with a medication and support group combination as they do in individual psychotherapy, whereas DAT caregivers may do better in psychotherapy than in other forms of treatment). This would involve careful study of individual difference variables (e.g., length of time as a caregiver, relationship to care-receiver, analysis of prior and current repertoire of coping strategies, and the like) to be as specific as possible when eventually recommending preferred mental health services for given subgroups of clients. This type of research would follow along the lines of the intervention research that has been going on in the psychotherapy field for some time. The reader is referred to a volume edited by Williams and Spitzer (1984) for a thorough review of this topic.

With family caregivers, some unique factors may have to be considered when conducting outcome research. For example, they may be unable to keep appointments on a regular basis—not because of "resistance" but because of caregiving emergencies at home. This may necessitate some changes in the structure of therapy so that the caregiver can be accommodated rather than dismissed from treatment (e.g., telephone counseling sessions to make up missed appointments).

Many caregivers do not have access to a respite-type program or to a paid or unpaid substitute caregiver who can monitor the Alzheimer's relative while they attend therapy or some other type of intervention program. Thus, programs may need to have a group of trained volunteers available to elder-sit while the caregiver attends sessions and/or be able to make referrals to low-cost sitters in the area. Such concerns do not typically fall within the purview of the psychotherapist or support group leader; however, it may be necessary to modify the usual roles and structures so that family caregivers can fully participate in the available treatment. Other unique aspects of intervention research with caregivers will come to light as the research proceeds.

Additional recommendations for the future involve research into measurement issues with family caregivers. Few valid and reliable measures of the predominant negative (and positive) emotions that older adults experience are available. Unless appropriate instrument development or refinement is undertaken, we will continue to have difficulty obtaining needed epidemiological and clinical data about the frequency and strength of these emotions.

In addition, we also need to broaden our concept of *what* is critical to measure in DAT caregivers. Most prior research has shied away from having caregivers complete a battery of interview or self-report measures, viewing this as an additional stress that might be inappropriate. Yet without a comprehensive battery of measures, many unanswered questions will remain. For example, we do not know the extent to which the experience of negative affects and/or depressive disorder can be offset by a strong repertoire of coping behaviors.

Since stress, coping, and emotional reactivity are so strongly interrelated in other groups (cf. Lazarus and Folkman 1984), they probably will be in DAT caregivers also. Study of the interrelationship of such variables as coping, burden, depression, anger, and anxiety should also be very fruitful.

We do not know how personality structure influences the style and effectiveness of caregivers' adaptation to their situations with minimal psychological distress. No published studies could be found that examined the personality structure of caregivers and/or attempted to relate these findings to mental health. Yet we must not lose sight of the fact that caregivers are human beings with full life histories and established personality styles than can predispose them to either effective or ineffective emotional responses to the situation. For example, how do childhood experiences with frail relatives affect later life decisions about caregiving? Does caregiving provide an opportunity for further growth through the resolution of old conflicts around "generativity" (see Erikson et al. 1986), or is nurturing the chronically ill too psychologically different from fostering the potential of young children? Do caregivers who experience a great deal of guilt and depression have a recognizable personality style (Rose 1984)? Do age-related changes in ego mastery (see Neugarten and Gutmann 1958) affect psychological readiness for caregiving?

To answer these kinds of questions, we have to recognize the need to incorporate the methodology of personality study into research on caregivers. One member of our research group (J. Rose) is doing this in a small substudy of female DAT caregivers. Using the Thematic Apperception Test (TAT) (Murray 1943) and the Shanan Sentence Completion Test (Shanan and Nissan 1961), he has begun to search for common and salient themes in the unconscious minds of caregivers. We hope this line of inquiry will help us understand how successful caregivers incorporate caregiving into the totality of their lives, and where unsuccessful caregivers get "stuck."

Our preliminary data suggest that strong identification with a devoted parent who put family before anything else may be one common element among unstressed caregivers. However, we have not collected enough data to say much more at present; we would encourage other researchers to incorporate this perspective into their work.

For those who prefer not to use projective measures to tap personality structure, a well-validated self-report measure of personality called the NEO personality inventory (Costa and McCrae 1985) is available. It yields scores for the domains of neuroticism, extroversion, openness to experience, antagonism, and conscientiousness. A large amount of research has been done with this instrument, and its predictive validity has been demonstrated with several samples of persons at risk for coronary heart disease (see Costa and McCrae in press). Thus, it seems to promise answers for some of the questions about correlates of caregivers' mental health. To our knowledge, it has not yet been used with this population.

At least two other factors undoubtedly exert an important influence on the emotional status of family caregivers: extent of social and familial support, and caregivers' actual or perceived physical health status. Much has been published on the stress-buffering role of social support in general adult populations (cf. Aneshensel and Stone 1982; Dean and Lin 1977), and some research has pointed to the importance of familial support for DAT caregivers' continuing to cope in their role (Horowitz 1985; Scott et al. 1986; Zarit and Zarit 1982). However, it is not known whether some optimal amount or type of social support will provide an effective buffer for the anger, dysphoria, and other negative affects we have been discussing in this chapter.

Even less is known about the interrelationship of caregivers' physical and mental health, and how problems in one area might lead to general or specific problems in the other. Pratt, Schmall, Wright, and Cleland (1985) surveyed 240 caregivers to study correlates of burden and found that perceived burden was significantly related to caregivers' self-reported overall physical health status; it was not related to such variables as caregiver age or membership in a support group. This study suggests that caregivers' health may be a very critical mediator of psychological distress. However, since depression, anger, and anxiety were not studied directly in that research (though they may be assumed to correlate highly with subjective burden), we do not know if health status and these emotional states are directly related.

The need for this type of research has been argued by Koin (this volume), particularly since caregiving so often results in stress, which in turn is implicated in the development and/or exacerbation of coronary heart disease and hypertension, two of the leading causes of death in this country. Thus, careful study of both the *actual* physical health status of caregivers and the impact of physical and mental health on each other seems to be a very important direction for future research. In fact, one might conclude this chapter by saying that the ideal programs of the future will be designed to maintain both the mental and physical health of caregivers. Caregivers need assistance to learn how to take better care of their psyches and their bodies; in all probability, only a truly comprehensive, multimodal approach to assessment and treatment will fulfill this need.

References

American Psychiatric Association. *Diagnostic and Statistical Manual of Mental Disorders*. 3d ed. Washington, DC: the Association, 1980.

Aneshensel, C., and Stone, J. Stress and depression: A test of the buffering model of social support. *Archives of General Psychiatry* 39:1392-1396, 1982.

Beck, A.T. *Depression: Clinical, Experimental, and Theoretical Aspects*. New York: Harper & Row, 1967. Republished as *Depression: Causes and Treatment*. Philadelphia: University of Pennsylvania Press, 1972.

Beck, A.T.; Ward, C.H.; Mendelson, M.; Mock, J.; and Erbaugh, J. An inventory for measuring depression. *Archives of General Psychiatry* 4:53-63, 1961.

Becker, D., and Williams, C.D. Epidemiology of dysphoria and depression in an elderly population. *American Journal of Psychiatry* 137:439-444, 1980.

Blazer, D.; Hughes, D.C.; and George, L. The epidemiology of depression in an elderly community population. *Gerontologist*, in press.

Brody, E.M. Parent care as a normative family stress. *Gerontologist* 25:19-29, 1985.

Burns, D. *Feeling Good: The New Mood Therapy*. New York: New American Library (Signet Books), 1981.

Cantor, M.H. Strain among caregivers: A study of experience in the United States. *Gerontologist* 23:597-604, 1983.

Chenoweth, B., and Spencer, B. Dementia: The experience of family caregivers. *Gerontologist* 26:267-272, 1986.

Cicirelli, V.G. *Helping Elderly Parents: The Role of Adult Children*. Boston: Auburn House, 1981.

Cohen, D.; Kennedy, G.; and Eisdorfer, C. Phases of change in the patient with Alzheimer's dementia: A conceptual dimension for defining health care management. *Journal of the American Geriatrics Society* 32:11-15, 1984.

Colerick, E.J., and George, L.K. Predictors of institutionalization among caregivers of patients with Alzheimer's disease. *Journal of the American Geriatrics Society* 34:493-498, 1986.

Coppel, D.B.; Burton, D.; Becker, J.; and Fiore, J. Relationships of cognitions associated with coping reactions to depression in spousal caregivers of Alzheimer's disease patients. *Cognitive Therapy and Research* 9:253-266, 1985.

Costa, P.T., and McCrae, R.R. *The NEO Personality Inventory Manual*. Odessa, FL: Psychological Assessment Resources, 1985.

Costa, P.T., and McCrae, R.R. Agreeableness vs. antagonism: Explication of a potential risk factor for CHD. *Journal of Personality*, in press.

Dean, A., and Lin, N. The stress-buffering role of social support. *The Journal of Nervous and Mental Disease* 165:403-417, 1977.

Dessonville, C.; Gallagher, D.; Thompson, L.W.; Finnell, K.; and Lewinsohn, P.M. Relation of age and health status of depressive symptoms in normal and depressed older adults. *Essence* 5:99-117, 1982.

Endicott, J., and Spitzer, R. A diagnostic interview for affective disorders and schizophrenia. *Archives of General Psychiatry* 35:837-844, 1978.

Erikson, E.H.; Erikson, J.M.; and Kivnick, H.Q. *Vital Involvement in Old Age*. New York: W.W. Norton, 1986.

Fengler, A.P., and Goodrich, N. Wives of elderly disabled men: The hidden patients. *Gerontologist* 19:175-183, 1979.

Gallagher, D. Intervention strategies to assist caregivers of frail elders: Current research status and future research directions. In: Lawton, M.P., and Maddox, G., eds. *Annual Review of Gerontology and Geriatrics*. Vol. 5. New York: Springer, 1985. pp. 249-282.

Gallagher, D. Assessment of depression by interview method and psychiatric rating scales. In: Poon, L.W.; Crook, T.; Davis, K.; Eisdorfer, C.; Gurland, B.; Kaszniak, A.; and Thompson, L.W., eds. *Handbook for Clinical Memory Assessment of Older Adults*. Washington, DC: American Psychological Association, 1986*a*.

Gallagher, D. The Beck Depression Inventory and older adults: Review of its development and utility. *Clinical Gerontologist* 5:149-163, 1986*b*.

Gallagher, D. Assessing affect in the elderly. *Clinics in Geriatric Medicine* 3:65-85, 1987.

Gallagher, D.; Rose, J.; Lovett, S.; and Silven, D. "Prevalence, Correlates and Treatment of Clinical Depression in Family Caregivers." Paper presented at the annual meeting of the Gerontological Society of America, Chicago, IL, Nov. 1986.

George, L.K., and Gwyther, L. Caregiver well-being: A multidimensional examination of family caregivers of demented adults. *Gerontologist* 26:253-259, 1986.

Goldman, L.S., and Luchins, D.J. Depression in the spouses of demented patients. *American Journal of Psychiatry* 141:1467-1468, 1984.

Groves, L.; Lazarus, L.W.; Newton, N.; Frankel, R.; Gutmann, D.; and Ripeckyj, A. Brief psychotherapy with spouses of patients with Alzheimer's disease: Relief of the psychological burden. In: Lazarus, L.W., ed. *Clinical Approaches to Psychotherapy with the Elderly*. Washington, DC: American Psychiatric Press, 1984. pp. 38-53.

Gurland, B.J. The comparative frequency of depression in various adult age groups. *Journal of Gerontology* 31:283-292, 1976.

Horowitz, A. Family caregiving to the frail elderly. In: Lawton, M.P., and Maddox, C., eds. *Annual Review of Gerontology and Geriatrics.* Vol. 5. New York: Springer, 1985. pp. 194-246.

Horowitz, M., and Kaltreider, N. Brief therapy of the stress response syndrome. *Psychiatric Clinics of North America* 2:365-377, 1979.

Horowitz, M.; Marmar, C.; Weiss, D.; DeWitt, K.; and Rosenbaum, R. Brief psychotherapy of bereavement reactions. *Archives of General Psychiatry* 41:438-448, 1984.

Kahan, J.; Kemp, B.; Staples, F.; and Brummel-Smith, K. Decreasing the burden in families caring for a relative with a dementing illness. *Journal of the American Geriatrics Society* 33:664-670, 1985.

Lazarus, R.S., and Folkman, S. *Stress, Appraisal, and Coping.* New York: Springer, 1984.

Lazarus, L.W., and Groves, L. Brief psychotherapy with the elderly: A study of process and outcome. In: Sadavoy, J., ed. *Treating the Elderly with Psychotherapy: The Scope of Change in Later Life.* London: International Universities Press, in press.

Murray, H.A. *Thematic Apperception Test.* Cambridge, MA: Harvard University Press, 1943.

Myers, J.K.; Weissman, M.M.; Tischler, G.; Holzer, C.; Leaf, P.; Orvaschel, H.; Anthony, J.; Boyd, J.; Burke, J.; Kramer, M.; and Stoltzman, R. Six-month prevalence of psychiatric disorders in three communities. *Archives of General Psychiatry* 41:959-967, 1984.

Neugarten, B.L., and Gutmann, D. Age-sex roles and personality in middle age: A Thematic Apperception Test study. *Psychological Monographs* 72(17):(whole no. 470). Washington, DC: American Psychological Association, 1958.

Norris, J.; Gallagher, D.; Wilson, A.; and Winograd, C. Assessment of depression in geriatric medical inpatients: The validity of two screening measures. *Journal of the American Geriatrics Society*, in press.

Novaco, R.W. *Anger Control: The Development and Evaluation of an Experimental Treatment.* Lexington, MA: D.C. Heath, 1975.

Novaco, R.W. Anger and its therapeutic regulation. In: Chesney, M., and Rosenman, R., eds. *Anger and Hostility in Cardiovascular and Behavioral Disorders.* Washington, DC: Hemisphere, 1985. pp. 203-226.

Oliver, R., and Bock, F.A. Alleviating the distress of caregivers of Alzheimer's disease patients: A rational-emotive therapy model. *Clinical Gerontologist* 3:17-34, 1985.

242

Pagel, M.; Becker, J.; and Coppel, D. Loss of control, self-blame, and depression: An investigation of spouse caregivers of Alzheimer's disease patients. *Journal of Abnormal Psychology* 94:169-182, 1985.

Pinkston, E., and Linsk, N. *Care of the Elderly: A Family Approach.* New York: Pergamon, 1984.

Plutchik, R. Conceptual and practical issues in the assessment of the elderly. In: Raskin, A., and Jarvik, L., eds. *Psychiatric Symptoms and Cognitive Loss in the Elderly.* Washington, DC: Hemisphere, 1979. pp. 19-38.

Powell, L.S., and Courtice, K. *Alzheimer's Disease: A Guide for Families.* Reading, MA: Addison-Wesley, 1983.

Pratt, C.; Schmall, V.; Wright, S.; and Cleland, M. Burden and coping strategies of caregivers to Alzheimer's patients. *Family Relations* 34:27-33, 1985.

Rabins, P.V.; Mace, N.L.; and Lucas, M.J. The impact of dementia on the family. *JAMA* 248:333-335, 1982.

Robins, L.N.; Helzer, J.E.; Croughan, J.; Williams, J.; and Spitzer, R. *NIMH Diagnostic Interview Schedule.* Version III. Rockville, MD: NIMH mimeo, 1981.

Robins, L.N.; Helzer, J.E.; Weissman, M.; Orvaschel, H.; Gruenberg, E.; Burke, J.; and Regier, D.A. Lifetime prevalence of specific psychiatric disorders in three sites. *Archives of General Psychiatry* 41:949-958, 1984.

Rose, J. "Guilt vs. Depression: Psychodynamic Understanding of the Wife of an Alzheimer's Patient." Paper presented at the annual meeting of the Gerontological Society of America, San Antonio, TX, Nov. 1984.

Rush, A.J., ed. *Short-Term Psychotherapies for Depression.* New York: Guilford Press, 1982.

Secretary's Task Force on Alzheimer's Disease, U.S. Department of Health and Human Services. *Alzheimer's Disease.* DHHS Pub. No. (ADM)84-1323. Washington, DC: Supt. of Docs., U.S. Govt. Print. Off., 1984.

Scott, J.P.; Roberto, K.; and Hutton, J.T. Families of Alzheimer's victims—Family support to the caregiver. *Journal of the American Geriatrics Society* 34:348-354, 1986.

Shanan, J., and Nissan, S. Sentence completion in personality assessment and diagnosis (in Hebrew). *Megamont* 11:232-252, 1961.

Snyder, B., and Keefe, K. The unmet needs of family caregivers of frail and disabled adults. *Social Work in Health Care* 10:1-14, 1985.

Spitzer, R.; Endicott, J.; and Robins, E. Research diagnostic criteria: Rationale and reliability. *Archives of General Psychiatry* 35:773-782, 1978.

243

Tensink, J.P., and Mahler, S. Helping families cope with Alzheimer's disease. *Hospital and Community Psychiatry* 35:152-156, 1984.

Teri, L., and Uomoto, J. "Treating Depression in Alzheimer's Disease: Teaching the Caregiver Behavioral Strategies." Paper presented at the annual meeting of the American Psychological Association, Washington, DC, Aug. 1986.

Thompson, L.W.; Gallagher, D.; and Breckenridge, J.S. Comparative effectiveness of psychotherapies for depressed elders. *Journal of Consulting and Clinical Psychology*, in press.

Thompson, L.W.; Davies, R.; Gallagher, D.; and Krantz, S. Cognitive therapy with older adults. *Clinical Gerontologist* 5:149-163, 1986.

Veith, R.C. Depression in the elderly: Pharmacologic considerations in treatment. *Journal of the American Geriatrics Society* 30:581-586, 1982.

Williams, J.B.W., and Spitzer, R., eds. *Psychotherapy Research: Where Are We and Where Should We Go?* New York: Guilford Press, 1984.

York, J.L., and Calsyn, R.J. Family involvement in nursing homes. *Gerontologist* 17:500-505, 1977.

Zarit, S.H.; Orr, N.; and Zarit, J.M. *The Hidden Victims of Alzheimer's Disease: Families Under Stress*. New York: New York University Press, 1985.

Zarit, S.H.; Reever, K.; and Bach-Peterson, J. Relatives of the impaired elderly: Correlates of feelings of burden. *Gerontologist* 20:649-655, 1980.

Zarit, S.H.; Todd, P.A.; and Zarit, J.M. Subjective burden of husbands and wives as caregivers: A longitudinal study. *Gerontologist* 26:260-266, 1986.

Zarit, S.H., and Zarit, J.M. Families under stress: Interventions for caregivers of senile dementia patients. *Psychotherapy: Theory, Research, and Practice* 19:461-471, 1982.

Zung, W.W.K. A self-rating depression scale. *Archives of General Psychiatry* 12:63-70, 1965.

Chapter 9

Caregiving, Mental Health, and Immune Function

Janice K. Kiecolt-Glaser, Ph.D., and Ronald Glaser, Ph.D.

In this chapter we briefly describe evidence suggesting that family caregivers of Alzheimer's disease victims are at high risk for depression. Studies that have linked both acute and chronic distress or dysphoria with alterations in immune function are discussed, including data from a cross-sectional study of caregivers. Finally, a conceptual framework that provides a structure for understanding these data is presented, emphasizing possible pathways through which psychological resources such as supportive interpersonal relationships might have an impact on health.

Caregiving as a Chronic Stressor

The process of providing care for a family member with Alzheimer's disease can be conceptualized as a chronic stressor (Fiore et al. 1983). The modal survival time after onset is approximately 8 years (Heston et al. 1981). The rapidity with which the disease will progress is unpredictable and uncontrollable; the only certainty is that the progressive cognitive impairments that are characteristic of Alzheimer's disease will lead to increasing needs for supportive care of afflicted individuals. The Alzheimer's disease victim's premorbid personality and intellectual capabilities will be gradually altered through the irreversible deterioration of brain tissue, culminating eventually in profound cognitive and behavioral changes including disorientation, incontinence, and an inability to provide any self-care (Heckler 1985). Caregivers have described the experience as one of repeated bereavement as they grieve for the loss of their family member, whose appearance has not changed but who is clearly not the person they knew.

In addition to these strains, caregiving frequently had adverse effects on a number of other facets of caregivers' lives. Caregivers have less time for their own interests and activities as the disease progresses and time demands become increasingly intense. Moreover, although the increased strains in caregivers' lives may enhance their needs for supportive relationships, the time that caregivers have available for such relationships frequently decreases as a function of caregiving time demands. Friends may visit caregivers less frequently because of the Alzheimer's disease victim's behavioral problems, and caregivers frequently become more reluctant to take the Alzheimer's disease family member to unfamiliar public places where they may become lost or upset (Barnes et al. 1981).

Other adverse changes are likely to occur in the lives of family members who are providing care. Caregivers' financial resources may be seriously strained. Family members are often reluctant to use their own limited financial resources, fearing that they may be needed to support the patient in a nursing home in the future. Respite care or home care services may be too expensive for retired individuals on fixed incomes (Barnes et al. 1981).

Thus, caregivers are faced with increasing time demands from an Alzheimer's disease patient whose functioning is deteriorating at the same time they face other stressors in their lives. These strains on caregivers' well-being may have a cumulative impact over time.

Mental and Physical Health
Correlates of Caregiving

Some progressive deterioration in caregivers' well-being over time may be related to the increasing impairment in the Alzheimer's disease family member. George and Gwyther (1984) found substantial deterioration in the well-being of those caregivers who provided continuous at-home care when measures were taken a year apart, including perceived decrements in health, decreased satisfaction with the amount of time available for social participation, decreased life satisfaction, and increased levels of stress-related psychiatric symptoms. These changes were particularly noteworthy because the baseline (time one) levels of well-being in these caregivers were already quite low in absolute terms. Similarly, Poulshock and Deimling (1984) found a "moderate-to-strong empirical link" between impairments of a dependent elder and perceptions of burden. Moreover, these perceptions of burden were related to changes in caregivers' lives, as well as those of their families.

There is good evidence that these chronic stresses associated with caregiving for a demented family member may have significant consequences for caregivers' mental health. Cross-sectional data from several laboratories suggest that the stresses of Alzheimer's disease caregiving leave family members at high risk for depression (Crook and Miller 1985; Eisdorfer et al. 1983). In one study of 44 spousal caregivers, 73 percent either currently met RDC criteria for depression or had met the criteria earlier in the spouse's illness (Fiore et al. 1983). Similarly, 81 percent of the caregivers in another sample met DSM-III criteria for major depression (Drinka and Smith 1983).

While these mental health consequences of caregiving have been well documented, the health-related consequences of this chronic stressor have not been studied as intensively. We found only three studies that assessed health. George and Gwyther's (1984) study found substantial deterioration in caregivers' self-rated health.[1] Sainsbury and Grad de Alarcon (1970) studied the effects of community care on the families of elderly psychiatric patients. Using psychiatrists' ratings of the impact of an elderly psychiatric patient (in a sample that included multiple psychiatric diagnoses) on the physical health of caregiving family members, they found substantial changes in health ratings. Brocklehurst, Andrews, Richards, and Laycock (1981) studied caregivers of another impaired population, stroke victims.

Using self-reports, they found that the number of caregivers reporting poor health tripled in the year after they began caregiving for a stroke patient, although those receiving medical treatment only increased from 33 percent to 40 percent.

Although these data suggest that caregiving responsibilities may be associated with self-reported health impairments, caregivers' health has not been studied using objective physiological measures. The relatively high incidence of depression among caregivers could have implications for their health, particularly in regard to the functioning of the immune system. Basic information on relevant aspects of immune system functioning and measurement is presented briefly, followed by a discussion of salient behavioral immunology studies.

---

1   A paper by George and Gwyther (1986) that reported data from the first of their two sample points showed no health differences between caregivers and age peers without caregiving responsibilities; the decline in self-rated health was clear, however, in the longitudinal data of the caregivers who provided continuous at-home care. Health changes may be more obvious in longitudinal studies.

Basic Information: Immune System Function

The immune system is the body's defense against infectious and malignant disease. There is no global measure of immune system function that can be used in isolation as a single measure. However, given the interdependence of the various components of the immune system, adverse changes in one aspect of immune function frequently have multiple repercussions.

Of particular relevance to this chapter is the fact that some declines in the functioning of the immune system are age-related (Goodwin et al. 1982); since the modal age of onset for Alzheimer's disease is 65-69, most Alzheimer's disease caregivers are middle-aged or older (Zarit et al. 1980). The significant functional immunological decrements that accompany aging are thought to be related to the increased morbidity and mortality of infectious disease in the elderly (Craig and Lin 1981; Roberts-Thomson et al. 1974).

There are a large number of different kinds of immunological assays. Those discussed in this chapter can be roughly divided into two classes: qualitative and quantitative. Qualitative assays provide information on functional aspects of immunity. i.e., information about relative efficacy under certain conditions. The quantitative or enumerative assays discussed are used to obtain information on the relative percentages of certain cell types. In general, the literature on age-related alterations in immune function shows larger and more reliable differences on qualitative assays, with very mixed evidence for age-related differences in quantitative aspects of immunity (Goodwin et al. 1982). Interestingly, we have found that qualitative assays are somewhat more reliably related to the psychosocial variables of interest than are quantitative assays.

Most components of the immune system change over days or weeks, not over minutes or hours. Thus, data to date suggest that a reasonably sustained period of distress or dysphoria (e.g., several days) is necessary for changes in most facets of immunity, rather than simply a bad afternoon.

Research on the relationships between the immune system and the neuroendocrine system provides evidence of physiological pathways through which distress may modulate immune function (O'Dorisio et al. 1985). Alterations in at least certain aspects of endocrine function can have an effect on immune function, and the responsiveness of the endocrine system to psychological states is well known. The central nervous system may also influence immune function through other pathways (Ader 1981).

248

Depression and Distress as Immunological Modifiers

Convergent data have linked depression with impaired immune function. For example, patients with a DSM-III major depression diagnosis have lower percentages of T-lymphocytes (Schleifer et al. 1985). T-lymphocytes are critical for the functioning of the cellular immune response; their activities are important for the body's defense against infectious viruses, transplanted tissue, cancer cells, fungi, and protozoans. Depressed patients also have lower percentages of one particularly important T-lymphocyte subpopulation, helper T-lymphocytes (Krueger et al. 1984). Helper T-lymphocytes are important because they stimulate a number of other immunological activities, e.g., helper T-cells stimulate the production of antibody by B-lymphocytes. Some data suggest that depressed patients have a poorer response to mitogen stimulation (Schleifer et al. 1984); blastogenesis, the stimulation of cell proliferation with a mitogen, is thought to provide an in vitro model for the body's proliferative response when challenged with a virus or bacteria.

High levels of depression in psychiatric inpatients are even associated with impairments at the molecular level, in the speed and quality of DNA repair. DNA repair is a primary defense against carcinogenesis, the development of certain kinds of cancer that occur through replication of transformed or mutant cells (Kiecolt-Glaser et al. 1985b).

It is not surprising that psychiatric patients with a major depression diagnosis have poorer immune function than matched nondepressed comparison subjects; even relatively commonplace events like academic examinations have been linked to transient changes in immunity. Data from blood samples taken from medical students during examinations show poorer cellular immune function than samples collected a month to 6 weeks earlier, when students were less distressed. Consistent with the data from depressed psychiatric patients, several studies with medical student subjects have shown lower percentages of total T-lymphocytes and helper T-lymphocytes during examinations when compared with baseline periods, as well as a poorer proliferative response in lymphocytes stimulated with two mitogens (Glaser et al. 1985b).

Natural killer (NK) cells are thought to be an important defense against certain kinds of viruses and possibly cancer as well (Herberman et al. 1982). We found lower levels of NK activity (using a functional assay) as well as lower percentages of NK cells using two different kinds of quantitative assays in medical student blood samples drawn during examination days, in comparison to samples obtained 1 month earlier (Glaser et al. 1986; Kiecolt-Glaser et al. 1986; Kiecolt-Glaser et al. 1984a). In addition, we found dramatic decrements in the production of gamma interferon by peripheral blood lymphocytes (white blood cells) that were stimulated with a mitogen (Glaser et al. 1986; Glaser et al. 1987). Interferon is important because it stimulates a number of immunological activities, including the growth and differentiation of NK cells (Herberman et al. 1982).

We were also interested in possible changes in antibody titers to latent herpesvirus, Epstein-Barr virus (EBV), the etiologic agent for infectious mononucleosis (Glaser et al. 1985a). Although somewhat counterintuitive, *higher* antibody titers to latent herpesviruses suggest that cellular immunity is less competent in controlling herpesvirus latency; the higher titers are thought to reflect a response to the replication of reactivated virus. Consistent data from immunosuppressed patients (either through an immunosuppressive drug regimen like chemotherapy or via an immunosuppressive disease like AIDS) show that poorer cellular immune function is associated with higher antibody titers to one or more of the herpesviruses (Glaser and Gotlieb-Stematsky 1982).

Evidence from seroepidemiological studies suggests that the geometric mean antibody titer (GMT) for EBV virus capsid antigen (VCA) in healthy adults is around 1:80 (Henle and Henle 1982). In contrast, the EBV VCA GMT for our 49 EBV seropositive medical students was over 1:560 in both the blood samples obtained 1 month before final examinations and those taken during examinations. The GMT dropped to 1:93 after the students' return from summer vacation. Similar stress-related changes occurred in antibody titers to two other herpesvirus: herpes simplex virus (the virus associated with cold sores) and cytomegalovirus (which produces a mononucleosis-like syndrome during the initial acute infection).

Interpersonal Relationships and Immune Function

A number of studies have provided evidence suggesting that alterations in interpersonal relationships may have immunological correlates. These data are consistent with the growing evidence that social support may have an impact on health (Cohen and Syme 1985).

Loneliness, Social Support, and Immunity

Lonelier students (those scoring above the median on the UCLA Loneliness Scale developed by Russell, Peplau, and Crutona, 1980) have poorer immune function than their fellow students who described themselves as less lonely (Kiecolt-Glaser et al., 1984a; Glaser et al. 1985a,b). Loneliness is associated with constricted and dissatisfying personal relationships (Jones et al. 1981), and the experience of being lonely is generally distressing (Peplau and Perlman 1982). While loneliness appears to result from perceived deficiencies in a person's social relationships, it is not synonymous with social isolation (Peplau and Perlman 1982).

Paralleling the pattern for the NK cell lysis data, lonelier students had significantly higher EBV VCA titers than their less lonely student colleagues (Glaser et al. 1985a). These data suggest that the cellular immune response in the former group was less competent in controlling herpesvirus latency.

We also found that lonelier psychiatric patients had significantly lower levels of NK cell activity than less lonely patients (Kiecolt-Glaser et al. 1984b). Lonelier inpatients showed a poorer proliferative response to one mitogen and also had higher levels of stress-related urinary cortisol.

Thomas, Goodwin, and Goodwin (1985) found low but statistically significant correlations between "satisfying confidant relationships" and two immunological indices, total lymphocyte count and mitogen responsiveness, among a sample of 106 women between the ages of 61 and 89 years of age, after correcting for psychological distress and other variables. The correlations were not significant for the 91 men in the sample. If, however, distress and support are causally treated, these limited data may underestimate the magnitude of the effects.

Bereavement

One of the earlier human psychoimmunology studies showed that bereaved spouses had a poorer proliferative response to mitogen stimulation 2 to 6 weeks after the spouse's death than nonbereaved controls (Bartrop et al. 1977). Similarly, in a prospective study of bereavement, Schleifer et al. (1983) followed 15 men whose wives were dying of breast cancer, with collection of blood samples before and after the wife's death. Men had a poorer blastogenic response after the wife's death than they did before bereavement, in spite of the fact that the death had been anticipated. Most of the men in their sample were back to their prebereavement immunological levels within a year.

251

Marital Disruption and Marital Quality

The loneliness data suggest that more chronic changes in immunity might be associated with the quality of interpersonal relationships. In a related vein, studies on marital disruption have examined acute changes in immune function in response to the loss of an important relationship, as well as subsequent adjustment. Moreover, data relevant to the issue of marital quality and health suggest that the simple presence of a spouse does not necessarily have positive psychological and physiological correlates.

Our laboratory's interest in the immunological correlates of marital disruption was fueled by the evidence that marital disruption was reliably associated with increased health risks in a number of epidemiological studies. We were also interested in a possible relationship between marital quality and immune function, since unhappy marriages are reliably associated with increased distress: on the average, unmarried individuals are less distressed than those in troubled marriages (Glenn and Weaver 1981; Pearlin and Lieberman 1979). Moreover, poorer marital quality has also been associated with poorer health. In a study by Renne (1971), unhappily married people reported poorer health than either divorced or happily married individuals of the same age, sex, and race.

Taken together, these studies suggest that both poorer marital quality and marital disruption are associated with greater distress and poorer health. We were interested in the possibility of concomitant immunological alterations in certain more vulnerable individuals. To test these speculations, we recruited 38 separated or divorced women and 38 sociodemographically matched married comparison women who completed questionnaires and allowed blood samples to be drawn (Kiecolt-Glaser et al. 1987a). The immunological assays included three qualitative or functional assays (blastogenesis with two mitogens and antibody titers to EBV) and three quantitative measures (percentages of NK cells, helper T-lymphocytes, and suppressor T-lymphocytes).

As predicted, poorer marital quality was significantly associated with greater depression and loneliness in hierarchical multiple regression equations, after entering subject's education, the husband's socioeconomic status, and the number of negative life events on previous steps. Similarly, poorer marital quality was significantly associated with a poorer response on the three qualitative measures of immune function after controlling for the above variables.

252

The predictions concerning psychological and immunological relationships in the 38 separated/divorced women were based on attachment theory, the primary conceptual framework used in the divorce literature to explain the differences in postseparation symptomatology (Bowlby 1975; Weiss 1975). Within this framework, continued preoccupation with the inaccessible spouse (including either positive or negative affect) leads to "separation distress" and the associated distress-related symptoms. Not surprisingly, attachment feelings are expected to decline as separation time increases. However, considerable variability occurs in the amount of continued attachment in separated and divorced individuals, even for those separated for similar time periods. Based on these factors, we expected that both shorter separation periods and stronger feelings of attachment would be significantly and inversely related to immune function, while both would be directly related to distress. These predictions were supported.

Two sets of comparisons were of interest. The separated/divorced group had separation times ranging from 3 months to 6 years, with a mean of 1.72 years. We found that the 16 women who had been separated a year or less had significantly poorer immune function on five of the six assays than 16 sociodemographically matched married women. Contrary to predictions, differences in distress were not statistically significant.

We did not predict overall group differences, since the average time since separation in our marital disruption group was almost 2 years. However, comparisons of data from all 38 separated/divorced women and 38 married women showed significantly poorer immune function across three of the six immunological assays in the former, with significantly greater distress in the former as well.

There are obvious problems in making inferences about causality using cross-sectional data such as these. However, data from Levenson and Gottman (1985) provide evidence of a pathway through which chronically abrasive relationships could mediate immune function. They found that greater autonomic arousal in interacting married couples was strongly predictive of larger declines in marital satisfaction 3 years later, and greater decrements in marital satisfaction were also strongly correlated with self-ratings of poorer health. If the presence of a spouse in a disturbed relationship is associated with relatively consistent physiological arousal, then there could be concurrent alterations in endocrine function that could have an impact on the immune response (O'Dorisio et al. 1985).

Chronic Stress and Immune Function in Alzheimer's Disease Caregivers

While acute stress has been associated with transient immunosuppression, little is known about the immunological consequences of chronic stress in humans. To investigate possible health-related consequences of a long-term stressor, we obtained psychological data and blood samples for immunological and nutritional analyses from 34 family caregivers of Alzheimer's disease victims (Kiecolt-Glaser et al. 1987b).[2] George and Gwyther (1986) argue that the measurement of caregiver burden can best be done by comparing caregivers' responses to those of their age-peers who do not have similar responsibilities. Thus, to better understand the health-related consequences of caregiving, we obtained comparable data from 34 sociodemographically matched (age, sex, and education) comparison subjects.

Family caregivers for Alzheimer's disease victims were more distressed than comparison subjects without similar responsibilities. In addition, greater impairment in the Alzheimer's disease victim was associated with greater distress and loneliness in caregivers. Caregivers had significantly lower percentages of total T-lymphocytes and helper T-lymphocytes than comparison subjects, as well as significantly lower helper/suppressor cell ratios. Caregivers also had significantly higher antibody titers to EBV than comparison subjects, presumably reflecting poorer cellular immune system control over the expression of this latent herpesvirus in the former group. There were no significant differences between the groups in the percentages of NK cells and suppressor T-lymphocytes. These data suggest that chronically stressed Alzheimer's disease family caregivers have lower levels of psychological or immunological adaptation than their well-matched peers.

We found no evidence that the observed differences were a function of nutrition, alcohol use, or caffeine intake. While the caregivers reported less sleep than comparison subjects, as would be expected from other studies (Barnes et al. 1981; Rabins et al. 1982), the amount of sleep was not reliably associated with immune function or mood in caregivers.

The differences in immune function between the caregiving and comparison subject groups are particularly noteworthy, because these caregivers are considerably less distressed than other caregiver

---

2   The study that examined caregivers' immune function was the direct result of a most helpful suggestion from Enid Light.

samples described in the literature (e.g., Drinka and Smith 1983; Fiore et al. 1983). These differences may be related to the fact that our caregivers were relatively well educated, and income data suggested that they had more financial resources than described in other similar samples (George and Gwyther 1986; Zarit et al. 1986). Given these relative advantages, it is reasonable to suggest that these data may well represent a "best case scenario" (Gwyther and George 1986). The persistence of significant physiological and psychological differences between our two cohorts in spite of these relative advantages strongly supports the hypothesized negative impact of caregiving responsibilities.

In contrast to data from other investigators (George and Gwyther 1986; Johnson and Catalano 1983), caregivers were not significantly more likely to become isolated from their usual companions and social activities because of the time demands than individuals without comparable responsibilities. However, greater impairment in the Alzheimer's disease victim was significantly correlated with fewer social contacts and greater depression and loneliness. If caregivers experience increased social isolation as their relative's condition deteriorates, it could have important consequences. Research with both older and younger adults suggests that social support may moderate stress-related depression or dysphoria, and may also be related to morbidity and mortality (Blazer 1982; Cohen et al. 1985).

The immunological data provide evidence of persistent alterations in cellular immune function associated with a chronic psychosocial stressor. These data are consistent with possible longer term immunological alterations suggested by the cross-sectional research on immune function, marital quality, and marital disruption described earlier (Kiecolt-Glaser et al. 1987a).

Psychosocial Enhancement of Immunity

Previous research with nursing home residents showed that increased attention was reliably associated with small but consistent improvements across a variety of mental and physical health indices (Schulz 1980; Rodin 1980). Simple interventions such as regular visits from college students have been associated with significant improvements in both physician- and self-ratings of physical and mental health, increased activity, and significant decreases in urinary cortisol. The data from medical students suggested that commonplace distress-producing events might be associated with sig-

255

nificant alterations in immune function; moreover, both lonelier medical students and lonelier psychiatric inpatients had poorer immune function than their counterparts who were presumably more satisfied with their interpersonal relationships. Based on these data, we were interested in the possibility that psychosocial interventions that reduced distress and/or loneliness might lead to an enhancement of immune function. Thus, 45 older adults were recruited from independent living facilities for an intervention study (Kiecolt-Glaser et al. 1985).

To evaluate the relative potency of relaxation and social contact conditions, our 45 older adult subjects were randomly assigned to a relaxation condition, a social contact condition, or a no-intervention condition. Subjects in the relaxation and social contact conditions were visited individually three times a week for a month. Blood samples and self-report data were collected at baseline before the interventions began, at the end of the 1-month intervention period, and at a 1-month followup.

Post hoc analyses of significant interactions showed discrete changes in the relaxation cohort. Relaxation subjects showed a significant increase in NK cell activity at the end of the intervention when compared to baseline, and a significant decrease in antibody titers to herpes simplex virus (HSV, using a Type 1 antigen). Taken together, the *increased* NK activity and *lower* HSV antibody titers are consistent with improved cellular immune system function at the end of the intervention. While NK cell activity did not differ significantly from baseline levels at the 1-month followup, HSV antibody titers were still significantly lower than baseline levels at followup.

Self-report distress data from the Hopkins Symptom Checklist showed discrete changes only for the relaxation group. Few subjects endorsed much distress-related symptomatology at baseline, so there was little room for decrements. Self-rated loneliness did not change significantly. Although relaxation was presented as a control-enhancing intervention, no significant changes were found in feelings of control.

Data from blastogenesis assays showed some general enhancement across the three experimental conditions. Significant improvement was also found in the self-rated quality of sleep across the three groups. Since the total sample comprised four cohorts who were drawn from four different facilities, and data were collected at four different times of year, these effects are unlikely to be the product of facility- or seasonal-related changes, and may reflect some more general enhancement associated with experimental participation.

The changes in the immunological variables suggested that relaxation might have some positive consequences for immune function.

256

While we did not find discrete differences associated with the social contact intervention, as suggested by previous studies, the residents of independent living facilities were used as subjects, rather than nursing home residents as in previous research (Rodin 1980; Schulz 1980). The greater environmental restrictions of the latter may increase the efficacy of social contact as a mood-altering intervention.

Behavioral Influences on Immunity: A Conceptual Proposal

It is important to highlight the conceptual paradigm for our behavioral immunology research program, since this model provides the basis for the interpretation and discussion of data in this chapter. We suggest that an increase in psychological distress, sustained over time, can lead to adverse immunological changes (Kiecolt-Glaser et al. 1984a; Kiecolt-Glaser et al. 1985; Glaser et al. 1985a,b; Glaser et al. in press). Thus, the distress that accompanies most negative major life changes presumably leads to immunological alterations in many individuals. These distress-related immunological alterations provide one physiological pathway through which major and minor life changes could lead to an increased incidence of infectious disease (Kiecolt-Glaser et al. 1987a,b; Glaser et al. 1986; Lynch 1977; Somers 1979).

However, most individuals undergoing even major life changes do not become ill, or they only experience short illness episodes. The prior health of the individual (particularly in regard to immune system function) and differential exposure to pathogens determine actual organically based illness episodes.

The probability of clinical illness and the intensity and duration of the illness episode are, at least in part, a product of the status of the individual's immune system when the person is exposed to an infectious agent such as a virus. Following this line of reasoning, the individuals who are presumably most likely to show changes in their health in response to stressors are those whose immune system function is already somewhat compromised, either by a natural process like aging (Braveman, in press), or by an immunosuppressive disease like AIDS. These individuals will most likely have poorer immunological defenses at the onset of a stressor, so that smaller stress-associated immunological decrements could have more important consequences. Illness episodes might also be more prolonged.

In addition, individuals who are chronically distressed may be at greater risk for infectious disease because of longer term immunologi-

257

cal changes. While some evidence shows that chronic physical stressors may produce immunological adaptation or even enhancement of immune function in rodents (Monjan and Collector 1977), we find that more chronically stressed groups such as Alzheimer's disease family caregivers appear to have poorer immune function than well-matched comparison subjects. Prolonged or chronic psychological stress in humans does not appear to lead to adaptation to the level of matched comparison subjects (Kiecolt-Glaser et al. in press a,b; Schaeffer et al. 1985).

More chronically distressed individuals might be at greater risk on a longer term basis in two additional ways. Data from Hammen, Mayol, deMayo, and Marks (1986) showed that a subset of individuals who had more depressive symptomatology initially continued to have both more depression and more high-impact stressful life changes over time; in contrast, those individuals who were initially non-symptomatic were relatively resistant, even when experiencing high-impact stressful events. Similarly, panel data from Mitchell and Moos (1984) suggested that perceived strain led to less perceived family support in a sample of depressed patients. Thus, individuals who are initially more distressed may simultaneously be more vulnerable to life changes while concurrently perceiving less family support over time. If the severity of depression is related to immune dysfunction, as suggested by some researchers (Schleifer et al. 1985), then chronically distressed individuals might show greater immunological changes in response to events than individuals who were less distressed initially.

Thus, we speculate that behavioral influences on immunity are likely to have an impact on health in certain more vulnerable individuals, either because their immune function is already compromised by a natural process like aging, or through more chronic stress-related alterations. We suggest that epidemiological data may provide some support for these speculations.

Individuals over 80 years of age with poorer immune function have higher rates of mortality (Roberts-Thomson et al. 1974). Pneumonia and influenza constitute the fourth leading cause of death among the elderly (Yoshikawa 1983). While pneumonia is an important factor in mortality in the elderly, it may be an even more deadly disease among more distressed older adults. Within the first year after psychiatric admission, 50 times more deaths occur from pneumonia among elderly psychiatric patients than among their age-matched general population counterparts. The ratio drops to 20 times that of their general population counterparts by the second year of hospitalization, suggesting that the hospital environment may be a less important factor than the transition (Craig and Lin 1981). Depression is

258

the modal reason for psychiatric hospitalization in the elderly (Solomon 1981). Moreover, it is reasonable to assume that community residents are less distressed than psychiatric inpatients, on the average.

Other epidemiological data are consistent with higher rates of morbidity and mortality in more distressed populations. For example, the mortality rates among psychiatric patients are $1^1/2$ to 2 times as high as among community residents, after removal of several obviously higher risk groups, including aged, chronically ill, and alcoholic patients (Babigian and Odoroff 1969). Psychiatric patients also have a higher incidence of cancer (Fox 1978).

If psychological resources like supportive interpersonal relationships moderate distress and concurrently attenuate adverse immunological changes, then individuals with less social support should be at higher risk. Blazer (1982) found that mortality was inversely related to three indices of social support (impaired frequency of social interaction, impaired roles and available attachments, and perceived social support) in a longitudinal study of older adults.

Another longitudinal study used an inner-city elderly population; their data showed that social networks exerted a direct effect on subsequent self-reported physical symptoms, after controlling for initial symptom levels. The maximal buffering effect was noted among those with greater numbers of life events (Cohen et al. 1985). Other investigators have also found evidence of lower morbidity and mortality associated with greater support (Cohen and Syme 1985).

Significantly higher mortality has been associated with bereavement, separation, and divorce. Bereavement has been linked to greater morbidity and mortality in epidemiological studies (e.g., Jacobs and Ostfeld 1977; Rees and Lutkins 1967), although many such studies have methodological limitations (Minkler 1985). Bereaved individuals have a higher incidence of cancer than similar nonbereaved adults (Ernster et al. 1979).

Other data suggest that separated and divorced individuals are at risk for both mental and physical illness (Bloom et al. 1978; Verbrugge 1979). Summarizing the evidence for differences in health, Verbrugge (1979) concluded: "Separated women are strongly disadvantaged, compared to married ones, for acute incidence [of illness], all short-term disability measures, major activity limitations, and partial work disability. . . . Divorced women are also strongly disfavored" (p. 283).

Separated and divorced individuals also have reliably higher rates of clinical depression than married persons (Bloom et al. 1978) and six times as many deaths from pneumonia as married adults (Lynch

1977). In addition, separated women have 30 percent more acute illnesses and physician visits than married women (Somers 1979).

These data provide evidence of health impairments in more distressed populations, in individuals whose marital relationships have been disrupted through divorce or death, and in older adults whose interpersonal relationships are less satisfactory and/or less numerous. Unfortunately, most of these studies do not specifically examine differences in infectious and malignant disease.

An Important Caveat: Objective Health Change Data

Factors other than distress might account for the observed differences in morbidity and mortality. For example, marital disruption or other major life changes might have adverse effects on health because of differences in risk-related health behaviors, e.g., distressed individuals might drink, smoke, or use drugs more than their less distressed counterparts, and/or they might have poorer diets and get less sleep (Verbrugge 1979). We normally use good health and the absence of prescription or nonprescription drug use as a screening criteria for all our subjects,[3] and we exclude subjects who drink more than 10 alcoholic drinks per week.

We have not found evidence of differences in sleep or nutritional status (Chandra and Newberne 1977) of sufficient magnitude to account for the observed differences in immune function in any of the populations we have studied to date. Thus, while some of the differences in the epidemiological literature may be a function of lifestyle vari-

---

3   While we normally limit our subject samples to those who are not taking medication, caregivers are primarily middle-aged or older, and the majority of older adults take some medication. We felt that limiting the sample to those who were not taking any medication would result in biased data, because only the healthiest of the population would be eligible. Thus, we excluded only those potential subjects who were taking medication known to have immunological consequences, with one exception; we matched Alzheimer's disease caregivers who were taking beta blockers, a widely prescribed medication among the elderly, with similarly medicated age-, sex-, and education-matched comparison subjects. Data from in vitro studies suggest that beta blockers adversely affect blastogenesis (Goodwin et al. 1979), and, while we were not aware of any similar in vivo data, we wished to have comparable subjects in our two cohorts.

We also matched female caregiver subjects who were taking estrogen supplements with similarly medicated comparison subjects. We are unaware of any evidence suggesting that estrogen may affect immunity; however, there is good evidence for multiple interactions between the endocrine system and the immune system (O'Dorisio et al. 1985).

ables, it is also possible that persistent distress-related physiological changes could contribute to the observed differences in health.

While both transient and more chronic immunosuppression may have adverse health consequences, the longitudinal studies essential for providing information on the magnitude of these effects and their association with the incidence, duration, and intensity of infectious disease are largely absent from the literature. The critical connections between stress-related immunosuppression and actual health changes are not well established. A recent longitudinal study from our laboratory suggested a confluence of increased distress, poorer immune function, and increased incidence of colds and flu in medical students (Glaser et al. 1987), and other studies have provided similar suggestive linkages (e.g., Kasl et al. 1979).

Longitudinal studies with chronically stressed at-risk groups like caregivers should provide valuable information on the contribution of psychosocial variables to morbidity and mortality. Alzheimer's disease presently affects 2 million older adults in this country, and the numbers are increasing as the number of older adults in the population increases. The majority of Alzheimer's disease patients live in the community, under the care of their relatives (Heckler 1985). Clearly, the health of caregivers is an important issue and one that deserves serious study.

References

Ader, R., ed. *Psychoneuroimmunology.* New York: Academic Press, 1981.

Babigian, H., and Odoroff, C.L. The mortality experience of a population with psychiatric illness. *American Journal of Psychiatry* 126:52-62, 1969.

Barnes, R.F.; Raskind, M.A.; Scott, M.; and Murphy, C. Problems of families caring for Alzheimer's patients: Use of a support group. *Journal of the American Geriatrics Society* 29:80-85, 1981.

Bartrop, R.W.; Luckhurst, E.; Lazarus, L.; Kiloh, L.G.; and Penny, R. Depressed lymphocyte function after bereavement. *Lancet* 1:834-836, 1977.

Blazer, D. Social support and mortality in an elderly community population. *American Journal of Epidemiology* 115:684-694, 1982.

Bloom, B.L.; Asher, S.J.; and White, S.W. Marital disruption as a stressor: A review and analysis. *Psychological Bulletin* 85:867-894, 1978.

Bowlby, J. Attachment and Loss: Attachment. New York: Basic Books, 1975.

Braveman, N. Immunity and aging: Immunological and behavioral perspectives. In: Riley, M.; Matarazzo, J.; and Baum, A., eds. *Perspectives on Behavioral Medicine.* New York: Academic Press, in press.

Brocklehurst, J.C.; Morris, P.; Andrews, K.; Richards, B.; and Laycock, P. Social effects of stroke. *Social Science and Medicine* 15A:35-39, 1981.

Chandra, R.K., and Newberne, P.M. *Nutrition, Immunity, and Infection: Mechanisms of Interactions.* New York: Plenum Press, 1977.

Cohen, C.I.; Teresi, J.; and Holmes, D. Social networks, stress, and physical health: A longitudinal study of an inner-city elderly population. *Journal of Gerontology* 40:478-486, 1985.

Cohen, S., and Syme, S.L., eds. *Social Support and Health.* New York: Academic Press, 1985.

Craig, T.J., and Lin, S.P. Mortality among elderly psychiatric patients: Basis for preventive intervention. *Journal of the American Geriatrics Society* 29:181-185, 1981.

Crook, T.H., and Miller, N.E. The challenge of Alzheimer's disease. *American Psychologist* 40:1245-1250, 1985.

Drinka, T., and Smith, J. Depression in caregivers of demented patients. *Gerontologist* 23:116, 1983.

Eisdorfer, C.; Kennedy, G.; Wisnieski, W.; and Cohen, D. Depression and attributional style in families coping with the stress of caring for a relative with Alzheimer's disease. *Gerontologist* 23:115-116, 1983.

Ernster, V.L.; Sacks, S.T.; Selvin, S.; and Petrakis, N.L. Cancer incidence by marital status: U.S. Third National Cancer Survey. *Journal of the National Cancer Institute* 63:585-587, 1979.

Fiore, J.; Becker, J.; and Coppel, D.B. Social network interactions: A buffer or a stress? *American Journal of Community Psychology* 11:423-439, 1983.

Fox, B.H. Cancer death risk in hospitalized mental patients. Letters, *Science* 201:966-967, 1978.

George, L.K., and Gwyther, L.P. "The Dynamics of Caregiver Well-Being: Changes in Caregiver Well-Being Over Time." Paper presented at the meeting of the Gerontological Society of America, San Antonio, TX, Nov. 1984.

George, L.K., and Gwyther, L.P. Caregiver well-being: A multidimensional examination of family caregivers of demented adults. *Gerontologist* 26:253-259, 1986.

Glaser, R., and Gotlieb-Stematsky, T., eds. *Human Herpesvirus Infections: Clinical Aspects.* New York: Marcel Dekker, 1982.

Glaser, R.; Kiecolt-Glaser, J.K.; Speicher, C.E.; and Holliday, J.E. Stress, loneliness, and changes in herpesvirus latency. *Journal of Behavioral Medicine* 8:249-260, 1985a.

Glaser, R.; Kiecolt-Glaser, J.K.; Stout, J.C.; Tarr, K.L.; Speicher, C.E.; and Holliday, J.E. Stress-related impairments in cellular immunity. *Psychiatric Research* 16:233-239, 1985b.

Glaser, R.; Rice, J.; Speicher, C.E.; Stout, J.C.; and Kiecolt-Glaser, J.K. Stress depresses interferon production concomitant with a decrease in natural killer cell activity. *Behavioral Neuroscience* 100:675-678, 1986.

Glaser, R.; Rice, J.; Sheridan, J.; Fertel, R.; Stout, J.; Speicher, C.E.; Pinsky, D.; Kotur, M.; Post, A.; Beck, M.; and Kiecolt-Glaser, J.K. Stress-related immune suppression: Health implications. *Brain, Behavior, and Immunity* 1:7-20, 1987.

Glenn, N.D., and Weaver, C.N. The contribution of marital happiness to global happiness. *Journal of Marriage and Family* 43:161-168, 1981.

Goodwin, J.S.; Messner, R.P.; and Williams, R.C. Inhibitors of T-cell mitogenesis: Effects of mitogen dosage. *Cellular Immunology* 45:303-308, 1979.

Goodwin, J.S.; Searles, R.P.; and Tung, K.S.K. Immunological responses of a healthy elderly population. *Clinical and Experimental Immunology* 48:403-410, 1982.

Gwyther, L.P., and George, L.K. Caregivers for dementia patients: Complex determinants of well-being and burden. *Gerontologist* 26:245-247, 1986.

Hammon, C.; Mayol, A.; deMayo, R.; and Marks, T. Initial symptom levels and the life-event-depression relationship. *Journal of Abnormal Psychology* 95:114-122, 1986.

Heckler, M.M. The fight against Alzheimer's disease. *American Psychologist* 40:1240-1244, 1985.

Henle, W., and Henle, G. Epstein-Barr virus and infectious mononucleosis. In: Glaser, R., and Gotlieb-Stematsky, T., eds. *Human Herpesvirus Infections: Clinical Aspects.* New York: Marcel Dekker, 1982. pp. 151-162.

Herberman, R.B.; Ortaldo, J.R.; Riccardi, C.; Timonen, T.; Schmidt, A.; Maluish, A., and Djeu, J. Interferon and NK cells. In: Merigan, T.C., and Friedman, R.M., eds. *Interferons.* London: Academic Press, 1982. pp. 287-294.

Heston, L.L.; Mastri, A.R.; Anderson, V.E.; and White, G. Dementia of the Alzheimer type. *Archives of General Psychiatry* 38:1085-1091, 1981.

Jacobs, S., and Ostfeld, A. An epidemiological review on bereavement. *Psychosomatic Medicine* 4:4-13, 1977.

Johnson, C.L., and Catalano, D.J. A longitudinal study of family supports to impaired elderly. *Gerontologist* 23:612-618, 1983.

Jones, W.H.; Freemon, J.A.; and Goswick, R.A. The persistence of loneliness: Self and other determinants. *Journal of Personality* 49:27-48, 1981.

Kasl, S.V.; Evans, A.S.; and Niederman, J.C. Psychosocial risk factors in the development of infectious mononucleosis. *Psychosomatic Medicine* 41:445-466, 1979.

Kiecolt-Glaser, J.K.; Fisher, L.; Ogrocki, P.; Stout, J.C.; Speicher, C.E.; and Glaser, R. Marital quality, marital disruption, and immune function. *Psychosomatic Medicine* 49:13-34, 1987a.

Kiecolt-Glaser, J.K.; Garner, W.; Speicher, C.; Penn, G.M.; Holliday, J.E.; and Glaser, R. Psychosocial modifiers of immunocompetence in medical students. *Psychosomatic Medicine* 46:7-14, 1984a.

Kiecolt-Glaser, J.K.; Glaser, R.; Dyer, C.; Shuttleworth, E.C.; Ogrocki, P.; and Speicher, C.E. Chronic stress and immune function in family caregivers of Alzheimer's disease victims. *Psychosomatic Medicine* 49:523-535, 1987b.

Kiecolt-Glaser, J.K.; Glaser, R.; Strain, E.C.; Stout, J.C.; Tarr, K.L.; Holliday, J.E.; and Speicher, C.E. Modulation of cellular immunity in medical students. *Journal of Behavioral Medicine* 9:5-21, 1986.

Kiecolt-Glaser, J.K.; Glaser, R.; Williger, D.; Stout, J.; Messick, G.; Sheppard, S.; Ricker, D.; Romisher, S.C.; Briner, W.; Bonnell, G.; and Donnerberg, R. Psychosocial enhancement of immunocompetence in a geriatric population. *Health Psychology* 4:25-41, 1985a.

Kiecolt-Glaser, J.K.; Ricker, D.; Messick, G.; Speicher, C.E.; Garner, W.; and Glaser, R. Urinary cortisol, cellular immunocompetency and loneliness in psychiatric inpatients. *Psychosomatic Medicine* 46:15-24, 1984b.

Kiecolt-Glaser, J.K.; Stephens, R.; Lipitz, P.; Speicher, C.E.; and Glaser, R. Distress and DNA repair in human lymphocytes. *Journal of Behavioral Medicine* 8:311-320, 1985b.

Krueger, R.G.; Levy, R.M.; Cathcart, E.S.; Fox, B.H.; and Black, P.H. Lymphocyte subsets in patients with major depression: Preliminary findings. *Advances* 1:5-9, 1984.

Levenson, R.W., and Gottman, J.M. Physiological and affective predictors of change in relationship satisfaction. *Journal of Personality and Social Psychology* 49:85-94, 1985.

Lynch, J. *The Broken Heart.* New York: Basic Books, 1977.

Minkler, M. Social support and health of the elderly. In: Cohen, S., and Syme, S.L., eds. *Social Support and Health.* New York: Academic Press, 1985. pp. 199-216.

Mitchell, R.E., and Moos, R.H. Deficiencies in social support among depressed patients: Antecedents or consequences of stress? *Journal of Health and Social Behavior* 25:438-452, 1984.

Monjan, A.A., and Collector, M.I. Stress-induced modulation of the immune response. *Science* 196:307-308, 1977.

O'Dorisio, M.S.; Wood, C.L.; and O'Dorisio, T.M. Vasoactive intestinal peptide and neuropeptide modulation of the immune response. *Journal of Immunology* 135:792s-796s, 1985.

Pearlin, L.I., and Lieberman, M.A. Social sources of emotional distress. In: Simmons, R., ed. *Research in Community and Mental Health*. Greenwich, CT: JAI Press, 1979. pp. 217-248.

Peplau, L.A., and Perlman, D., eds. *Loneliness: A Sourcebook of Current Theory, Research, and Therapy*. New York: John Wiley, 1982.

Poulshock, S.W., and Deimling, G. Families caring for elders in residence: Issues in the measurement of burden. *Journal of Gerontology* 39:230-239, 1984.

Rabins, P.V.; Mace, H.L.; and Lucas, M.J. The impact of dementia on the family. *JAMA* 248:333-335, 1982.

Rees, W.D., and Lutkins, S.G. Mortality of bereavement. *British Medical Journal* 4:13-16, 1967.

Renne, K.S. Health and marital experience in an urban population. *Journal of Marriage and Family* 23:338-350, 1971.

Roberts-Thomson, I.C.; Whittingham, S.; Youngchaiyud, U.; and MacKay, I.R. Aging, immune response, and mortality. *Lancet* 2:368-370,1974.

Rodin, J. Managing the stress of aging: The role of control and coping. In: Levine, S., and Ursin, H., eds. *Coping and Health*. New York: Plenum Press, 1980. pp. 171-202.

Russell, D.; Peplau, L.A.; and Cutrona, C.B. The revised UCLA Loneliness Scale: Concurrent and discriminant validity evidence. *Journal of Personality and Social Psychology* 39:472-480, 1980.

Schaeffer, M.A.; McKinnon, W.; Baum, A.; Reynolds, C.P.; Rikli, P.; Davidson, L.M.; and Fleming, I. Immune status as a function of chronic stress at Three Mile Island. *Psychosomatic Medicine* 47:85, 1985.

Schleifer, S.J.; Keller, S.E.; Camerino, M.; Thornton, J.S.; and Stein, M. Suppression of lymphocyte stimulation following bereavement. *JAMA* 250:374-377, 1983.

Schleifer, S.J.; Keller, S.E.; Meyerson, A.T.; Raskin, M.J.; Davis, K.L.; and Stein, M. Lymphocyte function in major depressive disorder. *Archives of General Psychiatry* 41:484-486, 1984.

Schleifer, S.J.; Keller, S.E.; Siris, S.G.; Davis, K.L.; and Stein, M. Depression and immunity. *Archives of General Psychiatry* 42:129-133, 1985.

Schulz, R. Aging and control. In: Garber, J., and Seligman, M.E.P., eds. *Human Helplessness: Theory and Applications*. New York: Academic Press, 1980. pp. 261-277.

Solomon, K. The depressed patient: Social antecedents psychopathologic changes in the elderly. *Journal of the American Geriatrics Society* 29:14-18, 1981.

Somers, A.R. Marital status, health, and use of health services. *JAMA* 241:1818-1822, 1979.

Thomas, P.D.; Goodwin, J.M.; and Goodwin, J.S. Effect of social support on stress-related changes in cholesterol level, uric acid level, and immune function in an elderly sample. *American Journal of Psychiatry* 142:735-737, 1985.

Verbrugge, L.M. Marital status and health. *Journal of Marriage and Family* 41:267-285, 1979.

Weiss, R.S. *Marital Separation*. New York: Basic Books, 1975.

Yoshikawa, T.T. Geriatric infectious diseases: An emerging problem. *Journal of the American Geriatrics Society* 31:34-39, 1983.

Zarit, S.H.; Reever, K.E.; and Bach-Peterson, J. Relatives of the impaired elderly: Correlates of feelings of burden. *Gerontologist* 20:649-655, 1980.

Zarit, S.H.; Todd, P.A.; and Zarit, J.M. Subjective burden of husbands and wives as caregivers: A longitudinal study. *Gerontologist* 26:260-266, 1986.

Chapter 10

A Model of Burden in Caregivers of DAT Patients

Peter P. Vitaliano, Ph.D., Roland D. Maiuro, Ph.D.,
Hans Ochs, M.D., and Joan Russo

The goal of this chapter is to encourage new research directions for studying family stress arising from caring for a victim of dementia of the Alzheimer's type (DAT). A theoretical model is offered to guide research on the biopsychosocial correlates of burden in caregivers of patients with DAT. The rationale for the model is presented along with the advantages of this multidisciplinary approach. Finally, ways to implement the model in caregiver research are presented along with preliminary data to support the model's utility.

DAT is characterized by a progressively downward clinical course with increasing cognitive and behavioral impairment. As the disease progresses, DAT patients are less and less able to care for themselves and become more and more dependent on their caregivers. The majority of early DAT victims reside in the home and are cared for by a family member, usually the spouse (Brody 1974). Over time, increased cognitive/behavioral decline in patients may result in increased psychosocial impairment (chronic stressful burden) in spouses (Morycz and Blumenthal 1983; Rabins et al. 1982).

In general, researchers have recognized the potential effect of DAT patients on the well-being of their spouses. Excellent discussions of the effects of DAT patients on caregivers have been prepared (Lawton 1978; Morycz and Blumenthal 1983; Rabins et al. 1982; Zarit 1985; Zarit et al. 1980); however, few studies have systematically related

NOTE: This research was supported by a grant from the National Institute of Aging, ROI AG06770-0. We wish to thank Dianne Williams, Nina Chin, and Roslyn Siegel for their valuable assistance.

patient characteristics to caregiver characteristics (Lauden-slager et al. 1982).

Description of the Model

Few studies have examined caregiver burden using theoretical models of distress to guide their research.

One distress model (Vitaliano et al. 1987) argues that:

$$\text{Distress} = \frac{\text{Exposure to stressors} + \text{Vulnerability}}{\text{Psychological resources} + \text{Social resources}}$$

When applied to caregiver burden, "exposure to stressors" is operationalized in terms of both the DAT patient's cognitive and behavioral impairment and the caregiver's general life stressors (e.g., problems with children, finances). "Distress" is defined as biopsychosocial responses (e.g., perceived burden, anxiety, depression, immune/cardiovascular reactivity) to stressors as well as such moderating factors as "vulnerability" (e.g., health, personality, and demographic variables) and "resources" (e.g., social supports and coping). In this model, individuals may improve their emotional state either by decreasing undesirable factors (numerator) or by increasing desirable factors (denominator) to strengthen themselves.

Such a model has two major advantages in caregiver research. First, the variables represented are well grounded in the theoretical stress literature (Appley and Trumbull 1967; Hinkle 1974; Kahn 1970; McGrath 1970). The emphasis on vulnerability and resources is supported by extensive research that has examined the importance of these variables in modifying or confounding relationships between stressful events and distress. Second, the model requires that, in examining caregiver burden, the researcher stratify on levels of vulnerability and resources present in the spouse (Mantel and Haenszel 1959; Miettinen 1974). Stratification improves the researcher's chances of detecting a relationship between stressors and burden when it is present (i.e., statistical power).

Exposure to Stressors

One way to objectively define exposure to stressors is to use an epidemiologic definition. In this scheme, caregivers are viewed as "exposed" and controls as "unexposed." Controls are individuals who have the potential for a similar problem but who have not experienced the demands of caregiving. For example, controls could be elderly individuals who live with other elderly persons. These latter individuals might have health concerns, other than DAT, that are common in aged groups (e.g., hypertension, arthritis).

Another objective measure of caregiver stress is the DAT patient's cognitive and behavioral impairment. Theoretically, one would expect that the more impairment in the patient, the more caregiver burden.

As with individuals in general, caregivers must contend with an entire host of life stressors. Hence, life changes provide additional objective measures of stress, which must be accounted for in a comprehensive assessment of caregiver burden.

Modifier Variables

Although many stress researchers assume that mere exposure to stressful life events may precipitate distress and illness, others have challenged this belief. In particular, Rabkin and Struening (1976) noted that interindividual and intraindividual differences exist in subjects' responses to stressors and that these variations must be accounted for in the relationship between life stress and illness (Johnsons and Sarason 1979). For this reason, recent life-stress research has focused on determining those personal socioenvironmental variables that can modify the impact of stressful experiences. Two sets of variables that have been studied are vulnerability (i.e., characteristics in subjects that make them more susceptible to stressful experiences and distress) and resources (e.g., social supports and coping).

Vulnerability. Two complementary areas of the vulnerability literature have special relevance to the study of caregivers. The first area focuses on enduring, less controllable influences on the individual. Zubin and Spring (1977) viewed vulnerability as a genetically inherited trait (Kallmann 1959; Rosenthal 1970) as well as propensities acquired through experience. According to this view, the degree of distress induced by "challenging events" is determined by whether the vulnerability threshold is crossed and maladaptation ensues (Mechanic 1967). Examples of this type of vulnerability are biological disposition and personality variables (e.g., values, beliefs).

The second area reflects a more global demographic approach and may permit a more immediate identification of caregivers at risk for burden. It is derived from the literature on psychiatric epidemiology (Leighton et al. 1963a, 1963b; Robins 1978; Segal 1973; Thoits 1982; Weissman and Klerman 1978). Research in this area suggests that demographic variables (e.g., age, residential location, socioeconomic status, marital status) may be predictors of psychiatric disorder and distress.

Social resources. One dimension, social support, has been examined both as a correlate of distress (a direct or main effect) and as a modifier of the relationship between stressful experiences and distress (an interaction effect). Studies have consistently shown a direct effect of social resources on distress, but evidence for a buffering effect has been less clear (Leavy 1983). The lack of social resources has been associated with increased distress among the aged (Moriwaki 1973; Trainer and Bolin 1975). Simultaneously, individuals with high levels of support have been shown to have less distress than those with low support (Andrews et al. 1978; Dean et al. 1980; Lin et al. 1979; Williams et al. 1981). To a lesser extent, data have suggested that in the presence of stressors, adequate social support has prophylactic properties, whereas weak social support is a risk factor for illness (for reviews see Cassel 1974; Cobb 1976; Dean and Lin 1977; Esser and Vitaliano in press; Gottlieb 1981).

Psychological resources. Individuals' cognitive styles (attitudes, expections) and behavioral responses interact with the roles that social supports play for them (Carson 1969; Hirsch 1980, 1981; Leary 1957; Sullivan 1953; Tolsdorf 1976). Pearlin and Schooler (1978) further suggested that coping styles significantly influence a subject's ability to use available resources. In Lazarus, Averill, and Opton's (1974) cognitive-phenomenological approach, the nature of the situation influences the degree to which one employs direct actions that change the objective situation or uses internal and cognitive (intrapsychic) modes of coping. The former includes problem-focused coping (making a plan of action and following it); examples of the latter include wishful thinking, self-blame, avoidance, and blaming others. Seeking social supports can involve both direct action and emotion-regulating forms of coping. Several researchers have observed relationships between distress and both direct action and emotion-focused coping (Billings and Moos 1981; Folkman and Lazarus 1981; Vitaliano et al. 1986).

Distress

The theoretical distress model presented here lends itself nicely to multidisciplinary research if one considers both psychosocial and biological outcomes of distress. Engle (1977) argued that health research could profit greatly from biopsychosocial models. In caregiver research, such models should provide a more systematic picture

270

of a caregiver's burden than either set of variables alone. Knowledge of biological distress also complements data on self-reports of emotional distress/burden. Biological markers allow a direct assessment of the impact of caregiver burdens on two major physiological systems known to be affected by stress: the cardiovascular and immune systems. Moreover, most spouses of DAT patients are at an age that, when combined with chronic stressors induced by caregiving, puts them at high risk for cardiovascular morbidity and immune degradation. The interrelationships of these two biological systems with psychosocial distress are discussed below.

Cardiovascular and psychosocial distress. One of the most fruitful avenues of interdisciplinary stress research was with the Type A behavioral pattern and its relationship to coronary heart disease (CHD). Friedman and Rosenman (1959) identified a common cluster of Type A characteristics, including a hard-driving need for achievement, a sense of time urgency, anger/hostility, and aggressiveness (Glass 1977). Using a structured interview, Type A men were found to have twice the incidence of CHD compared to other men, even when competing risk factors were controlled (Rosenman et al. 1976). An increased risk for CHD was found for both men and women in the Framingham study using a self-report measure of Type A (Haynes et al. 1980). Laboratory studies have reinforced these results and provided evidence that elevated Type A behavior can result in increased serum lipids and triglycerides (Friedman et al. 1970), reduced secretions of 17-hydroxycorticosteroids in reaction to ACTH injection (Friedman et al. 1969), as well as increases in blood pressure and urinary and serum catecholamines under challenging circumstances (Friedman et al. 1975; Glass et al. 1980).

Some investigators have suggested that anger and hostility may be the primary correlates in Type A cardiovascular risk studies (Dembroski et al. 1985; Matthews et al. 1977). Hostility has itself been directly related to CHD and mortality (Shekelle et al. 1983; Barefoot et al. 1983). Another indicator of biological distress, cardiovascular reactivity to stressors, has been associated with suppression or denial of emotions in subjects with a positive family history of hypertension (Jorgensen and Houston 1986). Blood pressure responses to stressors also have been implicated in both hypertension and CHD (Steptoe et al. 1984). Moreover, elevated diastolic and systolic blood pressure and hypertension have been shown to be related to chronic suppressed anger (Gentry et al. 1982).

The above results indicate that Type A personality and anger have a number of biological correlates and may play an important role in modifying cardiovascular risk in response to stress. However, in the

271

elderly, it is not clear whether Type A or Type B behavior is a vulnerability factor. For example, in contrast to the association between Type A and CHD found in men under 65, Type B behavior has been associated with myocardial infarction in men over 65 years of age with blue-collar job status (Haynes et al. 1980). Thus, the type of relationship observed in one sample may not be generalizable to samples that differ in demographics or stressors. Further research is needed to clarify the biopsychosocial effects of Type A behavior on elderly individuals who experience stress.

Immunocompetence and psychosocial distress. The effect of acute stress on the immune system has been studied extensively in animal models. Lymphocyte proliferation in response to mitogen stimulation is suppressed in mice that are exposed to loud noise (Monjan and Collector 1977), in rats exposed to high- and low-dose electrical shock (Keller et al. 1981), in bonnet monkeys during infant-mother separation (Laudenslager et al. 1982), and in pigtail monkeys during peer separation (Reite et al. 1981).

The observed effects of stressful conditions on lymphocyte proliferation may be due to depletion of unique functional lymphocyte subpopulations or to selective redistribution of lymphocyte subsets within lymphoid tissue. Alternatively, a variety of hormonal and neurosecretory systems may be involved in the stress-induced modulation of the immune system. Electrical shocks, frequently used as stressors, have been shown to induce increased plasma steroid levels (Ader et al. 1979; Keller et al. 1983), decreased norepinephrine levels (Weiss et al. 1980), or secretion of endogenous opioids (Drugan et al. 1981). Corticosteroids can suppress a variety of immune functions, including mitogen-induced lymphocyte proliferation (Monjan and Collector 1977; Keller et al. 1981). Lymphopenia associated with stress has been related to elevated levels of corticosteroids (Ahmed et al. 1974; Keller et al. 1983). Similarly, stressors that induce endogenous opioid secretion were found to be immune-suppressive, while conditions that did not induce opioid secretion were not immunosuppressive (Shavit et al. 1982). Using adrenalectomized rats, Keller et al. (1983) demonstrated that corticosteroid (adrenal) independent mechanisms participated in the stress-induced suppression of in vitro lymphocyte proliferation.

Several well-controlled studies demonstrate that acute or chronic stress, depression, and loneliness affect the immune system in humans. Persons who lost their spouses exhibited decreased mitogen-induced lymphocyte responses when compared to nonbereaved controls (Bartrop et al. 1977). In vitro mitogen responses were also depressed by 48 hours of sleep deprivation (Palmbald et al. 1979).

Using highly stressed trainees from a psychiatric training program who were taking their final oral examination, Dorian and colleagues (1982) found transiently elevated numbers of T and B lymphocytes, impaired in vitro antibody synthesis, and depressed mitogen responses when compared with low-stressed controls.

Another naturally occurring stress situation was explored by Kiecolt-Glaser et al. (1984) and Glaser et al. (1985). Medical students were studied prospectively 4-6 weeks before and on the first day of their final examination. Those with high scores on stressful life events and loneliness had significantly lower levels of natural killer (NK) cell activity; depressed mitogen-induced lymphocyte proliferation; lower percentages of T-lymphocytes, CD4 (helper) and CD8 (suppressor) T cells; and elevated serum IgA concentrations during the examination, as compared with the values of 4-6 weeks before when their stress scores were low. The loneliest students had the most severe immune depression.

The immunologic consequences of chronic psychosocial stress were studied in a group of 34 DAT family caregivers (Kiecolt-Glaser et al. 1987). Degree of distress and loneliness in caregivers was related to the extent of impairment of the DAT patients. Compared with matched controls, caregivers had significantly higher antibody titers to EBV-VCA, presumably reflecting depressed cell-mediated control of the virus. Percentages of both total and helper (CD4) T-lymphocytes were lower, and helper/suppressor (CD4/CD8) ratio was depressed in the caregiver group. This study supports the hypothesis that chronic psychosocial stress causes persistent alterations in cellular immunity. It is reasonable to assume that humoral immunity is also affected by chronic psychosocial stress, considering the regulatory role T-lymphocytes play in the antibody response to T-dependent antigens.

Immunocompetence may also be affected or modified by resources (coping). In carefully controlled animal experiments, Lauderslager and associates (1983) compared the effects of escapable shocks (that could be avoided/changed), identical inescapable shocks (not avoidable), or no shock on the mitogen-induced lymphocyte proliferation. Lymphocyte responses were severely suppressed in the inescapable shock group but not in the escapable shock group, supporting the hypothesis that the controllability of events (a manifestation of both coping and appraisal) is critical in modulating immune function.

In another study, Kiecolt-Glaser et al. (1986) demonstrated that stress-related transient immune deficiency in humans could be modulated by the use of relaxation techniques. The frequency of relaxation practice was a significant predictor of the percentage of CD4 cells but not of NK cell activity.

273

Questions have also been raised about the role of anger in immunocompetence. One study found that breast cancer patients who suppress anger had significantly higher levels of serum immunoglobin A than patients who express anger (Pettingale et al. 1977). Serum immunoglobin A appears to correlate positively with metastasis, suggesting a pathological risk associated with anger suppression and some types of cancer. Although some studies have suggested that both expressed and suppressed anger may be related to cancer development (Greer and Morris 1975), others have indicated that cancer patients are characterized by less anger expression (Morris et al. 1981). One group of researchers (Tobin and Lieberman 1976; Tobin 1980) found that the single most powerful predictor of morbidity and mortality for elderly individuals undergoing the stress of relocating was the dimension of passivityaggressivity. More negative outcomes were associated with passivity, a result that Tobin (1980) suggested might be related to either biological deterioration or heightened stress. In contrast, aggressive behavior (e.g., angry, irritating, and demanding) was positively associated with survival rates (Lieberman 1975).

Implementation of the Model

Ideally, an adequate realization of the model offered here should involve a design that includes exposed (caregivers) and nonexposed (noncaregivers) individuals along with repeated assessments of each group over time. In epidemiology, this is known as a multi-cohort longitudinal design. The cases and controls should preferably be matched according to relevant demographic variables (age, gender, and health status) at entrance to the study. Table 10-1 contains a list of the types of variables that should be useful in realizing the components of the model. The design and variables presented in the table are for studying caregivers who are also spouses of DAT patients. This is consistent with our current research (Vitaliano 1986).

The proposed design for implementing the model lends itself well to several hypotheses of interest in research on caregivers:

1. Both initially and at followup, spouses of DAT patients with mild dementia would be more distressed (biologically and psychosocially) than spouses of matched controls.

2. At followup, the mean distress scores of spouses of mild DAT patients would be greater than they were at initial assessment,

Table 10-1. Constructs, variables, and measures used to operationalize proposed distress (burden) model

Constructs in spouse distress model	Variables (indicators)	Measures
DISTRESS		
1. Immunocompetence	B and T lymphocytes, lympho-cyte proliferation, natural killer cells, helper cells, immunoglobulin synthesis	
2. Cardiovascular disease risk	Obesity, hypertension, cardiovascular reactivity, hyperlipidemia	Weight, height, DBP/SBP, pulse, HDL, LDL, triglycerides
3. Psychosocial	Anxiety	Symptom Checklist-90
	Depression severity	Beck Depression Inventory
	Perceived burden	Alzheimer's Spouse Burden Scale
	Marital adjustment	Dyadic Adjustment Scale
	Psychiatric illnesses (e.g., adjustment reaction)	Diagnostic Interview Schedule
	Loneliness	Revised UCLA Loneliness Scale
STRESSORS		
1. Having a DAT spouse	(yes, no)	
2. General life stressors	Nonsocial (e.g., financial debt)	Life Experience Survey (Dohrenwend)
	Social (e.g., friend's death)	
	Health (e.g., illness or injury)	
3. DAT patient/control characteristics		
a. Cognitive	(e.g., orientation, memory)	Mini-Mental Status
b. Behavioral	(e.g., toileting, feeding)	Record of Independent Living
c. Affective	Depression symptomatology (e.g., anorexia, insomnia)	Hamilton Depression Rating Scale
VULNERABILITY		
1. Demographics	(e.g., gender, age, education)	Screen and Psychosocial Interview
2. Health status/history	(e.g., no ailments, some hospitalization, family history of CVD)	Rosencranz Health Index, and Psychosocial Interview
3. Health behaviors	Exercise, diet, sleep, smok-ing, eating/drinking habits	Human Population Labora-tory Questionnaire
	Nutritional intake	4-Day Food Record
4. Psychiatric status/ history	(e.g., history/current presence of affective, anxiety disorders)	Diagnostic Interview Schedule
5. Personality	Anger/hostility	Spielberger Anger Expression Trait/State Anger
	Type A	Framingham Scale
	Emotional lability	Framingham Scale
	Daily stress	Reeder Daily Stress
RESOURCES		
1. Social Network	Number of available social supports–satisfaction with supports	Sarason Social Support Questionnaire
	Upset/helpful dimensions	Dunkel- Shetter UCLA Social Support Questionnaire
2. Coping	(e.g., problem-focused, wishful thinking)	Vitaliano et al. Revised Ways of Coping Checklist
	Change, accept, hold back, etc.	Vitaliano et al. Dimensions of Appraisal

whereas mean differences over time in spouses of control subjects would be less extensive.

3. Over time, increases in distress (e.g., immunocompetence, cardiovascular risk, and psychosocial impairment) among *DAT spouses* would be associated with increases in respective DAT patients' cognitive/functional decline. However, these relationships would be modified by spouse variables in the distress model. These would include life stressors not necessarily associated with the DAT patients' illness (e.g., finances, problems with children). Such variables would amplify caregiver distress/burden. Vulnerability (e.g., demographics, physical/psychiatric health history, personality) variables would also amplify distress among DAT spouses. In contrast, resources (e.g., coping and social supports) would ameliorate distress reactions among DAT spouses.

Empirical Support for the Model

Currently, a longitudinal study is underway that is empirically validating the utility of the distress model. Thus far, 63 dyads (spouse caregivers and DAT patients) have been examined. Criteria for patient inclusion were: (1) DSM-III diagnosis of Primary Degenerative Dementia (PDD) (no mixed dementias), (2) *mild-to-moderate stage of DAT* (i.e., Mini-Mental Status (MMS) score of 10-28 and Record of Independent Living (RIL) scores corresponding to "trouble with higher level activities"), and (3) living with one's spouse who is the caregiver.

In this study, distress is defined as caregiver burden using the Spouse Burden Scale (Vitaliano 1986). Exposure to stress is defined both as the DAT patient's cognitive impairment as measured by the MMS Exam (Folstein et al. 1975) and behavioral impairment on the RIL (Weintraub et al. 1982). Exposure to stress is additionally assessed by general life stressors (e.g., financial problems, problems with children).

Vulnerability is defined in four ways: (1) personality–anger held in and anger expressed out (Spielberger et al. 1985); (2) health–number of major illnesses, minor illnesses, and days in bed per year (Rosencranz and Pihlblad 1970); (3) emotion-focused coping–wishful thinking, avoidance, self-blame (Vitaliano et al. 1985); and (4) demographic variables–age, gender, education. Psychological resources are defined as problem-focused coping and seeking social supports (Vitaliano et al. 1985), and social resources are defined as number and satisfaction with social supports (Sarason et al. in press).

276

Results and Discussion

Spouse Burden

On the 21-item *Spouse Burden Scale*, the mean in our study was 18.3 (*SD* = 11.4; range 2-51). The items in which the spouses reported the most distress were "I have little control over my spouse's illness" (82.5 percent reported distress), "I have little control over my spouse's behavior" (77.8 percent), "My spouse is constantly asking the same questions over and over" (71.4 percent), "I am upset that I cannot communicate with my spouse" (55.6 percent), "I have to do too many jobs/chores that my spouse used to perform" (39.7 percent), "My spouse continues to drive when he/she shouldn't" (36.5 percent), "It is frustrating trying to find things that my spouse hides" (34.9 percent), "I worry that my spouse will leave the house and get lost" (31.7 percent), and "I am totally responsible for keeping our household in order" (33.3 percent).

Spouse Stressors

Patient characteristics are critical because they contribute greatly to the stress the spouse caregiver has to endure. Behavioral functioning such as *maintenance* (e.g., washing, eating, mobility) and *higher functioning* (e.g., talking, listening, hobbies) and cognitive deficits such as memory and attention problems are examples of such patient characteristics (Weintraub et al. 1982; Vitaliano et al. 1984).

Our patient data are in line with our inclusion criteria of only accepting participants in the earlier and milder stages of dysfunction. If we examine the mean item scores for patients on Maintenance and Higher Functioning, we find that the means are similar whether spouses or interviewers rated patients (*M* Maintenance is 0.84 for spouses and 0.95 for the interviewer; *M* Higher Functioning is 2.03 for spouses and 1.51 for the interviewer). These values indicate that on the Maintenance scale the patients lie between "no problem" (anchor point of 0) and "can do it alone, but needs more time" (anchor point of 1). On the Higher Functioning scale, the patients lie between "needs more time" (1) and "needs reminders, being told what to do ahead of time" (2). On the MMS, the *M* is 20.5 and the *SD* is 4.7 (range is 10-28), suggesting a relatively mild-to-moderate phase of cognitive deficit for most of the patients (only 14 percent had scores below 15).

In addition to spouse stressors related to the illness of the DAT patient, the spouses reported their distress due to several *general life stressors* appropriate to elderly samples. In order of prevalence of reported distress, these included change in family member's health (60.3 percent reported distress), change in relationship with spouse (51.6 percent), death of a family member or friend (47.6 percent), worry about children (45.2 percent), serious illness or injury of close family member (41.7 percent), and change in your (spouse's) physical health (33.3 percent). Moreover, 82.4 percent of the spouses chose one of these events as the major stressor in their life.

Vulnerability

Twenty (31.7 percent) of the spouses were men, and 43 (68.3 percent) were women. The mean age was 68.0 (SD = 7.6) with a range of 50 to 85 years. The mean educational level was 13.8 years (SD = 2.7), with a range of 8 to 24 years. In terms of spouse health, the six most prevalent *illnesses* were arthritis/rheumatism (52.4 percent), hypertension (41.3 percent), allergies (27.0 percent), sinus trouble (23.8 percent), tumor/cyst (22.2 percent), thyroid/goiter (19.0 percent), trouble with back/spine (17.5 percent), chronic gall bladder/liver (17.5 percent), and hernia/rupture (17.5 percent). Thirty-four percent reported that a health problem bothered them in the last 4 weeks. They also reported seeing a physician a mean of 2.3 times per year (SD = 2.0; median = 1.5); 59 of the 63 reported having a specific family doctor.

In terms of cardiovascular problems, 34 of the spouses had neither heart problems nor hypertension, and 29 had hypertension and/or other cardiovascular problems. A *Health Status* variable was developed following Rosencranz's scoring procedure; weights were provided for major/minor illnesses/ailments in the 4 weeks preceding testing (Rosencranz and Pihlblad 1970). On this index, the scores ranged from 0 to 38, M = 13.6 (SD = 9.2), and median = 10.4, suggesting a positively skewed distribution.

On anger held in (as a mode of expression), spouses had a mean score of 14.1 (SD = 3.0) and a range of 9 to 21, whereas on *anger out* they had a mean score of 11.9 (SD = 3.1) and a range of 8 to 22. Anger held in was shown to be a major vulnerability factor for spouse distress.

Spouse Resources

When the relative scores for the *Ways of Coping Checklist* scales were computed (Vitaliano et al. 1987), the group means and SDs on the percentages of efforts used were Problem-Focused (21.7 ± 6.9),

278

Wishful Thinking (20.6 ± 8.3), Seeks Social Support (20.2 ± 7.8), Avoidance (18.7 ± 7.4), and Self-Blame (18.8 ± 10.2).

In terms of their *appraisal* of the major stressor in their lives, 57.1 percent of the spouses believed they had some control over their major stressor (problem), 98.2 percent (all but 1 spouse) said it was very important to them, 81.0 percent believed it would always be a problem in their life, 74.6 percent believed it was threatening, 52.4 percent considered it to be ambiguous, and 93.5 percent said they had to accept their major stressor. Spouses reported a mean of 3.8 people (social supports) they could depend on (SD = 2.1, range = 0-9). Their mean satisfaction was 5.3 (SD = .65, range = 2-6), indicating that they were somewhere between "very satisfied" to "fairly satisfied" with their social supports.

Interrelationships of Burden and Other Variables

Table 10-2 contains zero-order correlations of burden with the other variables in the model. To reduce the number of correlations, summary scores for patient functioning were obtained by adding the Z scores of the cognitive and behavioral measures (this score was labeled total functioning). Patient functioning was rated independently by spouse caregivers and by a trained interviewer. This allowed us to determine whether the ratings were biased by spouse distress or spouse anger. Given these ratings, it was important that both spouse-assessed total functioning and interviewer-assessed total functioning be significantly related to burden. Note that the correlation of burden and patient functioning is -.41 (p<.001) for spouse-assessed functioning and -.27 (p<.05) for interviewerassessed functioning. Hence, direct relationships between patient functioning (exposure) and caregiver burden existed using both procedures.

The model predicts that, for a given level of functioning, some caregivers will experience more burden than others, based on their vulnerabilities and resources. Direct relationships between burden and these variables are shown in table 10-2. Caregivers who experienced more burden tended to be younger, have problems with their children, have higher scores on anger in and anger out as modes of expression, have less satisfaction with and use of social supports, and use more emotion-focused coping than caregivers who experienced less burden.

Our ultimate goal was to determine the degree to which multiple spouse variables could be used in conjunction with patient functioning and the interactions of patient functioning and spouse variables to predict burden. In this spirit, we examined each specific variable in the theoretical model in conjunction with patient functioning and

Table 10-2. Relationships of caregiver burden with caregiver stressors, vulnerability, and resources

Variable	Burden
Caregiver stressors	
Patient Mini-Mental Status score	-.13
Patient maintenance	
- Interviewer assessed	.27*
- Spouse assessed	.46***
Patient higher functioning	
- Interviewer assessed	.33**
- Spouse assessed	.40***
Patient total functioning	
- Interviewer assessed	-.41**
- Spouse assessed	-.27*
Problems with children	.26*
Caregiver vulnerability	
Anger held in	.34**
Anger out	.34**
Health	-.02
Emotion-focused coping	.67**
Age	-.33**
Gender	.06
Caregiver resources	
Number of social supports	-.08
Satisfaction with supports	.26*
Social support factor (number and satisfaction) . . .	-.19
Seeking social support coping	-.32**
Problem-focused coping	.14

Note: * = $p<.05$; ** = $p<.01$; *** $p<.001$

the interaction of that variable with patient functioning. However, we assessed the importance of spouse age and gender and DAT patient's depression (and their interactions with functioning) first to determine whether these variables needed to be included in subsequent models of burden. Only spouse age was significant, so it was included in all subsequent models.

Table 10-3 shows the results of these models (F value, p value, and R) for four vulnerability variables, three resources, and one life stressor. Only life stressors related to problems with children were used because the other stressors were either indirectly related to the DAT patient's illness (e.g., problems with spouse) or they had little variability. Models were developed in parallel for spouse and interviewer's ratings of patient functioning. All variables were significant, independent of functioning, except for health and problem-focused coping.

In testing interactions between the spouse variables and total patient functioning, only one variable yielded a significant interaction–anger held in. This was also significant in the two summary models (across all spouse variables). For spouse assessments, the model included spouse age (t (58) = 3.47, p<.001), total patient functioning (t (58) = -5.16, p<.001), anger in (t (58) = -4.01, p<.001), and the interaction of anger held in and functioning (t (58) = 2.63, p<.01). The model's overall F value was F(4,58) = 12.24; p< .001, R^2 adj = .42.

For interviewer assessments, the model included: spouse age (t (58) = 1.77, p<.08), total patient functioning (t (58) = -4.02, p<.001), anger out (t (58) = -2.68, p<.01), and emotion-focused coping (t (58) = -3.27, p<.002). The model's overall F value was F(4,58) = 9.62; p<.001, R^2 adj = .36.

The models indicate that high burden scores are associated with greater patient impairment (poorer functioning), greater anger out and greater anger held in, and greater emotion-focused coping. However, the relationship with burden and anger held in only occurs in spouses who are involved with DAT patients who have poorer functioning (higher impairment) scores and not in spouses involved with patients with higher functioning (low impairment) scores. This interaction is understandable because higher levels of DAT patient impairment are more likely to challenge the caregiver emotionally and be associated with anger management strategies.

Preliminary data on 63 spouse dyads indicate that the model of distress offered here for the study of caregivers has research utility. Burden is shown to be a function of both objective stressors (patient's cognitive and behavioral impairment) and spouse vulnerability. The global models provide a profile of those variables that make *unique*

281

Table 10-3. Single regression analyses for caregiver burden

Variable	df	Spouse assessed Δ F	Spouse assessed Δ R^{2a}	Interviewer assessed ΔF	Interviewer assessed ΔR^{2a}
Spouse age	1,61	7.3**	.09	7.3**	.09
Patient functioning	1,60	14.9***	.15	6.8*	.08
Caregiver vulnerability					
Anger held in	1,59^b	6.9**	.16	11.1**	.12
Anger out	1,59	5.2*	.05	8.0**	.09
Health	1,59	1.2	.00	.7	.00
Emotion-focused coping . .	1,59	10.0***	.10	11.6**	.13
Caregiver resources					
Problem-focused coping . .	1,59	2.2	.02	2.6	.02
Seeking social support coping	1,59	5.3*	.05	5.7*	.06
Social support factor	1,59	3.9*	.03	4.9*	.05
Other caregiver stressors					
Problems with children . . .	1,59	4.8*	.04	3.8*	.03

Note: $a = R^2$ adjusted for number of variables and sample size; b = main effect and interaction with functioning for spouse- assessed impairment (df = 2,59)
 $* = p<.05$; ** $p< .01$; *** $p<.001$

contributions to spouse burden. Interestingly, of the several spouse variables included in table 10-3, only three provide independent contributions to burden, and two of the three involve anger expression. Our literature review pointed out that anger expression has a major role in biological distress. As measured in this study, anger expression is not a mere byproduct of distress, but rather a dispositional mode of behavior and a vulnerability factor.

Our research with medical students indicated that scores on the Anger Expression Scale remain relatively stable (retest reliability of 0.7) over an 8-month interval, whereas scores on distress change markedly (reliability of .2-.3) (Vitaliano et al. 1987).

The demonstrated importance of anger in perceived caregiver burden also has implications for one of the longitudinal hypotheses in our current caregiver study. This study will prospectively assess 90 dyads over time. We expect that caregiver anger may be associated with a decline in DAT patients' functioning scores beyond what is expected from the patients' initial functioning scores. This proposition comes from research on schizophrenia and "expressed emotion." Researchers in the United States and the United Kingdom have studied the ways in which intrafamilial emotional communication influences the course of schizophrenic disorders. Expressed Emotion (EE) is assessed as either high or low on the basis of empirically derived cutting scores applied to a relative's expressions of criticism, hostility, and overinvolvement toward the patient during a structured interview, the Camberwell Family Interview (Vaughn and Leff 1976a). Ratings of a relative's EE near the time of a patient's hospital admission have been predictive of schizophrenic relapse in the 9 months following hospital discharge (Brown et al. 1972; Vaughn et al. 1982) and at a 2-year followup (Leff and Vaughn 1981). Patients returning to a family environment with high EE are four times as likely to relapse within 9 months of discharge as patients returning to families rated low on EE (Vaughn et al. 1982; Vaughn and Leff 1976b).

Although there are undoubtedly numerous differences in the cognitive, behavioral, and emotional experiences of DAT versus schizophrenic patients (to say nothing of major age differences), the EE literature suggests a potential link between the cognitive/behavioral processes of patients and the psychosocial characteristics of caregivers. Given the increasingly intensive interactions that exist between patients and caregivers over the course of DAT, it would appear that data on emotional and interpersonal dynamics may offer valuable sources of information for developing predictive models and designing intervention strategies.

Conclusion

In summary, we believe that to properly understand caregiver burden, multidisciplinary longitudinal studies need to be performed. Such studies should compare psychosocial, immunological, and cardiovascular distress in spouses of mild DAT patients to such distress in age-, sex-, and health status-matched spouses of controls. Attempts can also be made to match the controls to the DAT patients on age and depression. If measures such as those in table 10-1 are obtained on these samples, several provocative questions can be addressed: To what degree are spouses of DAT patients more distressed than spouses of controls at baseline and subsequent assessments? Do spouses of DAT patients become more distressed (e.g., more immune degradation, higher BP, depression) over time? If so, is the increase in distress explained in part by cognitive/functional decline in the DAT patient? Are certain types of spouses (e.g., hostile/angry, poor health) more affected by patients' cognitive and behavioral decline than other spouses? Finally, do biological and psychosocial variables correlate more highly over time? We believe that answers to these questions will improve our understanding of the interaction of family stress, coping strategies, and the management of DAT.

References

Ader, R.; Cohen, N.; and Gorta, L.J. Adrenal involvement in conditioned immunosuppression. *International Journal of Immunopharmacology* 1:141-145, 1979.

Ahmed, A.; Herman, C.M.; Knudsen, R.C.; Sode, J.; Strong, D.M.; and Sell, K.W. Effect of exogenous and endogenous glucocorticosteroids on the in vitro stimulation of lymphocytes from sedated and aware-restrained healthy baboons. *Journal of Surgical Research* 16:172-182, 1974.

Andrews, G.; Tennant, C.; Hewson, D.; and Vaillant, G. Life event, stress, social support, coping style, and risk of psychological impairment. *Journal of Nervous and Mental Disease* 166:307-316, 1978.

Appley, M.H., and Trumbull, R. On the concept of psychological stress. In: Appley, M.H., and Trumbull, R., eds. *Psychological Stress*. New York: Appleton-Century-Crofts, 1967. pp. 1-13.

Barefoot, J.C.; Dahlstrom, W.G.; and Williams, R.B. Hostility, CHD incidence, and total mortality: A 25-year follow-up study of 255 physicians. *Psychosomatic Medicine* 45:59-63, 1983.

Bartrop, R.W.; Luckhurst, E.; Lazarus, L.; Kiloh, L.G.; and Penny, R. Depressed lymphocyte function after bereavement. *Lancet* 1:834-836, 1977.

Billings, A.G., and Moos, R.H. The role of coping responses and social resources in attenuating the stress of life events. *Journal of Behavioral Medicine* 4:139-157, 1981.

Brody, E. Aging and the family personality: A developmental view. *Family Process* 13:23, 1974.

Brown, G.W.; Birley, J.L.T.; and Wing, J.F. Influence of family life on the course of schizophrenic disorders: A replication. *British Journal of Psychiatry* 121:241-258, 1972.

Carson, R.I. *Interaction Concepts of Personality*. Chicago: Aldine-Atherton, 1969.

Cassel, J. Psychosocial processes and "stress" theoretical formulation. *International Journal of Health Services* 4:471-482, 1974.

Cobb, S.B. Social support as a moderator of life stress. *Psychosomatic Medicine* 38:300-314, 1976.

Dean, A., and Lin, N. The stress-buffering role of social support. *Journal of Nervous and Mental Disease* 165:403-417, 1977.

Dean, A.; Lin, N.; and Ensel, W. The epidemiological significance of social support systems in depression. In: Simmons, R.G., ed. *Research in Community Mental Health*. Vol. 2. Greenwich, CT: JAI Press, 1980.

Dembroski, T.M.; MacDougall, J.M.; Williams, R.B.; Haney, T.L.; and Blumenthal, J.A. Components of Type A, hostility, and anger-in: Relationship to angiographic findings. *Psychosomatic Medicine* 47:219-233, 1985.

Dorian, B.; Garfinkle, P.; Brown, G.; Shore, A.; Dafna, G.; and Key-stone, E. Aberrations in lymphocyte subpopulations and function during psychological stress. *Clinical Experimental Immunology* 50:132-138, 1982.

Drugan, R.C.; Grau, J.W.; Maier, S.F.; and Marchas, J.D. Cross tolerance between morphine and the long-term analgesic reaction to inescapable shock. *Pharmacological Biochemical Behavior* 14:677-682, 1981.

Engel, G.L. The need for a new medical model: A challenge for biomedicine. *Science* 196:129-136, 1977.

Esser, S., and Vitaliano, P.P. Depression, dementia and social supports. *International Journal of Aging and Human Development*, in press.

Folkman, S., and Lazarus, R.S. An analysis of coping in a middle-aged community sample. *Journal of Health and Social Behavior* 21:219-239, 1981.

Folstein, M.F.; Folstein, E.; and McHugh, P.R. Mini Mental State: A practical method for grading the cognitive state of patients for the clinician. *Journal of Psychiatric Research* 12:189-198, 1975.

Friedman, M.; Byers, S.; Diamant, J.; and Rosenman, R.H. Plasma ACTH and cortisol concentration of coronary-prone subjects (Type A) to specific challenge. *Metabolism* 24:205-210, 1975.

Friedman, M.; Byers, S.; Rosenman, R.H.; and Elevitch, F.R. Coronary prone individuals (Type A behavior pattern): Some biochemical characteristics. *JAMA* 212:1030-1037, 1970.

Friedman, M., and Rosenman, R.H. Association of specific overt behavior pattern with blood and cardiosvascular findings. *JAMA* 169:1286-1296, 1959.

Friedman, M.; Rosenman, R.H.; and St. George, S. Adrenal response to excess corticotropin in coronary prone men. *Proceedings of the*

Society of Experimental Biology and Medicine 131:1305-1307, 1969.

Gentry, W.D.; Chesney, A.P.; Gary, H.E.; Hall, R.P.; and Harburg, E. Habitual anger-coping styles. I: Effect of mean blood pressure and risk for essential hypertension. *Psychosomatic Medicine* 44:195-202, 1982.

Glaser, R.; Kiecolt-Glaser, J.K.; Stout, J.C.; Tarr, K.L.; Speicher, C.E.; and Holliday, J.E. Stress-related impairments in cellular immunity. *Psychological Research* 16:233-239, 1985.

Glass, D.C. *Behavior Pattern, Stress and Coronary Heart Disease.* Hillsdale, NJ: Erlbaum, 1977.

Glass, D.C.; Krakoff, L.R.; Contrada, R.; Hilton, W.F.; Kehoe, K.; Mannucci, E.G.; Collins, C.; Snow, B.; and Elting, E. Effect of harassment and competition upon cardiovascular and plasma catecholamine response in Type A and Type B individuals. *Psychophysiology* 17:453-463, 1980.

Gottlieb, B. Social networks and social support in community mental health. In: Gottlieb, B., ed. *Social Networks and Social Support.* Vol. 4. Sage Studies in Community Mental Health. Beverly Hills, CA: Sage, 1981. pp. 11-42.

Greer, S., and Morris, T. Psychological attributes of women who develop breast cancer: A controlled study. *Journal of Psychosomatic Research* 19:147-153, 1975.

Haynes, S.G.; Feinleib, M.; and Kannel, W.B. The relationship of psychosocial factors to coronary heart disease in the Framingham Study: III, 8-year incidence of coronary heart disease. *American Journal of Epidemiology* 111:37-58, 1980.

Hinkle, L.E. The concept of stress in the biological and social sci-ences. *International Journal of Psychiatry in Medicine* 5:335-357, 1974.

Hirsch, B. Natural support systems and coping with major life changes. *American Journal of Community Psychology* 8:159-172, 1980.

Hirsch, B. Social networks and the coping process. Creating personal communities. In: Gottlieb, B., ed. *Social Networks and Social Support.* Vol. 4. Sage Studies in Community Mental Health. Beverly Hills, CA: Sage, 1981. pp. 149-170.

Johnson, J.H., and Sarason, I.G. Recent developments in research on life stress. In: Hamilton, V., and Warburton, D.M., eds. *Human Stress and Cognition.* London: Wiley, 1979. pp. 205-233.

Jorgensen, R.S., and Houston, B.K. Family history of hypertension, personality pattern, and cardiovascular reactivity to stress. *Psychosomatic Medicine* 48:102-117, 1986.

Kahn, R.L. Some propositions toward a researchable conceptualization of stress. In: McGrath, J., ed. *Social and Psychological Factors in Stress*. New York: Holt, Rinehart and Winston, 1970. pp. 97-103.

Kallman, F.J. The genetics of mental illness. In: Arieti, S., ed. *American Handbook of Psychiatry*. Vol. 1. New York: Basic Books, 1959. pp. 145-149.

Keller, S.E.; Weiss, J.M.; Schleifer, S.J.; Miller, N.E.; and Stein, M. Suppression of immunity by stress: Effect of a graded series of stressors on lymphocyte stimulation in the rat. *Science* 213:1397-1400, 1981.

Keller, S.E.; Weiss, J.M.; Schleifer, S.J.; Miller, N.E.; and Stein, M. Stress-induced suppression of immunity in adrenalectomized rats. *Science* 221:1301-1304, 1983.

Kiecolt-Glaser, J.K.; Garner, W.; Speicher, C.; Penn, G.M.; Holliday, J.; and Glaser, R. Psychosocial modifiers of immunocompetence in medical students. *Psychosomatic Medicine* 46:7-14, 1984.

Kiecolt-Glaser, J.K.; Glaser, R.; Shuttleworth, E.C.; Dyer, C.S.; and Speicher, C.E. Chronic stress and immunity in family caregivers of Alzheimer's disease victims. *Psychosomatic Medicine* 49:523-535, 1987.

Kiecolt-Glaser, J.K.; Glaser, R.; Strain, E.C.; Stout, J.C.; Tarr, K.L.; Holliday, J.E.; and Speicher, C.E. Modulaton of cellular immunity in medical students. *Journal of Behavioral Medicine* 9:5-21, 1986.

Laudenslager, M.L.; Reite, M.; and Harbeck, R.J. Suppressed immune response in infant monkeys associated with maternal separation. *Behavioral Neural Biology* 36:40-48, 1982.

Laudenslager, M.L.; Ryan, S.M.; Drugan, R.C.; Hyson, R.L.; and Maier, S.F. Coping and immunosuppression: Inescapable but not escapable shock suppresses lymphocyte proliferation. *Science* 221(1):568-570, 1983.

Lawton, M.P. Psychosocial and environmental approaches to the care of senile dementia patients. In: Cole, J.O., and Barrett, J.E., eds. *Psychopathology and the Aged*. New York: Raven Press, 1978. pp. 265-280.

Lazarus, R.S.; Averill, J.R.; and Opton, E.M., Jr. The psychology of coping: Issues of research and assessment. In: Coehlo, G.V.; Hamburg, D.A.; and Adams, J.E., eds. *Coping and Adaptation*. New York: Basic Books, 1974. pp. 249-315.

Leary, J. *Interpersonal Diagnosis of Personality*. New York: Ronald Press, 1957.

Leavy, R. Social support and psychological disorder: A review. *Journal of Community Psychology* 11:3-21, 1983.

Leff, J., and Vaughn, C. The role of maintenance therapy and relatives' expressed emotion in relapse of schizophrenia. *British Journal of Psychiatry* 139:102-104, 1981.

Leighton, D.C.; Harding, J.S.; Macklin, B.; Hughes, C.C.; and Leighton, A.H. Psychiatric findings of the Sterling County study. *American Journal of Psychiatry.* 119:1021-1026, 1963b.

Leighton, D.C.; Harding, J.S.; Macklin, B.; MacMillian, A.M.; and Leighton, A.H. *The Character of Danger.* New York: Basic Books, 1963a.

Lieberman, M.A. Adaptive processes in late life. In: Datan, N., and Ginsberg, L.H., eds. *Life Span Developmental Psychology: Normative Life Crises.* New York: Academic Press, 1975.

Lin, N.; Simeone, R.B.; Ensel, W.M.; and Kuo, W. Social support, stressful life events, and illness: A model and an empirical test. *Journal of Health and Social Behavior* 20:108-110, 1979.

Mantel, N., and Haenszel, W. Statistical aspects of the analysis of data from retrospective studies of disease. *Journal of the National Cancer Institute* 22:719-748, 1959.

Matthews, K.A.; Glass, D.C.; Rosenman, R.H.; and Bontner, R.W. Competitive drive, pattern A, coronary heart disease: A further analysis of some data from the Western Collaborative Group Study. *Journal of Chronic Diseases* 30:489-498, 1977.

McGrath, J., ed. *Social and Psychological Factors in Stress.* New York: Holt, Rinehart and Winston, 1970.

Mechanic, D. Invited commentary on self, social environment and stress. In: Appley, M.H., and Trumbull, R., eds. *Psychological Stress.* New York: Appleton-Century-Crofts, 1967. pp. 123-150.

Miettinen, D. Confounding and effect modification. *American Journal of Epidemiology* 100:350-353, 1974.

Monjan, A.A., and Collector, M.I. Stress induced modulation of the immune response. *Science* 196:307-308, 1977.

Moriwaki, S.Y. Self disclosure, significant other, and psychological well-being in old age. *Journal of Health and Social Behavior* 14:226-232, 1973.

Morris, T.; Greer, S.; Pettingale, K.W.; and Watson, M. Patterns of expression of anger and their psychological correlates in women with breast cancer. *Journal of Psychosomatic Research* 25:111-117, 1981.

Morycz, R.K., and Blumenthal, M.D. Late-life brain disease and family burden: Some theoretical perspectives. *Community Support Service Journal* 2:1-8, 1983.

Palmbald, J.; Petrini, B.; Wasserman, J.; and Akerstedt, T. Lymphocyte and granulocyte reactions during sleep deprivation. *Psychosomatic Medicine* 41:273-278, 1979.

Pearlin, L.I., and Schooler, C. The structure of coping. *Journal of Health and Social Behavior* 19:2-21, 1978.

Pettingale, K.W.; Greer, S.; and Tee, D.E. Serum IgA and emotional expression in breast cancer patients. *Journal of Psychosomatic Research* 21:395-399, 1977.

Rabins, P.; Place, N.; and Lucas, M. The impact of dementia on the family. *JAMA* 248:333-335, 1982.

Rabkin, J.G., and Struening, E.L. Life events, stress, and illness. *Science* 194:1013-1020, 1976.

Reite, M.; Harbeck, R.; and Hoffman, A. Altered cellular immune response following peer separation. *Life Science* 29:1133-1136, 1981.

Robins, L.N. Psychiatric epidemiology. *Archives of General Psychiatry* 35:697-702, 1978.

Rosencranz, H.A., and Pihlblad, C.T. Measuring the health of the elderly. *Journal of Gerontology* 25:129-133, 1970.

Rosenman, R.H.; Brand, R.J.; Sholtz, R.I.; and Friedman, M. Multivariate prediction of coronary heart disease during $8^{1}/2$ year follow-up in the Western Collaborative Group Study. *American Journal of Cardiology* 37:903-910, 1976.

Rosenthal, D. *Genetic Theory and Abnormal Behavior*. New York: McGraw-Hill, 1970.

Sarason, I.G.; Sarason, B.R.; Shearin, E.N.; and Pierce, G.R. A brief measure of social support: Practical and theoretical implications. *Journal of Social and Personal Relationships*, in press.

Segal, J., ed. *The Mental Health of Rural America: The Rural Programs of the National Institute of Mental Health*. DHEW Pub. No. 73-9035. Rockville, MD: Alcohol, Drug Abuse, and Mental Health Administration, 1973.

Shavit, Y.; Lewis, J.W.; Terman, G.W.; Gale, R.P.; and Liebeskind, J.C. *(Abstract.) Social Neuroscience* 8:71, 1982.

Shekelle, R.B.; Gale, M.; Ostfeld, A.M.; and Paul, O. Hostility, risk of coronary heart disease, and mortality. *Psychosomatic Medicine* 45:109-114, 1983.

Spielberger, C.D.; Johnson, E.G.; Russell, S.S.; Crane, R.J.; Jacobs, G.A.; and Worden, T.J. The experience and expression of anger: Construction and validation of an anger expression scale. In: Chesney, M.A., and Rosenman, R.H., eds. *Anger and Hostility in Cardiovascular and Behavioral Disorders*. New York: Hemisphere, 1985. pp. 5-30.

Steptoe, A.; Melville, D.; and Ross, A. Behavioral response demands, cardiovascular reactivity, and essential hypertension. *Psychosomatic Medicine* 46:33-48, 1984.

Sullivan, H.S. *The Interpersonal Theory of Psychiatry*. New York: Norton, 1953.

Thoits, P.A. Life stress, social support, and psychological vulnerability: Epidemiological considerations. *Journal of Community Psychology* 10:341-362, 1982.

Tobin, S.S., and Lieberman, M.A. *Last Home for the Aged: Critical Implications of Institutionalization*. San Francisco: Jossey-Bass, 1976.

Tobin, S.S. Institutionalization of the aged. In: Datan, N., and Lohmann, N., eds. *Transition of Aging*. New York: Academic Press, 1980.

Tolsdorf, C. Social networks, support and coping: An exploratory study. *Family Process* 15:407-417, 1976.

Trainer, P., and Bolin, R. "Models of the Reconstruction Process: Reconstruction of Familiar Coping." Paper presented at the Second Annual Invitational Conference on Natural Hazards, Boulder, CO, 1975.

Vaughn, C.E., and Leff, J.P. The measurement of expressed emotion in the families of psychiatric patients. *British Journal of Social Clinical Psychiatry* 15:157-165, 1976a.

Vaughn, C.E., and Leff, J.P. The influence of family and social factors on the course of psychiatric illness: A comparison of schizophrenic and neurotic patients. *British Journal of Psychiatry* 129:125-137, 1976b.

Vaughn, C.E.; Snyder, K.S.; Freeman, W.B.; Jones, S.; Falloon, I.R.H.; and Lieberman, R.P. Family factors in schizophrenic relapse: A replication. *Schizophrenia Bulletin* 8:425, 1982.

Vitaliano, P.P. Stress in Alzheimer's patient-spouse interactions. National Institute on Aging (R01-AG06770-02), 1986.

Vitaliano, P.P. Correlates of mental health in DAT spouses. National Institute of Mental Health (R01-MH43267-01), 1988.

Vitaliano, P.P.; Breen, A.R.; Albert, M.S.; Russo, J.; and Prinz, P.N. Memory, attention, and functional status in community-residing Alzheimer type dementia patients and optimally healthy aged individuals. *Journal of Gerontology* 39:58-64, 1984.

Vitaliano, P.P.; Katon, W.; Maiuro, R.D.; Russo, J.; Syrjala, K.; Becker, J.; Bateman, P.; and Dahlberg, S. "Relationships of Appraisal, Coping Distress in 12 Diverse Samples." Paper presented at the Western Psychological Association Annual Meeting, May 13, 1986.

Vitaliano, P.P.; Maiuro, R.D.; Bolton, P.; and Armsden, G. A psychoepidemiological model for the study of disaster. *Journal of Community Psychology* 15:99-122, 1987.

Vitaliano, P.P.; Maiuro, R.; Russo, J.; and Becker, J. Raw versus

290

relative scores for the assessment of coping strategies. *Journal of Behavioral Medicine* 10:1-18, 1987.

Vitaliano, P.P.; Maiuro, R.D.; Russo, J.; Mitchell, S.E.; Carr, J.E.; and Van Citters, R.L. A biopsychosocial model to explain personal sources of medical student distress. *Proceedings of the 26th Annual Conference on Research in Medical Education.* Washington, DC: Association of American Medical Colleges, 1987. pp. 228-234.

Vitaliano, P.P.; Russo, J.; Carr, J.E.; Maiuro, R.D.; and Becker, J. The ways of coping checklist: Revision and psychometric properties. *Multivariate Behavioral Research* 20:3-26, 1985.

Weintraub, S.; Barataz, R.; Mesulam, M. Daily living activities in the assessment of dementia. In: Corkin, S.; Davis, K.; Cravden, J.; Usdin, E.; and Wurtman, J., eds. *Alzheimer's Disease: A Report of Progress in Research.* New York: Raven Press, 1982. pp. 189-192.

Weiss, J.M.; Bailey, W.H.; Pohorecky, L.A.; Korzeniowski, D.; and Grillione, G. Stress-induced depression of motor activity correlates with regional changes in brain norepinephrine but not in dopamine. *Neurochemical Research* 5:9-22, 1980.

Weissman, M.M., and Klerman, G.L. Epidemiology of mental disorders. *Archives of General Psychiatry* 35:705-712, 1978.

Williams, A.; Ware, J.; and Donald, C. A model of mental health, life events, and social supports applicable to general populations. *Journal of Health and Social Behavior* 22:324-336, 1981.

Zarit, S.H. *The Hidden Victims of Alzheimer's Disease: Families Under Stress.* New York: New York University Press, 1985.

Zarit, S.H.; Reever, K.E.; and Bach-Peterson, J. Relatives of the impaired elderly: Correlates of feelings of burden. *Gerontologist* 20:649-655, 1980.

Zubin, J., and Spring, B. Vulnerability–A new view of schizophrenia. *Journal of Abnormal Psychology* 86:103-126, 1977.

Chapter 11

Caregiver Stress and Well-Being

Marcia Daniels, M.D., and Michael Irwin, M.D.

Introduction

Alzheimer's disease represents a major health problem in the aging population (Jenike 1986). This form of irreversible dementia affects an estimated 5-7 percent of persons older than 65 years, 20 percent of persons older than 80 years, and approximately half of all nursing home patients (Jenike 1986; Brothers 1986; Terry and Katzman 1983). While placement is often made to nursing homes or other institutions, the majority of older persons with Alzheimer's disease remain at home under the care of at least one family member (Rabins et al. 1982). Interestingly, the level of cognitive dysfunction in the patient with Alzheimer's disease is not the only factor in the decision to institutionalize, and demented individuals residing in nursing homes are not necessarily more functionally impaired than their counterparts living in the community (Fumich and Poulshock 1981).

Families appear to prefer home-based care and, possibly because institutionalization has been associated with both increased morbidity and mortality, they will go to great lengths to avoid institutionalizing their demented spouse or parent (Kahan et al. 1985; Bergmann et al. 1979; Schoor 1980). Consequently, family caregivers have become the major component of the primary health care delivery system for the individual with Alzheimer's disease (Gwyther and George 1986; Fitting et al. 1986; Schneck et al. 1982).

Caring for the demented person may represent a substantial stress for the identified caregiver(s), and the term "caregiver burden" has been used to refer to the physical, psychological, social, and financial problems experienced by these family members (George and Gwyther 1986). Most caregivers are wives and/or daughters of the demented patients, though, at times, husbands and/or sons have provided primary care for their demented family members (Fitting et al. 1986). Until quite recently, virtually all studies of caregiver burden aggregated males and females, though as we shall see, the caregiver role may be experienced differently depending upon gender. Similarly, the experience of caregiving can differ as a function of the age and blood/role relationship of the caregiver. In this chapter, we review what is known about caregiver burden, and we address the implications of the reviewed findings. We also comment on possible directions for future research efforts.

Caregiver Stress: Early Studies

Early research on caregiver stress, first conducted by Grad and Sainsbury in Great Britain in the 1960s, did not focus specifically on caregivers of demented persons, but rather included the family caregivers of psychiatric patients who were diagnosed with either functional psychiatric disorders or organic brain syndromes (Grad and Sainsbury 1963, 1968). Adverse effects on mental health were reported in 63 percent of these caregivers, while 58 percent reported deterioration in their physical health. Social and leisure activities were disrupted in half of these caregivers, and about 19 percent of them reported a decline in income. In addition, the relationship between the family caregiver and other family members became strained, and domestic routines were altered. The most severe burdens were reported among caregivers who experienced competing demands, such as poor personal physical health, or rejecting attitudes toward the infirm individual.

The problems reported by family caregivers were highly associated with the identified patient's age and duration of illness. Family caregivers of elderly psychiatric patients were twice as likely to report experiencing "severe burdens," as compared to caregivers of younger psychiatric patients. Further, the chronicity of the illness experienced by the infirm individual was also related to increased caregiver burden. While the sex of the infirm individual was not associated with caregiver burden, higher initial socioeconomic status appeared to buffer caregivers. Finally, caregiving adult children reported more burden than caregiving spouses.

Hoenig and Hamilton (1966) also studied elderly psychiatric patients and their family caregivers in the 1960s and found a high percentage of distressed caregivers. In their study, 80 percent of the family caregivers reported "significant burdens." These researchers conceptually differentiated "objective caregiver burden" and "subjective caregiver burden." Objective burden included adverse effects on the household of the caregiver, such as a decline in caregiver health and income. Subjective burden involved the caregiver's perception of the extent to which the infirm individual's illness burdened the caregiver. Both objective and subjective burden were highest among the family caregivers of persons who were demented or terminally ill. In this study, as well as subsequent studies, measures of objective caregiver burden were not correlated with subjective measures.

The contribution of these early studies lies in their documentation that some form of burden is experienced in an overwhelming majority of family members who take on the caregiving role. However, any conclusions about the unique role of Alzheimer's disease in the genesis of such caregiver stress are limited. The illnesses and demographics of those investigated were often aggregated or poorly described. Neither objective nor subjective measures of caregiver burden were well delineated. Despite these limitations, it appears that those who cared for the mentally impaired were more likely to experience stress and strain than those who cared for elderly and physically infirm persons.

Caregiver Stress: Recent Studies

Studies conducted in the 1980s have become increasingly sophisticated and focused. They have offered insights into the extent to which caregiver burden is related to behavioral impairment in the Alzheimer's patient, characterized the psychological distress of Alzheimer's caregivers, and explored the impact of caregiving on spouses, children, and other relatives.

Zarit and colleagues (1980) interviewed 29 demented individuals and their family caregivers to assess the caregivers' level of burden and the relationship between caregiver burden and behavioral impairment in the patient. Caregivers and their families, recruited from a geriatric training and research center, ranged in age from 42 to 82 years. Twenty-five caregivers were female, four were male. Eighteen were spousal caregivers, and the remaining eleven were adult children caregivers. While it was hypothesized that behavioral impairment in the demented individual would contribute to caregiver distress, level of burden was neither correlated with the frequency of memory and behavior problems nor with the level of cognitive or functional impairment. Indeed, only the frequency of family visits correlated with burden. As the frequency of family member visits to the demented individual increased, caregiver burden declined.

Rabins, Mace, and Lucas (1982) further documented the psychologic distress of Alzheimer's caregivers. In extensive interviews of primary caregivers of 55 patients suffering from irreversible dementia (60 percent of whom had Alzheimer's disease), these investigators demonstrated that 87 percent of the caregivers experienced chronic fatigue, anger, or depression, and that the caregivers often had difficulty differentiating between these feelings. Fifty-six percent reported family conflicts, and 55 percent reported loss of friends, hobbies, and personal time. Furthermore, 31 percent worried that they themselves would become ill, and 29 percent reported difficulty in assuming new roles and responsibilities as a caregiver for the demented. Only 7 percent reported that they did not experience significant caregiver psychologic distress.

Goldman and Luchins (1984) extended these observations by describing clinical depressions that occurred in primary caregivers of Alzheimer's patients. Specifically, they described three cases of major affective disorder in family caregivers, in which the caregivers required hospitalization for treatment of their depression. Although clinicians and researchers had previously described caregivers' emotional distress, including depressive symptomatology, Goldman and Luchins' work documented the first reported cases of severe clinical depression that appeared directly attributable to aspects of the relationship between a demented individual and his primary caregiver.

Cantor (1983), in a landmark study of four types of caregivers of the frail elderly, including spouses, children, other relatives, and friends/neighbors, documented how the strain and burden of caregiving was significantly different depending on the blood/role relationship between the frail elderly and the caregiver. Of the four types of caregivers, spouses were most troubled by financial issues and by the morale of their husband or wife. Spouses also reported the most significant physical and financial distress. Adult children, on the other hand, expressed relatively more distress over obtaining adequate help for the frail dependent than the other caregiver groups. While caregivers who were friends/neighbors expressed the least amount of burden, all caregivers expressed worry over the health of the frail elderly.

Cantor also examined the impact of caregiving on the everyday lifestyle of the caregiver. Caregivers were more likely to restrict their personal activities, such as socializing with friends or taking vacations, but were able to maintain job and familial responsibilities. Again, of the four groups of caregivers, spousal caregivers were most severely impaired in their personal activity sphere. Two factors—spousal caregiving and the degree of emotional closeness between the frail elderly and the caregiver—appeared to predict the distress of caregiving. Cantor's work underscored the importance of clearly defining the caregiver type and quality of relationship in any study of caregiver burden.

Fitting et al. (1986) compared differences in the health outcomes of 28 husbands who were caregivers to demented spouses and 26 wives who were caregivers to demented spouses. Increasing impairment in the demented partner was associated with an increased perceived health burden in the younger wives, aged 50 to 66, and the older husbands, aged 67 to 90. This association between level of impairment and caregiver burden had not been demonstrated by others, and Fitting and colleagues suggested that their findings might have differed because demented persons in their study were more disabled at the study onset than were patients in other studies. Also, different measures of impairment were used among the various studies. For example, in the study by Zarit et al. described above, specific cognitive and behavioral measures of impairment were used, while Fitting et al. used a generalized functional and neuropsychological severity rating scale.

Extending the observations of others who had documented the likelihood of depressive symptoms in caregivers, Fitting et al. found that wives were significantly more likely to report depressive symptoms than were husbands. While an increased number of depressed caregiver wives may have represented a true difference in prevalence of depression (providing further evidence of the generally higher rate of depression among women as compared to men), Fitting and colleagues (1986) suggested that depression in the caregiving setting might represent a demoralized state rather than a true disorder. Thus, depressive symptoms in spousal caregivers might be viewed as a response to the caregiver's feeling of powerlessness over the course of the mate's illness. Finally, Fitting et al. documented that caregiver wives, as compared to caregiver husbands, were more likely to experience a deterioration in the marital relationship with their demented spouse. Husbands possibly maintained a more positive view of their new role as caregiver and believed that they were appropriately repaying their spouse for her past nurturance. Female caregivers, on the other hand, may have resented their required return to the role of caregiver, after having already been a caregiver, albeit to a healthy spouse.

Zarit, Todd, and Zarit (1986) further elucidated the difference in distress experienced by male and female caregiver spouses. In a 2-year longitudinal study, Zarit and associates reported that wives initially experienced more burden than husbands, but these differences were no longer present after 2 years. While not directly studied, Zarit et al. suggested that female caregivers, by the end of the 2-year period, may have developed a coping style similar to male caregivers. Thus, their improved coping might have lessened their perceived burden.

Not all studies have demonstrated significant psychologic distress or depressive symptoms in Alzheimer's caregivers. For example, Gilhooly (1984) studied the impact of caring for a demented relative in 37 separate families. In 20 of the families, the caregiver resided with the demented relative ("coresident caregiver"), while in the other 17 families, the caregiver was a "nonresident caregiver." All spousal caregivers were also coresidents.

Coresident caregivers were significantly older than nonresident caregivers. The demented relative who lived with the coresident caregiver was also significantly more impaired than the demented relative that lived alone. While Gilhooly hypothesized that caregivers would show both low morale and poor mental health, their mental health overall was actually either good or only mildly impaired. None of the caregivers had significant psychiatric impairments, and all were capable of performing their usual daily routines without assistance.

Gilhooly's data revealed several factors that may have fostered relative well-being instead of burden among caregivers. Perceived satisfaction with social support, associated with good morale and mental health, was relatively high in this sample of caregivers. As other researchers had shown, she found that the level of impairment experienced by the demented individual was not associated with caregiver burden. Gilhooly also examined the relationship between caregiver demographic characteristics and caregiver burden. Male caregivers reported higher morale than females, but not greater mental health. Gilhooly suggested that improved morale in the male caregivers might be accounted for by less emotional involvement with their demented relative's illness, as well as their willingness to go out and leave the demented individual unattended at home.

Of note was the finding that when the relationship between any caregiver and demented relative was defined as "close," caregiver mental health was impaired. However, the blood/role relationship between the caregiver and the demented relative was not correlated with morale. Finally, Gilhooly unexpectedly documented that the longer the duration of caregiving, the better the caregiver's morale and mental health. Again, this improvement in caregiver mental health may have reflected better coping and adjustment on the part of the caregiver.

In sum, the findings from these studies suggest that the symptoms and behaviors of patients with dementia may be relatively less important in understanding caregiver burden and the characteristics of the caregivers, including their age, gender, and blood/role relationship. Some of these studies also suggested that an adaptive coping style and greater social support are associated with less burden and improved well-being among caregivers. These findings have obvious relevance when considering interventions to enhance the care received by patients with Alzheimer's disease, as well as when considering interventions to enhance the lives of the caregivers of such patients.

Alzheimer's Caregivers: Measures of Well-Being

The first account of both the level of well-being and of burden experienced by caregivers of demented adults as compared to age-matched peers without such caregiving responsibilities was reported by George and Gwyther (1986). Prior to their work, virtually all studies on caregiving had used instruments that might reliably measure caregiver burden, but that could not be used in any comparable way to assess noncaregiving adults. For example, Zarit's Burden Interview and Robinson's Caregiver Strain Index explored how caregiving per se influenced the caregiver's life (Zarit et al. 1980; Robinson 1983). While these two measures provided total scores of burden or strain along several health dimensions, they gave only limited information on more specific health parameters of well-being and burden.

George and Gwyther's work adapted measures of well-being that could be used to compare the lives of the caregivers with age-matched peers who were not involved in caregiving, thus significantly advancing the understanding of the consequences of caregiving. In their study of 512 caregivers from the Duke Family Styles Project, well-being was examined along several dimensions, including physical health, mental health, financial resources, and social participation. Multiple survey samples of age-matched cohorts were obtained and analyzed as comparison groups. The comparison samples came from the following data bases: Survey of the Well-Being of the Older People of Cleveland, Ohio; the Harris Survey of the Myth and Reality of Aging; and the Duke University Second Longitudinal Study (U.S. GAO 1977; Palmore 1974; Harris and Associates 1975).

In measures of physical health, including physician visits and self-reports, caregivers and noncaregivers were similar. On the other hand, the caregivers and the comparison groups differed significantly in terms of mental health status. Caregivers were less satisfied with life, reported three times as many stress-related symptoms, and used more psychotropic drugs than the noncaregiver comparison group. In addition, the caregiver group was characterized as having poor social health as compared to the comparison sample; they were less likely to pursue social activities and participate in social events. Only in terms of financial well-being was the caregiver group better off, reporting both a higher household income and greater perceived economic status than the comparison sample.

George and Gwyther also looked at specific caregiving role types, including spouses, children, and other relatives, and related these types to caregiver well-being. Overall, spousal caregivers experienced lower levels of well-being in all four dimensions of health status assessed, as compared to both adult children and other relative caregivers. Spousal caregivers were more likely to report stress symptoms, to have less life satisfaction, and to use psychotropic drugs. Their pursuit of and participation in social activities was significantly less than that of other caregivers. Finally, while not statistically significant, spousal physical health status, perceived health, and economic status were less than that of other family caregivers.

Such differences among different family caregivers had been previously documented by Cantor (1983), but not by others (Zarit et al. 1980; Robinson 1983). George and Gwyther suggested that these conflicting findings can be explained in part by differences in the sampling techniques used to select the caregiving cohort. Specifically, in some of the previous studies, the findings may have been due to an interaction effect between the caregiver/demented family member relationship and the demented family members' living arrangement. In contrast, in the study conducted by George and Gwyther, only 59 percent of the caregivers lived with the demented family member (the other 41 percent provided caregiving to institutionalized spouses). Thus, the potential interaction effect between the relationship and the living arrangement was lessened.

In sum, the work of George and Gwyther further documented that the level of impairment of the demented family member does not predict caregiver burden. Rather, the characteristics of the caregiver, more than the condition of the demented family member, are more likely to be associated with caregiver well-being.

Alzheimer's Caregivers: Coping and Social Support

The chronic mental deterioration of the Alzheimer's patient is a catastrophic, crisis-oriented trajectory, which can be viewed as both a chronic stressor and a crisis event causing acute stress. Two important determinants of whether severe adversities become translated into psychological and physical morbidity include style of coping and quality of social support (Dohrenwend and Dohrenwend 1978).

Recent research has focused on the buffering effects of coping strategies and social support in response to adverse events (Billings and Moos 1981; Haan 1982; Menaghen 1983). Work on coping and health, influenced by the research of Lazarus et al., suggests that coping responses can be considered in two general categories: problem focused and emotion focused (Lazarus and Folkman 1984; Lazarus 1981). Problem-focused coping involves such activities as information seeking, planning alternatives, and/or changing existing difficulties. Emotion-focused responses primarily serve to ease inner distress and may include emotional reactions, withdrawal, overeating, and substance abuse. Outcome appears to depend on the dominant coping strategy used. For example, Felton et al. (1984; Felton and Revenson 1984) demonstrated that problem-focused responses modestly improved adjustment among older adults suffering with chronic illnesses, whereas emotion-focused reactions such as fantasy, avoidance, or blame were associated with poorer adjustment and negative affect.

Pagel et al. (1985) extended these observations in caregiver spouses of Alzheimer's patients and found that self-blame combined with perceived loss of control significantly predicted worsened depression. In comparison, Levine et al. (1983) found that caregivers who were more highly skilled copers used problem solving, help seeking, and positive self-talk. Lower use of problem-focused coping and/or more negative life events appear to be significant predictors of depression (Mitchell et al. 1983).

Social supports and the periodic relief they provide for the caregiver also play an important part in maintaining the Alzheimer's patient in the family and community. In fact, Colerick and George (1986) found that the structure and characteristics of the caregiver's support system was a better predictor of institutionalization than the level of the patient's deterioration. Morcyz (1985) also demonstrated that the availability of social support predicted level of caregiver burden, with increased stress leading to a greater likelihood of institutionalizing the Alzheimer's patient. Apparently, respite care as a component of the support system serves as a resource in improving the caregiver's ability to cope and in ameliorating depressive symptoms (Scott et al. 1986; Phifer and Murrell 1986).

Immunity and Stress

Adverse life events can be associated with alterations in immune function. Natural killer (NK) cell activity is reduced among women whose husbands are terminally ill with lung cancer and those whose husbands have recently died of lung cancer (Irwin et al. 1986a, 1987a, b). In addition, elderly women who are experiencing severe and threatening life events have alterations in T-cell subpopulations (important in the regulation of the immune response) and reduced lymphocyte response to mitogens as compared to age-matched women who are not stressed (Irwin et al. 1986b). Bereaved men also appear to be susceptible to immunologic impairment, and their lymphocytes show reduced responses to mitogenic stimulation subsequent to their wives' deaths (Bartrop et al. 1977; Schleifer et al. 1983).

The relationship between reduced NK activity and health outcome is complex and remains largely unexplored. While reductions in NK function are relevant to morbid risk, especially viral illnesses, it may be too simplistic to suggest that decreases in one immune parameter may necessarily lead to increased illness susceptibility (Herberman and Ortaldo 1981). However, the values of NK function in several of the bereaved women were low (Irwin et al. 1987b). Reduced NK activity has also been reported in persons who either are at risk for recurrence of herpes simplex viral infection or suffering from lymphadenopathy or acquired immune deficiency syndrome (Rola-Pleszczynski and Lieu 1984; Creemers et al. 1985). Such reductions in NK activity appear to be temporarily associated with a rise in plasma viral titers to Epstein-Barr, cytomegalovirus, and herpes simplex (Kiecolt-Glaser and Glaser in press). Decrements in NK function might have health consequences in those individuals whose health is already impaired or in older persons who have age-related reductions in a variety of other immunologic functions (Makinodan and Kay 1980). Furthermore, in animal studies, stressors affect disease susceptibility. Foot shock stress, known to suppress NK activity, and lymphocyte response to mitogen stimulation are associated with decreased in vivo resistance to viral infections including herpes simplex, poliomyelitis, Coxsackie B, and polyoma viruses (Shavit et al. 1984; Marsh and Rasmussen 1960;

301

Rasmussen et al. 1957; Rasmussen 1969; Johnsson et al. 1963; Johnsson and Rasmussen 1965).

Psychologic states such as depression may mediate the reduction in NK activity and other measures of immune function in persons experiencing adverse life events. In a longitudinal study of NK activity in women during anticipatory and acute bereavement, Irwin et al. (1987b; Irwin and Weiner in press) demonstrated individual differences that might partly be explained by the spouse's psychologic response to the death of her husband. In that study, a subgroup of women were clinically observed to experience relief when their husbands died, ending their suffering from metastatic lung cancer. These wives' depressive symptoms resolved and NK activity significantly increased. In contrast, those women who remained distressed with active depressive symptoms had suppressed NK activity throughout bereavement. Others have also correlated severity of depressive symptoms with impaired immune function, including NK activity and lymphocyte responses to mitogenic stimulation (Irwin et al. 1987b; Kiecolt-Glaser et al. 1984; Locke et al. 1984; Schleifer et al. in press). Conversely, Kiecolt-Glaser and colleagues (1985) have shown that relaxation therapy, which presumably controls distress, is associated with significant increases in NK activity among geriatric persons.

Neuroendocrine Correlates of Stress

Since a vast literature has accumulated on neuroendocrine correlates of stress, only a few salient points will be made here. First, stresses of all sorts are capable of increasing secretion of cortisol, adrenocorticotropin (ACTH), and beta endorphin (Guillemin et al. 1977). Depressive symptoms are sometimes associated with a wide variety of hypothalamic-pituitary-adrenal (HPA) system abnormalities, including hypercortisolism (Kalin and Dawson 1986). These general observations have relevance to coping and health outcomes in Alzheimer's caregivers for two theoretically important reasons.

First, the neurohumoral factors released in response to stress may have effects on cognition, affect, and behavior, which may affect coping with the stress of caregiving. For example, animal research indicates that glucocorticoids may, on the one hand, facilitate habituation, but at the same time diminish an organism's ability to attend selectively to stimuli (McEwen and Parson 1982). In depressed humans, impairments in selective attention and other cognitive functions have been related to HPA overactivity (Rens and Miner 1985; Rubinow et al. 1984). In animal models, ACTH appears to produce increased exploration of the environment, may delay extinction in an active avoidance paradigm, may reduce aggressiveness and social interaction, and may have anxiogenic effects (File 1979; Velluci and Webster 1982). Beta endorphins appear to share many of these behavioral effects (DeWied and Joller 1982). The behavioral correlates of ACTH and beta endorphins in humans are poorly understood. In sum, it seems possible that elevation of certain neurohumors, in particular, cortisol, ACTH, and beta endorphin, may serve to mark the degree of physiologic arousal in caregivers and to be associated with changes in affect, motivation, and coping. Thus, neuroendocrine variables may be at once "outcomes" of caregiver stress and "modifiers" of further coping and long-term well-being.

Neuroendocrine Correlates of Immune Change

The second theoretically important role of neuroendocrine variables in Alzheimer's caregivers is in understanding immune changes coincident to stress. Recent work demonstrated concomitant hypercortisolemia and impaired NK activity in bereaved women as compared to controls. However, the reduction in NK activity is probably not mediated solely by adrenocortical activity. Low NK activity is present in anticipatory bereaved women, even though their levels of plasma cortisol are comparable to control levels (Irwin et al. 1987c, 1988). In depressed patients, decreases in lymphocyte response to mitogen are not associated with either an increased excretion of urinary free cortisol or dexamethasone nonsuppression (Kronfol and House 1985; Kronfol et al. 1986). Adrenal corticoids may contribute to, but apparently are not required for, stress-induced immune suppression.

Recent attention has focused on the role of neurotransmitters and peptides in the neural modulation of NK activity. Norepinephrine (NE), which reduces NK activity in vitro, may be elevated in the plasma of persons undergoing life changes (Cobb 1977; Hellstrand et al. 1985). Central corticotropin releasing factor (CRF), a neuropeptide that likely regulates neuroendocrine, physiologic, and behavioral responses to stressful stimuli in men and animals, reduces splenic NK activity in the rat (Irwin et al. 1987c). In addition, receptors to endogenous opioid peptides have been demonstrated on lymphocytes. The role of these receptors is not understood; however, at least one study showed that opioid peptides released with foot shock stress mediate the reduction of NK activity (Shavit et al. 1984).

Future Directions

Living with an Alzheimer's patient is a severely adverse life circumstance. Future studies are necessary to determine the impact of this stress on the caregiver and, particularly, on the spousal caregiver, who appears more likely to be distressed. Comparison of Alzheimer's caregivers with other persons caring for chronically ill patients might clarify differences between types of caregivers and the extent to which Alzheimer's caregiving is uniquely stressful. Furthermore, assessment of neuroendocrine and immune variables may provide physiological correlates for measures of the psychologic and somatic disturbances noted in caregivers.

A number of studies have now documented that the progression of Alzheimer's dementia does not solely influence the caregiver's burden. Rather, the ability of male and female caregivers to cope with the Alzheimer's patient may be a more important determinant of the psychological burden and the decision to institutionalize. Several factors might mediate the caregivers' coping ability, including the perceived stress of the caregivers, their physical and mental health, their age and financial status, and the type and amount of social support available.

The relation between Alzheimer's caregiver coping and health outcomes remains unexplored. Is caregiver coping associated with differences in the physical, psychologic, and physiologic status of caregivers? Furthermore, can interventions be developed that improve coping and maximize the health status of the caregivers? Factors posed in these questions are relevant to caregivers and probably to their ability to maintain and care for the Alzheimer's patient at home.

References

Bartrop, R.W.; Lazarus, L.; Luckherst, E.; Kiloh, L.; and Penny, R. Depressed lymphocyte function after bereavement. *Lancet* 1:834-836, 1977.

Bergmann, K.; Foster, E.M.; Justice, A.W.; and Mathews, V. Management of the demented elderly patient in the community. *British Journal of Psychiatry* 132:441, 1979.

Billings, A.G., and Moos, R.H. The role of coping responses and social resources in attenuating the stress of life events. *Journal of Behavioral Medicine* 4:139-141, 1981.

Brothers, L. The Sepulveda GRECC Method No. 12. *Geriatric Medicine Today* 5:87-94, 1986.

Cantor, M.H. Strain among caregivers: A study of experience in the United States. *Gerontologist* 23:597-604, 1983.

Cobb, S. Epilogue on psychosomatic medicine. In: Lipowski, Z.J.; Lipsitt, D.R.; and Whybrow, P.C., eds. *Psychosomatic Medicine.* New York: Oxford University Press, 1977. pp. 71-79.

Colerick, E.J., and George, L.K. Predictors of institutionalization among caregivers of patients with Alzheimer's disease. *Journal of the American Geriatrics Society* 34:493-498, 1986.

Creemers, P.C.; Stark, D.F.; and Boyko, W.J. Evaluation of natural killer cell activity in patients with persistent generalized lymphadenopathy and acquired immunodeficiency syndrome. *Clinical Immunology and Immunopathology* 36:141-150, 1985.

DeWied, D., and Joller, J. Neuropeptide derived from pro-opiocortin: Behavioral physiological and neurochemical effects. *Physiological Review* 62:3, 1982.

Dohrenwend, B.S., and Dohrenwend, B.P. Some issues in research on stressful life events. *Journal of Nervous and Mental Disease* 166:7-15, 1978.

Felton, B.J., and Revenson, T.A. Coping with chronic illness: A study of illness controlability and the influence of coping strategies on psychological adjustment. *Journal of Consulting and Clinical Psychology* 53:343-353, 1984.

Felton, B.J.; Revenson, T.A.; and Hinrichsen, G.A. Stress and coping in the explanation of psychological adjustment among chronically ill adults. *Social Science and Medicine* 18:889-898, 1984.

File, S.E. Effects of ACTH 4-10 in the social interaction tests of anxiety. *Brain Research* 171:157-160, 1979.

Fitting, M.; Rabins, P.; Lucas, M.J.; and Eastham, J. Caregivers for dementia patients: A comparison of husbands and wives. *Gerontologist* 26:248-252, 1986.

Fumich, J., and Poulshock, S.W. "Stress Provoking Tasks in Family Caregiving Situations." Paper presented at the meeting of the Gerontological Society, Toronto, 1981.

George, L.K., and Gwyther, L.P. Caregiver well-being: A multidimensional examination of family caregivers of demented adults. *Gerontologist* 26:253-259, 1986.

Gilhooly, M.L.M. The impact of caregiving on care-givers: Factors associated with the psychological well-being of people supporting a dementing relative in the community. *British Journal of Medical Psychology* 57:35-44, 1984.

Goldman, L.S., and Luchins, D.J. Depression in the spouses of demented patients. *American Journal of Psychiatry* 141:1467-1468, 1984.

305

Grad, J., and Sainsbury, P. Mental illness and the family. *Lancet* 1:544-547, 1963.

Grad, J., and Sainsbury, P. The effects that patients have on their families in a community care and a control psychiatric service: A two year followup. *British Journal of Psychiatry* 114:265-278, 1968.

Guillemin, R.; Vargo, T.; Rossier, J.; Minick, S.; Ling, N.; Rivier, C.; Vale, W.; and Bloom, F. Beta-endorphin and adrenocorticotropin are secreted concomitantly by the pituitary. *Science* 197:1367-1369, 1977.

Gwyther, L.P., and George, L.K. Caregivers for dementia patients: Complex determinants of well-being and burden. *Gerontologist* 26:245-247, 1986.

Haan, N. The assessment of coping, defense, and stress. In: Goldberger, L., and Breznitz, S., eds. *Handbook of Stress: Theoretical and Clinical Aspects*. New York: Free Press, 1982. pp. 461-470.

Harris, L., and Associates. *The Myth and Reality of Aging in America*. Washington, DC: National Council on the Aging, 1975.

Hellstrand, K.; Svante, H.; and Strannegard, O. Evidence for a beta-adrenoceptor-mediated regulation of human natural killer cells. *Journal of Immunology* 134:4095-4099, 1985.

Herberman, R.B., and Ortaldo, J.R. Natural killer cells: Their role in defenses against disease. *Science* 214:24-30, 1981.

Hoenig, J., and Hamilton, M.W. Elderly psychiatric patients and the burden on the household. *Psychiatria et Neurologia* (Basel) 154:281-293, 1966.

Irwin, M.; Daniels, M.; Bloom, E.; and Weiner, H. Life events, depression and natural killer cell activity. *Psychopharmacology Bulletin* 22:1093-1096, 1986a.

Irwin, M.; Daniels, M.; Bloom, E.; and Weiner, H. Depression and changes in T cell subpopulations. *Psychosomatic Medicine* 48:303-304, 1986b.

Irwin, M.; Daniels, M.; Risch, S.C.; Bloom, E.; and Weiner, H. Plasma cortisol and natural killer cell activity among bereaved women. *Biological Psychiatry* 24:173-178, 1988.

Irwin, M.; Daniels, M.; Smith, T.L.; Bloom, E.; and Weiner, H. Life events, depressive symptoms and immune function. *American Journal Psychiatry* 144:437-441, 1987a.

Irwin, M.; Daniels, M.; Smith, T.L.; Bloom, E.; and Weiner, H. Impaired natural killer cell activity during bereavement. *Brain, Behavior, and Immunity* 1:98-104, 1987b.

Irwin, M.; Vale, W.; and Britton, K.T. Central corticotropin releasing hormone suppresses natural killer cell cytotoxicity. *Brain, Behavior, and Immunity* 1:81-87, 1987c.

306

Irwin, M., and Weiner, H. Depressive symptoms in immune function during bereavement. In: Zisook, S., ed. *Biopsychosocial Dimension of Grief and Bereavement*. Washington, DC: APA Press, in press.

Jenike, M.A. Alzheimer's disease: Clinical care and management. *Psychosomatics* 27:407-416, 1986.

Johnsson, T.; Lavender, J.R.; Hultin, E.; and Rasmussen, A.F. The influence of avoidance-learning stress on resistance to coxsackie B virus in mice. *Journal of Immunology* 91:569-575, 1963.

Johnsson, T., and Rasmussen, A.F. Emotional stress and susceptibility to poliomyelitis virus infection in mice. *Archiv fuer die Gesamte Virusforschung* 17:392-397, 1965.

Kahan, J.; Kemp, B.; Staples, F.R.; and Brummel-Smith, V. Decreasing the burden in families caring for a relative with a dementing illness. *Journal of the American Geriatrics Society* 33(10):664-670, 1985.

Kalin, N., and Dawson, G. Neuroendocrine dysfunction in depression: Hypothalamic-anterior pituitary systems. *Trends in Neuroscience* 9:261-266, 1986.

Kiecolt-Glaser, J.K.; Garner, W.; Speicher, C.; Penn, G.M.; Holliday, J.; and Glaser, R. Psychosocial modifiers of immunocompetence in medical students. *Psychosomatic Medicine* 46:7-14, 1984.

Kiecolt-Glaser, J.K., and Glaser, R. Psychosocial influences in herpes virus latency. In: Kjvstak, E.; Lipowski, Z.J.; and Morozov, P.V., eds. *Viruses, Immunity and Mental Disorders*. New York: Plenum, in press.

Kiecolt-Glaser, J.K.; Glaser, R.; Williger, D.; Stout, J.; Messick, G.; Sheppard, S.; Ricker, D.; Romisher, S.C.; Briner, W.; Bonnel, G.; and Donnerberg, R. Psychosocial enhancement of immunocompetence in a geriatric population. *Health Psychology* 4:25-41, 1985.

Kronfol, Z., and House, J.D. Depression, hypothalamic-pituitary-adrenocortical activity, and lymphocyte function. *Psychopharacology Bulletin* 21:476-478, 1985.

Kronfol, Z.; House, J.D.; Silva, J., Jr.; Greden, J; and Carroll, B.J. Depression, urinary free cortisol excretion and lymphocyte function. *British Journal of Psychiatry* 148:70-73, 1986.

Lazarus, R. Personal dispositions related to the life stress process: The costs and benefits of denial. In: Dohrenwend, B.S., and Dohrenwend, B.P., eds. *Stressful Life Events and Their Contexts*. New Jersey: Rutgers University Press, 1981. pp. 130-157.

Lazarus, R.S., and Folkman, S. *Stress, Appraisal, and Coping*. New York: Springer, 1984.

Levine, N.; Dastoor, B.P.; and Gendron, C. Coping with dementia: A pilot study. *Journal of the American Geriatrics Society* 31:12-18, 1983.

Locke, S.E.; Kraus, L.; Leserman, L.; Hurst, M.W.; Heisel, J.S.; and Williams, R.M. Life change, stress, psychiatric symptoms, and NK activity. *Psychosomatic Medicine* 46:441-453, 1984.

Makinodan, R., and Kay, M.M.B. Age influences on the immune system. *Advances in Immunology* 29:307, 1980.

Marsh, J.T., and Rasmussen, A.F. Response of adrenals, thymus, spleen, and leucocytes to shuttle box and confinement stress. *Proceedings of the Society for Experimental Biology and Medicine* 104:180-183, 1960.

McEwen, B.S., and Parson, B. Gonodal steroid action in the brain neurochemistry and neuropharmacology. *Annual Review of Pharmacology and Toxicology* 22:555-598, 1982.

Menaghen, E.G. Individual coping efforts: Moderators of the relationship between life stress and mental health outcomes. In: Kaplan, H.B., ed. *Psychosocial Stress: Trends in Theory and Research*. New York: Academic Press, 1983. pp. 137-141.

Mitchell, R.E.; Cronkite, R.C.; and Moos, R.H. Stress, coping and depression among married couples. *Journal of Abnormal Psychology* 92:433-448, 1983.

Morcyz, R.K. Caregiving strain and the desire to institutionalize family members with Alzheimer's disease. *Research on Aging* 7:329-361, 1985.

Pagel, M.D.; Bicher, J.; and Coppel, D.B. Loss of control, self-blame, and depression: An investigation of spouse caregivers of Alzheimer's disease patients. *Journal of Abnormal Psychology* 94:169-182, 1985.

Palmore, E. Design of the adaptation study. In: Palmore, E., ed. *Normal Aging II*. Durham, NC: Duke University Press, 1974.

Phifer, J.F., and Murrell, S.A. Etiologic factors in the onset of depressive symptoms in older adults. *Journal of Abnormal Psychology* 95:282-291, 1986.

Rabins, P.V.; Mace, N.L.; and Lucas, M.J. The impact of dementia on the family. *JAMA* 248:333-335, 1982.

Rasmussen, A.F. Emotions and immunity. *Annals of the New York Academy of Sciences* 164:458-462, 1969.

Rasmussen, A.F.; Marsh, J.T.; and Brill, N.Q. Emotional stress and herpes susceptibility. *Proceedings of the Society for Experimental Biology and Medicine* 96:183-189, 1957.

Rens, V., and Miner, C. Evidence for physiological effects of hypercortisoleuria in psychiatric patients. *Psychiatry Research* 14:47-56, Jan. 1985.

Robinson, B.C. Validation of a caregiver strain index. *Journal of Gerontology* 38:344-348, 1983.

Rola-Pleszczynski, M., and Lieu, H. Natural cytotoxic cell activity linked to time of recurrence of herpes labialis. *Clinical Experimental Immunology* 55:224-228, 1984.

Rubinow, D.R.; Post, R.M.; Saward, R.; and Gold, P.W. Cortisol hypersecretion and cognition impairment in depression. *Archives of General Psychiatry* 41:279-283, 1984.

Schleifer, S.J.; Keller, S.E.; Bond, R.N.; Cohen, J.; and Stein, M. Major depressive disorder and immunity: Role of age, sex, severity and hospitalization. *Archives of General Psychiatry*, in press.

Schleifer, S.J.; Keller, S.E.; Camerino, M.; Thorton, J.C.; and Stein, M. Suppression of lymphocyte stimulation following bereavement. *JAMA* 250:374-377, 1983.

Schneck, M.K.; Reisberg, B.; and Ferris, S.H. An overview of current concepts of Alzheimer's disease. *American Journal of Psychiatry* 139:165-173, 1982.

Schoor, M. "...*thy father and thy mother*...": *A Second Look at Filial Responsibility and Public Policy*. SSA Publication No. 13-11953. Washington, DC: Supt. of Docs., U.S. Govt. Print. Off., 1980.

Scott, J.P.; Roberto, K.A.; and Hutton, J.T. Families of Alzheimer's victims: Family support to the caregivers. *Journal of the American Geriatrics Society* 34:348-354, 1986.

Shavit, Y.; Lewis, J.W.; Terman, G.W.; Gale, R.P.; and Liebskind, J.C. Opioid peptides mediate the suppressive effects of stress on natural killer cell cytotoxicity. *Science* 222:188, 1984.

Terry, R.D., and Katzman, R. Senile dementia of the Alzheimer type. *Annals of Neurology* 14:497-506, 1983.

U.S. General Accounting Office. *The Well-Being of Older People in Cleveland, Ohio*. Washington, DC: General Accounting Office, 1977.

Velluci, S.V., and Webster, R.A. Antagonism of the anticonflict effects of chlordiazepoxide by beta-carboline carboxylic acid ethyl ester RO-15-1788 and ACTH (4-10). *Psychopharmacology* (Berlin) 78:256-260, 1982.

Zarit, S.H.; Reever, K.E.; and Bach-Peterson, J. Relatives of the impaired elderly: Correlates of feelings of burden. *Gerontologist* 20:649-655, 1980.

Zarit, S.H.; Todd, P.A.; and Zarit, J.M. Subjective burden of husbands and wives as caregivers: A longitudinal study. *Gerontologist* 26:260-266, 1986.

Chapter 12

The Effects of Caregiver Stress on Physical Health Status

Diana Koin, M.D.

The term "caregiving" has assumed a special definition within the last 5 years. Among those working in the field of aging, no longer is the word only a general description of a person who provides care for another. A caregiver now is defined specifically as the person or family member who assumes responsibility and usually offers hands-on care for a frail and often demented old person. Interestingly, health professionals who care for this population are most often excluded from the definition of caregiver, an unfortunate oversight as our nascent understanding of the particular parameters which distinguish caregiving may well extend to the health care team as well as the family constellation.

Background: Caregiving

Of great importance is the fact that caregiving has multiple elusive qualities and components that make it difficult to accurately describe. This phenomenon may arise because caregiving is, by its very nature, a secondary existence, i.e., the primary focus is obviously on the frail elder. As Americans grow increasingly aware of their altering demographic profile, most students are certain to learn that 5 percent of those over 65 are institutionalized. Seldom emphasized, but crucial to our improved understanding of caregiving, is the fact that at least another 5 percent living at home are as frail, ill, and feeble as those institutionalized.

Data from the Veterans Administration Hospital-Based Home Care Project, which cares for frail veterans in their own homes, suggest that the functional status of the veterans living at home is actually more impaired than a comparable population being placed in nursing homes post discharge from acute hospitalization. Family caregivers are somehow expected to have the strengths and capability to handle these patients. Nurse's aides at nursing homes are given limited training to perform difficult, trying work; family caregivers have no training to perform the same kinds of difficult, trying work. We have come to accept all sorts of demonstrations of job dissatisfaction in aides, such as high turnover rate, frequent sick leave, and other kinds of absenteeism, but would be horrified if a caregiver demonstrated any of these behaviors. In fact, caregivers are often viewed as "difficult" if they attempt to ventilate their own sense of inadequacy and frustration to their doctors. Although limited progress has been made in delineating the etiology, prevention, and treatment of Alzheimer's disease and other chronic severely disabling diseases, the recent recognition of the importance of the caregiving role could have great impact on health care and public policy.

Fast upon the heels of the recognition of aging as a distinct and significant entity in the realm of medical specialties has come the requirement for certain health services for caregivers. Programs limit or triage their services to only those demented patients seeking care who have a caregiver. The assumption is that the ability to maintain independence in the community is jeopardized without a caregiver.

In the United Kingdom, frail and confused older people living in the community were at 50-percent greater risk of institutionalization than a like population with caregivers, raising discussion that prompt institutionalization for demented elders may help preserve the productivity and success of home care services (Arie 1985). Clearly, although caregivers have only recently been recognized as key figures in independent living, they may truly be the key to access to home or outpatient care.

In the medical care setting, the caregiver may regrettably be viewed from a negative perspective. In dealings with the patient's doctor, for example, the caregiver is expected to be the patient's spokesperson, as it is difficult and inappropriate to rely on a medical history from a demented person. If the caregivers interlace their historical accounts with frequent references to their own fatigue and despair, the caregivers' plight may be met with thinly veiled hostility. Not only is the physician unable to treat the patient's dementia, but views the caregiver's behavior as whining and troublesome. Thus, the caregiver's ability to serve as patient advocate is seriously compromised. The caregiver occupies a fragile and difficult position in the web of care. The financial impact of caregiving adds yet another layer of complexity to this issue. The caregiver is the gatekeeper who can save our nation billions of dollars that would otherwise be required for long-term institutionalization. Given current estimates that for every patient in a nursing home, at least one equally impaired person lives in the community, our long-term care expenditures would at least double without caregivers. Recent cutbacks in health care services that limit care to acute episodes strip caregivers of the help they need to provide chronic maintenance at home.

The Physical Health Status of Caregivers

Caregivers have been called "The Hidden Patients" in a landmark conceptual paper by Fengler and Goodrich (1979). Focusing on the mental health factors of caregiving, the authors found that morale scores of disabled husbands and their wives were associated. Low morale was linked to isolation, loneliness, economic hardship, and role overload. By alluding to a medical model by using the term "patients," the groundwork was established to add caregivers to the constellation of the afflicted in Alzheimer's disease and related disabling conditions.

Since that seminal paper, understanding about caregiving has grown in many respects. Investigators have developed measurement techniques to assess burden (Fitting et al. 1986; Robinson 1983; Zarit et al. 1980; Zarit et al. 1986). Programs to help caregivers cope have been described and evaluated (Gallagher 1985; Gallagher et al. 1986; Stafford 1980; Zarit and Zarit 1983) and the association of depression with caregiving has been reported (Gallagher et al. 1986).

Thus, although the psychosocial aspects of caregiving have received a growing amount of attention, the physical health status of caregivers has been only minimally studied. Those investigations which have addressed physical health used self-reports (George and Gwyther 1986; Rolando 1986). George and Gwyther also asked caregivers to report the number of visits to physicians during the last 6 months, but this indicator did not correlate with the perceived need for social support, whereas self-rated health did ($p < .01$). The lack of correlation with number of physician visits may well reflect the difficulty caregivers experience in leaving impaired patients even long enough for a necessary medical appointment and point to a need to measure physical health directly.

The stress of caregiving has not yet been linked as a risk indicator for any disease process by objective, longitudinal studies, although studies on immune functioning have recently been undertaken

(Kiecolt-Glaser in this volume). The epidemiology of the health status of caregivers requires a clear knowledge of their specific kinds of psychological liabilities as well as objective measures of their health. To compound the methodological difficulties, stress is a topic which requires careful delineation, as does risk.

Stress

The word "stress" is met with a spectrum of responses from scientists attempting to understand the association between stress and disease. As with other psychosocial factors, several hypotheses could be offered to explain the relationship between a disease indicator, such as hypertension, and stress. Marmot (1985) pointed out that the psychosocial factors may exert a direct effect on the neuroendocrine system, that groups that differ in sociocultural characteristics may differ in ways that affect blood pressure, or that psychosocial factors may alter the accessibility of health care services.

Marmot further points out the semantic difficulty of using the word stress because it describes both the stimulus and the response. Selye (1956) defined stress as the reaction of the body to a hostile person or environment. Other writers define stress as a mechanical engineer would, i.e., as a force applied from the exterior. Nonetheless, the precise distinguishing hallmarks of a stressful environment or situation as yet elude investigators in this field of research.

From one perspective, scientists attempt to take into account the large diversity of individual responses to an environment; measures must thus include an assessment of the individual's perception of the environment. If environments are a priori assessed as stressful or nurturing, individual differences are lost.

In the caregiving scenario, coping with caregiving varies greatly. Some caregivers unflinchingly assume responsibilities that would require around the clock, special-duty nursing in an institution, while other caregivers find a minimal duty overwhelming. In this area of research, it is important to attempt an objective assessment of the environment as well as an individual's response to it (Rose and Levin 1979).

Indicators of Physical Health Risk

Any attempt to investigate the relationship between caregiving and physical health status will need to carefully appraise the objective indicators to be used in the study. Risk factors differ from etiological determinants. The large epidemiological studies from which risk factors are derived are not laboratory experiments; no intervention is instilled into a population. Rather, risk factor studies attempt to link naturally occurring events in search of causes of disease. The traditional methods evolved for acute, episodic illness; chronic disease is not totally responsive to the acute disease model.

To further confound assessment of physical health status in caregivers, most caregivers are over 60 years old. Geriatric medicine recognizes that diseases vary with age, in terms of both their manifestations and their treatment. The sine qua non for elderly patients is nonspecific presentation of disease. Infections may present without fever or leukocytosis; myocardial infarction may present without chest pain. Investigators must therefore select objective criteria that universally reflect pathology and do not vary with age.

Cardiovascular and gastrointestinal diseases best fit the criteria for investigation of the relationship between the stress of caregiving and altered physical health. Peptic ulcer disease or irritable bowel syndrome would be examples of diseases that could be sought in a large caregiver population and that might demonstrate an association between stress and disease. Cardiovascular diseases are widespread in the elderly, and have been studied in a multitude of prior investigations attempting to link stress and disease. Cardiac risk factors are well delineated (Levy and Feinleib 1984) and provide discrete objective measures.

Cardiovascular Disease and Stress

Hypertension

One hypothetical construct states that psychosocial stimuli cause short-term elevation of blood pressure (Marmot 1985). The amount and duration of the hypertensive response will vary, depending on the nature of the stimulus and the responsiveness of the individual. If the stress is ongoing or repetitive, the blood pressure will increasingly remain elevated. Sympathetic stimulation is believed to be the mediator. Blood pressure response will also vary with other factors; sustained hypertension may be more likely with genetic predisposition or age. Although this construct is very appealing and quite plausible, it has yet to be proven.

Blood pressure rises with psychological stimuli, both in the clinical research center and in ambulatory monitoring. People with hy-

314

pertension have a greater response to these stimuli than do normotensives. In the short term, good evidence implicates the release of catecholamines. The role of renin is still being determined, as is potassium and calcium.

Several types of stressors have been investigated in attempting to unravel the relationship between stress and hypertension. Prolonged exposure to noise not only was linked with hearing loss but also with hypertension (Jonsson and Hansson 1977). Mental arithmetic and reaction time tests were evaluated along with orthostatic change (Drummond 1985). Schulte and colleagues (1984) combined noise and Kraepelin's arithmetic test in a study of essential hypertensives and stress. Suppressed anger in a study of occupational stress predicted hypertensive status (Cottington et al. 1986).

Many personality traits have been implicated in the attempt to identify stress as a risk factor for hypertension. Supersensitivity, tendermindedness, and submissiveness are examples of the personality characteristics examined. Anger, however, is the one characteristic that current investigation consistently relates to blood pressure. Dimsdale and colleagues (1986) found that systolic blood pressure was significantly related to suppressed anger ($p < .016$) in a population of white males, was suggestive of an association with black males, but had no predictive value in women.

The Tecumseh Community Health Study evaluated the relationship between anger-coping types, blood pressure, and all-cause mortality in a sample of 696 men and women (Julius et al. 1986). The mortality risk was twice as great in those who suppressed anger as in those who expressed it, when offered two hypothetical experiences. Interestingly, one of the scenarios offered to the subjects was reminiscent of a caregiving situation: "Imagine that your husband/wife/sweetheart yelled in anger or blew up at you for something that wasn't your fault." Suppressed anger interacted with elevated blood pressure to predict the highest mortality risk of the groups studied.

Preliminary results of an investigation evaluating the physical health status of caregivers not only demonstrated that 67 percent were hypertensive (defined as blood pressure greater than 140/90), but also noted that 25 percent of those subjects with known hypertension who were on a medication regimen were inadequately treated (Koin 1987).

Coronary Artery Disease

Stress and coronary artery disease have received widespread attention, as many researchers have attempted to find an association.

Today, psychosocial stress is recognized as a risk factor for ischemic heart disease, although methodological problems still persist. Historically, Morris was one of the first epidemiological workers to investigate heart disease in a stressed population, London bus drivers (Morris et al. 1966). The control group was conductors, who not only had exercise on the stairs of the double-deckers, but were more fit as documented by smaller sized trouser waists. At all increments of blood pressure, the stressed drivers had a higher annual incidence of ischemic heart disease than did the conductors.

The Framingham study evaluated the relationship of psychosocial factors to coronary heart disease (Haynes, Levine, et al. 1978; Haynes, Feinleib, et al., 1978, 1980). Framingham Type A behavior was evaluated by a 300-item questionnaire that addresses behavior types, situational stress, somatic strains, and sociocultural mobility. Women with coronary disease scored significantly higher on these measures than did subjects free of heart disease. In an 8-year followup, Type A women developed twice as much coronary heart disease and three times as much angina as did Type B women.

Type A behavior and heart disease has also been carefully investigated by Williams and colleagues (1980) and Friedman and colleagues (1984). Despite methodological difficulties, Type A behavior is widely held to be a risk factor for coronary heart disease. Recent investigation has attempted to identify the basic risk factors within the Type A personality; anger and hostility (Williams 1985) are implicated not only as risk indicators for cardiac disease but also for a much broader effect on survival (Shekelle 1983).

Currently, investigators are exploring silent ischemia and attempting to understand its relationship with coronary disease and mortality. Stress, elicited by mental arithmetic, has shown a correlation with increased episodes of silent ischemia (Darmely 1987).

Future Directions

The need for careful, objective research is clear if we are to understand the relationship between the stress of caregiving and physical illness. Although psychosomatic research has been hampered by methodological difficulties in designing a facsimile stress situation, the caregiver population offers a unique opportunity to gain knowledge and insight into stress. Precision will be needed in defining not only the psychosocial and physical measures, but also in measuring the severity of disability of the Alzheimer's victim. This avenue of research offers the possibility of developing a more humanistic approach to dementia patients and their families, as well as influencing public officials faced with allocating scarce resources.

Bibliography

Borhani, N.O. Prevalence and prognostic significance of hypertension in the elderly. *Journal of the American Geriatrics Society* 34:112-114, 1986.

Cottington, E.M.; Brock, B.M.; House, J.S.; and Hawtorne, V.M. Psychosocial factors and blood pressure in the Michigan statewide blood pressure survey. *American Journal of Epidemiology* 121:515-529, 1985.

Cottington, E.M.; Matthews, K.A.; Talbott, E.; and Kuller, L.H. Occupational stress, suppressed anger, and hypertension. *Psychosomatic Medicine* 48:249-260, 1986.

Diamond, E.L.; Schneiderman, N.; Schwartz, D.; Smith, J.C.; Vorp, R.; and Pasin, R.D. Harassment, hostility, and Type A as determinants of cardiovascular reactivity during competition. *Journal of Behavioral Medicine* 7:171-188, 1984.

Dimsdale, J.E.; Pierce, C.; Schoenfeld, D.; Brown, A.; Zusman, R.; and Graham, R. Suppressed anger and blood pressure: The effects of race, sex, social class, obesity and age. *Psychosomatic Medicine* 48:430-436, 1986.

Drummond, P.D. Cardiovascular reactivity in borderline hypertensives during behavioural and orthostatic stress. *Psychophysiology* 22:621-628, 1985.

Fengler, A.P., and Goodrich, N. Wives of elderly disabled men: The hidden patients. *Gerontologist* 19:175-183, 1979.

Fitting, M.; Rabins, P.; Lucas, M.J.; and Eastham, J. Caregivers for dementia patients: A comparison of husbands and wives. *Gerontologist* 26:248-252, 1986.

Friedman, M.; Thoresen, C.E.; Gill, J.J; Powell, L.H.; Ulmer, D.; Thompson, L.; Price, V.A.; Rabin, D.D.; Breall, W.S.; Dixon, T.; Levy, R.; and Bourg, E. Alteration of Type A behavior and reduction in cardiac recurrences in postmyocardial infarction patients. *American Heart Journal* 108:237-248, 1984.

Friedman, R. Experimental psychogenic hypertension. In: Wheatley, D., ed. *Stress and the Heart: Interactions of the Cardiovascular System, Behavioral State, and Psychotropic Drugs.* 2d ed. New York: Raven Press, 1981. pp. 209-228.

Gallagher, D.; Rose, J.; Lovett, S.; and Silven, D. "Prevalence, Correlates and Treatment of Clinical Depression in Family Caregivers."

Paper presented to the Gerontological Society of America, Chicago, Nov. 1986.

Gallagher, D. Intervention strategies to assist caregivers of frail elders: Current research status and future research directions. *Annual Review of Gerontology and Geriatrics* 5:249-282, 1985.

George, L.K., and Gwyther, L.P. Caregiver well-being, a multi-dimensional examination of family caregivers of demented adults. *Gerontologist* 26:253-259, 1986.

Grayboys, T.B. Stress and the aching heart. *New England Journal of Medicine* 311:594-595, 1984.

Harburg, E.; Gleiberman, L.; Gershowitz, H.; Ozgoren, F.; and Kulik, C. Twelve blood markers and measures of temperament. *British Journal of Psychiatry* 140:401-409, 1982.

Haynes, S.G.; Levine, S.; Scotch, N.; Feinleib, M.; and Kannel, W.B. The relationship of psychosocial factors to coronary heart disease in the Framingham study. I. Methods and risk factors. *American Journal of Epidemiology* 107:362-383, 1978.

Haynes, S.G.; Feinleib, M.; Levine, S.; Scotch, N.; and Kannel, W.B. The relationship of psychosocial factors to coronary heart disease in the Framingham study. II. Prevalence of coronary heart disease. *American Journal of Epidemiology* 107:384-402, 1978.

Haynes, S.G.; Feinleib, M.; and Kannel, W.B. The relationship of psychosocial factors to coronary heart disease in the Framingham study. III. Eight-year incidence of coronary heart disease. *American Journal of Epidemiology* 111:37-58, 1980.

Hypertension Detection and Follow-up Program Cooperative Group. Five-year findings of the hypertension detection and follow-up program: Reduction in mortality of persons with high blood pressure, including mild hypertension. *JAMA* 242:2562-2571, 1979.

Jenkins, C.D. Recent evidence supporting psychologic and social risk factor for coronary disease. *New England Journal of Medicine* 987-994, 1033-1038, 1976.

Jonsson, A., and Hansson, L. Prolonged exposure to a stressful stimulus (noise) as a cause of raised blood-pressure in man. *Lancet* 1:86-87, 1977.

Julius, M.; Harburg, E.; Cottington, E.M.; and Johnson, E.H. Anger-coping types, blood pressure, and all-cause mortality: A follow-up in Tecumseh, Michigan (1971-1983). *American Journal of Epidemiology* 124:220-233, 1986.

Kannel, W.B.; Wolf, P.A.; McGee, D.L.; Dawber, T.R.; McNamara, P.; and Castelli, W.P. Systolic blood pressure, arterial rigidity, and risk of stroke: The Framingham study. *JAMA* 245:1225-1229, 1981.

Kannel, W.B., and Sorlie, P. Hypertension in Framingham. In: Paul,

O., ed. *Epidemiology and Control of Hypertension.* New York: Stratton Intercontinental Medical Book Corp., 1975. pp. 553-592.

Koin, D.B. The physical health status of caregivers. (in progress).

Kreisberg, R.A., and Kasim, S. Cholesterol metabolism and aging. *American Journal of Medicine* 82(Suppl. 1B):54-60, 1987.

Levy, R.I., and Feinleib, M. Risk factors for coronary artery disease and their management. In: Braunwald, E., ed. *Heart Disease: A Textbook of Cardiovascular Medicine.* Vol. 2. Philadelphia: W.B. Saunders, 1984. pp. 1205-1234.

Marmot, M.G. Psychological factors and blood pressure. *Preventive Medicine* 14:451-465, 1985.

Marmot, M.G. Hypothesis-testing and the study of psychosocial factors. *Advances in Cardiology* 29:5, 1982.

Minaker, K.L. Aging and diabetes mellitus as risk factors for vascular disease. *American Journal of Medicine* 82(Suppl 1B):47-53, 1987.

Morris, J.N.; Kagan, A.; Pattison, D.C.; and Gardner, M.J. Blood pressure, exercise and ischaemic heart disease. *Lancet* 2:553-554, 1966.

Robinson, B.C. Validation of a caregiver strain index. *Journal of Gerontology* 38:344-348, 1983.

Rolando, J; Pett, M.A.; Laubacher, M.A.; et al. "Double Jeopardy: The Impact of Caring for a Demented Relative on the Health of Older Caregivers." Paper presented to the Gerontological Society of America, Chicago, 1986.

Rose, R.M., and Levin, M.A. The crisis in stress research; a critical reappraisal of the role of stress in hypertension, gastrointestinal illness, and female reproductive dysfunction. *Journal of Human Stress* 5:1-90, 1979.

Russel, H.I., Russel, L.G. Behavior patterns and emotional stress in the etiology of coronary heart disease: Sociological and occupational aspects. In: Wheatley, D., ed. *Stress and the Heart: Interactions of the Cardiovascular System, Behavioral State, and Psychotropic Drugs.* New York: Raven Press, 1981. pp. 15-24.

Schulte, W.; Neus, H.; Thones, M.; and vonEiff, A.W. Basal blood pressure variability and reactivity of blood pressure to emotional stress in essential hypertension. *Basic Research in Cardiology* 79:9-16, 1984.

Selye, H. *The Stress of Life.* New York: McGraw-Hill, 1956.

Shekelle, R.B.; Gale, M.; Ostfeld, A.M.; and Oglesby, P. Hostility, risk of coronary heart disease, and mortality. *Psychosomatic Medicine* 45:109-114, 1983.

Sowers, J.R. Hypertension in the elderly. *American Journal of Medicine* 82(Suppl 1B):1-8, 1987.

Stafford, F. A program for families of the mentally impaired elderly. *Gerontologist* 20:656-660, 1980.

Williams, R.B.; Haney, T.L.; Lee, K.L.; Kong, Y.H.; Blumenthal, J.A.; and Whalen, R.E. Type A behavior, hostility, and coronary atherosclerosis. *Psychosomatic Medicine* 42:539-549, 1980.

Working Group on Hypertension in the Elderly. Statement on hypertension in the elderly. *JAMA* 256:70-74, 1986.

Zarit, S.H.; Reeves, K.E.; and Bach-Peterson, J. Relatives of the impaired elderly: Correlates of feelings of burden. *Gerontologist* 20:649-655, 1980.

Zarit, S.H.; and Zarit, J.M. Families under stress: Interventions for caregivers of senile dementia patients. *Psychotherapy* 19:461-471, 1983.

Part III

Research Issues in the Treatment and Management of Alzheimer's Disease Patients

Research-validated clinical approaches are needed to address the immediate needs of Alzheimer's disease patients and their families. These chapters emphasize nonpharmacological approaches, due to the existence of several excellent pharmacologically oriented reviews.

Taken together, the chapters in this section suggest that clinical research on the treatment and management of Alzheimer's disease patients should focus on two areas: the *reduction of excess disability* and the *enhancement of spared capabilities*. The number of specific clinical research topics highlighted in these chapters include (1) an examination of treatment modalities relevant to the mental, behavioral, psychological, and physical problems associated with Alzheimer's disease and related dementias (e.g., the efficacy of different treatment modalities to reduce excess disability during different stages of the disease; (2) studies that identify the functional strengths of the Alzheimer's disease patient in terms of behavior, emotion, and language, which can be used as the basis for a treatment plan and the development of management for specific behavior problems; (3) studies that examine modification of the interpersonal and/or physical environment; (4) developing strategies for helping early stage Alzheimer's disease patients cope with their illness; and (5) the identification and design of interventions to alleviate the physical and emotional disabilities in Alzheimer's disease patients that are reversible or can be reduced. A major focus of these chapters is on the selection of appropriate outcome measures. Future studies might use large-scale validations of treatments and adopt systematic clinical observation.

Chapter 13

Behavior Problems in the Demented

Peter V. Rabins, M.D.

In the rush to study potential cures for the dementias (certainly a vitally important quest), we sometimes overlook the fact that many of the symptoms of dementia can be helped by appropriate intervention. This chapter focuses on the behavioral abnormalities commonly seen in persons with dementia and discusses currently available nonpharmacologic treatment approaches to these symptoms. The chapter presents a brief discussion of the principles of behavior therapy and identifies strategies for further research that might clarify how such care can be improved. This field has made little progress since the thoughtful 1977 articles of Harris and colleagues and Miller. Future advances will depend on the identification of specific problem behaviors, an appreciation of the behavior therapy approach to treating them, and the design of studies that adequately test their efficacy.

How Common Are Behavioral Disorders in the Demented?

The prevalence of disordered behavior in persons with dementia is unknown. Studies in nursing homes suggest that 60-75 percent of individuals (Rovner et al. 1986; Zimmer et al. 1984) suffer from at least one significant behavioral problem. These figures should not be extrapolated to all persons with dementia because the disordered behaviors may have led to institutionalization in many instances. Surveys of the prevalence and severity of behavior problems in persons who present for outpatient evaluations of dementia (Rabins et al. 1982) are likewise contaminated by ascertainment bias. In spite of this lack of adequate prevalence data, behavior disorders clearly are common in the demented, represent a source of caregiver and patient distress, and provide a currently available focus for relief of suffering.

Principles of the Behavioral Approach

The behavioral approach rests on several principles (Kuzdin 1980). Keeping these in mind when considering the specific problems associated with dementia can help both the clinician and the researcher use the strengths and avoid the weaknesses of this approach.

Behavior is defined as observable activity. Therefore, problem behaviors are directly observable and should be described as specifically as possible. This improves the definition of the problem (reliability) and can help identify *antecedents* (events that regularly occur before the behavior under scrutiny) and *consequences* (events that regularly occur after the problem behavior). For example, identifying a problem as "violence" is less helpful than "yells at staff" or "pushes staff in the bathroom."

Charting the frequency and time of occurrence of the behavior of interest is an important aspect of behavior analysis. It identifies specific places (e.g., in the bathroom), times (at mealtime, in the later afternoon), or patterns (when a lot of activity is occurring) and serves as a baseline for determining whether an intervention has worked (i.e., decreased or abolished a problem behavior or increased the frequency of a desired behavior).

The central tenet of the behavioral approach is that behavior is governed by its consequences. A positive (desired) reward following a behavior increases the frequency or length of the behavior. Removing a consequence or following a behavior with a negative or undesired consequence should decrease its occurrence. Thus, *positive reinforcement* should be instituted when one wants a behavior to increase in frequency; *negative reinforcement* should be used when the goal is to abolish a behavior.

An important question that has not been resolved is whether the behavioral paradigm is applicable to diseases that affect the ability to learn. The behavioral approach has made major contributions to the care of the mentally retarded (Neff et al. 1978), but the retarded do not suffer the disproportionate loss of learning ability common in Alzheimer's disease. Individual case reports suggest that the behavioral approach can be successfully used with the demented, but few studies allow generalization to the conclusion that this approach works better than chance or nonspecific interventions. Wider use of good research methodology is needed before the approaches outlined in the following section should be fully accepted.

Specific Behavior Problems

Memory Disorder

Memory is significantly impaired in almost every person with a dementia. Disordered memory is required to receive a DSM-III diagnosis of dementia, and memory systems seem to be most sensitive to disorders that globally affect brain function (i.e., the dementias). In spite of its universality, memory loss is rarely a prominent complaint of the ill person and often does not lead to significant behavioral disturbance. However, poor memory is a source of distress for some individuals.

The presence of dementia does not imply that all ability to learn has been lost. Repetition and constancy of environment may improve or capitalize upon the remaining memory abilities of a person and should be used when there is evidence that the patient can learn. Some mildly affected individuals can learn to keep a note pad available in a certain place, such as a shirt pocket or purse, and are able to remember to look at the pad when they are unsure of something. If the family or staff can remember to help such persons write down important upcoming facts, and they still have the ability to remember that they use such a pad, they might refer to it frequently and thus remind themselves of situations or current events. Clearly and simply labeling doors is not actually a learning aid but can allow individuals to find their way without relying on their memory. This can help the demented person remain independent and lessen the impact of forgetfulness and disorientation.

At times, other individuals–family, friend, professional, or stranger–are more distressed by memory impairment than the patient. The proper environmental intervention in this situation is for them to examine their own concern about the memory loss and their reaction to it. They may need to modify their own behavior (becoming angry, frustrated, or embarrassed) and not embarrass or frustrate the ill person.

While several studies have suggested that elderly individuals in nursing homes and State mental hospitals can learn (Cautela 1966; Mishara 1978; Frank et al. 1982), they often have not specified whether these individuals suffered from dementia. A recent study by McEvoy and Patterson (1986) demonstrated improvements in information, spatial orientation, communications, and activities of daily living using a behavioral paradigm in persons diagnosed as demented. Unfortunately, they had no control/untreated group so a Hawthorne effect (improvement related to a researcher's positive attitude about the intervention) cannot be ruled out. Their results suggest that improved cognition is a possibility with this approach.

Conceptual support for applying behavioral training/learning theory to memory-impaired individuals comes from work with Korsakoff's syndrome patients (Kaushall et al. 1981; Schacter 1983). This syndrome is characterized by an inability to learn verbally presented material. Careful testing of these patients has demonstrated ability to learn in nonverbal realms such as instrumental task learning. Because the deficits in Korsakoff's syndrome are more circumscribed than those in dementia, one must be cautious when extrapolating from Korsakoff syndrome patients to persons with the global cognitive impairment of dementia. The demonstration that some memory-impaired individuals can learn suggests that mildly affected dementia patients whose predominant cognitive symptom is memory loss might benefit more than severely impaired individuals whose cognitive disorder is more generalized. Unfortunately, memory training tasks that have been shown to be successful with the cognitively normal elderly do not work with the cognitively impaired (Yesavage and Jacob 1984).

The most widely applied behavioral approach to improving memory impairment is reality orientation. This technique consists of incorporating information about the day, date, weather, current events, etc., into the many conversations that staff members have with patients. Folsom developed the technique to increase verbal contact between the staff and patients of a State mental hospital (personal communication, 1982), but it has been widely applied in nursing homes to improve cognition. Some studies have confirmed that orientation improves after institution of a reality orientation program (Woods 1979) and have demonstrated that this improvement cannot be explained on the basis of increased frequency of contact alone (Hanley 1981), but there is no evidence that these improvements are clinically meaningful. No study has examined the clinical utility of reality orientation in carefully diagnosed persons with dementia.

Agitation, Violence, Explosiveness, Irritability

Behavior symptoms that make others feel threatened are distressing and can be dangerous. While violence, explosiveness, or irritability might seem easy to define, a recent careful analysis of "agitation" by Cohen-Mansfield and Billig (1986) revealed how difficult it can be to

325

develop a specific, concise definition. They define agitation as "inappropriate verbal, vocal or motor activity that is not explained by needs or confusion per se." This is a useful starting point, but its limitations are clear. For example, does this definition include putting on too many layers of clothing, as the authors suggest? How do we decide when an activity is "explained" by confusion?

We need to start with such definitions, but we are likely to end up quibbling as soon as we attempt to focus on its details. At times, it is more useful to describe the behavior in question in detail and to avoid passing judgment about its "appropriateness." The behavioral approach suggests that dissociating the description of the behavior (e.g., "becomes restless when dressing") from its presumed cause ("because he has forgotten how to dress" or "because he is apractic") allows the clinician to focus on changing the pattern or frequency of the behavior in question. On the other hand, recognition that a behavior is occurring because of the presence of another condition (e.g., weakness, apraxia, or depression) will suggest a specific intervention.

A concept related to agitation is that of *catastrophic reactions*, a term introduced by Kurt Goldstein (1952). These are sudden expressions of a negative emotion (such as crying or yelling). They may occur in the face of a task failure or request to do something the person cannot do. Catastrophic reactions can occur with overstimulation, for example, when too much noise is present or when an upsetting event occurs. The individual having the catastrophic reaction often develops a flushed face, appears to be upset, and seems, to an outside observer, ready to explode. Such behaviors are seen in persons with brain injuries of various etiologies and can have physical violence associated with them. This "violence" may range from attempting to escape the perceived threat by walking or running away to striking out at persons in the immediate vicinity.

The recognition that catastrophic reactions are occurring can lead to interventions aimed at *preventing* or *minimizing* them. An examination of the circumstances surrounding their occurrence might reveal that certain situations—e.g., large crowds, busy dining rooms, being bathed by a person of the opposite sex—precipitate them. If the situation can be modified to be less threatening, the upset may be prevented. If the activity is no longer in the patient's best interest, it is best to avoid it. For example, if the individual becomes upset by television, the simple solution is to remove the television from his room.

Distraction can often eliminate or minimize the catastrophic reaction once it has occurred. This distraction might be needed for only a few seconds, particularly in persons with severe memory impairment. However, even in persons with total loss of memory, the

326

emotional distress can last for hours, with significant behavior disorder.

The emotionally upset, brain-damaged individual is often quite sensitive to nonverbal cues (Buck and Duffy 1980). Therefore, it is important during a catastrophic reaction that persons around the patient *remain* as *calm* as possible. Repeatedly *reassuring* the individual that the family or staff member is in control of the situation and that things will be fine is often helpful as well.

Agitation can take the form of *pacing* or attempting to leave a confined space. A careful examination of the behavior can suggest different environmental interventions. The person who becomes restless and tries to leave a setting at certain times of day is different from the person who constantly paces. In the former situation the patient states he wants to return home and appears distressed. The aimless but constant wanderer or pacer, on the other hand, is less goal directed. Pacing itself appears to be the goal rather than the need to reach a specific place.

Wandering can sometimes be diminished by involving individuals in structured activities that are scheduled around the time the restlessness begins. This may engage and distract the ill person and thus diminish or abolish the behavior. Unfortunately, distraction does not always work, and the restlessness may continue. An alternative approach to wandering is to focus on the person's feeling state rather than on the behavior. Exploratory statements such as "you seem to miss your home," "you seem to miss your mother," or "why don't you tell me what you're going to do when you get home" can lead to an emotionally meaningful conversation about what it's like to be lonely and away from home, to miss one's parents, or to be in an unfamiliar setting. It might also lead to further discussion of a childhood home, description of one's parents, early school experiences, the first time away from home, etc. This environmental intervention engages the person on an affective level. In my opinion, it is especially useful because it both diminishes the behavior and establishes a relationship between the ill person and the caregiver.

Occasionally, it is better not to intervene in wandering. Some persons with dementia pace constantly and barely stop even to eat. Neither environmental nor pharmacologic interventions help, and they often make the situation worse. These driven, constant pacers are rare and generally do not cause direct distress to other individuals—unless one includes family or staff who are embarrassed by the constant pacing. An appropriate environmental intervention for the family or staff is to accept the symptom as part of the patient's condition and to recognize that their own reaction to it, rather than the distress of the ill person, needs to be relieved.

327

Dawson and Reid (1987) found that cognitive impairment and hyperactivity distinguished wanderers from nonwanderers. While "hyperactivity" and "wandering" seem redundant, their co-occurrence suggests that most problem wanderers engage in the behavior constantly, not occasionally. While different types of wanderers may respond to different interventions, no studies support this hypothesis.

The setting in which the agitated behavior occurs may provide clues to an appropriate environmental intervention. For example, agitation is common in bathrooms; if the person appears to become upset when assisted by a person of the opposite sex, then a same sex helper can be engaged whenever possible.

If the upset occurs over a specific activity, such as brushing one's teeth or sitting on the toilet, the ill person may have developed an apraxia and be unable to perform the activity. If the task can be carried out by another person (e.g., having someone else brush teeth), the agitation might be avoided. A facility in which a person can be wheeled into the shower and rinsed with a hand-held nozzle is less threatening to some people than standing in the shower or sitting in a tub.

Demonstrating or *modeling* a behavior is helpful to some mildly affected individuals. Others do best when the problem behavior or activity is broken down into simpler parts and the person is talked through.

Despite the most thoughtful and creative planning, at times these interventions do not work. If the individual who becomes very upset when bathed is not helped by a stepladder into the tub, new railings, improved lighting, an attendant of the same sex, and explanations about what is happening, the best that can be done is to work with all concerned to establish a schedule in which the stimulus (e.g., bathing) is kept to a minimal but acceptable frequency. Perhaps one bath per week, with accompanying agitation, would be enough. Pharmacologic interventions should be considered when environmental manipulations do not work.

Shouting is a disruptive behavior that can be difficult to manage. Patients should be examined to identify hidden sources of pain or unrecognized depression before behavior modification approaches are considered. Birchmore and Claque (1983) reported the successful treatment of constant vocalization in a patient with diagnosed senile dementia by rewarding his quiet periods with attention. In another case (Wisner and Green 1986), "yelling, cursing, and threatening" were diminished by a behavior plan with both negative and positive reinforcers as well as a 1-hour per week session in which alternative behaviors were discussed. Studies of this approach and other environmental interventions such as activity therapy, stimulation by music, or frequent visitors are warranted.

Sleep Disorders

Disordered sleep is common in many dementing illnesses and is associated with a variety of behavioral disorders. The patient may awaken in the middle of the night, wander around, search through dressers and rooms aimlessly, or make noise that awakens or frightens others. This can be especially difficult for the individual residing at home because the family often cannot sleep.

Environmental manipulations that might help include ensuring that the patient is up and active during the daytime. While some demented individuals seem to have a reversed sleep/wake cycle and are unable to stay awake in the daytime, many will stay awake if kept busy. The structured activities of a day center or an activity program in the nursing home appear to be clinically efficacious. Physical activity itself seems to be beneficial both by keeping the person alert and active during the day and by tiring him out so that he sleeps better at night. No studies have demonstrated the utility of this approach.

Sometimes the person arises at night to urinate. Fluid restriction after 7 p.m. might lessen this. Because the elderly may need less sleep and experience more awakenings than the young (i.e., sleep lighter), a quiet environment might be of some help. For some persons at home who do not respond to these interventions, closing the bedroom door may keep them in their rooms and lessen the disturbance to others. However, some patients become very upset by this and bang on the door, thus worsening the situation. When environmental interventions fail, pharmacologic intervention should be considered.

Language Disorder

Alzheimer's disease often affects a person's ability to express himself or to comprehend what is being said to him. Because communication difficulties underlie many of the behavioral disturbances of the Alzheimer's patient, it is imperative that clinicians and family recognize when verbal miscommunication is occurring. In some instances, the person is able to form words but unable to express himself meaningfully. The patient may say the opposite of what he means to say (no for yes), use an incorrect word (spoon for pen) or use words that are either combinations of other words (write downer for pen) or totally made up. These incorrect words are called *paraphasic errors* and are important indicators of aphasic language disorder.

Simplification of the language/communication process is most likely to help. Communication with nonverbal approaches such as sight or touch help also. However, McEvoy and Patterson (1986) reported that demented patients could improve "appropriate expression of pleasure and displeasure" after 1 month of a training module. Well-designed replication studies of this approach are needed. Clinical opinion suggests that patient comprehension can be improved with simplification and use of nonverbal communication, but improvement in patient expression of language is unlikely.

Paranoia, Suspiciousness, Making Accusations

Many patients with dementia feel they are being persecuted, believe that things are being taken from them, or are frightened because they believe that harm is about to occur (Miller 1977; Zimmer et al. 1984). Some accuse others of stealing things and occasionally verbally or physically attack them because of this (Rovner et al. 1986).

Accusations that things are being taken are especially common. In some instances, assessments reveal that demented persons are moving things and then becoming upset when they cannot find them. When this happens, they may be temporarily reassured when the object is found. At other times, patients develop persecutory *delusions*, that is, false ideas that they are convinced are true, which seem to have no basis in fact and from which they cannot be dissuaded. In either of these situations, the initial intervention should be environmental unless the situation is dangerous. Medication and drugs are generally not helpful, especially when misplacing things is the problem, and drugs often add problems by causing side effects. Several nonpharmacologic approaches to decreasing the behaviors associated with paranoia can be tried.

1. Distract the person or minimize the symptom. For example, one might say, "Let's look into that later. Why don't we go down the hall now and get dinner?" Similarly, one might engage the person in scheduled activities or conversation on other matters.

2. Address the underlying emotional concern of the individual rather than the content of the accusation. For example, one might say, "I understand you were a successful businessman. Were you always good with numbers?" When faced with a man who believes his bank books have been stolen, one might be able to get into a discussion of the individual's previous life work. For the patient who is afraid of being attacked, one might ask directly if he is frightened. If so, the source of the fear can be identified and discussed.

330

However, when accusations and false ideas become delusional or when they remain a constant or distressing preoccupation of the patient, pharmacotherapy is often necessary.

While several reports (Liberman et al. 1983), including one case study of an elderly person (Brink 1980), demonstrated that behavior therapy can induce a decrease in delusions and hallucinations, they did not show that patient well-being was improved. However, benefit to the patient was found in a case reported by Haley (1983). This "demented, paranoid older woman living with her family refused to leave her room" prior to treatment, but began participating in family activities when rewarded with involvement in meal planning.

It is important for caregivers (be they family or staff) to look at *their* emotional reaction to accusations. One of the ironies of caring for dementia victims is that accusations of mistreatment and thievery are often directed toward the person who is the most constant caregiver. It helps if the caregiver can recognize that these accusations are particularly distressing when they come from a person to whom one is devoting large amounts of physical, emotional, and financial support. A caregiver who recognizes his own frustration is less likely to verbally lash back at such a patient. Talking with others about the problem can help. Focusing both on the content (the accusation itself) and the feelings that it evokes ("I don't feel appreciated") are helpful.

Incontinence

Incontinence is an example of a symptom that can arise from the biology of the dementing illness, can have a variety of etiologies, and can respond to an environmental manipulation whatever the etiology. It is important to remember that persons with dementia may develop urinary tract infections, partial bladder outlet obstruction because of prostatic enlargement, or prostatic obstruction due to anticholinergic medications. Therefore, any incontinence should be evaluated for treatable causes.

If no reversible underlying cause of incontinence is identified, a strict schedule of going to the bathroom every 2 to 3 hours can be most helpful. This schedule should be made quite explicit to caregivers. I often suggest that the person be taken to the bathroom every 2 hours on the even hours (10 a.m., 12 noon, 2 p.m., 4 p.m., etc.). Some individuals resist this or have problems in the bathroom because they are fearful or apractic about sitting down, but many individuals can remain fully dry during the day on such a schedule. Minimizing fluid intake after 7 p.m. might help decrease urine volume and thus nighttime incontinence.

One study that used negative reinforcers was unsuccessful in

331

diminishing urinary incontinence in six demented males (Pollock and Liberman 1974). However, another study (Schnelle et al. 1983), which used random assignment and a nontreatment control group, reported a 45-percent improvement in correct toileting as the result of a program that featured hourly prompts, "social approval" for dry checks, and "social disapproval" for wet checks. Ninety-five percent of the subjects suffered from senile dementia. This study demonstrated that the frequency of incontinence can be diminished but did not identify whether the prompting, the reinforcers, or both led to the improvement. Prompting is probably a necessity because of the memory disorder.

Sexual Disorders

In our clinical experience (Rabins et al. 1982), sexual problems in the demented are not commonly reported but are distressing when they appear. Hypersexuality, hyposexuality, and public display of sexuality all occur.

Patients with an increased appetite for sexual activity have usually forgotten their recent sexual activity. Reminding them about their recent sexual relations may help. Several patients with this problem have not responded to redirection but have responded to neuroleptic drugs.

Inappropriate expression of sexual interest, for example, masturbating in public or disrobing in public, is often distressing. If the behavior occurs infrequently, the best approach is to direct the person to a more private place, such as his room. Becoming angry and upset with the person may precipitate a catastrophic reaction, so we encourage people to remain as matter of fact as possible. For the occasional persons who behave this way frequently, and for individuals who are disrobing, one must make sure that they understand their circumstances and are not confused about the setting.

For persons still remaining at home, sexual difficulties often arise because the spouse has lost interest. Here, the appropriate intervention is an exploration of these issues with the well spouse. Feelings of disinterest sometimes arise as a response to the change in the relationship. For example, some spouses feel that they have become care providers rather than loved ones, or the level of physical and directive care may have altered their feelings about sexual intimacy. Clearly identifying this can be helpful to the caregiver and may lead to an appropriate solution, be it resumption of sexual activity or sleeping in separate rooms.

Public expression of sexuality is occasionally explained as a demented patient's only remaining means of expression. Whether psychotherapy, activity therapy to improve self-esteem, or sexual activity itself can lead to nonpublic sexual expression is unknown.

Depression and Social Isolation

Depressed mood is present in 15-40 percent of patients with Alzheimer's disease (Rovner et al. 1986; Reiffler et al. 1982). No studies have addressed whether a behaviorally oriented approach might be useful in treating depression, apathy, or isolation in the demented, but a wide variety of studies suggest themselves. Activity therapy (Mace and Rabins 1984; Schwab et al. 1985), exercise, and positively reinforcing verbal interactions all deserve careful study.

Principles of Environmental and Behavioral Intervention

This chapter advocates merging the operant and classical conditional behavioral paradigms with a less theoretically based practical, problem-solving approach. Several generalizations can be made for the clinician or nonprofessional wishing to use this approach.

1. Be informed about dementia.

Designing interventions for the demented requires some knowledge of the dementing diseases themselves. Although most problems arise from a combination of the person's disease, his lifelong character traits, others in the environment, and the physical environment, it is helpful to identify the contribution that the disease itself makes. This approach avoids placing "blame" on the ill person, family, professionals, and environment and focuses the clinician on improving the quality of the interactions between the ill person and the caregivers.

This requirement should not suggest that "biologically based" symptoms be excluded from intervention. Rather, it suggests that the available behavioral repertoire is compromised in some individuals; this must be considered in designing the intervention and in choosing a desired goal. For example, if weight loss is a problem and there is no medical or psychiatric explanation, the patient may no longer be able to use silverware, chew and swallow meat, or find his way to the kitchen. Each of the potential etiologies must be explored before any intervention can be tried.

2. Focus on specific behavioral, cognitive, functional, and emotional problems.

Identify specific problems: Successful behavioral treatments rest on identification of specific behaviors, problems, and goals. The more a behavior can be broken down into its parts, the greater the likelihood of changing it. This is true whether or not a specific behavior modification approach is attempted. Furthermore, the identification of specific target symptoms and goals (for example, to decrease the frequency of incontinence or statements about persecution) allows the caregiver to gauge improvement or failure. As a generalization, the focus on narrow rather than broad problems makes it more likely that part of a problem will be solved.

Identify precipitants (antecedents): Once specific problems are identified, the caregiver should look for specific interpersonal or environmental precipitants. Some of these are discussed above under catastrophic reactions. Setting, time of day, people involved, and unusual changes in routine should all be examined. When possible, the identified precipitant should be modified or removed. If it cannot be absolutely avoided, one may be able to decrease how often it occurs (for example, bathing a person less often) or to make the setting less threatening.

Simplify the environment: Because persons with dementia are often more easily overwhelmed than they were prior to their illness, overstimulation can be as antitherapeutic as understimulation. The ability to tolerate stimulation and activity will vary from individual to individual, but environments can usually be established in which most people seem to do well. Extraneous noise should be kept to a minimum. A constantly running television, for example, is more likely to cause problems than to engage an occasional individual.

Daily schedules and routines help most individuals. Repetition builds on the person's remaining memory abilities. Routine makes the environment less stressful because it is more predictable. For example, if a person notices that he eats lunch every day after an exercise group, remembering this fact can be helpful by giving him a sense of orientation and a feeling that he knows what is coming. Scheduling activities also helps caregivers plan the day. Although some caregivers worry that repetition will induce boredom, this is rarely a problem. Indeed, many patients seem to derive pleasure from repeating activities.

For some individuals, a simplified environment means doing only one thing at a time. Step-by-step instruction and individual support is often helpful.

Encourage remaining abilities: Successful behavioral treatment works best by building on successes and strengths rather than by punishing weaknesses. This principle, extrapolated to the care of persons with dementia, means identifying the abilities that an individual still has and emphasizing them. The identification of remaining abilities, their inclusion in the treatment plan, and the construction of a program that emphasizes them is part of good environmental treatment.

Trial and error: Environmental care of persons with dementia is an art, and like all arts, failures are as informative as successes. The search for solutions to problems and attempts to maximize remaining abilities will inevitably overtax some individuals. The skilled caregiver develops the ability to recognize and identify when a person is being pushed too hard. These inevitable failures can be frustrating to families, professionals, and patients alike. Thus, the clinician may have to point out that some failures are necessary in order to succeed. Because the expectations of the caregiver are part of the patient's environment, unrealistic hopes can be a source of problems in themselves. Recognizing this and addressing these expectations directly is an intervention in and of itself. Other chapters in this book deal with the needs of families and professionals; these interventions, too, must be seen as part of the environmental care of dementia patients.

3. The interpersonal environment.

Unequivocally, the care of the demented can be most improved in the interpersonal environment. The approaches outlined here fall into that category, but other important modalities should not be overlooked. These include touch (Eaton et al. 1986), music, and family therapy.

Research Issues

The study of behavioral disorders in the demented and their nonpharmacologic treatment is in its infancy. The basic questions that still must be answered include: How common are specific problems? Do they occur in certain diseases, at certain times during the course of the disorder, or at certain times of the day? Do specific environmental circumstances increase their prevalence?

Adequately designed studies are sorely needed to determine if specific behavioral/environmental therapies can improve function and/or behavior or if nonspecific factors (being supportive, caring, encouraging, touching) are equally effective, additive, or more efficacious. To answer these questions, instruments that can reliably and validly identify specific behavior problems and can survey individuals in a variety of settings are needed. Unselected samples of individuals should be studied, not just those with behavior problems.

The effects of differing environments should be assessed. People in nursing homes, day care centers, or enrolled in Alzheimer's disease research centers are quite likely to have different problems than persons living at home. This is important, because intervention studies will probably need to be shaped by the environment in which the behavior occurs.

If being as specific as possible in defining behaviors is important, then multidisciplinary groups made up of persons with backgrounds in behavior description, behavior modification, clinical psychiatry, clinical psychology, and psychiatric nursing will be needed. Collaboration is necessary to decide how to identify the problem behaviors in individual patients, how to choose the behaviors to be focused upon, and how interventions and goals are best defined. The literature on behaviorally disordered children has grappled with such issues in the past and might be a place to start.

This chapter emphasizes the need to concentrate on specific problem behaviors. However, some researchers may choose to study overall behavioral impairment and assess whether general interventions such as activity therapy can bring improvement. Several instruments that globally rate behavioral disorders in persons with dementia can be found in *The Source Book of Geriatric Assessment* (Israel et al. 1984), published under the auspices of the World Health Organization. This compendium is helpful because it lists many of the available scales, provides copies of the scales, and critically reviews them. However, it focuses only on scales specifically derived for the elderly; it does not present other scales that might be useful. We found the PGDRS (Psychogeriatric Dependency Rating Scale) particularly helpful because it clearly defines specific problem behaviors and rates their severity. The N.O.S.I.E.(Nurses Observation Scale for Inpatient Evaluation) and the Brief Psychiatric Rating Scale (BPRS) should also be considered as measures of general behavioral impairment.

The currently available scales do not cover the whole range of behavioral difficulties. More specific and sensitive instruments should be developed. It would be useful, for example, to focus on agitation (perhaps as defined by Cohen-Mansfield and Billig) and to develop a scale that divides it into more specific behaviors. Such a scale should provide an algorithm or a list of definitions that show the clinician how to subcategorize the behavior.

The methodology of behavioral treatment trials in the demented must be improved. Single-case reports and small samples are useful beginnings, but now we need large, well-designed studies that meet rigorous scientific standards. It will be important to specifically identify the diagnoses of the individuals under study; the severity of their impairments; the degree of their neuropsychological, functional, behavioral, and emotional impairments; and the role of confounding variables such as medication or medical illness. Realistically, the ideal study will be quite difficult to carry out. One practical solution is for different studies to address a variety of specific behaviors. Consensual validity would then be a possibility.

Studies should also combine and compare behavioral and drug interventions. Medication may help some individuals respond better to environmental or behavioral treatments.

In summary, this chapter reviews the existing literature on behavior therapy approaches to disordered behavior in Alzheimer's disease and other dementias. Future study should validate these approaches, because they offer the prospect of help to the several million victims of dementia in the United States and to their family and professional care providers.

References

Birchmore, T., and Claque, S. A behavioral approach to reduce shouting. *Nursing Times* Apr. 20:37-39, 1983.

Brink, T.L. Geriatric paranoia: Case report illustrating behavioral management. *Journal of the American Geriatrics Society* 28:519-522, 1980.

Buck, R., and Duffy, R.J. Nonverbal communication of affect in brain-damaged patients. *Cortex* 16:351-362, 1980.

Cautela, J. Behavior therapy and geriatrics. *Journal of Genetic Psychology* 108:9-17, 1966.

Cohen-Mansfield, J., and Billig, N. Agitated behaviors in the elderly. I. A conceptual review. *Journal of the American Geriatrics Society* 34:711-721, 1986.

Dawson, P., and Reid, D.W. Behavioral dimensions of patients at risk of wandering. *Gerontologist* 27:104-107, 1987.

Eaton, M.; Mitchell-Bonair, I.L.; and Friedman, E. The effects of touch on nutritional intake of chronic organic brain syndrome patients. *Journal of Gerontology* 41:611-616, 1986.

Frank, P.J.; Klein, S.; and Jacobs, J. Cost-benefit analysis of a behavioral program for geriatric patients. *Hospital and Community Psychiatry* 33:374-377, 1982.

Goldstein, K. The effect of brain damage on the personality. *Psychiatry* 15:245-260, 1952.

Haley, E.W. A family-behavioral approach to the treatment of the cognitively impaired elderly. *Gerontologist* 23:18-20, 1983.

Hanley, I.G. The use of sign posts and active training to modify ward disorientation in elderly patients. *Journal of Behavior Therapy and Experimental Psychiatry* 12:241-247, 1981.

Harris, S.L.; Snyder, B.D.; Snyder, R.L.; and Magraw, B. Behavior modification therapy with elderly demented patients: Implementation and ethical considerations. *Journal of Chronic Diseases* 30:129-134, 1977.

Israel, L.; Kozarevic, D.; and Sartorius, N., eds. *The Source Book of Geriatric Assessment.* Geneva: World Health Organization, 1984.

Kaushall, P.I.; Zetin, M.; and Squire, L.R. A psychosocial study of chronic, circumscribed amnesia. *Journal of Nervous and Mental Disease* 169:383-389, 1981.

Kuzdin, A.E. *Behavior Modification in Applied Settings.* Rev. ed. Homewood, IL: Dorsey Press, 1980.

Liberman, R.P.; Teigen, J.; and Patterson, R. Reducing delusional speech in chronic paranoid schizophrenics. *Journal of Applied Behavior Analysis* 16:57, 1983.

Mace, N.L., and Rabins, P.V. *A Survey of Day Care for the Demented Adult in the U.S.* Washington, DC: National Council on the Aging, 1984.

McEvoy, C.L., and Patterson, R.L. Behavioral treatment of deficient skills in dementia patients. *Gerontologist* 26:475-478, 1986.

Miller, E. The management of dementia. A review of some possibilities. *British Journal of Clinical Psychology* 16:77-83, 1977.

Mishara, B.L. Geriatric patients who improve in token economy and general milieu treatment programs: A multivariate analysis. *Journal of Consulting and Clinical Psychology* 46:1340-1348, 1978.

Neff, N.A.; Iwata, B.A.; and Page, T.J. Public transportation training: In vivo versus classroom instruction. *Journal of Applied Behavior Analysis* 11:331-344, 1978.

Pollock, D.D., and Liberman, R.P. Behavior therapy of incontinence in demented inpatients. *Gerontologist* 14:488-491, 1974.

Rabins, P.R.; Mace, N.L.; and Lucas, M.J. The impact of dementia on the family. *JAMA* 248:333-335, 1982.

Reiffler, B.V.; Larson, E.; and Hanley, R. Coexistence of cognitive impairment and depression in geriatric outpatients. *American Journal of Psychiatry* 139:136-139, 1982.

Rovner, B.W.; Kafonek, S.; Filipp, L.; Lucas, M.J.; and Folstein, M.F. Prevalence of mental illness in a community nursing home. *American Journal of Psychiatry* 143:1446-1449, 1986.

Schacter, D.L. Amnesia observed: Remembering and forgetting in a natural environment. *Journal of Abnormal Psychology* 92:236-242, 1983.

Schnelle, J.F.; Traughton, B.; Morgan, D.B.; Embry, J.E.; Binion, A.F.; and Coleman, A. Management of geriatric incontinence in nursing homes. *Journal of Applied Behavior Analysis* 16:235-241, 1983.

Schwab, M.; Rader, J.; and Doen, J. Relieving the anxiety and fear in dementia. *Journal of Gerontological Nursing* 11:8-15, 1985.

Wisner, E., and Green, M. Treatment of a demented patient's anger with cognitive-behavioral strategies. *Psychological Reports* 59:447-450, 1986.

Woods, R.T. Reality orientation and staff attention: A controlled study. *British Journal of Psychiatry* 134:502-507, 1979.

Yesavage, J.A., and Jacob, R. Effects of relaxation and mnemonics on memory, attention and anxiety in the elderly. *Experimental Aging Research* 10:211-214, 1984.

Zimmer, J.A.; Watson, N.; and Treat, A. Behavioral problems among patients in skilled nursing facilities. *American Journal of Public Health* 74:1118-1121, 1984.

Chapter 14

Environmental Approaches to Research and Treatment of Alzheimer's Disease

M. Powell Lawton, Ph.D.

The attempt to apply behavioral principles to the design of environments for the aged, and specifically the dementia patient, could be said to date from 1964, the year Lindsley's chapter on geriatric behavioral prosthetics appeared. At that time, environmental psychology was starting to take shape, and other person-environment approaches to aging were beginning (Carp 1966; Rosow 1967). Since that time, the environmental psychology of later life has flourished both as an approach to theory and empirical research and as a field for application in such areas as housing (Howell 1980; Lawton 1975), planning (Newcomer et al. 1986), neighborhood study (Golant 1984), and transportation (Wachs 1979).

Lindsley's approach was highly specific, focusing on suggestions for environmental modifications targeted to very specific and limited behaviors. The promise of productive research leading to a splurge of empirically validated design directives was very encouraging at the time. After more than 20 years, that promise has yet to be fulfilled. The person-environment system has proved to be more complex than the behavioral-reinforcement arc, and we still have very few hard research findings leading to confidence in choosing one design alternative over another. What we do have is a generation of practitioners in both design and social services who have been exposed to some degree of sensitization regarding the possible relationships between environment and behavior.

Dissatisfied as we may be with the breadth of influence of person-environment thinking on the total array of building projects, we nonetheless see the highest quality projects routinely seeking professional and scientific consultation and a body of published material available to anyone wanting to look for it.

To write once more on this topic, in the absence of new knowledge, involves considerable repetition of material already abundantly available. Justification for doing so once more derives from several factors, however. First, a considerable amount of learning has occurred from informal observations of older dementia patients' behavior in a variety of new environments. Second, the emphasis on community-based long-term care as a parallel system to institutional long-term care has very recently occasioned thought about modifying home environments for dementia patients. Third, much of what has been written about designing for dementia has dealt with new construction. Modification of existing structures is at once the most feasible and the most neglected course. Finally, a number of subsidiary topics have emerged that require new thinking, such as how to generate design ideas, staff as an essential element in person-environment transactions, and the need for a technology to upgrade existing environments.

This chapter begins with a review of the theory underlying behavioral design and some guiding principles for applying behavioral knowledge to designs for the Alzheimer's patient. The bulk of the chapter discusses, as concretely as possible, how residential and institutional environments can be used to provide a positive milieu for the Alzheimer's patient. The chapter concludes with some suggestions on mobilizing direct-care staff to improve environmental quality.

The Theoretical Basis for Behavioral Design

The rationale for giving special attention to the environments of people of limited competence has been elaborated in detail elsewhere (Lawton 1982; Lawton and Nahemow 1973). Very briefly, the quality of the outcome of a person-environment transaction is a function of the degree of environmental demand, or "press" in Murray's (1938) terms, and the competence of the person. When the degree of demand is matched to the person's competence, a positive outcome in terms of affective response or adaptive behavior is the rule. When press is high in relation to competence, psychological disturbance in the form of strain is likely to occur. When press is low in relation to competence, sensory deprivation and atrophy of skills are likely.

The environmental docility hypothesis suggests that the less competent the person, the more strongly the environment determines the outcomes of the transactions. Stated another way, a given objective improvement in environmental quality may produce a disproportionately greater improvement in outcome for a person of low competence than for a person of high competence.

The original statement of this ecological model of person-environment relationships (Lawton and Nahemow 1973) noted that the same model fit many instances of low competence, such as health impairment, mental illness, or incomplete development (as in childhood). The argument suggests that highly impaired users may gain substantially from improved environments. Thus, the most general principle for discussing environments for the Alzheimer's patient will be identifying areas of major overdemand or underdemand where congruence may be reestablished by altering the environment. Such an approach has an obvious advantage in that environmental features are presumably in operation all the time, unlike human therapeutic interventions, which are time-limited and expensive.

An ideal therapeutic environment does not, of course, exist. In general, the fixed environment alone may prevent the occurrence of some behaviors and facilitate others. Rarely does the environment cause particular behaviors. Environmental determinism represents an oversimplified view of human ecology that is totally at variance with the reality of the person as an active, decisionmaking organism. People perceive the external environment, organize it cognitively, make choices regarding environmental options, change the environment to suit them, and make rules about the use of the environment that affect other people's behavior. These transactions with the environment may be called "environmental proactivity," that is, the person has an active role, rather than simply responding to environmental demands.

The ecological model suggests that no matter how impaired the person, some aspects of the environment may be used to satisfy the person's needs, thereby attaining a state of congruence between competence and press.

As we question the suitability of environments for the Alzheimer's patient, we need to apply three criteria. First, does the environmental aspect demand behavior (or a subjective response) that is within the person's ability to respond in an adaptive manner? Second, does the environmental aspect add some resource to the life space that could be potentially relevant to the person? Note that a potential resource is considered desirable even in the absence of present relevance. The objective environment is full of unused resources. The essence of an enriched environment is that people have the opportunity to discover something *new* in the environment to satisfy a need or arouse interest. Thus, we must be careful not to simply design for an average level of competence or preference, but to include resources that are surprising, puzzling, teaching, or leading. In fact, one other aspect of the Lawton and Nahemow (1973) model is that active enjoyment, novelty, new learning, and, ultimately, growth in competence are fostered when the level of environmental press is an increment above the level typical of total congruence, that is, perfect balance between competence and press. Thus, a third criterion for favorable design is whether the environment can provide "leading stimuli" that demand just a little more, but not too much more, than the demand level to which the users have become accustomed.

Designing for People, Older People, and Impaired Older People

Gerontologists working on the environmental psychology of later life have been major contributors over the past two decades to the general area of behavioral design. The strategy of beginning with a defined need of the user and then searching for an environmental way to satisfy that need represents a generic approach. In many instances, environmental features developed to serve the older user were found to be useful to people in general. For example, glare from a window placed at the end of a corridor causes disorientation in older institutionalized people, because it blots out details on the sides of the corridor. The problem is particularly bothersome to people with the visual problems of old age, but the glare is unpleasant and partially disorienting to people of any age. One early commentator on designing for the elderly expressed the same idea in a converse manner, agreeing that it was good to provide warm, resilient floors for nursing homes, but wondering who would be better off with cold, hard floors (Vivrett 1960)!

"Design for the aged" is, in fact, a rare phenomenon. The ecological model nowhere equates age per se with incompetence. The usual reasons for lowered competence are poor health, psychological maladjustment, deprivation, and social isolation. Although some of these negative conditions may become statistically more frequent as age increases, age alone does not intrinsically demand the alteration of design principles that apply to human beings in general.

Incompetence is, on the other hand, clearly implied by Alzheimer's disease and other irreversible organic conditions. The cognitive and behavioral manifestations of these conditions are unique and well known. Nonetheless, some people with dementia are also afflicted with a variety of unrelated physical symptoms or disabilities. Conversely, many Alzheimer's patients are relatively healthy, and some remain relatively competent in personal care.

343

Thus, environments for Alzheimer's patients must be designed to meet the needs of a heterogeneous group. Our approach emphasizes designs to counteract the disabilities associated with the organic brain disorders of old age. Inevitably, however, the goal of upgrading the environment will be served by innovations to counteract some of the physical problems frequent in nondemented older people, such as loss of visual acuity, muscle tone, or pulmonary endurance. In still other instances, improvements may be gained by altering the environment in ways that would benefit anyone. One of the latent benefits of a design approach targeted to a specific user group is that it helps sensitize people to a much broader variety of human considerations.

Environments Inhabited by Older Dementia Patients

Almost all published material on designing for the person with Alzheimer's disease assumes that the appropriate environment is the nursing home. To some extent this is an appropriate emphasis, since up to 60 percent of all institutionalized elderly, perhaps 800,000 individuals, suffer from some degree of judged cognitive impairment (National Center for Health Statistics 1977). The prevalence rate for similarly afflicted people living in community residences is around 3 percent, accounting for almost as many individuals as the institutional population. The great majority of these people live in households with a more competent person, usually a spouse or an adult child. Some unknown number of obviously vulnerable people live alone. Others live in mental hospitals, and an increasing number are found living in such locations as planned housing for older people, boarding homes, and shelters for the homeless.

Our thinking about environment as a therapeutic agent must take into account these diverse residences of older people with some element of dementia. The redesign of these dwelling units may well become a community-based service that will enable demented individuals to remain at home. Thus, our discussion deals with methods for improving the usability of community-based residences as well as institutions.

New Construction and Minor Alterations

Another emphasis of most published material in this area deals with basic structural characteristics of treatment facilities and other features in newly constructed buildings designed for the purpose. It is much more efficient to make all desirable facets of the treatment environment fit together from the beginning. While our society will undoubtedly need many new facilities over the next several decades, the great majority of Alzheimer's patients will always be residing in older units, built without the benefit of the behavioral-design perspective. Upgrading existing facilities is therefore as imperative as seeking the ideally designed new facility.

Very little has been written on a patchwork approach to design improvement in the nursing home. Because the State mental hospital is even less likely than the nursing home to be replaced by ideally designed new buildings, somewhat more attention has been given to bootstrap improvement in these settings (Whitehead et al. 1984; Mastroieni and Lawton 1983). A basic how-to manual suited for nursing home personnel, similar to the one written for the mental hospital by Mastroieni and Lawton, is badly needed.

A Research Base for Behavioral Design for Alzheimer's Patients

This entire volume's purpose is to organize existing knowledge and identify gaps in knowledge, research needs, and methods suited to filling such gaps. In some ways this chapter is an exception, concentrating as it does on theory and knowledge rather than a critical review of existing research.

Two reasons account for this difference. First, despite two decades of activity, very few relevant findings are available from traditional research. Second, this author suggests that research methods ideal for filling such gaps in knowledge are not yet even identified–not a very affirmative conclusion, to be sure. This section considers briefly the problems associated with using traditional research (see Lawton 1987 for a more extended discussion) and then gives a few suggestions for methods that can be used at present.

Traditional Research Methods

A majority of all psychological and social research in gerontology has surely been based on the verbal responses of people to examiner-determined questions. Aging or organic brain damage aside, the ability of people to recognize and verbalize their subjective responses to aspects of the external environment has been widely recognized as very limited. The environment is so taken for granted that people of any age find it difficult to isolate, and especially to introspect on, the possible influence of the environment on their thoughts, feelings, and actions.

345

Such useful introspections are more likely to be produced by sophisticated, articulate people, who are highly unrepresentative of the larger universe. In gerontological research, the problem is compounded because of the generally low education experience of today's older cohort. When the target group of older people suffers from an illness like Alzheimer's disease, the problem is obviously worse.

One is tempted to conclude out of hand that the most-available method, verbal report, has to be discarded. One tempering thought to such a hasty conclusion, however, is that we do not really know, from definitive research, that demented patients can tell us *nothing* about their environmental experiences and preferences. Thus, one research need is to test the limits of what people with measured degrees of cognitive impairment (for example, mildly and moderately impaired versus nonimpaired nursing home residents) can tell us. We may simply learn what most of us have assumed, that the yield of design-relevant information is so low as to preclude making the effort to question these users.

The other major generic method for gaining data is direct observation. Although the intent of this chapter is not to review such research exhaustively, good information has evolved from approaches that depend on (a) defining behaviors of interest, (b) developing criteria for the occurrence of these behaviors that enable them to be observed reliably, and (c) analyzing data based on these observations in traditional fashion. Some examples have been–

- Observing the seating locations and the views from these locations of nursing home residents (Archea 1974).
- Counting the social contacts, activity participation, shifts of gaze, and other behaviors of Alzheimer's patients (Lawton et al. 1984).
- Counting the patients who wander and the time they spend wandering (Robb and Mansour 1980).
- Counting and classifying the reinforcements given by patients and staff to independent and dependent behaviors of nursing home residents (Baltes et al. 1983).

Unquestionably, the best research on environment and the Alzheimer's-type patient used direct behavior observation. The major limitation is, first, that this method is very expensive, requiring hundreds of hours of trained-observer time. The yield may be very low as well. Many of the behaviors of particular therapeutic interest occur only sporadically against a background of the "null behavior" so characteristic of institutional life (Gottesman and Bourestom 1974). Finally, the meaning of directly observed behavior can never be made completely clear without some knowledge of the subjective interpretations of it made by the behaving subject. Without such a complementary view, the risk of accepting normative behavior as ideal becomes greater. A simple-minded example would be to conclude that people don't pay attention to an activity program because they don't comprehend it; a subjective consensus, were it possible to obtain, might be that the program is boring.

Despite the problems, much research can be performed productively by using the systematic observation of behavior and treating the observations in traditional statistical style. One inadequately used method is to offer residents an environmental choice and to interpret the outcome of the choice as a preference. Once again, many conclude that Alzheimer's patients cannot make rational choices, but that fact has not been established. Experiments offering systematic choices of clothing, food, seating location, or room furnishing would be simple to design. The outcome could be subjected to the prior test of whether a given person was consistent in choice across trials. The secondary test would be the content of the choice. As an example, Sheila Miller of Miami University (personal communication, December 1985) is exploring the limits to which nursing home residents can choose art from a "lending library" to display in their own rooms.

Another untried form of a traditional methodology is the "critical incident" technique (Flanagan 1979). In this method, a subject panel (in this case, staff serving Alzheimer's-type patients) would be asked to list, or collect over time, descriptions of patient behaviors that illustrated good and bad transactions with the environment. The large universe of such transactions would first be categorized by judges and then subjected to an evaluational analysis, resulting in a set of inductive principles or guidelines for design. Of course, the critical incident technique is not strictly limited to overtly observed and objectively coded behavior, since the incidents are reported selectively by observers and categorized in value-related style by judges.

Nontraditional Research Methods

Perhaps the most frequent method used is the judgment of the expert. The body of existing expertise for the design of environments for the mentally impaired is almost wholly composed of qualitative expert judgment. The literature in gerontology, long-term care, environmental design, and the professional specialties is full of analyses of environments for patients and clients based on knowledgeable direct contact with these types of settings. Typically, the conditions and extent of the observations are not specified, however. These reports vary tremendously in the extent of firsthand knowledge. On the other hand, the expertise represented in many such reports is the best that can be found.

347

Significant upgrading of the qualitative observer's report could be obtained if such reports included the following items as standard components:

- The role the writer plays in relation to the environment described
- The aggregate amount of direct exposure of the observer to the environment described
- The characteristics of the patients observed (diagnosis, diagnostic mix, age, physical health, ethnic background, etc.)
- The physical characteristics of the treatment setting
- The staffing and service characteristics of the treatment setting
- The social, physical, economic, and administrative characteristics of the larger organization in which the treatment environment is embedded
- The method used by the observer to process the observations (e.g., personal impressions only, discussion with others, use of archival supplementary information, systematic recording)
- Explicit statement of the goals of the treatment environment
- Explicit statement of the criteria or the indicators of favorable and unfavorable outcomes

Each of the above elements helps create a set in the observer away from subjectivity and toward external consensuality or validation. Such approaches have been discussed at length under the topic of "postoccupancy evaluation" (Reizenstein and Zimring 1980) or preconstruction planning (Lawton 1987).

Among the suggestions made for planning, Lawton (1987) recommended two approaches that may be applicable to qualitative research on the effects of environment on the Alzheimer's-type patient. First, a systematic series of observations by a team comprising the researcher, designer, and professional will put together several perspectives and inherently reduce subjectivity. These observer teams would identify critical places (e.g., the door entering an area, the dining table, the bedroom closet) and tasks (e.g., opening the door, sitting down, eating, getting up, obtaining a nightgown) and observe people engaging in these tasks. Problems may be easily identified in the physical uses of the environments, and sometimes evaluational or affective reactions of the user can be assessed.

A second approach is to reason that users of one environment who are similar to the users of the targeted environment may give clues relevant to design. For example, one of the phases of planning the Alzheimer's disease treatment area in the Philadelphia Geriatric Center involved assembling a group of nursing home residents who were cognitively intact enough to engage in a group discussion of the general question, "What do you like and what don't you like about this place?" (Lawton et al. 1984). This "focus group" format elicited a number of useful evaluations and succeeded better than observation at a distance in giving the planners the flavor of how residents respond to the institutional environment. The disadvantage, of course, is the uncertainty about whether the needs of the impaired resident differ from those of the intact resident.

Perhaps the most systematic attempt to distill knowledge from experts was performed by Zeisel, Epp, and Demos (1978). Although their studies dealt with planned housing rather than an institution, the method is quite applicable to, and should be performed on, the institutional environment for Alzheimer's-type patients.

This study began with a panel of experts who knew both the design and the behavioral research literature and themselves had firsthand knowledge of such housing environments. The project directors assembled a near universe of design issues, using their own expertise as well as the literature. Each design issue (for example, "Where should the window(s) be placed in the living room?") was responded to by each expert. For each response, the expert was asked the basis for the response: A research-validated fact; some research data to support the response; qualitative, systematic observation or experience to support the response; rational or a priori judgment; no basis for supporting one response versus another. Thus, they obtained not only the judgments of a panel of experts but also an indication of the degree of confidence the experts had in the firmness or validity of the conclusion.

As one might imagine, few responses could claim firm empirical research backing. Most were at best derived from qualitative observation and at worst from unsupported subjective judgment. Much of our knowledge is still based on such plausible but unvalidated conclusions.

A good sign is the increasing number of such reports appearing in the literature. This represents at least a primitive type of consensual validation. However, one has to be aware of how subject such reports are to preconceptions and personal ideological influence.

In any case, the nursing literature (Alverman 1979; Hall et al. 1986; Mace 1985; Schwab et al. 1985) and the institutional literature (Hiatt 1980, 1983; Sprague 1984) are showing increasing concern for the design of such environments, including concern over the methodology of such knowledge generation. Some research in this area was reviewed several years ago (Lawton 1986). By far the most complete treatment of this subject with respect to institutions may be found in Calkins (1988).

Application of Behavioral Design Principles

This section on application proceeds with full warning that any recommendations depend very much on good thinking and rational deduction, rather than hard data. To the extent possible, alternative positions are stated. Sensitization to the complexities of these issues is probably the best outcome of the discussion that can be expected. Certainly, a set of design prescriptions cannot be promised.

Approaches to Organizing Design-Relevant Suggestions

The most complete and systematic organization was described by Calkins (1988). She articulated and defined a set of "environment and behavior issues," which might also be thought of as goals for a treatment environment: way-finding, privacy and socialization, personalization, safety and security, and activities of daily living. Some or all of these goals may be pursued in physical areas present in most institutions: bedrooms, corridors, toilets, shared social spaces, dining spaces, kitchens, outdoor spaces, and nursing stations. Her discussion of the design issues related each relevant behavioral goal to the spaces in which the behaviors may occur. Such a cell-by-cell discussion covers the relevant material very systematically and gives an excellent picture of the complexities and tradeoffs between desired and undesired consequences of different design alternatives.

The present discussion cannot treat design application in such detail. Completeness in applying every criterion to every location is sacrificed in favor of dealing as completely as possible with the criteria for design, but limiting the applications to examples of how the criteria might affect design in a limited number of exemplary spaces.

This discussion is organized around a set of positive goals that may be applied to all person-environment transactions. In many instances, the specifics of the goals will be determined by the disabilities of the Alzheimer's patient. Where relevant, applications of the principles to home and institution and to new and existing facilities are discussed.

Positive Environmental Goals

Discussing the positive goals serves to emphasize the generality of human needs across all subgroups and pathologies. Viewed from this

350

vantage point, the universals are stressed, and the design guidelines that emerge are likely to be applicable to users beyond the targeted Alzheimer's disease group. The goals discussed are knowledge of the environment, negotiability, safety and health, activities of daily living, stimulation, social affordance, privacy, control, challenge, individuation, and cultural integration.

Knowledge of the environment is the first goal, and frequently the easiest to meet. To behave in either a life-preserving or a life-enriching manner, one has to be able to register and comprehend the environment. Yet, because most people comprehend most of the environment most of the time, we can easily lose track of the fact that impaired users may need help to understand the language of their environments.

Patients may have to be told the purpose of a space to use it properly. Thus, the presence of a well-known object, such as a dining table, may designate that the area is for eating. A sign ("bath") or a male or female bathroom symbol gives such knowledge. One of the problems of the institution is that all places look alike–knowledge of whose room is where may be conveyed through color coding, large numbers, different within-room decor, or large names or other personalized designation on the door.

Comprehension of the environment is easier in the home than in the institution. Yet the judicious use of some signs or arrows ("to the bathroom") may help even in a once-familiar environment. Very important are ways of maximizing the amount of information the homebound person gets about who is coming up the steps (a view from a favorite chair through window to porch), what the weather is like (curtains open in selected places), or communication with the outside world (handy phone, radio, television).

It is very easy to apply knowledge-enhancing features to an existing environment. Staff can usually come up with fruitful suggestions about what needs to be marked, where signs can be placed while maintaining an aesthetic atmosphere, etc. Less obvious but still quite remediable problems are such matters as illumination and inadequate differentiation of spaces. Some institutions are loath to use lamps of any kind. Where safe, these can do a great deal to make certain areas more easily comprehensible. If lamps cannot be installed, new wiring may be necessary to install a spotlight or lighten a dark corner. Do remember that, in moderation, shadows and variations in light intensity help orient people. Too often, ceiling fluorescent lights obliterate all such variation.

Negotiability is perhaps the most recognized human behavioral need in the designed environment, partly because of the success of the consumers' constituency for the handicapped in sensitizing us.

Most modern institutions are designed moderately well for pure physical accessibility. For the demented person, the problems are more with psychological accessibility. Such persons need to see a desired space or object rather than to remember that it exists. The Philadelphia Geriatric Center deliberately designed important functional areas to be visible from a resident's doorway to enhance psychological accessibility.

In the community dwelling unit, accessibility is a major problem. A few changes may be easy, such as moving the patient's bedroom closer to the toilet and keeping pathways free of objects. Almost any set of steps can be made more accessible by installing handrails on both sides of the staircase (maximum 28″ apart). Ramps are rarely satisfactory without help, however, given the muscular weakness of many of the people with whom we are concerned.

Safety and health are traditionally major concerns in the institution. Again, the best judgments of what constitutes a safety problem are often obtained by asking hands-on staff. One of the most frequent problems, because so easily overlooked, are small projections in places brushed by people's bodies or hands as they pass by, such as the door-latch plate, the corner of a paper-towel dispenser, or the unsanded underside of a chair.

From an opposite vantage point, however, concern for safety and health (especially through cleanliness!) can be overdone. This does not constitute an excuse for germ-breeding dirt, but on many occasions, overconcern for these issues is used to justify stripping an institution of any warmth. For example, a polished floor *looks* clean. It also disorients by the way it reflects hall ceiling light and further contributes to the unpleasant institutional look. Fabrics used as wall coverings or hangings do, indeed, pick up dirt. They also offer positive sensory experiences, and the best thing about them is that they can be cleaned or, if necessary, replaced.

The home is a well-known hazardous environment. However, in the hands of a good environmentally oriented inservice-training instructor, half a day would be sufficient to sensitize a whole in-home services staff in how to look for and remediate such conditions as trailing electric cords, unsteady furniture, loose rugs, slippery spots, dark hazards, and so on.

Activities of daily living are the behaviors most likely to show "excess disability," that is, a decline in adequacy for reasons other than true physical impairment. People caring for the impaired are frequently too quick to perform daily self-maintenance tasks for persons rather than waiting patiently while they do something for themselves. Sometimes the environment can help maintain the ability to perform such behaviors. In the institution, a primary prop for this

352

purpose is a broom, dust tray, and wastebasket handy to the person. The simple sight of these may motivate some people to do basic maintenance around their beds. For others, the combination of encouragement from staff and the environmental wherewithal may be necessary.

The clear marking of and direct access to the bathroom is a basic necessity. The mirror gives essential feedback for maintaining grooming skills. The placement of the mirror is frequently neglected. It must be at a height and location where the person can both look at it easily and get very close to it, and must be in a lighted area. Too often, no chair is near a low mirror, or the patient must sit back 20 inches or so from the mirror and look over the surface of a dresser. The way clothes are stored can affect the ease with which continued responsibility for one's dressing is maintained.

All these considerations apply to the home environment as well, where it may be easier to tailor the environment to the specific individual's needs. For example, safety locks can be installed on gas oven controls for periods when the demented person is unsupervised. With someone around to watch, however, the oven could be used by the person for special occasions.

Some clothes are easier to put on than others. Both over-the-head shirts and those that button are difficult. Substituting a friction fastener for zippers or buttons brings this task well within range. Socks and stockings are difficult to put on and the impaired individuals may require assistance. In the case of shoes, the slip-on variety requires less dexterity and leaves the patient feeling that he has completed the dressing task.

Dining implements, cups, and glasses are made in a variety of forms that may allow the patient with poor motor control or lack of concern for spillage to eat relatively unaided. A damp cloth always within reach may be used by the person who otherwise requires a complete cleanup from the caregiver. Even if the patient must be guided into a tub or shower, the act of self-washing may be initiated by putting a bar of soap or a washcloth in his hand.

The *stimulating quality* of an environment, being an abstract concept, is often unattended. The aesthetic quality is one such aspect. It is very heartening to observe over a period of years that even routine institutions are using a greater variety of colors, adorning walls with pictures, and so on. The auditory environment is less obvious. While nothing is worse than prolonged music or frequent public-address announcements, scheduled times for music or other auditory stimulation in limited areas help break the atmosphere of sensory deprivation. The pet idea has begun to catch on. Sometimes a wandering cat or rabbit can be tolerated by residents. More often, the exposure must be under limited conditions for a short time and with a staff person. Caged birds or totally enclosed aquariums are relatively problem free.

Most of these features can be managed easily by staff in existing environments. A particularly positive feature of such staff involvement is that change can be introduced as a goal in its own right, with the change being managed by staff. That is, part of maintaining continued stimulation is arranging for pictures or hangings to be exchanged, furniture rearranged, new paint colors chosen, and so on. Staff appreciate the task of trying to find out what patients want.

In the home, as everywhere else, change and other environmental stimulation have to be managed within a larger context of enough stability and tranquility to maintain a sense of security. In the home, particularly, long-owned objects and furnishings are very important sources of security. Sometimes such valued objects may be out of sight or forgotten. Conversation with persons about their possessions may help patients enhance this aspect of environmental quality.

Television in many ways has been a real boon to the shut-in. The future decade is certain to bring an explosion of closed-circuit and interactive television for enrichment, information, and training. These uses may be especially valuable for the Alzheimer's patient. All too often, however, the television runs unceasingly in the presence of an apparently uncomprehending, confused patient. Part of the problem is that unvarying stimulation of *any* kind pushes *all* people to "turn off" psychologically. If the best is to be obtained from television, the caregiver must try to learn what the patient enjoys and offer a mix of favorite programs, new programs, and *silence*! Radio alone may provide a bit of a change, but periodic absences of all such auditory stimulation are mandatory.

The term *social affordance* is meant to suggest that some situations are better than others for allowing social interaction to occur. Few situations can *cause* social behavior, but it is difficult without the presence of another person!

Some basic structural features of institutions may make social behavior more likely. Informal seating space in or near areas of high activity, such as a nurses station, a main doorway, or even the doctor's office, is likely to attract people. One level of social participation has clearly been shown to be "sitting and watching," where behavior may be vicarious but very subjectively active. The next level, real participation, is enhanced by physical proximity to another person or by being close enough to an ongoing activity to join in with minimal extra effort. Shared bedrooms, interestingly enough, do not seem to greatly enhance social behavior, possibly because space is shared by necessity, not by choice.

354

Short of making expensive, major structural changes, much can be done to arrange social behavior-inducing environments by combining placement of furniture and modification of the rules that govern the use of the environment. Often residents are discouraged from seating themselves in on-stage areas such as outside the front door or in the lobby, particularly if they engage in stereotypic or socially undesirable behaviors. Administrators sometimes justify such rules because of the image created in the eyes of relatives or the outside community. When this is true, then administrators, relatives, and the public should be educated about the relationship among the physical occupancy of space, watching the behavior of others, and the levels of social behavior appropriate to the Alzheimer's patient.

In the community, the family should thoughtfully consider their willingness to allow the social exposure of their impaired relative. Families are almost always embarrassed to have others see a relative with Alzheimer's and also misguidedly protective in shielding the relative from interactions with others. While a high level of exposure to complex social stimulation—for example, a large, 6-hour family reunion—may be stressful, measured doses of visits and contacts are almost guaranteed to be helpful. For example, when a workman or delivery person is expected, it is desirable to place the impaired person where the visitor may be seen, spoken to, and even observed at work. If relatives living outside the household do not visit spontaneously, it is good for both patient and relative to actively invite them to visit.

Even if the patient does not leave the home, degrees of isolation or social involvement are possible. The front porch is an inestimably positive resource for the impaired older person, and can be made secure if wandering is a problem. It allows the person to sit where a conversation may be held with a neighbor or passerby and, at the very least, offers the chance to watch behavior: pedestrians, deliveries, children at play, or just automobiles.

In some ways, the opposite side of social affordance is *privacy*, a very rare commodity in the institution. When even very impaired nursing home residents have a choice, good evidence shows that they construct their own most palatable mix of time alone in their rooms and time in the physical presence of others, as in halls or common spaces. In fact, for most residents, true physical privacy is hard to attain, so they develop psychological barriers to provide the functional equivalent of privacy in the presence of others (for discussions of this topic see DeLong 1970; Lipman 1968; Watson and Maxwell 1977).

Physical privacy is difficult and expensive to provide. Flexibility in providing privacy is best attained by managing the environment rather than its structure. Staff need to learn to arrange furniture to

355

serve both patients who wish to retire and those who might be stimulated toward social contact. Similarly, for some people at some times the gains of being able to sit behind their closed bedroom doors may override the need to maintain safety by surveillance. Training staff to knock, ask about going through closets and drawers, respect modesty, and so on are examples of environmental management in the service of privacy. Similar considerations apply to the way relatives, friends, and in-home service workers deal with impaired people living in their own homes.

Control is a much-invoked concept, sometimes seen as a universal cure-all (see Langer and Rodin (1976) and Schulz (1976) for some validation studies of the value of personal control in institutional settings). Personal control has very strong environmental aspects. Sometimes the environment offers the opportunity for patient control—regulation of heat, ventilation, and light; the choice of personal decor; the availability of physically private space for retreat or private visits; and so on. Very often the environment is controlled by administration and staff through rules about who can occupy which spaces at what time.

Residents often appropriate territory in common spaces and retain it as a place where their behavior can be more of their own choice than it is in "non-owned" space. DeLong (1970) observed that demented patients who owned seating spaces in the hall engaged in less hostile behavior than those who owned no such space. Staff sometimes find it hard to accept such behavior. Rules may either ease or make more difficult the personalization of space, the way one schedules a day, one's diet, and so on. Defining the conditions under which enhancing environmental control can benefit Alzheimer's residents remains to be done. Once more, hands-on staff, with consultation from professionals or administrators, are best suited for this task. Indeed, enhancing control depends entirely on the combined effort of all staff and their good thinking about how environmental features can contribute.

The behavioral world of impaired people living in the community is greatly shrunken, often consisting of the place were they sit and the area visible from that point. Maximum control is limited to what can be seen or reached, the "control center" (Lawton 1985). Personal control comes through exposure to information gained by viewing the front door, window, and street and through television, radio, and telephone, and ability to reach or see important objects such as photos, food, or reading material.

Environmental *challenge* is one of the most abstract attributes. How can one define a challenge in any way except for a single individual? One woman's challenge is another's barrier. To some

356

extent, challenge can be defined as a graded series of opportunities for behavior with differing demands. Clearly, one could introduce a stairway that everyone would have to traverse in order to eat. On the other hand, one could supply some elective activities that could only be accessed by the steps. For a few, exercising one's competence in the interest of a desired goal, for example, the opportunity to pet the rabbit that resided four steps up, can be programmed into the social and physical environment. It is, of course, easier to construct such a continuum in human-service terms than in physical environmental terms. That is what a behavioral-treatment milieu, based on reinforcement principles, is meant to do. In that approach, considerable emphasis is placed on making progress visible to both patient and staff. A graph or a tally of successes affords a reward to the viewer. Other more direct rewards are often an opportunity to engage in a desired behavior or a direct reinforcer like candy. The principle of the leading stimulus keeps the environmental demand just an increment ahead of the person's capability. Such a behavioral treatment context requires the total focusing of staff on such relevant behavioral principles.

In the community, a family caregiver or an in-home service worker may unconsciously reduce the number of challenges to which a demented person is exposed, assuming that once demented, the person cannot exert any effort. Thus, to urge the person to try to mount the steps, even part way and with help, is more desirable for the marginal person than to be too quick to move the bedroom to the ground floor. Some pathological behavior may be seen as a challenge matched to the competence of a person. For example, the act of wandering may well be a continued urge to exercise or explore more than is possible in that environment. Some evidence shows that wanderers may have needed to discharge tension through motor activity all their lives (Robb and Mansour 1980).

Even the most impaired appreciate unusual activities. Visits from outsiders and trips outside the dwelling unit are the most obvious breaks in the sameness of days. Day care centers have become more accessible in recent years; they offer the perfect respite for both patient and caretaker. In the home, small tasks that were learned in the past, such as knitting, may be possible for some. Ingenuity may be required to design others: cutting rags with scissors, polishing a table, sanding a toy. The important message of this section is that Alzheimer's disease does not mean the end of interest in things to do or immunity from boredom.

Individualization, or identity maintenance, suffers greatly from people's premature assumption of total incompetence in Alzheimer's patients. The rooms of demented nursing home patients are often stripped of anything personal, and the patients wear clothes provided en masse by the institution. For many patients, it is very easy to upgrade this deprived situation. In consultation with the patient, family and staff can work to learn what kinds of room adornments would remind them of who they are, who they were, their families, their former achievements and attachments, and so on. Photographs, pictures, mementos, a mirror, trophies, small collections, and even some articles of furniture help keep the continuity of self within awareness. The enemies of such a process are built-in furniture that consumes all floor space, prohibitions against attachments on the wall, fear of theft, problems caused by staff's having to dust around objects, and the overall conclusion, "Oh, he wouldn't know what all that stuff was anyway." Of course there are limits–too big pieces of furniture, valuable pieces, or fire hazards, for example.

The destructive or oral-incorporative person is a special problem, not only to his own objects but to those of others. Good judgment is clearly needed, but the error is too often made on the conservative side, that it is better to be safe. It may be possible to provide periodically a copy of a photograph or a second-rate picture that still might be meaningful, even if it eventually gets torn up. A favorite chair might have to be thrown away after a couple of months with an incontinent user, but isn't it better to have had it for 2 months?

Finally, *cultural integration* is rarely thought of as relevant to the environments of demented older people. However, symbols of one's belonging to a larger group may continue to communicate to the person. An American flag, a lodge symbol, a cross, or a mezuzah are a few objects that people in general use to deisolate themselves. Probably much could be learned about the persistence of such symbolic meanings and the ability of impaired people to express preferences for such props if given the choice and enough attention to discern whether a choice can be expressed.

It is worthwhile reiterating how tentative most of these suggestions must be. In fact, enough people are thinking about such interventions that directly opposite recommendations can be found. Take the instance of level of incoming stimulation which, according to the ecological model, could be a stressor (too high intensity) or a depriving environment (too low intensity). Much qualitative information supports the idea that the institutional environment is chronically understimulating, and many of the above suggestions would raise the intensity and complexity of stimulation. Yet we also know, for example from the clinical work of Goldstein and Scheerer (1941), that an overdemand is likely to result in a "catastrophic reaction" by the brain-damaged patient. Thus, highly experienced professionals have recommended a "low-stimulus unit," with no mirrors, neutral geometric designs instead of

358

pictures, and so on, in the interest of keeping stimulation within manageable bounds (Hall et al. 1986). Such a challenging reversal of recent thinking sets the stage for empirical research that should continue to advance the state of knowledge.

Human Actors as the Central Element in Environmental Treatment

Throughout the above discussion, the inertness of the physical environment and its dependence on decisions made by people are emphasized. A variety of specific suggestions are made about the Alzheimer's patient possessing some vestige of desire and capability for control; the central place of the administrator in making rules governing the use of the environment; the key role of direct-care institutional staff and in-home workers in facilitating the creative use of the environment; and the place of family household members in the same tasks.

In the institution, it is possible to go even further in supporting the growth of expertise and creative thought in staff. Everyone is a latent designer. The opportunity to indulge this whim is for many people a highly prized endeavor, though most people get no opportunity to allow that propensity to become manifest. A "therapeutic environment committee" is one way to activate such talent. If blessed by the administrator, given a small budget and channels to other decision-makers, such a group can make any care environment more therapeutic, whether the best-designed modern one or an eyesore from another century.

Such an endeavor can be structured in many ways. If the organization is large enough, a representative from each treatment area can participate in the large committee and, in turn, be the local expert on the direct-care team. In smaller institutions, the committee *is* the people who will broker the interventions. Whichever way that goes, it is essential to include the nurse's aides, housekeepers, and food-service workers who see the most of the residents. Fostering comfortable interchange between this direct-care staff and professionals is also a challenging task.

A therapeutic environment committee will do more than upgrade the treatment environment. It will just as certainly be a strong motivator for staff and an important contributor to staff morale, especially if the group is given periodic recognition for its efforts.

In conclusion, there is room for hope that traditional social-scientific research, systematic clinical observation, and qualitative user observation may converge on the task of moving beyond the speculative environmental design approach that has characterized this field for two decades. The most feasible first step is to have the clinicians exert themselves increasingly to record what they see, for only out of this material will the researchers be able to form hypotheses and the designers to create physical environments. Concurrently, the users of the environment need to be brought more closely into the research and design process, whether they be patient users or staff users.

References

Alverman, M.M. Toward improving geriatric care with environmental intervention emphasizing a homelike atmosphere. *Journal of Gerontological Nursing* 5:13-17, 1979.

Archea, J. Identifying direct links between behavior and its environment. In: Byerts, T.O., ed. *Environmental Research and Aging.* Washington, DC: Gerontological Society of America, 1974. pp. 117-153.

Baltes, M.M.; Honn, S.; Barton, E.M.; Orzech, M.; and Lago, D. On the social ecology of dependence and independence in elderly nursing home residents: A replication and extension. *Journal of Gerontology* 38:556-564, 1983.

Calkins, M.P. *Design for Dementia: Planning Environments for the Elderly and the Confused.* Owings Mills, MD: National Health Publishing, 1988.

Carp, F.M. *A Future for the Aged.* Austin: University of Texas Press, 1966.

DeLong, A.J. The microspatial structure of the older person. In: Pastalan, L.A., and Carson, D.H., eds. *Spatial Behavior of Older People.* Ann Arbor: University of Michigan Institute of Gerontology, 1970. pp. 68-87.

Flanagan, J.C. *Identifying Opportunities for Improving the Quality of Life of Older Age Groups.* Palo Alto, CA: American Institute for Research, 1979.

Golant, S.M. *A Place to Grow Old.* New York: Columbia University Press, 1984.

Goldstein, K., and Scheerer, M. Abstract and concrete behavior. *Psychological Monographs* 43:1-151, 1941.

Gottesman, L.E., and Bourestom, N.C. Why nursing homes do what they do. *Gerontologist* 14:501-506, 1974.

Hall, G.; Kirschling, M.V.; and Todd, S. Sheltered freedom–an Alzheimer's unit in an ICF. *Geriatric Nursing* 7:132-136, 1986.

Hiatt, L. Disorientation is more than a state of mind. *Nursing Homes* 29:30-36, 1980.

Hiatt, L. Effective design for informal conversation. *American Health Care Association Journal* 9:43-46, 1983.

Howell, S.C. *Designing for Aging: Patterns of Use.* Cambridge, MA: MIT Press, 1980.

Langer, E., and Rodin, J. The effects of choice and enhanced personal responsibility for the aged. *Journal of Personality and Social Psychology* 34:191-198, 1976.

Lawton, M.P. *Planning and Managing Housing for the Elderly.* New York: Wiley-Interscience, 1975.

Lawton, M.P. Sensory deprivation and the effect of the environment on management of the senile dementia patient. In: Miller, N., and Cohen, G., eds. *Clinical Studies of Alzheimer's Disease and Senile Dementia.* New York: Raven Press, 1986. pp. 227-249.

Lawton, M.P. Competence, environmental press, and the adaptation of older people. In: Lawton, M.P.; Windley, P.G.; and Byerts, T.O., eds. *Aging and the Environment: Theoretical Approaches.* New York: Springer, 1982. pp. 33-59.

Lawton, M.P. The elderly in context: Perspectives from environmental psychology and gerontology. *Environment and Behavior* 17:501-519, 1985.

Lawton, M.P. Strategies in planning environments for the elderly. *Journal of Independent Living* 1(3):1-14, 1987.

Lawton, M.P.; Fulcomer, M.; and Kleban, M.H. Architecture for the mentally impaired elderly. *Environment and Behavior* 16:730-757, 1984.

Lawton, M.P., and Nahemow, L. Ecology and the aging process. In: Eisdorfer, C., and Lawton, M.P., eds. *Psychology of Adult Development and Aging.* Washington, DC: American Psychological Association, 1973. pp. 619-674.

Lindsley, O.R. Geriatric behavioral prosthetics. In: Kastenbaum, R., ed. *New Thoughts on Old Age.* New York: Springer, 1964.

Lipman, A. A socio-architectural view of life in three homes for old people. *Gerontologia Clinica* 10:88-101, 1968.

Mace, N. Do we need special care units for dementia patients? *Journal of Gerontological Nursing* 11:37-38, 1985.

Mastroieni, M., and Lawton, M.P. *Designing a Therapeutic Environment in the State Mental Hospital.* Harrisburg, PA: Office of Mental Health, 1983.

Murray, H. *Explorations in Personality.* New York: Oxford, 1938.

National Center for Health Statistics. *Profile of Chronic Illness in Nursing Homes.* DHEW Publication No. (PHS) 78-1780, Series 13, No. 29. Hyattsville, MD: Department of Health, Education and Welfare, 1977.

Newcomer, R.J.; Lawton, M.P.; and Byerts, T.O., eds. *Housing an Aging Society*. New York: Van Nostrand Reinhold, 1986.

Reizenstein, J.E., and Zimring, C.M. Evaluating occupied environments. *Environment and Behavior* 12:427-558, 1980.

Robb, S.S., and Monsour, N. "Wandering Behavior in Old Age." Paper presented at the annual meeting of the Gerontological Society of America, San Diego, CA, Nov. 1980.

Rosow, I. *Social Integration of the Aged*. New York: Free Press, 1967.

Schulz, R. Effects of control and predictability on the physical and psychological well-being of the institutionalized aged. *Journal of Personality and Social Psychology* 33:563-573, 1976.

Schwab, M.; Rader, J.; and Doan, J. Relieving the anxiety or fear in dementia. *Journal of Gerontological Nursing* 11:8-15, 1985.

Sprague, G. Design considerations for the elderly. *Hospitals* 60:86-87, 1984.

Vivrett, W.K. Housing and community settings for older people. In: Tibbitts, C., ed. *Handbook of Social Gerontology*. Chicago: University of Chicago Press, 1960. pp. 549-623.

Wachs, M. *Transportation for the Elderly*. Berkeley: University of California Press, 1979.

Watson, W.H., and Maxwell, R.J. *Human Aging and Dying: A Study in Cultural Gerontology*. New York: St. Martins Press, 1977.

Whitehead, C.; Polsky, R.H.; Crookshank, B.A.; and Fik, E. Objective and subjective evaluation of psychiatric ward redesign. *American Journal of Psychiatry* 141:639-644, 1984.

Zeisel, J.; Epp, G.; and Demos, S. *Low-Rise Housing for Older People: Behavioral Criteria for Design*. Washington, DC: Office for Policy Development and Research, U.S. Department of Housing and Urban Development, 1978.

Chapter 15

Excess Disability in Dementia of the Alzheimer's Type

Burton V. Reifler, M.D., M.P.H., and Eric Larson, M.D., M.P.H.

Although dementia of the Alzheimer's type (DAT) cannot be cured, patients with DAT can be treated. Nothing is paradoxical about these statements, as the daily work of most health professionals includes treating patients with chronic incurable illnesses such as, to name just a few, emphysema, insulin dependent diabetes, and athero-sclerotic cardiovascular disease. The management of patients with DAT presents a similar situation but is not always seen that way by professionals or laymen, who often see DAT patients as hopeless and untreatable.

We believe the confusion that exists between incurability and untreatability of patients with DAT is due to bias on two counts: discrimination against the elderly and discrimination against in-dividuals with mental impairment. We begin this chapter by develop-ing this line of thinking, in the hope it will allow the reader to dispassionately evaluate the review of excess disability in DAT which follows, as our main point is that many patients with DAT have treatable components to their illnesses. A substantial body of re-search documents the existence of excess disability in DAT patients, but the biases mentioned continue to interfere with the proper application of this knowledge.

Discrimination Against the Aged

Everyday English reveals much about our culture's view of the aged: "old bags," "old geezers," "put out to pasture," and other, even less flattering, descriptions indicate that growing old makes one undesirable and useless. These messages are constantly reinforced. Two easily observed examples of such negative stereotypes are jokes and television programming.

Several authors, including Palmore (1971), Davies (1977), and Richman (1977), analyzed jokes and found them to negatively depict the elderly. Sheppard (1981) identified four categories of cartoons about the elderly–disparagement, ineffectuality, obsolescence, and isolation–and noted the frequent appearance of stereotyped characters, such as the dirty old man and little old lady. When the elderly are depicted as competent or energetic, the humor is often based on this being abnormal behavior for this age group. Even though stereotyping and caricatures are inherent to humor, these are used excessively when depicting the elderly.

On television programs, elderly characters are usually relegated to minor roles and in commercials are most often seen selling health-related products, including denture adhesives, hemorrhoidal preparations, or supplemental health insurance. Several authors, including Francher (1973) and Harris and Feinberg (1978) noted the frequent presence of strong stereotypes when the elderly are portrayed on television, and Bishop and Krause (1984) showed that we begin teaching this to our children at an early age. In their analysis of 106 Saturday morning cartoons broadcast on commercial television during a 6-week period, although old age was not a dominant theme, when it emerged it was typically framed in negative terms. For example, out of 21 offhand remarks related to old age made by the cartoon characters, 19 were negative, usually referring to loss of physical strength or mental ability, e.g., "Maybe Papa Smurf is losing his power–you know, getting old." Only two were positive: "wonderful old gal" and "wise old friends."

Discrimination against the aged has long been recognized. Almost 20 years ago, Butler (1969) published his celebrated paper on ageism in which he described the anti-old age biases held by our youth-oriented culture and, judging from the portrayal of the elderly in jokes and on television, even an optimist would have to concede that, at best, change has been coming slowly.

Discrimination Against the Mentally Ill

While the bias against individuals with mental illness has improved, there can be little doubt that such discrimination still exists.

While individuals who acknowledge a past history of mental illness are publicly regarded as courageous, they do so at risk to their careers (e.g., Senator Eagleton's brief candidacy for Vice President). All physicians are aware of patients who are concerned about listing a history of psychiatric treatment on a job application. (Unfortunately, their concerns are sometimes well founded.)

An eloquent account by a woman with a history of manic-depressive disorder recently appeared in *Lancet* (Anonymous 1986) in which she described the 40-year course of her illness. She commented that, "The worst difficulty one has to face on being discharged is the stigma attaching to mental illness. . . Most people regard mental illness with fear and wish to distance themselves from it." The irony is that the suffering from mental illness is great, but the compassion relatively small. On this account she comments, "Mental illness is far harder to bear than physical illness in my experience, yet it excites little sympathy, usually being attributed to lack of moral fibre." Her remarks leave little to add.

The Double Whammy

The cartoonist Al Capp created a character named Evil Eye Fleegle, whose eyes would bulge out when he applied the mysterious double whammy to his enemies. But there is nothing funny about the double whammy felt by those who have the double misfortune to be both old and mentally impaired.

To show how outrageous this discrimination is, let us describe how it exists even among psychiatrists, the physicians who should be most sympathetic to such patients, and how it is institutionalized by government via Medicare regulations and practice.

Ford and Sbordone (1980) examined the attitudes of psychiatrists toward elderly patients by analyzing the responses to questionnaires completed by 179 psychiatrists. The questionnaires contained four clinical vignettes constructed so the age of the patient was the independent variable and responses to three questions served as the dependent variables. The three questions, which required the respondents to place a mark on a 100-mm line continuum, were how well the patient met the physician's criteria for an ideal patient (the extremes were "not well" and "very well"), the estimated prognosis (ranging from "poor" to "excellent"), and preferred treatment (ranging from no treatment to various combinations of psychotherapy and/or pharmacotherapy). The four vignettes were identical except that in half the descriptions the patients were over 65 and in the other half, younger than 45.

The most striking finding was that the identical case histories, save for age, produced responses indicating that the psychiatrists saw the older patients as having a poorer prognosis and being less suitable for their practices. Statistically significant correlations were found in all four case vignettes between the physicians' estimates of "idealness" and patient prognosis, suggesting that psychiatrists use prognosis as a criterion for "idealness," and, in turn, older patients are less ideal because they are seen as having a poorer prognosis.

The data upon which the above paper was based were further analyzed by Ray et al. (1985) for evidence of ageism by psychiatrists, associated with gender, Board certification, and theoretical orientation. Characteristics associated with negative attitudes included psychoanalytic orientation, female gender, and certification by the American Board of Psychiatry and Neurology. The first of these three might have been predictable if one remembered Freud's view that psychoanalysis becomes less applicable with advancing age. The association between female gender and ageism is difficult to interpret, although the authors speculate on possible reasons, such as women feeling more threatened than men by contact with the elderly because of greater awareness of societal attitudes toward youthfulness and appearance. Finally, whatever the reason for stronger negative attitudes by Board-certified psychiatrists, a logical approach to correct this would be increased emphasis by the Board on geriatric psychiatry, both as part of the examinations and as a training requirement for Board eligibility.

A paper by Cohen (1976) provided evidence that the attitudinal problems noted above are reflected in delivery of mental health services. He found that, although elderly constitute 10 percent of the population, they make up only 4 percent of all psychiatric outpatients seen in private practice or mental health centers.

Our second example of the double whammy felt by those who are both old and mentally ill relates to Medicare regulations, both the regulations themselves and their interpretation. Financially, the only major category of illness subject to a 50-percent deductible and low annual maximum for outpatient treatment by a physician is mental illness. We thus see that the quotes from the anonymous patient cited earlier about mental illness exciting little sympathy, applies not only to the general public but to the nation's lawmakers. (We can hardly expect them to admit this; in fact, their public statements are quite the opposite, but their actions are clear.)

The Secretary of Health and Human Services established a Task Force on Alzheimer's Disease, and a hard-fought victory was the removal of the outpatient limitation for psychiatric management of a patient with DAT. An admirable goal, but based on our experience, it has simply not been put into practice by Medicare intermediaries. For example, claims for treatment of a patient with DAT who was receiving antipsychotic medication for control of paranoia were consistently denied on the basis of not representing active treatment (imagine a similar argument made about a diabetic whose insulin needed monitoring). This is precisely the type of situation for which the expanded coverage was intended, yet it was denied at the local level, despite detailed letters including copies of the appropriate references from the *Medicare Carrier's Handbook.*

The points raised above are directly related to the treatment of excess disability in DAT. The double whammy of being both old and mentally ill can make it difficult to find an interested physician, and even interested physicians are confronted with repeated, tangible evidence that both the legislative and administrative branches of government regard these problems as relatively unimportant.

We believe this will eventually change, for three basic reasons. The first is that families of DAT patients are determined to see this happen and will continue to pressure health professionals and governmental agencies for better care and better funding. Second, the satisfactions for health professionals are very great; few people are more appreciative for small improvements in a patient's condition than caregivers of DAT patients. The third reason is that education seems to work.

To expand on the last reason, a recent review of research on training programs in geriatric medicine (Reifler 1986a) showed that, although the amount of published research in this area is small, the results are encouraging. For example, Warren and coworkers (1983) investigated the effects of a 25-hour geriatrics educational program on the attitudes of third-year medical students toward older patients. The educational program included an introduction, 10 hours of contact with the elderly, two group discussions, and an exercise in sensory deprivation that required students to perform some activities of daily living while encumbered with sensory limiting devices. Students' attitudes improved in all four categories (personal anxiety toward aging, social value of the elderly, geriatric patient care, and stereotypes of the aged) and the percentage of students endorsing the statement "I will welcome old people into my practice" jumped from 50 percent to 90 percent.

A report by Wilson and Hafferty (1983) gives encouragement that the effects of educational programs for medical students are enduring and not forgotten as the course fades from memory. In their study, improvement in attitudes by first-year medical students taking a seminar on aging and health persisted when they were retested as fourth-year students. Wolf-Klein and associates (1983) found that 86 percent of general medicine residents on a 4-week geriatric rotation said it was a positive experience, and all of them felt the team approach could be applied to their future practices. Croen et al. (1984) had generally favorable comments about an interdisciplinary training program that included both medical and nursing students, concluding that such training leads to an increased understanding of the skills provided by other disciplines.

NIMH and NIA have identified specialized training in geriatric mental health and geriatric medicine as high priorities, and through various fellowships and academic awards, the numbers of academicians and clinicians are increasing. One can anticipate that if the funding for these programs continues, we will continue to see progress in the attitudes of physicians and other health professionals, and the lack of provision of mental health services noted earlier by Cohen (1976) should show increasing improvement.

From a conceptual point of view, we believe the most useful way to view the topic of excess disability in DAT is to clearly have in mind a disease model of dementia, free of bias concerning old age or mental illness. This perspective allows one to beneficially apply to dementia the points Beeson (1986) made in his excellent review of progress made in internal medicine over the past century.

He noted that internists have always regarded diagnosis as an end in itself, perhaps because formerly they had so little treatment to offer, and illustrates this by commenting on Osler's deserved reputation as a therapeutic nihilist, whose prescriptions often included measures such as good nursing care, adequate diet, fresh air, and sunlight. But there were some useful medications in those days, such as analgesics, digitalis, and iron. The therapeutic revolution we have seen since World War II includes, to name just a few, antibiotics, chemotherapy, organ and tissue transplants, antihypertensives, and neuroleptics such as antidepressants, antipsychotics, and lithium.

The analogy to DAT is simple: just as with many other illnesses, our current ability to make an accurate diagnosis of DAT is very good (Katzman (1986) commented that at many centers it is now diagnosed with 90-percent accuracy) and we have some useful measures to recommend, such as respite care, good diet, and proper hygiene. Also, medical therapeutics plays a clear role with selected patients. With the powerful research tools at our disposal, it is only a matter of time before DAT joins the list of diseases which have effective therapies. Rapid progress requires that we stay at the frontier, and in the clinical approach to DAT, this means recognition and treatment of excess disability.

368

Some Popular Concepts Revisited

Interpretations of the literature on diagnostic investigations of demented patients have often suffered the same fate as a tree at the hands of an inexperienced woodsman: sometimes on target but frequently off the mark. An example is the well-known paper by Marsden and Harrison (1972), which was clearly and conservatively presented, but which has often been interpreted incorrectly and also applied to groups of patients other than those they described. Their report was on 106 patients with presumed presenile dementia (regrettably, mean age and age range were not mentioned) who were hospitalized for evaluation. Thus, their report does not include geriatric outpatients, which includes the majority of DAT patients.

Nonetheless, their report was an important one, and perhaps their most valuable finding was that some of the patients referred for a dementia workup were not demented at all. They noted that "In 15 patients psychometry did not show any evidence of organic intellectual deterioration, and memory and learning were unimpaired." This group included cases of affective disorder, drug intoxication, and epilepsy. Among the demented patients, the authors reported that a clinical diagnosis was reached in 36 of 84 patients (43 percent). The most common diagnoses (and number of cases) were intracranial space-occupying mass (8), arteriosclerotic dementia (8), dementia in alcoholics (6), and possible normal pressure communicating hydrocephalus (5).

In their abstract, the authors concluded that a possible etiology for the dementia was found in 36 patients, and 15 percent of the whole series suffered from conditions amenable to treatment. It was worth reviewing the evidence they offered for these two figures, as these statements are not as straightforward as they first appear.

Marsden and Harrison stated that "In 48 of the 84 demented patients (57 percent), no firm diagnosis could be achieved." They presumed that many of these patients had Alzheimer's disease, or Pick's disease, but did not feel justified in making the distinction in the absence of histological confirmation and decided to classify these patients as "cerebral atrophy of unknown cause." It is interesting that they did not refrain from making other specific diagnoses, even in the absence of conclusive proof. For example, they listed Huntington's Chorea as the final diagnosis in three patients. But a recent report by Folstein et al. (1986) on the diagnosis of Huntington's Disease (HD) indicated that 15 percent of cases diagnosed as HD were found by the investigators to have some other condition, a figure greater than the 10 percent false positive es-

369

timate for DAT noted above by Katzman (1986). Furthermore, Marsden and Harrison noted that dementia in alcoholics is not a clearly defined entity, yet they diagnosed it in six cases, and the fact that three patients with dementia presumably due to communicating hydrocephalus did not improve after surgery did not stop them from making this diagnosis. It is not farfetched to wonder if their cases of arteriosclerotic dementia had evidence of strokes severe enough to positively account for the degree of dementia observed. This is not to imply any carelessness, but to make the point that many commonly used diagnostic categories are probabilities rather than certainties.

Back to this point in a moment, but first a look at their observations on treatment. They stated that 15 percent of their series consisted of patients with conditions amenable to treatment; this would be 17 individuals. They were not explicit about which 17 they referred to, but this group presumably included (among others) the 8 patients with space-occupying masses and the 5 with communicating hydrocephalus. But no treatment results are presented on the former, and of the latter group, ventriculoatrial drainage did not benefit four of the five patients, and we are not told how much it helped the fifth. A more accurate (though perhaps too harsh) wording than "condition amenable to treatment" might have been "condition for which a surgical procedure is available."

This is the second double whammy applicable to DAT: the mistaken beliefs that it cannot be diagnosed except by microscopic examination of brain tissue and, even if diagnosed, it cannot be treated. In fact, the diagnosis of DAT is no less certain than many of the other conditions with which the authors dealt. We have already commented twice on the diagnostic accuracy rates of 90 percent that are now the rule at major centers (Katzman 1986), a figure in agreement with our own experience comparing clinical diagnoses with autopsy findings. Second, the treatments described for the "conditions amenable to treatment" did not necessarily produce curative, or even beneficial, results. What constitutes treatment for a condition depends on one's point of view, but we favor a broader definition of treatment than Marsden and Harrison imply, and would include antihypertensive therapy and physical rehabilitation for arterial disease, cessation of drinking for alcoholism, and a wide range of treatment suggestions for DAT, including family counseling, referral to community programs such as day centers, and treatment of secondary symptoms and coexisting illnesses causing excess disability. Before going on, let us acknowledge that application of 1986 knowledge to a paper published in 1972 is unfair, but hidden assumptions in their report illustrate a way of thinking still very much with us, and on this basis it is justified.

370

DAT is no harder to accurately diagnose than many other causes of dementia, and treatment goals are similar to other incurable, progressive illnesses: accurate diagnosis, patient (and in this case, family) education, relief of suffering, preservation of function, avoidance of iatrogenic problems, and treatment of coincidental illnesses and sources of excess disability. But the double whammy of being old and mentally ill causes physicians to put on blinders and add their own double whammy of perceiving DAT to be undiagnosible and untreatable.

Marsden and Harrison, along with other investigators studying the differential diagnosis of dementia, made a very valuable contribution by simply pointing out the wide range of conditions that can cause cognitive impairment, and urging physicians to look for and treat these diseases, while remembering to first confirm that dementia is in fact present. However, an unfortunate result of their report, and others similar to it, was for physicians to note the finding that 15 percent of presenile demented inpatients had *potentially treatable* causes, and then to infer that 15 percent of *all* demented patients had *curable* causes. There has been an imbalance of effort, with great energy going into exhaustive and hopeful diagnostic evaluations and relatively little into the management of DAT, which in many cases extends over 5-10 years. The identification and treatment of sources of excess disability is a critical part of the long-term care for this chronic disease.

Identification and Treatment of Excess Disability in DAT

We discuss excess disability in DAT by reviewing our work at the University of Washington over the past 8 years, beginning in 1978 with the opening of the Geriatric and Family Services Clinic (Reifler and Eisdorfer 1980). Geriatric and Family Services, an outpatient clinic at the University of Washington Hospital, opened in response to requests from the public for evaluations of cognitively impaired elderly. We believe it was the first Alzheimer's clinic in the United States.

The evaluation at the clinic consists of a psychiatric assessment, general medical history and physical examination, social and environmental assessment (done in the patient's home when possible), and psychological testing. After these steps are completed (although some components can be waived if circumstances warrant, such as when cognitive impairment is so severe that psychological testing is unnecessary), there is a staff conference to review the findings and develop recommendations, followed by a family conference to discuss them. Recommendations are given to the family in writing and cover the following areas: (1) stop medications, (2) begin medications, (3) further medical evaluation or treatment, (4) move to new living situation, (5) modify current living situation, (6) regular treatment for patient, (7) further consultations with family, (8) additional in-home help, (9) participation in specific community programs, (10) respite for family, and (11) other. Each area is checked as strongly recommended, recommended, or not recommended, and space is provided for staff comments. Followup care is provided on a case-by-case basis.

Nothing was new about any of the components of this program; the novel aspects were to combine all of the features in a single administrative structure using an integrated data base (Cox et al. 1982), to place equal emphasis on both patient and family, and to pay close attention to program evaluation from the outset. Since its opening, the clinic has provided more than 1,500 assessments for mentally impaired elderly. The average age of our patients was 77 years; women were referred twice as often as men; most of the patients still lived at home; half were homeowners; the referring family member was usually a spouse, daughter, or son; and, as we expected, most of the patients had Alzheimer's disease, depression, or both. Appointment-keeping rates have consistently exceeded 90 percent.

The staff of Geriatric and Family Services now consists of six individuals, all working part-time—a psychiatrist, psychologist, intern-ist, social worker, nurse, and medical assistant. The clinic meets 2 full days each week. Apparently other institutions have found our model useful, as directors of several other programs have acknowledged that they either successfully replicated our program or that the experience from our clinic was useful in shaping their own. This confirms the need for clinics providing a comprehensive, family-oriented outpatient approach to the diagnosis and long-term management of Alzheimer's disease.

One important finding from our program is that many mentally ill elderly will see a psychiatrist when their family makes the necessary arrangements and then insists on it. (We have learned to advise the family members to request the evaluation for their own sake, acknowledging to the patient that they realize the patient may not feel it is necessary.) Although most of the patients would not have sought help on their own, they often looked forward to subsequent visits.

Our initial hopes, influenced by what we have come to call the folklore of reversible dementia (with its origins in the literature of the 1960s and 1970s referred to earlier), were to find substantial numbers of demented elderly who would prove to have curable underlying diseases accounting for their cognitive impairment. These hopes were raised higher when an early series of patients included several with folate deficiency (Reifler et al. 1981), but only one patient had cognitive improvement with treatment (a modest change perhaps due to episodic fluctuation in his DAT). We realized that folate deficiency did not cause the dementia; rather, the dementia probably caused the low folate (Larson et al. 1986), as some demented patients no longer ate the green leafy vegetables that provide this nutrient. We continue to recommend folate replacement therapy where indicated, but our rationale has shifted from hopes of a cure to treating a potential source of excess disability (for example, low folate could lead to anemia with resultant fatigue).

We have now had the opportunity to study, for almost a decade, both the diagnostic process in the evaluation of DAT and the results of followup of these patients, including those with potentially treatable conditions. We review here the results of diagnostic evaluations and followups in a series of 200 consecutive patients investigated for suspected dementia, then present our findings on the treatment of DAT patients who are also depressed, as depression appears to be the most commonly occurring cause of excess disability in DAT patients.

Evaluation for Dementia of 200 Elderly Outpatients, Including Followup

The findings summarized here have been published in more detail elsewhere (Larson et al. 1985), and the reader who wishes still more information on our work is also referred to Larson, Reifler, Canfield, and Cohen (1984), Larson, Reifler, Featherstone, et al. (1984), Larson, Featherstone, et al. (1985), Larson, Reifler, et al. (1986a), and Larson, Reifler, et al. (1986b).

All patients enrolled in this study were outpatients who met four criteria: (1) age greater than 60, (2) suspected global impairment on the basis of the patient or family complaining of symptoms such as forgetfulness, confusion, inability to care for self, or slow thought, (3) symptoms of at least 3 months duration, and (4) willingness to undergo diagnostic evaluation and to participate in followup for at least 1 year after evaluation.

Diagnoses were based on the results of the medical and psychiatric tests and were confirmed by a consensus group who reviewed the results of the history, physical and neurologic examination, laboratory tests including computed tomography scans, psychiatric evaluation, and psychometric tests. This consensus group included the internist who evaluated the patient, a psychiatrist, a psychologist, a neurologist/neuropathologist, and the public health nurses who coordinated the evaluation and followed the patients. All patients were followed for at least 12 months after evaluation, which included attempts at regular telephone followup and a patient visit approximately 12 months after the initial evaluation.

The sample had a mean age of 76 years and a range of 60 to 94. Most (72 percent) lived in their own homes or apartments, and mean duration of reported memory loss was 42 months. Only two were in nursing homes at the time of evaluation. The mean Mini-Mental State score (Folstein et al. 1975) was 19 (range 0 to 30 with higher score reflecting less impairment), a score indicating that the average patient had mild to moderate impairment.

The illness judged by the consensus group to be the primary cause of cognitive impairment included 129 (65 percent) with DAT, 10 (5 percent) with DAT and Parkinsonism, 10 (5 percent) with dementia due to drugs, 10 (5 percent) with alcohol-related dementia, 3 (2 percent) with myxedema, 2 (1 percent) with multi-infarct dementia, 13 (7 percent) with other known causes, 7 (4 percent) with unknown causes, 3 (2 percent) with benign forgetfulness, and 15 (8 percent) who were not demented, including 10 with depression.

A particularly important finding was the number of patients judged by the consensus group to have more than one illness contributing to the demented state. This situation occurred in 62 patients (31 percent), who had 69 other diagnoses judged to contribute to dementia. Some of the distinctions between primary and secondary causes of dementia were impossible to make with complete confidence and were simply matters of judgment. So-called secondary causes included depression (48 patients), drug toxicity (9 patients), and DAT (10 patients). Thus, a total of 19 patients had drug toxicity as a primary or secondary cause of dementia, and 149 patients had DAT. Three DAT patients also had coexisting hypothyroidism as a secondary cause of dementia.

The other noteworthy feature of the diagnostic evaluation was the number of other medical diseases detected. Just as it was sometimes difficult to be certain whether a given diagnosis was a primary or secondary cause of dementia, it was often hard to say with certainty that these other coexisting conditions were not contributing to the dementia; this could only be determined by observing the response to treatment of the other condition.

A total of 248 other medical diagnoses were made in 124 patients, diagnoses that included most of the diseases commonly seen in the elderly. Each of the following diagnoses were found in at least 10 patients: chronic obstructive pulmonary disease, hypertension, congestive heart failure, cerebrovascular accident, osteoarthritis, peptic ulcer disease, low serum folate level, and depression without DAT. Specific treatment recommendations were made in 115 of these 124 patients, including the following illnesses which led to new therapy: 5 patients with chronic bronchitis, 3 with iron deficiency anemia, and 2 with B12 malabsorption. Discontinuation and replacement of old therapies, including some that were possibly toxic, was accomplished in 16 patients with hypertension, 3 with congestive heart failure, and 3 with Parkinson's disease.

Outcome was determined for all 200 patients using clinical assessment and/or improvement in psychometric tests. Using explicit criteria to grade change (Larson et al. 1985), 55 patients (28 percent) experienced transient improvement (at least 1 month's duration) and of these, 28 (14 percent) had persistent improvement (at least 1 year). Even when evaluating cognitive improvement in DAT patients, 16 cases showed transient and 2 persistent improvement, an encouraging finding given the dismal prognosis usually attributed to DAT.

A simple rule-of-thumb for clinicians that summarizes some of our findings is the Rule of Halves: half of all elderly, demented outpatients will have one or more coexisting illnesses, half of these will have transient improvement of at least 1 month, and half of these will have persistent improvement of at least 1 year.

Given our experience with several hundred patients prior to starting this prospective study (Reifler et al. 1981; Larson et al. 1984), we were not surprised that only two patients experienced completely reversible dementia (one had possible cimetidine toxicity, which presented as acute psychotic depression, and the other had mild dementia due to chronic alcohol intoxication). Although it would be cavalier to suggest that severe, longstanding, gradually progressive dementia (i.e., a classical history for DAT) could not possibly have a completely reversible etiology, we have yet to see such a case, and as we have reported (Larson et al. 1985), autopsy results to date show a high (over 90 percent) accuracy rate for our clinical diagnoses of DAT. We were interested to note a recent report from Finland (Erkinjuntti et al. 1986), consistent with our observations, in which the investigators comment that "specific and potentially treatable causes of dementia were few in our series of unselected, moderately to severely demented medical inpatients."

Marsden and Harrison (1972) emphasized the importance of seeking treatable causes of dementia, but health professionals (and later, laymen as well) inferred that treatable meant curable, even in cases with what can now be recognized as classical presentations of DAT. From an historical perspective, our work is more in keeping with that of Williamson et al. (1964), who showed that careful examination of elderly patients revealed multiple, often previously undetected, problems contributing to their dysfunction.

Overemphasis on finding curable causes of dementia can have the unfortunate consequence, as reported to us by many families, of causing physicians to withdraw from cases of DAT in the sadly misguided notion that they have nothing further to offer. However, identifying and treating sources of excess disability in DAT helps to remind the physician that such patients require the same general approach as patients with any other chronic disease, namely to reduce suffering and enhance functional abilities (Larson et al. 1986).

DAT and Depression

We have studied in detail one specific cause of excess disability in patients with DAT–depression. What we have learned is obviously applicable to patients with coexisting DAT and depression and may also prove useful as a model for other conditions found in patients with DAT.

The early literature on the relationship between dementia and depression paralleled the general literature on investigations of demented patients; emphasis was placed on depression as a curable cause of dementia, rather than as a complication. A report by Kiloh (1961) used the term pseudodementia and included a case presumed to be that of a patient with depression who appeared demented, but was cured after receiving treatment for depression. However, a careful review of this case concluded that the short followup of 6 months and lack of objective confirmation of resolution of the dementia left room for doubt on the author's diagnostic impression (Reifler 1982), and this could well have been a case of mild DAT with coexisting depression.

The term pseudodementia illustrates our general point; considerable emphasis was placed on finding explanations other than DAT for cognitive impairment, and less attention was given to the far more common problem of depression causing excess disability in DAT. And just as Marsden and Harrison (1972) were misinterpreted, so was Wells (1979), even though he emphasized in his paper "Pseudodementia" that depression gives a very poor imitation of DAT, as patients' complaints of poor memory are generally unsubstantiated by objective assessment. The desire to find curable causes of dementia led to overutilization of both the term pseudodementia, which Reifler (1982) advocated abandoning, and probably caused unnecessary administration of antidepressant therapy to demented patients with absolutely no evidence of depression, in the hopes their cognitive impairment was being caused by an unrecognized variant of an affective illness.

In our first report on dementia and depression (Reifler et al. 1982), we commented on the 23 percent (20 of 88) of depressed patients within a group of cognitively impaired geriatric outpatients. Using the guidelines suggested by Wells (1979), and particularly keeping in mind his comment that "it is the totality of the clinical picture that is important," we determined that 17 of the 20 patients (85 percent) seemed to have depression superimposed on an underlying dementia, while only 3 (15 percent) had depression as their sole diagnosis. Depression was more common in milder cases of dementia, becoming less frequent as the dementia became more severe.

We wished to learn whether the depression seen in DAT patients could be treated and, if so, whether there would be cognitive improvement as well (in other words, to learn if the depression was contributing to the cognitive impairment). We began undertaking a retrospective review of our clinic patients' medical records (Reifler et al. 1986). In this sample of 131 patients with DAT, 41 (31 percent) also met DSM-III criteria for a major affective disorder. (We have consistently found about one-quarter to one-third of DAT patients to be depressed, consistent with Marsden and Harrison's (1972) comment that 25 percent of demented patients are depressed.)

Of the DAT plus depression patients whose records reflected treatment (usually with a tricyclic antidepressant), 85 percent (17 of 20) showed evidence of improved mood, vegetative signs, or activities of daily living (ADLs) based on a review of the medical record. An analysis of change in cognitive function as measured by the Mini-Mental State (Folstein et al. 1975) failed to reveal any difference between the depressed and nondepressed groups after a mean interval of 17 months, suggesting that depression was unrelated to change in patients' cognitive state.

A few DAT patients with depression had modest long-term cognitive improvement (given the poor prognosis associated with DAT, even modest improvements are encouraging) but no striking recoveries occurred among patients with longstanding dementia. We do not argue that depression is incapable of causing marked cognitive impairment, but agree with Rabins et al. (1984) that a subacute onset (weeks or months as opposed to years) is generally the hallmark of this situation.

The favorable impression gained from this review of medical records led to a double-blind study of the effectiveness of a tricyclic antidepressant (TCA) in mixed DAT and depression. While the data

377

analysis is still in progress, the preliminary findings are consistent with our earlier work.

The study design was an 8-week, double-blind, random assignment trial of imipramine or placebo in 61 outpatient volunteers from both sexes who had DAT with or without coexisting depression. Of 27 depressed subjects, 13 received imipramine and 14 placebo, and of 34 nondepressed subjects, 15 received imipramine and 19 placebo. At the completion of the study, mean dosage for the depressed DAT group on active medication was 83 mg per day, and serum level of imipramine plus desipramine was 119 ng/ml. For the nondepressed DAT group, comparable figures were 82 mg per day and 132 ng/ml. These dosages and serum levels are generally regarded as within the normal therapeutic range for this age group.

The most important finding was a significant interaction for diagnosis by time ($F(1,57) = 84.36$, $p < .001$), with depressed subjects in both treatment conditions (TCA and placebo) showing improvement in scores on the 17-item Hamilton Depression Scale (Hamilton 1976). The TCA group improved from a mean of 19.3 to 11.5, while the placebo group improved from a mean of 18.6 to 10.8. (The placebo group patients were seen weekly and received considerable personal attention; we do not believe similar improvements would have been seen simply by a waiting period.)

The improvement seen in many subjects was apparent to both the investigators and family members. An example of a very favorable comment by a relative was, "There very definitely has been a change in attitude. [She is] much more positive about the future. Even cooking some meals on her own."

Effects on cognitive function were more subtle and are undergoing additional analysis. Both improvements and declines were seen among the test measures, but these were changes of 10 percent or less. No subjects showed a striking return to normal cognitive function. On the positive side, we were unable to clinically detect cognitive worsening in DAT patients treated with TCAs, a concern due to the possibility of TCA's anticholinergic properties aggravating an underlying cholinergic deficit in DAT (Coyle et al. 1983).

We did not anticipate that the placebo and TCA groups would show comparable improvement. This has encouraged our group to begin testing a variety of pharmacologic and nonpharmacologic (e.g., behavioral) interventions to determine which treatment is best for depression in DAT. Also, the results from this study of moderately depressed outpatients are not necessarily generalizable to more severely depressed, hospitalized DAT patients; we do not know if treatment with a placebo would be as effective as a TCA in that setting.

To summarize the important findings relevant to the subject of excess disability, the treatment of depression in patients with DAT does not cure, or even noticeably improve, their cognitive impairment. But it does improve their mood, energy, and ability to participate in family life, and helps to ease the caregiver's feelings of burden. The likely outcome is not improvement of cognitive function, and if treatment is evaluated by this standard, it will be judged ineffective. Rather, the depression itself is the excess disability, and correcting this problem is often a great relief to patient and family.

Recommendation for Future Research

We have one simple recommendation for further research: interventions should be designed and tested for specific causes of excess disability in DAT, whether coexisting illnesses such as drug toxicity, hypothyroidism, or chronic obstructive pulmonary disease; or secondary symptoms such as paranoia, agitation, insomnia, or incontinence. Outcome measurements should include cognitive function, functional ability in terms of ADLs, affect, caregiver burden, and specific measures appropriate to the condition being studied.

Summary and Conclusions

DAT is an incurable disease, but patients with DAT can be managed using the same principles applicable to any other chronic illness: accurate diagnosis and provision of information, relief of suffering, preservation of existing function, avoidance of iatrogenic problems, and–the primary focus of this report–identification and treatment of sources of excess disability.

A set of unusual circumstances has delayed both research and its application in this area. First is society's double whammy against DAT patients, namely, powerful biases against both old age and mental impairment, causing their problems to be dismissed as unimportant. Second is the additional double whammy imposed by physicians who regard DAT as impossible to accurately diagnose (although no more so than many other common diagnoses not subject to this prejudice) and untreatable.

It is time to adjust the proportion of research effort related to the proper goals of the diagnostic process and ongoing management. (The search for etiology and definitive therapy must continue full speed ahead.) In our series of 200 patients (Larson et al. 1985), only two had complete reversal of symptoms. Over half had DAT with one or more coexisting diseases. This is 1-percent cure compared to more than 50 percent with excess disability. Yet studies related to finding curable conditions that might be mistaken for DAT have tended to dominate the literature. With at least 2 million victims of DAT in the United States, we are long overdue for increased research on identification and management of problems that needlessly add to these patients' difficulties and to the burdens of their families.

References

Anonymous. Manic-depressive illness. *Lancet* 505-506, Aug. 30, 1986.

Beeson, P.B. One hundred years of American internal medicine: A view from the inside. *Annals of Internal Medicine* 105:436-444, 1986.

Bishop, J.M., and Krause, D.R. Depictions of aging and old age on Saturday morning television. *Gerontologist* 24:91-94, 1984.

Butler, R.W. Ageism: Another form of bigotry. *Gerontologist* 9:243-246, 1969.

Cohen, G.D. Mental health services and the elderly: Needs and options. *American Journal of Psychiatry* 133:65-68, 1976.

Cox, G.B.; Hanley, R.S.; and Reifler, B.V. An integrated data base for an interdisciplinary geriatric clinic. *Journal of Psychiatric Evaluation and Treatment* 4:149-153, 1982.

Coyle, J.T.; Price, D.L.; and DeLong, M.R. Alzheimer's disease: A disorder of cortical cholinergic innervation. *Science* 219:1184-1190, 1983.

Croen, L.G.; Hamerman, D.; and Goetzel, R.Z. Interdisciplinary training for medical and nursing students: Learning to collaborate in the care of geriatric patients. *Journal of the American Geriatrics Society* 32:56-61, 1984.

Davies, L.J. Attitudes toward aging as shown by humor. *Gerontologist* 17:220-226, 1977.

Erkinjuntti, T.; Wikstrom, J.; Palo, J.; and Autio, L. Dementia among medical inpatients: Evaluation of 2000 consecutive admissions. *Archives of Internal Medicine* 146:1923-1926, 1986.

Folstein, M.F.; Folstein, S.E.; and McHugh, P.R. Mini-mental state: A practical method for grading the cognitive state of patients for the clinician. *Journal of Psychiatric Research* 12:189-198, 1975.

Folstein, S.E.; Leigh, J.; Parhad, I.M.; and Folstein, M.F. The diagnosis of Huntington's Disease. *Neurology* 36:1279-1283, 1986.

Ford, C.V., and Sbordone, R.J. Attitudes of psychiatrists toward elderly patients. *American Journal of Psychiatry* 137:571-575, 1980.

Francher, J.S. It's the Pepsi generation . . . Accelerated aging and the television commercial. *Aging and Human Development* 24:245-255, 1973.

Hamilton, J. Development of a rating scale for primary depressive illness. *The British Journal of Social and Clinical Psychology* 6:278-296, 1976.

Harris, A.J., and Feinberg, J. Television and aging: Is what you see what you get? *Gerontologist* 18:221-226, 1978.

Katzman, R. Alzheimer's disease. *New England Journal of Medicine* 314:964-973, 1986.

Kiloh, L.G. Pseudo-dementia. *Acta Psychiatrica Scandinavica* (Copenhagen) 37:336-351, 1961.

Larson, E.B.; Buchner, D.M.; Uhlmann, R.F.; and Reifler, B.V. Caring for elderly patients with dementia. *Archives of Internal Medicine* 146:1909-1910, 1986.

Larson, E.; Featherstone, H.J.; and Reifler, B.V. Medical aspects of care of elderly patients with cognitive impairment. *Developmental Neuropsychology* 1:145-171, 1985.

Larson, E.; Reifler, B.V.; Canfield, C.; and Cohen, G.D. The diagnostic evaluation in dementia: A reappraisal. *Hospital and Community Psychiatry* 35:425-428, 1984.

Larson, E.B.; Reifler, B.V.; Featherstone, H.J.; and English, D.R. Dementia in elderly outpatients: A prospective study. *Annals of Internal Medicine* 100:417-423, 1984.

Larson, E.B.; Reifler, B.V.; Sumi, S.M.; Canfield, C.G.; and Chinn, N.M. Diagnostic evaluation of 200 elderly outpatients with suspected dementia. *Journal of Gerontology* 40:536-543, 1985.

Larson, E.B.; Reifler, B.V.; Sumi, S.M.; Canfield, C.G.; and Chinn, N.M. Diagnostic tests in the evaluation of dementia: A prospective study of 200 elderly outpatients. *Archives of Internal Medicine* 146:1917-1922, 1986a.

Larson, E.B.; Reifler, B.V.; Sumi, S.M.; Canfield, C.G.; and Chinn, N.M. Features associated with potential reversibility in elderly outpatients with suspected dementia. *Western Journal of Medicine* 145:488-492, 1986b.

Marsden, C.D., and Harrison, M.J.G. Outcome of investigation of patients with presenile dementia. *British Medical Journal* 2:249-252, 1972.

Palmore, E. Attitudes toward aging as shown in humor. *Gerontologist* 11:181-186, 1971.

Rabins, P.V.; Merchant, A.; and Nestadt, G. Criteria for diagnosing reversible dementia caused by depression: Validation by 2-year follow-up. *British Journal of Psychiatry* 144:488-492, 1984.

Ray, D.C.; Raciti, M.A.; and Ford, C.V. Ageism in psychiatrists: Associations with gender, certification, and theoretical orientation. *Gerontologist* 25:496-500, 1985.

Reifler, B.V. Arguments for abandoning the term pseudodementia. *Journal of the American Geriatrics Society* 30:665-668, 1982.

Reifler, B.V. Training in geriatric mental health: Two innovative outpatient training sites. *Gerontology and Geriatrics Education* 6:65-73, 1986.

Reifler, B.V., and Eisdorfer, C. A clinic for the impaired elderly and their families. *American Journal of Psychiatry* 137:1399-1403, 1980.

Reifler, B.V.; Larson, E.; and Hanley, R. Coexistence of cognitive impairment and depression in geriatric outpatients. *American Journal of Psychiatry* 139:623-626, 1982.

Reifler, B.V.; Larson, E.; Hanley, R.; Cox, G.; and Featherstone, H. Treatment results at a multi-specialty outpatient clinic for impaired elderly and their families. *Journal of the American Geriatrics Society* 29:579-582, 1981.

Reifler, B.V.; Larson, E.; Teri, L.; and Poulsen, M. Alzheimer's disease and depression. *Journal of the American Geriatrics Society* 34:858-859, 1986.

Richman, J. The foolishness and wisdom of age: Attitudes toward the elderly as reflected in jokes. *Gerontologist* 17:210-219, 1977.

Sheppard, A. Response to cartoons and attitudes toward aging. *Journal of Gerontology* 36:122-126, 1981.

Warren, D.L.; Painter, A.; and Rudisill, J. Effects of geriatric education on the attitudes of medical students. *Journal of the American Geriatrics Society* 31:435-438, 1983.

Wells, C.E. Pseudodementia. *American Journal of Psychiatry* 136:895-900, 1979.

Williamson, J.; Stokoe, I.H.; Gray, S.; Fisher, M.; Smith, A.; McGhee, A.; and Stephenson, E. Old persons at home: Their unreported needs. *Lancet* 1:1117-1120, 1964.

Wilson, J.F., and Hafferty, F.W. Long term effects of a seminar on aging and health for first-year medical students. *Gerontologist* 23:319-324, 1983.

Wolf-Klein, G.P.; Libow, L.S.; Foley, C.J.; and Silverstone, F.A. Training internal medicine residents in geriatrics. *Journal of Medical Education* 58:583-584, 1983.

Chapter 16

Cognitive/Behavioral Therapy with Early Stage Alzheimer's Patients: An Exploratory View of the Utility of This Approach

Larry W. Thompson, Ph.D., Blake Wagner, Ph.D., Antonette Zeiss, Ph.D., and Dolores Gallagher, Ph.D.

The prevalence of emotional disorders in patients with early Alzheimer's disease has not been systematically documented, but clinical impressions suggest that both anxiety and depression are quite common in patients who are beginning to sense a loss in their cognitive and functional abilities (Caine 1981; McAllister and Price 1982; Reifler et al. 1982; Shraberg 1978). Recent papers, for example, have reported that depression coexists with dementia of the Alzheimer's type (DAT) in 25 to 30 percent of the patients examined (Reifler et al. 1982; Reifler et al. 1986).

Little has been reported about the nature of depression in patients with DAT. Based on the studies reported here, one could conclude that many of the common clinical symptoms of depression are clearly discernible in a substantial number of dementia patients. However, there is uncertainty whether many of the symptoms are a direct result of organic changes in the central nervous system, or if they occur as a secondary effect of the dementia process, most likely as a result of perceived losses. For example, personality and behavioral changes commonly associated with the dementing process include such characteristics as progressive indifference, apathy, and a loss of initiative.

NOTE: Preparation of this chapter was supported in part by grants MH37196-04 and MH40041-03 (Alzheimer's Disease Clinical Research Center) from the National Institute of Mental Health, and by grant #AG04572 from the National Institute on Aging.

In our clinical experience, depressive features in DAT patients often are consistent with such personality changes. Frequently, a tendency toward social withdrawal, disinterest, and apathy occurs, often without subjective report of distress or sadness.

The manifestations of depression might possibly vary as a function of the level of dementia. Clinical symptoms of depression with accompanying dysphoria have been reported to occur more frequently in patients with a mild degree of dementia than in patients with more severe forms (cf. Reifler et al. 1982). There are several possible explanations for this phenomenon. First, during the initial stages of illness, individuals generally have awareness of their diminished capabilities and some insight into the progressive and debilitating effects of the dementia process. However, a decrease in self-awareness and a consequent decrease in perceived losses appear to be concomitant with the progression of the dementia. This, in turn, could lead to a decrease in dysphoria as well as some of the other symptoms of depression.

Second, in the more severely demented patient, depressive symptoms may become obscured by cognitive deficits and therefore manifest as "simpler equivalents." For example, instead of expressing psychological distress verbally, patients may show agitation and a variety of regressed, stereotyped behaviors (DeMuth and Rand 1980). Finally, a substantial number of pseudodementia patients, who are actually depressed and receive an inaccurate diagnosis of dementia, might be included in the category of early dementia patients with depression. All three of these explanations would lead one to expect that active treatment of depression, when it is observed in early dementia patients, would be very appropriate. In addition, the second explanation implies that treatment of observed behavioral changes possibly representing simple expressions of depressive symptoms may be worth attempting.

Treatment Interventions for Depression in DAT Patients

The value of treating depression and other emotional disorders in patients with dementia is mentioned with increasing regularity in the recent literature (Katzman 1987; Reifler 1982). Despite the irreversible and progressive nature of DAT, there is conservative optimism about the possible benefits of appropriate clinical interventions to improve affective status in those who have depression.

384

Beyond improvements in mood, concomitant effects may be expected on specific aspects of cognitive and behavioral functioning that have been negatively affected by the mood disturbance. Along these lines, substantial evidence shows that psychological distress factors can impair cognitive functioning in elderly patients without dementia (Fraser and Glass 1980; Gibson 1981; Hilbert et al. 1976; Miller 1975; Raskin et al. 1982; Raskin 1987; Whitehead 1973). Patients with early signs of dementia are in no way exempt from this negative impact.

In all likelihood, emotional distress results in additional cognitive impairment and disturbance in behavioral functioning, which may be reversible with appropriate treatment (Reifler et al. 1982). Thus, if such patients could achieve relief from their psychological problems, they might function at a more optimal level for a longer time, which would probably increase quality of life for both the patient and the family.

Very little substantive information stemming from controlled studies details appropriate treatments for emotional disorders in patients with early DAT. A trial of antidepressants is frequently employed, sometimes with striking results (cf. Shraberg 1978). Reifler et al. (1986) reviewed medical records of patients with mixed DAT and depression who received tricyclic antidepressants and reported that approximately 85 percent of the cases reviewed had significant improvements in mood, vegetative signs, and/or activities of daily living. Although no changes were found in the patients' cognitive functioning, this was measured only by brief screening procedures. In addition, absolute levels of functioning were not reported, making it difficult to determine the proportion of patients that might have been in the early stages of the disease process. Small doses of neuroleptics have also been used with some success in patients with more severe behavioral disturbances (Katzman 1987).

An alternative to drug treatment would be helpful in working with older patients who have DAT, since a substantial proportion may not be able to take psychoactive drugs. Further, many of the drugs used to treat affective disorders have anticholinergic effects, which could conceivably have a negative effect on higher level cognitive processes.

Despite the potential benefits of psychotherapeutic interventions with early DAT patients, a review of the literature failed to uncover any controlled outcome studies. In addition to our own observations of the positive effects of structured psychotherapeutic interventions, Teri and Gallagher (in press) have reported successful applications of cognitive and behavioral treatments with depressed outpatients who were judged to be in the initial stages of a progressive dementing process.

Less direct support for the position that psychotherapy can be a viable alternative approach for lessening dysphoria among early DAT patients can be taken from the research findings on the treatment of depression in the elderly. In recent years, a small number of controlled trials have been conducted on the efficacy of psychotherapy alone for the treatment of nonpsychotic unipolar depressive disorder in the elderly. Fairly strong positive effects with individual therapeutic approaches were reported at our own center (Thompson et al. in press). Significant positive impact was also reported for the use of group psychotherapies with elderly patients (Gallagher 1981; Steuer et al. 1984; Yost et al. 1986).

Our current data indicate that 50 to 55 percent of elderly depressed patients can be expected to remit, and an additional 15 to 20 percent will show great improvement in their level of depression after a 4-month course of structured, skill-building therapy (e.g., cognitive or behavioral therapy). These findings are particularly relevant for this book because a sizable portion of the treatment sample complained of impairment in cognitive processes. Moreover, neuropsychological testing prior to treatment provided objective evidence of cognitive slippage in some of the patients who benefited from the therapy program. This suggests that short-term therapies may be effective in reducing depression in patients who are experiencing some mild losses in the early phases of a progressive degenerative dementia.

The considerable body of controlled research using behavioral interventions with institutionalized dementia patients lends additional indirect evidence to the potential value of psychotherapeutic treatments. A variety of target behaviors have been effectively modi- fied through operant procedures, showing that some dementia patients can learn adaptive behaviors when the training is highly focused and structured. For example, MacDonald and Butler (1974), Baltes and Zerbe (1976), and Blackman, Howe, and Pinkston (1976), among others, reported improvement in specific behaviors (e.g., walking, eating, and prosocial activity) as a result of contingent reinforcement. Berger and Rose (1977) were moderately successful in modifying more complex social interaction patterns in nursing home residents through a brief individualized social skills training program.

While these studies have limited applicability to outpatient samples, whose problems are more heterogeneous and where less control over intervening variables is possible, they nevertheless highlight the potential plasticity of behavior in patients with organic pathology. Furthermore, noninstitutionalized dementia patients would generally tend to be in less advanced stages of illness, and would bring greater cognitive/behavioral capacity to the therapy process.

386

Overview of Cognitive/Behavioral Therapy

The cognitive/behavioral (CB) model (Beck et al. 1979) is based on the assumption that the root of depression lies in the cognitive set (or bias) of the patient; this is characterized by an interactive triad of negative views of the self, experience, and the future. Depressive or dysphoric affect develops from this basic ground. Beck (1967) argued that, although depressive episodes may be externally precipitated, individuals' distorted perceptions and idiosyncratic appraisals of their circumstances induce depression.

Initially, the cognitive triad revolves around the patient's negative self-perceptions (as deficient, inadequate, or unworthy), along with attributions of adverse experiences associated with presumed inherent physical, mental, or moral defects. For example, following marital separation, depression-prone individuals ascribe the cause to shortcomings in themselves such as "I am unlovable," despite the fact that more plausible alternatives are available.

The second aspect of this negative triad is the patient's interpretation of current and past experiences. Such persons view the world as making inordinate demands or presenting insurmountable obstacles, and interpret interaction with the environment as representing defeat or deprivation. The last component is the depressed person's belief that the future will simply be a continuation of current difficulties, with frequent failures ahead.

These three components structurally interact to form what Beck (1963) terms a "schema" or framework for classification and evaluation of new information. In most depression, the overriding conceptual schema leads to a typical "downward spiral." Thus, "the more negatively the patient thinks, the worse he feels; the worse he feels, the more negatively he thinks" (Beck 1967, p. 289).

More importantly for dementia sufferers, the patient's systematic negative bias against self both originates and is maintained through topological and formal distortive thinking processes, such as arbitrary inference, selective abstraction, and overgeneralization. These automatic distortions, particularly overgeneralization, may occur more readily and function more powerfully when individuals have difficulty with such cognitive processes as remembering, reasoning, abstracting, and sustaining focused attention. Stylistically, for example, one might expect even greater exaggeration in magnifying negative and minimizing positive events. Semantically, persons would be more inclined toward inexact labeling of events, leading to personalization and affective overreaction. Formally, the automatic nature of these cognitive responses would increase. These ideas would probably be extremely plausible to the patient with impaired cognitive processes, even in the face of disconfirming evidence.

In contrast to normal negative feelings such as grief, depression occurs when the person is particularly sensitive to specific situations (e.g., if a current situation is analogous to prior experiences of developmental significance such as chronic rejection by peers or significant others). Depression can also develop when a predepressive cognitive constellation is present, such as lowered self-esteem that increases vulnerability to stress. In this instance, the ingredients are right for the "downward spiral," and clinical depression is likely to result. For example, imagine a patient with early stage dementia who has become sensitive about his inability to perform certain tasks efficiently, such as helping with financial planning. His wife has trouble balancing her checkbook, and turns to an adult child for help. The patient may believe he was not asked to help because of a defect in himself. This may lead to preoccupation with the kinds of distortions described above, such as reasoning that he is no longer loved, exaggerating the financial problems caused by his illness, etc. If this scenario is repeated often enough, eventually most of the patient's encounters with other people would generate some kind of negative evaluation of self.

Beck and his colleagues (1979) advocate that therapy for depression should focus on modification of these hypothesized internal events that mediate depressive behaviors. This position is not to be confused with the psychoanalytic model, although Beck used the psychoanalytic method in forming his theory and therapy, and does maintain some intrapsychic focus. Cognitive therapy departs significantly from psychoanalysis in the use of time-limited treatment, a highly directive role for the therapist, and behavioral techniques (such as self-monitoring of distorted cognitions) to aid in the cognitive restructuring essential for progress.

CB Therapy for Early DAT Patients

Rationale

The cognitive changes experienced by early DAT patients present some obvious difficulties for successful psychotherapeutic interventions. While DAT patients differ in their specific pattern of cognitive fallout, most show declines in short-term memory, disruption of ability for new learning, and impaired abstract reasoning. Thus, they typically have trouble comprehending concepts, and acquiring and retaining the information presented.

CB therapy, with some modifications, can be a useful treatment modality for depression in patients with early DAT. Those most likely to benefit would have sufficient insight and cognitive capability to utilize training in basic coping skills. As a general guideline, this might include patients in the "mild" dementia phase on the Clinical Dementia Rating Scale (Hughes et al. 1982) or who rate a 3 or possibly a 4 on the Global Deterioration Scale (Reisberg et al. 1982). CB therapy may be particularly well-suited for early DAT patients, because it (1) is short term; (2) is highly structured, so the therapist can play an active, directive role; (3) focuses on current problems and practical issues; (4) emphasizes strengthening or relearning of basic problem-solving skills, which are likely to be impaired; and (5) is multimodal to maximize the learning process.

Application

The CB treatment protocol developed by Beck and his associates has been outlined in detail elsewhere (e.g., Beck et al. 1979). Slight modifications of this procedure for use with cognitively intact elderly patients have also been described in a recent paper (Thompson et al. 1986). We found the following general considerations to be helpful in conducting effective therapy with patients experiencing mild dementia.

First, the clinician should be very sensitive to the actual cognitive capabilities (strengths as well as weaknesses) of the patient, in order to know what the patient is capable of and to understand how the patient is compensating for deficits. Often, this means that therapy will begin with a review of existing neuropsychological evaluation data. If these are not available, then neuropsychological testing should be completed early in treatment.

Knowledge of a patient's relative cognitive strengths and weaknesses can be of considerable value in designing an individualized therapeutic strategy. An approach should be developed that takes full advantage of remaining abilities and compensates for areas of deficit. Moreover, this knowledge enables the therapist to judge whether a particular negative thought or self-appraisal is accurate (i.e., reflects true deficits) or a distortion. For example, a DAT patient may have difficulty with word-finding but not with other aspects of verbal expression. By learning to discriminate intact skills (compared to skills that really are compromised), depression may be reduced and overgeneralization about deficits can be minimized.

Second, the therapist must provide a great deal of structure to the

389

therapy sessions. This means that a very specific agenda needs to be routinely set and followed carefully, so that time is used efficiently. Also, structure helps engender hope and positive expectancies in patients, who often believe that Alzheimer's disease is a "death knell" for their ability to function and participate adequately in relationships. By learning that they can respond well to structure, patients also learn that progress can occur by compartmentalizing problems, breaking them down into component parts, and trying to solve them incrementally. In other words, the way time is used and the way problems are approached in the therapy session provide a model that the patient can follow at home, as well as after therapy is concluded.

Third, therapists must use all methods at their disposal to facilitate learning on the part of the patient. In particular, patients should continuously learn, indirectly, that they can think and do at least some things well, despite their diagnosis. Some specific techniques include (1) scheduling brief sessions to offset reduced attentional capacities (e.g., 30 minutes); (2) scheduling frequent sessions; (3) involving family members so that appropriate prompting and structure can be encouraged in the home, enhancing generalization from therapy to other settings; (4) frequent repetition of therapeutic themes and interventions; (5) having the patient keep a simple record of key issues worked on in therapy, homework assignments and their results, and important information for future sessions; (6) providing patients with audiotapes of sessions to play back between sessions to facilitate memory and learning; and (7) encouraging the patient and family to use the external prompts and aids they have learned about whenever possible (keeping a diary, asking people to speak slowly or repeat information, etc.).

The importance of continually monitoring the patient's comprehension of the therapeutic content and assignments cannot be overemphasized. It is imperative to avoid overtaxing the patient's abilities, which will likely be more frustrating and stressful than therapeutic. Specifically, the therapist must determine an appropriate pace for each individual, frequently pause to ensure that points are grasped by the patient, and provide ample opportunity throughout sessions for questions and clarifications.

Beck's model emphasizes identifying and challenging dysfunctional thoughts. Many skills are needed for this type of activity. First, patients must be able to monitor their thoughts and feelings and note the situational context in which they occur. Second, patients must be able to remember things well enough to recreate the sequence by describing the specific situation, and the kinds of feelings experienced, and then listing in detail the kinds of thoughts occurring at or immediately after the event.

Third, patients must be able to label dysfunctional thoughts. Fourth, patients must be able to challenge the dysfunctional aspect of their thinking. Finally, the patient should develop the ability to use this process in new situations.

It is highly unlikely that DAT patients will be able to complete all of these steps. Therefore, the process must be made extremely concrete for the patient. For example, the therapist and client might identify a prominent dysfunctional thought or distortion that can be addressed repeatedly. External aids that can facilitate this process in settings outside therapy should be brought into play whenever possible. For example, we frequently suggest that memory-impaired patients carry cue cards (e.g., in a shirt pocket), on which is written an adaptive response to a particularly troublesome and frequent distortion.

The therapist must take a highly directive role in this therapeutic approach. Beck generally recommends the Socratic method, which relies on questioning and active collaboration of the patient in identifying distortions and generating challenges. However, with DAT patients, the therapist needs to be more didactic than Socratic.

A common pattern of distortion seen among DAT patients is overgeneralizing their disabilities and "catastrophizing" perceived limitations. For example, an inability to balance the checkbook may lead to an immediate chain of thoughts about other functions or tasks the patient presumably can't do (e.g., make change at the store, toss a salad, or write down phone messages), which then leads to the conclusion that "I am completely incompetent–I am worthless."

A critical feature here is that these thoughts occur so automatically that patients are unaware of the process and typically accept the distortions as based on fact. The therapist must work diligently with DAT patients to help them learn to monitor this process so they can identify distortions and challenge them with more accurate constructions. This is extremely difficult to do with individuals who are experiencing a progressive loss of function and are well aware of the endpoint. Nevertheless, calm and supportive efforts by the therapist and family alike can help the patient learn the value of this technique in reducing dysphoric episodes.

Any number of other behavioral/cognitive strategies can be used that are inherently more concrete and didactic than the technique described above. For example, priming, so-called because of its similarity to "priming the pump," is a concrete technique to facilitate the flow of positive thoughts. It involves writing down numerous positive thoughts, particularly about oneself, on 3 x 5 cards (one to a card). This deck of cards is then carried about, and periodically during the day, the patient reads one of the cards and tries to pay particular attention to its contents. For persons with memory problems, these thoughts can be displayed at critical places where they will cue the patient to read and consider them.

Other techniques that make relatively minor demands on information processing abilities include thought interruption, worry time, blowup, etc. For further information about these and other such strategies, the reader is referred to a recent publication by Lewinsohn and his colleagues (1986) entitled *Control Your Depression*.

The Reality of Loss

One tragic feature of Alzheimer's disease is the relentless occurrence of undeniable evidence of a progressive deteriorative process. Almost daily, patient and family are confronted with new indications that the patient is functioning less well–he or she forgets to turn off the stove, fails to write down an important telephone message, makes a serious error in balancing the checkbook, behaves inappropriately in front of friends or other guests, etc. CB therapy cannot change the underlying disease course, nor will it provide permanent remedies to preclude devastating events. However, learning to curtail over-generalization and catastrophizing can help. While both patients and caregivers may experience sadness on occasion as they are confronted with the reality of what is happening, recognizing and dealing with the cognitive distortions may prevent a devastating depression. This will help patients and caregivers alike function better, and will prolong the remaining capacities of the patient.

Many patients will accurately perceive their diminished functioning. CB therapy does not attempt to explain away accurate negative perceptions but, rather, helps the patient recognize and learn to stop negative distortions. Other consequences of the true loss that may be evident include (a) intense sadness leading to a need for support and caring from the therapist, the caregiver, and significant others in the community; (b) a need for increased problem-solving with caregivers and other health providers to maximize benefits from health programs; and (c) a need for increased positive activities for the patient to balance the inevitable increase of negative experiences.

Setting Realistic Goals

One important aim of CB is to encourage patients to form realistic views of their disabilities rather than unduly distorted ones. A secondary aim of treatment is to teach patients cognitive and social skills for maintaining as high a level of functioning as possible, along with ways to compensate for their deficits. Both patients and caregivers should be informed of these aims, so that unrealistic expectancies of the outcome do not occur.

With respect to cognitive objectives, it is often most useful to isolate one or two central distortions or patterns of dysfunctional thinking and continue to focus heavily on them throughout the therapy to maximize the patient's learning potential. Behavioral objectives that shift from difficult activities that cannot be managed to easier ones that are equally satisfying and pleasurable can be extremely helpful to the patient in learning to check overgeneralization. For example, a patient who no longer can handle the complexities of a stove may be able to prepare a salad.

Therapists face considerable difficulties in working with the DAT population. There is the pain of watching the inevitable decline. This is different from working with other populations of depressed persons, who can reasonably be expected to recover completely and return to optimal functioning. There may well be unacknowledged fears of the disease itself, since so little is known. A paucity of research is available to guide one's efforts through the treatment process. Therapists are, for the most part, pulling themselves (and their patients) up by their bootstraps.

Therapists can do a number of things to address such issues. They should turn to colleagues for consultation and support frequently. They should be very explicit about setting goals for themselves as well as their patients, and they should be liberal with the rewards to themselves as well as the patient for meeting even minimal goals.

Therapists must avoid cognitive distortions in themselves. For example, being ineffective with a patient on a specific task might lead to the conclusion that this patient can't be helped at all, or that CB therapy is ineffective with this type of patient, or, perhaps worst of all, that "I'm not an effective therapist." Finally, it may be useful for the therapist to view working with such patients as an opportunity to collect valuable data and contribute to knowledge (whether the therapy is effective or not).

Conclusions

Our analysis of the literature indicates that depression among early DAT patients is a serious clinical problem that has received only minimal attention. It would seem that the challenge of intervening with cognitively impaired patients who are experiencing an inexorable pattern of decline has been viewed with pessimism, and there can be little doubt that this has contributed to the paucity of systematic studies in this area. Yet it would be difficult to overestimate the value of careful research focused on the development of effective therapeutic procedures for use with this patient population. Aside from the important clinical goal of alleviating pain and suffering, any effort that optimizes adaptive capacities of these unfortunate individuals is likely to delay the burden of intense caregiving activities which, in turn, may prolong that day when inpatient services are required. Thus, there are both psychological and economic consequences that may stem from the development of effective treatment programs.

Preliminary clinical experiences offer encouragement that structured therapeutic techniques currently available, such as Cognitive/Behavioral Therapy, can be applied effectively in the treatment of these patients with only minor modifications. Several factors deserve particular attention when working with impaired patients. Keeping sessions highly structured and focused on only one or very few issues greatly facilitates the acquisition of useful skills, as does multimodal presentation of ideas and techniques. Repetitions of material frequently assures better learning, and concrete illustrations emphasizing generalization of points to many different situations tends to increase skill utilization in situations outside therapy. Despite presumably obvious benefits observed in clinical settings, there remains a glaring need for controlled research efforts to systematically develop and evaluate the effectiveness of potentially useful psychotherapeutic interventions. Research efforts should pay particular attention to process measures of the patients' comprehension of material presented in order to determine whether the concepts presented are in fact being retained. Outcome measures need to be carefully selected to distinguish between depressive symptoms and symptoms of the dementia process. As a final measure, it is important to assess the possible impact of therapy interventions on the well-being and functioning of family caregivers. Hopefully, research efforts in this direction will elucidate increasingly effective techniques of therapy, as well as strengthen the interest in applying psychotherapeutic interventions to improve the lot of patients with this tragic disease.

References

Baltes, M., and Zerbe, M. Independence training in nursing home residents. *Gerontologist* 16:428-432, 1976.

Beck, A.T. Thinking and depression: I. Idiosyncratic content and cognitive distortions. *Archives of General Psychiatry* 9:324-333, 1963.

Beck, A.T. *Depression: Clinical, Experimental and Theoretical Aspects.* New York: Harper and Row, 1967.

Beck, A.T.; Rush, A.J.; Shaw, B.; and Emery, G. *Cognitive Therapy of Depression.* New York: Guilford Press, 1979.

Berger, R.M., and Rose, S.D. Interpersonal skill training with institutionalized elderly patients. *Journal of Gerontology* 32:346-353, 1977.

Blackman, D.; Howe, M.; and Pinkston, E. Increasing participation in social interaction of the institutionalized elderly. *Gerontologist* 16:69-76, 1976.

Caine, E.D. Pseudodementia: Current concepts and future directions. *Archives of General Psychiatry* 38:1359-1364, 1981.

DeMuth, G.W., and Rand, B.S. Atypical major depression in a patient with severe primary degenerative dementia. *American Journal of Psychiatry* 137:1609-1610, 1980.

Fraser, R.M., and Glass, I.B. Unilateral and bilateral ECT in elderly patients. *Acta Psychiatrica Scandinavica,* 62:13-21, 1980.

Friedman, A.S. Minimal effects of severe depression on cognitive functioning. *Journal of Abnormal and Social Psychology* 69:237-243, 1964.

Gallagher, D. Behavioral group therapy with elderly depressives: An experimental study. In: Upper, D., and Ross, S., eds. *Behavioral Group Therapy.* Vol. 3. Champaign, IL: Research Press, 1981.

Gibson, A.J. A further analysis of memory loss in dementia and depression in the elderly. *British Journal of Clinical Psychology* 29:179-185, 1981.

Hilbert, N.M.; Niederehe, G.; and Kahn, R.L. Accuracy and speed of memory in depressed and organic aged. *Educational Gerontology* 1:131-146, 1976.

Hughes, C.P.; Berg, L.; Danzinger, W.L.; Coben, L.A.; and Martin, R.L. A new scale for the staging of dementia. *British Journal of Psychiatry* 140:566-572, 1982.

Kahn, R.L.; Zarit, S.H.; Hilbert, N.M.; and Niederehe, G. Memory complaint and impairment in the aged: The effect of depression and altered brain function. *Archives of General Psychiatry* 32:1569-1573, 1975.

Katzman, R. Alzheimers disease: Advances and opportunities. *Journal of the American Geriatrics Society* 35:69-73, 1987.

Kranzler, G. *You Can Change How You Feel.* Eugene, OR: University of Oregon Press, 1974.

Lewinsohn, P.M.; Munoz, R.F.; Youngren, M.A.; and Zeiss, A.M. *Control Your Depression.* New York: Prentice Hall, 1986.

MacDonald, M., and Butler, A. Reversal of helplessness in nursing home wheelchair residents using behavior modification procedures. *Journal of Gerontology* 29:97-101, 1974.

McAllister, T.W., and Price, T.R. Severe depressive pseudodementia with and without dementia. *American Journal of Psychiatry* 139:626-629, 1982.

Miller, W.R. Psychological deficit in depression. *Psychological Bulletin* 82:238-260, 1975.

Miller, E., and Lewis, P. Recognition memory in elderly patients with depression and dementia: A signal detection analysis. *Journal of Abnormal Psychology* 86:84-86, 1977.

Niederehe, G., and Camp, C.J. Signal detection analysis of recognition memory in depressed elderly. *Experimental Aging Research* 11:207-213, 1985.

Raskin, A. Partialing out the effects of depression and age on cognitive functions: Experimental data and methodologic issues. In: Poon, L.W.; Crook, T.; Davis, K.; Eisdorfer, C.; Gurland, B.J.; Kaszniak, A.W.; and Thompson, L.W., eds. *Handbook for Clinical Memory Assessment*. Washington, DC: American Psychological Association, 1987.

Raskin, A.; Friedman, A.S.; and DiMascio, A. Cognitive and performance deficits in depression. *Psychopharmacology Bulletin* 18:196-202, 1982.

Raskin, A., and Jarvik, L.F., eds. *Psychiatric Symptoms and Cognitive Loss in the Elderly: Evaluation and Assessment Techniques*. Washington, DC: Hemisphere Publishing Corporation, 1979.

Reifler, B.V. Arguments for abandoning the term pseudodementia. *Journal of the American Geriatrics Society* 30:665-668, 1982.

Reifler, B.V.; Larson, E.; and Hanley, R. Coexistence of cognitive impairment and depression in geriatric outpatients. *American Journal of Psychiatry* 139:623-626, 1982.

Reifler, B.V.; Larson, E.; Teri. L.; and Poulsen, M. Dementia of the Alzheimer type and depression. *Journal of the American Geriatrics Society* 34:854-859, 1986.

Reisberg, B.; Ferris, S.H.; DeLeon, M.J.; and Crook, T. The global deterioration scale for assessment of primary degenerative dementia. *American Journal of Psychiatry* 139:1136-1139, 1982.

Salzman, C., and Shader, R.I. Clinical evaluation of depression in the elderly. In: Raskin, A., and Jarvik, L.F., eds. *Psychiatric Symptoms and Cognitive Loss in the Elderly: Evaluation and Assessment Techniques*. Washington, DC: Hemisphere Publishing Corporation, 1979.

Shraberg, D. The myth of pseudodementia and the aging brain. *American Journal of Psychiatry* 135:601-603, 1978.

Steuer, J.; Mintz, J.; Hammen, C.; Hill, M.A.; Jarvik, L.F.; McCarley, T.; Motoike, P.; and Rosen, R. Cognitive-behavioral and psychodynamic group psychotherapy in treatment of geriatric depression. *Journal of Consulting and Clinical Psychology* 52:180-189, 1984.

Teri, L., and Gallagher, D. Cognitive behavioral interventions for depressed patients with dementia of the Alzheimer's type. In: Sunderland, T., ed. *Depression in Alzheimer's Disease: Component or Consequence?* New York: Grune & Stratton, in press.

Thompson, L.W.; Davies, R.; Gallagher, D.; and Krantz, S.E. Cognitive therapy with older adults. *Clinical Gerontologist* 5:245-279, 1986.

Thompson, L.W.; Gallagher, D.; and Breckenridge, J.S. Comparative effectiveness of psychotherapies for depressed elders. *Journal of Consulting and Clinical Psychology*, in press.

Whitehead, A. Verbal learning and memory in elderly depressives. *British Journal of Social and Clinical Psychology* 13:201-208, 1973.

Yost, E.B.; Beutler, L.E.; Corbishley, M.A.; and Allender, J.R. *Group Cognitive Therapy: A Treatment Approach for Depressed Older Adults.* New York: Permagon Press, 1986.

Part IV

Issues and Directions for Mental Health Services Research

What is the optimal range of community and institutional services for individuals with Alzheimer's disease and related disorders and their families throughout the course of this disease with regard to service design, staffing, and the time of such services during the progression of the disorder? What is the best way to combine formal support services provided by health care professionals for individuals with Alzheimer's disease and related dementias and informal support services provided by families, friends, and neighbors? How can methods be improved for delivering services to individuals with Alzheimer's disease and their families, including outreach services, comprehensive assessment and care management services, out-patient treatment services, home care services, respite care services, adult day care services, partial hospitalization services, and nursing home services? How best can individuals with Alzheimer's disease who do not have informal support available be identified and receive services? Questions such as these highlight the important role services research can play in advancing the development of validated services and clinical approaches for the immediate care needs of Alzheimer's disease patients and their families.

While the development of reliable, generalizable services of high quality can only be accomplished within a services research context, the history of Alzheimer's disease services research has been limited. In the past, the growth of the services research base was delayed by fragmented research efforts that were largely atheoretical and did not always represent the state-of-the-science. However, with the rapid burgeoning of scientific literature on Alzheimer's disease patient assessment and management, as well as increased understanding of the stresses of caregiving, the directions and the capacity of the field to conduct new and improved services research studies has been enhanced.

The following chapters address many of the methodological and theoretical issues that have previously burdened the field. These chapters confirm the need to examine service delivery within the context of the changing course of the disease and the needs of the Alzheimer's disease patients and their families; the utmost need for clarity and precision in describing services; the need for a diversity of service research studies that address the broadest range of issues; and the need to pay careful attention to the findings of basic and clinical research in both designing services and selecting appropriate variables for research.

Chapter 17

Services Research: Research Problems and Possibilities

Linda K. George, Ph.D.

Mental health services research is in its relative infancy; geriatric mental health services research is embryonic. The formative status of geriatric mental health services research is evidenced by two related conditions. First, the extant research base is very small; we know little about geriatric mental health services because very little research has been done. Second, the methodological quality of much of the extant research base is problematic. As a consequence, we cannot be confident about the validity and generalizability of results from most available studies of geriatric mental health services.

The above statements should not be viewed as indictments of the field of geriatric mental health services research or its investigators. The current state of affairs is understandable precisely because of the topic's early stage of development. The natural histories of scientific problems suggest that new areas of investigation are characterized by the slow accumulation of knowledge, heavy startup costs associated with the development of measuring instruments and other methodological tools, and the emergence of a research base adequate for developing experience-based quality control criteria.

This volume focuses specifically on Alzheimer's disease. However, investigators studying services in the context of Alzheimer's disease and those studying geriatric mental health services in general confront the same major methodological issues. The purpose of this chapter is to provide an overview of these methodological issues.

The chapter is organized into three major sections. First, a typology of mental health services research is presented. The purpose of the typology is to highlight major methodological similarities and differences underlying the numerous research questions subsumed under the rubric of mental health services research. The second and major section examines several specific methodological issues in the context of geriatric mental health services research in general, and services for Alzheimer's Disease in particular. The issues examined have been frequently ignored or compromised in previous research and pose common difficulties in research based on Alzheimer's patients. The third section offers some final thoughts about future research in this important area.

Typology of Mental Health Services Research

The term "mental health services research" subsumes a multitude of specific research topics. It is important to recognize this diversity because different research questions imply different research designs and methodological concerns. Nonetheless, some form of aggregation is needed for efficiency (i.e., every substantive topic cannot be discussed separately in a chapter of reasonable length) and to note the methodological similarities that often underlie studies on different substantive topics.

Figure 17-1 presents a typology of mental health services research based on two major research design characteristics. Research topics are cross-classified in this matrix along two dimensions: unit of analysis (i.e., individual versus group/population) and overall purpose (i.e., description versus explanation). Explanatory studies are further divided into experimental and nonexperimental designs. Each cell of the matrix has two examples of substantive topics that fulfill design characteristics. As these illustrations demonstrate, substantively diverse topics may share fundamental similarities in unit of analysis and/or overall purpose.

This matrix is not unique to geriatric mental health services. The sample topics in the cells of the matrix are relevant to mental health services research, but are not inherently geriatric. At an even broader level, the dimensions that define the rows and columns of the matrix are not specific to mental health services research–they could easily be applied to numerous other topics. Nonetheless, the matrix is a useful starting point for examining methodological issues relevant to geriatric mental health services research.

Unit of Analysis

Health services research appropriately includes studies at both the

Figure 17-1. Typology of mental health services research with examples

| | Unit of analysis | |
Purpose of study	Individual	Group/population
Description	Natural history of mental health services	Prevalence of unmet need for mental health services
	Patterns of mental health service use	Prevalence of psychotropic drug use
Explanation, nonexperimental	Determinants of help-seeking	Impact of health insurance on mental health service use
	Determinants of referrals to mental health specialists	Impact of supply of mental health services on demand
Explanation, experimental	Treatment efficacy studies	Impact of DRG's on psychiatric outcomes
	Impact of prevention efforts	Cost/benefit studies

micro (i.e., individual) and macro (i.e., group/population) levels of analysis. Both are appropriate, but the choice is rarely a matter of investigator preference. Instead, unit of analysis should be determined by the nature of the research question. For example, consider the following research questions: What is the prevalence of benzodiazepine use among persons age 65 and older in the United States? What are the determinants of benzodiazepine use among older adults? Appropriate units of analysis for these research questions are clear and straightforward. Prevalence estimates are by definition population-based. The question concerning the predictors of drug use clearly states that comparisons are to be made among individuals.

In some cases, however, the appropriate unit of analysis is less clear. For example, should the impact of milieu therapy be assessed in terms of changes in individual functioning or changes in the wards where it is implemented? What is the appropriate unit of analysis in an examination of urban/rural differences in mental health service use? On one hand, place of residence is a characteristic of individuals; on the other hand, the prevalence of mental health service use can be compared for urban and rural populations.

In both these illustrations, difficulty in determining an appropriate unit of analysis results from ambiguity in the research question. In the study evaluating milieu therapy, the investigator must be able to specify the outcomes that the intervention is expected to affect—such specification is part of defining the research problem. If the outcomes are individual characteristics (e.g., symptom levels), the unit of analysis is the individual. If the outcomes are properties of the ward (e.g., staff turnover rates across wards), the ward is the unit of analysis.

The same logic applies to the issue of urban/rural differences in mental health service utilization. A micro study might involve examination of differences in help-seeking between rural and urban residents. A population-based study might involve comparison of per capita State hospital admissions between urban and rural counties. If the investigator defines the research question clearly, the appropriate unit of analysis is readily identifiable.

The unit of analysis has several implications for research design. The most important is sampling. It should be obvious that individuals are the elements to be sampled in micro studies; groups or other aggregates are sampled in macro studies. Although this concept seems straightforward, in practice a surprising amount of confusion surrounds this issue. Most problems occur in macro studies, where investigators sometimes confuse individuals within groups with the groups per se. For example, if an investigator wishes to examine the impact of a change in reimbursement policies on nursing home staffing patterns, the unit of analysis is the nursing home—not residents or staff of the nursing homes. Concomitantly, the sample size is the number of nursing homes, not the number of nursing home residents or staff. Another difficulty in some macro studies is obtaining a sample of sufficient size to permit stable estimates and tests of statistical significance. Thus, sampling strategy and size must be directly linked to the unit of analysis.

In some cases, it is appropriate and valuable to include both individual and aggregate outcomes in the same study. Thus, an investigator may wish to examine the impact of milieu therapy upon both individual and ward outcomes. This is perfectly acceptable, but both individuals and wards must be sampled systematically and in sufficient numbers to permit meaningful data analysis.

One special type of multilevel study merits brief mention: studies of contextual effects. In these studies, the outcomes examined are properties of individuals, but the independent variables include both personal characteristics and measures of aggregates or the environmental context. One example would be a study of the effects of demographic variables (e.g., personal characteristics of nursing staff) and measures of environmental context (e.g., local labor market conditions) upon turnover and retention of nursing staff in long-term care facilities. Studies of contextual effects impose both sampling and statistical complexities on the investigator. Nonetheless, these multilevel studies are a potentially rich and, as yet, untapped arena for geriatric mental health services research.

Descriptive Versus Explanatory Studies

The distinction between descriptive and explanatory studies is simple and straightforward. Descriptive studies systematically describe phenomena of interest. Explanatory studies make causal inferences about the effects of one or more independent variables on a dependent variable of interest.

Descriptive studies are especially important in the early stages of a research tradition, when information is needed about the nature, prevalence, and distribution of a phenomenon. For example, given the recent public health danger posed by AIDS, large amounts of effort are being devoted to generating epidemiological and clinical portraits of this disease. Indeed, it is difficult to imagine launching major explanatory studies in the absence of a solid base of descriptive information about the phenomenon.

Even more established research traditions, however, can often be advanced by appropriate descriptive analyses. Regier and associates, for example, used descriptive analyses to introduce the "de facto mental health service system"–a concept that greatly enhanced our understanding of help-seeking for and treatment of mental disorders in the United States (Regier et. al 1978). Similarly, epidemiologists continue to generate estimates of the prevalence of treated and untreated psychiatric conditions. Prevalence figures are, by definition, descriptive. Thus, descriptive studies are an integral part of mental health services research.

Explanatory studies generally are viewed as the pinnacle of medical science because they focus on the causes of, consequences of, and cures for disease. Studies of risk factors for disease onset; biological, social, and psychological sequelae of illness; and the development and evaluation of social and clinical interventions are explanatory studies. In addition to telling us about the mechanisms underlying phenomena of interest, explanatory studies also make greater methodological demands on investigators. Most of the methodological issues discussed in this chapter are relevant to both descriptive and explanatory studies. Systematic sampling, careful choice of measuring instruments, adequate definition of the research question, and efforts to control bias, for example, are all equally important to both types of studies. Explanatory studies, however, also require that the research design warrant causal inference.

Inferences about causality rest on three criteria: (1) evidence of concomitant variation, (2) evidence of temporal order, and (3) evidence that competing hypotheses have been taken into account (Selltiz et al. 1976). First, the criterion of concomitant variation requires that the independent and dependent variables vary together or are correlated. Second, to make a causal inference, the independent variable must precede or occur simultaneously with the dependent variable. Causal inference is obviously precluded if the hypothesized independent variable occurs after the dependent variable. Third, and most difficult, the investigator must convincingly demonstrate that the independent variable directly affects the dependent variable and that the dependent variable is not solely due to other, unmeasured and/or unestimated factors. A variety of methods can be used to rule out competing hypotheses or estimate the effects of alternate predictors of the dependent variable.

Some studies, especially correlational studies, appear to fit neither the descriptive nor the explanatory label. Consider, for example, a study of the correlates of seeking mental health services from public agencies. Is that descriptive or explanatory? In fact, correlational studies often straddle the descriptive versus explanatory distinction. Because concomitant variation is one of the three criteria required for causal inference, many correlational studies have an explanatory flavor. Nonetheless, causal inference is inappropriate unless evidence documenting temporal order and ruling out competing hypotheses also is presented. It is both acceptable and useful to determine whether correlational relationships support one's causal hypotheses. It is unacceptable, however, to make causal inferences on the basis of correlational data alone–an all too frequent mistake in health services research.

Experimental and Nonexperimental Studies

The classical experiment holds special status in social science (and other types of) research. Of all research designs, it is best equipped to meet the requirements of causal inference (Selltiz et al. 1976). The basic design of the classical experiment is familiar:

1. Research participants are randomly assigned to at least one experimental group and at least one control group.

2. The outcome of interest is measured at least twice: prior to manipulation of the independent variable/intervention (the pretest) and after manipulation of the independent variable/intervention (the posttest).

3. Both the experimental and control groups are subjected to identical conditions, except that the experimental group is exposed to the independent variable/intervention and the control group is not.

This simple but elegant design ensures that the criteria required for causal inference are established. Concomitant variation and temporal order are experimentally manipulated. Competing hypotheses are ruled out by randomization of subjects to experimental and control groups and by experimenter control ensuring that the independent variable/intervention is the only difference experienced by experimental and control groups. From a purely methodological perspective, the most rigorous explanatory studies are based on classical experiments.

In health services research, it is often appropriate to expose the control group to a placebo (i.e., to provide an intervention, but one that lacks the "active ingredient" hypothesized to affect the outcome of interest). Placebo designs are most frequently used in clinical trials where the proverbial "sugar pill" can appear to be identical to the therapeutic agent under investigation.

The logic of the placebo control group can often be translated into health services research. If an investigator wishes to examine the efficacy of cognitive therapy for late-life depression, for example, the experimental group can be administered cognitive therapy and the control group can be given nonspecific social interaction on the same schedule. In some methodology texts, control groups receiving as much attention as the experimental group (but not receiving the treatment under study) are called attention control groups. The placebo/attention control group is a useful addition to the research design, permitting the investigator to rule out one important competing hypothesis: that the simple belief that one has received treatment fully accounts for improvement.

The classical experiment has been described in its simplest form (i.e., one experimental group and one control group). Space limitations preclude a review of more complex research designs. However, a variety of more complex classical experiments are available to investigators. Multiple experimental groups can be used to examine varying quantities of the independent variable (e.g., varying dosages of drugs), to compare qualitatively different kinds of interventions (e.g., drug therapy versus psychotherapy) or to estimate the effects of multiple independent variables. Multiple control groups can be used to quantify the effects of various factors of methodological interest, such as measurement effects. Reviews of more complex experimental designs and their purposes are available in several methodological texts (cf. Selltiz et al. 1976; Keppel 1973).

For a number of reasons, classical experiments are precluded in many research studies. In some cases, research participants cannot be randomly assigned to experimental and control conditions, i.e., the investigator cannot manipulate the independent variable and must study persons who are and are not exposed to it "in nature." Inability to randomly assign subjects seriously compromises the ability to rule out competing hypotheses—the investigator can never be sure that differences observed between experimental and control groups do not reflect predisposing characteristics of the subjects in those groups.

In other cases, the researcher cannot control the conditions under which experimental and control groups operate during the experimental intervention (e.g., the study cannot be completed under controlled conditions in the laboratory). The investigator is therefore unable to eliminate certain competing hypotheses because extraneous factors may interact with the independent variable or affect the experimental and control groups differently.

In still other cases, ethical issues regarding acceptable procedures for human subjects preclude implementation of one or more features of the classical experiment (e.g., random assignment of subjects to the independent variable, withholding treatment from the control group).

Although the classical experiment cannot always be implemented, it should be approximated as closely as possible in all explanatory studies. A number of methodological techniques have been developed to assist in approximating these conditions. Most important among these are statistical techniques that can be used to evaluate and control for predisposing characteristics and extraneous factors that threaten to confound results in nonexperimental studies (provided that these competing hypotheses are anticipated and measured).

Classical experiments have been criticized as being less adequate than nonexperimental studies in at least one area. Some researchers object that experimental conditions (especially laboratory-based studies) are artificial and overly controlled and, therefore, are not generalizable to the "real world." Without question, generalizability is an important issue. What some critics fail to recognize, however, is that the classical experiment is not necessarily a *laboratory* experiment; many classical experiments have been performed in natural environments. The setting in which research is performed should not be confused with the design of the study. Although it is appropriate to criticize studies that are performed in inappropriate settings–and many studies have been deficient on those grounds–this issue is separate from the logic of the classical experiment.

Major Methodological Issues in Geriatric Mental Health Services Research

In this section, a number of methodological issues relevant to geriatric mental health services research are examined. Seven issues are relevant to both descriptive and explanatory studies; the other three apply only to explanatory studies. The issues examined are admittedly selective; they were chosen because they frequently pose problems for investigators and are critical components of high-quality research. None of these issues is unique to geriatric mental health services research–most are relevant to all research, regardless of substantive topic. The issues are not discussed exhaustively; rather, each issue is embedded in the context of geriatric mental health services research. Statistical and data analysis issues are not examined.

Defining the Research Problem

The first task confronting any investigator is defining the research problem. The importance of this task cannot be overstated. An adequately defined research problem is a prerequisite for a successful research project. Both methodological and theoretical or conceptual criteria must be met.

Methodologically, the research problem must be specific, testable, and appropriate in scope. A well-designed study addresses a specific research question or a limited number of interrelated research questions. The research question(s) must be specific, because the adequacy of a research design can be evaluated only by examining it in relation to the question(s) to be answered.

An adequate research question is testable. In this context, testable should be interpreted in a relatively broad sense–i.e., the research question can be addressed using some kind of empirical data. This broad definition is obviously quite inclusive. Nonetheless, some questions cannot be addressed using empirical data; such questions fall outside the boundaries of science.

Finally, the scope of the research question(s) must be reasonable. On the one hand, the question cannot be so narrow as to be substantively trivial. On the other hand, the scope of the research question cannot be too broad or the research design becomes unwieldly (e.g., competing hypotheses become difficult to rule out, data collection becomes excessive and a burden on respondents).

Conceptual issues relate to an adequately defined research question in two ways. First, in all but the most exploratory studies, adequately defined research questions are based on formal theory or an extant knowledge base. The conceptual foundation thus forms the rationale for a research project. Second, the findings generated by research should refine, extend, or otherwise contribute to a body of theory. Thus, theory is both the launching pad and the end-point of science.

Insufficient attention to theoretical issues can seriously compromise research efforts. Failure to base a research problem on a state-of-the-art conceptual foundation leads to a number of problems that are observed all too frequently in practice: studies that "reinvent the wheel" because investigators were apparently unaware of previous work, studies that are incapable of making scientific or practical contributions, and studies that waste human and economic resources.

Cross-Sectional Versus Longitudinal Studies

Once the research question is defined, the investigator must develop an appropriate research design. An important initial task is determining whether a cross-sectional or longitudinal study is required. If the research question is adequately framed, this decision is relatively straightforward. In general, cross-sectional studies are appropriate when a snapshot in time is needed. Longitudinal studies are required when the research questions focus upon change or process and/or when temporal order must be established to support a causal inference. The choice of a cross-sectional or longitudinal design is generally made with little difficulty. Beyond this basic decision, however, are more complex issues.

Two important elements of longitudinal designs are the interval(s) between test dates and the number of measurements. Unfortunately, these issues are treated in a cavalier or arbitrary manner in many studies. The major purpose of most longitudinal studies is to monitor change–either naturally occurring change or change generated by intervention. To accurately characterize change, measurements must be made at appropriate intervals. But how is the investigator to identify an appropriate interval between measurements? The length of the interval between test dates should be based on a theoretical rationale or the results of previous research. Unfortunately for many research issues, extant theory and research do not provide adequate guidelines for choosing the interval between test dates.

The number of measurements to be made in longitudinal studies also merits careful consideration. Decisions should be based on theory, previous research, and the nature of the research question. But, again, theory and previous research are often inadequate for this purpose. In intervention studies, multiple followup measurements are often advantageous for monitoring both the short- and long-term effects of intervention and for assessing possible lagged effects. Similar logic can be applied to studies of transitions or life events. Methodological issues may also influence decisions about the number of measurements. There are statistical advantages, for example, in having three or more measurements when modeling the trajectory of change (cf. Heise 1969, 1975).

Because of the limited base of theory and research in geriatric mental health services, researchers are at somewhat of a disadvantage in deciding about number of measurements and measurement intervals in longitudinal studies. The creative investigator may be able to find alternate sources of information useful for those decisions. Depending upon the research question, consultation with clinicians or health administrators may produce valuable insights about the process to be studied. Medical records may also be a source of relevant information. Thus far, however, few efforts have been made to mine these sources.

Cross-sectional studies are appropriate for some research questions. They can also serve as important precursors to longitudinal efforts. A cross-sectional study can be an important first step in investigating a hypothesis about the relationship between independent and dependent variables. In the logic of experimentation, cross-sectional data can provide information about concomitant variation and can be implemented so that at least some competing hypotheses are eliminated. While the third criterion for causal inference—temporal order—cannot be adequately established with cross-sectional data, these results are often useful to support the decision to launch a longitudinal study.

Cross-sectional studies can also be used to obtain retrospective data by having respondents report about past as well as current circumstances. Retrospective data have been strongly criticized because they are subject to bias and/or inaccuracy due to forgetting or distortion when accounts of the past are unwittingly affected by current situations or reinterpretation (cf. Selltiz et al. 1976; Kerlinger 1973; Ridley et al.

411

1979). These criticisms are well taken; thus, retrospective data can seldom be used to meet the criterion of temporal order in explanatory studies. Nonetheless, retrospective data can be useful for examining the plausibility of a hypothesis prior to launching a longitudinal study. Indeed, creative investigators often use retrospective data as a simple check of whether the presumed independent variable occurred before the presumed dependent variable.

Retrospective data often generate information from respondents who experienced a given event (e.g., institutionalization) or exposure to the independent variable at differing intervals prior to measurement. Given sufficient sample size, such data can be used to construct "synthetic cohorts" based on length of time since exposure to the independent variable. Synthetic cohorts can be used to project a possible trajectory of the dependent variable at varying times subsequent to the independent variable. Ultimately, research questions concerning process or change must be examined with longitudinal data, but cross-sectional studies can be used to refine hypotheses about change and to inform decisions about the value of launching a prospective study.

Measuring Instruments

The backbone of science is empirical data. Thus, the quality of any research effort depends heavily on the adequacy of the methods used to obtain data. Data collection modalities can be usefully classified into four categories: observational techniques, surveys, interviews, and use of archival data. All four methods are frequently employed in geriatric mental health services research. Even archival data, which are infrequently used in most research areas, are commonly used in health services research because many studies use data from medical records. Space limitations preclude descriptions of specific instruments, general measurement strategies, or the relative advantages and disadvantages of particular measurement strategies. Rather, three issues of particular importance to geriatric mental health services research, including services for Alzheimer's patients, are briefly discussed.

Psychometric properties. A critical factor in the appropriateness of measuring instruments is psychometric adequacy. More specifically, measures must be reliable and valid. A reliable instrument is free of random error. Evidence for reliability usually is assessed via tests of replicability (as in test-retest reliability and interrater reliability), equivalence (as in split-half reliability), and/or internal consistency (as in the use of coefficient alpha to estimate the reliability of multi-item scales) (cf. Bohrnstedt 1969; Nunnally 1967).

The potential reliability of any measurement is constrained by forces outside the investigator's control. In mental health services research, this is best illustrated, perhaps, by self-report measures of health service use. Considerable evidence shows, for example, that respondents cannot reliably report volume of health service use for longer than about 3 months previous to the test date (cf. U.S. Department of Health, Education, and Welfare 1972a, 1972b, 1973). Although detailed questions and probes can increase reliability of such self-reports, reliability is ultimately restricted by memory limitations. Thus, the appropriate goal of psychometric efforts should be to develop measures that maximize reliability within the constraints imposed by the realities of the measurement context.

A truism in psychometric literature says that a measure is valid to the extent that it measures the phenomenon that the investigator intends to measure (cf. Nunnally 1967). Ideally, the validity of an instrument is assessed by comparing that measure to a "gold standard," a perfect measure of the phenomenon of interest. In reality, this kind of direct validity assessment is rarely used, for two reasons. First, there simply is no "gold standard" for many phenomena of interest. Second, if a "gold standard" existed, there would be little need for another measure of that phenomenon.

In most cases, validity assessment must be conducted using indirect evidence. Examples of validity tests based on indirect evidence include convergent validity (measures of the same phenomenon should be highly correlated), discriminant validity (measures of different phenomena should not be highly correlated), and tests of predictive validity (a valid measure of a phenomenon should predict theoretically relevant outcomes). Concepts relevant to geriatric mental health services research vary in the degree to which validity assessment can be based on direct evidence or must rely upon indirect evidence. For example, it should be possible to assess the validity of information concerning the cost of mental health services directly. In contrast, the validity of measures of psychiatric status and social functioning can be validated only against indirect evidence.

A final threat to validity merits brief mention: bias or other forms of systematic error. Though random error is a threat to reliability, systematic error jeopardizes validity. All forms of data collection are at risk; consequently, a variety of methods must be used to rule out systematic error. Mental health services research has a number of sources of potential bias or systematic error. For example, the ability of mentally ill and cognitively impaired respondents to report reliable and valid data cannot be taken for granted. Similarly, service providers have clear incentives to report their behaviors in a manner consistent with standard clinical practice.

Sensitivity to change. Much geriatric mental health services research focuses upon change–both naturally occurring and induced by intervention. In any analysis of change, it is critical that the phenomenon of interest be measured with an instrument that is sensitive (or reactive to) change (George and Bearon 1980). Sensitivity to change is frequently overlooked by researchers.

One of the complicating factors surrounding sensitivity to change is the frequent failure of theories to provide guidance about the degree to which phenomena are *changeable* (George 1979). When we are uncertain about the extent to which a phenomenon is changeable, it is almost impossible to assess the degree to which a measure is sensitive to change. If a measure is observed to be very stable over time, the stability may reflect either insensitivity of the measure or the nature of the phenomenon. Clearly, numerous phenomena relevant to geriatric mental health services research merit longitudinal observation simply to determine whether they are changeable–and, if so, the timeframe within which detectable change can be expected.

It may be tempting to conclude that unchangeable phenomena are inappropriate candidates for intervention studies. Such a conclusion is premature, however. Almost always, some facet of the phenomenon of interest *is* changeable–and is, therefore, a suitable candidate for intervention. Consider Alzheimer's disease. As is well known, it currently has no cure nor an effective method of slowing its progression. Nonetheless, it may be possible to develop interventions that effectively alter some of the important sequelae of Alzheimer's disease–sequelae that range from behavioral problems such as wandering to inappropriate use of medications and health services. Thus, an important strategy in designing intervention studies is to focus upon changeable components of the phenomenon of interest.

Use of medical records. Medical records are a potentially important source of data for mental health services research. They also pose significant problems, as do all archival data. Those problems merit attention–especially because some investigators seem to view medical records as a "gold standard" source of information about diagnosis, service use, and treatments received. This assumption is rarely tenable.

The major problem with archival data in general, and data from medical records in particular, is that the data are not recorded with the primary goal of meeting scientific standards (Selltiz et al. 1976). As a consequence, such data often are characterized by incompleteness, high levels of random error, and systematic error. In addition, because the data are not intended for research purposes, it often is not possible to measure variables in the format desired by the investigator.

The incompleteness of medical records is well documented (cf. Andersen et al. 1976; U.S. Department of Health, Education and Welfare 1973). Clinicians simply do not record all the information available to them about patients' symptoms, treatment decisions, and provider-patient interaction. Medical records also are not governed by concerns about reliability. Consequently, random error is likely. Interrater reliability (i.e., reliability across different providers in the same service setting) is especially problematic in medical records. Evidence shows that medical records are often subject to several kinds of systematic error. For example, it is commonly acknowledged that the diagnoses recorded may be affected by policies concerning reimbursement by third-party payers (Houpt et al. 1979). Similarly, clinicians fail to record psychosocial treatments (including reassurance and brief counseling) more frequently than psychophar- macological treatments (Orleans et al. 1985).

In a good research project, data collection is highly standardized, issues of validity and reliability are confronted directly, and quality control mechanisms are applied at multiple stages. These factors rarely characterize medical records. Thus, medical records must be used judiciously in geriatric mental health services research.

Controlling Bias

Eliminating bias is a critical component of research design. Bias is minimized during data collection by using standardized measures of documented reliability and validity that minimize the subjective evaluations of observers/investigators and by implementing quality control checks throughout the data collection procedures. Other facets of the research design are also vulnerable to bias. Two of these potential sources of bias are discussed in this section. The first issue, sampling, is familiar to most investigators–though the quality of sampling remains problematic in many studies. The second issue, ceiling or floor effects, is less frequently acknowledged although its effects can be devastating.

Sampling without bias. Generalizability of research results depends upon obtaining data from a representative sample of the population of interest. A representative sample is best obtained by using some form of probability sampling technique (cf. Kish 1965). In practice, it is difficult to obtain probability samples of populations of interest. An obvious obstacle to random sampling is expense–especially if the population of interest is large and/or geographically

415

dispersed. Another common problem is difficulty in assembling a complete sampling frame of all the elements in the population–and, of course, the investigator must have a complete sampling frame to ensure that each member of the population has a known probability of selection into the sample.

Poor quality samples are, unfortunately, very common in mental health services research in general, and geriatric mental health services research in particular. In part, this reflects the very real obstacles to obtaining probability samples (e.g., expense). In addition, however, investigators often are simply sloppy about sampling issues. Often no explicit attempt is made to define the population of interest. Investigators also often fail to caution readers about limitations concerning the quality and/or representativeness of their samples.

Two sampling biases are particularly common in mental health services research. The first is selecting research subjects from the patient population of a single health care delivery setting. This strategy inevitably introduces bias, because patients do not select health care settings on a random basis (Houpt et al. 1979). Inpatients are more seriously ill than outpatients. Users of fee-for-service settings and, especially, enrollees in health maintenance organizations, are of higher socioeconomic status and more likely to have insurance coverage–and the latter have more positive attitudes toward prevention. In contrast, users of public clinics are of lower socioeconomic status and often lack private health insurance. These selection effects severely compromise the generalizability of results obtained from such samples.

The second common bias is introduced into mental health services research by the use of inclusion and exclusion criteria. For example, a particular study may include only patients with certain disorders and exclude persons with a previous history of psychiatric disorder. These criteria are used for good reasons–because of the research design (e.g., to rule out competing hypotheses) or for good medical practice (e.g., in clinical trials, medications may be counterindicated among persons with multiple disorders). On the other hand, each inclusion or exclusion criteria added to a research project further narrows the generalizability of findings. This tradeoff between homogeneity and generalizability needs to be more explicitly noted in geriatric mental health services research.

Ceiling and floor effects. In intervention studies, a primary goal is to determine the ability of the intervention to improve an outcome of interest. To demonstrate positive effects resulting from an intervention, several conditions must be met: (a) the intervention must be efficacious, (b) the instrument used to measure the depend-

416

ent variable must be sensitive to change, and (c) the sample must allow "room for" or a reasonable probability of change. The first criterion is obvious and the second has already been discussed. The last criterion is the matter at hand.

In a standard intervention study using a classical experiment design, pretest scores are obtained prior to administration of the independent variable to the experimental group(s). Ceiling effects occur when the intervention is expected to increase scores on the dependent variable, but respondents, prior to intervention, already score at or near the top of the range for the dependent variable. Floor effects are the exact opposite. Ceiling and floor effects clearly introduce an unwelcome bias into intervention studies–and the bias operates against the investigator (George and Bearon 1980). Clearly, sampling should be focused upon appropriate target groups so that ceiling and floor effects are avoided. In addition, prettest scores can be used to ensure sufficient room for change in the anticipated direction.

Pilot Data

A much underrated component of research, including geriatric mental health services research, is pilot data. Pilot data serve several useful purposes. First, and most obvious, pilot data can be used to determine whether a research question is sufficiently promising to merit investment in a full-scale study. Such information is important both to investigators (who wish to avoid long-term commitment to projects that do not hold promise for scientific payoff) and to review panels (who wish to ensure that research funds are invested wisely). Although sample size is usually small, pilot data can be used to bolster the scientific rationale for a proposed project.

Second, and perhaps most important, pilot data are invaluable for testing the feasibility of research procedures. In an optimal pilot study, the total research process is subjected to a trial run–sampling techniques, data collection procedures, data entry and processing strategies, and quality control procedures. To obtain maximal information about feasibility, the same types of research participants and project staff should be used in the pilot as will be used in the full-scale study. It is inappropriate, for example, to use colleagues or students as pretest subjects. Techniques that are feasible for these subjects may be too complex or require too much time when transferred to patient populations or even representative community samples. Similarly, a semistructured interview that can be administered and reliably coded by the investigator designing the study may not generate the same positive outcomes when administered by a data technician or student assistant.

417

Third, and less commonly recognized, pilot studies provide important opportunities to explore major concepts in a more qualitative manner than often is possible in surveys or experiments. For example, participants in the pilot study can be asked, in a debriefing session, to identify confusing questions or procedures or to elaborate their reasons for particular responses. Interviewers or experimenters can be asked to make detailed notes about the extraneous comments volunteered by participants and/or their opinions concerning the meaning and quality of data collected. In a pilot study, subjects and support staff can be involved in a more flexible and open-ended way than is usually possible or desirable in a full-scale study. Information gained by that kind of involvement can be used to modify the research design and/or interpretation of findings.

Pilot studies also offer some unique benefits when the research question involves older and/or demented respondents. A variety of procedures and measuring instruments with documented validity for young and middle-aged adults are either inappropriate or must be modified for use with older adults (e.g., older adults are known to refuse telephone surveys more often than younger persons, the amount of time required to administer standardized instruments may be longer for older than younger adults). Similarly, many instruments that are suitable for use with cognitively intact older adults cannot be used in studies of cognitively impaired older adults. When previous experience is based on research with the nonelderly or the cognitively intact, pilot data can be particularly useful.

Aged and/or Demented Research Participants

Throughout this chapter, care has been taken to explicate the relevance of standard methodological issues for geriatric mental health services research. Also important, however, are the special demands posed by research on older and/or demented research subjects.

A substantially larger proportion of older than younger adults are incapable (because of physical and/or mental impairment) of participating in research projects. Depending on the population of interest, the proportion of incompetent subjects will vary greatly—but in all populations, the prevalence of incompetence is typically higher among older adults. When investigators exclude incompetent persons from their samples, generalizability is compromised and bias is clearly introduced.

In some cases, incompetent subjects must be excluded because they are the only source of data about themselves. Under such circumstances, investigators should caution readers about the limitations posed on results by the nature of the sample. In other cases, a knowledgeable informant or "proxy" can be used to obtain relevant information about the respondent. The kinds of information that proxy respondents can provide with adequate reliability and validity are limited to data about current or recent experiences and relatively objective information. Thus, proxy respondents are not always valuable. Gerontological investigators should always consider the issue of respondent incompetence, however, and develop a rationale for deciding whether to use proxy respondents.

In studies of demented older adults, the issue of competence is clearly relevant: respondents are nearly always incapable of participating in conventional interviews and/or providing reliable data about themselves. In most studies, formal or informal caregivers serve as proxy respondents for at least some data. Again, investigators must realize that proxy respondents generally can provide reliable and valid data about only relatively recent and objective experiences. Caregivers may find it difficult to provide objective information about the patients to whom they provide care.

To secure respondent cooperation and collect high-quality data, investigators must design research procedures that minimize respondent's burden. In general, older respondents are at greater risk of respondent burden than younger participants—both because older people are more likely to tire easily or be physically frail and because it usually takes longer for older persons to complete the research protocol (i.e., older respondents require longer to complete a survey, interview, or performance task). Thus, older persons are less efficient research participants than younger adults and are more likely to terminate participation in a study because of fatigue. Consequently, investigators should exercise increased vigilance with regard to respondent burden in studies that rely upon older participants.

Respondent burden is especially likely in studies of demented older adults. Persons with Alzheimer's disease and other dementing disorders often become frustrated when they face demands they cannot meet. Caregivers often shield their patients from research participation because of concern that the patients will become upset or fatigued. Investigators must develop their protocols for demented patients with extra sensitivity to respondent burden—and be prepared to answer caregivers' questions about the value of exposing their patients to the demands of research.

Attrition is a potential problem in all longitudinal studies, but can be of even greater concern in studies of older samples (Norris 1985). Attrition results in two problems. First, as attrition increases, the sample size available for longitudinal analysis decreases. In some studies, attrition has been so great as to preclude confident estimates

419

of change over time and/or preclude multivariate data analysis. Second, attrition is rarely random among study participants (cf. Criqui 1980; Goudy 1976). Consequently, dropout can—and often does—lead to bias in longitudinal studies.

Four major sources of attrition occur in longitudinal studies: (a) refusal to participate further, (b) relocation of or inability to locate project participants, (c) incidence of disability sufficiently severe to preclude continued participation, and (d) death of participants. These sources of attrition are not equally distributed across age groups (Dohrenwend and Dohrenwend 1968). In general, younger subjects are more likely to refuse participation or be unavailable for further study; older respondents are at greater risk of disability or death. Absolute attrition rates tend to be higher among older participants.

Investigators can use a variety of procedures to decrease attrition among all participants in longitudinal studies, regardless of age (cf. Crider et al. 1971; Freedman et al. 1980). Overall, however, gerontological investigators need to pay particular attention to attrition and plan sample sizes sufficiently large to accommodate a relatively large attrition rate, estimate the bias introduced by selective dropout, and take knowledge about attrition into account when interpreting results.

Longitudinal studies of demented older adults are subject to especially high levels of attrition. Mortality rates are elevated among demented older adults, compared to their cognitively intact age peers. Rates of institutionalization are also very high among Alzheimer's patients and older persons with dementing diseases. In some research, institutionalization renders participants ineligible for further study.

Ethical Considerations

Protection of the health, mental health, privacy, and dignity of human subjects is the responsibility of all investigators. Prescriptions for ethical research protocols are well documented in many sources and need not be reviewed here. Three ethical issues particularly relevant to geriatric mental health services research, however, are briefly noted.

Competence of participants to provide informed consent. Informed consent is one of the major mechanisms by which investigators protect the rights and well-being of research participants. An adequate informed consent procedure includes a description of the research procedures, an accurate assessment of the benefits and risks associated with participation, assurance that participation is

420

voluntary and can be terminated at the discretion of the subject, and the assurance of confidentiality (Galliher 1973). By definition, informed consent is meaningful and appropriate only if the potential participant is capable of understanding the conditions of participation and making a rational decision. Though the vast majority of older adults are capable of understanding informed consent, a nontrivial minority of older adults are not (Strain and Chappell 1982; Yordi et al. 1982). And in studies of demented older adults, incompetence to provide informed consent is nearly universal.

Competence to provide informed consent usually rests on cognitive status. That is, evidence of severe cognitive impairment is the major mechanism by which incompetence is identified. If, for example, an adult woman is disoriented about time and place, she is unlikely to be capable of providing informed consent.

Most sophisticated studies of older populations routinely use cognitive screening tests to determine whether respondents are capable of giving informed consent and reporting reliable and valid data. Screening tests such as the Mini-Mental State Examination (Folstein et al. 1975) and the Short Portable Mental Status Questionnaire (Pfeiffer 1975) are good choices for screening cognitive status because they are short, easy to administer, and easily scored "on the spot".

One practical problem with cognitive screening tests is that respondents dislike them–the items obviously comprise a test. Cognitively intact subjects find them degrading; cognitively impaired respondents find them frustrating and upsetting. A partial solution to the problem is to administer cognitive screening tests only if respondents seem disoriented or show other evidence of incompetence, or if the study is focused on a sample of demented older adults.

The use of incompetent adults as research subjects raises at least two ethical considerations. First, how are investigators to determine competence for purposes of informed consent? Second, if an investigator wishes to include older adults incapable of providing informed consent in a research protocol, who should give the consent? Both questions are difficult and lack clear-cut answers. Nonetheless, from an ethical perspective, it is critical that competence be considered in relation to informed consent. From a scientific perspective, it also is important that a set of *standardized* procedures be used to make decisions about competence.

In some studies (e.g., drug trials), investigators wish to include incompetent participants or even focus exclusively upon incompetent older adults (e.g., persons with Alzheimer's disease). This is acceptable provided that ethically adequate informed consent procedures can be implemented. In these circumstances, informed consent is complicated by the fact that most incompetent older persons do not have legal guardians or other officially appointed caretakers, but informed consent must be obtained from someone. For incompetent community-dwelling respondents, the best source of informed consent is a close family member. For incompetent institutionalized respondents, a staff member of the institution is the best source. Inclusion of incompetent participants clearly complicates the research process. Ethically, however, the necessity for such complexities is clear-cut: special precautions must be taken when obtaining data from persons incapable of protecting their own interests.

Access to medical records. Medical records are a common source of data in health services research, but the issue of informed consent is especially ambiguous when using them. On the one hand, medical records are in the custody of service providers, who must be willing to make them available. On the other hand, medical records include personal information about patients, and patients are unlikely to assume that their records will be used for research purposes. Ethical standards are best met by obtaining permission to access records from both the providers who generated the records and the patients whose records are to be used. This recommendation has clear implications for the complexity and cost of obtaining data from medical records. Contacting patients and obtaining release forms for accessing their medical records is very expensive. Nonetheless, this is the most ethical strategy and, therefore, an expense that investigators and funding agencies must be willing to bear.

Two exceptions to the need to obtain consent from patients should be noted. If the investigator wishes to obtain (a) only aggregate data or (b) data from which all identifiers have been removed by the health care setting, the confidentiality implied by the provider-patient relationship is retained. Under these conditions, patient consent is unnecessary.

Withholding treatment. From a scientific perspective, the most rigorous therapeutic intervention studies compare subjects receiving the intervention with subjects who receive no intervention (or who receive only a placebo). Using this design, the unique effect of the intervention can be isolated and quantitatively estimated. From an ethical perspective, however, withholding treatment from a control group is a complex and thorny issue. Indeed, this issue is so controversial that many human subjects review boards will not approve withholding of treatment even if research participants are willing to be randomly assigned to treatment and no-treatment conditions and will sign informed consent documents to that effect.

Two kinds of objections to withholding treatment arise, though this distinction is seldom recognized in texts on methodology and clinical trials. In some cases, the objection is not that the experimental intervention is withheld from control subjects, but that other kinds of treatments are not administered. One response to this kind of concern is to compare distinctly different interventions (e.g., comparing Drug X and Drug Y or comparing cognitive therapy to behavioral therapy). Another variation of this approach is to compare "standard treatment" to "standard treatment plus the experimental intervention." Overall, these are scientifically acceptable research designs, but they are not without cost. These approaches preclude quantified estimates of the unique effect of the experimental intervention. In the comparative design, only relative differences in impact can be observed. In the "standard treatment plus" strategy, it cannot be determined whether observed differences are additive or interactive (i.e., dependent upon the presence of the standard treatment).

A second kind of concern occasionally raised in intervention trials is more difficult to overcome. Some critics of intervention trials proposing experimental and control conditions argue that the *experimental treatment* should not be withheld from any research participants. These critics argue that, if there is sufficient rationale to justify use of the experimental intervention, then the intervention should not be withheld from anyone. These criticisms frankly put the investigator in the proverbial "Catch-22" position: on the one hand, the investigator must show sufficient rationale for the intervention to reasonably seek permission to administer it to research subjects; on the other hand, the investigator must express sufficient doubt about the efficacy of the intervention to justify withholding it from members of the control group.

In my opinion, withholding an untested (or relatively untested) experimental intervention from control subjects does not constitute an ethical problem. Experimentation is required to document efficacy, and experimentation requires comparison groups. If human subjects boards insist on administration of the experimental treatment to all research subjects, however, investigators have no choice but to rely upon weaker experimental designs such as pre- and posttest comparisons of a single (experimental) group.

Choice of Control/Comparison Groups

All causal studies involve comparison of some kind—either between groups that are and are not exposed to the independent variable or between groups that are exposed to varying amounts of the independent variable. Because of the fundamental importance of comparison in causal inference, appropriate choice of control or comparison groups is a key element of research design.

423

In classical experiments, choice of control/comparison groups is relatively straightforward. The investigator must, of course, determine the number of levels of the independent variable to be examined, decide whether to include a control group, and, if so, what kind (e.g., absence of any intervention versus placebo). After those decisions are made, however, randomization is used to assign research subjects to experimental and control conditions.

When the investigator is unable to randomly assign participants to experimental and control conditions, however, choice of comparison groups becomes much more difficult. Without the classical experimental design, causal inferences are less certain because it is harder to rule out competing hypotheses.

An example may help to illustrate the nature of the difficulty. Assume that Researcher X is interested in determining whether sexual assault is a risk factor for depression. One possible research strategy is to compare women who have never experienced sexual assault with women who were sexually assaulted in the past 6 months. If the latter report significantly more depressive symptoms than the former, Researcher X might conclude that sexual assault is indeed a risk factor for psychiatric disorder. But other kinds of comparisons might further elucidate the nature of the link between sexual assault and depression. It might be useful, for example, to compare women who experienced sexual assault with women who experienced physical assault without a sexual component—this comparison might help to separate the effects of physical violence from those of forced sexual activity. Or, sexual assault might be compared with other stressful events (e.g., bereavement, physical illness) to determine whether the link between sexual assault and depression is unique (in presence/absence or magnitude) or reflects a more generalized stress response.

As this example demonstrates, choice of appropriate comparison subjects depends on the nature of the research question. In theory, the specificity of the research question is equally important in experimental and nonexperimental designs. In practice, however, choice of appropriate comparison groups appears to be more problematic in nonexperimental studies. I believe that this reflects the differential extent to which the investigator is directly involved in manipulating the independent variable. In experimental studies, investigators "create" the independent variables and administer them to randomly assigned participants. Investigators of nonexperimental topics must measure phenomena as they occur in nature. Because they do not "create" their independent variables, nonexperimental investigators focus less attention on careful delineation of the independent variable. Whether or not my attribution is correct, a common problem in nonexperimental studies is inadequate attention to comparison groups.

In research with older populations, choice of appropriate comparison groups is often problematic—an issue of special relevance to geriatric mental health services research. Confusion is particularly acute over when older persons should be compared to members of other age groups and when comparisons should be based on sources of variation within the older population. Again, the solution to the problem lies in careful specification of the research question.

Ruling Out Competing Hypotheses

In explanatory studies, the most difficult criterion to meet is ruling out competing hypotheses. To some extent, no study can "prove" causality because it is not possible to eliminate every alternative hypothesis. Nonetheless, the best explanatory studies rule out as many competing hypotheses as possible and take particular care to eliminate the most theoretically plausible competing hypotheses.

Research designs vary widely in the strategies used to rule out competing hypotheses. In the classical experiment, most competing hypotheses are assumed to be eliminated via research design—an assumption that is much more tenable in laboratory experiments than in field experiments. In laboratory experiments, experimental and control groups are known to experience identical conditions (except for exposure to the independent variable), thus ruling out the impact of extraneous factors. In field experiments, experimental and control groups are at considerable risk of differential exposure to extraneous factors that may jeopardize group comparisons. In nonexperimental studies, in which subjects are not randomly assigned to the independent variable, it is even more difficult to rule out competing hypotheses because "experimental" and "control" groups may differ in both exposure to extraneous factors and predisposing characteristics.

Fortunately, statistical analysis techniques are sufficiently sophisticated to provide powerful tools for ruling out competing hypotheses. If the investigator can *measure* the occurrence of extraneous factors and/or predisposing characteristics, methods of statistical control can be used to estimate the relationship between the independent and dependent variables net of the influences of possible competing hypotheses. Indeed, the development of multivariate statistical procedures (primarily, but not exclusively, analysis of variance and regression techniques) has made two major contributions to explanatory research: (a) the ability to isolate the effects of independent variables with other factors (i.e., competing hypotheses) statistically controlled and (b) the ability to examine the effects of multiple independent variables on a dependent variable in an efficient and non-biased manner. Because of these powerful multivariate statistical techniques, causal inference is possible in many situations where the logic of experimentation cannot be implemented in the research design.

Although multivariate statistical techniques have revolutionized causal inference, they also impose greater demands upon our theories. Investigators can statistically control possible confounding factors (i.e., extraneous variables and predisposing characteristics) only if those variables are measured. Thus, investigators must be able to identify potential confounding variables prior to designing the data collection procedures and must collect valid information about those confounding factors. The ability to identify major competing hypotheses depends most heavily upon the complexity and quality of the theory upon which the research question is based. That is, the theoretical development needed to design an adequate explanatory study demands not only a rationale for hypothesizing a relationship between the independent and dependent variables of interest, but also consideration of possible confounding factors. In my experience, the statistical procedures available often outstrip the theoretical complexity needed for compelling evidence of causality.

Two types of competing hypotheses are especially relevant to geriatric mental health services research and are frequently neglected or handled improperly. Hypotheses about the causal impact of age upon various outcomes pose unusual problems in the research design. At the heart of the matter is the age-period-cohort issue—an issue that is well-documented in many sources and will not be reviewed here in detail. The bottom line is that (a) cross-sectional studies, which can be used only to discern age differences, confound age effects and cohort effects, and (b) longitudinal studies, which are used to identify age changes, confound age effects and period effects (cf. Baltes 1968; Schaie 1965). Although significant advances have been made in terms of both research design and statistical analysis to permit accurate estimation of age, period, and cohort effects (cf. Mason et al. 1973; George et al. 1981), the problem remains a significant one. And, in practical terms, studies of age differences and age changes cannot resolve the age-period-cohort confound, although they must acknowledge its potential impact.

Other, more manageable confounds affect both longitudinal and, especially, cross-sectional studies in which age is an independent variable of interest. For example, in any study of age differences, compositional differences between older and younger cohorts comprise competing hypotheses and must be taken into account. Compared to younger cohorts, older cohorts have higher proportions of females and the unmarried (especially the widowed), and have lower levels of socioeconomic status. Consequently, compositional differences in the characteristics of older and younger cohorts must be statistically controlled when testing for age differences in a phenomenon of interest. It also is important to rule out competing hypotheses in longitudinal studies, because not all changes observed over time are age changes. To use a simple example, a longitudinal study examining the impact of age on income clearly would generate inaccurate conclusions if the investigators failed to take employment status into account. Precisely because so many factors are correlated with age, it is critical to rule out the effects of those factors when examining age as an independent variable.

In health services research, a surprising number of studies fail to consider the impact of services received from other service settings, as well as services received from informal sources of social support. For example, studies of change in psychiatric status before and after receiving services from a community mental health center (CMHC) *must* take into account services that patients receive from other service settings (including primary care physicians) and from social support networks. Otherwise, the investigator cannot know whether the CMHC services lead to positive outcomes, whether improvements in psychiatric status reflect the effects of other services received by patients, or whether both CMHC and other services have significant effects upon psychiatric status. It is critical that studies of the impact of particular services or treatments rule out the competing hypothesis that services from other sources account for the observed change in the dependent variable.

Documenting the Intervention

The term "intervention" is used in two major ways in the research literature. At the broadest level, it refers to an experimentally manipulated independent variable. In more restricted form, it refers to treatments or services intended to have a positive impact upon recipients' levels of health or well-being. In this section, I use the term intervention in the narrower, therapeutic sense. A significant proportion of mental health services research consists of intervention studies (i.e., evaluations of the effects of treatments or services).

All interventions (a) have the possibility of risk (i.e., noxious effects), (b) require commitment of time and resources by both those giving and receiving the intervention, and (c) involve subjects in need of assistance. Because of these conditions, it is not ethical to provide intervention unless the intervention has a reasonable likelihood of improving patient status. Thus far, a rationale for expecting positive results sounds like an ethical and practical issue. It is, but ultimately it is also a theoretical issue. The strongest rationale for intervention is theoretical—and it is almost impossible to justify an intervention in the absence of a theoretical rationale for why and how the intervention is likely to be effective.

A common problem in mental health services research is failure to adequately specify and measure the intervention. This is frequently referred to as the "black box" problem—i.e., the intervention is a black box, the contents of which are not readily apparent. Failure to adequately specify and measure the intervention is problematic in both scientific and practical terms. Scientifically, it is important that interventions be standardized across subjects and accurately measured in detail. Unless the intervention is standardized, random and/or systematic variance will be introduced into the research design, making it more difficult to detect positive results. Interventions must be measured in detail for analyses to identify the "active ingredient(s)" within the intervention. Another reason to specify and standardize the nature of the intervention is to ensure replicability. The ability to replicate results is scientifically critical (i.e., all valid results are replicable rather than idiosyncratic); but replicability is also of practical importance. Clinical practice is advanced only to the extent that effective intervention can be transferred to and used by other clinicians.

In addition to adequately specifying and measuring the intervention, three related issues merit brief examination: (a) specifying the therapeutic dose, (b) the importance of implementation checks, and (c) the importance of checking for unanticipated noxious effects. Each of these is briefly described.

Specifying the therapeutic dose. Given evidence that an intervention has positive effects, it is also important to specify the optimal therapeutic dose. Although the term "therapeutic dose" connotes pharmacologic intervention, the concept of an optimal amount of intervention extends beyond the realm of pharmacology. For efficient resource utilization and cost containment, patients should receive the optimal level of treatment needed to maximize therapeutic response. Suboptimal intervention wastes resources and precludes maximal therapeutic response; overuse of intervention is also wasteful.

In mental health services research, many treatments/services that are known to be beneficial have not yet had an optimal therapeutic dose identified. Thus, controversy continues about the optimal length of hospitalization for particular psychiatric disorders, the conditions under which brief versus long-term psychotherapy is warranted, and the length of time that psychoactive medications must be ad-

428

ministered to maximize therapeutic response while minimizing side effects. As these examples illustrate, there is rarely *a single* optimal therapeutic dose. Rather, research is needed to specify the conditions under which specific amounts of particular interventions are optimal. In addition, the age of the patient may be one of the factors affecting standards for optimal therapeutic doses.

Implementation checks. Research investigators typically measure interventions in terms of the behaviors of the person administering the intervention. Thus, investigators will measure the number of sessions of cognitive therapy provided to subjects, the amount of medication prescribed to participants in clinical trials, or the nature of the stress-reduction techniques presented to group therapy participants. A very common problem, however, is failure to measure the extent to which subjects "receive the message" or implement the strategies that the investigator has "sent them." Rather, investigators often naively assume that subjects understand the principles of cognitive therapy to which they have been exposed, take the medications they have been prescribed, and master the stress-reduction techniques they have seen demonstrated.

Implementation checks refer to techniques that investigators can use to determine whether research participants in intervention studies are, in fact, implementing the intervention. Different types of interventions obviously require different kinds of implementation checks. In a drug trial, investigators can ask participants about compliance and/or check drug supplies to determine that compliance has taken place. In studies of cognitive therapy or stress-reduction, part of the sessions can be used to test comprehension of the principles offered in the intervention or participants can be required to demonstrate their ability to apply the principles they have learned.

The information gained by implementation checks can be used in two ways. If the implementation checks are performed throughout the intervention, corrective efforts can be made to ensure that participants implement the intervention. If implementation checks are performed only once, they should be performed at the end of intervention, just prior to posttests on the dependent variable. In this situation, information about implementation success can be used as a control variable in analyses of treatment response. Overall, implementation checks offer important information about the effects of interventions and individual differences in response to treatment. Investigators should include implementation checks in all intervention studies.

Checking for noxious effects. For both ethical and scientific reasons, all intervention studies must include investigation of possible noxious effects caused by the intervention. To again paraphrase the language of drug trials, it is incumbent upon the investigator to explore the possibility of side effects. Noxious effects of interventions can occur in two ways. First, the intervention may have a negative effect on the dependent variable. This rarely happens, but when it does, the nature and magnitude of the noxious effect is obvious. Second, and less visible, an intervention may have a positive effect on the dependent variable of interest, but have a negative impact in another area. This is the classic side effect condition.

The ability to identify side effects depends upon measuring dimensions of well-being or functioning other than the primary dependent variable of interest. The ideal intervention study includes multiple dependent variables, covering several areas of functioning. The major emphasis of the study may be a specific dependent variable, but inclusion of multiple dependent variables is useful for two purposes. First, this design is best-suited to detecting noxious effects. Second, the use of multiple dependent variables permits the investigator to identify possible unanticipated *positive* effects of the intervention. For example, congregate meal programs for older adults were designed as nutritional interventions. Research evidence indicates that congregate meal programs do, in fact, improve the nutritional status of participants; but they also facilitate social interaction of frail older adults at-risk of social isolation—an initially unexpected benefit. Thus, use of multiple dependent variables offers the investigator opportunities to learn about both positive and negative unexpected effects of the intervention.

Final Thoughts

The major methodological issues relevant to geriatric mental health services research in general, and services research in the context of Alzheimer's disease in particular, are generic issues. They are simply the methodological criteria relevant to any high-quality research initiative. In addition, however, this review highlights a number of issues that are particularly or, in some cases, uniquely, relevant to services research based on samples of demented older adults. These issues include difficulties in obtaining data from severely cognitively impaired older adults, greater reliance on proxy respondents and the limitations associated with informant data, increased rates of respondent attrition, and the need for special procedures to obtain informed consent.

430

Although this chapter focuses on methodological issues, it is prudent to reiterate the importance of theory and substantive knowledge for successful research. Methodological sophistication, by itself, is insufficient for producing high-quality research. Indeed, the quality and utility of any research project is constrained by the significance of the research question being addressed. Asking important questions is as crucial as implementing an appropriate research design; all methodological decisions must be based upon the substantive realities of the phenomenon under investigation as well as upon the logic of scientific inquiry. Both theory and methodology should–often must be–supplemented by direct observation of the phenomenon of interest and immersion in its experiential reality. Indeed, one of the wisest investments investigators can make is to intensely observe, in a broad and inductive sense, the phenomenon they want to describe or explain. The richness of this intense observation frequently leads clinicians to be excellent sources of information about potential hypotheses and confounding factors.

Geriatric mental health services research is in a very early stage of development. Services research focused specifically on Alzheimer's patients and their caregivers is even more rare. At the simplest level, these research fields will be advanced by a greater volume of research. But the growth of the knowledge base will be faster, and research investments will have greater payoff, if the expanded volume of research also is methodologically sound.

A number of methodological issues are reviewed in this chapter. Though none of the issues examined are unique to geriatric mental health services research, all are relevant to it, and not all have simple, straightforward resolutions. But all of them can be tackled in productive ways. One of the messages I have tried to convey in this methodological review is that the standard methodological tools used in clinical, gerontological, and social science research are largely transferable to geriatric mental health services research. Thus, though little is known about geriatric mental health services in general, or services for Alzheimer's patients in particular, a powerful arsenal of methodological tools is available for remedying that situation.

References

Andersen, R.; Kasper, J.; and Frankel, M. *Total Survey Error: Bias and Random Error in Health Survey Estimates*. Chicago: Center for Health Administration Studies, 1976.

431

Baltes, P.B. Longitudinal and cross-sectional sequences in the study of age and generation effects. *Human Development* 11:145-171, 1968.

Bohrnstedt, G.W. A quick method for determining the reliability and validity of multiple-item scales. *American Sociological Review* 34:542-548, 1969.

Crider, D.; Willets, F.; and Bealer, R. Tracking respondents in longitudinal surveys. *Public Opinion Quarterly* 32:74-83, 1971.

Criqui, M. Potential errors by non-response bias. *American Journal of Public Health* 70:1301-1302, 1980.

Dohrenwend, B.S., and Dohrenwend, B.P. Sources of refusal in surveys. *Public Opinion Quarterly* 32:74-83, 1968.

Folstein, M.F.; Folstein, S.E.: and McHugh, P.R. "Mini-mental state:" A practical method for grading the cognitive state of patients for the clinician. *Journal of Psychiatric Research* 12:189-198, 1975.

Freedman, D.; Thornton, A.; and Camburn, D. Maintaining response rates in longitudinal studies. *Sociological Methods and Research* 9:87-99, 1980.

Galliher, J.F. The protection of human subjects: A re-examination of the professional code of ethics. *American Sociologist* 8:93-100, 1973.

George, L.K. The happiness syndrome: Substantive and methodological issues in the study of psychological well-being in adulthood. *Gerontologist* 19:210-216, 1979.

George, L.K., and Bearon, L.B. *Quality of Life in Older Persons: Meaning and Measurement.* New York: Human Sciences Press, 1980.

George, L.K.; Siegler, I.C.; and Okun, M.A. Separating age, cohort, and time of measurement: Analysis of variance or multiple regression? *Experimental Aging Research* 7:297-314, 1981.

Goudy, W. Nonresponse effects on relationships between variables. *Public Opinion Quarterly* 40:360-369, 1976.

Heise, D.R. Separating reliability and stability in test-retest correlations. *American Sociological Review* 34:93-101, 1969.

Heise, D.R. *Causal Analysis.* New York: John Wiley and Sons, 1975.

Houpt, J.L.; Orleans, C.S.; George, L.K.; and Brodie, H.K.H. *The Importance of Mental Health Services to General Health Care.* Lexington, MA: Ballinger, 1979.

Keppel, G. *Design and Analysis: A Researcher's Handbook.* Englewood Cliffs, NJ: Prentice-Hall, 1973.

Kerlinger, F.N. *Foundations of Behavioral Research.* 2d ed. New York: Holt, Rinehart, and Winston, 1973.

Kish, L. *Survey Sampling.* New York: John Wiley and Sons, 1965.

Maddox, G.L., and Douglass, E.B. Aging and individual differences:

432

A longitudinal analysis of social, psychological, and physiological indicators. *Journal of Gerontology* 29:555-563, 1974.

Mason, K.O.; Mason, W.M.; Winsborough, H.H.; and Poole, W.K. Some methodological issues in cohort analysis of archival data. *American Sociological Review* 38:242-258, 1973.

Norris, F.H. Characteristics of older nonrespondents over five waves of a panel study. *Journal of Gerontology* 40:627-636, 1985.

Nunnally, J.C. *Psychometric Theory.* New York: McGraw Hill, 1967.

Orleans, C.T.; George, L.K.; Houpt, J.L.; and Brodie, H.K.H. How primary care physicians treat psychiatric disorders: A national survey of family practitioners. *American Journal of Psychiatry* 142:52-57, 1985.

Pfeiffer, E. A short, portable mental status questionnaire for the assessment of organic brain deficit in elderly patients. *Journal of the American Geriatrics Society* 23:433-441, 1975.

Regier, D.; Goldberg, I.; and Taube, C. The de facto mental health system. *Archives of General Psychiatry* 35:685-693, 1978.

Ridley, J.C.; Bachrach, C.A.; and Dawson, D.A. Recall and reliability of interview data from older women. *Journal of Gerontology* 34:106-115, 1979.

Schaie, K.W. A general model for the study of developmental problems. *Psychological Bulletin* 64:92-107, 1965.

Selltiz, C.; Wrightsman, L.W.; and Cook, S.W. *Research Methods in Social Relations.* 3d ed. New York: Holt, Rinehart, and Winston, 1976.

Strain, L.A., and Chapell, N.L. Problems and strategies: Ethical concerns in survey research with the elderly. *Gerontologist* 22:526-531, 1982.

U.S. Department of Health, Education, and Welfare. Reporting health events in household interviews: Effects of reinforcement, question length, and reinterviews. *Vital and Health Statistics.* Series 2, No. 45. Washington, DC: U.S. Govt. Print. Off., 1972a.

U.S. Department of Health, Education, and Welfare. Reporting health events in household interviews: Effects of an extensive questionnaire and a diary procedure. *Vital and Health Statistics.* Series 2, No. 49. Washington, DC: U.S. Govt. Print. Off., 1972b.

U.S. Department of Health, Education, and Welfare. Net differences in interview data on chronic conditions and information derived from medical records. *Vital and Health Statistics.* Series 2, No. 57. Washington, DC: U.S. Govt. Print. Off., 1973.

Chapter 18

Applied Services Research:
Clinical Issues and Directions

Kathleen Coen Buckwalter, R.N., Ph.D.

Introduction

To date, the bulk of the research on Alzheimer's disease has focused on biomedical approaches designed to discover the cause of the disorder. Very little study has been directed toward improving the situation confronted by the more than 2 million older persons currently afflicted with the disease and their families. This chapter argues that what is also needed is an applied services research focus to stimulate the development of research-validated clinical and services approaches to address the immediate needs of the Alzheimer's disease patients and their families. To that end, the chapter highlights some of the many clinical issues related to applied services research on this population.

The development of appropriate, effective, and safe services for the care and support of Alzheimer's disease patients and their families is a particular challenge because of the complex nature of the illness. Designers of services and interventions must keep in mind that Alzheimer's disease has a progressively deteriorating clinical course, and the anatomical and neurochemical changes that occur in the brains of its victims are accompanied by impairments in behavior, cognition, emotions, and psychosocial functioning. The nature and range of services, and the amounts and the providers of those services, needed by patients and their families throughout the full course of the illness can vary dramatically at different stages. Further, an understanding of the behavioral problems that accompany Alzheimer's disease, such as wandering, sleeplessness, agitation, suspicion, and depression can illuminate the nature of the chronic stressors with which caregivers contend.

The nature of the clinical progression of Alzheimer's disease and its consequences for the patient and family provides direction for addressing research and training issues. We suggest focusing on the development, implementation, and testing of interventions and services designed to control the changing mental, behavioral, and psychological problems that are the fundamental characteristics of those with Alzheimer's disease. In addition, we must design interventions and service delivery patterns that assist caregivers in maintaining Alzheimer's disease victims at an optimal functional level and, at the same time, help caregivers cope with their own intense feelings and stress-related responses.

At present, the services research knowledge base is limited and reflects fragmented research efforts that do not always represent the state of the science. Many of the studies currently in the literature are atheoretical, allowed inadequate time for followup measures, and employed psychometrically questionable instrumentation that is non-cumulative, thus leading to a paucity of comparative studies.

Further, many model service delivery programs were not developed from a research perspective, rendering them difficult to evaluate and impossible to compare with other programs in terms of their effectiveness.

Yet another problem for consumers, service providers, researchers, and policymakers is the fact that community-based, inpatient, and home health services are often assumed to refer to some specific standardized caregiving model (e.g., respite care), when in actual practice the services vary substantially in terms of provider expertise, environmental considerations, and therapeutic emphasis. Thus, a fundamental concern is that the lack of clearly defined, research-validated approaches and training could lead consumers of services unknowingly to place themselves or their family member in a treatment setting that, at best, does not meet their needs or live up to their expectations and, at worst, is potentially harmful. The range and variability of these inpatient, community-based, and home care services are examined in this chapter from the perspective of continuity of care.

Continuity of Care

From a clinical perspective, all services provided to Alzheimer's disease patients and their families must be evaluated against the overall criteria of continuity of care, a concept that mandates access to a variety of medical and supportive services over an unpredictable and changing clinical course. Alzheimer's disease patients and their families should be treated together, because change in the status of one affects the other. Too often, studies that describe the impact of caregiving and the effectiveness of various interventions in relieving caregiver stress fail to identify patient deterioration as a significant variable. However, Farran (1986) developed a conceptual model that considers the impact of both caregiver characteristics and stage of patient deterioration on caregiver functioning. This model is in keeping with the notion of continuity of care throughout the caregiver's career as well.

Currently, continuity of care is more an ideal than a reality. Most service delivery systems are fragmented and characterized by unrelated agencies variously involved in the care of Alzheimer's disease patients and their families. And yet, as Bachrach noted, continuity of care can be achieved "only when there exists true access to needed services" (1986, p. 171). She set forth four dimensions that are essential to continuity of care and relevant to this discussion of applied services research: (1) longitudinal access—because of the long-term nature of Alzheimer's disease, services must be available over long periods of time; (2) psychological access—systems of care must be easily accessible, helpful, and leave Alzheimer's disease patients and their families with positive feelings about using them: (3) financial access—Alzheimer's disease patients and their families must be able to pay for needed services; and (4) geographical access—Alzheimer's disease patients and their families must be able to get to places where needed care is provided, or the services must be taken to them, as is the case with outreach models (Bachrach 1986, p. 171). Achievement of these access dimensions is one yardstick against which current and proposed service delivery systems can be measured. We might add that Alzheimer's disease patients and their families must also have access to quality care that is appropriate to the stage of the illness and that respects and works with the informal caregiving network.

Continuity of services is achieved through the development of appropriate services and the coordination (e.g., case management) of those services, so that Alzheimer's disease patients and their families don't "fall between the cracks of the service delivery system" (Bellack and Mueser 1986, p. 186). Ideally, health services for Alzheimer's disease patients and their families will be comprehensive and include an array of residential and treatment settings and services that complement, rather than impede, the efforts of informal support networks (Bachrach 1986, p. 172). Treatment for Alzheimer's disease, like that

436

for many chronic mental illnesses, must be "multidimensional, multidisciplinary, and long-term" (Bellack and Mueser 1986, p. 178) and should integrate patient and family needs with treatment programs (Shern et al. 1986, p. 191). A chronic illness model that focuses more on symptom management and quality of life, rather than an acute disease model with its more curative focus, seems more appropriate when considering health services for the Alzheimer's disease victim. However, as discussed by Reifler in this volume, Alzheimer's disease victims often have coexisting medical disorders, and for these persons, an acute model may also be applicable.

But even in those rare situations where an integrated continuum of services exists, health care providers often remain uncertain about what specific treatments and services are best for particular patient symptoms or family problems. Thus, applied services research on Alzheimer's disease must be broadly focused—on needs, costs, quality, and access issues, as well as on Alzheimer's disease patients and their families, throughout the progressively downward course of the disease. We also need to critically evaluate currently available inpatient, outpatient, and in-home services, as well as to design, implement, and evaluate new models of care. Only through such systematic and coordinated research efforts can we hope to improve care for Alzheimer's disease patients and their families. The remainder of this chapter highlights some of the clinical issues related to applied services research in a variety of treatment settings, beginning with a discussion of research as shaped by the downward course of Alzheimer's disease.

Disease-Related Issues

Alzheimer's disease patients experience a decline in mental status, which includes alterations in most of the components of cerebral function, such as memory, language, praxis, mood state, concentration, cooperation, and thought processes, both perceptions and content. Memory deficits are both recent and remote and are accompanied by progressive disorientation. Language and speech deteriorate; early word-finding difficulties eventually progress to a loss of all verbal abilities. Praxis, the ability to conceptualize and perform motor tasks, also deteriorates, and Alzheimer's disease victims often display difficulty pursuing a complex task or become so obsessed with certain aspects of an act that they are unable to complete it (Reisberg 1983; Rosen et al. 1984; Semple et al. 1982).

Mood changes may be characterized by emotional lability or by blunted and/or exaggerated emotional responses. Expressions of anxiety, fear, sadness, tearfulness, or anger may occur until the disease progression renders the Alzheimer's disease victim relatively passive (Reisberg 1983). These mood changes have been related to both physiological changes in the brain and the patient's reactions to the disease process (Cohen et al. 1984; Iqbal and Wisniewski 1983).

Persons with Alzheimer's disease also lose their ability to concentrate and may appear uncooperative to family members or other caregivers. Moreover, a variety of psychotic symptoms may develop as cerebral function declines. Psychotic symptoms represent alterations in thought perception and content, and may include hallucinations, delusions, depression, mania, catastrophic reactions, and physical and verbal abusiveness (Lucas et al. 1986; Reisberg 1983). These symptoms are often stressful, frightening, and disruptive to the lives of caregivers, and their influence on placement decisions needs to be evaluated. In many cases, psychotic symptoms are amenable to psychopharmacological treatment and environmental manipulations, and their alleviation in terms of outcome measures and program success needs to be considered.

The nature of the behaviors displayed by an individual with Alzheimer's disease often varies depending on how far the disease has progressed (Reisberg 1983; Semple et al. 1982). While a number of stages of decline have been described in the literature, a three-stage model offers a useful framework for describing the progressive decline in Alzheimer's disease patient function and for testing the effectiveness of stage-specific clinical interventions. These stages include the forgetfulness phase, the confusional phase, and the dementia phase (Reisberg 1983; Schneck et al. 1982; Semple et al. 1982; Williams 1986). Although based on clinical observations, it must be noted that persons with Alzheimer's disease progress through the stages at different rates and seldom experience identical symptoms. For this reason, service systems often focus on individual symptoms rather than on "stage-of-decline" phenomena, although the staging process is conceptually helpful.

The forgetfulness phase is characterized by subjective cognitive deficit that does not interfere appreciably with day-to-day functioning. In this first phase, affective changes are characterized by anxiety. The cognitive deficit may be objectified in psychological testing, but the presence of forgetfulness alone does not necessarily indicate a diagnosis of Alzheimer's disease. Individuals who never progress beyond the forgetfulness phase are often said to have age-associated memory impairment, while those who progress on to the confusional phase are presumed to have Alzheimer's disease (Reisberg 1983; Schneck et al. 1982). Diagnosis of Alzheimer's disease is still basically one of exclusion (Rathmann and Connor 1985; Williams 1986). Generally, other causes of dementia must be ruled out through neurological, physical, and psychiatric examinations, and other tests and procedures, including computer-assisted tomography (CAT) scans, electroencephalogram, spinal fluid studies, complete blood counts, serological count for syphillis, serum thyroxine, vitamin levels, a metabolic test battery, and a chest x ray (Williams 1986).

The second phase, the confusional stage, is characterized by more severe impairments in cognitive functioning. Individuals tend to experience severe recent memory deficits, appear increasingly disoriented, and may lack concentration. Language deficits may appear; word recall becomes noticeably impaired. Both anxiety and denial can be observed in this phase (Reisberg 1983; Schneck et al. 1982), and functional deficits first become apparent. The care needs of those with mild dementia have not been well defined and should be examined. In addition, more research is needed on ways to support the informal care network in early stages of the illness.

Late in the illness (the third, or dementia phase) the person becomes severely impaired. The patient is very disoriented, and cognitive and memory deficits worsen (Mace and Rabins 1981). Anxiety may remain, alterations in thought processes and content become common, and functional abilities deteriorate. During this stage, many families are forced to consider placing the patient in a long-term care facility (Reisberg 1983; Schneck et al. 1982). Research is needed to determine if Alzheimer's disease patients are institutionalized because of the deficits associated with dementia, or if other disabilities and management problems such as wandering contribute to their placement.

At present, the exact cause(s) of the changes in mental status noted above are unknown. They have been linked to alterations in brain structure and function, although a causal relationship has not yet been empirically demonstrated. Health services research efforts must be focused on determining which clinical strategies and approaches are most beneficial in managing behavioral symptoms as they occur during the individual course of illness. Further, the relationship between severity of the illness (stage) and service use patterns must be documented and described. The efficacy of new services for Alzheimer's disease patients at different stages of the disease must be determined, and their long-term care needs (e.g., medical treatment, behavioral management, and personal care) identified, and optimal approaches to meet these diverse needs developed and tested.

Inpatient Issues

After enduring years of unrelenting strain, many families place their loved one in a nursing home. In fact, approximately 60 percent of nursing home residents have dementing illnesses like Alzheimer's disease (Brody et al. 1984). Long-term care placement often follows months or years of agonizing for the Alzheimer's disease patients and their families and may precipitate a period of crisis (Buckwalter and Hall 1987). The stress associated with placement and the changes inherent in giving up the primary caretaker role need more study. Often families feel they have "abandoned" their loved one to the nursing home staff and, thus, should no longer participate in any aspect of caregiving other than bringing in needed supplies. Or, they may try to recreate their primary caregiver role in the long-term care facility, with extended daily visits that tend to both aggravate the nursing staff and effectively prohibit them from "getting on" with their own lives. Regrettably, the family and staff may develop a competitive or even adversarial relationship in trying to protect and care for the newly admitted Alzheimer's disease patient (Buckwalter and Hall 1987).

The absence of any well-defined societal role for the unaffected Alzheimer's disease spouse following institutionalization gives rise to what has been termed the "neither wife nor widow" syndrome. Often, female caregivers, in particular, will feel they have no role to fulfill. Their primary role of caretaker, which they may have assumed for many years, has now been assumed by the inpatient staff. And yet they feel guilty engaging in social activities or dating because they are still technically married.

While conducting bereavement groups for divorced and widowed elderly at Senior Centers, I have frequently seen the members reject Alzheimer's disease spouses from inclusion in their group on the grounds that they are still married to a "living" spouse. The value of both individual and group logotherapy approaches for Alzheimer's disease spouses, which stress the rediscovery of meaning in life, needs to be systematically evaluated. Other therapeutic approaches that deal with issues of loss of intimacy, anger, feelings of abandonment, and guilt, and that help families accept the decision for long-term care placement, need to be developed and tested as well.

Whether former caregivers have appropriate roles in collaborative staff-family efforts needs to be examined (Buckwalter and Hall 1987). For example, Alzheimer's disease spouses have effectively served as

440

co-group leaders in nursing homes for remotivation, movement and music groups, and other rehabilitative strategies that do not require professionals. The effects of this type of family involvement, in an adjunct staff capacity, on patient, staff, and family morale poses some interesting research questions.

With institutionalization, the burden is placed on the nursing home staff to deliver highly skilled care to patients who are frequently unable to articulate their needs. The educational and training needs of inpatient staff, as well as optimal staff-to-patient ratios and the multidisciplinary mix necessary to meet this enormous health care challenge, have yet to be determined. The notion of staff stress, low morale, and high attrition rates associated with inpatient care of the Alzheimer's disease patient is only beginning to be addressed. Studies that prospectively investigate the effect of work stress on indicators of psychological well-being (e.g., burnout, depression, work involvement, and job satisfaction) among nursing home employees are essential (Curry 1987). Similarly, research that compares the effects of traditional integrated units versus specialized Alzheimer's disease units on staff outcomes (Maas et al. 1986) will have important implications for caregiving sites.

Little research on Alzheimer's disease has focused on how to improve care. Burnside (1983) identified the need for research that concentrates on the management of Alzheimer's disease symptoms. Thus, along with issues related to environmental characteristics, staffing patterns, professional roles, and coordination of services, interventions designed to treat the problems associated with caring for Alzheimer's disease patients must be identified and tested.

The gerontological literature has recently included descriptions of special care units (SCUs) for persons with Alzheimer's disease (Ackermann 1985; Hall et al. 1986; Laxton 1985; Peppard 1985). These SCUs separate persons with Alzheimer's disease and the staff who care for them from the other residents of the long-term care facility. They are often constructed with environmental modifications intended to prevent wandering, support patient functioning, and decrease sensory overload while providing enough environmental cues to encourage orientation (Maas et al. 1986). Environmental modifications aimed at reducing noxious or confusing stimuli might include removing prints and patterns from floors, walls, and furniture, or covering floors with carpet to reduce glare. Intercom systems and mirrors are also frequently removed in an effort to keep extraneous noise and frightening reflections to a minimum.

One study reported on a low-stimulus unit (N=12 patients) containing many of these environmental modifications, emphasizing individualized patient care, and maintaining a consistent routine to decrease patient stress (Hall et al. 1986). After 3 months, the authors observed the following functional changes: increased socialization, weight gain in six residents, decreased use of psychotropic medications, and improved sleep (Hall et al. 1986). Although this study provided some important descriptive information on the potential value of SCUs, it suffers from many of the methodological limitations cited earlier, including lack of controls and systematic, long-term followup with valid instruments. Further, patient severity or illness stage was not documented, and many of the measurements were based on anecdotal staff reports.

Special care units are also designed to encourage individualized interventions geared to the needs of the demanding Alzheimer's disease population (Mace 1985). Despite the description of care strategies in the literature, relatively little data indicate which strategies are currently being used in caring for persons with Alzheimer's disease or which ones are most effective. For example, while most authors discourage the use of restraints in management of agitation and wandering (Pajk 1984; Rader et al. 1985; Ridder 1986), one pilot study in an 800-bed long-term care facility reported that Alzheimer's disease patients were physically restrained between 8.5 and 14 hours per day while awake (Maas and Buckwalter 1986). This suggests the need for further research to determine if descriptions of preferred care strategies in the literature actually match the realities of caregiving situations.

Besides determining the types of strategies used, caregivers need to document the success of their interventions. For example, although most authors caution that medications should not be overused in managing mental and functional decline in Alzheimer's disease patients, there is little evidence that other care strategies are more effective and a lack of research validation to compel clinicians to adopt other approaches to care (Lucas et al. 1986; Tunik 1987). These areas represent gaps in the literature on care of Alzheimer's disease patients that need to be addressed by systematic health services research efforts.

Debate exists as to whether SCUs for Alzheimer's disease patients are beneficial. Those individuals who oppose SCUs state that confused patients remain better oriented and function at higher levels when residing with nondemented patients (Salisbury and Goehner 1983). Proponents of SCUs disagree with this contention and point out the disadvantages to both the confused and nonconfused residents of integrated facilities such as invasion of privacy, disrupted sleep patterns, and increased numbers of socially unacceptable be-

442

haviors (Hall et al. 1986). Still other issues include the cost of SCUs, the need for special training to care for Alzheimer's disease patients, the potential stress to staff in caring exclusively for Alzheimer's disease patients, and appropriate patient mix.

In many SCUs, Alzheimer's disease victims are divided on the basis of ambulatory status (e.g., able to walk, even with assistance, versus bedfast). For example, to qualify for admission to the ambulatory unit of one SCU (Maas et al. 1986), patients must be rated at Stage 5 (moderately severe decline) or Stage 6 (severe cognitive decline) on the Global Deterioration Scale (GDS) for Age Associated Decline and Alzheimer's Disease (Reisberg et al. 1982). Alzheimer's disease patients must also score above 20 on the cognitive subscale and above 10 on the noncognitive subscale on the Alzheimer's Disease Assessment Scale (Rosen et al. 1984).

Many SCUs do not have such standardized admission criteria, and certainly, optimal patient mix–level of functional and cognitive impairment and presence of behavioral symptoms–has yet to be determined. Clearly, this debate will continue until services research is conducted that documents the effects and replicability of these SCUs on Alzheimer's disease patients, their families, and the inpatient staff.

The essential components of SCUs must be identified and their effectiveness determined for different stages of the illness. Examining the efficacy of SCUs is clearly an important line of research. Under Public Law 99-660, Alzheimer's Disease and Related Dementias Services Research Act of 1986, Congress specifically requested that the National Institute of Mental Health provide for research concerning "the efficacy of various special care units in the United States for individuals with Alzheimer's disease, including an assessment of the costs incurred in operating such units, appropriate standards to be used by such units, and the measurement of patient outcomes in such units" (Section 944b iv). Finally, to determine the efficacy of various inpatient approaches, consistent and valid outcome-oriented measures must be applied across studies.

Although most demonstration projects are community based, a few involve institutional settings and attempt to link nursing home residents with the community, or to ease the transitional process for those elderly who can be discharged back to the community with appropriate supportive services (Haber 1986). These demonstration projects must be replicated and evaluated from a research perspective for effectiveness, ability to bridge the gap between inpatient and community-based services, and applicability to Alzheimer's disease populations.

Community-Based Service Issues

Approximately one-half to two-thirds of all dementia patients live at home (Rabins 1984). The goal of in-home and community-based long-term care services is

> to maintain persons in a self-determining environment . . . that provides the most homelike atmosphere possible, allows maximum personal choice for care recipients and caregivers, and encourages optimal family caregiving involvement without overwhelming the resources of the family network. (Haber 1986, p. 39)

Families of Alzheimer's disease patients report needing more respite and in-home supportive services (ADRDA regional conference, 1986). And yet, at present, these services are not widely available and are of variable quality, and most of the cost must be borne by the family. Somewhere between a fifth to more than one-half of all nursing home placements have been projected to be inappropriate (Knight and Walker 1985) on the basis of optimum level of care. Despite these statistics, which services are most effective in preventing inappropriate placement and the identified causes of inappropriate placement have not been adequately addressed by research. This section examines some of the many community-based and in-home services available to Alzheimer's disease patients and their families, from the perspective of this much needed services research.

Respite care, which provides "short-term, intermittent substitute care for impaired family members on behalf and in the absence of the family caregiver" (Gwyther 1986, p. 4), provides an excellent example of the lack of uniformity typical of community-based services for Alzheimer's disease patients and their families. Respite services may be offered under a variety of auspices, including voluntary, private, public, or private nonprofit. Programs also vary in the nature of their setting (e.g., home, day care center, institution), duration of services, level of care, eligibility criteria, and staffing patterns (Gwyther 1986, p. 4.). There is little comparability between programs offered, for example, by church groups who provide in-home hourly relief for a homebound caregiver, respite admissions to hospitals or nursing homes, respite provided by long-term care agencies, and day care centers serving 20 or more demented elderly for a full day. Even in the more specialized day care centers, staff are often untrained in caring for Alzheimer's disease patients, and programs are not always appropriate for Alzheimer's disease patients with different levels of intellectual and memory ability (French 1986, p. 19).

444

Some specialized day care centers, such as the one at the Suncoast Gerontology Center in Tampa, Florida, provide specialized interventions for Alzheimer's disease clients, such as unique programming; increased volunteer-to-client ratios; enhanced staff training, support, and staffing patterns; and increased caregiver support (Haber 1986). This program is being evaluated in terms of its impact on institutional placement rates, client functioning, and family member morale (Pfeiffer 1985). Specialized centers of this nature need to be further assessed for effectiveness and replicability.

As Gwyther noted, "The uneven distribution, inflexible hours, difficulties with transportation/escort, and the patient's own reluctance to try anything new, all contribute to make this option (day care centers) less available or acceptable to many family caregivers" (1986, p. 4). Research needs to be conducted on reducing barriers to the use of day care and examining optimal day care program strategies.

Just as currently available respite services vary greatly, so, too, do family needs for those services, ranging from the need for highly skilled professional nursing care to companion/sitter services. The duration of service needed is also highly variable, ranging from a period of several hours to do marketing to several weeks for a family vacation. The value of respite services early in the disease process also deserves the attention of researchers and clinicians.

The level of training needed by respite workers has not been determined. The advanced level of disability of most Alzheimer's disease patients by the time their families seek respite services suggests that skilled health care professionals such as social workers and nurses can best provide the necessary array of assessment, supervisory, and referral services. And yet the current reimbursement mechanisms do not facilitate long-term professional intervention. The majority of respite care is still provided by untrained members of the informal care network (e.g., family, friends, neighbors). In the absence of affordable and accessible help from formal community agencies, these caregivers require education and training in order to provide even minimal levels of safe care and to prevent crises and reduce their caregiving burden. Mutual help groups provide yet another option for caregivers to share experiences, coping strategies, and knowledge of community resources, and to be supportive of the efforts of others (Haber 1986). However, much more rigorous research on characteristics of these support groups is needed.

The diversity and innovativeness of the respite programs that are developing gives some cause for optimism. Haber (1986, p. 41) noted that the more flexible and accessible programs include respite exchanges between families (Berger 1984), volunteer respite placements (Lewis 1985), and respite centers that link trained respite workers

445

with provider agencies (Haber 1986). Before these innovative programs can be recommended for adoption nationwide, they must be replicated and rigorously evaluated in a variety of settings.

Services research is critically needed in the area of community-based services. As Gwyther argued, "Reimbursement is not likely to become available until the effectiveness of mutually agreed upon outcomes of respite services can be demonstrated and until more is known about appropriate auspices, organization and delivery mechanisms" (1986, p. 5). Current evaluation efforts of most respite and day care programs are positive, yet largely anecdotal (see French 1986, p. 26).

Some of the many service-related questions that must be addressed through high-quality research include: What are the best methods of delivering community-based services (e.g., respite care, adult day care, partial hospitalization, outreach programs, case management, or outpatient treatment)? What is the relationship between the availability of these community-based services and institutionalization; that is, do community-based services delay or prevent nursing home placement of Alzheimer's disease patients? How is access to community-based services influenced by geographic (rural/urban), racial, and socioeconomic factors? Are some Alzheimer's disease patients excluded from community-based service programs? If so, based on what criteria? How can formal community-based support services best complement and support informal caregiving interventions, and do their roles change throughout the progression of the disease? How should quality-assurance mechanisms be structured for community-based services to ensure quality standards of care? What additional types of community-based services are needed to provide a continuum of care for the noninstitutionalized Alzheimer's disease patient? Do characteristics of the service delivery system affect the therapeutic modality; that is, are there advantages to training caregivers in behavioral management techniques in the home versus in an outpatient setting?

In-Home Services

Home care services can play a key role in community-based care of Alzheimer's disease patients. If the ideal of home care providers teaching self-care and essential caregiving skills to the family members of Alzheimer's disease patients is realized, this could serve as a tremendous resource for decreasing caregiver stress and improving their quality of life. Although many home care agencies exist (an estimated 11,000), and more are being formed all the time, home care is not always available or of consistent quality for the Alzheimer's disease victim. Contributing to this variability is the number of distinctly different providers of home care services, including: visiting nurse associations (VNAs), homemaker/home health aide services, institutionally based agencies, government agencies (e.g., VAs, county health departments), community service organizations, hospices, and a recent proliferation of commercial firms (Nassif 1986-87). Not surprisingly, the services provided run the gamut from nonskilled, supportive services to those requiring trained health professionals providing sophisticated high-technology services such as chemotherapy and parenteral nutrition. Some home care agencies provide a full range of services, including medical equipment dealerships and social service case management (Nassif 1986-87).

Quality assurance, given the great diversity of services, is made even more difficult by the current lack of uniform national standards of care or mandatory regulatory mechanisms to ensure compliance (Nassif 1986-87, p. 8).

For Alzheimer's disease patients and their families, home care can be a valuable option only if services are available that can meet both their acute medical needs and their long-term maintenance needs (Holt 1986-87). Too often, home care agencies restrict their services (in large part because of Medicare reimbursement patterns) to acute, skilled services, thus limiting their usefulness for the Alzheimer's disease patient and others suffering from chronic diseases. As Holt (1986-87) noted, "To achieve a system of long-term care in the home approaching a continuum requires a broader view of client needs and funding sources" (p. 9).

Holt (1986-87, pp. 10-12) cited a number of barriers to building service systems that can be responsive to the home care needs of long-term care clients, such as Alzheimer's disease patients, including (1) Federal and State patterns of reimbursement for home care that favor intermittent, acute, skilled nursing care; (2) lack of management information systems to coordinate diverse services; (3) difficulty recruiting, training, supervising, and retaining qualified service delivery personnel; (4) need for increased case management capabilities to coordinate multiple providers; (5) diversification and reimbursement problems associated with the necessity to mix a number of funding sources in long-term care service systems; (6) the inability of many agencies to finance service diversification into the long-term care market; (7) the need to change the acute care bias currently imposed by Medicare to one that provides for continuous nonskilled supportive services as well; and (8) inappropriateness of some clients for home care.

447

This last barrier may be particularly important for Alzheimer's disease patients, many of whom will require a level of care that can best be provided in institutional settings over a long term. On a more optimistic note, a recent review of 30 projects for in-home and community-based services funded by the Administration on Aging (AOA) suggested that a number of different approaches are being tried to promote self-determination at different levels of environmental restrictiveness (Haber 1986).

One home-based alternative to the more traditional congregate site was implemented in Idaho, with the original objective to "enhance the living space of the frail elder by utilizing the home of a paraprofessional as the site of the day-care program" (Haber 1986, p. 45). Although an interesting option, this care approach was unsatisfactory to many clients and their families, and the majority of placements were eventually made in the client's, rather than the provider's, home (Cohen et al. 1984).

Haber (1986) suggested that regardless of the care setting, home-based alternatives such as the Adult Residential Day Care Program described above may have particular usefulness in rural areas where geographic distance and transportation problems can make access to congregate adult day care sites difficult. However, a similar program implemented in Pennsylvania was unsuccessful in attracting rural clients. Staff speculated that their rural clients may be more resistive to such nontraditional care approaches (Hack 1984). Clearly, the impact of cultural, geographic, and other sociodemographic factors on the acceptability and availability of service programs must be established through systematic services research.

Another innovative and promising service development for Alzheimer's disease patients and their family members is the concept of a Nursing Home Without Walls (NHWW). Recent descriptions of two such programs, in New York (Lombardi 1986-87) and Hawaii (Goto and Braun 1987), suggest that NHWWs may provide a much needed cost-effective, quality care alternative to institutionalization for patients in need of a variety of long-term care services. Alzheimer's disease patients in either the second or third stage of their illness could be eligible for NHWW services, which require that patients be medically eligible for care in a residential health care facility.

The Hawaii NHWW program, for example, provides a comprehensive array of assessment and treatment services for Medicaid recipients who need nursing home care, but who wish to receive long-term care services in their own home. An important aspect of the attractiveness of this care alternative is that the NHWW concept encourages the continued involvement of informal caregivers, as well as strives to prevent or delay institutionalization (Goto and Braun

448

1987). Among the many home-based services offered are speech and recreational therapies, social services, day care, environmental modifications and housing maintenance or home-delivered meals, homemaker/home health aide services, transportation, medical supplies and equipment, and emergency services (Goto and Braun 1987; Lombardi 1986-87). In the New York NHWW program, the great variety of services are coordinated and available round-the-clock, every day of the week.

As mandated by the program, costs for the NHWW cannot exceed 75 percent of the average cost of nursing home care. Data from the Hawaii program indicate that costs run at 61 percent of those of institutional care (Goto and Braun 1987), and the New York program reports that the average cost per patient has consistently been about half the cost of care in a skilled nursing facility (Lombardi 1986-87).

Providers in the New York NHWW program must be hospitals, residential health care facilities, or home health care agencies that have met specified criteria (Lombardi 1986-87). Nurses play a critical role in the supervision of care in these programs, assisted by social workers and a variety of paraprofessional staff. The nature and extent of the geriatric training of NHWW providers need to be more fully described.

Although, in theory, the NHWW concept appears to meet the criteria for true continuity of care, reports in the literature are still largely anecdotal and descriptive. Rigorous evaluation research needs to be conducted on the effectiveness of these promising programs in terms of cost-effectiveness, replicability, patient outcomes, and patient and family satisfaction measures.

Among the many service research issues related to home care is the question of whether Alzheimer's disease patients and their families would use in-home long-term care services not currently provided under Medicaid and Medicare, if those services became more widely available and less costly. Further, would these home care services help to delay or prevent institutionalization? How can we best assure quality of home-care services? To what extent do home-care services support the informal caregiving network of family, friends, and neighbors? Do home-care services substitute for informal caregiving and thus add to the financial burdens of local, State, and Federal governments (Haber 1986)?

Hospice care is a relatively new service delivery option. According to Federal regulations, hospice services must provide a "homelike atmosphere" and "private space" for terminally ill patients and their families (HCFA 1983), both in their own homes or through short-term hospice inpatient care units. However, operationalization of somewhat vague terms like "homelike atmosphere" could potentially lead to great variability among hospice services as well. Ideally, hospice services include medical, psychological, and social assistance by "an integrated team of professional caregivers" (Taylor 1987, p. 22).

Descriptions of model hospice programs are available in the recent gerontological literature (Taylor 1987), and preliminary descriptive and evaluative evidence suggests that hospice care may be a viable service system for Alzheimer's disease patients and their families. However, most of the hospice data are on cancer patients, and this service approach needs to be validated for an Alzheimer's disease population. Data from the National Hospice Study showed that older hospice patients in their survey had approximately the same level of functional impairment on admission to the hospice program as did younger patients. Further, hospices do not tend to draw from institutionalized elderly populations with chronic impairments such as Alzheimer's disease (Mor 1987). Part of the problem with Alzheimer's disease patients may be the unpredictability of their lifespan, and Medicare reimbursement is prospective, with a cap of $6884 per patient. Most of the research on hospice services, like that on community-based services, is anecdotal in nature, uses setting-specific instruments that are not generalizable, and in general lacks methodological rigor. Clearly, the feasibility and costs associated with hospice care for terminally ill Alzheimer's disease patients must be explored, as well as the impact of this service option on family caregivers and hospice workers.

Other Caregiver Issues

The U.S. Department of Health and Human Services Task Force on Alzheimer's Disease (1984) charged the research community to

> Identify the most effective coping strategies and interventions used by caregivers; and identify the kinds of information, education, support, and treatment that best reinforce or increase coping abilities of families with Alzheimer's disease members. (p. xiii)

Sanford (1975) classified research on the problems faced by Alzheimer's disease caregivers into three categories: (1) problematic aspects of the Alzheimer's disease patient's behavior, such as wandering, incontinence; (2) adverse effects on the caregiver's social life and environment, such as financial constraints and disrupted social activities; and (3) problems resulting from the caretaker's emotional responses to caregiving, such as depression, embarrassment, or

450

anxiety. Findings related to caregiver burden are often inconsistent, in part because of variations in definitions of caregiver stress or burden and the use of different instruments to assess burden across studies. Further, some theorists have urged a distinction between objective and subjective aspects of caregiver burden (Poulshock and Deimling 1984; Thompson and Doll 1982). Objective burden refers to disruptions in caretakers' lives due to the Alzheimer's disease patients' condition, whereas subjective burden is related to the caregivers' emotional reaction to caregiving, which could easily be influenced by such factors as their level of depression. The development of reliable and valid measures of caregiver burden, which can be discriminated from measures of depression and social desirability, are essential to future studies of caregiver stress (Russell and Cutrona 1987).

Failure to specify caregiver characteristics and experience with the disease process has also compromised the ability of researchers and clinicians to distinguish the appropriateness of interventions designed to reduce caregiver stress. However, longitudinal studies, such as those conducted by Farran (1986), Pearlin (1986), and Gallagher (1986), are now underway, seeking to identify the most effective coping strategies used by caregivers and to identify the kinds of educational and support programs that most effectively assist caregivers in their efforts to postpone nursing home placement of the Alzheimer's disease patient.

Certainly, many types of community-based groups are now available to Alzheimer's disease caregivers. These include self-help groups, such as those sponsored by the Alzheimer's Disease and Related Disorders Association (ADRDA), which provide ongoing informal groups in which caregivers support and educate each other by sharing experiences. Often professionals will present more formal educational sessions as part of the ADRDA group meeting as well. Other group approaches have included time-limited unstructured supportive and informative groups led by professionals (Clark and Rakowski 1983), and intensive structured supportive and educational groups (Glosser and Waxler 1985; Kahan et al. 1985). And yet, at present, we do not know to what extent these various types of groups meet or do not meet caregiver needs, reduce stress, or postpone nursing home placement (Mace 1985). In addition, we need more research, such as that being conducted by Farran (1986), that explicates why some caregivers do not participate in groups or withdraw from them prematurely and that identifies the degree of patient impairment and characteristics of caregivers who participate in different kinds of educational and support programs available in the community.

To design services and therapeutic modalities that minimize stress on caregivers, it is essential to examine their impact on different

451

caregivers. For example, Grunow (1986) is examining personal care aspects of caregiving such as nutrition, activities of daily living, bowel and bladder functioning, and medications. Further research is needed to identify factors associated with success and failure in caregiving activities, such as change in health status or degree of dependency of the Alzheimer's disease patient, and the strategies most useful to caregivers in coping with stressors associated with meeting the personal care needs of these patients.

One final area of needed research related to caregiver stress is derived from the work of Seligman (1975) on "learned helplessness." Recently, Pagel et al. (1985) published research on spouse caretakers of Alzheimer's disease patients suggesting that a high percentage (40 percent) of them were depressed. Further, the beliefs of these caregivers about their ability to control significant aspects of their spouse's unpredictable behavior predicted the development or continuation of depressive status over time. The role of helplessness cognitions in the development of caregiver depression warrants further examination, in caregivers of both institutionalized and community dwelling Alzheimer's disease patients.

Learned helplessness offers a viable theoretical model for examining affective changes in the caregivers of patients whose clinical course is one of unpredictability and inexorable deterioration. (See Schultz in this volume for a more indepth discussion of this paradigm.) From the perspective of services research, this paradigm may be particularly useful. Although the clinical course of Alzheimer's disease may remain unpredictable and uncontrollable, the service delivery system, if well designed and providing true continuity of care, may, in fact, be able to offer "predictable" help. The role of service delivery in structuring a predictable environment should be examined.

Service providers and researchers need to pay close attention to the findings of basic and clinical researchers. For example, the research cited by Gallagher et al. (this volume) indicating that caregivers may experience high levels of anger suggests that services research should focus on effective ways to deliver therapies involving anger management and expression.

The effectiveness of services delivery should be measured in ways that clearly reflect findings from early caregiver studies as well as measures suggested by current theory. Certainly, any assessment of the outcome of services on caregivers must include both an array of psychological (e.g., level of depression, anxiety, anger, guilt) and physical (e.g., cardiovascular and immunological) variables.

Both community-based and institutionalized Alzheimer's patients and their families have been adversely affected by gaps in the service delivery system. How to best fill those gaps to meet the special and changing needs of Alzheimer's disease patients and their families should be the focus of current and future health services research efforts. The development of a truly comprehensive and coordinated system of care, embodying the principles of continuity of care, requires better epidemiological data, more research related to the nature of Alzheimer's disease, evaluation of a variety of treatment and service setting approaches, and a better understanding of the role of the informal caregiving network vis-a-vis formal agencies (Secretary's Task Force 1984, p. 55).

To assume a static need for services in a progressively deteriorating disease is unrealistic. Rather, research is needed to determine the spectrum of services needed to individualize care at different stages of the illness, and the optimum training and staffing patterns of the various professionals and paraprofessionals who provide these services.

Acknowledgments

Trish Tunick, R.N., M.A., for assistance with sections of the manuscript dealing with clinical progression and inpatient issues.

Joan Crowe for help with manuscript preparation.

References

Ackermann, J. Separated not isolated–As basic as administrative, backing, and commitment. *Journal of Long-Term Care Administration* Fall:90-94, 1985.

"ADRDA Regional Conference Report." Paper presented at St. Paul's Lutheran Church, Cedar Rapids, IA, November 1, 1986.

Bachrach, L.L. The challenge of service planning for chronic mental patients. *Community Mental Health Journal* 22(3):170-174, 1986.

Bellack, A.S., and Mueser, K.T. A comprehensive treatment program for schizophrenia and chronic mental illness. *Community Mental Health Journal* 22(3):175-189, 1986.

Berger, D. *Family Cooperative Respite Demonstration Program.* New York: United Cerebral Palsy Association, 1984.

Brody, E.; Lawton, M.P.; and Liebowitz, B. Senile dementia: Public policy and adequate institutional care. *American Journal of Public Health* 74:1381-1383, 1984.

Buckwalter, K.C., and Hall, G.R. Families of the institutionalized older adult: A neglected resource. In: Brubaker, T.H., ed. *Aging, Health and Family: Long Term Care.* Newbury Park, CA: Sage, 1987.

Burnside, I. If I don't worry, who will? *Journal of Gerontological Nursing* 9(2):72, 1983.

Clark, N.M., and Rakowski, W. Family caregivers of older adults: Improving helping skills. *Gerontologist* 23:637-642, 1983.

Cohen, D.; Kennedy, G.; and Eisdorfer, C. Phases of change in the patient with Alzheimer's dementia: A conceptual dimension for defining health care management. *Journal of the American Geriatrics Society* 32:11-15, 1984.

Curry, J.P. "Work Stress and Morale Among Nursing Home Employees." NIMH grant #5 R01 MH42915-02, 1987.

Farran, C.J. "Examination of Caregiver Characteristics and Need for Services." Research proposal submitted to College of Nursing, Rush University, 1986.

French, C.J. The development of special services for victims and families burdened by Alzheimer's disease. *Pride Institute Journal of Long Term Health Care* 5(3):19-27, 1986.

Gallagher, D.; Wrabetz, A.; Lovett, S.; Del Maestro, S.; and Rose, J. Depression and other negative affects in family caregivers. In: (this volume).

Glosser, G., and Wexler, D. Participants' evaluation of educational/support groups for families of patients with Alzheimer's disease and other dementia. *Gerontologist* 25:232-236, 1985.

Goto, L., and Braun, K. Nursing home without walls. *Journal of Gerontological Nursing* 13(1):7-9, 1987.

Grunow, J.L. "Alzheimer Caregivers: Management of Personal Care." Nursing Research Individual National Research Service Award Application to Department of Health and Human Services, Rush University, 1986.

Gwyther, L. Introduction: What is respite care? *Pride Institute Journal of Long Term Home Health Care* 5(3):4-6, 1986.

Haber, D. In-home and community-based long-term care services: A review of recent AOA projects involving self-determination. *Journal of Applied Gerontology* 5(1):37-50, 1986.

Hack, C. *Accessing Existing Resources to Develop a Community-Based Adult Day Care Program in a Rural Community.* Lewistown, PA: Mifflin-Juniata Area Agency on Aging, 1984.

Hall, G.R.; Kirschling, M.; and Todd, S. Sheltered freedom: The creation of an Alzheimer's unit in an intermediate care facility. *Geriatric Nursing* 7:132-136, 1986.

Healthcare Financing Administration. Medicare program: Hospice care; Final rule. *Federal Register* 48(243, Part 7):56008-36, 1983.

Holt, S.W. The role of home care in long term care. *Generations* 11(2):9-12, 1986-87.

Iqbal, K., and Wisniewski, H. Neurofibrillary tangles. In: Reisberg, B., ed. *Alzheimer's Disease*. New York: Free Press, 1983. pp. 48-57.

Kahan, J.; Kemp, B.; Stamples, F.R.; and Brummel-Smith, K. Decreasing the burden in families caring for a relative with a dementing illness. *Journal of the American Geriatrics Society* 19:465-480, 1985.

Knight, B., and Walker, D.L. Toward a definition of alternatives to institutionalization for the frail and elderly. *Gerontologist* 25(4):358-363, 1985.

Laxton, C. The John D. French Center for Alzheimer's disease. *Caring* 22-24, Dec. 1985.

Lewis, P. *Camp Fire's Special Sitters Respite Care Program*. Seattle, WA: Seattle-King County Council of Camp Fire, 1985.

Lombardi, T. Nursing home without walls. *Generations* 11(2):21-24, 1986-87.

Lucas, M.; Steele, C.; and Bognanni, A. Recognition of psychiatric symptoms in dementia. *Journal of Gerontological Nursing* 12(1):11-15, 1986.

Maas, M., and Buckwalter, K. "Evaluation of a Special Alzheimer's Care Unit." Unpublished manuscript, University of Iowa, Iowa City, IA, 1986.

Maas, M.; Buckwalter, K.; and Russell, D. "Nursing Evaluation Research: Alzheimer's Care Unit." Unpublished manuscript, University of Iowa, Iowa City, IA, 1986.

Mace, N. Do we need special care units for dementia patients? *Journal of Gerontological Nursing* 11(10):37-38, 1985.

Mace, N., and Rabins, P. *The 36-Hour Day*. Baltimore, MD: Johns Hopkins University Press, 1981.

Mor, V. Hospice. *Generations* 11(3):19-22, 1987.

Nassif, J.Z. There's still no place like home. *Generations* 11(2):5-8, 1986-87.

National Institute of Mental Health. *Alzheimer's Disease: Report of the Secretary's Task Force on Alzheimer's Disease*. DHHS Pub. No. (ADM)84-1323. Washington, DC: Supt. of Docs., U.S. Govt. Print. Off., 1984.

Pagel, M.D.; Becker, J.; and Coppel, D.B. Loss of control, self-blame, and depression: An investigation of spouse caregivers of Alzheimer's disease patients. *Journal of Abnormal Psychology* 94:169-182, 1985.

Pajk, M. Alzheimer's disease inpatient care. *American Journal of Nursing* 84(2):216-222, 1984.

Pearlin, L.; Turner, H.; and Semple, S. Coping and the mediation of caregiver stress. In: (this volume).

Peppard, N. Alzheimer special-care nursing home units. *Nursing Homes* 34(5):25-28, 1985.

Pfeiffer, E. *The Impact of Specialized Alzheimer's Disease Day Care Programs on Patients and Family Caregivers*. Tampa, FL: Suncoast Gerontology Center, University of South Florida, 1985.

Poulshock, S.W., and Deimling, G.T. Families caring for elders in residence: Issues in the measurement of burden. *Journal of Gerontology* 39:230-239, 1984.

Rabins, P.V. Management of dementia in the family context. *Psychosomatics* 25:369-375, 1984.

Rader, J.; Doan, J.; and Schwab, M. How to decrease wandering, a form of agenda behavior. *Geriatric Nursing* 6:196-199, 1985.

Rathmann, K.L., and Connor, C.S. Recent advances in Alzheimer's disease. *Pharmacy International* 5:193-195, Aug. 1985.

Reifler, B.V., and Larson, E. Excess disability in dementia of the Alzheimer's type. In: (this volume).

Reisberg, B. An overview of current concepts of Alzheimer's disease, senile dementia, and age associated cognitive decline. In: Reisberg, B., ed. *Alzheimer's Disease*. New York: Free Press, 1983. pp. 3-20.

Reisberg, B.; Ferris, S.H.; de Leon, M.J.; and Crock, T. The global deterioration scale (GDS): An instrument for the assessment of primary degenerative dementia. *American Journal of Psychiatry* 139(9):1136-1139, 1982.

Ridder, M. Nursing update in Alzheimer's disease. *Journal of Neurosurgical Nursing* 17:190-200, 1986.

Rosen, W.; Mohs, R.; and Davis, K. A new rating scale for Alzheimer's disease. *American Journal of Psychiatry* 141:1356-1357, 1984.

Russell, D.W., and Cutrona, C.E. "Development and Validation of a Caregiver Burden Questionnaire." Aging Seed Grant Proposal, University of Iowa, Committee on Aging, 1987.

Salisbury, S., and Goehner, P. Separation of the confused or integration with the lucid? *Geriatric Nursing* 4:231-233, 1983.

Sanford, J.R.A. Tolerance of debility in elderly dependents by supporters at home: Its significance for hospital practice. *British Medical Journal* 23:471-473, 1975.

Schneck, M.; Reisberg, B.; and Ferris, S. An overview of the concepts of Alzheimer's disease. *American Journal of Psychiatry* 139:165-173, 1982.

Seligman, M.E.P. *Helplessness: On Depression, Development, and Death*. San Francisco: W.H. Freeman, 1975.

456

Semple, S.; Smith, C.; and Swash, M. The Alzheimer's disease syndrome. In: Corklin, S.; Davis, K.; Growden, J.H.; Usdin, E.; and Wurtman, R., eds. *Alzheimer's Disease: A Report of Progress in the Literature.* New York: Raven Press, 1982. pp. 93-108.

Shern, D.L.; Wilson, N.Z.; Ellis, R.H.; Bartsch, D.A.; and Coen, A.S. Planning a continuum of residential/service settings for the chronically mental ill: The Colorado experience. *Community Mental Health Journal* 22(3):190-202, Fall 1986.

Taylor, J. Hospice house: A homelike inpatient unit. *Generations* 11(3):22-26, 1987.

Thompson, E.H., and Doll, W. The burden of families coping with the mentally ill: An invisible crisis. *Family Relations* 379-388, July 1982.

Tunik, P.M. "Persons with Alzheimer's disease: A descriptive study of problematic behaviors and the care strategies used in the home and in community nursing homes." Unpublished master's thesis, University of Iowa, College of Nursing, 1987.

Williams, L. Alzheimer's: The need for caring. *Journal of Gerontological Nursing* 12(2):21-28, 1986.

Chapter 19

Issues and Directions in Family Intervention Research

Steven H. Zarit, Ph.D.

Introduction

Planned evaluations of interventions with families of dementia patients address the most critical social issue associated with the dementing illnesses—to what extent can families assume long-term responsibility for the care of patients without harming their own health or well-being. While many dementia patients are institutionalized, community studies continue to show that the majority live outside institutions with the support of family members or other caregivers. Community care is often in the patient's best interests, except in abusive or otherwise troubled family situations, because it minimizes the demands on them for new learning and adaptation to new routines and environmental cues. Home care may also be in the public interest, if it is associated with lower overall costs for long-term care. But it has now been clearly documented that home care can have substantial costs for family caregivers in terms of decreased physical or emotional well-being, diminished participation in work or social activities, and increased problems in the caregiver's marital and family relationships, as well as financial costs (Brody 1985; Cantor 1983; Fitting et al. 1985; George and Gwyther 1986; Gilhooly 1984; Grad and Sainsbury 1963, 1968; Morycz 1980, 1985; Poulshock and Deimling 1984; Rabins et al. 1982; Sainsbury and Grad de Alarcon 1970; Zarit et al. 1980; Zarit et al. 1986). The critical question for research is to what extent can planned programs and services directed toward patients and their families relieve the negative consequences associated with caregiving so that the costs to family caregivers are not excessive.

While there is considerable public interest in developing interventions to relieve some of the stress experienced by caregivers, clinical programs and research on their effectiveness are still in preliminary stages. The current literature primarily consists of impressionistic descriptions of programs, or of data presented on program participants but with no contrast or comparison groups (see Zarit and Anthony 1986 for a review).

The investigator who wants to conduct intervention research, however, faces obstacles at every step. There is no consensus on major research questions concerning subject selection, design, and, especially, measurement. This chapter focuses on the methodological issues involved in conducting intervention research, particularly issues of measurement and design, in the hope of stimulating more and better studies of innovative treatment programs. The chapter is organized into three major sections: (1) assessment of patient variables relevant to subject selection and outcome; (2) assessment of caregiver variables; and (3) research design issues.

Patient Variables

Intervention research should include diagnosis and severity of impairment of the patient as variables. Even though the focus of interventions may be on the family, clarification of these patient variables makes replication possible and enables researchers to consider whether the intervention's effectiveness depends on the type and/or severity of the patient's problems.

Diagnosis

The degree of imprecision and uncertainty that surrounds diagnosis of dementing illnesses can be a major stumbling block for intervention research. Because diagnosis of Alzheimer's disease can only be confirmed definitively at post mortem, any sample is likely to have some heterogeneity of underlying pathology. Yet reliable diagnosis is relevant for questions about the relative value of interventions for different disease groups, for example, Alzheimer's versus other dementias, or more broadly, cognitively impaired versus cognitively intact but physically frail elders.

Several possible approaches to diagnosis can be taken by the intervention researcher, each involving a tradeoff between the degree of precision in determining probable diagnosis and the cost involved, with more precise strategies generally involving more expense. Three major strategies for dealing with inclusion criteria can be identified: targeting families of patients with Alzheimer's disease, targeting families of patients with dementia of varied etiology, and targeting caregivers broadly without limiting the sample to those with cognitive impairment typical of dementia. The costs and benefits of each of these strategies is discussed below.

The ideal situation would be to have each patient assessed according to current research diagnosis criteria (RDC), to rule out treatable disorders and to identify probable type of dementia. The framework for conducting this type of diagnostic evaluation has been developed (McKhann et al. 1984), although the caveat that diagnosis can be definitively made only at autopsy remains. Research on interventions, however, is likely to be developed in psychosocial settings in which the comprehensive neuropsychiatric examination needed to apply the RDC is not readily available. Requiring such an examination adds considerably to the cost of evaluating psychosocial interventions. An equally problematic strategy is to require families to pay for a new medical evaluation of the patient. Counting on Medicare to pay for most or all of the cost may be unrealistic, especially since many families seeking help from a psychosocial intervention will already have taken the patient for one or more diagnostic evaluations.

The critical question, of course, is whether this type of diagnostic assessment is needed to ensure the internal validity of the research. When testing the benefits of psychosocial approaches to patients and families, it may be more important to concentrate on developing a good model and testing it well, than to devote a lot of time and resources toward determining diagnosis. Some consistent criteria, however, should be employed. The questions that seem most important are: (1) does the patient meet some operational criteria for dementia; (2) has the possibility of reversible disorder been ruled out; and (3) what is the probable type of dementia?

Adequate operational criteria for determining the presence of dementia is especially important. While diagnosis is a slippery issue, it is possible to determine that patients meet certain functional criteria consistent with a diagnosis of dementing illness. Moreover, these functional criteria will identify families who are coping with the type of problems that are targeted by the intervention, regardless of whether the underlying pathology is of the Alzheimer's type or some other condition. These criteria can be implemented without excessive costs and in nonmedical as well as medical settings.

Criteria should include a global assessment of cognitive deficit and history. Cognitive assessment can be conducted by using any of the commonly available mental status tests, such as the Mini-Mental State Examination (Folstein et al. 1975), the Short Portable Mental

Status Questionnaire (Pfeiffer 1975), or the Kahn-Goldfarb Mental Status Questionnaire (Kahn et al. 1960). Each procedure has criteria for identifying cognitive deficits consistent with a diagnosis of dementia (though, of course, none is sufficient by itself in establishing diagnosis). The Mini-Mental State is probably the most widely used and accepted procedure currently, although on some items, such as serial subtraction of 7s, effects of aging and dementia are clearly confounded. A more extended test, the Blessed Dementia Scale, has been used in British research for some time (Blessed et al. 1968) and now has been adapted for American samples (Fuld et al. 1982).

History is also a very important criterion for establishing the presence of dementia (Gurland 1980). The history should show progressive deterioration over an extended period to be consistent with a diagnosis of dementia. Patients who have experienced recent and sudden changes (even after a long period of decline), or whose conditions have been stable for an extended period, should be referred for a medical evaluation to clarify their condition before including them in a dementia sample.

The second criterion is that reversible disorders have been ruled out. When the researcher does not have the means of conducting a new medical evaluation at the time of entry into the study, it should be determined that the patient was evaluated at some point in the course of the illness. Also, any recent changes in the course and pattern of symptoms should be evaluated for possible reversible causes. While community standards for these evaluations clearly vary and it will not be possible to rule out all treatable dementias, the researcher should be able to keep the number of incorrectly diagnosed individuals to a minimum.

The third criterion, determining the probable type of dementia, is the most problematic. The patient's physician may be unreliable, since the approaches used by community practitioners for identifying type of dementia are highly variable. It is still rare for the diagnosis of Alzheimer's disease to be made according to the criteria proposed by McKhann et al. Other approaches are equally problematic. While the criteria developed by Hachinski and his colleagues (Hachinski et al. 1974; Hachinski 1983) use historical data provided by the family and the medical history, serious questions about the validity of this approach have been raised (Liston and LaRue 1983).

Some preliminary studies have used patterns of performance on psychological tests to differentiate Alzheimer's disease from other dementias (Storandt et al. 1984). However, the findings should be viewed as tentative, especially as pathological confirmation was not obtained. In addition, the differentiation was made for mildly im-

461

paired subjects. As the dementia worsens, patterns of impairment among the different illnesses could begin to converge.

While precise diagnosis is preferable, researchers should ask to what extent it is necessary for carrying out the study. Although the early symptoms and course of Alzheimer's disease and multi-infarct dementia differ slightly, by the time the patient has a moderate degree of impairment, a preliminary study found few behavioral differences and no overall difference in impact on the family (Hassinger et al. 1982). More attention should be paid to this question of the implications for families of whether the dementia is Alzheimer's, multi-infarct, or some other type. Interventions with families would seem to address a common core of functional problems that overlap sufficiently between diagnostic groups. For the purposes of intervention research, adequate documentation of the presence of what the researcher believes to be critical functional problems or demands on the family is more important than precise diagnosis.

Finally, the question can be raised whether determining the presence of dementia is necessary at all. Some studies of the stress on caregivers have used samples that included physically and mentally frail elders. While several of these studies comment on apparent relations between symptoms of dementia and caregiver stress, only one study to date (Birkel 1987) systematically examined the impact of cognitive versus physical impairments. Using sampling criteria that established groups that were homogeneous for cognitive or physical deficits (rather than mixed characteristics), he found that dementia caregivers reported significantly more emotional distress. Furthermore, factors in the household situation that mediated the stress on caregivers operated differently in the two groups. Caregivers of dementia patients who had more people in the household reported lower stress, while the reverse was true for caregivers of physically disabled elders. While this issue requires further investigation, the demands placed on caregivers by physically versus mentally frail elderly may differ sufficiently to require that dementia be treated as either an independent or exclusionary variable, depending on the nature of the intervention.

In summary, while systematic medical evaluation of all patients can provide a high degree of rigor in establishing diagnosis, this step may not be feasible in most studies of community-based psychosocial interventions. In fact, requiring that diagnosis be established in that way would slow down the development of practical knowledge about interventions. The approach recommended here is to identify persons with cognitive impairment and history consistent with dementia, with reversible causes ruled out by a prior medical evaluation. Furthermore, researchers would be advised to describe their sample as having dementia, rather than Alzheimer's disease, unless the RDC for Alzheimer's disease have been consistently applied. If caregivers of physically disabled but mentally intact elders are included, the presence or absence of dementia should be treated as an independent variable in the design.

Severity of Impairment

Severity of the patient's impairments is an important variable for intervention studies. The demands placed on caregivers clearly change over time as the dementia worsens. The degree of impairment should be documented to indicate the problems with which caregivers are coping, and to permit replication. The researcher should also consider whether specific interventions for families or patients work best when the patient is at a particular level of severity. It could be argued, for example, that day care or overnight respite would be more effective early in the course of the disease, because patients would have more ability to adjust to the new surroundings, and families would not have reached a point of exhaustion before turning for help. To cite another example, clinical reports about support groups suggest that caregivers of patients with mild deficits may not benefit as much because they are not ready to accept the implications of the diagnosis, while caregivers with severely impaired patients might not benefit because the level of demands on them is too high. Also, a critical subset of behavioral problems may be particularly difficult for caregivers, for example, when patients keep family members awake at night. If the researcher has a specific hypothesis about the effects on treatment outcome of the patient's overall severity of impairment, or about the effect of particular problems, these factors should be included as independent variables in the design.

Several options exist for rating severity, and the choice should depend on how that particular approach serves the objectives of the research. Since the focus of interventions with families is primarily on the family, measurement of patient characteristics can be brief, unless identifying particular information is important for research design and/or designing the intervention program, or measuring outcome. Possible approaches include characterizing the stage of dementia, measuring cognitive deficits, and assessing functional deficits.

Stage of dementia. Several simple frameworks for staging the severity of dementia have been proposed. Perhaps the most widely used has been the system developed by Riesberg and his colleagues (1982). Their approach combines measures of cognitive deficit and impairment in activities of daily living (ADL) to yield a rating of severity of deficits. A stage model of severity is appropriate when the study calls for a quick characterization of patients, or for matching patients on broad categories of impairment.

These measures also have some limitations. A stage measure will provide less information about individual differences in the patients' behavior than procedures that provide a more extensive profile of behavioral and cognitive deficits. Questions also remain about the validity of stages of dementia or of Alzheimer's disease. While the face validity of Riesberg's model is high, no studies have determined the extent to which symptoms actually cluster together in the manner indicated by the measure or estimated the number of people who follow unusual patterns. Clinical impressions suggest at least some variability in the type and progression of impairment, and some individuals follow a highly atypical course. Certainly, a sample with a heterogeneous etiology for dementia would likely be even more variable.

Stage models have also been proposed for characterizing the reactions of caregivers to the patient. These models have been drawn from classic psychoanalytic approaches to loss (e.g., Lindemann 1944; Kubler-Ross 1969). To date, however, no empirical attempts have been made to validate stages of caregivers' reaction. This is, in fact, likely to be a formidable task, because caregivers probably vary more among themselves in their reactions than do patients in their symptoms.

Cognitive deficits. Another approach to the measurement of severity is to determine the extent of cognitive deficit through mental status testing and/or more extensive neuropsychological testing. The use of mental status tests has several advantages. They can be administered to determine the presence of dementia-related deficits, so the data needed for estimating severity in this way will already be available. Second, the commonly used procedures all have adequate documentation of their overall validity; for example, subjects who score more poorly on mental status tests generally have more functional problems (Whitlatch et al. 1986), are at higher risk for mortality (Goldfarb et al. 1966), and have more extensive cerebral pathology at post mortem (Blessed et al. 1968).

These measures have some limitations, however. First, the sample of cognitive behavior is brief and limited to a few domains, usually information and memory. Even the Mini-Mental State Examination, which assesses constructional and naming abilities, only includes a couple of items. As a result, the variance among subjects will be decreased, compared to more extensive testing. These measures are sensitive to gross differences in severity, but do not permit finer distinctions such as whether some abilities are more affected than others. Although dementia has been characterized as a global deficit, recent studies have pointed to more selective patterns of changes, especially in the early stages of Alzheimer's disease (Storandt et al. 1984).

Second, these measures have a floor effect. Severely impaired subjects will be unable to answer any items correctly, even though performance on other abilities, particularly functional tasks, can be somewhat intact. Thus, these tests provide little differentiation among the most severely impaired patients.

Third, cognitive tasks are only an approximate indicator of the extent of functional impairment, which may be the more relevant variable for the intervention researcher. In a recent study, three mental status tests (Kahn-Goldfarb MSQ, Mini-Mental State Examination, Dementia Rating Scale) showed moderate degrees of correlation (in the range of .30 to .44) with ADL and behavioral impairment measures (Whitlatch et al. 1986). For one subset of behavioral disturbance items—patient's emotional symptoms, which was found to be an important predictor of caregiver distress by Niederehe and his associates (1983)—the relationship with mental status scores was negligible.

More extensive neuropsychological testing provides more precise estimates of the extent and types of cognitive deficits present. Neuropsychological testing may also generate information useful for planning interventions. If a prominent naming deficit is identified, for example, the patient's functional problems can be reviewed to determine if and how the naming deficit may be a contributing factor to everyday problems, and appropriate strategies for management developed. As this example indicates, more extensive neuropsychological assessment would be expected to predict the degree of functional impairment better than mental status tests.

Strong associations between neuropsychological test performance and functional status of Alzheimer's patients have been reported (Vitaliano et al. 1984). While neuropsychological assessments provide better estimates of overall severity than mental status tests, the researcher whose primary interest is in documenting the presence and magnitude of common functional problems would do better to assess those directly, rather than inferring a level of impairment from cognitive performance.

One standardized measure of neuropsychological performance, which was developed specifically for this population, is the Mattis Dementia Rating Scale (Coblentz et al. 1973). This measure provides brief assessments in several domains: initiation and perseveration, memory, attention, constructional abilities, and conceptualization.

The time needed to complete this instrument is not excessive, and it provides a broader range of information than standard mental status examinations.

Functional problems. The patient's behavioral deficits in carrying out everyday activities and the behavioral disturbances that affect family life represent the most direct demands placed on caregivers. Several measures of functional problems have been reported in the literature, with considerable overlap among the behaviors sampled (Greene et al. 1982; Haycox 1984; Niederehe and Fruge 1984; Poulshock and Deimling 1984; Riesberg et al. 1981; Weintraub et al. 1982; Zarit and Zarit 1983; Zarit et al. 1986). These measures assess failure to carry out typical activities of daily living and the extent to which problematic or troubling behavior is present.

Following Lawton (1971), most measures include indicators of impairment in physical activities of daily living (P-ADL) including dressing, bathing, and toileting, and instrumental activities of daily living (I-ADL), such as handling money, shopping, and housework. While some researchers have omitted instrumental activities, that domain is affected earlier in the disease and can place major demands on caregivers.

The various measures also differ in their scaling of the degree of impairment. ADL scales were originally developed and validated on physically impaired samples, and the scaling reflects gradations of incapacity to perform activities, such as partially dependent and totally dependent. More than with physical disabilities, dementia involves the interface of physical and mental impairments. Early in dementias, patients may be physically able to carry out some activities, but lack the attention or memory to complete the sequence of activities involved. In some situations, caregivers may find they can get the patient to perform the activity by supervising it and providing step-by-step instructions. In other instances, the patient may become obstinate and refuse to carry out the activity, or become combative, for example, if the caregiver tries to dress the patient. Later in the disease, physical impairment may account for the inability to carry out activities, although even then, cognitive factors may still be more important. Clinical experience, for example, suggests that even fairly late in the course of Alzheimer's disease, incontinence can be reversed by setting up a regular schedule of toileting. To date, none of the available scales have fully addressed these problems in scaling impairments in ADLs.

For the purposes of intervention research, it seems critical to determine which tasks require the caregiver to provide partial or complete assistance, which tasks require supervision, and which are problematic because of the patient's resistance. It should be pointed out that level of impairment measured in this way represents an interaction between the patient's illness and the caregiver's coping responses. Some caregivers may decide to dress a patient, when supervision alone would be sufficient, thereby creating an "excess disability" (Kahn 1975) and, in some cases, provoking a certain amount of resistance.

Measures of behavioral disturbances have been developed generally from clinical experience. Factor analysis has sometimes been conducted to develop subscales of items. This approach is problematic because data were obtained from samples that were heterogeneous with respect to diagnosis, and also quite varied in extent of impairment. Because Alzheimer's disease and the other dementing illnesses are progressive disorders, it is possible that the relations among disabilities change over time. Furthermore, factor analysis based on cross-sectional data may yield scales that depend on the particular mix of patients in that sample, rather than an underlying pattern of disability.

Niederehe and Fruge (1984) took another approach. On an a priori basis, they divided items on their TRIMS Behavioral Problems Checklist into five subscales that they believed reflected major subtypes of disability, including cognitive symptoms, self-care deficits (ADLs), emotional behavior, management problems, and other behavior problems that represented changes in the person but did not require the caregiver to monitor or intervene. They tested the subscales for internal consistency and then used a principle components factor analysis to confirm the subscale structure. Although this approach is still limited by the cross-sectional nature of the data, it proceeds from a conceptual to a statistical model, rather than just providing a mathematical solution to the researchers' dilemma of reducing large amounts of discrete behavioral items to more manageable units.

Another aspect of the psychometric properties of these measures is their reliability and validity. Most researchers have reported internal reliabilities that are in acceptable ranges. No studies have looked at interrater reliability or, since most measures depend on the reports of caregivers, the extent to which their ratings correlate with an independent observer's. The validity of these measures has also been estimated through correlations with other indicators of severity, such as cognitive test scores. While there is generally a strong association, the total scores do not continue to increase as the dementia progresses, because some behavioral problems no longer occur (Zarit et al. 1986). Wandering and paranoid accusations are two examples of behaviors that tend to lessen as the disease progresses. To use a functional measure as an index of overall severity of the disease, it is necessary to modify the scaling to indicate if behavioral disturbances had occurred in the past, even if they are no longer evident. For purposes of estimating the current demand on caregivers, however, this modification is not necessary.

When designing an intervention study, the researcher needs to consider whether to target caregivers who are coping with particular problems. As examples, the intervention might focus on families who are coping with agitated patients or those who are awake at night.

A broader issue is whether specific problems or deficits are especially troublesome or upsetting to families. Some studies have addressed this issue, although without reaching a consensus. One problem is that the behavior categories used in some studies are very broad (e.g., confusion, memory loss) so that it is difficult to determine what behaviors were specifically troublesome. In one interesting approach, Sanford (1975) asked families to rate the degree to which they could tolerate various behaviors and reported that tolerance was lowest for sleep disturbance, immobility, daytime wandering, aggressive or dangerous behavior, and fecal incontinence. Haley and his associates (Haley et al. in press) had families rate stressfulness of various problems. They found that I-ADL problems had a high prevalence, but were generally rated least stressful; ADL problems were judged to be somewhat more stressful; and a set of behavioral problems similar to those noted by Sanford, including agitation, embarrassing behavior, hallucinations, hiding things, engaging in potentially dangerous activities, and incontinence, were the most stressful. In a somewhat surprising outcome, Niederehe and his associates (1983) reported that the patient's emotional behavior (e.g., crying, irritability, emotional lability) was highly correlated with their measures of family stress. This finding is noteworthy since most other studies have not looked at this dimension of the patient's behavior.

Family Variables

Certainly, the most important issue for intervention research is what family or caregiver variables should be measured to adequately select subjects for treatment and/or evaluate outcome. Such variables would assess the common experiences of caregivers (burden, strain, depression) and the specific goals and objectives targeted by the intervention. These two areas can overlap, but typically an intervention addresses the broader problems of caregiving, for example, reducing burden through some intermediate action, such as increasing social support. The outcome, then, needs to be evaluated at both levels–did social support change specifically and did the caregiver's global assessment of burden improve? A third dimension is subjects' evaluations of the intervention, including their overall satisfaction and ratings of what aspects of the treatment they found helpful.

While there is widespread agreement that caregiving is stressful, no consensus has emerged about the best way to characterize the impact or stress on family members. This problem has been exacerbated by a considerable degree of semantic confusion (to which this author has been one of several contributing parties). The terms burden, strain, and stress, in particular, are defined and operationalized in different ways by different researchers. Disagreement has also arisen over whether summary measures or separate factors are more appropriate.

To address the problems created by confusing terminologies, several major papers on caregiving issues were reviewed. What emerges is, despite differences in terminologies, a general agreement about the areas that should be measured to study the impact on families. In discussing the overlap among constructs used in these studies, I have avoided using those terms (e.g., burden) that were defined and operationalized in different ways by researchers.

Three areas were consistently identified by most researchers: demands on the caregiver (or family), the caregiver's perception of demands as stressful, and the consequences of those demands. Patient care demands and the consequences of those demands need to be clearly differentiated. Demands involve the objective tasks or events caregivers must cope with, while the consequences are the impact of those events on the caregiver's life. Some researchers also propose an intervening dimension, the extent to which a particular task, event, or behavior is perceived by the caregiver to be stressful. How these three areas have been named and operationalized is summarized in table 19-1.

Besides these three main areas, potential mediators of burden were identified, especially coping response, social supports, and the quality and type of relationship (e.g., spouse, parent-child) between patient and caregiver. A model of stress associated with caregiving that appears to underlie most studies is summarized in figure 19-1. Each area is discussed below.

A major variation on this model should be noted. Poulshock and Deimling (1984) characterized depression as both contributing to the consequences of caregiving (in their framework, disturbed elder-caregiver and caregiver-family relationships) and indicating outcome. This formulation is consistent with current models of depression. Poulshock and Deimling do not, however, expand on the specific ways depression may contribute to other negative outcomes. The other

Table 19-1. Current perspectives and terminology on measuring the dimensions of caregiving

	Demands on caregiver	Caregiver's perception of demands as stressful	Consequences for caregiver
George & Gwyther (1986)			Normative measures of WELL-BEING; Physical health, Mental health, Social participation, Financial resources
Montgomery, Gonyea, & Hooyman (1985)	ADLs. Tasks performed by the caregiver		Changes in the time, energy, family life, health and activities of caregivers, called OBJECTIVE BURDEN
			Affective responses to changes changes in the patient or in one's lifestyle, called SUBJECTIVE BURDEN
Morycz (1985)	Tasks involving physical labor (e.g., ADLs); Tasks involving vigilance (e.g., wandering)—called OBJECTIVE STRESS		". . . (burden is) manifested by feelings of depression, anger, embarrassment, fatigue, perception of poor health, sleep disturbance, reduction of leisure and social activities, or simply in more generalized feelings that the present overall situation is not managed well, is unsatisfactory, and is burdensome." (p. 333)—called BURDEN or STRAIN Likelihood of institutionalization as a consequence of burden
Niederehe & Fruge (1984)	TRIMS Behavior Problems Checklist, Subgroups— Cognitive symptoms, Self-care deficits, Emotional behavior, Management problems, Behavioral changes.	Caregiver's reaction to behavior problems ("how upsetting the problem is")	Caregiver's mental health, physical health, social role functioning, subjective sense of caregiving (called SUBJECTIVE STRAIN), and perception of the quality of their family life
Poulshock & Deimling (1984)	Impairment of elder; ADL impairment, and Mental impairment	The extent to which ADL or mental impairment was found tiring, difficult, or upsetting by caregiver—called BURDEN	Negative changes in elder caregiver and caregiver-family relationships; Restrictions in caregivers' activities—called IMPACT (NOTE—Depression is seen both as a contributing factor and consequence)
Zarit & Zarit (1982); Zarit, Todd, & Zarit (1986)	Memory and Behavior Problems Checklist; Frequency of ADL impairments and behavioral disturbances	The extent to which behavioral deficits are perceived as difficult to tolerate or upsetting by caregiver	Perceived impact of caregiving on several domains, including, physical and emotional well-being, family life, personal activities, and finances, called BURDEN; Psychiatric symptoms; Institutionalization as an outcome of burden

Figure 19-1. A model of the dimensions of caregiver stress

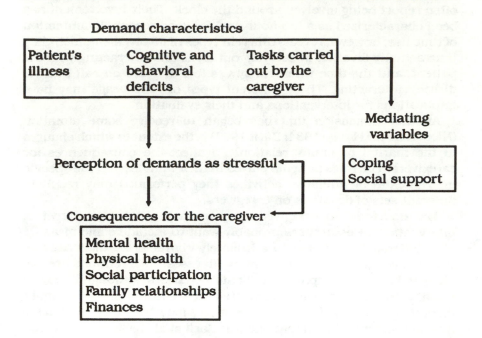

articles reviewed treat mental health variables such as depression as outcomes rather than antecedent variables.

Demands on the Caregiver

The demands on the caregiver were measured by characterizing the functional impairment of patients in the major caregiving studies shown in table 19-1. The measures used include several reviewed earlier in the discussion of assessment of the patient, but here the focus is on the caregiver. A potentially important distinction is between all the care demands presented by the patient and those for which the caregiver being studied is actually responsible. Both dimensions are interesting from the perspective of quantifying the demands in the caregiving situation. Preliminary data suggest that having help with some of the caregiving demands reduces the emotional strain experienced by family members (Zarit et al. 1980; Birkel 1987).

Demands may be characterized in ways other than the number of tasks caregivers carry out. One area is the amount of time the caregiver actually devotes to activities. When the primary caregiver does not live in the same household, estimating time of involvement is fairly straightforward. In shared households, however, caregivers often report being involved around the clock. Their involvement has been characterized as a "36-hour day" for good reason. Examination of time use, however, reveals different types of involvement, including time actually involved in carrying out tasks and interacting with the patient, and the time when caregivers feel they are on call but not directly interacting. These different types of time usage may have implications for interventions and their evaluation.

Another dimension that has begun to receive some attention (Niederehe and Fruge 1984; Zarit 1982) is the extent to which changes in the marital or family relationship affect the consequences for caregivers. The roles patients played in their families and the specific instrumental or affiliative activities they performed may result in different sets of demands on caregivers.

The demands on caregivers may or may not be the target of interventions. Researchers probably want to include some measure of functional impairment to adequately characterize their sample. Because of the nature of dementing illnesses, interventions are not likely to have large impact on patients' behaviors, although it may be possible to modify specific behaviors that are troubling to the family. Incontinence and agitation, for example, may be partly modifiable through behavioral interventions (see Zarit et al. 1985; Pinkston and Linsk 1984). If that is one goal of the intervention, then the specific behaviors being targeted and the extent to which caregivers or other persons actually implement the treatment should be measured in a reliable way. Self-reports of caregivers about how they carried out a plan and its results have unknown reliability, but may be the best obtainable data because of the expense and intrusiveness of in-home observations. The number of tasks caregivers carry out may change even though the patient's behavior has not been modified, if more assistance becomes available as the result of the intervention. Again, the optimal strategy is to identify the specific goals of the treatment and to measure change in those areas. As an example, an in-home respite program might want to relieve caregivers of the responsibility for certain tasks (e.g., dressing the patient) and to increase the amount of time caregivers have for personal activities. Both those objectives, then, would be directly assessed.

Caregiver's Perceptions of Demands

Caregivers' idiosyncratic responses to the behavioral disturbances and other demands caused by the patient's disease have been considered an important intervening variable by several researchers

472

(Sanford 1975; Poulshock and Deimling 1984; Zarit and Zarit 1982; Zarit et al. 1986). Changes in this dimension may reflect treatment effects. Caregivers' estimates of the stressfulness of behaviors may change if they adopt more effective strategies for managing these problems, if they receive periodic relief from the demands of care, or if they reappraise how they view the problem (Zarit et al. 1986).

Reappraisals of the patient's behavior may be especially important. Different caregivers may appraise the same behaviors in different ways. One may view incontinence as a terrible problem, while another can take it in stride. Similarly, some caregivers change their appraisals over time and are better able to tolerate impairments that previously were upsetting (Zarit et al. 1986). Although it would be desirable to measure the particular mechanisms—coping and support—believed to underlie changes in caregivers' perceptions of the stressfulness of events, there may not always be straightforward ways of measuring them.

Consequences of Caregiving

The most critical area for intervention research, and the one that causes the most disagreement, is evaluation of the consequences or impact of caregiving. Controversy exists over whether special measures should be utilized with this population, whether global or factor-derived measures of impact are better, and whether objective and subjective indicators of impact should be treated separately. The various approaches used for measuring consequences are summarized in table 19-1.

Several domains of life are potentially affected by being a caregiver. Early studies were concerned with changes in the health and mental health of caregivers and in the financial impact (Lowenthal et al. 1967). Other consequences include negative changes in family relationships that result from caregiving activities, negative changes in the caregiver-elder relationship, and changes in work or social activities (see table 19-1). Most studies, however, did not systematically evaluate all of these domains simultaneously, but concentrated on one or two areas or used a summary measure that relies on a small number of items to indicate changes in a domain.

The measurement strategies used for evaluating consequences for caregivers included development of new scales to reflect specific effects of caregiving and the use of measures that have been normed on other populations. George and Gwyther (1986) have been the primary advocates of the use of normed measures for evaluating the stress on caregivers. They proposed that the relative impact of caregiving can be assessed more clearly if scores of caregivers are compared to appropriate normative and stressed populations. Are the burdens of caregivers, for example, more severe than those of single parents?

The relative burden of caregiving has important policy implications. If the impact is no greater on the family than for other stressful situations, then it becomes problematic to argue that special resources and policies are necessary. In their study, George and Gwyther compared caregivers to normative populations on measures of physical health, mental health, social participation, and financial resources. Major differences were found on the mental health and social participation variables. The lack of significant differences on the financial measures needs to be viewed with caution, however. The financial obligations of spouses and children are quite different, with the former faced with bearing the cost of nursing home care. This difference was not explored in the study. Differences in measures of mental health between caregivers and normative populations that were matched for age were also reported by Anthony, Zarit, and Gatz (1986).

Normed measures also have some disadvantages, namely, that they may not be specific enough to identify some of the consequences of caregiving. Measures developed especially for the caregiving situation, such as changes in elder-caregiver or caregiver-family relationships, or restrictions in leisure or personal activities, may be better choices in an intervention study if those areas have been targeted for the intervention. Also, while normed measures indicate differences from a reference sample, they do not provide an estimate of intra-individual differences; that is, a caregiver may not score worse on a mental health measure than average respondents, but still might have experienced a decline compared to previous or characteristic level of functioning. This perceived sense of decline may have considerable relevance for understanding how caregivers make decisions about the care situation, for example, when thinking about institutionalization. Furthermore, this approach frees caregiver research from a focus solely on pathology. While depression or health problems are important for many caregivers, the primary concern for others may be the sense that their quality of life has changed for the worse. Interventions may choose to focus on these perceived changes, rather than on a construct like depression, especially if subjects' depression scores are not consistently elevated.

A related issue in choice of measures is whether global or domain-specific measures should be used. George and Gwyther (1986) and Poulshock and Deimling (1984) argued that total scores do not allow for examination of different antecedents of impact or the relative impact on different domains. Responding to this position, Montgomery,

Stull, and Borgatta (1985b) wrote that . . . "there is no notion of a single measure of burden, but this should not preclude the notion that there are summary and cumulative measures" (p. 142). A summary measure is justified if it is assumed that the accumulation of stress, rather than any particular set of problems, leads to the breakdown of the family care system. A related assumption is that caregivers can tolerate different types of stress, and that caretaking breaks down when the changes are significant to that particular caregiver. In other words, some caregivers may willingly tolerate changes in social activities, while others do not. A cumulative score provides a comparison across subjects while allowing for these individual differences.

This assumption that the accumulation of strain across domains, rather than strain in one particular area, is the best predictor of breakdown of family care can be tested empirically. One preliminary study looked at factors related to institutionalization and found that a combination of the severity of the patient's functional impairment and the caregiver's total score of subjective burden predicted institutionalization (Hassinger and Zarit 1986).

Factor scores derived from the burden measure improved the prediction slightly, with subscales indicating caregiver anger, patient dependency, and caregiver lack of privacy as the best predictors. The model tested was improved only slightly (75 percent of cases correctly identified versus 63 percent by using the factor-derived scales).

The choice of a global or domain-specific measure, then, may depend on the research question being asked. For identifying the nature and severity of consequences of caregiving, domain-specific measures are more appropriate. But when considering the cumulative effects of all the negative changes caregivers have experienced, a global measure that sums across several areas may be more useful.

A related issue is what criteria to use for choosing measures within a particular domain. One consideration for intervention studies is that the measure needs to be sensitive to change. If a scale measures a characteristic that is likely to be stable, it is unreasonable to expect any effects from treatment. Personality traits are a good example of stable characteristics, while mood or morale is more likely to change. Similarly, health-seeking behavior (e.g., visits to the doctor) may be more stable than the amount of stress-related symptoms.

One way of characterizing this diverse information is to consider the direct impact that caregiving has had on several domains of life, the degree of acceptability associated with each area of impact, and the extent to which health and well-being change. This model of consequences builds on the work of Montgomery and her associates (Montgomery et al. 1985a, b). They proposed a distinction between objective and subjective burden. Objective burden is defined as the specific "events, happenings, and activities resulting from caregiving" (Montgomery et al. 1985a, p. 21), including such things as changes in time for one's self, privacy, finances, energy, and family relationships. Subjective burden, in contrast, represents an affective dimension of the impact of objective burdens on the caregiver. This distinction is similar to the one made above between specific behavioral disturbances and caregivers' perception of them as stressful. In this case, however, each area of objective burden is not assessed for its subjective impact; rather, global scores for objective and subjective burden are obtained. The value of this distinction was supported by their findings, which suggested different predictors for objective and subjective burden. Objective burden was more strongly related to tasks that restricted the caregiver, while subjective burden was associated with characteristics of the caregiver (e.g., income, age).

Underlying the distinction between objective and subjective burden is the assumption that caregivers will react in variable ways to the restrictions imposed upon them. One caregiver may look at restrictions on leisure or social activities as an acceptable sacrifice with negative consequences, while for another, they may produce strong feelings of hardship or other adverse consequences. Similarly, tasks that take time and effort may present unacceptable demands, because of their impact on health and/or mental health, for some caregivers but not others. The literature makes assumptions about which types of sacrifices are unacceptable to caregivers, but this point has not been tested empirically.

These three broad areas—changes in the caregiver's life, the sense that these changes are unacceptable or burdensome, and the potential for negative changes in health and mental health—represent a promising framework for evaluating the consequences of caregiving. The choice of specific measures for an intervention study depends on several factors, including the objectives of the intervention and characteristics of the sample of caregivers being studied.

In deciding on measures, careful consideration should be given to the impact of the intervention. A global burden measure may be misleading in that several domains are sampled without considering the areas most likely to be affected by the intervention. For example, one objective of day care is to provide respite for caregivers so they can rest and/or carry out personal activities. These areas need to be assessed directly to evaluate the outcome of the intervention. In fact, although it seems reasonable to assume that caregivers will benefit from increased free time, clinical impressions suggest that this may not always be the case. Sometimes, aspects of the program may minimize its effectiveness, for example, if the patient is away for a brief time, or the caregiver has to provide transportation. In other cases, the caregiver may have difficulty accepting this type of help. When interventions target different consequences of caregiving, those areas should be specifically measured.

Other Issues

Five additional issues pertaining to caregiver variables are relevant to the planning of intervention studies: use of specific entry criteria, limitations of self-report measures, measurement of hypothesized mediators of consequences, assessment of caregivers' perceptions of the intervention, and relation of caregiver and patient behaviors.

Entry criteria. The use of entry criteria that select particular caregivers for an intervention may be important, depending on the goals of the intervention. This is particularly true when the researcher believes the treatment will have a specific effect on a domain. Caregivers who are not having problems in that domain would then be inappropriate for the intervention.

This issue can be best illustrated by looking at mental health variables. Although evidence is accumulating that caregiving has negative consequences for mental health, it cannot be assumed that all caregivers entering a study will have elevated scores on the measures being used to assess treatment effects. Caregivers may have considerable concern about their situations because of unacceptable changes in some domains of life, but these may not include decreased mental health. If an intervention targets mental health measures, such as depression, for change, the inclusion of subjects whose depression scores are not elevated will reduce the likelihood of demonstrating change (Zarit et al. 1987; Haley et al. in press).

An additional problem arises from including subjects whose scores are in normal ranges on mental health or morale scales. These measures may not be as sensitive in showing changes within normal ranges of functioning. As a result, the researcher will not be able to assess any changes that may occur.

This problem can be overcome by using specific entry criteria that select a sample appropriate for the intervention in the first place. If the treatment is intended to reduce feelings of depression or the occurrence of stress-related health symptoms, for example, then entry criteria need to be developed to ensure that caregivers who receive treatment have the problem targeted by the intervention. The criteria should be operationalized as clearly as possible. Impressions, such as the caregiver sounded stressed on the telephone, should be avoided because of their lack of precision.

477

A weakness of this approach is that it may limit the intervention to a subset of caregivers, while others might benefit in different ways. If the costs of caregiving can vary from one caregiver to another, then a different approach would be to determine individually what domains each subject feels have been affected, and to use measures of those areas as the dependent variables. This strategy, however, limits researchers' ability to demonstrate comparability across subjects.

Entry criteria would differ if the purpose of the intervention were primarily preventative. In that case, it would be optimal to identify subjects before these negative changes occur. The hypothesis would be that the intervention would minimize some set of potentially harmful consequences to health, mental health, or some other domain.

Use of self-report measures. Researchers and clinicians frequently observe that at least some caregivers significantly underreport their level of distress (Gallagher et al. 1986). It may be useful, therefore, to use multimodal methods of assessment, for example, combining self-reports with observer ratings of key variables.

Measurement of mediating variables. Treatments may focus on mediators of the impact of the dementia on caregivers, for example, by teaching new coping strategies or increasing utilization of social resources. If changing these potential mediators is the focus, then it is desirable to measure them as part of the research protocol. Social support and coping, however, are complex constructs, and straightforward measurement strategies do not exist. Social support has many dimensions, including number of people in the social network, frequency of interactions, types and closeness of relationships, geographic proximity of key people, and the specific types of assistance provided. To the extent that a specific domain of support is targeted in the treatment—for example, increasing the assistance the caregiver receives—then that area should be measured.

The measurement of coping is more difficult, but some promising conceptual and measurement approaches have been developed (e.g., Pearlin and Schooler 1979; Lazarus and Folkman 1984; Billings and Moos 1981, 1985). The value of these approaches either for planning or evaluating treatment has not been established. These measures may not, in fact, be sensitive to the type of change targeted in interventions, which focus on increasing specific sets of responses rather than changing overall coping style. The problem facing researchers in this area may be a chicken-and-egg dilemma—there is no agreement on better coping responses and no existing measure of optimal responses.

478

Subjects' impressions of the intervention. Two other areas of measurement for intervention studies are subjects' satisfaction with the program or treatment, and their perception of what elements of the intervention were helpful to them. These types of evaluations may be quite positive, even in the absence of changes in other domains (Haley et al. in press; Zarit et al. in press). By considering the elements that caregivers find helpful, the researcher will be able to construct better measures for treatment outcome for subsequent studies.

Impact of changes on the patient. Patients as well as caregivers are involved in interventions and the impact should be measured on both of them. Change or well-being among patients is difficult to measure, however. Their overall cognitive and behavioral abilities are not likely to change much as the result of psychosocial interventions, although some small improvements may be possible. Patients are also not reliable reporters of their own affective states, so that self-report measures can present a misleading picture. New approaches to evaluations of patients are needed that operationalize quality of life issues in ways that can be assessed with cognitively impaired individuals.

Design Issues

Major design issues for intervention studies include the choice of an appropriate control group and the need to account for other variables that may influence the outcome measures.

Control Groups

Control groups are a necessary, and almost universally neglected, part of an adequate research design in intervention studies with the frail elderly. Because of the complexity of conducting applied research, it may not always be possible to have truly random assignment into treatment and control groups, but a number of methods are available for evaluating the effects of interventions with appropriate comparison groups.

Random assignment into treatment and no-treatment groups provides the researcher with the most control. The use of no-treatment control groups, however, presents several problems. While it is possible to provide minimal treatment to control group subjects for a short period of time, withholding treatment over longer periods raises ethical and public relations problems. The ethical issues are

479

especially critical if some subjects are experiencing clinically significant depression or health problems.

Another problem, well documented in the psychotherapy literature, is that subjects in a no-treatment condition are not necessarily passive. They may be making significant changes in their situation that affect the dependent measures. This problem is especially true for longer control periods, but even during a short waiting-list period, caregivers were found to make changes in their situation which had been targeted by the treatment being offered, including using more social services (Zarit et al. 1987).

One way around this problem is to compare caregivers in two treatments that have theoretically different effects. This strategy also controls for the possibility that nonspecific factors, such as the attention and concern of other people, is the major source of change. A comparison of two or more treatments, however, does not allow for comparison of long-term benefits with an untreated group.

A more practical approach in many situations is to use a quasi-experimental design, in which subjects in one community receive an experimental intervention, while residents of a comparable community are evaluated but do not receive any specific services other than what is normally available. This approach has some risks, for example, subjects in the two communities might differ in some important characteristics, such as SES, or the presence of an intervention in one community might lead to some selection bias, that is, a particular subgroup of caregivers seek out the treatment. If these problems can be controlled, this design offers the potential for an adequate, long-term comparison group, against which the benefits of a particular treatment can be evaluated. The researcher should not view the control subjects as inactive, however, but should determine what services or treatments they use during the control period.

Another approach that may be especially appropriate for pilot studies is the single-case experimental design, in which subjects serve as their own controls (Barlow and Hersen 1984). The classic single-case design is A-B-A—a baseline period followed by treatment followed by a reversal. The major problem with this design is the need for reversal. While the reversal demonstrates that the observed changes are due to the intervention, rather than to extraneous variables, it may not be feasible for ethical reasons or because subjects will not cooperate. For example, caregivers who are trained to use a behavioral management approach for controlling problem behaviors might continue to employ those procedures in the reversal period, especially if they have proven effective. There may be instances in which the reversal can be achieved. At the least, however, a baseline which precedes treatment (A-B) offers more potential control for pilot studies than if the first measurements occur at the start of treatment.

One strategy that should be avoided is to use samples of convenience as control groups, such as subjects who refuse to participate in the intervention or who drop out during treatment. These groups are important to consider as part of the overall evaluation of the intervention, but their reasons for dropping out are likely to be related to some aspects of the intervention. That makes them inappropriate as an untreated control group, even if they do not differ from other subjects on demographic or dependent measures.

Other Variables That Might Affect Outcome

Depending on the researcher's question and characteristics of the sample, it may be necessary to control other variables that might be related to outcome measures. Issues that need to be considered include diagnosis, family structure, and SES.

The need to control for diagnostic indicators depends on the hypothesized effects of the intervention and characteristics of the sample. When the patient population includes cognitively impaired and cognitively intact individuals, it is critical to control for this dimension and to test for differential effects of the treatment within each patient-caregiver group and for interactions. In a sample composed only of dementia patients, it would be desirable to control for the diagnosis of Alzheimer's disease versus other types of dementia, although this difference may not be as critical for psychosocial studies. Severity of the patients' deficits, however, may be an important dimension affecting response by caregivers to the intervention. Severity should be treated as an independent variable whenever the researcher has hypotheses about its effects on response to treatment.

As with diagnosis, family structure raises complex problems for the design of intervention studies. Perhaps the most important dimensions of family structure in caregiving research are whether the patient lives with the caregiver and the relationship of caregiver and patient. Since the impact of the illness is likely to be significantly different depending on whether the patient lives with the caregiver or not, the effect of living situation should be evaluated. Relationship is also likely to have a significant effect on dependent variables and, therefore, on response to treatment (Boutselis 1985; Zarit et al. 1987).

SES variables as well as culture and ethnicity could also affect response to intervention. Most intervention studies will not have a sample large enough to test in a systematic way for main effects or interactions of all these variables. If the researcher has a hypothesis about the effects of SES or ethnicity, then that variable needs to be

481

included in the design. Generally, however, it may only be possible to assess the correlation of these variables with dependent measures, and to determine if dropouts or other nonresponders differ from other subjects in SES or ethnicity.

Summary

This chapter reviews major issues that pertain to conducting research on interventions with caregivers of dementia patients. In developing a research protocol, the investigator needs to consider patient variables, caregiver variables, and appropriate strategies for design. Although considerable disagreement exists over measurement approaches, a consensus is gradually emerging on conceptualizations of caregiver stress. Well-designed studies that measure critical variables are needed to clarify the problems faced by caregivers and to test hypotheses about the effectiveness of various interventions.

References

Anthony, C.R.; Zarit, S.H.; and Gatz, M. Symptoms of psychological distress among caregivers of dementia patients. *Psychology and Aging*, in press.

Barlow, D.H., and Hersen, M. *Single Case Experimental Designs*. 2d ed. New York: Pergamon, 1984.

Billings, A.G., and Moos, R.H. The role of coping responses and social resources in attenuating the stress of life events. *Journal of Behavioral Medicine* 4:139-157, 1981.

Billings, A.G., and Moos, R.H. Psychosocial stressors, coping, and depression. In: Beckham, E., and Leber, W., eds. *Handbook of Depression: Treatment, Assessment, and Research*. Homewood, IL: Dorsey, 1985. pp. 940-974.

Birkel, R.C. Toward a social ecology of the home-care household. *Psychology and Aging*. 2:294-301, 1987.

Blessed, G.; Tomlinson, B.; and Roth, M. The association between quantitative measures of dementia and of senile change in the cerebral gray matter of elderly subjects. *British Journal of Psychiatry* 114:797-811, 1968.

Boutselis, M.A. "The Effects of Gender and Relationship on Caregiver Burden, Distress and Responsivity to Intervention." Unpublished dissertation, University of Southern California, Los Angeles, 1985.

Brody, E.M. Parent care as a normative family stress. *Gerontologist* 25:19-29, 1985.

Cantor, M.H. Strain among caregivers: A study of experience in the United States. *Gerontologist* 23:597-604, 1983.

Coblentz, J.M.; Mattis, S.; Zingesser, L.H.; Kassof, S.S.; Wisniewski, H.M.; and Katzman, R. Presenile dementia. *Archives of Neurology* 29:299-308, 1973.

Fitting, M.; Rabins, P.; Lucas, M.J.; and Eastham, J. Caregiver for dementia patients: A comparison of husbands and wives. *Gerontologist* 26:248-252, 1986.

Folstein, M.F.; Folstein, S.E.; and McHugh, P.R. "Mini-mental state": A practical method for grading the cognitive state of patients for the clinician. *Journal of Psychiatric Research* 12:189-198, 1975.

Fuld, P.A.; Katzman, R.; Davies, P.D.; and Terry, R.D. Intrusions as a sign of Alzheimer dementia: Chemical and pathological verification. *Annals of Neurology* 11:155-159, 1982.

Gallagher, D.; Rose, J.; Lovett, S.; and Silven, D. "Prevalence, Correlates, and Treatment of Clinical Depression in Family Caregivers." Paper presented at the meetings of the Gerontological Society of America, Chicago, IL, Nov. 1986.

George, L.K., and Gwyther, L.P. Caregiver well-being: A multidimensional examination of family caregivers of demented adults. *Gerontologist* 26:253-259, 1986.

Gilhooly, M.L.M. The impact of caregiving on caregivers: Factors associated with the psychological well-being of people supporting a dementing relative in the community. *British Journal of Medical Psychology* 57:35-44, 1984.

Goldbarb, A.I.; Fisch, M.; and Gerber, I. Predictors of mortality in the institutionalized aged. *Diseases of the Nervous System* 27:21-29, 1966.

Grad, J., and Sainsbury, P. Mental illness and the family. *Lancet* 1:544-547, 1963.

Grad, J., and Sainsbury, P. The effects that patients have on their families in a community care and a control psychiatric service: A two year follow up. *British Journal of Psychiatry* 114:265-278, 1968.

Greene, J.G.; Smith, R.; Gardiner, M.; and Timbury, G.C. Measuring behavioural disturbance of elderly demented patients in the community and its effects on relatives: A factor analystic study. *Age and Aging* 11:121-126, 1982.

Gurland, B. The assessment of the mental status of older adults. In: Birren, J.E., and Sloane, R.B., eds. *The Handbook of Mental Health and Aging.* Englewood Cliffs, NJ: Prentice-Hall, 1980.

Hachinski, V.C. Differential diagnosis of Alzheimer's disease: Multi-infarct dementia. In: Riesberg, B., ed. *Alzheimer's Disease: The Standard Reference.* New York: Free Press, 1983.

Hachinski, V.C.; Lassen, N.; and Marshall, J. Multi-infarct dementia: A cause of mental deterioration in the elderly. *Lancet* 2:207-210, 1974.

Haley, W.E.; Brown, S.L.; and Levine, E.G. Experimental evaluation of the effectiveness of group intervention for dementia caregivers. *Gerontologist,* in press.

Haley, W.E.; Brown, S.L.; and Levine, E.G. Family caregiver appraisals of patient behavioral disturbance in senile dementia. *Clinical Gerontologist,* in press.

Hassinger, M.J.; Zarit, J.M.; and Zarit, S.H. "A Comparison of Clinical Characteristics of Multi-infarct and Alzheimer's Dementia Patients." Paper presented at the meetings of the Western Psychological Association, Sacramento, CA, 1982.

Hassinger, M.J., and Zarit, S.H. "Predicting Institutionalization of Community-residing Dementia Patients: A Clinical Study." Paper presented at the meetings of the American Psychological Association, Washington, DC, 1986.

Haycox, J.A. A simple reliable clinical behavioral scale for assessing demented patients. *Journal of Clinical Psychiatry* 45:23-24, 1984.

Kahn, R.L. The mental health system and the future aged. *Gerontologist* 15(1, Part 2):24-31, 1975.

Kahn, R.L.; Goldfarb, A.I.; Pollack, M.; and Peck, A. Brief objective measures for the determination of mental status in the aged. *American Journal of Psychiatry* 117:326-328, 1960.

Kubler-Ross, E. *On Death and Dying.* New York: Macmillan, 1969.

Lawton, M.P. The functional assessment of elderly people. *Journal of the American Geriatrics Society* 19:465-481, 1971.

Lazarus, R.S., and Folkman, S. *Stress, Appraisal, and Coping.* New York: Springer, 1984.

Lindemann, E. Symptomatology and management of acute grief. *American Journal of Psychiatry* 101(2):141-148, 1944.

Liston, E.H., and LaRue, A. Clinical differentiation of primary degenerative and multi-infarct dementia: A critical review of the evidence. Part II. Pathological studies. *Biological Psychiatry* 12:1467-1483, 1983.

Lowenthal, M.F.; Berkman, P.; and Associates. *Aging and Mental Disorders in San Francisco.* San Francisco: Jossey-Bass, 1967.

McKhann, G.; Drachman, D.; Folstein, M.; Katzman, R.; Price, D.; and Stadlan, E.M. Clinical diagnosis of Alzheimer's disease. *Neurology* 34:939-944, 1984.

Montgomery, R.J.V.; Gonyea, J.G.; and Hooyman, N.R. Caregiving and the experience of subjective burden. *Family Relations* 34:19-26, 1985*a*.

Montgomery, R.J.V.; Stull, D.E.; and Borgatta, E.F. Measurement and the analysis of burden. *Research on Aging* 7:137-152, 1985*b*.

Morycz, R.K. An exploration of senile dementia and family burden. *Clinical Social Work Journal* 8:16-27, 1980.

Morycz, R.K. Caregiving strain and the desire to institutionalize family members with Alzheimer's disease. *Research on Aging* 7:329-361, 1985.

Niederehe, G., and Fruge, E. Dementia and family dynamics: Clinical research issues. *Journal of Geriatric Psychiatry* 17:21-56, 1984.

Niederehe, G.; Fruge, E.; Woods, A.M.; Scott, J.C.; Volpendesta, D.; Nielsen-Collins, K.E.; Moye, G.; Gibbs, H.; and Wiegand, G. "Caregiver Stress in Dementia: Clinical Outcomes and Family Considerations." Paper presented at the meetings of the Gerontological Society of America, San Francisco, CA, 1983.

Pearlin, L.I., and Schooler, C. The structure of coping. *Journal of Health and Social Behavior* 19:2-21, 1979.

Pfeiffer, E. A short portable mental status questionnaire for the assessment of organic brain deficit in elderly patients. *Journal of the American Geriatrics Society* 23:433-439, 1975.

Pinkston, E.M., and Linsk, N.L. *Care of the Elderly. A Family Approach.* New York: Pergamon, 1984.

Poulshock, S.W., and Deimling, G.T. Families caring for elders in residence: Issues in the measurement of burden. *Journal of Gerontology* 39:230-239, 1984.

Rabins, P.V.; Mace, N.L.; and Lucas, M.J. The impact of dementia on the family. *JAMA* 248:333-335, 1982.

Riesberg, B.; Ferris, S.H.; de Leon, M.J.; and Crook, T. The Global Deterioration Scale for the assessment of primary degenerative dementia. *American Journal of Psychiatry* 139(9):1136-1139, 1982.

Riesberg, B.; Ferris, S.H.; Schneck, M.K.; de Leon, M.J.; Crook, T.; and Gershon, S. The relationship between psychiatric assessments and cognitive test measures in mild to moderately cognitively impaired elderly. *Psychopharmacology Bulletin* 17:99-101, 1981.

Sainsbury, P., and Grad de Alarcon, J. The psychiatrist and the geriatric patient: The effects of community care on the family of the geriatric patient. *Journal of Geriatric Psychiatry* 4:23-41, 1970.

Sanford, J.F.A. Tolerance of debility in elderly dependents by supporters at home: Its significance for hospital practice. *British Medical Journal* 3:471-473, 1975.

Storandt, M.; Botwinick, J.; Danziger, W.L.; Berg, L.; and Hughes, C.P.

Psychometric differentiation of mild senile dementia of the Alzheimer type. *Archives of Neurology* 41:497-499, 1984.

Vitaliano, P.P.; Breen, A.R.; Albert, M.S.; Russo, J.; and Prinz, P.N. Memory, attention, and functional status in community-residing Alzheimer type dementia patients and optimally healthy aged individuals. *Journal of Gerontology* 39:58-64, 1984.

Weintraub, S.; Baratz, R.; and Mesulam, M. Daily living activities in the assessment of dementia. In: Corkin, S.; Davis, K.L.; Growdon, J.H.; Usdin, E.; and Wurtman, R.J., eds. *Alzheimer's Disease: A Report of Research in Progress.* New York: Raven Press, 1982.

Whitlatch, C.J.; Zarit, S.H.; and Mack, W. "Functional Correlates of Mental Status Tests." Paper presented at the meetings of the Gerontological Society of America, Chicago, IL, 1986.

Zarit, J.M. "Predictors of Burden and Stress for Caregivers of Dementia Patients." Unpublished doctoral dissertation, University of Southern California, Los Angeles, 1982.

Zarit, J.M., and Zarit, S.H. "Measuring Burden and Support in Families with Alzheimer's Disease Elders." Paper presented at the meetings of the Gerontological Society of America, Boston, MA, Nov. 1982.

Zarit, S.H., and Anthony, C.R. Interventions with dementia patients and their families. In: Gilhooly, M.L.M.; Zarit, S.H.; and Birren, J.E., eds. *The Dementias: Policy and Management.* Englewood Cliffs, NJ: Prentice-Hall, 1986. pp. 66-92.

Zarit, S.H.; Anthony, C.R.; and Boutselis, M. Interventions with caregivers of dementia patients: A comparison of two approaches. *Psychology and Aging* 2:225-235, 1987.

Zarit, S.H.; Orr, N.K.; and Zarit, J.M. *The Hidden Victims of Alzheimer's Disease: Families Under Stress.* New York: New York University Press, 1985.

Zarit, S.H.; Reever, K.E.; and Bach-Peterson, J. Relatives of the impaired elderly: Correlates of feelings of burden. *Gerontologist* 20:649-655, 1980.

Zarit, S.H.; Todd, P.A.; and Zarit, J.M. Subjective burden of husbands and wives as caregivers: A longitudinal study. *Gerontologist* 26:260-266, 1986.

Zarit, S.H., and Zarit, J.M. Cognitive impairment of older persons. Etiology, evaluation and intervention. In: Lewinsohn, P.M., and Teri, L., eds. *Coping and Adaptation in the Elderly.* New York: Pergamon, 1983.